Personnel/ Human Resource Management

Sixth Edition

Personnel/ Human Resource Management

Sixth Edition

Robert L. Mathis
UNIVERSITY OF NEBRASKA AT OMAHA

John H. Jackson
UNIVERSITY OF WYOMING

West Publishing Company
St. Paul   New York   Los Angeles   San Francisco

Copyediting:	Elaine Levin
Art:	John and Jean Foster
Composition:	Parkwood Composition
Cover Art:	Miyake Illustration

A study guide has been developed to assist students in mastering the concepts presented in this text. It reinforces chapter material presenting it in a concise format with review questions. An examination copy is available to instructors by contacting West Publishing Company. Students can purchase the study guide from the local bookstore under the title *Student Resource Guide: Cases, Exercises, and Study Questions to Accompany Personnel/Human Resource Management, Sixth Edition* prepared by Sally Coltrin, University of North Florida, and Roger Dean, Washington and Lee University.

COPYRIGHT © 1976, 1979,
    1982, 1985, 1988   By WEST PUBLISHING COMPANY
COPYRIGHT © 1991   By WEST PUBLISHING COMPANY
                     610 Opperman Drive
                     P.O. Box 64526
                     St. Paul, MN 55164-0526

Printed in the United States of America

98 97 96 95 94 93 92   8 7 6 5 4 3

Library of Congress Cataloging-in-Publication Data:

Mathis, Robert L., 1944-
        Personnel/human resource management/Robert L. Mathis, John H. Jackson.—6th ed.
        p.   cm.
        Includes Index.
ISBN 0-314-77009-7 (hard)
        1. Personnel management. I. Jackson, John Harold. II. Title.
HF5549.M3349 1991
658.3—dc20   90-42782
                          CIP

To

Jo Ann Mathis who manages me

R.D. and M.M. Jackson
who have been successful managers of
people for many years

Contents in Brief

Contents

Chapter 4   Individual Performance and Job Design   73

Preface

"The future has suddenly and dramatically become the present."

Roger Babson

Managers of organizations today face a rapidly changing world, and many of their past practices are having to be adapted in light of a myriad of changes. Many of these changes are impacting the management of human resources in organizations. Every week numerous newspaper articles, television special reports, and special seminars describe such issues as changing work force demographics, labor shortages, family-work balancing, and equal employment concerns. The thrust of this book is to cover relevant ideas and developments that managers will face by the year 2000 in the field of personnel/human resource management (P/HR).

This sixth edition continues the tradition established in the past, but the authors firmly believe that this book must change in order to remain one of the leading P/HR texts. Consequently every line and word of content of the fifth edition has been reviewed and major revisions made in many areas. Therefore, we believe that this edition continues the high standards of current ideas, readability, and excellence associated with the previous editions.

Certainly not everyone who reads this book will become a P/HR manager. In fact, many students who take a P/HR course will not become P/HR generalists or specialists. However, anyone who works in any organization will come in contact with P/HR management—both good and bad. Those who become managers must be able to manage P/HR activities because every manager's P/HR actions can have major consequences for an organization. One continuing feature of the book is the specification of the areas of contact between operating managers and the P/HR unit. Throughout the book these "interfaces" will describe typical divisions of P/HR responsibilities even though some variations will occur depending on the size of the organization, its technology, history, and other factors.

Organization of the Book

Each chapter begins with an example of a P/HR problem, situation, or practice in an actual organization illustrating a facet of the content that follows in the chapter. Within each chapter, vignettes, entitled "P/HR Practice and Research," capsule specific practices by employers and/or highlight research studies on P/HR topics. New to this edition is the identification of ethical issues in P/HR management, reflecting a growing concern about the need to educate students and professionals on business ethics. The end of chapter cases are "real-life" problems and situations using actual organizations as examples. The section cases, which were valued highly by reviewers, have been retained, and four new cases have been provided.

A special feature in this edition is the new comprehensive case on the evolution of the P/HR function at Federal Express, a company well-known to readers of the text. Prepared specially for this text, the case shows how integral P/HR management has been to Federal Express as it has built its "absolutely, positively" culture and operations.

The sixth edition opens with an examination of some of the major P/HR forces of change faced by managers and organizations. In Chapter 1 the impact of shifts and changes are discussed. The areas highlighted include changes in economic and employment patterns, demographic and work force composition, work patterns and contingent workers, social values, and family-work issues. Chapter 2 discusses P/HR management as a field of study and work. The third chapter examines the strategic role of P/HR management and why that strategic role is growing in importance. Chapter 4 concludes the first section by focusing on individual performance and job design. The components of individual performance and motivation are discussed in relation to absenteeism, turnover, job satisfaction, and job design.

Major revisions have been made in Chapters 5 and 6, comprising Section II, on equal employment opportunity. A detailed review of the content by several prominent employment attorneys ensured that coverage of changes in legislation and recent court decisions is accurate and current.

Section III on Analyzing and Staffing Jobs begins with Chapter 7, which covers job analysis and provides details on preparation and use of job descriptions and job specifications. Chapter 8 on recruiting has been upgraded to include more material on recruiting planning and evaluation. The ninth chapter continues its solid coverage of the employment process and selection activities.

Chapter 10 on training contains several revised sections, while maintaining comprehensive coverage on employee orientation. Chapter 11 discusses employee development and career planning and the importance of P/HR activities in these areas. The final chapter of Section IV on performance appraisal has been reorganized to include additional research and practice information.

Section V on Compensating Human Resources covers pay administration, incentives, and benefits. More information has been included on pay-for-performance, gainsharing and other incentive programs presented in Chapters 13 and 14. Major changes in content have been made in Chapter 15 on benefits in order to highlight the growing cost concerns facing managers and organizations. Special coverage of mandated benefits, health-care cost management, and family-related benefits highlight current challenges, while discussion of flexible benefits systems identifies one response of employers to these challenges.

Employee and labor relations activities are covered in Section VI. In Chapter 16, health and safety, additional coverage has been included on hazard communications, fetal protection, and other evolving issues. Chapter 17 discusses the various issues associated with employee rights and discipline, such as employment-at-will, privacy rights, and substance abuse. The coverage of union-management relations in Chapters 18 and 19 highlights the legal framework for unionism, emerging trends in unionism, collective bargaining, and effective grievance management.

The final section contains two chapters that cover a variety of topics of importance to P/HR management. Chapter 20 discusses P/HR management in international environments and the necessary adaptation of international P/HR management when organizations operate in two or more cultures and countries. Also discussed in Chapter 20 is P/HR management in small, entrepreneurial organizations and in public sector entities. Finally, the text concludes with a chapter on assessing P/HR effectiveness. Significant revisions have been made in this chapter in order to incorporate coverage of human resource information systems. The focus of the final chapter is on what is needed in order to determine how effectively the P/HR activities are being performed in an organization.

The instructor's manual, prepared by Jack A. Hill (University of Nebraska at Omaha) represents one of the most exciting, professionally useful instructor's aids available. The test bank contains approximately 2000 test questions prepared by Jack Hill and Diane Lloyd Gillo (University of Wisconsin—Stevens Point). It is available in computerized form also from West Publishing, as are over 60 transparencies. An excellent student resource guide, prepared by Sally A. Coltrin (University of North Florida) and Roger A. Dean (Washington and Lee University), contains sample test questions, cases, and exercises to enhance the learning potential of the text.

Acknowledgments

Producing any book requires assistance from many others. The authors are especially grateful to those individuals who provided reviews and numerous helpful comments for this edition. The authors particularly wish to thank Lee P. Stepina (Florida State University) for his extensive comments and content organization ideas. The following colleagues also provided extensive review input:

Philip G. Benson, New Mexico State University
Douglas A. Benton, Colorado State University
James H. Cox, Jefferson Community College
Naomi Berger Davidson, California State University, Northridge
Diane Lloyd Gillo, University of Wisconsin, Stevens Point
Allen K. Gulezian, Central Washington University
Sylvia Keyes, Bridgewater State University
Jerry L. Sellentin, University of Nebraska-Lincoln
Jeffery D. Stauffer, Ventura College
Cary D. Thorp, Jr., University of Nebraska-Lincoln
Elzberry Waters, Jr., Marymount University

In addition, many others have provided ideas and assistance. Practicing P/HR executives in a variety of organizations provided suggestions to ensure that theory and practice were well integrated. Too numerous to mention specifically, thanks are expressed to all of them. A special thanks goes to James A. Perkins of Federal Express for his willingness to describe the evolution of the P/HR function at his firm. Contributors of section cases and case ideas were Marjorie A. Amato, Mary J. Jaderborg, Donald Krause, and Ann E. Oasen.

Those involved in changing messy scrawls into printed ideas deserve special recognition. At the top of that list are JoAnn Mathis and Carolyn Foster. Others who assisted with many miscellaneous but necessary details include Nancy Hess and Maureen Bittner. Special thanks for her support and encouragement throughout the production process go to Carole Balach of West Publishing.

The authors are confident that this edition will continue to fill the need for a relevant and interesting text for those learning more about P/HR management. We are optimistic that those who use the book will agree.

Robert L. Mathis (SPHR)   John H. Jackson
OMAHA NEBRASKA   LARAMIE, WYOMING

Perspectives on Personnel/ Human Resource Management

Section I

New challenges in the management of human resources have emerged. This text provides perspectives on important traditional, current, and emerging practices in organizations in order to help you develop a practical, realistic, and modern view of the field. Some of the challenges in managing people at work in the 1990s are highlighted in Chapter 1.

This first section introduces you to personnel/human resource (P/HR) management as a field of study and practice, including strategic planning, which sets the stage for P/HR activities. The relationship of individual performance to motivation and organizational efforts is discussed.

Chapter 2 identifies P/HR management's role in organization. P/HR generalists and specialists, as well as operating managers, are required to ensure effective management of employees. Eleven

major P/HR activities that must be performed in any organization are identified. Also, P/HR management as a career field is examined.

Chapter 3 identifies the P/HR unit's responsibilities for strategic planning. External environmental scanning as it relates to P/HR management is presented and an examination is made of how organizations forecast supply and demand for employees and how they deal with shortages and surpluses.

Chapter 4 focuses on individual performance and motivation within organizations. Analyzing human behavior helps organizations to improve existing working environments and to address issues associated with job satisfaction, turnover, absenteeism, and loyalty. How jobs are designed also is examined in light of motivation theory.

Managing Human Resources In the 1990s

Chapter 1

After you have read this chapter, you should be able to:

1. Discuss three economic and employment shifts that will affect organizations in the 1990s

2. Identify how the demographic and work force shifts of women, minorities, and older workers will affect organizations in the 1990s

3. Define contingent workers and discuss the growth in temporary, part-time, and job-sharing employment

4. Discuss three alternative working patterns

5. Explain how family-work balancing and employee rights issues are affecting the management of human resources

P/HR: Today *and* Tomorrow	Human Resources Shortages

In the decade from 1990 to the year 2000, obtaining, retaining, and developing human resources may be the biggest challenge facing managers and organizations in the United States. A wide range of economic, demographic, and social forces have converged to intensify the pressures on acquiring a sufficient number of workers with the necessary knowledge and skills.

Some of the specific indicators of the dramatic adjustments occurring in the U.S. work force are as follows:[1]

■ Because of educational deficiencies only 15 of every 500 applicants at one bank in New York City are qualified.

■ Over half of all nursing homes surveyed reported that they have severe or moderate difficulties in filling nursing aide jobs.

■ Approximately 40 percent of the 20 million new jobs to be created in the United States from 1988 to 2000 will require at least one year of college.

■ The fastest-growing segment of the U.S. work force will be minorities, with Hispanics and Blacks being the primary groups adding workers. However, those groups have among the highest high-school dropout rates.

■ There will be fewer people between ages 18–25 in 1999 than in 1988, which means fewer teen workers available to fill entry-level jobs.

■ A shortage of over 1 million workers will exist for jobs requiring computer knowledge between 1990 and 2000.

■ The food service/restaurant industry will need 11.5 million workers by 1995, up from 8.3 million in 1990, resulting in severe pressures on industry employers in attracting workers.

■ Over 1 million women per year are entering or re-entering the U.S. work force.

■ Over 50 million workers will have to receive training from 1988 to 2000, including over 30 million current workers to be retained and 20 million new employees requiring training.

■ Older individuals who retired are taking more part-time jobs, with 45 percent of all men and 60 percent of all women over age 65 holding part-time jobs of some type during a year.

■ Almost half of all college faculty members in the United States will retire between 1995 and 2010; a 30 percent shortage of faculty members is anticipated because of a shortage of people with doctorates who will go into college teaching.

As the preceding examples suggest, some of the pressures are due to demographic shifts. Lower birthrates in the 1970s mean fewer young persons will be available to work in the 1990s. At the same time, the number of persons over age 55 will grow. More women are working and more people have part-time or temporary jobs. Service industry jobs, which tend to be very labor-intensive, are growing, but the number of manufacturing jobs are declining. Jobs that will be created between 1990 and the year 2000 increasingly will require higher knowledge and skills, while the educational level of many people will be inadequate.

Scarcity of human resources with appropriate knowledge and skills is the single biggest human resource challenge for the 1990s. How well that challenge is met will determine the future viability and growth of many organizations.

"The changes are so deep and far reaching that there are no simple descriptions or answers as to the real nature of work and employment in the 21st century."

Jeffrey J. Hallett

The management of people at work is one of the primary keys to organizational success. Increasingly, managers in organizations recognize that *people* are *human resources* to be managed effectively, just like money and other organizational resources. Many employers have discovered that better management of human resources can be a major source of productivity improvement and growth. Corporate public relations documents often refer to people as "the most valuable resource" in an organization.

Yet, as the chapter-opening discussion indicates, the availability and composition of those human resources today is dramatically different from previous decades. Likewise, various shifts in the United States and other economies are forcing changes in many industries. Finally, a wide range of political forces and social trends are having significant impact on the policies and practices used by employers to manage their human resources. With all of these changes impacting organizations at the same time, managers during the 1990s must be prepared for many challenges in obtaining, retaining, and developing their human resources.

■■ ■ TO THE YEAR 2000

Many managers operate as if their organizations are still facing the problems and challenges of the 1970s. But the decade of the 1990s demands different strategies, policies, and practices from those of the past.[2] The major changes affecting the management of human resources for the future can be grouped into four general categories. A brief discussion highlights some of the human resource pressures in each of the following areas:

- Economic and employment shifts
- Demographic and work force shifts
- Changing work patterns and contingent workers
- Changes in social values and issues

Economic and Employment Shifts

Several economic shifts have been occurring that will affect employment and occupational patterns in the United States. A major one is the shift of jobs from manufacturing and agriculture to service industries and telecommunications. Additionally, pressures from global competitors have forced many U.S. firms to close plants, adapt their managment practices, and increase productivity. A look at some of these forces for change is in order.

GLOBAL COMPETITION.   Truly, the world has become a global economy. Events in Eastern Europe, Japan, and Latin America create both opportunities and challenges for U.S. firms. Numerous examples can be cited, but a few illustrate the world economic linkages.

Consider the events in Europe beginning very recently. The opening of the Eastern European countries such as Poland and Czechoslovakia gives U.S.-based and other firms dramatically expanded opportunities to sell products and services. Also, the ample supply of workers available in those countries, whose wage rates are relatively low, means that manufacturing facilities can be started up to tap the available labor pools. In Europe, efforts to create a unified European economic market, labeled "Europe 1992," has led to cross-country mergers of firms and greater cooperation by European governments. At the same time, those efforts may have the effect of limiting the import of U.S. and Japanese-made goods to the participating European countries. Therefore, U.S. and Japanese firms have added offices and production facilities in Europe to avoid potential trade restrictions.

On the other side of the world in Asia, Japan's economy has been maturing, and Japanese society has been changing because of a rapidly aging population. Also, younger Japanese are becoming more "westernized" and they are buying more imported goods. Gradually, the Japanese government has had to open up its markets and make changes in its economy in response to pressure from the U.S. and other countries. Economic relations between U.S. firms and those in countries such as Taiwan, South Korea, Singapore, and Malaysia have become more complex as the latter's exports to the United States have increased, while U.S. firms have established production operations in those countries.

Many U.S. firms receive a substantial portion of their profits and sales outside the United States. Estimates are that the largest 100 U.S. multinational firms have foreign sales of more than $500 billion in one year. For firms such as Colgate and Coca-Cola, foreign sales and profits account for over 60 percent of total sales and profits. Other U.S. firms have substantial operations in other countries as well.

Worldwide economic forces have affected the competitiveness of U.S. firms. As a result, the number and types of jobs in those firms have changed. The impact of global competition can be seen in many industries. The automobile, steel, and electronics industries have had to close facilities or reduce employment because of competition from firms in Japan, Taiwan, Korea, West Germany, and other countries. At the same time, foreign-owned firms have been investing in plants and creating jobs in the United States. In one year, foreign-owned firms invested about $58 billion in plant, equipment, and services in the United States.[3]

The growth in employment resulting from foreign investments helps to replace jobs lost at U.S. firms. In addition, these foreign-owned firms are affecting the policies and practices of human resource management. A prime example is the Toyota manufacturing facility in Kentucky. In a departure from traditional American practice, management instituted a team approach whereby assembly-line employees work in teams of six. To staff the plant, Toyota used a different selection process than that typically used at U.S. automobile manufacturers. Group and team leaders were selected and then trained in Japan. Part of the training was to prepare the leaders to interview and select their team members at the U.S. plant.[4] Similar approaches have been used at other plants, including the joint Toyota/General Motors plant in Fremont, California.

OCCUPATIONAL AND INDUSTRY SHIFTS. The U.S. economy increasingly has become a service economy (for example, about 80 percent of the new jobs created in California over a ten-year period were in service industries),[5] and that shift is expected to continue, as Figure 1–1 indicates. Approximately 75 percent of U.S. jobs are in service industries, and most new jobs created by the year 2000 also will be in services. It is estimated that manufacturing jobs will represent only 12 to 15 percent of all U.S. jobs by this date.

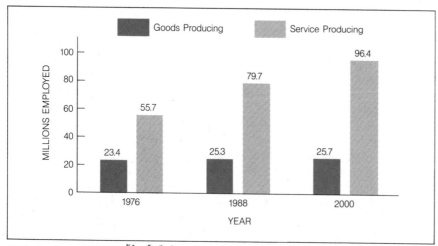

Figure 1–1
Employment Projections (goods producing vs. service producing)

SOURCE: Adapted from the *Monthly Labor Review,* November, 1989.

Although service industries employ white-collar workers, professionals, and unskilled entry-level employees, the main growth is anticipated to be in the computer, medical, engineering, and clerical fields. The fastest-growing occupations in these fields will be paralegals (104 percent increase), medical assistants (90 percent), physical therapists (87 percent), physical therapy aides (82 percent), data-processing equipment repair technicians (81 percent), and home health aides (80 percent).[6]

Occupational growth also will occur in computer-related jobs. For instance, according to the U.S. Bureau of Labor Statistics, the demand for computer programmers and systems analysts is expected to increase over 70 percent for the years 1988–2000. The telecommunications industry also anticipates continued economic growth as advances in fiber optics, lasers, and other technologies occur. At the same time, less-skilled jobs in food service, building maintenance, and retail sales clerical positions will increase.

Jobs in the agriculture, mining, and printing industries face the sharpest declines. For example, over half of all employed people over age fifteen who live on farms do not having farming as their primary economic occupation. Also, only about 2 percent of the U.S. population lives on farms.[7] Many individuals who live on farms work in towns and cities and farm part-time. To tap the human resources available in rural areas, particularly the 76 percent of farm women who work off the farm, firms in a variety of industries have established facilities in several smaller towns. For instance, many telemarketing firms have opened up operations centers employing 100 or fewer employees in smaller towns throughout the Midwest and Plains states, where wage costs are low and there is a pool of potential workers available.

Another facet of change is the pattern of job growth and shrinkage in firms of varying sizes. Whereas many large firms have cut jobs by reducing their work forces, many smaller firms have continued to create jobs. One study by the Hudson Institute found that over a seven-year period, more jobs were created by firms with fewer than 20 employees than by firms with over 500 employees.[8] The number of entrepreneurially-oriented individuals who start small businesses also has been growing.

EDUCATION AND "KNOWLEDGE" JOBS.   Changing patterns in many occupational groups and industries will require more educated workers. The number of jobs requiring advanced knowledge is expected to grow at a much more rapid rate than other jobs. This growth means that people without high school diplomas are at an increasing disadvantage, as their employment opportunities are confined to the lowest-paying service jobs.

There is a growing gap between the knowledge and skills required by jobs and those possessed by employees and applicants. Several different studies and projections all point to a crisis in the ability of employers in many industries to obtain sufficiently educated and trained workers. One study divided jobs into six levels of knowledge and skills, with level one being the lowest level required. When examining work force education and skill competencies, the study found that only 22 percent of all new workers entering the work force from 1988 to 2000 will be able to function at a level higher than level two. Another indicator of deficiencies in knowledge and skills is seen in the experience of New York Telephone Company. That firm had to test about 60,000 applicants in order to hire 3,000 qualified individuals. Many of the applicants were minority-group members who had insufficient basic reading and writing skills.[9] Some employers are dealing with the problems of inadequate knowledge and skills of individuals already employed by teaching basic literacy skills.

Knowledge and skills deficiencies affect some minority groups more than others. For example, in the 21 to 25 year age group, about 60 percent of whites, 40 percent of Hispanics, and less than 25 percent of Blacks could perform such tasks as locating basic facts in a newspaper or balancing a checkbook.[10] Unless major efforts are made to improve educational systems, especially those serving minorities, employers will be unable to find enough qualified workers for the growing number of "knowledge" jobs.

Demographic and Work Force Shifts

The shifting characteristics of the U.S. work force will have another significant impact on employers in the 1990s. The work force of the 1990s and beyond will be dramatically different from the work force of the 1970s and 1980s. According to the U.S. Bureau of Labor Statistics, several significant population and work force changes are:[11]

- The total labor force will grow more slowly during the 1990s than during the 1980s.
- In the 1990s, women will account for a greater proportion of growth in the labor force than they did over the past decade.
- Hispanics, Blacks, and other minority groups will account for about one-quarter of the overall growth in the labor force during the 1990s.
- Younger members of the labor force, age 16 to 24, will decline in absolute numbers.
- Average age of the U.S. population will increase, but work force participation rates will decline for workers over 55, as more older individuals retire earlier.

As a result of these shifts, employers in a variety of industries will face shortages of qualified workers. A more detailed look at some of these changes follows.

WOMEN IN THE WORK FORCE.   The influx of women into the work force is a major social change that affects P/HR planning. The number of women in the work force increased from 21 million in 1960 to 55 million in 1989. As Figure 1–2 indicates, women are expected to represent 47 percent of the U.S. work force by the year 2000. Further, about half of all working women are single, separated,

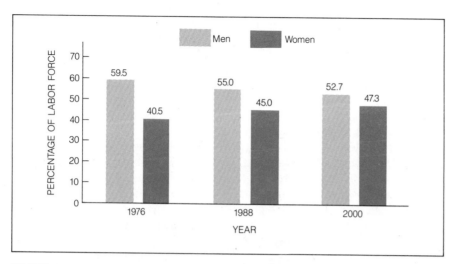

SOURCE: Adapted from the *Monthly Labor Review*, November 1989.

Figure 1–2
Civilian Labor Force Projections by Sex

divorced, or widowed, so they are "primary" income earners, not co-income providers. Forecasts are that over 80 percent of women from 25 to 40 years old will be working or looking for work in 1995.

As more women work, traditional earnings and employment patterns will continue to change. A growing number of women are entering jobs traditionally held by men. The P/HR: Research discusses a study that examined the job satisfaction of women in nontraditional occupations. Earnings patterns for women will improve if more women shift into higher-paying professional and technical fields. Women's average pay still is significantly lower than men's (about 79 percent of men's), although more than 5 million women earn more than their husbands (about 18 percent of all working couples).

Changes in P/HR activities are another consequence of more women in the work force. Benefit programs increasingly are adapting to employee demands for child-care aid and parental-leave programs. More flexible work scheduling, another way to accommodate the multiple needs of employees, is being used by a growing number of employers. A third response has been to establish relocation programs for dual-career couples by helping working spouses find jobs if their mates are transferred. In 1990, about 50 percent of all married couples, about 30 million households, had dual careers, and that number is projected to increase.[13] Many women are no longer willing to leave their jobs if their husbands are transferred, because they themselves have good positions in the organizations for which they work. Men married to women who are being considered for transfer face the same problem. Rather than reject a promotion that requires one mate to locate, some couples have chosen to have a "commuter marriage."

MINORITIES IN THE WORK FORCE.   The fastest growing segments of the U.S. population are minority groups—especially Hispanics, Blacks, and Asians. Projections indicate that the Black labor force will grow about twice as fast as the white labor force from 1990 to 2000. Workers of Hispanic and Asian origin also will increase faster than white workers because of higher birthrates.

Immigration also is increasing the percentage of minority individuals. Approximately 85 percent of all immigrants to the United States in a recent year were from Asia, Latin America, and the Caribbean.[14] Annually, about 400,000 legal,

P/HR: Practice *and* Research

Job Satisfaction of Women in Nontraditional Occupations

As more women enter the work force, many of them are taking jobs that traditionally have not been held by women in large numbers in the United States. To determine the job satisfaction of women who have nontraditional jobs, Hester R. Stewart conducted a study of women employed in a cross section of nontraditional jobs in Delaware businesses. The study appeared in the *Journal of Employment Counseling*. Stewart defined a nontraditional occupation as one in which 25 percent or fewer women are employed. In her study, the women held such jobs as mechanic, lot attendant, engineer, and carpenter.

Stewart mailed a questionnaire to 527 women that contained questions relating to eighteen job factors and several demographic classifications. Responses were received from 217 women, a 44 percent return rate.

The results showed that the highest satisfaction ratings were on (a) opportunity to do things for others, (b) geographic location of the job, and (c) chance to work alone. The greatest dissatisfaction was found on (a) opportunity for advancement, (b) salary earned, and (c) supervisor's manner of handling people. When asked about combining work and family roles, 69 percent of the respondents indicated that their jobs allowed them to meet both work and family demands. Almost half of the respondents said that they were totally responsible for financial support of their households.

Stewart concluded that the nontraditional occupations held by women did offer opportunities that might not be available in jobs more traditionally held by women. At the same time, the lack of advancement opportunities and the low pay are issues that must be addressed by employers attempting to attract women to nontraditional occupations.[12]

permanent immigrants enter the United States. Another 300,000 arrive under temporary work arrangements for periods of up to a year of more.[15]

AGING OF THE WORK FORCE.   The U.S. population is gradually aging, according to U.S. Census Bureau data. The median age of all U.S. citizens in 1986 was 31.5 years, and it is expected to increase to 39 by the year 2000. This increase is due to people living longer and a falling birthrate. Further, evidence suggests that workers over age 55 will decline as the group swells with members past retirement age.

Figure 1–3
Labor force projections for 16–24-year-olds

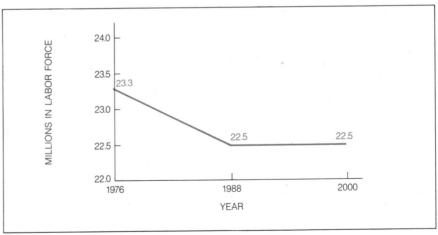

SOURCE: Adapted from the *Monthly Labor Review*, November, 1989.

The aging of the U.S. work force should be viewed from the other end of the spectrum as well. Workers in the 16–24 year age bracket decreased from 1976 to 1988. As Figure 1–3 on the previous page shows, little growth in this age group is projected from 1988 to the year 2000.

One of the major implications of the age shift is that employers who usually fill large numbers of entry-level jobs with teens and other younger workers will have to look to other labor sources. In particular, service-sector employers such as hotels, fast-food chains, retailers, and military branches of the government will face significant staffing difficulties. Some employers are trying new approaches to this problem. To generate additional applicants for workers, McDonald's hired a service to distribute the mini-application form pictured in Figure 1–4, placing them on door handles in neighborhoods near local McDonald's restaurants. It had some success, and illustrates the creativity being used by service-industries to obtain workers.

Another consequence is that employers will have to attract more senior citizens back into the work force through the use of part-time and other work-scheduling options. For example, the Traveler's Insurance Company has retirees listed in a job bank who are contacted to provide temporary clerical, secretarial, or other work assistance.[16]

Figure 1–4
McDonald's Mini-Application

Contingent Workers and Changing Work Patterns

Other important changes in the work force are the result of workers' changing lifestyles and work patterns. Many of today's employees require temporary or part-time employment at certain stages in their work life, and many firms find they are able to cut costs by employing such workers. Consequently, employers are offering greater variety in work patterns and schedules.

Individuals classified as **contingent workers** are those who are employed as temporary or regularly scheduled part-time workers. Estimates are that there are up to 30 million contingent workers, representing about 25 percent of the total U.S. civilian work force.

A CONTINGENT WORKER is one who is employed as a temporary or part-time worker.

TEMPORARY WORKERS.   Temporary employees can be obtained by an employer hiring its own "temporary staff" or by using a temporary worker agency. Such agencies supply workers on a rate-per-day or per week basis. The increasing use of temporary help has been impressive. Since 1986, the payrolls of temporary help suppliers have grown approximately 18 percent per year. Many employers use temporary workers at some time to augment their staffing needs.

Originally developed to provide clerical and office workers to employers, temporary agencies now provide temporary accountants, lawyers, systems analysts, nurses, and many other occupations. Approximately 12 percent of the temporary workers in the United States are in professional and technical fields.[17] Another 10 percent are in medical fields.

For a variety of reasons, the use of temporary workers may make sense. If an organization has work that is subject to seasonal or other fluctuations, hiring temporary help may be more efficient than hiring permanent employees. Using temporary workers may be less costly than hiring full-time employees, paying their benefits, then releasing them when they are no longer needed. Many firms have found temporary workers to be more efficient and productive because those workers know that they will be doing a job for only a limited period of time. Some firms staff their mail rooms completely with temporary people because of the high turnover of full-time workers.

But there are some disadvantages to using temporary workers.[18] Temporary workers who enter a company for a short time often do not understand how an organization operates, what its policies are, and what the management styles and expectations are. Also, temporary workers may not have as much commitment to the organization and its productivity goals because they know they will be gone shortly. Finally, temporary workers may be treated as social outcasts by the regular employees in the organization.

PART-TIME EMPLOYMENT.   Many U.S. workers actually put in fewer than 35 hours a week; they are considered part-timers. However, it is important to clarify that there are two part-time subgroups:

- Voluntary part-time workers.
- Involuntary part-time workers (who normally work full time but are employed part time because of economic conditions).

VOLUNTARY PART-TIME WORKERS are individuals who wish to work less than 35 hours per week.

Voluntary part-time workers are individuals who wish to work less than 35 hours per week. They represent an important segment of the U.S. labor force. According to the U.S. Bureau of Labor Statistics, about 13 percent of all employed people in the United States are voluntary part-time workers.[19] Part-time employment is concentrated mainly in retail trade and service industries, and about half of all part-timers hold managerial, professional, or technical positions. Attorneys, chemists, engineers, technical medical specialists, accountants, and computer experts are among those professions particularly adaptable to part-time work. [20]

Many employers increasingly are using part-time workers on a regular basis. However, relatively few managers work as regular part-time employees. Regular part-time employment sometimes has been referred to as "permanent part-time" in the past, but the word *permanent* is not recommended by labor attorneys because such terminology can cause difficulties if an employee is terminated.

Regular part-time employment has some pluses and minuses for an organization. The advantages include savings on overtime payments, greater work assignment flexibility, increased productivity, reduced fatigue, and lower absenteeism. Also, many employers do not offer the full range of benefits, such as medical insurance and pension plans, to part-time employees, so part-time employment can produce significant cost savings to an organization. Potential disadvantages include increased administration costs, increased training costs, and more communication problems. In addition, unions often oppose part-time employment because it increases job competition and may damage the interests of their full-time members. Part-timers may be willing to work for less pay or fewer benefits.

Involuntary part-time workers are persons who work less than 35 hours per week, but normally would be working full time if possible. These individuals may be working fewer hours for two reasons: (1) inability to find full-time employment, and (2) accepted reduction in full-time hours because of unfavorable conditions faced by their employers.

The second reason reflects that, historically, when U.S. employers have suffered serious economic downturns, they have had to reduce their work forces. To prevent layoffs, organizations can use **work sharing,** in which an employer reduces work hours and total pay for all or a segment of the employees. This alternative permits individual employees to maintain their jobs, although with reduced hours and wages. In times of recession, this practice fills the need for job security by maintaining a full complement of employees and spreading out the available benefits among the entire work force. For example, when Motorola, Inc. had to cut production in its Phoenix, Arizona, plant, management chose work sharing over releasing employees, by cutting hours from every employee's work week. [21]

JOB SHARING.   A different work pattern is **job sharing,** whereby two part-timers share one full-time job. The potential advantages of job sharing include reduced turnover, increased efficiency, greater continuity, and higher productivity. Turnover rates are high in jobs that are tedious or stressful, but the sharing of such jobs may result in a reduction in turnover. Many times a full-time job does not suit a worker's personal needs. Job sharing offers one way of recruiting and maintaining a highly capable employee who might otherwise choose other employment. This attraction has been particularly strong for women who want more time to spend with their children and work as well. For example, two women may have a job and perform their childrearing duties by splitting a nursing position. Other examples of job sharing appear in the P/HR Practice.

ALTERNATIVE WORK SCHEDULES.   One type of working arrangement that has been in transition is the regular full-time, 8-hour-a-day, five-day-work-week schedule. Organizations have been experimenting with many different possibilities for change: the four-day, 40-hour week; the four-day, 32-hour week; the 3-day week;

INVOLUNTARY PART-TIME WORKERS are individuals who work less than 35 hours per week, but normally would be working full time if possible.

WORK SHARING occurs when an employer reduces work hours and total pay for all or a segment of the employees.

JOB SHARING is a work arrangement in which two part-time workers share one full-time job.

P/HR:	Practice *and* Research	Job Sharing

Job sharing is in use in many different types of firms, and there are different ways that job sharing is done. At Steelcase, Inc., a Grand Rapids, Michigan, manufacturer of office furniture, only current employees with good work records can request job sharing. Office job sharers must have at least one year of service, and production workers two years of service. Also, the sharing employees must report to the same supervisor or manager. Steelcase has found that the most common job-sharing schedule is for one person to work full time for five days (Wednesday through the following Tuesday), and then have a week off. That schedule means that both individuals work every week and the transitions in work do not occur over a weekend, allowing for better continuity. In addition, each person can get some Friday or Monday holidays.

Job sharers note the importance of communication between the sharing employees. At Aetna Life & Casualty (Hartford, Connecticut), Dotty Black and Sue Townsend share a secretarial job. They have created a series of folders that contain specific types of work, and they write each other notes to leave instructions and give status reports. They also regularly call one another at home to maintain contact and ensure coordination.

As is true in any continuing relationship between people, the compatibility of the job sharers is critical. Each job sharer must have the necessary skills and a commitment to quality work performance.

Key to making job sharing work is having well-defined guidelines among managers, supervisors, and job sharers. These guidelines address such issues as how many hours each job sharer will work, what employee benefits will be provided, how heavy work-load situations will be handled, and what the goals and performance requirements of managers are. Once those issues are decided and agreed to by all parties, job sharing is off to a good start.[22]

and flexible scheduling. Changes of this nature require some major adjustments for organizations, but in some cases they have been very useful.

FLEXTIME
refers to variations in starting and ending times but assumes that a constant number of hours (usually 8) is worked each day.

Flextime is a type of schedule redesign in which employees work a set number of hours but vary starting and ending times. The traditional starting and ending times of the 8-hour work shift can vary up to one or more hours at the beginning and end of the normal workday. Flextime allows management to relax some of the traditional "time clock" control of employees. One study of 50 companies found that a majority of the P/HR managers indicated that flextime helped with recruiting, and 66 percent said that productivity was higher.[23] Flextime is discussed in more detail in Chapter 4.

A COMPRESSED WORK WEEK
is one in which a full week's work is accomplished in fewer than five days.

Compressed work weeks are another way to change work patterns. In a compressed work week, a full week's work is accomplished in fewer than five days. Common schedules used include:

- Four days with 10-hour days
- Three days with 12-hour days
- Four-and-one-half days with four 9-hour days and one 4-hour day (usually Friday)
- The 5/4-9 plan whereby the employee alternates five-day and four-day work weeks, working 9 hours per day
- The work weekend of two 12-hour days, paid at premium rates

Although work hours are condensed in each of these plans, the total time worked is not significantly changed in most of them. Compression simply alters the number of hours per day per employee on any given day, and usually results in a longer working day and a decreased number of days worked per week.

Greater flexibility in staffing and better or longer job coverage are two major reasons why employers use compressed work weeks or other flexible scheduling options.[24] The appeal for individuals is that they have more flexibility to meet family or other personal responsibilities.

Work at Home and Telecommuting

A growing number of workers in the United States do not leave home to go to work. One estimate is that about 27 million U.S. workers work at home on job-related work at least part-time, about 60 percent of whom are white-collar workers. About 5 million workers earn all of their income at home. Estimates are that the number of at-home workers is growing at a rate of 7 to 9 percent per year.[25]

The at-home workers are in many job categories, including computer programmer, commodity broker, interior decorator, mail order telephone operator, architect, book copy editor, beautician, and child-care provider. A particularly fast-growing segment of at-home workers are those who telecommute to work.

Telecommuting is the process of going to work via electronic computing and telecommunications equipment. Over 300 U.S. employers have telecommuting employees or are experimenting with them, including such firms as American Express, Travelers Insurance, Pacific Bell, and J.C. Penney Co.

Professionals and self-employed workers find telecommuting particularly useful. These individuals in a variety of fields work at home a large part of the time. Some telecommuters are software developers, real estate developers, writers, advertising designers, accountants, engineers, psychologists, and financial planners. Some prisoners in penal institutions even telecommute. For example, a joint program between an airline and the California Youth Authority uses inmates as reservation sales agents. In Arizona, prisoners in the women's prison take reservations for several hotel chains. In addition, telecommuting allows handicapped individuals, who might not otherwise be able to hold a job, to work at home. In sum, the advantages of at-home work and telecommuting for individuals are numerous: better use of time, more flexible hours, and cost reduction or elimination of frequent physical commuting are a few.

The ability to attract workers who might otherwise be restricted from working is a major advantage for employers. Individuals with small children, many of whom are women, can continue careers and still be at home to care for children or aging relatives with health problems. Many firms use at-home workers as independent contractors so that they do not have full-time staffing commitments and associated costs. The flexibility of staffing and using at-home workers as work loads shift also gives employers some productivity advantages.

But not all the news about at-home work and telecommuting is positive.[26] The difficulties in restructuring jobs and tasks to make them suitable for at-home work or telecommuting have discouraged some employers. Also, problems about how to supervise the work and how to pay at-home workers, particularly those performing clerical tasks, must be worked out.[27] For individuals, some at-home workers report they miss the social interactions associated with working in an office with others. Additionally, labor unions are adamantly opposed to telecommuting because their leaders fear that workers will be exploited. They fear that employers will pay less than minimum wage rates and that they generally use at-home work as a means to avoid paying benefits.

In spite of these problems, work at home–telecommuting is predicted to grow. There even is a National Association for the Cottage Industry to address the problems of at-home and "electronic cottage" workers. If such growth continues, it is possible

TELECOMMUTING
is the process of going to work via electronic computing and telecommunications equipment.

that more future workers will complain about a "tough day at the terminal," even though they never left home.

■■ ■ CHANGES IN SOCIAL VALUES AND ISSUES

When managing human resources in the 1990s, employers are facing a wider range of pressures and problems compared with those faced in the 1970s, because of changes in social values and new social issues. Until the early and mid-1980s, employers were not subject to pressures for smoke-free workplaces, AIDS policies, drug testing, employer-sponsored child-care assistance, and many others. Yet today, those issues call for action by employers of all sizes and in all industries. Although many changes in values and issues have occurred, two major ones are growing in prominence: (1) family/work balancing and (2) employee rights. A brief look at each of these areas follows.

Family/Work Balancing

For many workers in the United States, balancing family responsibilities and work demands is a significant challenge. While always a concern in the past, the decade of the 1980s saw major growth in the number of women working and dual-career couples. About 65 percent of all married women were employed in 1990, and that figure is projected to increase to 75 percent by 2000.[28]

One implication of the increase in the number of working women is that there are more pressures on both men and women workers to be caregivers to sick children or ailing relatives. Currently, about 57 percent of all women with children under six years of age work full time, and 60 percent of all women having babies work during pregnancy. Also, the absenteeism rate for women with children was 11.7 days per year, compared with women with no children of 9.6 days per year, men with children of 9.4 days, and men with no children of 7.4 days.[29]

On the other end of the caregiving continuum, surveys of workers in large companies have found that about 30 percent of all workers have significant responsibilities for caring for elderly relatives, and these responsibilities can detract from job performance and increase absenteeism.[30] In recognition of this problem, some employers have offered elder-care benefits.

Family composition also is changing (see Figure 1-5). A majority of all U.S. households have no children under the age of eighteen living at home. But of those households with children at home, many are headed by unmarried women. Census Bureau data indicate that women head 6 million households with children under eighteen years of age.[31] One-parent households are less prevalent with whites than racial/minority groups.[32]

Public recognition of these problems has put growing pressure on employers to provide various forms of child-care assistance ranging from maintaining referral services on care providers to setting up on-site employer-sponsored child-care centers. It also is clear that child-care arrangements affect the ability of individuals to hold jobs and build careers.[33]

There has been considerable publicity surrounding a view of women's work roles dubbed the "mommy track." According to Felice Schwartz, many women with children, particularly those holding managerial and professional jobs, should be set on a different career track than women without children. Instead of having a

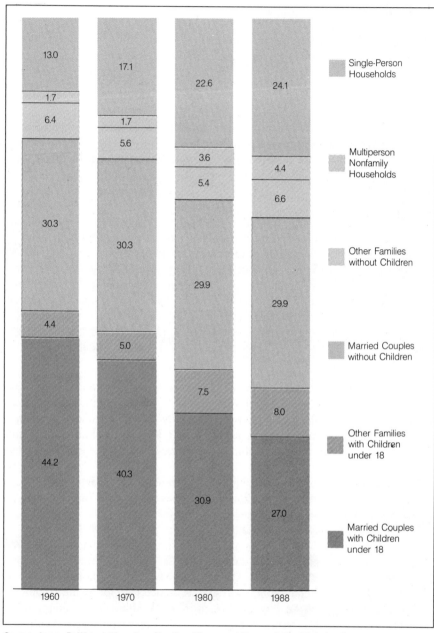

Figure 1–5
Composition of American households, selected years, 1960–88 (in percentages)

Source: James R. Wetzel, "American Families: 75 years of Change." *Monthly Labor Review*, March 1990, 10.

career as the primary track, this "career and family" (or mommy track) approach is appropriate because many women with children will forego promotions or career moves for family reasons. However, "career primary" women, whether they do or do not have children, should have the same career advancement opportunities as men.[34] As would be expected, this dual-track view has been very controversial. Nevertheless, views such as these indicate that balancing family and work will continue to be an issue affecting the management of human resources throughout the 1990s.

Employee Rights

Other major social shifts impacting the management of human resources in the 1990s have to do with employee rights. Some of the most common employee rights issues are restrictions on smoking at work, drug testing, and employee privacy and due process concerns.

SMOKING.   Many employers, either voluntarily or in response to state or local laws, have banned or severely restricted smoking at work. These local and state laws have imposed various requirements on employers, including the following:[35]

- Policies designating workplace areas as either smoking or nonsmoking
- Posting of smoking/non-smoking signs
- Establishment of smoking complaint procedures

Nonsmokers have welcomed these restrictions because it restores their rights to clean air at work. But the rights of those who smoke have been reduced. Often, employers must balance the rights of both groups, while still operating their organizations productively. Approaches used by employers have ranged from refusing to hire smokers and banning all smoking at work to establishing smoking-cessation clinics. One study found that 60 percent of all companies restrict smoking. Once a smoke-free environment is established, some employers have had to deal with smokers taking longer breaks in order to go outside or off-premise to smoke.[36]

SUBSTANCE-ABUSE TESTING.   More employers are using drug testing of workers. Estimates are that drug use by employees costs U.S. employers $33 billion a year because of higher absenteeism and lower productivity. According to some estimates, drug and alcohol substance abusers represent over 38 percent of all construction workers, 17 percent of all manufacturing employees, and 21 percent of all retail industry employees.[37]

The Drug-Free Workplace Act of 1988 requires that most federal government contractors notify workers of drug-free workplace requirements and take steps to punish or rehabilitate drug abusers. Otherwise, the firms can be penalized by having contract payments delayed or by being banned as a government contractor.[38]

To combat abuse problems, employers have resorted to two strategies. The first is to offer aid to employees with substance-abuse problems through employee assistance programs (EAP). In an EAP, an employee with emotional, health, or other problems can get counseling and other assistance paid for by the employer.

The other strategy is to use drug tests to identify users. Although questions remain about the accuracy of drug testing through urinalysis, many employers test potential applicants in order to screen out abusers. Also, many firms require drug testing of employees who are involved in work-related accidents. Some firms even use random drug testing to ensure that employees are drug-free. All of these uses of drug testing raise some concerns about violating employees' personal privacy rights. Court decisions have generally supported employer use of drug testing, particularly for certain high-risk safety-related jobs such as train engineer and air traffic controller. Because this area is one in which the legal and judicial requirements are evolving, it is important for employers to keep abreast of local, state, and federal court decisions and legislation.

EMPLOYEE PRIVACY.   Privacy at work can be an issue in several ways. What records are maintained on employees and who has access to them is one area.

Another is the measurement of productivity. Through such means as electronic monitoring of performance, and listening in on telephone calls to and from customers, managers can track the performance of employees. Some have suggested these practices are an unfair invasion of personal privacy and place inordinate stress on employees to work faster.

EMPLOYMENT-AT-WILL.   To protect their rights, employees have become more willing to sue their employers. Many of these suits charge that employers did not exercise "due process" when taking action against workers. These suits strike at the "employment-at-will" idea, which says that employees work at the will of the employer, and they can be released at any time for any reason or no reason at all. Workers from all fields and all organizational levels have won wrongful discharge suits, and the number of these suits is growing. One study found that over 25,000 wrongful discharge cases were pending in state and federal courts in 1989.[39]

These and other issues are examined in the following chapters. For now, it is important to keep in mind that the management of human resources in the 1990s will be different in character and more challenging than in any decade in the past because of the breadth and impact of new issues, pressures, and changes.

SUMMARY

- Shortages of human resources will be a major concern for organizations and managers during the 1990s.
- Significant change forces will impact the management of human resources from 1990 to the year 2000.
- The change forces can be categorized into: economic and employment shifts, demographic and work force shifts, changing work patterns, and changes in social values and issues.
- Economic and employment changes include the increase in global competition, shifts in employment from manufacturing to service industries, and the growth of jobs requiring higher knowledge and education levels.
- Major demographic and work force shifts affecting employers are the increasing number and percentages of women workers, the growing minority population, and the aging of the population and work force.
- Contingent workers, those who are employed as temporary or part-time workers, are a major way that organizations are staffing their jobs.
- Part-time workers can be classified as either voluntary or involuntary.
- Job sharing is a work arrangement in which two part-time workers share one full-time job.
- Work patterns and schedules have become more varied. Growing use is being made of flextime and compressed work weeks.
- Individuals in many different fields are working at home and telecommuting.
- Changes in social values and issues are affecting employers in the areas of family/work balancing and employee rights.
- Family/work balancing issues include dual-careers, child care, elder care, and the careers of women.
- Employee rights concerns include rights of both smokers and nonsmokers, substance abuse testing, employee privacy, and employment-at-will.

REVIEW AND DISCUSSION QUESTIONS

1. Discuss the following statement: "Shifts in the types of jobs and the industries in which jobs are gained or lost reflect global competition and other economic shifts that are occurring in the United States."
2. What are the major work-force-related shifts that will have an impact on organizations between now and the year 2000?
3. What are the reasons for the growth in contingent workers and alternative work schedules?
4. Of the different working patterns discussed in the chapter, (job sharing, flextime, compressed work week, etc.) which one is most appealing and which one is least appealing to you? Why?
5. Comment on the following statement: "Family/work issues and employee rights will be the dominant issues that organizations must face once individuals have been hired."

CASE	Wanted: Telemarketing Workers

One industry that has been affected by the shortage of workers is the telemarketing industry. The industry includes both firms that receive inbound calls on 800 numbers and those whose employees call out to businesses and individual consumers to sell products and services. Inbound telemarketing includes catalog orders, hotel and other travel industry reservations, product orders from cable television commercials, and many others. Outbound telemarketing often is done by service bureaus, which are firms hired to call customers to market such products as credit cards, auto club memberships, photography services, financial investments, and the like.

Generally speaking, the industry makes use of a large number of part-time employees. One reason for this is the legal restrictions that exist on calling hours for outbound telemarketing. Outbound telemarketing firms have had more difficulty hiring and retaining workers than inbound firms because calling consumers to sell product or services is less appealing than taking calls from customers who wish to buy.

The city that was the first to develop telemarketing as an industry is Omaha, Nebraska. Beginning in the early 1970s, several firms started in Omaha, and those firms have grown and spread throughout the country. In Omaha, a city of about 350,000, approximately 12,000 to 15,000 people are employed in the telemarketing industry. Some of the reasons for the growth of this industry in Omaha are:

■ Central time zone location of the city
■ Good telephone communications systems with ample room for additional lines for expansion
■ Midwestern work ethic in a relatively union-free state
■ Neutral speaking accent by most residents
■ Lower cost of living and wage structures, when compared with larger cities in the Midwest and East.

In addition to small- and medium-sized local firms, major corporations such as American Express, Marriott, and Hyatt have reservation and telemarketing centers in Omaha. Most of the workers in the industry are part-timers working fewer than

25 hours per week. The wage rates have risen over the last few years so that starting rates of $5.00 per hour for inbound telemarketers are common, and the starting wage rates for employees whose jobs require outbound calling have increased to over $6.00 per hour.

The problem faced by the industry in Omaha is simple: a shortage of workers willing to do telemarketing part-time. The telemarketing companies in Omaha are finding the competition for the same labor pool becoming severe. Some companies are adding jobs in other cities instead of Omaha. Others are considering relocating to smaller cities to find an untapped pool of part-timer workers. Those located in Omaha are having to become more aggressive in attracting and retaining workers. Some firms are paying hiring bonuses of $100 if employees complete training successfully. Others are offering tuition and up to $1,000 if employees stay with the firm for a year.

The shortage of telemarketing workers is not limited to Omaha. As the industry has grown in other cities, similar shortages have appeared. At a recent meeting of the American Telemarketing Association, over 70 percent of the telemarketing executives and managers indicated that they could increase their sales by at least 25 percent if they had enough workers.

QUESTIONS

1. How have the economic and work force changes discussed in the chapter contributed to the worker shortage in the telemarketing industry?
2. What specific suggestions to telemarketing executives would you make to aid them in locating and attracting additional workers?

NOTES

1. Many of the statistics on work force composition and trends are taken from U.S. Department of Labor, Bureau of Labor Statistics and Census Bureau data widely reported in various reference and news media sources. Other sources include *Forbes*, October 16, 1989, 138–139; *Business Week*, September 25, 1989, 91; and *USA Today*, February 6, 1989, D1.

2. Gareth Morgan, *Riding the Waves of Change* (San Francisco: Jossey–Bass Co., 1988).

3. "The 100 Largest Foreign Investments in the U.S.," *Forbes*, June 24, 1989, 313.

4. Bill Stack, "Toyota in Bluegrass Country," *Industry Week*, June 5, 1989, 30–33.

5. Nancy Yoshihara, "State's Service Sector Goes Up Scale," *Los Angeles Times*, November 21, 1988, CC 1–2.

6. U.S. Department of Labor, Bureau of Labor Statistics, *Occupational Outlook Handbook* (Washington, D.C.: U.S. Government Printing Office, 1988).

7. U.S. Census Bureau, 1989.

8. Office of Advocacy, U.S. Small Business Administration unpublished data, in *Workforce 2000* (Indianapolis: Hudson Institute, June 1987), 60.

9. Aaron Bernstein, "Where the Jobs Are Is Where the Skills Aren't," *Business Week*, September 19, 1988, 104–108.

10. "Specialists Call for 'Revolution' in Education," *Omaha World-Herald*, September 24, 1989, 1G.

11. Throughout the following section, various statistics on work force composition and trends are taken from U.S. Department of Labor, Bureau of Labor Statistics and Census Bureau data widely reported in various reference and news media reports. For additional details, pertinent issues of the *Monthly Labor Review* can be consulted, but specific reference sources are not presented.

12. Hester R. Stewart, "Job Satisfaction of Women in Nontraditional Occupations," *Journal of Employment Counseling*, March 1989, 26–34.

13. U.S. Census Bureau, 1990.

14. "The Latest Huddled Masses," *Business Week*, September 25, 1989, 106.

15. "U.S. Immigration Law Frustrates Some Firms Seeking Foreign Talent," *Omaha World-Herald*, July 9, 1989, 1G.

16. David V. Lewis, "Make Way for the Older Worker," *HR Magazine*, May 1990, 75–77.

17. "A Booming Market," *Industry Week*, August 17, 1989, 20.

18. Michael A. Verespej, "Part-Time Workers: No Temporary Phenomenon," *Industry Week*, April 3, 1989, 13.

19. Thomas J. Nardone, "Part-Time Workers: Who Are They?" *Monthly Labor Review*, February 1986, 13–19.

20. "The Flexible Work Force—What Organizations Think," *Personnel Administrator*, August, 1986, 36–39.

21. "Shorter Workweeks: An Alternative to Layoffs," *Business Week*, April 14, 1986, 77–78.

22. Adapted from Michael A. Verespej, "Care to Share?" *Industry Week*, November 6, 1989, 20–21.

23. Marilyn Elias, "Flextime Gives Employees Muscle," *USA Today*, October 11, 1989, D1.

24. Barrey Olmsted, "Flex for Success," *Personnel Journal*, June 1989, 50–55.

25. Donald C. Bacon, "Look Who's Working At Home," *Nation's Business*, October 1989, 20–31.

26. David C. Farwell and Barbara M. Farwell, "Telecommuting," *Encyclopedia of Library and Information Science 43*, Supplement 8 (1988): 202–213.

27. Joseph F. McKenna, "Have Modem, Don't Travel," *Industry Week*, November 20, 1989, 26–30.

28. Jewel Gregory, "The Spouse Seeks a Job," *National Relocation Magazine*, July 1988, 58–61.

29. "The National Report on Work and Family," (Washington, D.C.: Bureau of National Affairs, 1988).

30. "Elder-Care Benefit Is Coming of Age," *Omaha World-Herald*, June 18, 1989, 1G.

31. William Dunn, "Figures Show Altered Profile for Families," *USA Today*, September 20, 1988, 3A.

32. U.S. Census Bureau, February 1989.

33. David E. Bloom and Todd P. Steen, "Why Child Care Is Good for Business," *American Demographics*, August 1988, 22–27, 58.

34. Felice Schwartz, "The Mommy Track," *Harvard Business Review*, January/February 1989.

35. Robert J. Nobile, "Putting-Out Fires with a No-Smoking Policy, *Personnel*, March 1990, 6–10.

36. Fred Williams, "Firm's Rules Put Smokers Under Fire," *USA Today*, May 1, 1990, 1B.

37. Shelley Liles-Morris, "Drugs in the Work Place," *USA Today*, October 11, 1989, B1–2.

38. Janet Deming, "Drug-Free Workplace Is Good Business," *HR Magazine*, April 1990, 61–62.

39. Milo Geylin, "Fired Managers Winning More Lawsuits," *Wall Street Journal*, September 7, 1989, B1.

Introduction to Personnel/Human Resource Management

After you have read this chapter, you should be able to:

1. Define and clarify the two roles of P/HR management
2. Identify how P/HR professionals and managers must share P/HR responsibilities
3. Explain briefly the historical evolution of the P/HR field
4. List and define each of the eleven P/HR activities
5. Discuss P/HR management as a career field including job levels, career outlooks, and preparation

P/HR: Today *and* Tomorrow

Revitalizing the HR Department at CalComp

By 1987, it was apparent that changing the role and activities of the human resources (HR) function at CalComp was essential for the firm's future. Cal-Comp, a worldwide wholly-owned subsidiary of Lockheed Corporation, produces and sells computer graphics equipment. The company had 2,700 employees working in offices located in 14 countries. Consequently, the firm and its HR department faced problems on both the domestic and international fronts.

Employee morale was low and the HR department was viewed simply as a "traffic cop" that told employees and managers why they could not do something. It was difficult to recruit workers at corporate because the firm is located in Orange County in the Los Angeles area, which was a highly competitive labor market.

To lead the change, Charles Furniss was hired as vice president of human resources in July 1987. Furniss first called the twenty-two-person HR staff together to develop a strategic plan for the HR department. He conducted interviews with the HR staff and all top-level managers in the firm to determine what the HR department needed to do to become more "customer-focused" internally. Following the interviews, a strategic plan for the HR future for a two-year period was prepared. The plan was titled "World-Class Human Resources." Once the plan was developed and endorsed by top management, the HR staff marketed it by making presentations to employees, managers, and local professional associations in order to communicate that CalComp was going to have a progressive and responsive HR department.

Some of the initial activities taken to implement the plan included redesigning the employee publications and publishing them more frequently. Also, motivation and training services were offered to all employees in the headquarters office. One program was so successful that it was duplicated at the CalComp plant in Scottsdale, Arizona, by closing the plant for a full day so that all 250 employees could participate. Shortly after, the HR department sponsored an open house for employees to show off newly refurbished department offices and to encourage employees to meet with HR staff members. Also, management development training was expanded; over 300 managers and supervisors attended programs over a six-month period of time.

While a more active and responsive image of the HR department was being established, Furniss and his staff members moved to implement some of the other components of the World-Class Human Resources Plan by setting specific strategies, goals, and timetables for various HR activities. For instance, one goal was to reduce turnover 4 percent and recruiting costs 20 percent during 1988, both of which were accomplished. In addition, measures for assessing the performance of the HR department were set and a regular reporting process was established for five major HR areas: staffing, compensation, benefits, training and development, and employee relations.

As a result of all of those efforts, the HR department at CalComp today has a different image with employees and managers. More importantly, the HR department is playing a vital role for the corporation as it faces the challenges of the 1990s.[1]

"It is fashionable these days to give the Personnel Department a new name, such as the 'Department of Human Resources.' But a good deal more is needed than a new name."

Peter Drucker

Effective management of human resources is vital in all types and sizes of organizations and by all managers. As the opening discussion about the HR department at CalComp reveals, the progressive management of personnel/human resource activities also has strategic implications for organizational performance for the 1990s.

■■ ■ WHAT IS PERSONNEL/HUMAN RESOURCE (P/HR) MANAGEMENT?

The definition of the field of personnel/human resource management is not as easy as it might appear because the field is in such a transitional period. This transition is reflected in the problem of terminology. Neither writers and scholars nor practitioners can agree on what these departments should be called: "personnel departments" or "human resource departments." One survey of over 820 practitioners revealed that 60 percent use "human resources" as the title of the department. However, "human resources" was used more often in firms with more than 2,500 employees, whereas "personnel" was used by a majority of the employers with fewer than 100 employees.[2]

Whatever term is employed, this transition represents one of the most dramatic changes in a major organizational function in the last two decades, somewhat similar to the shift of the field of "data processing" to "management information systems." External pressures in the form of additional laws restricting the actions of employers and numerous court decisions expanding the rights of employees have forced many of the shifts. The debate over nomenclature has been an attempt to define the nature of the field. For instance, the debate over the "correct" name for the field even extends to whether the term should be "human resources management" (plural) or "human resource management" (singular).

Nature of Personnel/Human Resource Management

At the heart of the name confusion is the fact that there are two types of roles associated with the management of human resources in organizations:

■ Operational
■ Strategic

OPERATIONAL FOCUS.   Operational activities are tactical and administrative in nature. An operational emphasis is concerned with a variety of specific activities. Compliance with equal employment and other laws must be ensured, applicants must be interviewed, new employees must be oriented to the organization, supervisors must be trained, safety problems must be resolved, and wages and salaries must be administered. In short, the activities typically associated with the day-to-day management of people in organizations must be performed efficiently and appropriately. It is this collection of activities that often is referred to as "the personnel function." But that "personnel management" role is insufficient for the organizations of the 1990s.

STRATEGIC FOCUS. The strategic focus is concerned with the planning and attainment of organizational objectives with a longer-term time horizon.[3] The chief executive officer of Shell Oil Company highlights the need for the strategic focus when he says:

> The process of human resource management is an integral part of our company's strategic planning efforts. Key business plans, as well as the external environment, are considered in light of human resource implications.[4]

In the 1990s, the strategic focus is leading to an expanded role for those who manage human resources in organizations.[5] As discussed in Chapter 1, in such service industry organizations as fast-food restaurants, telemarketing communications, and computer software operations, shortages of adequately qualified help have made P/HR managers become strategic organizational planners. It is through planning and involvement with strategic issues affecting the organization that the strategic human resource dimension is added to the traditional set of personnel activities.

Figure 2–1 characterizes each focus. It illustrates that personnel management primarily is concerned with administrative and operational activities, whereas a human resource focus is strategic. However, *both facets are necessary and must exist together*. So management of human resources today has an expanded function that includes both personnel and human resource (P/HR) management. The strategic view of human resources in an organization is an integral part of overall organizational strategic planning.[6]

Figure 2–1
Human Resource Management Activities

AREA	FOCUS	MOST OFTEN REPORTS TO	TYPICAL ACTIVITIES
Human Resource Management (strategic)	Global, long-run, innovative	CEO/President	■ Human resource planning ■ Evolving legal issues ■ Work force trends and issues ■ Community economic development ■ Cost containment and benefit options ■ Employee advisory boards ■ Compensation planning and strategies
Personnel Activities (operational)	Administrative short-term maintenance	Corporate Vice President of administration	■ Recruiting and selecting ■ Conducting employee orientation ■ Reviewing safety and accident records ■ Resolving employee complaints/grievances

P/HR UNIT	MANAGERS
■ Develops legal, effective interviewing techniques ■ Trains managers in selection interviewing ■ Provides interviews and testing ■ Screens applicants and sends them to managers, who want to do final interview ■ Checks references ■ Does final interviewing and hiring for certain managers and job classifications	■ Decide whether to do own final interviewing ■ Receive interview training from P/HR unit ■ Do final interviewing and hiring where appropriate ■ Review reference information ■ Provide feedback to P/HR unit hiring/rejection decisions

Figure 2–2
The Selection Interviewing Interface Between the P/HR Unit and Other Managers

DEFINING THE FIELD.   Both roles are captured in the following definition of the field: **Personnel/human resource** (P/HR) **management** is the strategic and operational management of activities focusing on the human resources in an organization.

Throughout this text the acronym P/HR will be used. Designations such as P/HR department, P/HR professionals, and P/HR management all reflect the dual facets of personnel and human resource management.

PERSONNEL/HUMAN RESOURCE (P/HR) MANAGEMENT
is the strategic and operational management of activities focusing on the human resources in an organization.

Managing Personnel/Human Resource Activities

As an applied field, P/HR management requires the use of judgment and intuition to know what actions to take, based on prior experience or research in various situations. At the same time, the view often held by those outside the field that a "concern for people" is all that is necessary for success in P/HR matters is inadequate. The importance of having a strategic focus on human resource management expands the demands placed on professionals in the field. Unfortunately, many practitioners are not performing the strategic role of human resource management, partly because of individual limitations and partly because of top management's lack of desire for an expanded P/HR role.

SHARING P/HR RESPONSIBILITIES.   Cooperation among people who specialize in P/HR management and other managers is critical to organizational success.[7] This cooperation requires contact, or **interface,** between the two groups. These points of contact represent the "boundaries" that determine who does what in the various P/HR activities. In all organizations, decisions must be made to manage the "people-related" activities; they cannot be left to chance. P/HR staff and other managers must have a *situational perspective* that blends research and theories from the behavioral sciences with intuition and experience when making decisions about the problems faced by people in organizations. For example, Figure 2–2 illustrates how some of the responsibilities in the process of selection interviewing might be divided between the P/HR unit and other managers.

Clearly, P/HR management is a concern of *both* the managers *and* the P/HR unit in an organization, and the P/HR managers must train other managers on performing P/HR activities effectively.[8] The division of various P/HR responsibilities is outlined in each chapter, illustrating P/HR responsibilities in an area and who typically performs what portion of them. However, these illustrations are not attempts to indicate "the one way" all organizations should perform P/HR activities,

INTERFACES
are areas of contact between the P/HR unit and managers within the organization.

but only how these activities can be divided. For example, in one medium-sized bank, all new nonmanagement employees are hired by the P/HR department. In another equally successful company, applicants are screened by the P/HR department, but the new employees actually are selected by the supervisors for whom they will work.

Ethics and P/HR Management

As the issues faced by P/HR managers have increased in number and complexity, so have the pressures and challenges of acting ethically. Ethical issues in P/HR management are ones that pose fundamental questions about fairness, justice, truthfulness, and social responsibility.[9] As a result of numerous news media reports, valid concerns have been raised about the ethical standards used in organizations, particularly business organizations.

WHAT IS ETHICAL BEHAVIOR?   Ethics deals with what "ought" to be done. For the P/HR manager, this means that there are ethical ways in which a manager "ought" to act relative to human resource issues and decisions. But specifically *how* one should act is not always clear. There is apparently no *single* guideline to channel decisions in ethical directions. Perhaps the closest to a general guideline is "deal with people honestly," a general ethic of truth. But even that is not always clear, because frank and direct comments may not be kind or even beneficial in all cases.

Ethics involves motivation and behavior. Motivation deals with why an action was taken. Behavior deals with consequences of that motivation as it affects others. For a decision to have ethical implications, two elements must be present: (1) an *intent* to act and (2) the potential for *harm* to someone.

The Greek philosopher Aristotle said that only two factors diminish the responsibility to act in an ethical manner. If we are truly ignorant of the consequences of our actions, we are certainly not as responsible as if we *know* someone would be hurt and continued to act anyway. Second, if we have no capacity to behave in any other way, our responsibility is limited. For example, if we are truly powerless to change a situation, ethical responsibility cannot be placed at our doorstep. The complete study of ethics is philosophical, complex, and beyond the scope of this book. The intent here is to provide some basic guidelines and highlight the ethical aspects of P/HR management.

ETHICAL ISSUES IN P/HR MANAGEMENT.   Some of the ethical issues that P/HR managers must face were mentioned in Chapter 1, such as how much information on employees should be retained. But there are many others that must be addressed, such as the following:

- How much information on a problem employee should be given or withheld from another potential employer?
- Should an employment manager check credit agency records on applicants, but not disclose those checks to the individuals?
- What obligations are owed a long-term employee who has become an ineffective performer because of changes in the job skills required?
- What impact should an employee's personal lifestyle have on promotion decisions if work performance has been satisfactory?
- Should employees who smoke be forced to stop smoking when new no-smoking restrictions are implemented by an employer?

■ How much accommodation should be made for employees with family problems that affect their work performance?

■ Should an otherwise qualified applicant be refused employment because a dependent child has major health problems, which would raise the employer's insurance costs?

These and many other situations pose both ethical and legal questions in which there may be a variety of conflicting facts, concerns, and options. With P/HR management in an international environment, other ethical pressures arise. Such practices as gift giving and hiring practices vary in other countries, but some of those practices would not be accepted as ethical in the United States. Consequently, all managers in the 1990s, including P/HR managers, must be sensitive to ethical issues and how they interplay with P/HR activities. Throughout the text ethical issues are discussed in boxed features.

■■ ■ PERSONNEL/HUMAN RESOURCE MANAGEMENT IN ORGANIZATIONS

P/HR management as a specialized field of study, and research on work in organizations has evolved since its beginning about 1900. Today it is undergoing significant changes also. To understand those changes, a historical review is useful.

Evolution of P/HR Management

Figure 2–3 highlights the major shifts that have occurred in the field. Before 1900, improving the working life of individuals was a major concern of reformers. Some employees attempted to start unions or strike for improved conditions. As far back as 1786, the Philadelphia Cordwainers (shoemakers) went on strike to obtain a $6 per week minimum wage.

P/HR management as a specialized function in organizations began its formal emergence shortly before 1900. Before that time most hiring, firing, training, and pay adjustment decisions were made by individual supervisors. Some organizations adopted programs to benefit some employees, such as American Express which established a pension plan in 1875. Also, the Scientific Management studies conducted by Frederick. W. Taylor and others, beginning in 1885, helped management identify ways to make work more efficient and less fatiguing, thus increasing worker productivity.

As organizations grew larger, many managerial functions such as purchasing and personnel begun to be performed by specialists. The first employment agents were hired by B. F. Goodrich Company in 1900. Some firms offered English language classes to their many immigrant workers. Also, because many employees lived in tenements in crowded, unsanitary conditions, health and social workers were hired to help and instruct employees in good hygiene practices.[10] Concerns about unsafe working conditions and child labor led to the enactment of some state laws protecting workers beginning in 1908. Some corporations hired specialists to interpret the laws and ensure compliance.

The growth of organizations also led to the establishment of the first personnel departments about 1910. Work by individuals such as Frank and Lillian Gilbreth dealt with task design and efficiency. The Hawthorne Studies, conducted by Elton Mayo in the mid-1920s, revealed the impact of work groups on individual workers.

Figure 2–3
Changing Concerns of P/HR Management

TIME PERIOD	SUBJECT OF PRIMARY CONCERN TO MANAGEMENT	MANAGERIAL PERCEPTIONS OF EMPLOYEES	P/HR ACTIVITIES
Before 1890	Production technologies	Indifference to needs	Discipline systems
1890 to 1910	Employee welfare	Employees need safe conditions and opportunity	Safety programs, English language classes, inspirational programs
1910 to 1920	Task efficiency	Need high earnings made possible with higher productivity	Motion and time studies
1920 to 1930	Individual differences	Employees' individual differences considered	Psychological testing, employee counseling
1930 to 1940	Unionization	Employees as management adversaries	Employee communication programs, anti-unionization techniques
1940 to 1950	Economic security	Employees need economic protection	Employee pension plans, health plans, fringe benefits (pensions, etc.)
1950 to 1960	Human relations	Employees need considerate supervision	Foremen training (role playing, sensitivity training)
1960 to 1970	Participation	Employees need involvement in task decisions	Participative management techniques (MBO, etc.)
1970 to 1980	Task challenge	Employees need work that is challenging and congruent with abilities	Job enrichment, integrated task teams, etc.
1980 to 1990	Employee displacement	Employees need jobs—lost through economic downturns, international competition, and technological changes	Outplacement, retraining, restructuring
1990 to 2000	Work force changes and shortages	Employees need more flexibility in schedules, benefits, policies	Strategic HR planning, employee rights, training, flexible benefits, computerization, etc.

SOURCE: Adapted from Stephen J. Carroll and Randall S. Schuler, "Professional HRM: Changing Functions and Problems," in *Human Resources Management in the 1980s*, edited by Stephen J. Carroll and Randall S. Schuler (Washington D.C.: Bureau of National Affairs, 1983), 8–10. Used with permission.

Ultimately, these studies led to the development and use of employee counseling and testing in industry.

In the 1930s the passage of several major labor laws, such as the National Labor Relations Act of 1935, led to the growth of unions. The importance of collective bargaining and union–management relations following the labor unions' rise to power in the 1940s and 1950s expanded the responsibilities of the personnel area in many organizations, especially those in manufacturing, utilities, and transportation. Such work as keeping payroll and retirement records, arranging stockholder visits, managing school relations, and organizing company picnics were often the major tasks of personnel departments. The role of the P/HR department in the organization as a staff function to support operational (line) departments (discussed later in this chapter) started during this period, and line–staff issues grew to influence P/HR departments in the following decades.

Increased legal requirements and constraints arising from the social legislation of the 1960s and 1970s forced dramatic changes in the P/HR departments of most organizations. P/HR departments had to become much more professional and more concerned about the legal ramifications of policies and practices. Also, organizations took a new look at employee involvement and quality of work as a result of concerns about the impact of automation and job design on worker productivity.

With the advent of the 1980s, the strategic role of P/HR management became essential as organizations reduced staff, closed plants, or "restructured," often because of economic pressures and the need to remain competitive. The ability of foreign firms from Japan, Korea, and other countries to outsell U.S.-based manufacturing companies forced U.S. organizations to become "lean and mean."

During the 1980s P/HR management turned to issues raised by the wave of mergers and acquisitions of firms. Common problems during a merger or acquisition included how to combine the benefits of the two companies into one coordinated plan, how to restructure departments, how to determine which employees would be offered relocation or have their jobs eliminated, and many others. Outplacement of employees and retraining of those kept became prime concerns of P/HR departments. Also, containment of P/HR costs such as health-care costs became more important.

For the 1990s, it appears that one major area of emphasis in P/HR management will be dealing with the shifting work force composition (as discussed in Chapter 1) and the shortages of workers caused by those shifts. Also, computerization of P/HR activities, even in small firms, will continue to receive attention. Finally, the growth of employee rights issues such as drug testing and smoking restriction will affect how P/HR activities are managed. All these changes, and others, reflect the exciting nature of the field.

P/HR Management as an Organizational Function

As an organization grows so does the need for a separate P/HR department. One survey of 433 organizations examined the number of P/HR departmental employees for every 100 workers in an organization.[11] The survey also revealed differences in the number of P/HR unit employees by industry. The average bank/finance industry organizations have more P/HR unit employees per 100 workers than nonbusiness or health-care organizations, for example. Organizations with fewer than 250 employees have a higher average of P/HR unit employees per worker (1.8 per 100 workers) than larger organizations. As might be expected, the number of P/HR unit employees needed to serve 200 employees is not significantly different from the number needed to serve 300 or 400 employees. The same activities simply must be provided for more people.

The cost of having a P/HR department is greater in organizations with fewer than 250 employees, as Figure 2-4 shows. For those firms, the P/HR departmental budgetary medians are 3.5 percent of total payroll and benefit costs, but for large firms (over 1,000 employees) the median drops to 1.8 percent of total payroll. An interesting finding is that 29 percent of the organizations surveyed do not have a

EMPLOYER SIZE	MEDIAN TOTAL P/HR STAFF PER 100 EMPLOYEES	MEDIAN COST PER EMPLOYEE
Up to 250 employees	1.8	$1,235
250–499 employees	1.2	918
500–999 employees	.8	688
1,000–2,499 employees	.8	569
2,500 or more employees	.8	415

SOURCE: Adapted from SHRM–BNA Survey #54 "Personnel Human Resources Department: 1989–1990," *Bulletin to Management,* June 28, 1990.

Figure 2–4
Costs of the P/HR Function

Figure 2–5
Functional Organization Chart

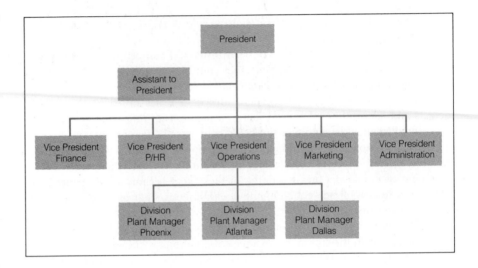

separate P/HR budget,[12] which may mean that P/HR activities are budgeted with another department, that the organization does not have a formal budget, or that the organization does not see the P/HR function as a separate entity.

In a growing number of organizations, some specialty activities are being contracted to outside providers and consultants. For example, one firm with 1,500 employees has many processing activities related to employee benefits performed by a service bureau instead of hiring two full-time benefits technicians. Likewise, temporary help firms can provide recruiting, selection, and training for temporary or "leased" employees.

Once a P/HR department is established, it takes its place along with other departments in the organization. Figure 2–5 contains a simplified organization chart for a typical manufacturing firm. Notice that the P/HR unit is only one of other functional entities. One of these entities is the line part of the organization, while others are staff in nature.

LINE FUNCTION
generally is the operating branch of the organization or that part directly concerned with producing the product or service.

STAFF FUNCTIONS
refer to people or positions that provide an advisory, control, or support role to the organization.

LINE AND STAFF.   The traditional distinction between line and staff refers to types of work performed and to the assignment and type of *authority*, which gives someone the right to use resources to accomplish goals. The **line function** generally is the operating branch of the organization or that part directly concerned with producing the product or service.

Staff functions commonly refer to people or positions that provide an advisory, control, or support role to the organization. In Figure 2–5 the president, vice president of operations, and division plant managers make up the line organization, while the others are staff units. It is important to note that the titles associated with line or staff may vary from organization to organization, depending on the primary business of the organization.

The type of authority that line and staff have varies. *Line authority* gives someone the right to make decisions and command subordinates. This type of authority is more superior–subordinate related. The traditional view of *staff authority* is that it is advisory in nature. Consequently, staff gives advice or assists line managers, but staff people do not command and direct line managers to follow their advice.

Typically, line officials consult staff people for their expertise when a decision is to be made. The real authority or influence of a staff department emerges from its ability to make worthwhile and significant contributions to solving the problems facing line employees.

Traditionally, the P/HR unit was seen as a staff function. Its role was to support and advise line managers, but it could not command their actions. However, that view has changed greatly because P/HR specialists have the responsibility to enforce compliance with equal employment regulations, wage and hour laws, and many other externally imposed concerns. Thus, in many organizations the P/HR specialists are given *functional authority* to make P/HR decisions affecting legal issues and others. For example, if a manager is sexually harassing an employee, the P/HR department can tell the manager to cease or disciplinary action will result.

Consequently, the line–staff dichotomy is a fuzzy one that is becoming less clear as organizations adapt to rapid changes. Although the P/HR unit may still perform some advisory and supportive staff activities, the P/HR management role is operationally integral to the organization.[13]

Centralized versus Decentralized P/HR Departments

How P/HR activities are coordinated and structured varies considerably from organization to organization. Some organizations have centralized P/HR departments, whereas these departments are decentralized in other organizations.

Centralization and **decentralization** are the end points on a continuum. Organizations are seldom totally centralized or decentralized. The degree to which authority to make P/HR decisions is concentrated or dispersed determines the amount of decentralization that exists. With centralization, decision-making authority/responsibility is concentrated upward in the organization; whereas with decentralization, decision-making authority/responsibility is distributed downward throughout the organization.

How large a P/HR staff is or should be or the extent of centralization or decentralization of P/HR decision-making in organizations is determined by such factors as size of the organization, management style of the executives, geographic location, industry patterns, extent of unionization, and others.[14]

CENTRALIZATION is the extent to which decision-making authority/responsibility is concentrated upward in the organization.

DECENTRALIZATION is the extent to which decision-making authority/responsibility is dispersed downward through the organization.

■■ ■ PERSONNEL/HUMAN RESOURCE MANAGEMENT ACTIVITIES

The preceding discussion of P/HR management has focused on defining the field and placing it in an organizational context. With those areas as background, the specific activities that compose P/HR management can be examined.

Figure 2–6 shows that P/HR management is affected by a number of different external environmental forces. These forces impact all organizations. Beginning at the top of the figure, the major activities comprising the management of human resources are:

- Strategic human resource planning
- Equal employment opportunity compliance
- Job analysis
- Staffing (recruitment and selection)
- Training and development
- Performance appraisal
- Compensation and benefits
- Health and safety
- Employee relations
- Union relations
- HR information and assessment systems

Figure 2–6
P/HR Management Activities

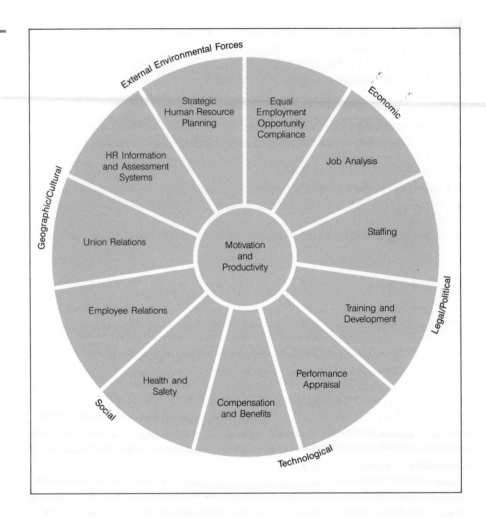

Strategic human resource planning identifies external forces and changes and their impact on the organization, and then responds to them. Equal employment compliance is also a major activity. The remaining activities are those that require significant administrative and operational efforts. At the core are employee motivation and productivity, the twin dimensions to which all other P/HR activities are directed. The nature of motivation and its impact on job satisfaction, turnover, absenteeism, and job design are examined in Chapter 4. The P/HR activities and their scope and significance are discussed next.

Strategic Human Resource Planning

Through human resource planning, the management of human resources becomes a top-level, strategic concern. The overall strategic planning process in an organization attempts to anticipate changes and their effects on the organization. Given all of the demographic and other changes discussed in Chapter 1, the importance of *human resource planning* in preparing an organization for the future will increase.

Only by anticipating the future needs for employees and developing specific human resource plans to obtain the appropriate number and types of employees can organizations meet the future with a reasonable expectation of success. Strategic human resource planning is examined in Chapter 3.

Equal Employment Compliance

Managers and organizations today face an expanding and shifting array of governmental rules and regulations that require employers to provide equal employment opportunity (EEO) for many different groups. Beginning with an initial focus on racial discrimination, EEO regulations now include women, people over age 40, disabled individuals, and many other groups.

Equal employment compliance affects all other P/HR activities. For instance, when strategic human resource plans are made, one component must be how to have sufficient availability of protected group individuals to meet *affirmative action* requirements. In addition, when recruiting, selecting, and training individuals, all managers must be aware of EEO requirements. Other P/HR activities are affected likewise by EEO concerns. The nature of EEO and implementation processes for equal employment compliance are discussed in Chapters 5 and 6.

Job Analysis

Job analysis focuses on a job as a unit of work. It is the most basic P/HR activity because it is the foundation for so many other P/HR efforts. From job analysis information, *job descriptions* and *job specifications* can be prepared. They are used in recruiting and selecting employees, in orienting new employees, and in appraising how well employees are fulfilling the identified job requirements and expectations. In addition, comprehensive analyses of jobs are used in establishing pay systems. The basic activity of job analysis is discussed in Chapter 7.

Staffing

Staffing concerns the recruitment and selection of human resources for an organization. *Recruiting* precedes the actual selection of people for positions in organizations. Choosing the best person for the job involves the use of such data sources as *application blanks, interviews, tests, background investigations,* and *physical examinations.* All managers have to staff their jobs with people in ways that are compatible with current legal and social expectations. Staffing activities are discussed in Chapters 8 and 9.

Training and Development

Training and development includes the *orientation* of new employees, the *training* of employees to perform their jobs, and the *retraining* of employees as their job requirements change. Encouraging the *development* and *growth* of employees and managers is another aspect.

Assessment of training needs, training evaluation, career planning, and *management development* are growing activities. It is estimated that employers in a recent year spent over $5 billion on training and development of employees. Large companies with over 5,000 employees annually budgeted for training and development an average of $521,300; medium-sized firms (500–5,000 employees), $234,000; and smaller firms, with fewer than 500 employees, $92,400.[15]

But with training costs increasing, management wants to know whether it is receiving at least a dollar's worth of benefit for every dollar spent in training. Consequently, P/HR staff members must be able to evaluate training effectiveness. Activities associated with training and development are examined in Chapters 10 and 11.

Performance Appraisal

Performance appraisal assesses how well employees are doing their jobs. Appraisals are useful in making compensation decisions, in specifying areas in which additional training and development of employees is needed, and in making placement decisions.

Managers in many organizations do not do an effective job of conducting performance appraisals, for a variety of reasons. But appraisals often are needed as evidence in equal employment and termination disputes that end up in court. In addition, more effective ways to relate performance appraisals to pay are necessary to establish true "pay-for-performance" systems. Appraisal of employees is examined in Chapter 12.

Compensation and Benefits

Compensation rewards people through *pay, incentives,* and *benefits* for performing work within the organization. Organizations must develop and refine their basic wage and salary systems to ensure that pay-for-performance policies are followed. Other employers have been experimenting with new ideas, such as holding employee base pay steady but giving merit raises as lump-sum bonuses.

The rapid increase in benefit costs, especially for health-related benefits, will continue to be a major issue. Changing lifestyles and increased governmental pressures are leading to new and improved benefit options for employees. One trend to watch is the use of *flexible benefit systems* within organizations, which offer employees more options in using their benefit dollars. Compensation and benefit activities are discussed in Chapters 13, 14, and 15.

Health and Safety

The physical and mental health and safety of employees are vital concerns. The Occupational Safety and Health Act of 1970 (OSHA) has made organizations more responsive to *health and safety* concerns. The traditional concern for *safety* has focused on eliminating accidents and injuries at work. Newer concerns are *health* issues arising from hazardous work with certain chemicals and other possibly harmful substances, largely in response to OSHA regulations and management's increasing awareness of its social responsibilities to its employees and the general public.

Through a broader focus on health, management can assist employees with substance abuse and other problems through *employee assistance programs* (EAP) in order to retain otherwise satisfactory employees. Employee *wellness programs* to promote good health and exercise are becoming more widespread. Health and safety activities are examined in Chapter 16.

Employee Relations

The formal relationship between employees and their employers must be managed for the benefit of both. To facilitate good employee relations, it is important to develop and communicate P/HR *policies and rules* so that managers and employees alike know what is expected, as well as to update these policies and rules. Concerns about *employee rights* and *privacy protection* must be incorporated into policies and practices. Issues of drug testing, honesty testing, and workplace rights of smokers and nonsmokers are faced by many managers and organizations. All these issues are examined in Chapter 17.

Union Relations

Union-related activities are important because they affect employees, managers, and the performance of many P/HR activities. Contact between a union and an employer occurs at two levels. At the formal organizational level, the union is the agent representing a group of employees in an organization. After successful *union organizing* of workers in a firm, a labor contract must be negotiated through union–organization discussion and *collective bargaining*—a process in which behavioral considerations play a vital role. At another level, a continuing union–organization relationship focuses on *grievance management* to address individual grievances that arise during the term of the labor agreement. Legal requirements and other facets of union–management relations are discussed in Chapters 18 and 19.

HR Information and Assessment Systems

Information, communications, and research systems are vital to the coordination of P/HR activities. The development and use of computerized *human resource information systems* are necessary for P/HR departments to do better record keeping and P/HR research. Creating and maintaining P/HR data bases and systems are critical aspects of the strategic role of P/HR management.[16] Employers use various methods to keep employees informed about organizational developments and policies. Upward communication through suggestion systems is an appealing strategy for a growing number of employers.

Measuring P/HR effectiveness is done by evaluating how well P/HR activities are being performed in an organization. Various means can be used, ranging from attitude surveys to formal HR audits.[17]

P/HR activities take place in varied organizational environments. There are some differences associated with managing human resources in small-sized, public sector, and international organizations. Chapters 20 and 21 examine these areas.

■■■ PERSONNEL/HUMAN RESOURCE MANAGEMENT AS A CAREER FIELD

Effective management of human resource activities requires professionals. As the activities become more and more important, the demands placed on individuals who make the P/HR field their career specialty will increase.

Figure 2-7
P/HR Generalists and Specialists

GENERALISTS	SPECIALISTS
Vice President of Personnel	Employment Manager
Human Resources Director	Training Director
Director of Industrial Relations	Compensation Analyst
Personnel Assistant	Benefits Clerk
Personnel Clerk	Job Analyst
Personnel Technician	Personnel Interviewer
Employee Relations Administrator	Labor Relations Specialist
Personnel Representative	EEO/Affirmative Action Coordinator
Corporate Personnel Director	Human Resource Information Systems Specialist
	Safety Coordinator
	Career Planning Specialist
	Testing Technician
	College Recruiter
	Pension/ERISA Compliance Manager

Types of P/HR Jobs

The levels of P/HR jobs range from executive to clerical.[18] Here are some examples of each level:

- Executive: vice president of human resources, personnel director
- Managerial: employment manager, personnel manager
- Technical/specialist: job analyst, interviewer, benefits specialist
- Clerical: personnel clerk, personnel secretary

A wide variety of jobs can be performed in P/HR departments. The common job titles listed in Figure 2–7 illustrate the number of areas in which career P/HR professionals can work. There are job opportunities in specific P/HR areas and for P/HR generalists who are knowledgeable in several areas.

P/HR GENERALIST
is a person with responsibility for performing a variety of activities.

P/HR GENERALISTS.   As a firm grows large enough to need someone to focus primarily on P/HR activities, the role of the P/HR generalist emerges. A person who has responsibility for performing a variety of P/HR activities is a **P/HR generalist.**

Generalists may be specialists who entered the P/HR field and have "grown up" with a company. Or they may be individuals who transferred into the field from some other area such as sales, accounting, or operations. Regardless of background, generalists must maintain an adequate knowledge of numerous activities as P/HR programs become more complex. As the duties of the generalist increase, so does the need for specialists to support the generalists.

P/HR SPECIALIST
is a person with in-depth knowledge and expertise in a limited area.

P/HR SPECIALISTS.   Individuals who have in-depth knowledge and expertise in a limited area are **P/HR specialists.** Intensive knowledge of an activity such as benefits, testing, training, or affirmative action compliance typifies the work of P/HR specialists. Because of the in-depth knowledge required of specialists, they may need to have advanced education in a specialty area.

Growth in organization size and complexity is one factor contributing to the need for specialists. Another is the proliferation of laws and regulations affecting

P/HR activities. Consider a midwestern telemarketing firm which started in 1975 with 5 employees. By 1980, the firm had 80 employees, and had hired a recent college graduate to manage recruiting, employee benefits, and personnel record keeping. That P/HR manager added staff to her own department and many others until, by 1984, the P/HR department had recruited, selected, and trained almost 200 employees out of the firm's 260 employees. By then the P/HR director had a staff of 5 people, including a full-time employment specialist, a compensation–benefits specialist, and a training specialist. By 1990, the firm had 500 employees, a P/HR staff of 6, and a human resources vice president. Except for the director (now promoted to vice president), a generalist by virtue of her growth with the firm, the others in the department were specialists.

Career Outlook

The number of P/HR jobs has increased as the field has grown in importance. Projections made by the U.S. Bureau of Labor Statistics indicate that P/HR jobs will grow through the mid-1990s about as fast as the average for all occupations.[19] Most P/HR job needs will be in the private sector. Even though the number of jobs in the field will increase some, most job openings will be for replacements. An abundant supply of candidates is foreseen. Consequently, entry into the field will be very competitive and salary levels likely will not increase significantly because of a plentiful supply of qualified experienced workers and the growing number of college-trained graduates.

Salaries

P/HR salary levels, as do the salary patterns in other fields, vary by geographic area, educational level, and experience. Individuals in large metropolitan areas generally are more highly paid. Having some international P/HR responsibilities often leads to higher salaries at managerial and executive levels. The educational level of a P/HR professional also affects salary. Finally, there is a direct relationship between experience and pay, especially at managerial- and executive-level positions.

Top P/HR jobs in manufacturing organizations generally pay more than those in nonmanufacturing organizations. As would be expected, P/HR practitioners in small organizations generally are paid less than their counterparts in large organizations.

Career Factors

P/HR management as a career field is highlighted in the P/HR: Research discussion. The results of that study should be kept in mind when thinking about a career in P/HR.

"Liking to work with people" as the major qualification necessary for success in P/HR is one of the greatest myths about the field. This simplistic view glosses over the technical knowledge and education needed. Depending on the job, P/HR professionals must have some knowledge about tax laws, finance, statistics, and computers. Extensive knowledge about equal employment regulations, wage and want to succeed in the field must work at preparing themselves educationally by continually updating their knowledge. Reading P/HR publications, such as those listed in Appendix A, is another way to update P/HR knowledge.

P/HR: Practice *and* Research

P/HR Career Tracks

One of the ways to assess a career field is to examine the career tracks of individuals already in it. Fortunately, a study sponsored by Right Associates, a human resource management consulting firm, gives some perspectives for individuals considering P/HR management as a career field.

A survey of approximately 800 P/HR professionals was conducted at a national convention of the American Society for Personnel Administration (now called Society for Human Resource Management). The pattern of respondents closely reflected the actual membership profile of ASPA at the time.

Senior human resource managers/executives who were members of the society made up 38 percent of survey respondents. Of the remaining nonmanagers, 36 percent indicated that they were human resource generalists, another 19 percent responded that they were human resource specialists of one kind or another, and 9 percent placed themselves in the "other" category. Almost one third of the survey respondents (30 percent) worked for very large organizations, employing over

5,000 employees. An almost equal number (28 percent) worked for small organizations (less than 500 employees). Almost half of the survey respondents had been in the P/HR field more than ten years. Over half of the respondents also had more than five years' experience with their current employer.

Males represented 55 percent of the respondents and females 45 percent. There were major differences in responses between males and females answering the survey. Women tended to work for smaller employers, were less likely to be managers, and had less experience as human resource professionals than the male respondents. As a result, the compensation level of women respondents was found to be lower than that of the male respondents. The median salary for the women in the survey was $39,100; for the men it was $52,500.

Some of the findings are of special interest to those thinking of P/HR as a career. The decision to enter the human resource field was a conscious one for the majority of respondents. Those entering the field right out of college numbered 27 percent,

while another 40 percent entered through a self-directed career change. Also, 27 percent entered the field through a company-initiated action such as job rotation or transfer into the field. When asked about the factors that influence advancement in their companies, survey respondents indicated that the top five criteria were *job performance, credibility with senior management, interpersonal skills, ability to manage,* and *skill in a specialty.*

Only one-third of the respondents reported that they were very satisfied that their current employers would be able to meet their career needs. Of those who were somewhat or very dissatisfied with their employers' ability to meet their career needs (24 percent of the total respondents), almost 70 percent reported that they were searching for another position.

Although research on other professional fields might find similar concerns, the results of this study should be reviewed by anyone seriously considering a career in P/HR management. The salary levels, types of organizations, satisfactions, and frustrations all must be weighed.[20]

EDUCATIONAL PREPARATION.   The breadth of issues and activities faced by professionals in the field requires that they be well educated in a broad range of business and other topics. Experts have suggested knowledge in three areas, with special emphasis in the fields noted:

1. General education: English, mathematics, psychology, social sciences
2. Business core: accounting, finance, computers, marketing, economics, business law, statistics, operations management
3. Personnel/human resource management: P/HR management, labor law, human behavior, compensation administration, collective bargaining, industrial psychology

A study of 173 P/HR professionals who were asked to identify their majors and the specific P/HR courses they had taken showed that P/HR management, general management, and general business were the three most frequent majors. As would be expected, an introduction to P/HR management was the most frequently taken course. Courses focusing on the behavioral aspects of management were two of the top four courses identified.[21]

As P/HR has become more professionalized, many colleges and universities have developed undergraduate degree programs in P/HR management. Also, graduate degrees in P/HR management have become more prevalent. Relevant graduate degrees (M.B.A., M.S., M.A.) are offered in a variety of departments within colleges and universities.

EXPERIENCE.   Although about one-fourth of the individuals enter the P/HR field directly from schools, P/HR is not a career field that is as easily entered as are other fields. Individuals with experience in other jobs and areas in the organization who have interests in P/HR management are often selected to move into the P/HR jobs. Results of one survey found that present employees in an organization are more likely to have an advantage in obtaining entry-level P/HR jobs than individuals with only college preparation.[22] Those sincerely interested in P/HR management as a career field should obtain some experience in a P/HR department while in college, even if it is clerical in nature. Part-time jobs, summer internships, or other means can help individuals gain experience.

PROFESSIONAL INVOLVEMENT.   As with many other professions, interaction with other professionals is critical. It is possible to be a member and participate in a variety of professional associations in the P/HR field.

To reflect the transitions in the field, the leading professional association changed its name from the American Society for Personnel Administration (ASPA) to the Society for Human Resource Management (SHRM). Among the approximately 40,000 members of SHRM are both P/HR generalists and specialists, but a majority are generalists from private sector firms. Opportunities for involvement are nationwide: SHRM has over 400 professional chapters and more than 250 student chapters throughout the United States.

There are a number of other organizations that are more specialized. For example, the International Personnel Management Association (IPMA), an organization with both generalists and specialists, is made up mostly of members from public sector organizations. For various P/HR specialties there are organizations such as the American Compensation Association (ACA), the American Society for Training and Development (ASTD), and Employment Management Association (EMA). Also, many industries have P/HR management associations. If you are interested in contacting any of these organizations, you can locate the addresses in Appendix B.

CERTIFICATION.   One of the characteristics of a professional field is having a means to certify the knowledge and competence of members of the profession. The C.P.A. for accountants and the C.L.U. for life insurance underwriters are well-known examples. Through the Human Resource Certification Institute, affiliated with SHRM, P/HR generalists can obtain basic- or senior-level certification, as described in the accompanying P/HR Practice.

Other professional associations in specialized areas of P/HR also have developed certification programs. For example, compensation professionals can become accredited or certified through programs offered by the American Compensation Association (ACA). Addresses for these entities are available in Appendix B.

P/HR: Practice *and* Research

Human Resource Certification Institute

One characteristic of a profession is some type of program for certifying professional knowledge and competence. Because P/HR management as a profession is much younger and less defined than many, certification is not as widely used. Nevertheless, a program that certifies P/HR professional competence is available through the Human Resource Certification Institute (HRCI), which is affiliated with SHRM. Over 7,000 P/HR professionals have become certified through the institute program since its beginnings in 1972. Although some changes and refinements in the program have been necessary, the current certification program has met with growing acceptance. The program is two-tier: basic certification of Professional in Human Resource (*PHR*) and advanced certification as a Senior Professional in Human Resources (*SPHR*).

Special provisions are available for college students. Degree candidates and recent college graduates may take the basic-level examination even though they currently do not meet the work experience requirements. If they pass the examination, they receive a letter certifying examination results. Then they have three years in which to complete the specific experience requirements to earn certification. Full certification is granted as soon as they submit evidence of meeting the work experience requirements.

All certified individuals must demonstrate that they have continued their professional learning and competence by meeting recertification requirements every three years. For information on P/HR certification, contact the Human Resource Certification Institute, 606 North Washington St., Alexandria, VA 22314 (703-548-3440).

SUMMARY

- Successful management of human resources is essential to organizational success. The field has expanded to include both human resource management and personnel management.
- P/HR management is the strategic and operational management of activities focusing on the human resources in an organization.
- A sharing of P/HR responsibilities between the P/HR manager and an operating manager creates an interface on P/HR activities.
- Ethical issues in P/HR management have proliferated, and must be faced in all types and sizes of organizations.
- P/HR management over the past 100 years has paralleled general social changes and has evolved into a complex and multifaceted field.
- P/HR management traditionally has been viewed as a staff function, but its operational role has been increasing.
- P/HR departments can be highly centralized or decentralized, depending on size, management philosophy, geographic dispersion, and industry differences.
- The activities focusing on the effective management of human resources in an organization are *strategic human resource planning, equal employment opportunity compliance, job analysis, staffing, training and development, appraisal, compensation, health and safety, employee relations, unions,* and *HR information and assessment systems.*

- P/HR jobs can be grouped into clerical, technical, specialty, managerial, and executive levels.
- P/HR departments are composed of generalists and specialists. A generalist has broad knowledge of a number of P/HR activities, whereas a specialist has intensive knowledge of a limited set of activities.
- Salaries in the P/HR field differ by job level and type, industry and size, regional area, educational background, and experience.
- Preparation for a career in P/HR management includes broad and specialized education, experience, professional involvement, and certification.

REVIEW AND DISCUSSION QUESTIONS

1. What are the two major roles of P/HR management and why are both necessary in organizations?
2. Discuss why the concepts of line and staff have become less significant as P/HR departments have evolved.
3. Discuss the changing issues and emphases in P/HR management over the last 100 years.
4. What are the eleven major sets of P/HR activities and how could you describe them?
5. Would P/HR management be a possible career field for you? Why or why not?

CASE | Progressive P/HR Management Pays Off

Many organizations recognize the importance of personnel/human resource management. At least in theory, firms with better P/HR practices should see some payoffs in their financial and operating results. It was such a link that Dr. Dennis Kravetz found through research on the 500 largest publicly held U.S. corporations.

Kravetz developed an "HR Progressiveness Index" to give each of the 150 responding firms a score. Each firm answered a questionnaire that described its current practices in each of the fifty areas of HR activities that were identified as "leading edge." Examples of those areas include:

- Communications progressiveness
- Company culture emphasizing people
- Participative management style
- Emphasis on workplace creativity and excellence
- Extent of career development and training
- Effective ways to maximize employee job satisfaction
- Extent of recognition and rewards for good performance
- Use of flextime, at-home work, and part-time employment
- Degree of flatness and decentralization of the management structure

The HR index was computer scored based on the responses of each firm. The ten firms with the highest HR progressiveness scores were as follows:

Company	HR "Progressiveness Score"
IBM	211
Tandem Computers	207
Tektronix	204
American Medical International	195
Rockwell International	194
General Mills	193
Merck	192
Perkin–Elmer	191
Hospital Corporation of America	189
3M	188

Once these HR index scores had been computed, Kravetz compared each firm's index with financial performance as reported in financial statements in the firm's annual reports. The HR index was correlated with eight different financial measures over a five-year period. The analyses showed that the highly progressive firms had significantly higher annualized growth in sales profits, equity, earnings per share, and dividends.

In summary, this research effort indicated that having "progressive" P/HR practices and activities was strongly related to organizational financial performance and success. As Kravetz says, "A company that is high in human resources progressiveness understands the critical contribution people make to the bottom line and operates with this in mind."[23]

QUESTIONS

1. Look at the P/HR areas Kravetz examined and discuss why these may or may not be good indicators of progressiveness.
2. How would you rate the firms for whom you have worked on the progressiveness factors?
3. What does the link between HR progressiveness scores and financial performance of firms indicate about the strategic side of P/HR management?

NOTES

1. Adapted from Larry K. Kromling, "CalComp Reshapes HR for the Future," *Personnel Journal*, January 1990, 57–63.

2. Dave Stier, "More Use of Human Resource Title," *Resource*, October, 1989, 2.

3. Jac Fitz-Enz, "HR, Inc.," *Personnel Journal*, April 1986, 34–41.

4. David Ulrich and Arthur Young, "A Shared Mindset," *Personnel Administrator*, March 1989, 38–45.

5. Edward E. Lawler III, "Human Resources Management: Meeting the New Challenges," *Personnel*, January 1988, 22–27.

6. Cynthia A. Lengnick-Hall and Mark L. Lengnick-Hall, "Strategic Human Resources Management: A Review of the Literature and a Proposed Typology," *Academy of Management Review* 13 (1988): 454–470.

7. Abraham Zaleznik, "What's Wrong with HRM?" *Harvard Business Review*, November-December 1988, 170–171.

8. Barbara W. Shimek, "All Managers are H.R. Managers," *HR Magazine*, January 1990, 67–70.

9. M. A. Hitt, R. D. Middlemist, and R. L. Mathis, *Management: Concepts and Effective Practice* (St. Paul: West Publishing Co., 1989,) 68–76.

10. Peter B. Petersen, "A Pioneer in Personnel," *Personnel Administrator*, June 1988, 60–64.

11. SHRM-BNA Survey #54, "Personnel/Human Resources Department: 1989–1990," *Bulletin to Management*, June 28, 1990.

12. Ibid.

13. William H. Wagel, "On the Horizon: HR in the 1990's," *Personnel*, January 1990, 11–16.

14. James W. Walker, "How Large Should the HR Staff Be?" *Personnel*, October 1988, 36–42.

15. Morton E. Grossman and Margaret Magnus, "The $5.3 Billion Tab for Training," *Personnel Journal*, July 1989, 54–56.

16. Laura M. Herren, "The New Game of HR: Playing to Win," *Personnel*, June 1989, 19–22.

17. Jack J. Phillips and Anson Seers, "Twelve Ways to Evaluate HR Management," *Personnel Administrator*, April 1989, 54–59.

18. William J. Traynor, *Opportunities in Personnel Management* (Lincolnwood, Ill.: National Textbook, 1989).

19. Bureau of Labor Statistics, U.S. Department of Labor, *Occupational Outlook Handbook*, Bulletin No. 2250 (Washington, D.C.: U.S. Government Printing Office, April 1990), 46–58.

20. Adapted from *Staying on the Right Career Track: A Perspective and Introspection of Human Resource Professionals* (Philadelphia: Right Associates, 1989); and Virginia M. Lord, "Men and Women on the HR Career Track," *Human Resource Professional*, September/October 1989, 18–23.

21. O. Jeff Harris and Art L. Bethke, "HR Professionals Two Decades Later," *Personnel Administrator*, February 1989, 66–71.

22. T. J. Bergmann and M. J. Close, "Preparing for Entry–Level Human Resource Management Positions," *Personnel Administrator*, April 1984, 95–99.

23. Adapted from Dennis J. Kravetz, *The Human Resource Revolution* (San Francisco: Jossey-Bass, 1989); and *Ideas & Trends in Personnel*, April 19, 1989, 65, 68–71.

Strategic Human Resource Planning

Chapter 3

After you have read this chapter, you should be able to:

1. Define human resource planning and discuss management and P/HR unit responsibilities for it

2. Outline the strategic human resource planning process

3. Discuss why external environmental scanning is an important part of human resource planning

4. Explain how auditing current jobs and skills relates to human resource planning

5. Identify factors to be considered when forecasting the supply and demand for human resources in an organization

6. Discuss several ways to manage both a surplus and a shortage of human resources

7. Define organizational culture and identify how it affects human resource planning

P/HR: Today *and* Tomorrow

Downsizing:Trend for the 1990s?

The 1980s saw the introduction of a trend that very likely will accelerate in the 1990s. Downsizing, (reducing the size of the work force) became an often painful necessity in many American firms as a wave of merger and acquisition activity swept the country, often leaving the new combination companies with redundant departments, plants, and people. Managers in the current decade face the same necessity but for different reasons. The merger craze has slowed, but foreign competition, a smaller concern at the beginning of the 1980s, has become a major concern for the 1990s. Often, bloated American firms have faced lower-cost competitors across shrinking oceans and trade barriers.

Downsizing has led to a variety of innovative ways to remove people from the payroll, some on a massive scale. For example, at Exxon more than 40,000 employees were given the option of leaving the company voluntarily or taking a chance that their jobs would be among the ones retained. To encourage volunteers, an early retirement buy-out plan was offered to anyone over fifty years of age who had at least fifteen years' service with Exxon. Improved pensions were offered to people who took retirement. For those not eligible for the early retirement buy-out, a lump-sum settlement of approximately two weeks' pay for each year of service was offered. Further, those entitled to regular pensions would still get them when they became eligible later in life. For both the volunteers who chose to leave and the employees laid off, employee relations specialists developed retirement counseling seminars, outplacement assistance to aid former employees in finding other jobs, and stress counseling. Ultimately, 6,200 employees elected to leave under the program.

The first major reduction-in-force (RIF) of Exxon workers ever undertaken gave a major jolt to the way in which employees viewed Exxon. Bitterness, anger, disbelief, and shock were common reactions. For those who survived the cuts, Exxon's paternalistic culture and image as a "lifetime" employer were gone forever.

IBM Corporation has had a policy of not laying off employees since Thomas Watson founded the company. However, to avoid layoffs, the company has invented a variety of approaches: a hiring freeze on full-time employees, a drastic cut in its use of temporary workers and summer student help, and a decrease in overtime hours to reduce payroll expenditures. Employees have been encouraged to take unused vacation time so that others could continue to work. In addition, workers were asked to move to other jobs at other company locations; people were shifted to sales positions from factory and staff jobs; and early retirement buy-outs were offered.

As IBM's business has grown more slowly, the company has made a series of cutbacks; to date the tradition of no layoffs is intact. However, as Chairman John Akers noted, "It's impossible to guarantee for all time full-time employment under any and all circumstances."[1]

Downsizing will be a fact of the 1990s. With it comes a host of ethical and business issues that will require increasing attention to human resource planning. Organizations of all kinds will face changing conditions in the last decade of the twentieth century; the problem is to anticipate human resource needs and respond to them. The P/HR segment of an organization is no different from any other: Planning is crucial to avoid problems associated with unanticipated events.

"Thorough planning is an open road to great accomplishments."

A. L. Romanoff

■■ ■ STRATEGIC PLANNING

This chapter deals with two levels of planning: strategic planning at the level of the organization and its subset, human resource planning. **Strategic planning** is the process of identifying organizational objectives and the actions needed to achieve those objectives. Strategic planning involves such areas as finance, marketing, and human resources to determine the capacities of the organization to meet its objectives. Strategic planning must include planning for human resources to carry out the rest of the plans. Thus, a key element of overall strategy is an effective human resources strategy.[2] Conversely, the business strategy of an organization and what it is trying to accomplish affects the strategies and activities in the P/HR area.[3]

STRATEGIC PLANNING
is the process of identifying organizational objectives and actions needed to achieve those objectives.

The Strategic Planning Process

The strategic planning process can be thought of as a narrowing process.[4] As Figure 3–1 shows, the process begins with identification and recognition of the philosophy and mission of an organization. This first step addresses the most fundamental questions about an organization:

■ Why does the organization exist?
■ What is the unique contribution it makes?
■ What are the underlying values and motivations of key managers and owners?

Once the philosophy and mission of the organization are identified, the next requirement is "environmental scanning." **Environmental scanning** is the process of studying the environment in which the organization exists to pinpoint opportunities and threats. Environmental scanning provides information about the ex-

ENVIRONMENTAL SCANNING
is the process of studying the environment of the organization to pinpoint opportunities and threats.

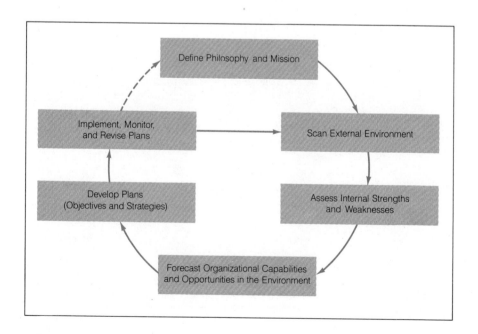

Figure 3–1
The Strategic Planning Process

ternal forces and pressures that impact the organization and the people in it. Work force patterns, economic conditions, social values and lifestyles, and technological developments are some factors discussed later in this chapter.

After the pressures in the world outside the organization are examined, an internal assessment is made of what the organization *can* do. Internal strengths and weaknesses must be identified while also considering the philosophy and culture of the organization. Factors such as current work force skills, retirement patterns, and demographic profiles of current employees are items that relate to human resource capabilities.

Next is forecasting organizational capabilities and future opportunities in the environment to specify organizational objectives and strategies. The objectives are specific, desired outcomes, and the strategies identify the allocation of resources needed to attain the objectives. The objectives and strategies that are set attempt to match external opportunities and threats with internal strengths and weaknesses.

Finally, specific plans are developed to identify how strategies will be implemented. Details of the plans become the bases for implementation and later adjustments. As with all plans, they must be monitored, adjusted, and updated continually. The strategic planning process is circular since the environment is always changing and the steps in the process must be repeated over and over again. Using this overview as a base, the human resource planning component can be discussed.

■■ ■ HUMAN RESOURCE PLANNING

In planning for human resources, an organization must consider the allocation of people to jobs over long periods—not just for the next month or even the next year. **Human resource planning** (hereafter called *HR planning*) is the process of analyzing and identifying the need for and availability of employees. Factors to consider include the current level of skills in an organization and the expected vacancies due to retirement, promotion, transfer, sick leave, or discharge. Human resource planners also try to foresee any expansions or reductions in operations and technological changes that may affect the organization. On the basis of such analyses, plans can be made for shifting employees within the organization, laying off or otherwise cutting back the number of employees, or retraining present em-

HUMAN RESOURCE PLANNING consists of analyzing and identifying the need for and the availability of the human resources required for an organization to meet its objectives.

Figure 3–2
Competitive Strategy and HR Strategy

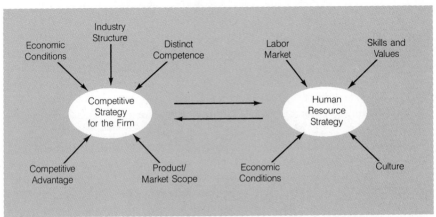

SOURCE: Adapted from C. A. Lengnick-Hall and M. Lengnick-Hall, "Strategic Human Resources Management: A Review of the Literature and a Proposed Typology," *Academy of Management Review 13* (1988), 467.

P/HR UNIT	MANAGERS
<ul><li>Prepares objectives for HR planning</li><li>Participates in strategic planning process for overall organization</li><li>Designs HR planning data systems</li><li>Compiles and analyzes data from managers on staffing needs</li><li>Identifies HR strategies</li><li>Implements HR plan as approved by top management</li></ul>	<ul><li>Identify supply and demand needs for each division/department</li><li>Review/discuss HR planning information with P/HR specialists</li><li>Integrate HR plans with departmental plans</li><li>Monitor HR plan to identify changes needed</li><li>Review employee succession plans and career paths in line with HR plan</li></ul>

Figure 3–3
Human Resource Planning Responsibilities

ployees, as well as for recruiting and hiring new people. Because of its focus on organizational needs, HR planning must be related to the overall strategic planning process in an organization. Since the HR planning process is a part of the organizational planning process, the two are considered together in this chapter. Figure 3–2 shows how they interact.

To support the organizational strategy the P/HR area also must have appropriate strategic direction. The pay system has to fit with the performance appraisal system, which must fit with selection decisions, and so on. If the different activities in the P/HR area are in tune with the general business strategy, as well as with one another, the P/HR group will be able to provide support for business goals.

Human Resource Planning Responsibilities

In most organizations that do HR planning, the top P/HR executive and subordinate staff specialists have most of the responsibilities for this planning. However, as Figure 3–3 indicates, other managers must provide data for the P/HR specialists to analyze.

Top management is responsible for overall strategic planning. Top managers usually ask the P/HR unit to project the necessary human resource support to implement overall organizational goals. The P/HR: Practice shows how business-level planning and HR planning were linked at one organization.

■■ ■ ORGANIZATIONAL PHILOSOPHY AND MISSION

The philosophy and mission of an organization are the core of its existence and the place to begin strategic planning. Together they define the *values* of the company and identify the reason the organization exists. The P/HR policies of a firm are shaped by the philosophies of its key managers. For example, a powerful founder with a clear set of values regarding his/her employees is more likely to encourage a consistent culture. Over time that culture will influence new managers who, in turn, will continue to promote the philosophy in their interaction with employees.

The mission statement clarifies how this organization is different from competing entities. The specific components of a mission statement are:[6]

- Purpose
- Principal business goals
- Corporate identity
- Policies of the organization
- Values

P/HR: Practice *and* Research

How HR Planning Worked at People's Bank

In the mid-1980s, changes in the environment of regional banks had shaken the industry to the core. Deregulation, growing competition, and large increases in expenses led one of these—People's Bank—to alter its strategic direction to minimize risks in its new environment and take advantage of new opportunities. The bank is headquartered in Connecticut and has over $4 billion in assets and sixty branches. People's objectives, growth and a market orientation would require aligning all of its human resources to support the business objectives.

First, the bank analyzed its current situation to decide what changes were needed. Growth would require new jobs and perhaps a new structure for the organization. A market orientation required a diversified product portfolio of services. As areas of the bank expanded or contracted there would be shifts in the numbers and kinds of people needed.

Following the analysis, the bank generated a series of action plans to address the specific needs that were identified. New positions were first filled with internal management talent. The company found it had outgrown its own human resources data system and few people were being transferred across divisions. The bank's talent pool was "inventoried" and a new internal recruitment strategy was implemented. The inventory pinpointed needs for more people with skills in marketing, sales, and general management.

The audit revealed much more as well, but the primary interest was the plan the bank used to link HR planning with business planning from that time forward. People's now conducts HR planning in conjunction with its business planning process. Both human resources and department managers are responsible for various parts of the process, as the following chart shows.[5] This approach helped refocus many of the bank's efforts and address its human resources requirements in an ongoing way.

Component	Accountability
I. Situation Analysis	Human Resource Department
External:	
Labor market pool/availability of key skills	
Industry trends (compensation, benefits, etc.)	
Internal:	
A. Organizational implications of business plans:	Management
Required changes in structure	
Number/types of key positions	
B. Human resources implications of business plans:	Management
Demand (number and kinds of skills required)	
Supply (turnover, skill levels and productivity of current work force)	
Actions to assure supply meets demand (recruitment, training, etc.)	
C. Management process implications of business plans:	Management
Compensation/other reward systems	
Communication process	
D. Culture implication of business plans:	Management
Current attitudes and behavior compared to desired culture	
II. Plan Development	Management and Human Resource Department
Objectives and strategies to ensure that organizations, people, process, and culture support business plans	
Actions to ensure human resources supply meets demand (recruitment, training, downsizing, productivity programs, etc.)	
III. Evaluation	Management and Human Resource Department
Costs and expected payoffs associated with human resource strategies	

▨ ▩ EXTERNAL ENVIRONMENTAL SCANNING

At the heart of strategic planning is scanning the external environment for changes.[7] Scanning especially affects HR planning because an organization must draw from the same labor market that supplies all employers. One measure of organizational effectiveness is the ability of an organization to compete for critical human resources. Many factors can influence the supply of labor available to an employer and to the general economy. The reputation of the organization is one factor, but labor market conditions and the HR plan also must be considered. Some more significant environmental factors are identified in Figure 3–4. Management must scan the environment in each of these areas to see how the labor supply and HR planning will be affected. Points for scanning include work force composition, work patterns and schedules, governmental influences, and economic, geographic, and competitive conditions.

Work Force Composition and Work Patterns

Chapter 1 dealt with the major changes influencing the work force in the United States and changing work patterns. Changes in the age, sex, racial, and educational composition of the work force combine with the use of contingent workers, alternative work schedules, and family/work balancing to create a very different work place from that of a generation ago.

Strategic planners must consider work force composition and work patterns in the environment to see their effects on organizational labor needs. Another major element that affects labor supply is governmental influences.

Governmental Influences

Today, managers are confronted with an expanding and often bewildering array of governmental rules and restrictions that have a tremendous impact on their organizations. Governmental regulation of P/HR activities has occurred for many years, but more restrictions continue to be added. For example, the Equal Employment Opportunity Commission (EEOC) can require employers to alter their hiring and promotion practices to assure that certain groups of people, such as women, are

Figure 3–4
**External Environmental Factors
Affecting Labor Supply**

provided equal chances for employment. As a result, HR planning must be done by individuals who know the numerous legal requirements of various equal employment regulations. Government trade policies and restrictions can affect HR planning in other ways. For example, government policies on importing Japanese cars affect the plans of automakers like General Motors, Ford, Chrysler, and American Motors because, under a "closed-import" policy, foreign firms may establish more American-based manufacturing operations. An "open-import" policy, on the other hand, creates an entirely different economic environment.

One industry that has experienced wrenching changes in the past five years is the hospital industry. Many hospitals have had to close wings, reduce staff, or offer new services just to survive. Many of those changes can be traced to a change in the federal government's reimbursement regulations for medical costs through Medicare.

Tax legislation at local, state, and federal levels also affects HR planning. Pension provisions and Social Security legislation may change retirement patterns and funding options. Elimination or expansion of tax benefits for job-training expenses might alter some job-training activities associated with work force expansions. Employee benefits may be affected significantly by tax law changes. Tax credits for employee day care and financial aid for education may affect employer practices when recruiting and retaining workers. In summary, an organization must consider a wide variety of governmental policies, regulations, and laws when doing HR planning.

Economic Conditions

The general business cycle of recessions and booms also affect HR planning. Such factors as interest rates, inflation, and economic growth can affect both organizational plans and objectives and the availability of workers. Economic conditions help determine wages, the need for overtime, and hiring or layoff decisions. Unemployment levels are influenced by economic conditions as well.[8] There is a considerable difference between finding qualified applicants in a 5 percent unemployment market and in a 9 percent unemployment market. In the 5 percent unemployment market, significantly fewer qualified applicants are likely to be available for any kind of position. Those who are available may be less employable because they are less educated, less skilled, or unwilling to work. As the unemployment rate rises, the number of qualified people looking for work increases.

Geographic and Competitive Conditions

One geographic factor affecting the supply of human resources is the *net migration* into a particular region. For a time after World War II, the population of northern U.S. cities grew rapidly and provided a ready source of labor. The shift of population growth to the Sunbelt is an important HR planning concern. The *demand* for workers by *other employers* in a geographic region also affects the labor supply. If, for example, a large military facility is closing or moving to another geographic location, a large supply of good civilian labor, previously employed by the military, may be available for a while. On the other hand, the opening of a new plant may decrease the supply of potential employees in a labor market for some time

Within the last decade, there has been a growing reluctance on the part of many workers, especially those with working spouses, to accept geographic *relocation* as a precondition of moving up in the organization. This trend has forced organizations to change their development policies and practices.

Competitors are another important external force in staffing. Failure to consider the competitive labor market and to offer pay scales and benefits competitive with organizations in the same general industry and geographic location may be a mistake. Underpaying or "undercompeting" may result in a much lower quality work force. The impact of *international competition*, as well as numerous other external factors, must be considered as part of environmental scanning.

■■ ■ INTERNAL STRENGTHS AND WEAKNESSES

After scanning the external environment, strategic planning requires that management assess the internal strengths and weaknesses of the organization. By taking input from a cross-section of the organization, strategists can identify organizational strengths and weaknesses. Auditing the jobs to be done and the skills available to do them is the first step in this assessment process.

Auditing Jobs

The starting point for evaluating internal strengths and weaknesses is an audit of jobs to be done. A comprehensive job analysis of all current jobs provides the base on which to build an internal evaluation. By knowing what jobs are currently being performed, a planner can examine the following questions:

■ What jobs now exist?
■ What are the reporting relationships of jobs?
■ How many individuals are performing each job?
■ How essential is each job?

Much of the data on these questions should be available from existing organization charts. However, the last question about the essential nature of each job may require some judgment on the part of planners. Once planners obtain an understanding of current jobs, they can make a detailed audit of current employees and their skills.

Auditing Skills

The basic source of data on employees and their skills is the P/HR records of the organization. Increasingly, employers make use of computerized human resource information systems (HRIS). The specifics of developing and using an HRIS are discussed in Chapter 21.

INDIVIDUAL EMPLOYEE DATA.   Personal data on individual employees for planning include the following:

■ Individual employee demographics (age, length of service in organization, time in present job)
■ Individual career progression (job held, time in each, promotions or other job changes, pay rates)
■ Individual performance data (work accomplishment, growth in skills)

EMPLOYEE SKILLS INVENTORY is a compilation of data on the skills and characteristics of employees.

Performance data form an integral part of an **employee skills inventory,** which is a compilation of data on the skills and characteristics of employees. Data typically included on an individual employee are:

- Education and training
- Mobility and geographic preferences
- Specific aptitudes and abilities
- Areas of interest and internal promotion ladders
- Promotability ratings
- Anticipated retirement

An employee skills inventory can be as simple as a five-item form or as sophisticated as a computerized information system. One caution should be kept in mind: All information that affects a person's promotability or selection for promotion must meet the same standards of job-relatedness and nondiscrimination as those used when the employee is initially hired. Security of such information is important to ensure that sensitive information is available only to those who have specific use for it.

In using a skills inventory (or skills bank) for long-range HR planning, planners make a comparison between the skills available now and the skills required in the future. That comparison can give planners an idea of needs for recruiting, selection, and training and the feasibility of making bids for new work.[9]

AGGREGATE WORK FORCE PROFILES.   Once the data are available, they must be aggregated into a profile of the current work force. This profile specifically addresses the strengths and weaknesses of the current work force. The absence of some skills, such as computer skills, may affect the ability of an organization to take advantage of new technological developments. If a large group of skilled employees are all in the same age bracket, their retirement plans or group turnover rate may leave a major void in the organization. For example, eight skilled line workers of a small rural electric utility were due to retire within a three-year period of time. Yet it takes seven years of apprenticeship and on-the-job training for a person to be qualified for a senior skilled job within that company.

Other areas often profiled include turnover, anticipated retirements, mobility restrictions of current workers, and specialization of workers by group. A number of these factors are ones over which the organization has little control. Some employees will die, leave the firm, retire, or otherwise contribute to a reduction in the current employee force. Charts giving an overview of the employee situation may be plotted for each department in an organization. When overall data are charted, the accumulated information can show which departments may need external candidates to fill future positions. Likewise, the inventory may indicate where there is a reservoir of trained people that the employer can tap as it meets future conditions.

■■ ■ FORECASTING

The data and information gathered during both the external environment scanning and the assessment of internal strengths and weaknesses can be evaluated and used to develop human resource supply and demand forecasts in light of organizational objectives and strategies.

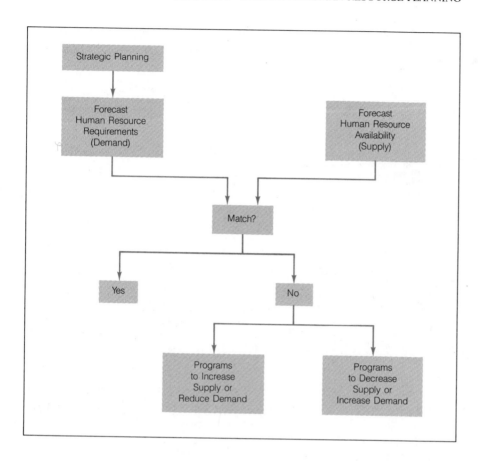

Figure 3–5
Human Resource Forecasting

Forecasting uses information from the past and present to identify expected future conditions. Figure 3–5 shows the place of HR forecasting in the planning process. A wide variety of forecasting methods is available to individuals doing HR planning.

FORECASTING
uses information from the past and present to identify expected future conditions.

Forecasting Methods

Models for forecasting human resources range from a manager's best guess to a rigorous and complex computer simulation. Simple models may be quite accurate in certain instances, but complex models may be necessary in others.

Figure 3–6 identifies four different types of forecasting models and their uses. It is beyond the scope of this text to discuss in detail the numerous methods available, but a few of the more prominent ones are highlighted.

The most common forecasting methods used are judgmental and subjective.[10] *Judgmental* means that knowledgeable individuals, such as managers and P/HR experts, make estimates. With the *Delphi technique*, a group of experts provide independent input via questionnaires on what forecasted situations will be. These expert opinions are then aggregated.

RULE-OF-THUMB FORECASTS. Rule-of-thumb forecasts rely on general guidelines applied to a specific situation within the organization. For example, a guideline of one operations manager per five reporting supervisors aids in forecasting the number of excess supervisors in a division. However, it is important to adapt the guidelines in order to recognize widely varying departmental needs.

Figure 3–6
Forecasting Models and Applications

TYPE OF MODEL	TECHNIQUES	APPLICATIONS
Simple forecasting models	Judgmental forecasts	Rudimentary forecasts of available supply and demand under stable conditions
	Rules of thumb Staffing standards Ratio-trend analysis Time series Delphi technique	Long-range forecasting
Organizational change models	Succession analysis Markov/stochastic processes Renewal models Regression analysis	Replacement analysis and blockages Probability-based flow forecasts Correlations to project changes
Optimization models	Linear programming Nonlinear programming Dynamic programming Goal programming Assignment models	Future needs defined by constraints Future needs identified to achieve defined objectives Matching individuals with anticipated vacancies
Integrated simulation models	Corporate models: combined techniques	Total entity simulation linked with corporate planning

SOURCE: James W. Walker, *Human Resource Planning* (New York: McGraw-Hill, 1980), 132.

Forecasters using *trend projections and analysis* generally take historical data and project them into the future. This method is adequate, but forecasters should remember that historical data are based on trends that may be changing.

SUCCESSION ANALYSIS.   Succession analysis is a widely used method to forecast the supply of people for certain positions. It relies on *replacement charts*. These charts are succession plans developed to identify potential personnel changes, select backup candidates, promote individuals, and look at attritions (resignations, retirements) for each department in an organization. A survey of 264 organizations revealed that development of replacement charts was the most widely used forecasting technique in HR planning.[11]

STATISTICAL FORECASTING.   *Regression analysis* makes a statistical comparison of past relationships among various factors. For example, a statistical relationship between gross sales and number of employees in a retail chain may be useful in forecasting the number of employees needed in the future if the retailer's sales increase 30 percent. *Simulations* are representations of real situations in abstract form. External factors examined often include available economic models and labor market workers. Numerous other methods and techniques are available also, but surveys reveal that the more complex techniques are used by relatively few firms.[12]

Forecasting Periods

Human resource forecasting should be done over three planning periods: *short-range*, *intermediate*, and *long-range*.[13] The most commonly used planning period is short-range, usually a period of six months to one year. This level of planning is routine in many organizations because very few assumptions about the future are necessary for such short-term plans. These short-term forecasts offer the best estimates of the immediate personnel needs of an organization. Intermediate and long-range forecasting are much more difficult processes. Intermediate plans usually project one to five years into the future, and long-range plans extend beyond five years.

Forecasting the Supply of Human Resources

Based on analysis of external and internal factors, management can forecast the supply of workers for the future. Forecasters should consider both internal and external supply sources and identify the specific skills of workers, not just an aggregate number of workers.

A "supply-push" approach considers that employees move from their current jobs into others through promotions, lateral moves, terminations, etc. For example, if a loading dock has two basic job classifications—loaders and drivers—and there are two levels of each, the following situation exists:[14]

	Loaders	Drivers	
Level II	15	6	
Level I	25	10	
			Total
			56

Now suppose that to the 25 loaders in Level I the following happens:

```
 25 (Beginning number)
 −8 (Promoted to Level II)
 −1 (Promoted to Driver Level II)
 −1 (Fired)
 +1 (Transferred in from Driver Level I)
 +5 (New Hires
 ‾‾
 21
```

The proportion of the beginning pool of 25 loaders (Level I) that was promoted, fired, or transferred can be estimated from this historical data for next year.

The supply of potential loaders available outside the organization can be estimated by considering the following factors:

- Net migration in/out of area
- Individuals entering/leaving work force
- Individuals graduating from schools and college
- Changing work force composition and patterns
- Economic forecasts for the next few years
- Technological developments and shifts
- Actions of competing employers
- Governmental regulations and pressures
- Factors affecting persons entering/leaving the work force

Forecasting Human Resource Demand

To identify the demand for human resources, two basic approaches can be used: (1) calculating the demand for people on an organization-wide basis and (2) considering the needs of individual units in the organization rather than the organization as a whole. For example, to forecast that the firm needs 125 new employees next year might mean less than to forecast that the corporation needs 25 new people in sales, 45 in production, 20 in accounting, 5 in personnel, and 30 in the warehouse. This unit breakdown obviously allows for more consideration of the specific skills needed than the aggregate method does.

A "demand-pull" approach to forecasting considers specific openings that are likely to occur. The openings (or demands) are created when employees leave a position because of promotions, transfers, terminations, etc. The analysis always begins with the top positions in the organization because from those there can be no promotions to a higher level. Consider the example of loaders and drivers on the loading dock again:

	Loaders	Drivers	
Level II	50	30	
Level I	90	60	
			Total
			230

Decision rules (or "fill rates") are developed for each position or level. (For example, 50 percent of loaders Level II will come through promotions from loader Level I, 25 percent from promoting drivers Level I, and 25 percent will be filled with new hires).

Then anticipated openings are estimated:

+8 Openings due to predicted turnover
+6 Added loaders due to expansion
14 openings

Since 50 percent of loader (Level II) jobs are to be filled by promotions from loader Level I, it is forcasted that 7 will come from that source, and so on. Forecasters must be aware of chain effects throughout, because as people are promoted, their old positions open up.

Unfortunately, the accuracy of forecasts for human resources demand has been relatively weak. In one survey of 5,000 firms, only 35 percent of the forecasts were correct within 1 percent, whereas about one-third were off by more than 25 percent. The troubling part of this survey is that the forecasts were only for one year, not the three years commonly projected in HR planning.[15] Good HR planning is not easy and more precision comes from more precise figures; however, it is wrong to conclude that HR planning is useless. More effort to get good data and more flexibility in living with variation in the data are key.

▬ ▬ COMPILING A HUMAN RESOURCE PLAN

With all the data collected and forecasts done, an organization has the information for an HR plan. An HR plan can be extremely sophisticated or rather rudimentary. Regardless of how complex a plan is desired, the ultimate purpose of the plan is to enable managers in the organization to match the available supply of labor with the forecasted demands in light of the strategies of the firm. If the necessary skill level does not exist in the present work force, employees may need to be trained in the new skill or outside recruiting may need to be targeted. Likewise, if the plan identifies that there are too many people, work force reductions may be necessary.

The HR plan provides a "road map" for the future. This map should identify where employees are likely to be obtained, when employees will be needed, and what training and development employees must have. Through career and succession planning, employee career paths can be tailored to individual needs that are consistent with organizational requirements. A discussion of career planning appears in Chapter 11.

Some potential benefits of an effective HR planning system are:

■ Upper management has a better view of the human resource dimensions of business decisions.
■ P/HR costs may be less because management can anticipate imbalances before they become unmanageable and expensive.
■ More time is provided to locate talent because needs are anticipated and identified before the actual staffing is required.
■ Better opportunities exist to include women and minority groups in future growth plans.
■ Development of managers can be better planned.

■■ ■ IMPLEMENTING AN HR PLAN

All efforts involved in HR planning will be futile unless management takes action to implement the plans. A key reason for doing HR planning is to achieve a match between the identified needs for workers and the internal and external supply of workers. Managerial actions vary depending on whether there is a surplus or a shortage of workers forecasted.

Managing a Human Resources Surplus

There are a variety of ways that a surplus of workers can be managed within an HR plan. But regardless of the means, the actions are difficult because they require that some current workers be removed from the organization. **Downsizing** is a term that has grown in use in recent years and refers to the reduction in size of an organizational work force.[16] Attrition, early retirement/buy-outs, and layoffs are the most frequently used ways of downsizing an organization. Outplacement helps displaced employees find new jobs.

DOWNSIZING
is reducing the size of an
organizational work force.

ATTRITION.   Through "attrition," individuals who quit, die, retire, or otherwise leave an employer are not replaced. With this approach, no one is cut out of a job, but those who remain must handle the same work load with fewer people. Unless turnover is high, attrition will eliminate only a relatively small number of employees.

EARLY RETIREMENT/BUY-OUTS.   Early retirement is a means of encouraging more senior workers to leave the organization early. To provide this voluntary incentive, employers make additional payments to employees so that they will not be penalized too much economically until their pensions and Social Security benefits take effect.

Voluntary termination programs entice an employee to quit with financial incentives. They are widely viewed as ways to accomplish force reduction without the general ugliness of layoffs and individual firings.

Buy-outs appeal to employers because they can reduce payroll costs significantly over time. Although there are some upfront costs, the organization does not incur the continuing payroll costs. One hospital saved $2 for every $1 spent on early retirees.[17] Early retirement buy-outs are a more humane way to reduce staff than just terminating long-service, loyal employees. In addition, as long as buy-outs are truly voluntary, the organization is less exposed to age discrimination suits.

Most early retirement buy-out programs offer a one-time "window." Employees must decide on early retirement during that window, typically 60 to 90 days, or take their chances that their jobs will not be eliminated in future restructuring efforts. Both employees whom the company wishes would stay and those it wishes would leave can take advantage of the buy-out. Consequently, some individuals whom the employer would rather have retained will take the buy-out.

Ford Motor dealt with that problem by targeting specific groups (such as accounting or technical support) for reduction. But instead of offering resignation incentives to the entire group, individual managers made offers only to certain employees within that group. Ford also made it clear there would be no retaliation against any employee who turned down the offer. Ford's goal was to cut 20 percent of the employees in the targeted groups over 5 years.[18]

LAYOFFS.   Layoffs occur when employees are put on unpaid leave of absence. If business improves for the employer, then employees can be called back to work. Careful planning of layoffs is essential. Managers must consider the following questions:

- How are decisions made about whom to lay off (seniority, performance records)?
- How will call-backs be made if all workers cannot be recalled at the same time?
- Will any benefit coverage be given workers laid off?
- If workers take other jobs, do they forfeit their call-back rights?

Layoffs may be an appropriate downsizing strategy if there is a temporary downturn in an industry. Companies have no legal obligation to provide a financial cushion to laid-off employees; however, many do so. When a provision exists for severance pay, the most common formula is one week's pay for every year of employment.[19] Larger companies tend to be more generous. Loss of medical benefits are a major problem for laid-off employees. But under federal law displaced workers can retain their medical group coverage for up to eighteen months and thirty-six months for dependents if they pay the premiums themselves.

Bell Atlantic Corporation devised a variation on the layoff theme. The company gave 160 surplus managers unpaid leaves of 12 to 24 months. The managers could do whatever they wanted, including working for a noncompeting company. At the end of the leave they could return to a job with the same status and pay (but not necessarily at the same location).[20]

Surplus Human Resources and Mergers/Acquisitions

During the 1980s in the United States, a large number of firms acquired or merged with other firms. Some of these mergers were large, such as General Electric acquiring RCA, or Texas Air Corporation merging with Continental, People Ex-

P/HR: Practice *and* Research

Survey of the Effects of Restructuring

In one a study looked at the HR issues and HR participation in corporate restructuring. The survey of HR professionals occurred in two stages. First, 6,000 HR professionals were surveyed and asked if they had been involved in restructuring, and if so, what kind. Of these, 80 percent indicated they had been. This group was then sent the second-stage questionnaire requesting more specific information. Most restructuring had occurred as a result of either merger/acquisition activities or downsizing (76 percent).

Results indicated the following:

■ Permanent work force reduction is present in two-thirds of the restructuring situations.
■ Companies were successful in reducing labor costs.
■ Downsizing goals were more frequently accomplished than merger and acquisition goals.
■ Integrating pay systems and management structures were a major problem.
■ Morale, company image, and management credibility suffered frequently.
■ However, low morale did not necessarily lead to more tangible difficulties with a union or to individual employee lawsuits.
■ Productivity often improved.

---

press, Frontier, and Eastern Airlines. Others were smaller, such as the merger of two local hospitals. But a common result of most mergers and acquisitions is an excess of employees once the firms have been combined. Because much of the rationale for combinations is financial, elimination of expensive overlapping employees in both entities is a primary concern. The natural response of employees is anxiety about their future: Who will be eliminated? What operations will be closed? Who will be required to relocate or lose employment? Stress follows anxiety because the climate and culture of the organization are strained.[21]

At the same time, P/HR specialists must be involved in identifying and planning how the combined firms will operate. They must evaluate surplus reduction options and implement the selected options. Different P/HR policies, benefit programs, compensation plans, and personnel record systems must be integrated. One study revealed that seven of the twelve top factors to be considered after a merger are related directly to human resources.[22]

Five out of six bought-out companies have undergone restructuring and consequent staff cuts, according to one study.[23] A number of approaches have been tried to minimize the adaptation of employees in both organizations after merger has occurred.[24] However, research suggests that this has not been well done in many cases and special attention should be paid to merging the cultures of the organizations effectively.[25] The P/HR: Research describes a survey on the effects of restructuring.

Outplacement

Outplacement assistance is advantageous for employees who lose their jobs through downsizing, especially those involuntarily removed because of plant closing or elimination of departments, Outplacement services typically offered workers include personal career counseling, resume preparation and typing services, interviewing workshops, and referral assistance.

OUTPLACEMENT
is a group of services provided displaced employees to give them support and assistance.

There are several reasons why a company should consider such a seemingly costly and time-consuming program even though employees are terminated because of financial burdens:[26]

1. *Cost:* It may not be as great as it seems. For example, helping workers find jobs more quickly can cut down on unemployment benefits.
2. *Company image:* Outplacement efforts typically show the image of the company as a caring employer.
3. *Legal issues:* The longer employees are out of work, the more likely they are to consider suing for damages.
4. *Social responsibility:* Certainly not everyone agrees that there is a moral or ethical obligation to former employees, but some argue there is such an obligation.

Figure 3–7 shows the kind of outplacement services provided by the "Fortune 1000" companies that have undergone restructuring.

▬ ▬ ORGANIZATIONAL CULTURE

ORGANIZATIONAL CULTURE
is a pattern of shared values and beliefs giving members meaning and providing them with rules for behavior.

An issue that affects strategic HR planning is organizational culture. Just as nations and regions have unique cultural characteristics, so do organizations. **Organizational culture** is a pattern of shared values and beliefs giving members meaning and providing them with rules for behavior.[27] These values are inherent in the ways organizations and their members view themselves, define opportunities, and plan strategies. Much like the way personality shapes an individual's response, organizational culture shapes its members' responses.

The culture of an organization is seen in the norms of expected behaviors, values, philosophies, rituals, and symbols used by its employees. Culture evolves over a period of time. Only if an organization has a history in which people have shared experiences for years does a culture stabilize.[28] A relatively new firm, such as a business existing for less than two years, probably would not have developed a stabilized culture.

An excellent example of how philosophy, mission, and culture are interrelated can be seen in the breakup of AT&T and its subsidiaries. Before the divestiture required by the federal government, AT&T and its "Baby Bell" subsidiaries provided telecommunications services in a regulated environment. Consequently, the over-

Figure 3–7
Outplacement Services Provided Most Frequently (in percent)

	Senior Management	Middle Management	Administrative Staff	Hourly Workers
Outplacement services using an outside firm	87	69	57	31
Severance pay above normal allowance	83	69	59	43
Outplacement through company	17	60	66	57
Retraining/transfer	39	66	83	71
On-site career center	38	67	79	67
Medical benefits continuation	92	94	90	71
Job search assistance	72	89	78	59
Stay-to-the-end bonuses	50	88	79	36
Early or enhanced retirement benefits	87	90	85	54
Other	100	100	50	50

SOURCE: Adapted from H. Pines and P. deLisser, "Restructuring Is Worth the Cost," *Human Resource Professional,* May/June 1989, 44.

riding culture at AT&T was one of stability and routine, with high value placed on loyalty, conformity, and length of service. However, after the divestiture, the "Baby Bells" took new names (Nynex, Ameritech, U.S. West, Pacific Telesis) and began to compete with one another and AT&T in certain market segments. Other competitors, such as MCI and U.S. Sprint, got access to long-distance customers. AT&T, previously a very stable and highly structured organization, faced an extremely competitive environment in which old strategies no longer applied.

The new AT&T mission focused on "information technologies," not just on telephone communications. Its strategies shifted to a market orientation, to encouragement of risk taking, and to anticipation of competitive changes. As one AT&T executive commented, "Basically, we have had to change bureaucrats into entrepreneurs and marketers."

The organizational culture at AT&T inhibited the change process. Loyalty and length of service did not do the firm much good when many existing employees lacked the ability and temperament to vie for customers in an extremely competitive external environment. AT&T has undertaken a series of early retirement and layoff retrenchments, as have the Baby Bells, to better adapt to the environment. For example, U.S. West, the Denver-based communications company that resulted from the breakup, has eliminated thousands of jobs since it was created from Mountain Bell. In 1990, it offered early retirement incentives to about 20,000 managers. For a 50-year-old manager with 25 years of service, retirement would normally result in payments of $740 per month if taken before age 55. However, in an effort to get people to leave, the company offered $1,470 per month for the first 5 years, dropping to $1,200 per month after that. U.S. West hoped the plan would produce big savings in salaries as it faced stiffer competition, tough regulation, and a turbulent regional economy. The company's culture required that early retirement be tried to reduce its work force rather than layoffs.[29]

Culture is important because it tells people how to behave (or not to behave). It is relatively constant and enduring over time. Newcomers learn the culture from the senior employees and the rules of the games are perpetuated.[30]

Levels of Culture

Analysts have identified three levels of organizational culture.[31] Figure 3–8 shows examples of each of the elements of culture. The first level—*artifacts*—is made up of consistent behavioral patterns and the results of those behaviors. The written and spoken language, office layout, dress codes, and behavioral norms are included here. These are relatively easy to see, but may not make much sense without an understanding of the other two levels.

The second level—*values and beliefs*—has to do with what people in the organization feel "ought to be." This level of culture provides reasons for the behaviors at the first level. Ethical and moral codes are the formal expression of these behaviors.

Level three includes *underlying basic assumptions*, completely accepted and deeply ingrained ideas that actually guide behavior. They differ from values in that basic assumptions are more abstract and perhaps not even operating at a conscious level.

Measuring Organizational Culture

If organizational culture is defined as beliefs, values, and artifacts, rather straightforward research tools are available with which to measure it. They include ques-

Figure 3–8
Examples of Elements of Organizational Culture

I. ARTIFACTS (tangible/visible things)	II. VALUES (beliefs)	III. BASIC ASSUMPTIONS (subconscious agreement)
Celebrations (a retirement party)	Feelings (loyalty to the company is good)	Widely agreed-upon fundamentals
Managing practices (firing for stealing)	Ethical codes (we value honesty)	The glue that holds the organization together
Organizational stories (the "old man" could do every job in the place)	Knowledge (broad knowledge is good)	The nature of human relationships
Symbols (sizes of office)	Purpose (if you know where you are going and work hard you will get your reward)	Mind-set
Informal rules (you don't leave if your work isn't done)	Commitment to excellence (keep at it until you do it right)	Spirit

SOURCE: Adapted from J. Ott, *The Organizational Culture Perspective* (Pacific Grove, Calif.: Brooks/Cole, 1989).

tionnaires, interviews, and observations. If culture is defined more abstractly as basic assumptions, then it is more difficult to measure.

For example, observing physical settings, going through organizational archives and records, and observing language, jargon, and stories are fruitful approaches to studying artifacts. Questionnaires often are appropriate to identify values. But measuring basic assumptions requires observers knowledgeable about the organization who can make reliable deductions by observing the more tangible parts of organizational culture.

Effect of Culture on Strategy

When doing strategic planning, managers must consider the culture of the organization because the appropriate strategies may be negated by an incompatible culture. For example, AT&T has had to try and shift from a process culture to a results-oriented culture in the aftermath of company restructuring.

Another example is an insurance firm whose culture was highly stable, resistant to innovation, and low on customer service and marketing. The firm wanted to start a financial services unit, an action identified by its strategic planning process. To be successful, an extensive number of service contracts and rapid financial marketing adjustments were necessary. But because of the mismatch between culture and strategy, the firm decided it could not implement this strategy, even though it was a viable possibility from a business standpoint.[32]

The culture of an organization also affects the way external forces are viewed. In one culture, external events are seen as threatening, whereas another culture views risks and changes as challenges requiring immediate responses. The culture of an organization also can be a source of competitive advantage, especially if it is unique and hard to duplicate.[33] For example, IBM's culture gives the company and its people a valuable competitive edge. A directory of ex-IBMers, similar to an alumni association of a university, shows the impact of IBM's culture on people even after they leave IBM. Figure 3–9 illustrates the relationship among planning, culture, and life cycle of the company. Life cycle is discussed next.

▬ ▬ ORGANIZATIONAL LIFE CYCLE AND HR PLANNING

An organization needs different human resource strategies at different times in its life, and the plans flowing from these strategies reflect these differences.[34] For example, a small, three-year-old high-tech software firm will have differing needs from a large computer company. Apple Computer is a good illustration. At one time Apple, founded by Steven Jobs and Stephen Wozniak, was a laid-back, entrepreneurial organization. But as the company grew, the need for more structure and formalization of plans and policies became evident. A new president, John Scully, was hired from Pepsi Cola, and within two years the founders left Apple. Scully reduced staff to eliminate duplicate jobs and instituted more formalized policies throughout the company. Apple had passed from the growth to the maturity stage of its life cycle.

Life Cycle Stages and Planning Needs

The relationships among the life cycle of an organization and its P/HR activities are capsuled in Figure 3–10. A discussion of each follows.

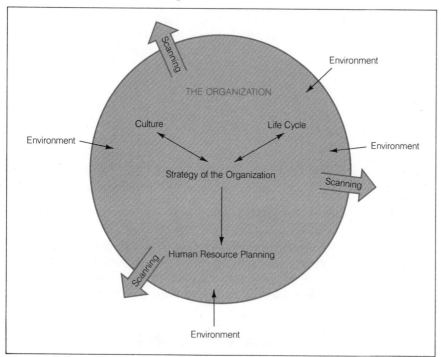

Figure 3–9
Interaction of Culture, Life Cycle, Strategy and Human Resources Planning

SOURCE: Adapted from Thomas A. Kochan and Thomas A. Barocci, *Human Resource Management and Industrial Relations: Text, Readings, and Cases,* p. 105. Copyright © 1985 by Thomas A. Kochan and Thomas A. Barocci. Adapted by permission of Scott, Foresman and Company.

Figure 3–10
Organizational Life Cycle, Culture, and P/HR Activities

LIFE CYCLE STAGE	Staffing	Compensation	Training and Development	Labor/Employee Relations
Introduction	Attract best technical/professional talent	Meet or exceed labor market rates to attract needed talent	Define future skill requirements and begin establishing career ladders	Set basic employee relations philosophy and organization
Growth	Recruit adequate numbers and mix of qualified workers. Plan Management succession. Manage rapid internal labor market movements	Meet external market but consider internal equity effects; establish formal compensation structures	Mold effective management team through management development and organizational development	Maintain labor peace, employee motivation, and morale
Maturity	Encourage sufficient turnover to minimize layoffs and provide new openings. Encourage mobility as reorganizations shift jobs around	Control compensation	Maintain flexbility and skills of an aging work force	Control labor costs and maintain labor peace; improve productivity
Decline	Plan and implement work force reductions and reallcation	Tighter cost control	Implement retraining and career consulting services	Improve productivity and achieve flexibility in work rules; negotiate job security and employment adjustment policies

SOURCE: Thomas A. Kochan and Thomas A. Barocci, *Human Resource Management* (Boston: Little, Brown, 1985), 105. Used with permission (as adapted).

INTRODUCTION.   At the introduction stage, a high-risk and entrepreneurial spirit pervades the organization.[35] The founders often operate with limited financial resources; consequently, P/HR activities are handled reactively and training seems less important. When skills are needed, the organization recruits and hires individuals who are already trained.[36]

GROWTH.   The growth stage requires that the organization continue to take risks and invest in marketing and operations. The organization needs investments to expand facilities, marketing, and personnel to take advantage of the demand for its products and services. Often backlogs and scheduling problems indicate that the organization has grown faster than its ability to handle the demand. One study revealed that the decisions made during the growth stage have a critical impact on the organization as it moves into maturity.[37] Consequently, just as in the Apple Computer situation, some formalization of policies and rules must occur. Inadequate staffing becomes a major concern, so the organization begins to focus on recruitment and selection of workers. It recognizes the need for some HR planning, not just for reacting to immediate pressures, and institutes some simplified HR planning procedures.

MATURITY.   In the maturity stage the organization and its culture are stabilized. The organization's size and success enable it to develop even more formalized plans, policies, and procedures. It now reaps the fruits of its past risky labors. Often, organizational politics flourish and P/HR activities expand. At the same time, managers are concerned about keeping the organization and its costs under control. Compensation programs become a major focus for P/HR efforts. Human resource planning becomes vital, especially for work force shifts, as demand for some products and services slows.

DECLINE.   The organization in the decline stage experiences resistance to change: rules and policies have hardened into a structure. Numerous examples can be cited in the manufacturing sectors of the U.S. economy. Steel manufacturing firms have had to reduce their work forces, close steel mills, and use their accumulated profits from the past to diversify into other industries. During the decline stage, employers try certain P/HR practices, productivity enhancement, and cost and reduction programs to slow the decline. Unionized workers resist the decline by demanding no pay cuts and greater job security provisions in their contracts. Nevertheless, employers are compelled to reduce their workforces through attrition, early retirement incentives, and major facility closings.

SUMMARY

- Human resource planning focuses on analyzing and identifying the future needs for, and availability of, human resources for the organization.
- The P/HR unit has major responsibilities in HR planning, but managers must provide supportive information and input. HR planning is tied to the broader process of strategic planning, beginning with identification of the philosophy and mission of the organization.
- Assessment of internal strengths and weaknesses as a part of HR planning requires that current jobs and employee skills be audited and aggregate work force profiles be developed. Using information on the past and present to identify expected future conditions and forecasting the supply and demand for human resources can be done with a variety of methods for differing periods of time.
- "Supply-push" and "demand-pull" approaches to forecasting help identify specific needs.
- Management of human resources surpluses may require downsizing and outplacement.
- Organizational culture is a pattern of shared values and beliefs giving members meaning and providing them with rules for behavior.

■ In developing an HR plan, strategists must consider the stage in the organizational life cycle: introduction, growth, maturity, decline.

REVIEW AND DISCUSSION QUESTIONS

1. What is HR planning and what differences exist in the responsibilities between managers and P/HR specialists?
2. Why must HR planning be seen as a process flowing from the organizational strategic plan?
3. Assume you have to develop an HR plan for a local hospital. What specific external factors would be important for you to consider? Why?
4. At a hospital, how would you audit the current jobs and skills of employees?
5. Why are the time frame and methods used to forecast supply and demand for human resources so important?
6. Assume that as a result of HR planning, a hospital identifies a shortage of physical therapists, but a surplus of administrative workers. Discuss what actions might be taken to address these problems and why they must be approached carefully.
7. Discuss how organizational culture, organizational life cycle, and P/HR activities are interrelated.

CASE | **Culture Clash and Change at General Motors**

For many years General Motors Corporation (GM) had been one of the largest and most successful firms in the United States. However, the 1980s were not outstanding years for GM. For example, from 1980–1986, GM dropped almost 5 percent in its share of the U.S. auto market. In some years, earnings dropped up to 15 percent over the year before.

To address GM's long-term survival, Chairman Roger Smith made some bold moves to change GM's structure, products, and corporate culture. The Saturn project represented one such attempt. By targeting a new automobile slated for production in a new factory in Tennessee, GM hoped to use advanced production methods, including robotics, and Saturn employees were to use significantly different staffing and work methods. Unfortunately, the plant has run into difficulties that have caused delays and changes.

Additionally, to enhance its technological capabilities, GM spent billions to buy Hughes Aircraft Company. Another costly purchase was Electronic Data Systems (EDS), a Dallas-based computer service and information-processing firm founded by H. Ross Perot. Each of these firms had its own unique corporate culture; blending them has represented one of Smith's major challenges. Perot captured the essence of the cultural differences when he commented, "Revitalizing GM is like teaching an elephant to tap dance. You find the sensitive spots and start poking."

The culture clashes between GM and EDS employees are legendary. For example, EDS had a required dress code and made rules against employees drinking alcohol at lunch. When 10,000 data-processing employees were transferred from GM to EDS, rampant dissatisfaction spread. Over 600 GM data-processing employees quit and others filed for union elections. At the same time, the EDS employees became frustrated with some GM managers' efforts to use a bureaucratic approach. Perot commented, "The first EDSer to see a snake kills it. At GM the first thing you do is organize a committee on snakes. Then you bring in a consultant who knows about snakes. Third thing you do is talk about it for a year." Perot was later bought out and removed from the scene.

To reduce culture clashes between Hughes and GM, Smith learned from the EDS problem. Consequently, he insulated divisions in each by setting up independent subsidiaries.

One of the major changes facing GM and Smith is redefining and reemphasizing GM's mission and philosophy. To emphasize the shifts, Smith had GM "culture cards" printed up and distributed. On the card, GM's mission is stated as follows:

> "The fundamental purpose of General Motors is to provide products and services of such quality that our customers will receive superior value, our employees and business partners will share in our success, and our stockholders will receive sustained, superior return on their investment.[38]"

GM 's future will be determined, in large, by the changes made at GM to enable it to fulfill its mission. Whether the changes succeed will have to be determined around 1999.[38]

QUESTIONS

1. Regarding the different types of organizational cultures that have had to be merged at GM, what are they and what are the implications of the differences?
2. What external and internal factors do you believe contributed to Smith's determination to change many facets of GM?
3. If you had to blend two totally separate organizations with different cultures, life cycle stages, and strategies, what general approaches would you use?

NOTES

1. P. Coy, "IBM To Cut 10,000 Jobs," *Laramie Daily Boomerang*, December 6, 1989, 18.
2. Russell G. Roberts and Martin G. Wolf, "Human Resources Strategy," in *The Strategic Management Handbook*, ed. K. J. Albert (New York: McGraw-Hill, 1983), 15. 1–15. 8.
3. A Tsui and G. Milkovich, "Personnel Department Activities: Constituency Perspectives and Preferences," *Personnel Psychology*, 40 (1987): 519–539.
4. Adapted from the process discussed in James W. Walker, *Human Resource Planning* (New York: McGraw–Hill, 1980), 78–79.
5. Adapted from S. M. Coleman, M. Leshner, and C. Hewes, "HRP: A Tool for Strategic Change," *The Banker's Magazine*, November/December 1986, 39–44.
6. Jerome H. Want, "Corporate Mission: The Intangible Contributor to Performance," *Management Review*, August 1986, 46–50.
7. E. Burack and N. Mathys, "Environmental Scanning Improves Strategic Planning," *Personnel Administrator*, April 1989, 82.
8. D. J. Mitchell, *Human Resource Management: An Economic Approach* (Boston: PWS-Kent Publishing, 1989), 410.
9. A. Sharon, "Skills Bank Tracks Talent, Not Training," *Personnel Journal*, June 1988, 49.
10. C. R. Greer and D. M. Armstrong, "Human Resource Forecasting and Planning: A State-of-the Art Investigation," *Human Resource Planning* 3 (1980): 67–78.
11. Stella M. Nkomo, "The Theory and Practice of HR Planning: The Gap Still Remains," *Personnel Administrator*, August 1986, 71–84.
12. Ibid.
13. Walker, *Human Resource Planning*, 104–105.
14. The following examples of supply-push and demand-pull analysis were adapted from T. Bechet and W. Maki, "Modeling and Forecasting Focusing on People as a Strategic Resource," *Human Resource Planning* 10, (1987): 214–217.
15. "Businesses Are Naive Forecasters," *Dun's Business Month*, October 1985, 82.

16. C. Albrecht Jr., "The Upside to Downsizing," *Human Resources Professional*, May/June 1989, 19.

17. *Hospitals*, April 5, 1986, 90.

18. D. Machan, "The Hidden Cost of Golden Handshakes," *Forbes*, February 20, 1989, 131.

19. "Layoff Policies Left for Firms to Determine," *Omaha World-Herald*, August, 27, 1989, 1G.

20. J. Solomon, "Temporary Leave Rather than Permanent," *Wall Street Journal*, June 12, 1989, B1.

21. David L. Schweiger and John M. Ivancevich, "Human Resources: The Forgotten Factor in Mergers and Acquisitions," *Personnel Administrator*, November 1985, 47–61.

22. David Robino and Kenneth DeMeuise, "Corporate Mergers and Acquisitions: Their Impact on HRM," *Personnel Administrator*, Novemvber 1985, 33–44.

23. D. Attany, "Just Pawns in the Takeover Game," *Industry Week*, July 17, 1989, 30.

24. N. Gilbert, "Post-Merger Personnel at Prime Computer," *Human Resources Professional*, May/June 1989, 23. F. Lavoir "Surviving the Corporate Merger," *Modern Office Technology*, September 1988, 80.

25. A. Nahavandi and A. Malekyadeh, "Acculturation in Mergers and Acquisitions," *Academy of Management Review 13* (1988): 79–90.

26. L. Lancaster and T. Li-Ping Tang, "Outplacement Offers Safety Net for Displaced Workers," *Personnel Administrator*, April 1989, 60–63.

27. Stanley M. Davis, *Managing Corporate Culture* (Cambridge, Mass.: Ballenger, 1984), 1.

28. Edgar H. Schein, "What You Need to Know about Organizational Culture," *Training and Development Journal*, January 1986, 30–33.

29. F. Allen, "US West to Set Pension Plan to Cut Costs," *Wall Street Journal*, December 1, 1989, A6.

30. D. Dalton and C. Enz, "Absenteeism in Remission: Planning, Policy, Culture," *Human Resource Planning 10* (1987): 85.

31. J. S. Ott, *The Organizational Culture Perspective* (Pacific Grove, Calif.: Brooks/Cole, 1989), 59.

32. Robert C. Ernest, "Corporate Cultures and Effective Planning," *Personnel Administrator*, March 1985, 49–60.

33. Jay B. Barney, "Organizational Culture: Can It Be a Source of Sustained Competitive Advantage?" *Academy of Management Review 11* (1986): 656–665.

34. Thomas A. Kochan and Thomas A. Bariocci, *Human Resources Management and Industrial Relations* (Boston: Little, Brown, 1985), 101–109.

35. Rohit Deshpande and A. Parasuraman, "Linking Corporate Culture to Strategic Planning," *Business Horizons*, May/June 1986, 28–37.

36. Kochan and Barocci, *Human Resource Management*, 104–105.

37. Carl R. Anderson and Carl P. Zeithaml, "Stage of the Product Life Cycle, Business Strategy, and Business Performance," *Academy of Management Journal 27* (1984): 5–24.

38. Adapted from, "Roger Smith's Campaign to Change the GM Culture," *Business Week*, April 7, 1986, 84–85; "Ross Perot's Crusade," *Business Week*, October 6, 1986, 60–65.

Individual Performance and Job Design

Chapter 4

After you have read this chapter, you should be able to:

1. Explain three components of individual performance
2. Discuss how productivity, innovation, and loyalty are interrelated
3. Define motivation and discuss problems encountered in identifying the factors that motivate employees
4. Describe four views about why people behave as they do
5. Diagram and discuss the relationship between job satisfaction and turnover and absenteeism
6. Identify three absenteeism and turnover control alternatives
7. Define job design and describe its nature
8. Explain the difference between job enrichment and job enlargement
9. Identify the five components of the job characteristics model

P/HR: Today *and* Tomorrow

The New Work Force: Performance Without People?

One fact driven home to U.S. managers in the last several years is that people cost money and there are some jobs that machines can do just as well as people. As a result, the shift toward replacing people with machines, especially in those jobs that are routine, has accelerated.

Unions, understandably, have been concerned about automation taking jobs. This concern is not new, but the current emphasis on raising productivity through automation promises to spread the "robot revolution" much more widely. White-collar jobs also are being affected. Lexicons, machines that type directly from speech, are coming into use. Ultimately, they may eliminate 50 percent of all clerical and stenographic jobs.

There has been much speculation about how people would cope with the loss of some of their work in the robotized future. But researchers who have examined the kinds of jobs generated after automation has been implemented suggest that more interesting jobs are a likely result, which should increase employee motivation. At Ford Motor Company's Livonia, Michigan, transmission plant, machines do the "go-fer" jobs. Computers on the lines summon unmanned vehicles that glide across the factory floor bringing parts as needed. Unskilled labor is history in this 80 percent automated factory. Unskilled workers have been replaced with better-educated employees who have stronger voice in decision making.

Ford autoworker Bob McCallum, who started making cars twenty-two years ago, saw the handwriting on the wall and hit the books. After 360 hours of instruction in robotics and other subjects, he now trains others. He says: "With this training, our chances of keeping the doors open on this building are 100 percent better. If my sons want a job in the auto industry, at least Livonia will still be here."

New jobs are being created by new technology. Many managers have been slow to realize that workers *can* learn new skills associated with the new equipment. One college professor points out that in the 1880s it was thought that only mechanics could drive cars—but the average person soon learned to operate an automobile.

The picture that is likely to emerge is one of evolution rather than revolution. Industry must be able to afford robots before buying them, a fact that will lengthen the time before robots make much impact on a work force of 100 million.

Previous waves of automation have caused unemployment in the short term, but they have forced corresponding changes in the work force. Increased education, shorter workweeks and workdays, longer training, earlier retirement, child labor laws, and welfare and unemployment payments have all had roles in easing our adjustments to new technologies. Americans have been successful in translating productivity gains from automation into higher standards of living instead of into less work.

However, automation brings about requirements for the organization that are somewhat different from those in the past. Automated solutions require an investment in the organizational and human capabilities needed to use them. High levels of skill and motivation on the part of employees are a part of the inseparability of technology and human resources.[1]

"The perception used to be that Human Resources thought about the happiness of employees. . . . Now we realize the overriding concern is the yield from employees.

Jean Coyle

Effective organizations remain competitive by innovatively managing all of their resources. Human resources are both a major expense and a major plus for any organization. Within this resource, individual performance must be sufficiently high if the organization is to compete successfully. Individual performance depends on: (1) an employee's willingness to put forth the *effort* necessary, (2) the employee's *training,* and (3) the employee's *ability* to do what is required (Figure 4–1).

Employers tend to place a high premium on "motivated" employees. Motivation and the effort component of the equation in Figure 4–1 go together. In fact, in a survey done by Dun and Bradstreet, business owners listed finding qualified, motivated employees as their third biggest problem, ahead of controlling business costs. Only cash-flow problems and liability insurance difficulties were more important concerns.[2]

This chapter looks at factors influencing people's performance at work. The intent is not to provide an all-inclusive review of the literature, but rather to look at the performance most employers want from employees and key issues associated with that performance. Job attitudes and absenteeism and turnover behaviors are examined because they also can impact individual performance. Finally, job design is considered as one way in which human resources can be matched with jobs to improve performance.

■■ ■ INDIVIDUAL PERFORMANCE: THREE PERSPECTIVES

There are three kinds of individual performances that organizations need to prosper: *productivity, innovation,* and *loyalty.* Productivity on an individual level can be equated with efficiency: the amount produced divided by the person hours required to do it. Many managers *mean* productivity when they speak of "motivation." Is the person willing to put forth the effort to get a job done?

Innovation—new ways of doing work, new products, new services—is another important performance variable in many jobs. Many organizations need innovation to continue to compete successfully.

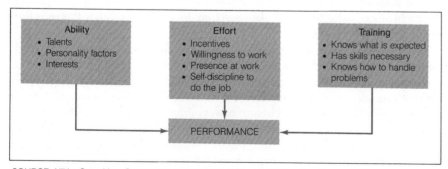

Figure 4–1
Components of Individual Performance

SOURCE: Nikko Securities, Competitive Manufacturing Research, Houston, Texas, 1989.

Loyalty to the organization is the third performance factor desired by many employers. While there may be practical limits to loyalty, a loyal work force is beneficial to the organization. Each of these factors—productivity, innovation, and loyalty—is discussed next.

Productivity

PRODUCTIVITY
is most often defined as the ratio of output to input.

Productivity is most often defined simply as the ratio of output to input. For measuring *labor productivity*, hours of work that went into a product could be an input. The amount of product produced, for example, bushels of wheat, could be the output. Productivity then could be expressed as 2 hours of labor per bushel of wheat produced.

This example of productivity is a bit oversimplified, because the assumption is that labor is the only input that influences the amount of wheat produced. Such is seldom the case, regardless of the product. In the wheat example, the fertility of the soil, the amount of money spent on fertilizer and on farm equipment to plant and harvest the wheat, and even the weather would affect productivity— probably even more than the hours of labor invested.

Individual productivity (the amount a given individual can produce in a given time) depends on the *effort* that a person puts forth, but that is by no means the only determinant. Education and experience on the job can increase productivity over time as people design more efficient and effective ways to to the job. Further, the tools individuals have to work with make a difference. A ditch digger with a power backhoe can dig a ditch in 20 minutes that might take a person with a shovel all day.

Productivity is a concern at three levels—the level of the individual, the level of the organization, and the level of the nation as a whole. Many of the activities undertaken in a P/HR system deal with individual productivity. Pay and appraisal systems, training, selection, and incentives are concerned with productivity very directly. Controlling turnover and absenteeism affects productivity as well.[3]

Productivity at the level of the organization ultimately affects profitability and competitiveness in a for-profit organization and total costs in a nonprofit organization. Decisions to close (or open) plants often are the result of productivity concerns. A useful way to measure productivity is by **unit labor cost,** or the total

UNIT LABOR COST
is the total labor cost per unit of output. The unit labor cost is equal to the average wage divided by the level of productivity.

labor cost per unit of output, which is computed by dividing the average wage of workers by their level of productivity. Using the unit labor cost it can be seen that a company paying relatively high wages still can be economically competitive *if* it can also achieve an offsetting high productivity level.[4] The automobile industry worldwide is an interesting study in how one industry has attempted to cope with the problems of individual- and plant-level productivity. (See P/HR Practice: Productivity in the Auto Industry.)

At the national level, productivity is of concern for several reasons. First, high productivity leads to high standards of living, as symbolized by a greater ability for a country to pay for the things it wants. Next, increases in national wage levels without increases in national productivity lead to inflation; this means an increase in costs and a decrease in purchasing power. Finally, lower rates of productivity make for higher unit labor costs and a less competitive position for a nation's products in the world marketplace. Figure 4–2 shows the trend in productivity figures for several major producing nations.[5]

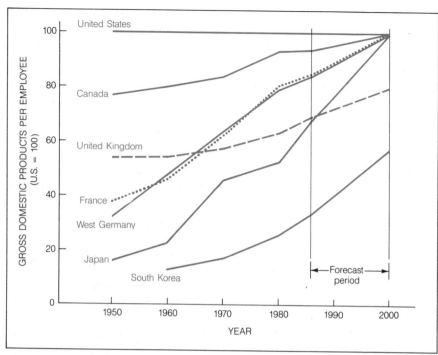

Figure 4–2
Trends in Productivity

SOURCE: American Productivity Center

QUALITY CONCERNS.   Related to productivity is the issue of the quality of the products and services produced. Currently, many American goods suffer from an image of poor quality. Some observers state that the quality problems stem overwhelmingly from the failure of U.S. manufacturers to make quality a first priority. W. Edwards Deming, an American quality expert, says, "Fifteen to forty percent of the cost of almost any American product you buy is for the waste embedded in it."[6] Deming advocates "getting the job done right the first time" through pride in craftsmanship, vigorous training, and an unwillingness to accept delays, defects, and mistakes. U.S. companies are proceeding on the quality front in many different ways, ranging from general training of workers on quality to better engineering of products prior to manufacturing.[7] The consensus seems to be that it takes a company-wide dedication from the top to the bottom to strive for perfection. Productivity without quality has proved costly.

PRODUCTIVITY IN SERVICE ORGANIZATIONS.   Service workers account for an increasingly large percentage of the work force in the United States. Although improving productivity in this segment of the economy clearly is important, there are some special problems with productivity measurement in service organizations.[8] Outputs for service workers are not easy to measure. Many cannot even define *output* in specific terms, because often little physical product is produced. Paperwork, ideas, "coordination," machine monitoring or caring for sick a person, are hard to quantify as outputs.

Of course, some services are immune from increased productivity. "It still takes two person-hours to perform a half-hour Mozart string quartet. You aren't going to change that."[9] Service companies often raise productivity (just as on the shop

P/HR: Practice *and* Research

Productivity in the Auto Industry

In the early 1980s, productivity became a major concern of U.S. automakers. Japanese automobile imports were priced well below American products. The U.S. auto companies, feeling the crunch of foreign competition, looked closely at output per employee. Then a wide variety of techniques to improve productivity, ranging from automation and work redesign to "motivation programs" and attempts at psychological "involvement" were tried, but the results were mixed.

One example is the General Motors assembly plant in Fremont, California. In the early 1980s, the absenteeism rate was about 20 percent. There were 5,000 outstanding grievances, frequent wildcat strikes, and constant feuds between management

and labor. Finally, General Motors shut the plant down and turned it over to Toyota Motor Corporation as part of a joint venture called New Unit Motor Manufacturing, Inc. (NUMMI). Adding little new technology, Toyota implemented a typical Toyota production system with just-in-time delivery of parts and components and flexible assembly lines run by teams of workers in charge of their own jobs. The firm hired back the United Auto Workers (UAW) members who wanted to work, including their militant leaders.

As a result, 2,500 employees assemble what it formerly took 5,000 people to produce with GM. Significantly, absenteeism decreased to

about 2 percent, and outstanding grievances averaged only about two at a time.

Productivity (and quality) in U.S.-owned plants in the United States still is below Japanese plants (both in Japan and in the United States) but better than in European-owned plants in Europe.

U.S. automakers have not been the only ones to learn from the Japanese. Volvo of Sweden has redesigned its traditional assembly-line jobs to incorporate teams of workers who can handle all assembly jobs. Volvo claims the plant using this approach already produces cars with fewer hours of labor and better quality than its three other Swedish plants.[10]

floor) with a new machine such as installation of computers to replace manual paper work processing. Lasting gains in productivity come when service or nonprofit organizations confront the problem directly, investing in technology, education, and job restructuring so that each worker can do substantially more.[11]

Innovation

Innovation requires creative behavior. Stimulating and maintaining innovation is an important goal for all organizations facing a changing competitive environment. For example, American Express, the financial service organization, used task forces to develop an innovative method that reduced the time needed to process applications for personal credit cards. The company was concerned because delays in approving credit applications led to lost revenue, unhappy clients, and lost customers in the competitive credit card industry. The firm asked members of the task force to describe and measure each step of the application review process. By carefully identifying each step, the task force targeted and removed the obstacles. Average application review time was cut 60 percent (from 35 to 14 days). Thus, this innovation resulted in improved productivity, customer satisfaction, employee involvement, and organizational performance.[12]

The need for innovation must overcome human problems and limitations. First, there is the tendency to *resist change*. Not all innovations will be accepted by employees or customers, yet creative ideas must be both accepted and implemented to be successful. Second, some innovative attempts may prove to be unproductive or costly, yet these results cannot be prevented. Innovation contains a clear element of *risk*, which concerns many managers, although people who do not take risks cannot innovate.

Certain companies seem to be more adept at innovation than others. 3M, Merck, Hewlett-Packard, and Rubbermaid are considered among the best currently. 3M spins out new products better than almost anyone. In a recent year 32 percent of 3M's $10.6 billion in sales came from products introduced in the previous 5 years.[13] The simple rules that 3M relies on are similar to those used in other innovative companies. 3M's vice president for human resources summarizes employees' feelings this way: "Our studies have shown that the biggest reward they can receive is to be given the opportunity to be innovative many times during their careers. We have never paid our technical people on the basis of what they actually invented. It might get reflected in a merit increase but we don't give them a specific bonus."[14]

INTRAPRENEURSHIP.   Gifford Pinchot III coined the term **intrapreneuring** to describe an employee who works within an organization in an independent, innovative manner. Such innovative behavior, while critical to many organizations, can cause problems unless the organization is flexible and has a human resource system geared to handling the unusual. Still, not all innovation requires such flexibility. IBM's success with the PC can be attributed to its innovative techniques carried out within a large and presumably inflexible company.

INTRAPRENEURING
describes employees acting in an independent manner within an organization.

Loyalty

The long-term economic health of most organizations depends on a stable, skilled, work force. Loyalty is an ingredient in that stable work force. There are many definitions of loyalty, but as used here, **loyalty** is commitment and allegiance to an organization.

LOYALTY
is commitment to and allegiance with an organization.

Most managers want loyal performance from their employees. Lack of loyalty usually shows up in relatively minor P/HR matters, such as refusal to relocate, but sometimes in more expensive problems, such as turnover. In some industries, defection from individual firms is widespread. In Central California's Silicon Valley, turnover rates at 231 electronics companies averaged more than five times the rate for all U.S. manufacturing companies.[15]

Polls about employee loyalty provide a mixed picture. One poll showed 80 percent of corporate middle managers still were "deeply committed" to their company,[16] while another found that 65 percent of salaried workers are less loyal to their companies than they were 10 years ago.[17]

Turnover is one possible result where loyalty is missing, but disloyal employees who cannot leave might resort to less effort, sabotage, theft, and absenteeism. In high-tech work and professional occupations, loyalty is more likely to be to the profession or to the technology used than to one's employer.

One question asked by managers is what motivates loyalty? IBM is known for having a fiercely loyal work force, which the company fosters in two ways. First, it selects people who share company values and beliefs. Second, the company has tried not to lay off employees.

In many ways loyalty appears to be an exchange. The employee supplies effort, loyalty, and productivity to the organization and in return *expects* loyalty from the organization. As organizational mergers and employment cutbacks have swept the country, resulting in layoffs and restructuring, more and more employees seem convinced that companies will not return their loyalty. The "exchange" is not completed.

As can be seen from the Silicon Valley example above, the "one-company-for-life" attitude that prevailed from before World War II until the early 1970s has changed. Employees are changing jobs twice as frequently as they did 20 or 30 years ago. Job tenure in the 1960s averaged 20 years. Today, the average is below 8.75 years.[18] One researcher notes that, although it is a complex relationship, education level (which has been increasing) is negatively related to organizational commitment.[19] Some suggest that firms seriously consider job redesign to emphasize the instrinsic rewards in a job for motivating more highly educated employees to stay with an organization.

Many companies are apparently concerned about the lack of loyalty in today's work force. However, "they should be looking at themselves," according to one HR consultant.[20] Several suggestions to improve the organizational side of the equation include:

- Encourage employee involvement in decisions
- Stress face-to-face communication
- Give competitive compensation and emphasize rewarding excellence
- Provide training
- Promote from within
- Maintain adequate career paths
- Reduce distinctions of rank

Increased mobility and different values have brought about a change in this traditional element of work performance. Yet organizations continue to seek loyal employees and the advantages that occur in productivity, stability, and knowledge.

■■ ■ MOTIVATION

P/HR professionals are interested in the topic of motivation because many of their responsibilities (compensation, incentives, discipline, job design, career planning, and appraisal, to name a few) require assumptions about what motivates people. Motivation is concerned with the "whys" of human behavior. It attempts to account for the drives and wants of an individual, rather than focusing just on the individual's actions.

MOTIVATION
is derived from the word *motive* and is an emotion or desire causing a person to act.

Motivation is an emotion or desire within a person causing that person to act. People usually act for one reason: to obtain a goal. Thus, motivation is a goal-directed drive and, as such, it seldom occurs in a void. The words *need, want, desire,* and *drive* are all similar to *motive.*

Importance of Motivation

Most managers agree that the success of any organization is determined by the efforts of the people in it. Also, managers often say that problems relating to employee behavior are the most preplexing.[21] Questions that arise include "How do you get people to do what you want them to do?" and "How can one be sure that people will do their work without a supervisor constantly watching them?" Because the human resources in an organization are an important part of how well it performs, these questions are of major concern to managers.

Understanding Motivation

It is often difficult to determine why employees behave as they do simply by observing their behavior. People's actions are not always directly related to their conscious or subconscious thoughts. Nor are these actions always related to obvious daily occurrences. For example, if an employee has an argument with a supervisor and fails to report to work the next day, it may appear that behavior is a result of the confrontation. However, the worker's behavior may actually be motivated by a combination of factors including overwork, family illness, or some other problems.

MULTIPLE CAUSES.   Different people may have different reasons for behaving in the very same manner. For example, one manager joins a service club because it is a good place to make business contacts; another joins because of the social environment; still another joins because of the interesting programs and speakers at the club. Thus, different "whys" can underlie the same behavior, further complicating the process of inferring motivation from behavior. The motivations people have to pursue a certain career can spring from quite different sources. Personality, background, experiences, group effects, or many other factors can impact a person's career choice.

MULTIPLE BEHAVIORS.   In addition, the same motive may result in different behavioral patterns. For example, if an individual wants a promotion, she may concentrate on performing her job exceptionally well. But another worker who also wants a promotion, may try to "apple polish" the boss to get the promotion. Another manager, who also wants the promotion, may be afraid to do anything at all for fear he will fail. These three managers have the same motive but behave differently to obtain what they want.

MOTIVATION AS A SUBJECT.   Approaches to understanding motivation differ because many individual theorists have developed their own views and theories of motivation. They approach motivation from different starting points, with different ideas in mind, and from different backgrounds. No one approach is considered to be the "correct" one. Each has made its contribution to the understanding of human behavior.

Many managers' views of motivation are based on assumptions about what goals they expect people to achieve as employees. For example, if a manager says he wants to "motivate" employees, he is really saying he wants his employees to select the goals that *he* wants them to seek—goals that he considers best for salespeople in his division. His employees are undoubtedly motivated, but perhaps not toward doing what he would have them do. Figure 4–3 illustrates such a manager's model of motivation. This view, although widely held by managers, is too restrictive because it does not consider the needs of employees.

The study of motivation over the last century has been focused partly on answering the question "What is the basic goal of humans?" Managers have operated with their own preconceived ideas about these goals. Over time, four major assumptions about human nature and the mainsprings of motivation have emerged. These assumptions have been translated into managerial philosophies and views of employee motivation. One long-lived approach is based on the assumption that people are rational-economic beings.

Figure 4–3
Managerial Model of Motivation

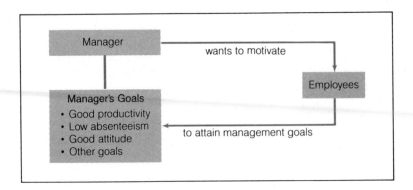

Rational-Economic View

The rational-economic view suggests that humans reasonably, logically, and rationally make decisions that will result in the most economic gain for themselves. Therefore, employees are motivated by the opportunity to make as much money as possible and will act rationally to maximize their earnings. The assumption is that money, because of what it can buy, is the most important motivator of all people.

This explanation of human motivation is weak because a great deal of behavior does not reasonably follow from the rational-economic assumption made about human nature. For example, if employees are primarily interested in maximizing their economic return, why do some turn away from the potential profits of piece-rate production and others refuse to take overtime? Obviously, the rational-economic assumptions have some limitations.

Social View

The social view of human nature suggests that all people can be motivated to perform if a manager appeals to their social needs. A predominant emphasis of this viewpoint is "Happiness and harmony in the group lead to productivity," or "A happy worker is a productive worker."

HUMAN RELATIONS.   The social view of human nature has led to the human relations approach, in which people are viewed as a bundle of attitudes, sentiments, and emotions. Managers are told that to be effective they should convince workers of their importance to the company. Employee participation in the decision-making process (as long as it cannot harm the operation) is supposed to lead to feelings of harmony, loyalty, and satisfaction.

Unfortunately, proponents of this view often have gone to extremes to explain motivation from just one variable, as earlier proponents of money as a motivator had done. In fact, not everyone is motivated primarily by harmony and cooperation, and many are suspicious of the sincerity of the human relations approach.

Some organizations purport to believe in employee participation, but they actually involve employees in decisions that management already has made. Such tactics can lead to total dissatisfaction. For example, a well-respected organization recognized that people were spending long lunch hours drinking coffee, so it asked employees to work on a new lunch policy. However, management paid no attention to the employees' policy and eventually introduced the plan it had developed before employee involvement.

Self-Actualizing View

During the late 1950s and early 1960s, the ideas of another group of management thinkers, many of whom were trained in the behavioral sciences, became very popular. They assumed that each person strives to reach self-actualization, that is, to reach his or her full potential.

MASLOW.   This concept was developed by a clinical psychologist, Abraham Maslow, whose theory of human motivation continues to receive a great deal of exposure in management literature. Maslow classified human needs into five categories that ascend in a definite order. Until the more basic needs are adequately fulfilled, a person will not strive to meet higher needs. Maslow's well-known hierarchy is composed of: (1) physiological needs, (2) safety and security needs, (3) belonging and love needs, (4) self-esteem needs, and (5) self-actualization needs.[22]

An assumption often made by those using Maslow's hierarchy is that workers in modern advanced societies have basically satisfied their physiological, safety, and belonging needs. Therefore, they will be motivated by the need for self-esteem, esteem of others, and self-actualization. Consequently, conditions to satisfy these needs should be present at work; the job itself should be internally meaningful and motivating.

MCGREGOR.   Douglas McGregor, using the self-actualization view as a point of departure, presented two opposite sets of assumptions about people's work motivation that he believed were held by most managers. Summarized in Figure 4–4, one set (which is negative) was labeled Theory X and the other (which is positive) Theory Y.[23] McGregor felt that managers typically held one of these sets of assumptions about human nature and acted in keeping with those assumptions. However, McGregor argued that people are really more like Theory Y than Theory X. A key point in McGregor's Theory Y is that work itself is a motivator of most people.

HERZBERG.   In the late 1950s, Frederick Herzberg and his research associates conducted interviews with 200 engineers and accountants who worked in different

THEORY X	THEORY Y
■ People dislike work and will attempt to avoid it. ■ People have to be coerced and threatened with punishment if organizational goals are to be met. ■ Most workers like direction and will avoid responsibility. ■ People want security above all in their work.	■ People do not inherently dislike work. ■ People do not like rigid control and threats. ■ Under proper conditions, people do not avoid responsibility. ■ People want security but also have other needs, such as self-actualization and esteem.

Figure 4–4
A summary of Theory X and Theory Y (McGregor)

SOURCE: Douglas McGregor, *The Human Side of Enterprise* (New York: McGraw-Hill, 1960), 33–45.

organizations. The result of this research was a theory that, like Maslow's, has been widely discussed in the management literature.[24] Maslow identifies basic human needs, while Herzberg's work relates factors in the job to a person's motivation.

Herzberg's motivation/hygiene theory assumes that one group of factors, *motivators*, accounts for high levels of motivation to work. Another group of factors can cause discontent with work. These factors are labeled *hygiene*, or maintenance, factors. Figure 4–5 compares Herzberg's motivators and hygiene factors with Maslow's need hierarchy.

The implication of Herzberg's research for management and P/HR practices is that although managers must carefully consider hygiene factors to avoid employee dissatisfaction, even if all these maintenance needs are addressed, people may not necessarily be motivated to work harder. Only motivators cause employees to exert more effort and thereby attain more productivity.

The self-actualizing school of thought, with its sometimes moralistic requests to improve the job and let the individual achieve self-actualization, has given way to the recognition that everyone is somewhat different and that job situations vary. To understand motivation and human behavior, one must understand the interactions between individual characteristics and the characteristics of the situation. The fourth approach to motivation and human behavior recognizes this complexity.

Complex View

The complex view suggests that, because each person is different, a variety of items may prove to be motivating, depending on the needs of the individual, the situation the individual is in, and the rewards the individual expects for the work done. Theorists who hold to this view do not attempt to fit people into a single category, but rather accept human differences.

People act to obtain goals. But Victor Vroom noted that whether they will act at all depends on whether they believe their behavior will help them achieve their goal.[25] In charting a path to a goal, people choose among various actions based on their prediction of the outcome of each action. For example, does hard work lead to more money in the pay envelope? Some people think that it does, and others think that it does not, depending on past experiences with hard work and earning more money.

Figure 4–5
Maslow's and Herzberg's Ideas Compared

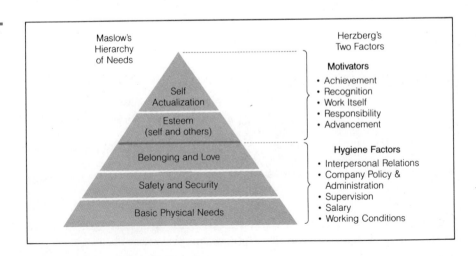

Another critical element is how much the person wants the expected outcome. To put it another way, a person's motivation depends on (1) his or her expectation that a particular behavior will result in a desired outcome or goal and (2) the value the person assigns to that outcome.

Another approach, by Lyman Porter and E. E. Lawler, contends that a person's desired goal and the value placed on the goal should be expanded to include the person's perceived equity or fairness as a factor that influences his or her job behavior. *Perception* is the way an individual views the job. Figure 4–6 contains a simplified Porter and Lawler model. This view is further affected by what people *expect* to receive from jobs. If their *expectations* are not met, they may feel that they have been unfairly treated and consequently become dissatisfied.[26]

Suppose that a salesclerk is motivated to expend effort on her job. From this job she expects to receive two types of rewards: intrinsic (internal) and extrinsic (external). For this salesclerk, intrinsic rewards could include a feeling of accomplishment, a feeling of recognition, or other motivators. Extrinsic rewards might be such items as pay, benefits, good working conditions, and other hygiene factors. The salesclerk compares her performance with what she expected and to both types of rewards she receives. She then reaches some level of job satisfaction or dissatisfaction. Once this level is reached, it is difficult to determine what she will do. If she is dissatisfied, she might put forth less effort next time, she might work harder to get the rewards she wants, or she might just accept her dissatisfaction. If she is highly satisfied, it does not always mean she will work harder. She may emphasize quality, or may say, "I got what I wanted."

The essence of the Porter and Lawler view of motivation is perception. In addition, if a feedback loop is present, performance leads to satisfaction rather than satisfaction leading to performance.

EQUITY AS A MOTIVATOR.   People want to be treated fairly, not just in the rewards they receive, but also in such areas as vacations, work assignments, and penalties assessed. Fairness in management literature is referred to as **equity,** which relates to inputs and outcomes. Inputs are what a person brings to the organization. They include educational level, age, experience, productivity, and other skills or efforts. The items received by a person, or the outcomes, are the rewards obtained in exchange for inputs. Outcomes include pay, benefits, recognition, achievement, prestige, and any other rewards received. Note that an outcome can be either

EQUITY
is the perceived fairness of what the person does (inputs) compared with what the person receives (outcomes).

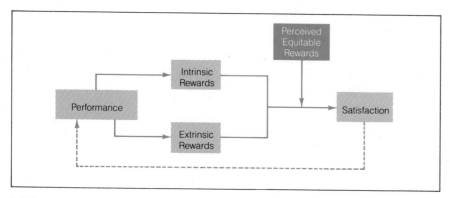

Figure 4–6
Porter and Lawler Motivation model

SOURCE: Adapted from Edward E. Lawler III and Lyman W. Porter, "The Effect of Performance on Job Satisfaction." *Industrial Relations* 7 (1966).

Figure 4–7
Equity Evaluations

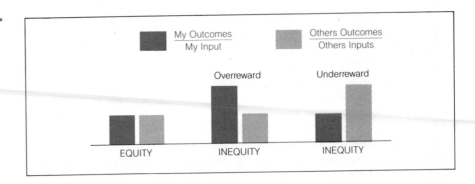

tangible (such as economic benefits) or intangible (internal rewards such as recognition or achievement).

The individual's view of fair value is critical to the relationship between performance and job satisfaction because one's sense of equity is an exchange and comparison process. Assume you are a laboratory technician in a hospital. You exchange talents and efforts for the tangible and intangible rewards the hospital gives. Then you compare your inputs (what you did) and your outcomes (what you received) with what other people did and received to determine the equity of your compensation. As Figure 4–7 shows, the comparison process includes the individual's comparison of inputs/outcomes to the inputs/outcomes of other individuals. Thus, you also will compare your talents, skills, and efforts to those of other laboratory technicians or other hospital employees. Your perception—correct or incorrect—significantly affects your valuation of your inputs and outcomes. A sense of inequity occurs when the comparison process results in an imbalance between inputs and outcomes.

IF INPUTS EXCEED OUTCOMES.   One view of equity theory research suggests that if an employee is underrewarded (more inputs than outcomes), the employee will tend to reduce his or her inputs. If, in your job as a lab technician, you feel that your rewards have been fewer than your inputs, you will attempt to resolve the inequity. Your reactions can include some or all of the following: increasing dissatisfaction, attempting to get compensation raised, quitting the job for a more equitable one, changing your perceptual comparison, or reducing your productivity. All these actions are attempts to reduce the inequity.

IF OUTCOMES EXCEED INPUTS.   One way a person may attempt to resolve being overrewarded is by putting forth more effort. If you feel that you receive more rewards than you deserve, you might work harder to justify the "overpayment." Or you might process the same number of laboratory samples, but do so more accurately and produce higher quality results. Another action could include a recomparison, whereby you might decide that you evaluated your efforts inaccurately and that you really were not overpaid.

Regardless of what action you take, you will make some attempt to relieve the inequity tension. Research evidence on the type of action you are most likely to take is mixed.[27] Because they can affect motivation, feelings of inequity have important implications for the design and administration of compensation programs, staffing, training, and performance appraisal. Motivation may lead to satisfaction with a job well done; however, job satisfaction is both an outcome and a process related to, but separate from, motivation.

P/HR: Practice *and* Research	Genetics and Job Satisfaction

Industrial psychologist Richard Arvey, studying identical twins who grew up in different families, found evidence that genes may influence employees' satisfaction with their job. The study, reported in the *Journal of Applied Psychology*, focused on 34 pairs of identical twins who had been separated when younger than 6 months and raised apart. They had been reunited at an average age of thirty-two.

Each twin completed a 20-item questionnaire about satisfaction with the major jobs in his or her life. Comparing jobs held by twins, Arvey found that twins tended to hold jobs similar in degree of mental complexity, physical demands, and coordination requirements.

Twins also tended to be similar in their satisfaction with their jobs. Some pairs generally were happy with what they did, whereas others seemed to have trouble finding satisfying work.

Personality, which many believe has a genetic basis, is a very likely mechanism affecting satisfaction. Therefore genes may influence what people focus on in their jobs (such as supervision), or perhaps genes affect what people want from a job and, as a result, their satisfaction.[29]

JOB SATISFACTION

In its most basic sense, **job satisfaction** is a pleasurable or positive emotional state resulting from the appraisal of one's job experiences.[28] Job *dissatisfaction* occurs when these expectations are not met. For instance, if you expect clean and safe working conditions on the job, you are likely to be dissatisfied if your work place is dirty and dangerous.

Job satisfaction is determined by an individual's evaluation of his or her work experiences. The evaluation may be personal and internal or it may be partly external, influenced by manager, co-workers, or the like; but the individual is the final determinant of the positive (or negative) feeling that results.

Job satisfaction has many dimensions. Some include satisfaction with the work itself, wages, recognition, rapport with supervisors and co-workers, and organizational culture and philosophy. Each dimension contributes to an overall feeling of satisfaction with the job itself, but the "job" is defined differently by different people.

Comparisons and expectations influence job satisfaction. To form a measure of job satisfaction, the worker looks at many elements of the job. There is no simple formula for predicting every worker's satisfaction. The relationship between productivity and job satisfaction is not entirely clear. It *is* clear that "happy workers" are not always more productive workers. For example, concern with a generally low level of productivity in the United States is coupled with a generally high level of job satisfaction. In a nationwide poll, Media General-Associated Press found that:

- Nine out of ten people said they liked their jobs.
- Sixty-three percent said they were paid fairly.
- Of those who liked their jobs, 33 percent liked the work best, 25 percent liked their co-workers best, 12 percent liked the money best.
- White-collar workers liked their jobs better than blue-collar workers.
- Older workers liked their jobs better than younger workers.[30]

JOB SATISFACTION
is a pleasurable or positive emotional state resulting from the appraisal of one's job experiences.

Job satisfaction depends on characteristics of the individual (see P/HR: Research on genetics and job satisfaction) and characteristics of the job. Research evidence indicates that satisfaction with one's job leads to commitment to the organization, which helps determine absenteeism and turnover[31] (Figure 4–8). Although job satisfaction itself is interesting and important, perhaps the "bottom line" is the effect job satisfaction has on employee absenteeism and turnover.

▬ ▬ ABSENTEEISM

Being absent from work may seem like a small matter to an employee. But if a manager needs twelve people to work in a unit to get the work done, and four of the twelve are absent most of the time, the unit's work will probably not get done or additional workers will have to be hired.

Not all absence is bad, nor can absenteeism be reduced to zero. People do get sick and there are circumstances that make it impossible for people to attend work. This is usually referred to as involuntary absenteeism. However, much absenteeism is avoidable, and a relatively small percentage of individuals in the workplace is responsible for a disproportionate share of the total absence.

Cost of Absenteeism

Absenteeism is expensive. Certain elements of labor overhead continue for an employer even though the employee is absent. For example:

- *Benefits.* Most organizations continue to pay benefits for employees who are absent on a long-term basis.
- *Worker's compensation premiums.* Employers who use a private insurer for worker's compensation are likely to face an increase in premiums as a result of a long-term work-related absenteeism.
- *Lost productivity.* With both short- and long-term absenteeism, a certain amount of production will be lost.[32]

Figure 4–8
Causal Model: Job Satisfaction, Absenteeism, and Turnover

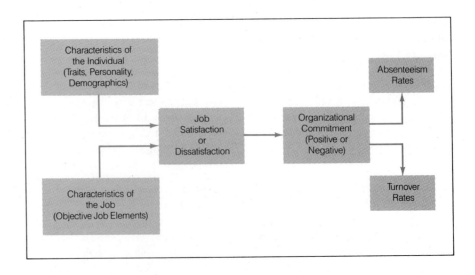

P/HR: **Practice *and* Research**   Creative Reasons for Being Late or Absent

Robert Half, an employment recruiter, surveyed P/HR executives from 100 of the largest companies for their favorite excuses for tardiness or absence from work. Here are some that are hard to top.

"My pet chicken froze to the driveway and I had to wait around to thaw it loose."

"My six-year-old son set all the clocks in the house back an hour as a joke."

"I thought Halloween *was* a national holiday."

"The dog hid my toupee."

"I fell asleep over breakfast and the waitress didn't wake me up till 9:30."

"I thought I saw a flying saucer and followed it 50 miles down the highway."

"Someone stole one of my shoes on the bus."

"A spider cornered me in the bathroom."

"I was up half the night looking for Halley's Comet."

"When you work as hard as I do, you're entitled."[35]

Organizations consistently have noted that there are more absences on Fridays and Mondays than on other days because some employees like to stretch the weekend to three or four days. Employees with higher job satisfaction will probably be absent less often than those who are dissatisfied with their jobs. (See the P/HR: Practice and Research on creative reasons for being late or absent.)

Absenteeism Control

Controlling absenteeism would be easier if managers understood the causes more clearly, but a solid theory of absenteeism has not yet emerged. One theory that has some support is that absence occurs when people do not cope well with certain aspects of their jobs, so voluntary absence is a way of *avoiding* such a situation.[34]

Controlling or reducing absenteeism must begin with continuous monitoring of absenteeism statistics in work units. Monitoring helps managers pinpoint employees who are frequently absent and departments that have excessive absenteeism. Offering rewards for good attendance, giving bonuses for missing fewer than a certain number of days, and "buying back" unused sick leave are all positive methods of reducing absenteeism. If absenteeism is excessive, the problem employees can be dismissed.

Organizational policies on absenteeism should be clearly stated in an employee handbook and stressed by supervisors and managers. Counseling and discussing the matter with employees may correct some problems that make people reluctant to come to work. Positive actions to avoid being absent should be suggested. Absenteeism control options fall into three categories: (1) discipline, (2) positive reinforcement, or (3) a combination of both.

DISCIPLINARY APPROACH. Scott, a large paper company, used the disciplinary approach in its Mobile, Alabama, plant to good effect. People who were absent first received an oral warning, but subsequent absences brought written warnings, suspension, and finally dismissal. In five years under this system, 70 workers were fired; the absenteeism rate dropped from 7 percent to around 4 percent.[36]

The Research Institute of America estimates that a one-day absence by a clerical worker costs the company up to $100 in reduced productivity and increased supervisory work load. Cumulatively, absenteeism drains the U.S. economy by at least $40 billion per year.[33] Absenteeism often varies from 2 to 12 percent per month.

Employees can be absent from work for several reasons. Illness, death in the family, or other personal reasons are unavoidable and understandable. Consequently, many employers have sick-leave policies that allow employees a certain number of paid absent days per year. Employees who miss fewer days are reimbursed with sick pay.

A formula for computing absenteeism rates, suggested by the U.S. Department of Labor, is as follows:

$$\frac{\text{Number of person-days lost through job absence during period}}{(\text{Average number of employees}) \times (\text{Number of work days})} \times 100$$

(Note: The rate can be computed based on number of hours instead of number of days.)

POSITIVE REINFORCEMENT. Positive reinforcement includes such methods as giving employees cash, recognition, time off, or other rewards for meeting attendance standards. In one firm, employees with perfect attendance records were given the opportunity to participate in a lottery with a cash reward. The program reduced absenteeism.

COMBINATION APPROACH. Combination approaches ideally reward desired behavior and punish undesired behavior. At some firms, including some hospitals, each employee gets a time-off "account," against which vacations, holidays, and sick days are drawn. If employees run out of days in their accounts, they are not paid for the days missed. However, they can accrue sick time yearly.

Impact of Absence Policies

The policies and rules an organization uses to govern absenteeism may provide a clue to the effectiveness of that control. Studies indicate that absence rates are highly related to the control policies used for absenteeism. Policies can encourage attendance or absence. For example, one examination concluded:[38]

- Organizations that pay more have higher absence rates.
- Employees can afford to "buy" leisure.
- Companies that require a doctor's certificate when ill have lower absence rates.
- Organizations that accrue sick leave faster have higher absenteeism (some people feel sick leave is to be used).
- Organizations that *do not* reimburse unused sick leave have higher absenteeism rates.

■■ ■ TURNOVER

TURNOVER
occurs when employees leave the organization and have to be replaced.

Turnover occurs when employees leave an organization and have to be replaced. This can be a very costly problem. One firm had a turnover rate of more than 120

Figure 4–9
A Study of Factors Associated with Turnover

EXTERNAL FACTORS	WORK-RELATED FACTORS	PERSONAL CHARACTERISTICS
■ Other job alternatives available ■ No union present ■ Low unemployment rate	■ Low pay ■ Low job satisfaction ■ Low job performance ■ The job is unclear	■ Young age ■ New employee ■ High education level ■ Few dependents ■ Female ■ Expectations not met

SOURCE: Adapted from J. Colton and J. M. Tuttle, "Employee Turnover: A Meta Analysis and Review with Implications for Research," *Academy of Management Review* 11, (1986): 55–70.

percent per year! It costs the company $1.5 million a year in lost productivity, increased training time, increased employee selection time, lost work efficiency, and other indirect costs.

It is the cost that makes turnover a common indicator of the P/HR performance of a company. But cost is not the only reason turnover is important. Lengthy training times, interrupted schedules, overtime for others, mistakes, and not having a knowledgeable employee in place are some of the frustrations associated with excessive turnover.

The turnover rate for an organization can be computed in a number of different ways.[39] The following formula from the U.S. Department of Labor is widely used. (*separations* are people who left the organization).

$$\frac{\text{Number of employee separations during the month}}{\text{Total number of employees at midmonth}} \times 100$$

Common turnover figures range from 2 to 35 percent per year. Note that normal turnover rates vary among industries. Organizations that require little skill for entry-level employees are likely to have a higher turnover rate among those employees than among managerial personnel. As a result, it is important that turnover rates be computed by work units. For instance, one organization had a company-wide turnover rate that was not severe—but 80 percent of the turnover occurred within one department. This imbalance indicated that some action was needed to resolve problems in that unit.

Causes of turnover are varied: lack of challenge, better opportunity, pay, supervision, geography, pressure, and so on. Certainly, not all turnover is negative. (Some work force losses are quite desirable, especially if those who leave are lower performing, less reliable individuals.)

Turnover often is classified as *voluntary* or *involuntary* and/or *avoidable* or *unavoidable*. Involuntary turnover occurs when an employee is fired. Voluntary turnover occurs when an employee leaves by his or her own choice, and can be caused by many factors. The obvious ones are those that cause job dissatisfaction.

Figure 4–9 shows the results of a comparison of 120 different turnover studies. Three classes of variables (external factors, work-related factors, and personal characteristics) were considered. In each classification, certain items were reliably related to a person's likelihood to leave the organization.

New employees are more likely to leave than employees who have been on the job longer. One estimate is that a company is likely to lose 16 to 20 percent of its employees during the first year, 8 to 9 percent during the second year, and only 1 percent of those remaining after ten years.[40] Studies of new employee turnover suggest that if people view their job performance as based on unstable factors such as luck, they are more likely to leave. If luck is the explanation for one's early performance, it may not give the employee enough feeling of achievement to persist through the anxious first few months of work. Turnover also shows something of a "snowball" effect—that is, turnover itself causes more turnover.[41]

Turnover Control

Turnover can be controlled in several ways. Because it is related to job satisfaction, matching an employee's expectations of rewards and satisfaction to what is actually provided by the job may help reduce turnover problems. A good way to eliminate turnover is to *improve selection* and to better match applicants to jobs. By fine-tuning the selection process and hiring people who are more likely to stay, managers can decrease the chances that employees will leave.

Good *employee orientation* also will help reduce turnover. Employees who are properly inducted into the company and are well-trained tend to be less likely to leave. If people receive some basic information about the company and the job to be performed, they can determine early whether they want to stay. If individuals believe that they have no opportunity for career advancement, they may leave the organization. Consequently, *career planning* and *internal promotion* can help an organization keep career employees.

In addition, a fair and equitable *pay system* can help prevent turnovers. An employee who is underpaid relative to employees in other jobs with similar skills may leave if there is an inviting alternative job available. An awareness of employee problems and dissatisfaction may provide a manager with opportunities to resolve them before they become so severe that employees leave.

In extreme cases in which there is a shortage of qualified workers, companies may spend heavily on training only to have competitors "pirate" away employees. Such situations have led to "payback agreements" whereby an employee must repay training, relocation, and even some salary costs if he or she leaves within a certain time.

■ ■ JOB DESIGN

JOB DESIGN
refers to a conscious effort to organize tasks, duties, and responsibilities into a unit of work.

Job Design refers to a conscious effort to organize tasks, duties, and responsibilities into a unit of work. The way people look at work and jobs has evolved gradually over the years. The design of many jobs has changed and others are now in the process of change. *Job design* considers the *content* and the effect of jobs on employees. Today more attention is being paid to job design for three major reasons:

1. Job design can impact *performance* in certain jobs, especially in those jobs in which employee motivation can make a substantial difference. Lower costs through reduced turnover and absenteeism also seem related to good job design.
2. Job design can affect *job satisfaction*. Because people are more satisfied with certain job configurations than with others, it is important to be able to identify what makes a "good" job.
3. Job design can affect both *physical and mental health*. Problems such as hearing loss, backache and leg pain can be directly traced to job design, as can stress and related blood pressure and heart disease.

P/HR UNIT	MANAGERS
■ Monitors need for job redesign company-wide ■ Researches and provides information on effects of job designs on performance, satisfaction, and health ■ Identifies experts in various kinds of redesign to help when needed	■ Design jobs with help from P/HR unit and employees ■ Supervise performance on job as designed and make needed adjustments ■ Monitor productivity, turnover, and other factors as indicators of need for redesign ■ Identify new jobs for initial design

Figure 4–10
Job Design Responsibilities

Designing and redesigning jobs requires cooperation by P/HR professionals and operating managers. Figure 4–10 shows how a large organization that has a separate P/HR unit divides the duties. In a small organization, the operating managers have to perform all activities.

The managers are mainly responsible for developing work procedures, identifying performance standards, and designing and supervising the performance of work in jobs. The P/HR unit attempts to determine the effects of job design and to suggest changes when research reveals that job design is having negative effects.

What Is a Job?

Every job is composed of *tasks*, *duties*, and *responsibilities*. Although the terms "position" and "job" are often used interchangeably, there is a slight difference in emphasis. A **position** is a collection of tasks, duties, and responsibilities performed by one person. A **job** may include more than one position. Thus, if there are two persons operating postage meters in a mailroom, there are two positions (one for each person) but just one job (postage meter operator).

A **task** is composed of motions and is a distinct identifiable work activity, whereas "a **duty** is composed of a number of tasks and is a larger work segment performed by an individual." Because both tasks and duties describe activities, it is not always easy or necessary to distinguish between the two. If one of the employment supervisor's duties is to "interview applicants," one task associated with that duty would be "asking questions."

Responsibilities also go with jobs, and they are obligations to perform certain tasks and duties. Because managerial jobs carry greater responsibilities, they are usually more highly paid.

Person/Job Fit

Not everyone would be happy as a physician, as an engineer, or as a dishwasher. But certain people like and do well at each of those jobs. The person/job fit is a simple but important concept that involves matching characteristics of people with characteristics of jobs. Figure 4–11 depicts the person/job fit. Obviously, if a person does not fit a job, either the person can be changed or replaced, or the job can be altered. In the past, it was much more common to make the round person fit the square job. Titles such as farmhand or factory hand suggested that *hands* were hired, not whole people. However, successfully "reshaping" people is not easy to do. By redesigning jobs, the person/job fit can be more easily improved. Jobs may be designed properly when they are first established or redesigned later.

POSITION
is a collection of tasks, duties, and responsibilities performed by one person.

JOB
is a grouping of similar positions having common tasks, duties and responsibilities.

TASK
is a distinct identifiable work activity composed of motions.

DUTY
is a larger work segment composed of several tasks that are performed by an individual.

RESPONSIBILITIES
are obligations to perform certain tasks and duties.

Figure 4–11
Person/Job Fit

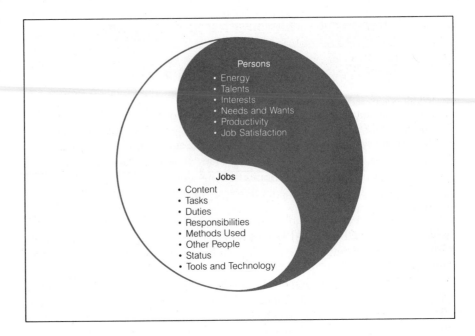

Nature of Job Design

Identifying the components of a given job is an integral part of job design. Designing or redesigning jobs encompasses many factors, and a number of different techniques are available to the manager. Job design has been equated with job enrichment, a technique developed by Frederick Herzberg, but job design is much broader than job enrichment alone.

Job design must consider:

- *Content* of the job
- *Methods*, *tools*, or *technology* used
- Their combined *effects* on the people during the job
- *Relationships* with other people at work that are likely to develop through interpersonal contact

Job design has not always been as comprehensive as the list suggests. A brief review of the history of job design shows how it has evolved.

History of Job Design

With the industrial age, people found employment outside agriculture, and many jobs evolved into simply machine-tending jobs. People were controlled by rules, and management's job was to enforce those rules. The idea that jobs could be satisfying to people's needs was not widely held. The prevailing work ethic led most people to associate hard work with morality, regardless of the nature of the work.

SCIENTIFIC MANAGEMENT.   The concept of scientific management developed by Frederick W. Taylor, approached job design from the standpoint of trying to achieve maximum efficiency—the greatest amount of work in the least amount of time. It was built on three major ideas:

1. *Division of labor*. Jobs were broken into their smallest component parts because small parts could be done with greatest efficiency. A person was then put in charge of each small job. These smaller jobs required only unskilled workers because the jobs could be learned quickly.
2. *Standardization*. The "one best way" to do a particular job was discovered through study, then everyone performed it that way. Advantages were gained in efficiency, ease of training, and reduction of wage and training costs.
3. *Specialization*. Specialization results from division of labor. As people specialize on narrow tasks, they become more proficient. Specialization has continued to increase as organizations have become larger and more complex.

Specialization can result in some problems. Among these problems are an inability to communicate with specialists in other areas and a shortage of people trained to see the entire picture of the organization. Further, petty jealousies, territoriality, stereotyping, boredom, and a low sense of achievement also can result from specialization. However, specialization may have major economic advantages and can be satisfying when it allows a person to develop expertise in a particular area.

When the concepts of scientific management are used to design jobs, common characteristics seem to develop:

- Work speed is determined by the machine.
- Employees do the same small task over and over.
- Skill requirements are low.
- Each job is only a tiny fraction of the finished product.
- People cannot develop relationships because of noise and physical separation.
- Staff specialists control any meaningful job changes.

Unfortunately, because many workers do not like jobs designed in this manner, they often perform at minimum levels.

Job Enlargement/Job Enrichment

Attempts to alleviate some of the problems encountered in excessive job simplification fall under the general headings of job enlargement and job enrichment. **Job enlargement** involves broadening the scope of a job by expanding the number of different tasks to be performed. **Job enrichment** means that the depth of a job is increased by adding responsibilities for planning, organizing, controlling, and evaluation.

An assembly-line worker is very restricted in choosing what is done and when it is done, and therefore has very little *depth* in the job. The vice president of purchasing has a wide job *scope* because that position has a great variety of managerial duties. Enlarging job scope means adding more similar operations to a job.

JOB ROTATION. The technique known as **job rotation** can be a way to break the monotony of an otherwise routine job with little scope by shifting a person from job to job. For example, one week on the auto assembly line, John Williams attaches doors to the rest of the body assembly. The next week he attaches bumpers. The third week he puts in seat assemblies, then rotates back to doors again the

JOB ENLARGEMENT
is broadening the scope of a job by expanding the number of different tasks to be performed.

JOB ENRICHMENT
is increasing the depth of a job by adding employee responsibility for planning, organizing, controlling, and evaluating the job.

JOB ROTATION
is the process of shifting a person from job to job.

following week. Job rotation need not be done on a weekly basis. John could spend one-third of a day on each job or one entire day, instead of a week, on each job. It has been argued, however, that rotation does nothing to solve the problem of employee boredom. Rotating a person from one boring job to another may help somewhat in the short term, but the jobs are still perceived to be boring. The advantage is that job rotation does develop an employee who can do many different jobs.

INCREASING JOB DEPTH.   Increasing job depth means increasing the influence and control employees have over their jobs. A manager might increase job depth by promoting variety, requiring more skill and responsibility, providing more autonomy, and adding opportunities for personal growth. Giving an employee more planning and control responsibilities over the tasks to be done also increases job depth. However, simply adding more similar tasks does not increase job depth.

Examples of actions that increase job depth include:

- Giving a person an entire job rather than just a piece of the work
- Giving more freedom and authority so the employee can perform the job as he or she sees fit
- Increasing a person's accountability for work by reducing external control
- Expanding assignments so employees can learn to do new tasks and develop new areas of expertise
- Giving feedback reports directly to employees rather than to management only

Supporters of increased job depth contend that the additional challenge and responsibility lead to higher productivity, lower absenteeism, and increased motivation. However, while job enrichment may result in substantial improvements in employee attitudes, it may not necessarily lead to greater productivity.

Job Characteristics and Job Design

Individual responses to jobs vary. A job may be fascinating to you but not to someone else. It is useful for a manager to know what effect a job has on different people.

Depending on how jobs are designed, they may provide more or less opportunity for employees to satisfy their job-related needs. For example, a sales job may furnish a good opportunity to satisfy social needs, whereas a training assignment may satisfy a person's need to be an expert in a certain area. A job that gives you little latitude to do anything *your* way may not satisfy your creative or innovative needs.

The job characteristics model developed by Hackman and Oldham identifies five important design characteristics of jobs [42] Figure 4–12 shows that *skill variety*, *task identity*, and *task significance* stimulate meaningfulness of work. *Autonomy* stimulates responsibility, and *feedback* provides knowledge of results. The following is a description of each:

- *Skill variety*. The extent to which the work requires several different activities for successful completion. The more skills involved, the more meaningful the work.
- *Task identity*. The extent to which the job includes a "whole" identifiable unit of work, carried out from start to finish, with a visible outcome. It is more meaningful to make a pair of shoes from start to finish than simply to nail on the heels, even though the skills may be about equal in difficulty.

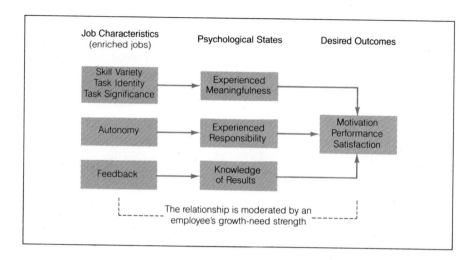

Figure 4–12
Job Characteristics Model

■ *Task significance*. The amount of impact the job has on other people. A job is more meaningful if it is important to other people for some reason. For instance, a soldier may experience more fulfillment when defending his or her country from a real threat than when merely training to stay ready in case such a threat arises.

■ *Autonomy*. The extent of individual freedom and discretion in the work and its scheduling. More autonomy leads to a greater feeling of personal responsibility for the work.

■ *Feedback*. The amount of clear information received about how well or poorly one has performed. Feedback leads to a greater understanding of the effectiveness of one's performance and contributes to the overall knowledge an employee has about the work.

Jobs designed to take advantage of these important job characteristics are more likely to be positively received by employees. Such characteristics help distinguish between "good" and "bad" jobs.

SUMMARY

■ Productivity at individual, organizational, and national levels has serious implications for organizational ability to compete.

■ Employers want "motivated" employees, which usually means productivity, innovative behavior, and loyalty to the organization.

■ Motivation deals with the "whys" of human behavior.

■ Four major views of human nature are rational-economic, social, self-actualizing, and complex.

■ The complex view of motivation includes the expectancy and equity theories and recognizes the current situations people in organizations face.

■ Job satisfaction affects organizational commitment, which affects absenteeism and turnover.

■ Absenteeism is expensive, but it can be controlled by discipline, positive reinforcement, or some combination of the two.

■ Turnover has been studied extensively and appears to be strongly related to certain external, work-related, and personal factors.

- A job is a grouping of similar positions.
- Job design affects the performance, satisfaction, and health of the job holder.
- Matching people and jobs is important, but sometimes, when there are mismatches, jobs are more easily changed than are people.
- Job design began formally with scientific management, which was based on division of labor, standardization, and specialization.
- Job enlargement, job enrichment, and job rotation all have been used to redesign jobs.
- The job characteristics model suggests that five different characteristics of jobs (skill variety, task identity, task significance, autonomy, and feedback from the organization) affect motivation, performance, and satisfaction.

REVIEW AND DISCUSSION QUESTIONS

1. Explain why managers often are never willing to look only at the effort portion of the performance model to explain performance.
2. How is productivity in organization affected by the absence of innovation and a lack of loyalty by employees?
3. Why is it difficult to identify what motive is operating on a person at a given time?
4. Of the four views about human behavior, which one/ones are most congruent with your own values and beliefs? Why?
5. "Job satisfaction is a prime way to affect absenteeism and turnover." Discuss.
6. Contrast the use of control and discipline with rewards and positive reinforcement as ways to reduce absenteeism and turnover.
7. Why is job design important to productivity and loyalty?
8. Compare and contrast job enlargement with job enrichment.
9. Use the job characteristics model (Figure 4–12) to analyze a job you have had.

| CASE | I Won't Give at the Office |

Terri Ware got a message from the boss: "Give to the United Way, or else." She refused, so she was fired from her part-time job as a bank teller. The president of the company said, "I've had 100 percent participation from my employees for years and I'll be damned if one person is going to come along and change that." He offered her the job back only after the firing received publicity. This incident, which occurred at First Federal Savings and Loan in Cumberland, Maryland, may or may not be unusual.

Employees may not be dismissed over fundraising conflicts, but they are subjected to more subtle forms of pressure. Of course, organizations can apply pressure because they do have power over jobs and salaries. At Chase Manhattan Bank many employees fill out their contribution cards in front of a supervisor who reads the donation amounts in the employee's presence. At AT & T workers are rewarded if the levels are reached. The 100 percent participation goal receives significant emphasis at AT & T, where 96 percent employee participation is the average and many units end the drive at or over 100 percent of the targeted amounts.

At Chase Manhattan "team captains" call meetings to give employees payroll deduction cards. One participant watched as his supervisor read every card turned in. The supervisor called several people to the front to "correct" their cards when they indicated they were not giving.

Some workers rebel. A Union Carbide workers said, "Last year I gave money because they called me into a meeting and gave me the pitch and then handed me the card. This year I just skipped the meeting, and I won't give either."

Although many workers resent the United Way, the organization actually evolved to protect them. Its nearly exclusive right to collect money at the workplace was meant to protect workers from an onslaught of outstretched hands. Instead, one hand—the United Way—collects and distributes money. The United Way says it discourages coercion, but acknowledges it has no control over how the money is raised. It hired a pollster who studied donor attitudes and found that 15 percent of workers felt coerced into giving.

Experts say image promotion is behind the emphasis on giving at most companies. "Companies want to look good in comparison with their competitors in the industry. It just looks better to say that all the employees gave."[43]

QUESTIONS

1. Describe the motives of management and the motives of different employees in situations such as those described in the case.

2. How might the treatment Terri Ware received affect the organizational commitment of other employees?

NOTES

1. J. P. Macduffie, "The Japanese Auto Transplants: Challenges to Conventional Wisdom," *ILR Report 26*, (Fall 1989): 12.

2. Dun and Bradstreet Survey, reported in *Wall Street Journal*, November 12, 1986, 35.

3. T. Rollins and J. R. Bratkovich, "Productivity's People Factor," *Personnel Administrator*, February 1988, 50–57.

4. D. J. Mitchell, *Human Resource Management: An Economic Approach* (Boston: PWS–Kent Publishing, 1989).

5. D. Altany, "Global Trends Color 90's Outlook," *Industry Week*, April 18, 1988, 79.

6. K. R. Sheets, "Showdown on the Dollar," *U.S. News and World Report*, February 2, 1989, 20.

7. G. Skarow, "Zero Defects," *Industry Week*, July 17, 1989, 35; D. Bacon, "How the Baldridge Winners Did It," *Nation's Business*, January 1989, 32; J. Hoerr, "The Payoff from Teamwork," *Business Week*, July 10, 1989, 56–62. S. Kaufman, "Quest for Quality," *Business Month*, May 1989, 61; R. Harris, "McDonnel Tries New Tack on Quality," *Wall Street Journal*, April 24, 1989, B4.

8. J. E. Ross and E. Shaw, "Improving the Productivity of Service Organizations," *IM*, September/October 1989, 21.

9. D. Wessel, "Working Smart," *Wall Street Journal*, June 1, 1989, 1.

10. G. Gardner, "Japanese Playing Tough Game in U.S. Auto Industry," *Omaha World Herald*, December 28, 1989, 21; W. J. Holstein et al., "Japan U.S.A.," *Business Week*, July 14, 1986, 47. J. Kapstein, "Volvo's Radical New Plant," *Business Week*, August 28, 1989, 92.

11. Ibid, A16.

12. B. Johnson, "Boosting Productivity at American Express," *Business Week*, October 5, 1989, 62–63.

13. R. Mitchell, "Masters of Innovation," *Business Week*, April 10, 1989, 58.

14. S. Vittolino, "3M Stuck on Creativity," *Human Resource Executive*, April 1989, 26.

15. T. F. O'Boyle, "Loyalty Ebbs at Many Companies as Employers Grow Disillusioned," *Wall Street Journal*, July 11, 1985, 29.

16. J. Dresang, "Company Loyalty Remains Strong," *USA Today*, January 9, 1989, B1.

17. M. Giallourakis, "Reforming Corporate Loyalty," *SAM Focus on Management*, April 1988, 1.

18. P. Sherrod, "Workers Now Seminomadic, Ethic of Loyalty to Firms Ebbs," *Arizona Republic*, November 16, 1986, E9.

19. C. J. Mottaz, "An Analysis of the Relationship between Education and Organizational Commitment in a Variety of Occupational Groups," *Journal of Vocational Behavior* 28 (1986): 214–228.

20. M. Goldstein, "Loyalty's Death," *Industry Week*, September 7, 1989, 83.

21. For example, see Kenneth M. Dawson and Sheryl N. Dawson, "How to Motivate Your Employees," *HR Magazine*, April 1990, 78–80.

22. A. H. Maslow, *Motivation and Personality* (New York: Harper & Row, 1954).

23. Douglas McGregor, *The Human Side of Enterprise* (New York: McGraw-Hill, 1960), 33–45.

24. F. Herzberg, B. Mausner, and B. Snyderman, *The Motivation to Work* (New York: John Wiley & Sons, 1959).

25. Victor H. Vroom, *Work and Motivation* (New York: John Wiley & Sons, 1964).

26. Edward E. Lawler, III, and Lyman W. Porter, "The Effect of Performance on Job Satisfaction," *Industrial Relations* 7 (1966).

27. R. Griffeth, J. W. Logan, and R. Vecchio, "Equity Theory and Interpersonal Attraction," *Journal of Applied Psychology* 74, (1989): 394–401.

28. Edwin A. Locke, "The Nature and Causes of Job Satisfaction," in *Handbook of Industrial and Organizational Psychology*, ed. M. Dunnette (Chicago: Rand McNally, 1976), 1,300.

29. R. Arvey, L. Abraham, T. Bouchard, and N. Segal, "Genetic Influences on Job Satisfaction," *Journal of Applied Psychology*, 74 (1989): 234–246.

30. "For Some, Challenging Work Outranks Pay," *Chicago Tribune*, January 22, 1989, 1G.

31. L. J. Williams and J. T. Hazen, "Antecedents and Consequences of Satisfaction and Commitment in Turnover Models: A Reanalysis Using Latent Variable Structural Equation Methods," *Journal of Applied Psychology* 71 (1986): 219–231.

32. F. Kuzmits, "What to Do about Long-Term Absenteeism," *Personnel Administrator*, October 1986, 93–101.

33. "Expensive Absenteeism," *Wall Street Journal*, July 29, 1986, 1.

34. G. P. Latham and C. A. Frayore, "Self-Management Training for Increasing Job Attendance," *Journal of Applied Psychology* 74, (1989): 411–416; or D. A. Harrison and C. L. Hulin, "Investigations of Absenteeism: Using Event History Models," *Journal of Applied Psychology*, 74, (1989): 300–316.

35. *CPA Client Bulletin*, April 1986, 3.

36. T. H. Stone, "Absence Control: Is Your Company a Candidate?" *Personnel Administrator*, September 1988, 81.

37. J. Putzier and F. Nowak, "Attendance Management and Control," *Personnel Administrator*, August 1989, 58–61.

38. D. Dalton and C. A. Enz, "Absenteeism in Remission: Planning, Policy, Culture," *Human Resource Planning*, 10 (1987), 82.

39. Robert P. Steel, Guy S. Shane, and Rodger W. Griffeth, "Correcting Turnover Statistics for Comparative Analysis," *Academy of Management Journal* 33 (1990): 179–187.

40. M. J. Major, "Turning Over the Odds to Your Favor," *Modern Office Technologies*, October 1986, 112.

41. D. Krackhardt and L. W. Porter, "The Snowball Effect: Turnover Embedded in Communications Networks," *Journal of Applied Psychology* 71, (1986): 50–55.

42. J. R. Hackman and G. R. Oldham, *Work Design* (Reading, Mass.: Addison-Wesley, 1980), 72–73.

43. Adapted from D. J. Blum, "Donor's Backlash," *Wall Street Journal*, January 12, 1982, 1.

Equal Employment Opportunity

Equal Employment Opportunity (EEO) permeates all facets of an organization and its operations. There are a variety of groups which have been identified for special protection against discrimination by various laws. Therefore, you should be aware of EEO ramifications before considering other P/HR management activities. For example, recruiting advertisements often contain notations that employers are "equal opportunity employers." Employment processes, including application blanks, interviews, and tests, should be free of discriminatory references and effects. Training programs and performance appraisal practices also can be affected by equal employment concerns and regulations.

Chapter 5 examines the legal constraints presented by EEO in the staffing process of an organization. Title VII of the Civil Rights Act of 1964, various other laws, and numerous landmark court cases all must be considered in order to achieve compliance. The two major strategies for complying with EEO regulations identified in the 1978 Uniform Selection Guidelines are covered. The chapter concludes with a discussion of several concepts of validity.

Chapter 6 looks at issues associated with implementing EEO in an organization. Legal requirements directed by the Equal Employment Opportunity Commission and the Office of Contract Compliance Programs often require that affirmative action programs be established. The nature of affirmative action and EEO record-keeping requirements must be understood as well. Sex discrimination, employment practices related to disabled individuals, religious discrimination, and seniority are a few of the specific areas discussed.

Equal Employment

Chapter 5

After you have read this chapter, you should be able to:

1. Briefly explain five legislative acts that deal with equal employment issues
2. Discuss how to identify when illegal discrimination occurs
3. Identify three cases associated with preferential selection, or reverse discrimination
4. Describe the two most important equal employment enforcement agencies
5. Discuss the two strategies that can be used to comply with the 1978 Uniform Selection Guidelines
6. Define validity and reliability
7. Explain three means of validating employment tests

P/HR: Today *and* Tomorrow

Paying for Discrimination

Discrimination can be expensive, as a number of employers have discovered. Whether the discrimination was based on age, sex, race, or other factors, a variety of U.S. employers have paid for such acts. Some examples are:

■ State Farm Insurance Co. agreed to settle a sex discrimination suit that will cost it an estimated $300 million over several years. The suit charged that about 85,000 women were discouraged from, or not allowed to, apply for insurance sales jobs in California from 1974 to 1987.

■ The former circulation manager for the *Orange County Register* (California) newspaper was awarded $885,000 because of sex discrimination, which occurred when she was twice passed over for promotion and less-qualified males were selected. The newspaper announced it would appeal the jury decision.

■ Chrysler Corporation had to pay $8 million to older workers who were forced to retire involuntarily or who were required to sign retirement agreements containing illegal age discrimination provisions.

■ A $14 million payment for back pay to thousands of minority and female employees was made by Harris Trust and Savings Bank of Chicago to settle discrimination complaints filed by the federal government.

■ Volkswagen of America and the United Auto Workers union paid a total of $718,000 to settle a six-year-old case involving discrimination against minority employees.

■ Iowa-based Hy-Vee Food Stores was ordered by the Iowa Supreme Court to pay a Vietnamese woman checker $2,500 in damages and back pay for discriminating against her in failing to allow her to work more hours and for not granting her promotions.

■ Burlington Northern Railroad agreed to pay $5.7 million and offer up to 450 jobs with retroactive seniority and up to 200 promotions to settle sex discrimination charges brought by women employees and those women who applied but were not hired by the railroad.

■ United Airlines paid 145 pilots approximately $10.2 million in back pay and damages to settle an age discrimination suit. The suit grew out of a United policy that forced pilots to retire at age sixty. The policy was later changed to allow captains and first officers to accept a downgrade to flight engineer and work until age seventy.

■ A former policewoman in Grand Island, Nebraska, received over $22,000 in back pay and $24,000 in lieu of being reinstated as a police officer. A federal court found that she was sexually harassed and retaliated against for filing a discrimination complaint.

■ A budget analyst in Broward County, Florida, filed a suit for being fired three months after he was diagnosed with AIDS. Ultimately, the individual, whose annual pay was $20,000 a year, received an out-of-court settlement of $196,000 for being discriminated against as a handicapped person.

■ Wendy's International settled a class-action suit for sex discrimination in which it was charged that Wendy's failed to promote female managers. The food chain agreed to: (1) pay approximately 700 women a total of $1.4 million; (2) fill 40 percent of upper management and 50 percent of lower management vacancies with women; (3) establish a scholarship fund for women; and (4) hold EEO seminars for all managerial employees.

■ An employee, a member of the Jehovah's Witness religious group, refused to answer a company telephone with the greeting "Merry Christmas," because such a request by her employer violated her religious beliefs. She was fired, filed suit, and won her case in Kentucky. She received back pay and the firm was assessed a $250 fine.[1]

"Our equality lies in the right for each of us to grow to our full capacity."
Pearl Buck

As these examples of the costs of discrimination indicate, the days are past when employers can manage their work forces in any manner they wish. Federal, state, or local laws have been passed prohibiting unfair discrimination against individuals on the following bases:

- Race/ethnic, origin/color (Black, Hispanic, Oriental, Pacific Islander, American Indian, Eskimo)
- Gender (women, including those who are pregnant)
- Age (individuals over forty)
- Handicapped (physically and mentally disabled and limited)
- Military experience (Vietnam veterans)
- Religion (special beliefs and practices)
- Sexual preferences (gay rights)

The term *discrimination* has been used in many ways. The dictionary definition is neutral; it identifies discrimination as the ability to recognize the difference between, or the ability to differentiate between, items or people. Thus, discrimination involves choosing among alternatives. For example, employers must discriminate (choose) among applicants for a job on the basis of job requirements and each candidate's qualifications. However, discrimination can become illegal in situations in which either (1) two different standards are used to judge individuals, or (2) the same standard is used but more individuals in certain groups are adversely affected.

Individuals who are covered under equal employment laws are referred to as "members of a protected class" or **protected group members.** To implement laws barring discrimination, several regulatory agencies have developed guidelines and regulations. Because of the important EEO (equal employment opportunity) requirements mandated by federal, state, and local governments, this chapter and the next one focus on the nature and impact of equal employment on P/HR practices.

A PROTECTED GROUP MEMBER
Is an individual who falls within a group identified for protection under equal employment laws.

■■ ■ EQUAL EMPLOYMENT LAWS AND REGULATIONS

Over the past three decades, various laws have been passed that require employers to provide equal opportunity for people to be employed and to progress in their employment. Figure 5–1 contains a listing of the major EEO laws and regulations affecting employers. Although there are other laws with EEO implications, those listed have the greatest impact on P/HR practices. The subject and specific coverage of each law given in Figure 5–1 is highlighted in the discussion that follows.

Equal Pay Act of 1963

As a part of amendments to the Fair Labor Standards Act (FLSA) in 1963, 1968, and 1972, the Equal Pay Act attempts to prohibit wage discrimination on the basis of sex. As the Wage and Hour Division of the U.S. Labor Department states:

The equal pay provisions of the FLSA prohibit wage differentials based on sex, between men and women employed in the same establishment on jobs that require equal skill, effort, and responsibility and which are performed under similar working conditions[2]

Figure 5–1
Major Federal Laws Related to Equal Employment Opportunity

ACT	YEAR	PROVISIONS
Equal Pay Act	1963	Requires equal pay for men and women performing substantially the same work
Title VII, Civil Rights Act	1964	Prohibits discrimination in employment on basis of race, religion, color, sex, or national origin
Executive Orders 11246 and 11375	1965, 1967	Requires federal contractors and subcontractors to eliminate employment discrimination and prior discrimination through affirmative actions
Age Discrimination in Employment Act (as amended in 1978 and 1986)	1967	Prohibits discrimination against persons over age 40 and restricts mandatory retirement requirements, except where age is a "bona fide occupational qualification"
Executive order 11478	1969	Prohibits discrimination in the U.S. Postal Service and in the various government agencies on the basis of race, color, religion, sex, national origin, handicap, or age
Vocational Rehabilitation Act, Rehabilitation Act of 1974	1973, 1974	Prohibits employers with federal contracts over $2,500 from discriminating against handicapped individuals
Vietnam-Era Veterans Readjustment Act	1974	Prohibits discrimination against Vietnam-era veterans by federal contractors and the U.S. government and requires affirmative action
Pregnancy Discrimination Act	1978	Prohibits discrimination against women affected by pregnancy, childbirth, or related medical conditions; requires they be treated as all other employees for employment-related purposes, including benefits
Immigration Reform & Control Act	1986	Establishes penalties for employers who knowingly hire illegal aliens; prohibits employment on basis of national origin or citizenship
Americans with Disabilities Act	1990	Requires employer accommodation of disabled individuals

To qualify, jobs must be "substantially" the same but not necessarily identical. For example, one midwestern department store chain was required to pay women who managed women's ready-to-wear departments a cumulative total of $750,000 in back pay because these women received less than males managing men's departments.

Pay differentials on the basis of seniority or performance are not prohibited if they are not based on sex discrimination. The most common acceptable reasons for differences are more seniority or better job performance. However, the lower pay that women traditionally have received for the same jobs that men perform cannot be justified on the basis of future promotability. Paying a man more because the employer believes the man to have greater possibility of staying with the organization is not allowed. Some employers also felt that women should be paid less because they might quit to marry, become pregnant, or move because their spouses were transferred. However, such concerns often are not true; in any event, they cannot be used to justify pay differences.

COMPARABLE WORTH ISSUE.   Discussed in more detail in Chapter 6, the issue of comparable worth builds upon the Equal Pay Act. The idea behind comparable worth is that jobs having relatively equal "worth" to the organization should be paid equally. Worth is determined through comparison of the knowledge, skills, and abilities required to perform various jobs.

Some feel that it is discriminatory to give unequal pay for jobs of comparable worth even though the jobs clearly have different tasks, duties, and responsibilities. Others feel that supply and demand, rather than discriminatory actions by an employer who pays according to market rates, are what create such disparities. Whatever the merits of the concept, the U.S. Supreme Court has ruled that comparable worth is not required by law, but some states have passed laws addressing "pay equity." Nevertheless, employers must be mindful of future cases and rulings on this issue when developing pay systems.

1964 Civil Rights Act, Title VII

Discrimination against many groups is now clearly prohibited by law. The keystone of the structure of antidiscrimination legislation is the Civil Rights Act of 1964. Title VII, Section 703(a) of the act states:

> It shall be unlawful employment practice for an employer (1) to fail or refuse to hire or to discharge any individual, or otherwise to discriminate against any individual with respect to his compensation, terms, conditions, or privileges of employment, because of such individual's race, color, religion, sex, or national origin; or (2) to limit, segregate, or classify his employees in any way which would deprive or tend to deprive any individual of employment opportunities or otherwise adversely affect his status as an employee because of such individual's race, color, religion, sex, or national origin.[3]

The Civil Rights Act was passed by Congress to bring about equality in hiring, transfers, promotions, access to training, and other employment-related decisions. As is often the case, the law contains ambiguous provisions giving considerable leeway to agencies that enforce the law.

WHO IS COVERED?   Title VII, as amended by the Equal Employment Opportunity Act of 1972, covers most employers in the United States. Any organization meeting one of the criteria listed below is subject to rules and regulations that specific government agencies set up to administer the act:

- All private employers of 15 or more persons who are employed 20 or more weeks per year
- All educational institutions, public and private
- State and local governments
- Public and private employment agencies when functioning as employers
- Labor unions with 15 or more members
- Joint (labor-management) committees for apprenticeships and training[4]

Executive Orders 11246, 11375, and 11478

Beginning with President Franklin D. Roosevelt and continuing through the passage of the Civil Rights Act of 1964, numerous executive orders have been issued that require employers holding federal government contracts to be nondiscriminatory on the bases of race, color, religion, national origin, and sex. An executive order is issued by the president of the United States to provide direction to government departments on a specific issue or area.

During the 1960s, by executive order, the Office of Federal Contract Compliance Programs (OFCCP) in the Labor Department was established and given responsibility for enforcing nondiscrimination in government contracts. Under Executive Order 11246 issued in 1965, amended by Executive order 11375 in 1967, and updated by Executive Order 11478 in 1979, the Secretary of Labor was given the power to:

- Publish the names of noncomplying contractors or unions
- Recommend suits by the Justice Department to compel compliance
- Recommend action by Equal Employment Opportunity Commission (EEOC) or the Justice Department to file suit in federal district court
- Cancel the contract of a noncomplying contractor or blacklist a noncomplying employer from future government contracts

These orders have required employers to take *affirmative action* to overcome the effects of past discriminatory practices. A detailed discussion of affirmative action is given in Chapter 6.

Americans With Disabilities Act (1990)

People who are disabled or limited due to various physical and mental disabilities face special discrimination problems because they often are not considered for jobs they could perform. Since the first legislation to deal with their concerns in 1973, other conditions have been determined to be disabilities, including those of AIDS victims, rehabilitated drug users, and others that are discussed in the next chapter.

The Americans with Disabilities Act (ADA) was built upon the Vocational Rehabilitation Act of 1973 and the Rehabilitation Act of 1974. Generally, the effect of the law in the employment area, which becomes effective in 1992, is as follows:

- Federal contractors and subcontractors with contracts valued at more than $2,500 must take affirmative action to hire qualified handicapped people.
- The ADA covers all employers with 15 or more workers.
- Discrimination is prohibited against individuals if they can perform the *essential* job functions with *reasonable proficiency*, a standard that is somewhat vague.
- A covered employer must make "reasonable accommodation" for persons with disabilities, so that they can function as employees unless "undue hardships" would be placed on the employer.
- Preemployment medical examinations are prohibited except after an employment offer is made, conditional upon passing the physical examination.
- Buildings financed with public funds must be accessible to the disabled.

Age Discrimination in Employment Acts

The Age Discrimination in Employment Act (ADEA) of 1967, amended in 1978 and 1986, makes it illegal for an employer to discriminate in compensation, terms, conditions, or privileges of employment because of an individual's age. The later amendments first raised the minimum mandatory retirement age to 70, and then eliminated it completely.

The ADEA applies to all individuals above the age of 40 working for employers having 20 or more workers. Under the 1986 amendments, a seven-year exemption for public employers and colleges/universities was included to allow them to adjust to the elimination of mandatory retirements for police and fire officers and faculty members, respectively.[5] However, the act does not apply if age is a job-related occupational qualification. For example, a bus company has the legal right not to hire an entry-level driver 45 years or older because of training, experience, and licensing requirements.

Prohibitions against age discrimination do not apply when an individual is disciplined or discharged for good cause, such as poor job performance. Older workers who are poor performers can be terminated just as anyone else. However, numerous suits under ADEA have been filed involving workers over 40 who were forced to take "voluntary retirement" when organizational restructuring or work force reduction programs were implemented.

Vietnam-Era Veterans Readjustment Act of 1974

Concern about the readjustment and absorption of Vietnam-era veterans into the work force led to the passage of the Vietnam-Era Veterans Readjustment Act. The act requires that affirmative action in hiring and advancing Vietnam-era veterans be undertaken by federal contractors and subcontractors having contracts of $10,000 or more.

Pregnancy Discrimination Act of 1978

In 1978, the Pregnancy Discrimination Act (PDA) was passed as an amendment to the Civil Rights Act of 1964. This act requires that women employees "affected by pregnancy, childbirth, or related medical conditions will be treated the same for all employment-related purposes."[6] The major impact of the act was to change maternity leave policies and employee benefit systems. Under the PDA, pregnancy must be treated just like any other medical condition. The same provisions regarding disability insurance and leaves of absence must apply to pregnant employees as to all other workers. A more detailed discussion of the impact of the PDA is contained in the next chapter.

A 1986 Supreme Court decision did allow states to pass laws that require employers to give pregnant employees maternity leave and reinstate them in their same jobs at their same pay once the women can return to work. Leave for adoptions also was covered under the California law reviewed by the Supreme Court.[7] Attempts to pass a federal law requiring provisions similar to the California law have been resisted by employers, but continuing efforts are being made.

Immigration Reform and Control Act of 1986

To deal with the myriad problems arising from the continued flow of aliens to the United States, the Immigration Reform and Control Act was passed in 1986. In one of the act's major provisions, employers are prohibited from knowingly hiring illegal aliens. Those employers who violate the law can be fined from $250 for the first offense to $10,000 for subsequent offenses, and those guilty of a repeat pattern or practice of employing illegal aliens can be fined up to $3,000 and/or sentenced up to six months in prison.

The act requires employers to examine applicant's identification documents; new employees also must sign verification forms about their eligibility to work legally in the United States. Further, discrimination on the basis of national origin or citizenship status is illegal. A special section of the U.S. Department of Justice was established to handle relevant claims of discrimination.[8]

State and Local Employment Laws

In addition to federal laws and orders, many states and municipalities have passed their own laws prohibiting discrimination on a variety of bases. Often these laws are modeled after federal laws; however, the state and local laws sometimes provide greater remedies, require different actions, or prohibit discrimination in areas beyond those addressed by federal law. Also, state and local enforcement bodies have been established to enforce EEO compliance.

■ ■ MAJOR ISSUES AND COURT CASES

Laws establishing the legal basis for equal employment opportunity generally have been written in a broad manner. Consequently, only through application to specific organizational situations can the laws truly affect employers. The broad nature of the laws has led enforcement agencies to develop guidelines and to enforce the acts as they deem appropriate. However, agency rulings and the language of those rulings have caused confusing and differing interpretations by employers. Interpretation of the ambiguous provisions in the laws also changes as the membership of the agencies change. The court system is left to resolve the disputes and issue interpretations of the laws. Even the courts, especially the lower courts, have issued conflicting rulings and interpretations. The ultimate interpretation often has rested on decisions by the U.S. Supreme Court, although Supreme Court rulings, too, have been interpreted differently.

Equal employment opportunity is a dynamic, evolving concept that often appears confusing because of conflicting decisions and rulings by courts and agencies. Also membership changes in the U.S. Supreme Court have led to decisions that alter or reverse previous ones. The areas and cases discussed next are regarded as major precedent-setting decisions.

When Does Illegal Discrimination Occur?

A major area that first must be decided by courts and regulatory authorities is to identify if and when illegal discrimination has occurred. In making their decisions the courts have had to consider several issues:

■ Employer intentions
■ Unequal treatment
■ Results of employer actions
■ Burden of proof

P/HR:	Practice *and* Research	Unequal Treatment and Racial Discrimination

The impact of unequal treatment of racial minority individuals was studied by Greenhaus, Parasuraman, and Wormley. As reported in the *Academy of Management Journal*, the researchers focused on "treatment discrimination." This type of discrimination "occurs when subgroup members receive fewer rewards, resources, or opportunities on the job than they legitimately deserve on the basis of job-related criteria."

The authors developed a survey that was distributed through the company mail systems of three firms in the eastern United States. One firm was in communications, another in banking, and the third in electronics. Surveys were sent to about 800 blacks and 800 whites, all of whom were managers. Also, surveys were sent to those to whom those managers reported. The surveys were returned by 828 managers and their supervisors. Questions on the managerial survey asked for details on race, gender, organizational experiences, job performance ratings, and career outcomes. Each of the manager's supervisors was asked how the supervisor viewed the manager's performance and career promotability.

Analyses of the data revealed that race did appear to be a factor in a number of areas. Regarding job performance, blacks tended to be rated lower than whites by their supervisors. Also, the supervisors viewed blacks less favorably for promotion than whites. Whether the lower performance ratings and promotions possibilities of blacks in the study were due to lower actual performance or to racial bias could not be determined by the researchers. Blacks also had lower career satisfaction scores than whites did, presumably because of their reported perceptions that they had less job discretion and autonomy.

The authors of this study concluded that some treatment discrimination on the basis of race did exist, but they were cautious about generalizing these results to other organizations and industries. Even with those cautions and the need for more research on race and treatment discrimination, the study does raise issues about the impact of unequal treatment of protected group members who are managers.[9]

EMPLOYER INTENTIONS AND DISPARATE TREATMENT. It would seem that when considering whether discrimination has occurred, motives or intentions of employers might enter into the determination. The courts consistently have ruled that the motives and intentions of employers should not be a factor in this determination. Regardless of whether the employer intended to discriminate or not, it is the outcomes of the employer's actions that will be considered when deciding if illegal discrimination occurred.

A factor that is considered when determining if illegal discrimination has occurred is unequal treatment of protected group individuals. Called **disparate treatment,** this concept means that protected group members are treated differently from other employees. For example, if different requirements are placed on women than on men, then disparate treatment may be occurring. The P/HR Research discusses a research study that examined the issue of unequal treatment of managers based on race.

DISPARATE TREATMENT
occurs when protected group members are treated differently from other employees.

RESULTS OF EMPLOYER ACTIONS. An issue on which court decisions have shifted over the years has been concerned with the results of employer actions. In many of the decisions a major question has been the following: If employers use job-related "tests" for making employment-related decisions, are they guilty of illegal discrimination if the results of their tests mean that protected group members are disproportionately and negatively affected? For example, is it illegal for an employer to terminate employees for attendance violations if a greater percentage of minorities lose their jobs as a result? Or, if an employer is located in a geographic area in which a minority group is 25 percent of the population, is the employer guilty of illegal discrimination if only 10 percent of the employees in the firm are in that group? The answers to such questions have shifted over time. One reason for the change of direction of court decisions is the changing composition and ideology of the judges and U.S. Supreme Court justices appointed by various presidents, governors, and others.

BURDEN OF PROOF.   A final issue is the determination of which party has the burden of proof when illegal discrimination is alleged. At issue is what must the individuals who are filing suit against employers prove to establish that illegal discrimination has occurred. For instance, in 1973, in *McDonnell-Douglas v. Green* the U.S. Supreme Court addressed the question of whether a qualified black individual could be rejected for employment. The Court ruled that a preliminary *(prima facie)* case of discrimination existed by showing that: (1) the person (Green) was a member of a protected group, (2) the person applied for and was qualified for a job but was rejected, and (3) the employer (McDonnell-Douglas) continued to seek other applicants after the rejection occurred.[10]

This case indicates that once a court rules that a *prima facie* case has been made, the burden of proof shifts to the employer to show that it did not discriminate illegally. Also, assuming that a *prima facie* case of discrimination has been made, the courts have had to decide what employers must do to refute the allegations.

Key Cases on Illegal Discrimination

Some key court decisions on these issues are discussed next. They concern initial selection, promotion, layoff, and termination actions by employers.

GRIGGS V. DUKE POWER (1971).   In March 1971, the Supreme Court's decision in the case of *Griggs v. Duke Power Company*[11] put some teeth in the Civil Rights Act. As a result, companies must be able to prove that their selection procedures do not tend to discriminate. The Griggs case dealt with a promotion and transfer policy that required individuals to have both a high school diploma and to obtain a satisfactory score on two professionally developed aptitude tests. One of the tests was the Wonderlic Intelligence Test, on which blacks scored lower as a group than whites. In addition, fewer blacks had high school diplomas than whites.

The U.S. Supreme Court ruled that Title VII of the Civil Rights Act prohibits not only overt discrimination but also practices that are fair in form but discriminatory in operation. This decision established two major points: (1) It is not enough to show a lack of discriminatory intent if the selection tool results in a *disproportionate effect* that discriminates against one group more than another or continues a past pattern of discrimination; (2) The employer has the burden of proving that an employment requirement is directly job-related. Consequently the use of the intelligence test and the high school diploma requirements was ruled to be not related to the job.

ALBERMARLE PAPER V. MOODY (1975).   The 1975 Supreme Court case of *Albermarle Paper v. Moody*[12] reaffirmed the idea that any "test" used for selecting or promoting employees must be a valid predictor or performance measure for a particular job. The term *test* includes such items as performance appraisals used for promotion decisions. If any selection test has an adverse impact (for instance, evidenced by hiring or promotion, that does not result in a pattern similar to minority representation in the population), the burden of proof for showing that the test is valid falls on the employer. Employment tests also must be sound predictors of a person's future job success.

WASHINGTON V. DAVIS (1976).   A 1976 Supreme Court decision in a case involving the hiring of police officers in Washington, D.C., represents a slightly different emphasis. In this case, the issue was reading comprehension and aptitude test given to all applicants for police officer positions. The test contained actual material that the applicants would have to learn during a training program. The city could show a relationship between success in the training program and success as a police officer, although a much higher percentage of women and blacks than white men failed this aptitude test.

The court ruled that the city of Washington, D.C., did not discriminate unfairly because the test was definitely job related. If a test is clearly related to the job and tasks performed, it is *not* illegal simply because a greater percentage of racial minority persons or women do not pass it. The crucial outcome is that a test must be specifically job-related and cannot be judged solely on its adverse impact against protected group members.[13]

TEXAS DEPARTMENT OF COMMUNITY AFFAIRS V. BURDINE (1981).   The 1981 U.S. Supreme Court case focused on sex discrimination. Joyce Burdine was denied a promotion that was given to a male, and then she was terminated during staff reduction. Consequently, Burdine charged sex discrimination was a basis for the actions against her.

The court decision dealt with the burden of proof required by individuals charging discrimination and by employers who must defend their actions. According to the decision ruling against Burdine, the employer only needs to establish a business-related nondiscriminatory reason for not hiring or promoting a member of a protected group. The employer does not have to prove that the hired individual was more qualified than the protected group person. Thus, the individual charging illegal discrimination has the burden of establishing that intentional discrimination occurred.[14]

CONNECTICUT V. TEAL (1982).   In this case, the U.S. Supreme Court ruled that Title VII focused on the individual instead of the protected group as a whole. When ruling for Teal, the Court said that an employer must ensure that each part of a multiple-step selection process is nondiscriminatory, even though the overall results are nondiscriminatory.[15]

PRICE WATERHOUSE V. HOPKINS (1989).   In this 1989 case, the U.S. Supreme Court ordered a lower court to rehear Ann Hopkins's charges that the large accounting firm for which she worked had been guilty of sex discrimination. Hopkins charged that she was denied a partnership at Price Waterhouse because of "sexual stereotyping" in which she was viewed as being too macho and aggressive. The Supreme Court ruled that when an employment discussion is based on both legitimate and impermissible factors, the employer has the burden of proof to show that the same employment decision would have been made if the illegal factors had not been considered.[16]

WARDS COVE PACKING V. ATONIO (1989).   This case was brought by Filipino and Alaskan individuals against an Alaskan salmon cannery firm. The individuals claimed that the packing company illegally discriminated against them by failing to hire them into higher-skilled cannery jobs. The evidence submitted by the plaintiffs suing the company was based on a statistical study that showed a higher percentage of nonwhite workers in the unskilled jobs and a lower percentage in the more skilled, higher-paying positions.

The Supreme Court, by a five-to-four vote, ruled that the statistical imbalance between job groups was not a sufficient basis for establishing a *prima facie* case of illegal discrimination.[17] Instead, the appropriate statistical comparisons should be made between the racial percentage of jobs in question to the racial composition for the local labor market. The end result of this decision was that the ruling made it more difficult for protected group individuals to use statistics to show that illegal discrimination occurred.[18]

Preferential Selection or Reverse Discrimination?

Probably the most volatile equal employment issue concerns preferential selection and reverse discrimination. At the heart of the conflict is the role employers have in selecting, training, and promoting protected group members when they are underrepresented in numbers in various jobs within an organization. At issue in many of these cases is the concept of **affirmative action,** through which employers identify problem areas, set goals, and take positive steps to guarantee equal employment opportunities for people within a protected group. Affirmative action focuses on the hiring, training, and promoting of protected groups where they are deficient within an organization. An affirmative action plan (AAP) is a formal document that the organization makes available for review by employees and enforcement officers. More on these plans is contained in Chapter 6.

By having preferential selection for protected group members, individuals not in that group may complain that they are being discriminated against in reverse.[19] The concept of **reverse discrimination** implies that a person is denied an opportunity because of preferences given to a member of a protected group who may be less qualified. Some of the key court cases that have dealt with preferential selection and reverse discrimination follow.

AFFIRMATIVE ACTION
requires employers to identify problem areas in the employment of protected group members and to set goals and take steps to overcome those problems.

REVERSE DISCRIMINATION
may exist when a person is denied an opportunity because of preferences given to protected group individuals who may be less qualified.

KAISER ALUMINUM V. WEBER (1979).   Brian Weber, a white steelworker, charged Kaiser Aluminum and his union, the United Steelworkers, with "reverse discrimination." Weber sued because he was denied admission to a training program even though he had more seniority than some black workers admitted to the program. Because blacks were underrepresented in crafts jobs at Kaiser, a voluntary quota system and special crafts training programs were agreed to by the company and the union. Under the agreement, 50 percent of the slots in a crafts training program were reserved for blacks.

The U.S. Supreme Court ruled against Weber and said that the plan did not violate the Title VII provisions because the company and union *voluntarily agreed* to the affirmative action plan that gave preference to blacks. Because the preference policy did not require discharging white workers and replacing them with black workers, the plan was a temporary measure used to eliminate racial inequality.[20]

WYGANT V. JACKSON BOARD OF EDUCATION (1986).   This case arose after the Jackson, Michigan, school board agreed to a layoff provision tied to the racial composition of the teaching force. When the school board experienced a reduction in force, white teachers with more seniority were laid off in favor of less senior black teachers. The white teachers sued, claiming that the layoffs violated their constitutional rights as guaranteed under the equal protection clause. By a five-to-four vote, the U.S. Supreme Court ruled that an affirmative action layoff plan between a school board and the union representing the teachers unlawfully violated the rights of nonminority teachers.[21]

JOHNSON V. SANTA CLARA COUNTY TRANSPORTATION AGENCY (1987). Undoubtedly, the most significant decision affecting affirmation action and reverse discrimination was handed down by the U.S. Supreme Court in 1987. In this case, a male scored higher on a selection test, but a female was given the job under an affirmative action plan that Santa Clara County had enacted voluntarily, even though no one proved past discriminatory practices. By a six-to-three vote, the Supreme Court endorsed giving preferential treatment to protected group members if they are underrepresented and if the employer has a voluntary affirmative action plan.[22]

MARTIN V. WILKS (1989).   The somewhat confusing stand of the Supreme Court on affirmative action evolved further with a five-to-four decision that held that nonminority employees can challenge affirmative action provisions agreed to by an employer and minority employees. In this case, the City of Birmingham, Alabama, agreed to settle a discrimination charge brought by some black fire fighters. The consent decree settled on provided for affirmative action by the city on the hiring and promotion of fire fighters. However, a group of white fire fighters filed suit charging reverse discrimination. The U.S. Supreme Court ruled that the white fire fighters could challenge the affirmative action consent decree in court.[23]

OVERVIEW.   As the composition of the U.S. Supreme Court has changed, decisions have reflected a shift in the legal views of preferential selection and reverse discrimination. Past rulings have not given a clear consistent direction.[24] At the time of the writing of this text, there appears to be a trend in court decisions to restrict the use of preferential selection and affirmative action for protected group members. Whether the U.S. Supreme Court will continue to make decisions reflecting that approach must be evaluated as future decisions are issued. What all of these court cases illustrate is that equal employment is a dynamic, evolving, and multifaceted area that must be monitored continuously by P/HR professionals and enforcement agencies alike.

■ ENFORCEMENT AGENCIES

Government agencies at several levels have powers to investigate illegal discriminatory practices. At the state and local levels, various commissions have enforcement authority. At the federal level, the two most prominent agencies are the Equal

Employment Opportunity Commission (EEOC) and the Office of Federal Contract Compliance Programs (OFCCP).

Equal Employment Opportunity Commission (EEOC)

The EEOC, created by the Civil Rights Act of 1964, is responsible for enforcing the employment-related provisions of the act. The agency initiates investigations, responds to complaints, and develops guidelines to enforce Title VII regulations.

The EEOC has been given expanded powers several times since 1964 and is the major agency involved with employment discrimination. When the courts have upheld EEOC findings of discrimination, they have ruled that remedies include back pay and remedial "affirmative action." Over the years, the EEOC has been given the responsibility to investigate equal pay violations, age discrimination, and handicapped discrimination, in addition to areas identified by Title VII of the Civil Rights Act.

COMMISSION MEMBERSHIP.   As an independent regulatory agency, the EEOC is composed of five members appointed by the president and confirmed by the Senate. No more than three members of the commission can be from the same political party. Members serve for seven years. In addition, the EEOC has a staff of lawyers and investigators who do investigative and follow-up work for the commission.

Office of Federal Contract Compliance Programs (OFCCP)

Whereas the EEOC is an independent agency, the OFCCP is part of the Department of Labor. The OFCCP was established by executive order to ensure that federal contractors and subcontractors have nondiscriminatory practices. A major thrust of OFCCP efforts focuses on requirements that federal contractors and subcontractors take affirmative action to overcome the effects of prior discriminatory practices. Affirmative action plans are discussed in detail in the next chapter.

Enforcement Philosophies and Efforts

Since 1964, the various U.S. presidential administrations have viewed EEO and affirmative action enforcement efforts from different philosophical perspectives. Often, the thrust and aggressiveness of enforcement efforts vary depending on whether a Republican or Democratic president and Congress is in office. For example, under the Carter administration (1977–1980) the appointees to the EEOC tended to be activists who believed strongly that protected group members be given opportunities to move ahead through affirmative action programs. Enforcement efforts from both the EEOC and the OFCCP were wide and varied. However, under the Reagan administration philosophical disagreements with affirmative action efforts led to appointees who had differing views from those appointed by Carter.

The purpose of this discussion is not to identify who is right or wrong but rather to emphasize that laws are enforced by agencies staffed by presidential appointees. Differing degrees of activism and emphasis result, depending on the philosophical beliefs and priorities held by a particular administration.

■■ ■ EQUAL EMPLOYMENT GUIDELINES

To implement the provisions of the Civil Rights Act of 1964 and the interpretations of it based on court decisions, the EEOC and other federal agencies developed their own compliance guidelines and regulations, each having a slightly different set of rules and expectations. Finally, in 1978, the major government agencies involved agreed upon a set of uniform guidelines.

Uniform Guidelines on Employee Selection Procedures

The 1978 guidelines apply to the EEOC, the Department of Labor's OFCCP, the Department of Justice, and the Office of Personnel Management.[25] The guidelines provide a framework used to determine if employees are adhering to federal laws on discrimination.

These guidelines affect virtually all phases of P/HR management because they apply to test and other selection procedures used in making employment decisions, including but not limited to the following:

- Hiring (qualifications required, application blanks, interviews, tests)
- Promotions (qualifications, selection process)
- Recruiting (advertising, availability of announcements)
- Demotion (why made, punishments given)
- Performance appraisals (methods used, how used for promotions and pay increases)
- Training (access to training programs, development efforts)
- Labor union membership requirements (apprenticeship programs, work assignments)
- Licensing and certification requirements (job requirements tied to job qualifications)

The guidelines apply to most employment-related decisions, not just to the initial hiring process. Within the guidelines two major means of compliance are identified: (1) no-adverse-impact strategy, and (2) job-related validation strategy.

No-Adverse-Impact Strategy

Generally, when courts have found discrimination within organizations, the most important issue concerns the *effect* of employment policies and procedures, regardless of the *intent*. A practice, however harmless in intent, that results in an adverse impact on members of a protected group is considered discriminatory. The *Griggs v. Duke Power* decision is an example of such a ruling.

Adverse impact occurs when there is a substantial underrepresentation of protected group members in employment decisions. The Uniform Guidelines identify the "no adverse impact" strategy in the following statement: "These guidelines do not require a user to conduct validity studies of selection procedures where no adverse impact results."[27]

Under the guidelines, adverse impact is determined with the **4/5ths "rule."** If the selection rate for any protected group is less than 80 percent (4/5ths of the selection rate of the majority groups) or if there is proportional underrepresentation in relation to the relevant labor market, discrimination exists. Thus, the guidelines have attempted to define discrimination in statistical terms.[28] Adverse impact can be checked in two ways: external or internal.

ADVERSE IMPACT
occurs when there is a substantial difference in employment decisions (hiring, laying off, promoting) that works to the disadvantage of members of protected groups.[26]

THE 4/5THS RULE
states that discrimination generally occurs if the selection rate for a protected group is less than 80 percent of their representation in the relevant labor market or 80 percent less than the majority group.

Figure 5–2
External Adverse Impact at Orbus Company

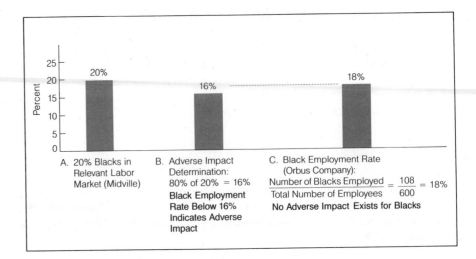

EXTERNAL.   Adverse impact is checked externally by comparing the percentage of employed workers in a protected group in the organization to the percentage of protected group members in the surrounding relevant labor market. External comparisons also are made on the percentage of protected group members who are recruited and who apply for jobs to ensure that the employer has drawn a "representative sample" from the surrounding labor market. Although employers do not have to have exact proportionate equality, they must be "close," as defined by the 4/5ths rule.

As an example, Figure 5–2 shows how one phase of a firm's employment practices are evaluated for adverse impact. In Midville (the relevant labor market), the labor force is 20 percent black. In Orbus Company, which has 600 employees, 108 of the employees (18 percent) are black. Consequently, there is no adverse impact because there is 18 percent black representation in the company, and the firm must have only 16 percent (20 percent × 4/5) to avoid adverse impact.

INTERNAL.   Checking for adverse impact internally requires that employers compare the treatment received by protected group members to that received by non-protected group members. Assume, for example, that Standard Company interviewed both men and women for manufacturing assembly jobs. Of the men who applied, 40 percent were hired; of the women who applied, 25 percent were hired. As show in Figure 5–3, the selection rate for women is less than 80 percent (4/5) of the selection rate for men (40% × 4/5 = 32%). Consequently, Standard Company does have "adverse impact" in its employment process.

P/HR activities for which internal adverse impact can be checked by comparing the treatment and results of protected and non-protected group members include:

- candidates selected for interviews of those recruited
- performance appraisal ratings as they affect pay increases
- promotions, demotions, or terminations
- pass rates for various selection tests

EFFECT OF THE NO-ADVERSE-IMPACT-STRATEGY.   The 4/5ths rule is a yardstick that employers can use to determine if they have adverse impact on protected group members. However, to meet the 4/5ths compliance requirement, employers must have no adverse impact at *all levels* and in *all job classes* for *each protected group.*

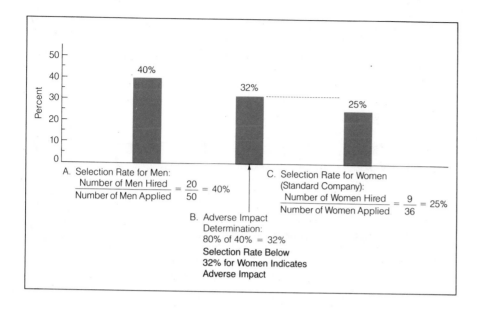

Figure 5–3
**Internal Adverse Impact at
Standard Company**

A. Selection Rate for Men:
$$\frac{\text{Number of Men Hired}}{\text{Number of Men Applied}} = \frac{20}{50} = 40\%$$

B. Adverse Impact
   Determination:
   80% of 40% = 32%
   **Selection Rate Below
   32% for Women Indicates
   Adverse Impact**

C. Selection Rate for Women
   (Standard Company):
$$\frac{\text{Number of Women Hired}}{\text{Number of Women Applied}} = \frac{9}{36} = 25\%$$

Some skeptics have suggested that this approach comes down to "getting your numbers in line." Consequently, using this strategy is not really as easy or risk-free as it may appear.

The U.S. Supreme Court also has raised questions about using statistics to prove or disprove illegal discrimination. For example, in a case involving Sears, Roebuck, the U.S. Supreme Court said that using statistics alone to determine illegal sex discrimination is grossly unfair to an employer.[29] A partial rejection of the idea that discrimination can be avoided simply by meeting "bottom line" (total employment) quotas was voiced in a 1982 U.S. Supreme Court decision in *Connecticut v. Teal*.[30] The Court said that because Title VII focused on the individual instead of on a protected group as a whole, arriving at the proper *"bottom-line"* results does not eliminate the discrimination suffered by individuals. Another case, which questioned the use of adverse impact statistics internally unless they are compared with the qualified work force in the relevant labor market, was the *Wards Cove Packing v. Atonio* case. Because of these varied court decisions, employers may want to turn to the other compliance strategy of validating that their employment decisions are based on job-related factors.

Job-Related Validation Strategy

The idea that employment practices must be valid includes such practices and tests as job description, educational requirements, experience requirements, work skills, application forms, interviews, paper and pencil tests, and performance appraisals. Virtually everything used to make employment-related decisions—recruiting, selection, promotion, termination, discipline, and performance appraisal—must be shown to be specifically job-related. Hence, the concept of validity affects many of the common tools used to make P/HR decisions.

Validity simply means that a "test" actually measures what it says it measures. As applied to employment settings, a test is any employment procedure used as the basis for making an employment-related decision. For a general intelligence test to be valid, it must actually measure intelligence, not just a person's vocabulary. An employment test that is valid must measure the person's ability to perform the job for which he or she is being hired.

VALIDITY
means that a "test" actually measures what it says it measures.

A test is said to be valid for selection purposes if there is a significant statistical relationship between performance on the test and performance on the job. The better a test can predict satisfactory and unsatisfactory performance on the job, the greater its validity. Applicants' scores on valid tests can be used to predict their probable job performance by computing *correlation coefficients*. Correlation coefficients identify the extent to which any two measures, in this case test scores and job performance, change together.

The ideal condition for employment-related "tests" is to be both valid and reliable. **Reliability** is a consistency measure. For a test to be reliable an individual's score should be about the same every time the individual takes it (allowing for the effects of practice). Unless a test measures a trait consistently (or reliably), it is of little value in predicting job performance. Acceptable reliability coefficients are quite high—a correlation of .80 or better.

Reliability can be measured by several different statistical methodologies. The most frequent ones are test–retest, alternate forms, and internal consistency estimates. A more detailed methodological discussion is beyond the scope of this text; those interested can consult appropriate statistical references.[31]

RELIABILITY
refers to the consistency with which a test measures an item.

■ ■ VALIDITY AND EQUAL EMPLOYMENT

If a charge of discrimination is brought against an employer and adverse impact is established, the employer must be able to demonstrate that its employment procedures are valid. To be valid, employment tests must relate to the job and the requirements of the job.

General aptitude and psychological tests, such as those dealing with mental abilities, are difficult to validate because a test must measure the person for the job, not the person in abstract, as emphasized in *Griggs v. Duke Power*. The 1978 Uniform Selection Guidelines recognize the three types of validity discussed next:

1. Criterion-related (concurrent and predictive) validity
2. Construct validity
3. Content validity

Criterion-Related Validity

Employment tests of any kind attempt to predict how well an individual will perform on the job. The test is labeled the *predictor* and the desired job knowledge, skills, abilities, and measures of job performance are called the *criterion variables*. Careful analysis of the jobs for which the test is being used as a predictor is necessary. Job analysis determines as exactly as possible what knowledge, skills, abilities, and behaviors are needed for each task in the job. Tests are then devised and used as predictors to measure different dimensions of the criterion-related variables. Examples of tests are requiring a college degree, scoring a required number of words per minute on a typing test, or having five years of banking experience. These predictors are then validated against the criteria used to measure job performance, such as performance appraisals, sales records, or absenteeism rates. Some court cases, such as *Albermarle Paper v. Moody*, have pointed out the difficulty in using subjective performance appraisals by supervisors as the criteria against which the tests are validated. However, if the predictors do satisfactorily predict job performance behavior, they are legally acceptable and quite useful in selection.[32]

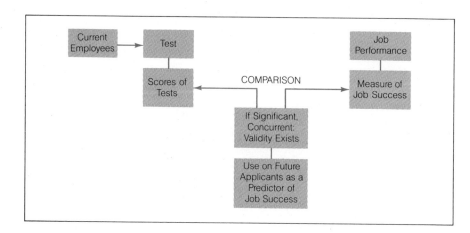

Figure 5–4
Concurrent Validity

Within criterion-related validity there are two different approaches: (1) concurrent validity and (2) predictive validity. Concurrent validity represents an "at-the-same-time" approach to validity, while predictive validity is a "before-the-fact" approach.

CONCURRENT VALIDITY. Concurrent means "at the same time." As shown in Figure 5–4, when an employer uses concurrent validity, current employees instead of newly hired employees are used to validate the test. The test is given to these employees and the scores are correlated with their performance ratings, determined by such measures as accident rates, absenteeism records, or supervisory performance appraisals. A high correlation suggests that the test is able to differentiate between the better and the poorer employees.

A major potential drawback of concurrent validity is that those employees who performed poorly in their jobs are no longer with the firm and therefore cannot be tested, and the extremely good employees may have been promoted or may have left the organization for a better job. Thus, the firm does not really have a representative range of people to test. Also, the test takers may not be as motivated to perform well on the test because they already have jobs. Any learning that has taken place on the job influences the test score, presenting another problem. Therefore, applicants taking the test without the benefit of on-the-job experience might score low on the test, but might be able to do the job well.

PREDICTIVE VALIDITY. This method of validating employment practices is calculated by giving a test and then comparing the test results with the job performance of those tested. Figure 5–5 outlines the predictive validity process.

The following example illustrates how a predictive validity study might be designed. A retail chain, Eastern Discount, wants to establish the predictive validity of requiring one year of cashiering experience, a "test" it plans to use in hiring cashiers. Obviously, the retail outlet wants a test that will do the best job of separating those who will do well from those who will not. Eastern Discount first hires thirty people, regardless of their cashiering experience or other criteria that might be directly related to their experience. Sometime later (perhaps six months) the performance of employees who joined the company with and without cashiering experience is compared with the thirty employees' job success. Success on the job is measured by such yardsticks as absenteeism, accidents, errors, and performance appraisals. If those employees who had one year of experience demonstrate better

Figure 5–5
Predictive Validity

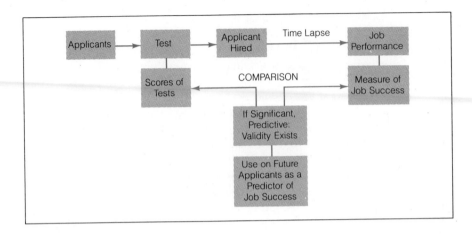

performance, as statistically compared with those without such experience, then the experience requirement is considered a valid predictor of performance and may be used in the hiring of future employees.

In the past, predictive validity has been preferred by EEOC because it is presumed to give the strongest tie to job performance. However, predictive validity requires (1) a fairly large number of people, and (2) a time gap between the test and the performance. As a result, it is not useful in many situations. Because of these and other problems, other types of validity often are used.

Construct Validity

Construct validity is based on an abstract idea or characteristic inferred from research. Those researchers who have studied behavior have given various characteristics (such as personality traits) names like as introversion, agression, or others. These are called *constructs*. When a test measures an intangible or abstract construct, such as intelligence quotient (IQ), it has construct validity. Other common constructs for which test have been devised are creativity, leadership potential, and interpersonal sensitivity. Because a hypothetical construct is used as a predictor in establishing this type of validity, personality tests and other such constructs are more likely to be questioned for their legality and usefulness than other measures of validity. Consequently, construct validity is used less frequently in employment selection than the other types of validity.

Content Validity

Content validity is logical and nonstatistical. A test is said to be content-valid if a person performs an *actual sample* of the work done on the job. Thus, an arithmetic test for a cashier contains some calculations that a cashier would have to make on the job. Content validity is especially useful if the work force is not large enough to accommodate better statistical designs. Content validity is a solid alternative because its basic requirement is a good analysis of what tasks one performs in a job.

GROWTH OF CONTENT VALIDITY.   Many practitioners and specialists see content validity as a way to validate staffing requirements with a commonsense approach that focuses on job requirements rather than statistically-oriented methods. In the *Washington v. Davis* case discussed earlier, the Supreme Court also appeared to support the content validity approach because the training course test given by the police department represented actual training materials used by police officers.

The legislation and court decisions mentioned in this chapter are forcing employers to make changes that should have been made earlier. Using an invalid instrument to select, place, or promote an employee has never been a good management practice, regardless of its legality. Management also should be concerned with using valid instruments from the standpoint of operational efficiency. Invalid tests may result in screening out individuals who might have been satisfactory performers or in hiring less satisfactory workers.

Many organizations are increasing the use of instruments that have been demonstrated to be valid. In one sense, the current requirements have done management a favor because they force employers to do what they probably should have been doing previously—using job-related employment procedures.

Validity Generalization

Paper-and-pencil selection tests are the means behind validity generalization and are gaining renewed interest from employers. At the heart of this concept is the idea that the validity of ability tests is relatively stable for a variety of jobs and organizations. Through the methodological technique called metanalysis, a way was identified to adjust or correct the historical inconsistencies in test-validation studies. Although the approach is controversial,[35] it has been adopted by the U.S. Employment Service, a federal agency, and is being implemented throughout the United States in state and local job service offices.

The General Aptitude Test Battery (GATB) is the means for validity generalization used by the job service offices. First developed in the early 1940s, the GATB has been used and evaluated for research purposes for many years. The GATB is composed of twelve parts, eight of which are paper and pencil in nature and four apparatus and mechanical, all timed. These tests give aptitude scores in eight areas: verbal, numerical, spatial, form perception, clerical perception, motor coordination, finger dexterity, and manual dexterity. A general learning ability or intelligence score also can be derived from the GATB. Individuals who take the tests can then be matched to the basic abilities needed for various jobs; thus, job counseling and placement can be more efficient.

The validity generalization approach combines the eight specific aptitude results into three general ability scores, which are weighted and combined to give overall aptitude measures for five general job families. Applicants at individual job service offices are tested, receive a test report, and then are matched to a job family and job order submitted by employers to the job service. Once a general match is made, other employer requirements, such as experience, specific training or education, and hours of work, are considered and applicants are referred for job interviews.

The value of validity generalization testing can be seen from the results obtained in local job service offices. For example, in one year over 73,000 applicants in Michigan were tested, and 26,000 of those were identified through validity generalization and referred to employers. A major employer found that employees hired with the validity generalization approach had significantly better training success than those hired without the approach. As more and more state and local job services adopt the approach, more detailed records of results can be obtained. Anyone interested in learning more about the GATB and validity generalization should contact the job service office in a specific locale to find out how it is used[36]

SUMMARY

- Equal employment opportunity laws prohibit discrimination against protected-group individuals.
- The 1964 Civil Rights Act, Title VII, is the most significant equal employment law, but there are several others that address specific discrimination problems:
  - Equal Pay Act
  - Executive Order 11246, 11375, and 11478
  - Age Discrimination in Employment Acts
  - Americans with Disabilities Act
  - Vietnam-Era Veterans Readjustment Act
  - Pregnancy Discrimination Act
  - Immigration Reform and Control Act
- There have been a number of issues addressed by landmark cases concerning discrimination in P/HR practices. The major issues are employer intent, unequal treatment, results of employer actions, and burden of proof.
- Whether preferential selection is legal or is reverse discrimination has been the subject of several landmark court cases.
- The Equal Employment Opportunity Commission (EEOC) and the Office of Federal Contract Compliance Programs (OFCCP) are the major federal equal employment enforcement agencies.
- The 1978 Uniform Guidelines are used by the enforcement agencies to examine hiring, promotions, recruiting, and other employment practices.
- Under the 1978 guidelines, two alternative compliance strategies are identified: (1) no adverse impact strategy; and (2) job-related validation strategy.
- Adverse impact is determined through use of the 4/5ths rule.
- Job-related validation requires that tests measure what they are supposed to measure (validity) in a consistent manner (reliability).
- There are three types of validity—criterion related, construct, and content.
- The two approaches of criterion-related validity are, concurrent validity and predictive validity. Whereas predictive validity is a "before-the-fact" measure, concurrent validity uses tests and criteria measures available at the same time.
- Construct validity shows a relationship between a measure of an abstract characteristic, such as intelligence, and job performance.
- Content validity is growing in use because it shows the job-relatedness of a measure based on the fact that it is a sample of the actual work to be performed.

REVIEW AND DISCUSSION QUESTIONS

1. Various laws have been passed to provide equal employment protection for a number of groups of people. Identify five protected groups and briefly describe the appropriate laws.
2. If you were asked by an employer to review an employment decision to determine if discrimination had occurred, what factors would you consider and how would you do so?
3. Identify your personal views on the debate over preferential selection versus reverse discrimination, and cite some case rulings to support your view.

4. What are the differences in enforcement responsibilities of the EEOC and the OFCCP?
5. Why is validation considered to be a more business-oriented strategy than a no-adverse-impact strategy in complying with the 1978 Uniform Selection Guidelines?
6. Explain what validity is and why content validity is growing in use compared with the construct and criterion-related types.

| CASE | Noncompliance at U.S. Steel |

U.S. Steel Corporation (renamed USX Corporation) had the unique experience of being found in violation of both equal employment compliance strategies because of its employment practices at its Fairless Hill, Pennsylvania, plant. To understand the decision, one must first understand the employment situation.

Between 1972 and 1982, U.S. Steel had approximately 50,000 applicants for the 7,000 to 10,000 positions at the plant, most of which were for entry-level laborer jobs. Most applicants met the job specifications in terms of physical condition, literacy, and age. As jobs became available, applicants were called for interviews, and U.S. Steel kept a running tally to see what percentage of minority persons were hired. If more minority employees were needed, more blacks were called for interviews. A group of black applicants who were not hired filed suit claiming race discrimination because the black hire rate (18 percent) should have been in proportion to the black applicant rate (26 percent), even though the work force in the area was 9.5 to 11.5 percent black.

The ruling in a federal district court in Pennsylvania was for the applicants. The court decision said that the actual applicant flow rate of 26 percent should have been used as the target percentage because it represented the actual available work force, not a hypothetical one in the area. Consequently, the no-adverse-impact strategy used by the company was rejected.

U.S. Steel also claimed that it used valid hiring procedures to identify the most qualified candidates, and the lower rate of blacks selected was due to the inferior qualifications of the black applicants. Determination of who was the most qualified was made by supervisors who conducted the interviews. However, the court ruled that the interviewers had not been trained in interviewing and the hiring criteria of education, experience, no prior criminal record, attitude, personality, alertness, and initiative were too vague and subjective. Consequently, the hiring procedures were ruled to be too subjective, open to bias, and nonsystematic.

As a result of a U.S. Court of Appeals for the Third Circuit decision, U.S. Steel is projected to have to pay approximately $30 million to about 8,000 blacks denied employment at its Fairless Works. A spokesman for the company in 1990 indicated that the decision would be appealed to the U.S. Supreme Court.[37]

QUESTIONS

1. Identify, specifically, how the employment practices at U.S. Steel violated the two compliance strategies in the 1978 Uniform Guidelines.
2. What needs to be done to develop a content-valid interviewing process at U.S. Steel?

NOTES

Author's note: Appreciation for assistance with Chapters 5 and 6 is expressed to Herbert E. Gerson, attorney at law; McDonnell, Boyd, Smith, and Salmson; Memphis, TN.

1. *Personnel Journal,* May 1989, 20–26; *Los Angeles Times,* April 20, 1989, Part I–22; *New York Times,* April 19, 1989, A20; *Omaha World-Herald,* January 25, 1990, A34; *Omaha World-Herald,* August 10, 1986, 10B; *Wall Street Journal,* July 2, 1986, 14; *Omaha World-Herald,* August 5, 1986, 11; *Resource,* February 1987, 16; *Employment Practices Review,* October 1987, 2; and *Resource,* November 1987, 19.

2. Wage and Hour Division, U.S. Department of Labor, *Handy Reference Guide to the Fair Labor Standards Act* (Washington, D.C.: U.S. Government Printing Office, 1983), 4.

3. Civil Rights Act of 1964, Title VII, Sec. 703A.

4. U.S. Equal Employment Opportunity Commission, *Affirmative Action and Equal Employment* (Washington, D.C.: U.S. Government Printing Office, 1974), 12–13.

5. *U.S. News & World Report,* November 3, 1986, 60.

6. Public Law 95–555, 92 Stat. 2076, October 31, 1978.

7. *California Federal Savings and Loan Association v. Guerra,* 197 S.Ct. 683 (1987).

8. *Resource,* March 1987, 1, 6.

9. Jeffrey H. Greenhaus, Saroj Parasuraman, "Effects of Race on Organizational Experiences, Job Performance Evaluations, and Career Outcomes," *Academy of Management Journal* 33 (1990): 64–86.

10. *McDonnell Douglas v. Green,* 411 U.S. 972 (1973).

11. *Griggs v. Duke Power Co.,* 401 U.S. 424 (1971).

12. *Albermarle Paper Co. v. Moody,* 74–389 (1975).

13. *Washington, Mayor of Washington D.C. v. Davis,* 74–1492 (1976).

14. *Texas Department of Community Affairs v. Burdine,* 25 FEP Cases 113 (1981).

15. *Connecticut v. Teal* 457 U.S. 440 (1982).

16. *Price Waterhouse v. Hopkins,* 87–1167 (1989).

17. *Wards Cove Packing Co. v. Atonio,* 87–1837 (1989).

18. Robert M. Preer, Jr. "This Hidden Impact of *Wards Cove,*" *Labor Law Journal* 41 (1990): 45–50.

19. Janet Maleson Spencer, "When Preferential Hiring Becomes Reverse Discrimination," *Employee Relations Law Journal* 14 (1989): 513–529.

20. *Kaiser Aluminum and Chemical Corp. v. Brian F. Weber,* 78–435 (1979).

21. *Wygant v. Jackson Board of Education,* 106 S.Ct. 1842 (1986).

22. *Johnson v. Santa Clara County Transportation Agency,* 107 S.Ct. 1442 (1987).

23. *Martin v. Wilks,* 87–1614, (1989).

24. For details, see Paul S. Greenlaw, "Reverse Discrimination: The Supreme Court's Dilemma," *Personnel Journal,* January 1988, 84–89.

25. "Adoption by Four Agencies of Uniform Guidelines on Employee Selection Procedures (1978)," *Federal Register,* August 15, 1978, Part IV, 38295–38309.

26. Ibid, Sec. 16B, P38307, as adapted.

27. Ibid, Sec. 1B, P38296.

28. Kenneth R. White and James A. Xander, "Minimizing Discrimination Practices," *Personnel Administrator,* August 1988, 92–95.

29. *EEOC v. Sears, Roebuck and Co.,* 504 F.Supp. 241 (1986).

30. *Connecticut v. Teal.*

31. For a discussion in the context of employment selection, see Robert D. Gatewood and Hubert S. Feild, *Human Resource Selection,* 2nd ed. (Chicago: Dryden Press, 1990), 117–196.

32. For a review of the issues, see Lawrence Kleiman and Robert H. Foley, "The Implications of Professional and Legal Guidelines for Court Decisions Involving Criterion-Related Validity: A Review and Analysis," *Personnel Psychology* 38 (1985): 803–833.

33. Adapted from J. T. McGowan, "Trash Test Fight Keeps Women Out," *USA Today,* July 14, 1986, 3A.

34. Wayne F. Cascio, Ralph A. Alexander, and Gerald V. Barrett, "Setting Cutoff Scores: Legal, Psychometric, and Professional Issues and Guidelines," *Personnel Psychology* 41 (1988): 1–24.

35. See *Personnel Psychology* 38 (1985): 697–801, for questions, commentary, and discussion on validity generalization and meta-analysis.

36. Adapted from Robert M. Madigan et al., "Employment Testing: The U.S. Job Service is Spearheading a Revolution," *Personnel Administrator,* September 1986, 102–112.

37. "USX Loses Appeal in Discrimination Suit," *Wall Street Journal,* February 28, 1990, B4; *Green v. U.S. Steel,* ED PA. No. 76–3673 (1983); and *Omaha World-Herald,* August 5, 1986, 11.

Implementing Equal Employment

After you have read this chapter, you should be able to:

1. Identify typical equal employment opportunity (EEO) record-keeping requirements and those records used in the EEO investigative process

2. Define affirmative action and what is contained in an affirmative action plan (AAP)

3. Explain the importance of bona fide occupational qualifications (BFOQs), "business necessity," and job-relatedness

4. Give examples of three sex-based discrimination issues

5. Discuss the two types of sexual harassment

6. Identify two age-related discrimination issues

7. Apply the "reasonable accommodation" idea to discrimination on the grounds of disability and religion

8. Identify two other bases of discrimination that have been the subject of lawsuits

P/HR: Today *and* Tomorrow	Combating Sexual Harassment

Sexual harassment in the workplace is a major issue addressed by equal employment regulations and court decisions. The following statistics indicate the extent of the problem:

■ Approximately 5,000 sexual harassment charges were filed with the Equal Employment Opportunity Commission in one year.
■ A 1987 sexual harassment case against K-Mart resulted in a $3.2 million judgment.
■ In California, over a five-year period, the median jury verdict awarded in sexual harassment cases was $183,000, ranging from $45,000 to almost $495,000.
■ One estimate is that sexual harassment costs the average large firm over $6 million annually through higher turnover, increased absenteeism, and lower productivity.
■ Well over 90 percent of the sexual harassment charges are filed by women, with about two-thirds of all sexual harassment complaints being made against immediate supervisors and top management individuals.

In a survey of U.S. government workers, 42 percent of the women employees reported that they had been sexually harassed within the previous two years. The most frequent sexual harassment situations included:

■ Sexual teasing and telling of sexually explicit jokes
■ Sexually suggestive looks or gestures
■ Being asked repeatedly for dates or to meet outside of work
■ Actual touching, fondling, or pinching
■ Physically cornering, "trapping," or leaning over a worker

Yet only 500 sexual harassment complaints had been filed. This low number of actual complaints indicates that the women either took steps personally to stop the harassment or felt that filing complaints would do little good or might affect their careers.

To counter sexual harassment in the federal government, the Office of Personnel Management has developed a training course for managers and supervisors. But because attendance at courses is not mandatory, relatively few managers have participated.

Other organizations have been more aggressive. Chase Manhattan Bank has a two-hour sexual harassment awareness program for all managers. Firms that offer specific mandatory training include Douglas Aircraft, AT&T, DuPont, and many others.

As the percentage of women in the work force grows, there will be more potential situations in which sexual harassment can occur, and consequently a greater need for organizations to implement both preventive and corrective measures. In summary, combating sexual harassment will be a major EEO challenge for organizations and managers in the 1990s[1].

"There are, in every age, new errors to be rectified and new prejudices to be opposed."

Samuel Johnson

The issues covered by equal employment regulations do not deal just with the initial employment of individuals. As the opening discussion on sexual harassment illustrates, employers must take steps to implement equal employment opportunity in a variety of areas. However, many employers do not have the necessary understanding of equal employment requirements to take such steps. It is important for those employers to know how to comply with the regulations and requirements of various EEO enforcement agencies.

▬ ■ EEO COMPLIANCE

Employers must comply with all regulations and guidelines covered in Chapter 5. To do so, managers should be aware of what specific administrative steps are required and how charges of discrimination are investigated.

EEO Records

Through several enforcement agencies, the federal government has required employers to survey work forces and maintain records on the distribution of protected group members in their organizations. All employers with twenty or more employees are required to keep records that can be requested by the Equal Employment Opportunity Commission (EEOC). If the organization meets certain criteria, then reports and investigations by the Office of Federal Contract Compliance Programs (OFCCP) also must be addressed.

Under various laws, employers also are required to post an "officially approved notice" in a prominent place where employees can see it. This notice states that the employer is an equal opportunity employer and does not discriminate.

EEO RECORDS RETENTION.   All employment records must be maintained as required by the EEOC, and "employer information reports" must be filed with the federal government. Further, any personnel or employment record made or kept by the employer must be maintained for review by the EEOC. Such records include application forms and records concerning hiring, promotion, demotion, transfer, layoff, termination, rates of pay or other terms of compensation, and selection for training and apprenticeship. Even application forms or test papers completed by unsuccessful applicants may be requested. The length of time documents must be kept varies, but generally three years is recommended as a minimum time period.

Keeping good records, whether required by the government or not, is simply a good P/HR practice. Complete records are necessary for an employer to respond when a charge of discrimination is made and a compliance investigation begins.

ANNUAL REPORTING FORM.   The most basic report that must be filed with the EEOC is the annual report form EEO-1 (Figure 6–1). All employers with 100 or more employees (except state and local governments) or subsidiaries of another company that would total 100 employees must file this report. Also, federal contractors who have at least 50 employees and contracts of $50,000 or more and

Figure 6–1
Annual Report Form EEO-1

EQUAL EMPLOYMENT OPPORTUNITY
EMPLOYER INFORMATION REPORT EEO-1

Standard Form 100
(Rev. 12-76)
Approved GAO B-180541 (R0077)
Expires 12-31-78

Joint Reporting Committee

- Equal Employment Opportunity Commission
- Office of Federal Contract Compliance Programs

Section A — TYPE OF REPORT
Refer to instructions for number and types of reports to be filed.

1. Indicate by marking in the appropriate box the type of reporting unit for which this copy of the form is submitted (MARK ONLY ONE BOX).

(1) ☐ Single-establishment Employer Report

Multi-establishment Employer:
(2) ☐ Consolidated Report
(3) ☐ Headquarters Unit Report
(4) ☐ Individual Establishment Report (submit one for each establishment with 25 or more employees)
(5) ☐ Special Report

2. Total number of reports being filed by this Company (Answer on Consolidated Report only) _____

Section B — COMPANY IDENTIFICATION *(To be answered by all employers)*

OFFICE USE ONLY

1. Parent Company
   a. Name of parent company (owns or controls establishment in item 2) omit if same as label

   Name of receiving office | Address (Number and street)

   City or town | County | State | ZIP code | b. Employer Identification No.

2. Establishment for which this report is filed. (Omit if same as label.)
   a. Name of establishment

   Address (Number and street) | City or town | County | State | ZIP code

   b. Employer Identification No. | (If same as label. skip.)

   (Multi-establishment Employers:
   Answer on Consolidated Report only)

3. Parent company affiliation
   a. Name of parent—affiliated company | b. Employer Identification No.

   Address (Number and street) | City or town | County | State | ZIP code

---

Section C — EMPLOYERS WHO ARE REQUIRED TO FILE   *(To be answered by all employers)*

☐ Yes ☐ No 1. Does the entire company have at least 100 employees in the payroll period for which you are reporting?

☐ Yes ☐ No 2. Is your company affiliated through common ownership and/or centralized management with other entities in an enterprise with a total employment of 100 or more?

☐ Yes ☐ No 3. Does the company or any of its establishments (a) have 50 or more employees AND (b) is not exempt as provided by 41 CFR 60-1.5, AND either (1) is a prime government contractor or first-tier subcontractor, and has a contract, subcontract, or purchase order amounting to $50,000 or more, or (2) serves as a depository of Government funds in any amount or is a financial institution which is an issuing and paying agent for U.S. Savings Bonds and Savings Notes?

NOTE: If the answer is yes to ANY of these questions, complete the entire form; otherwise skip to Section G.

Figure 6-1 Continued

Section D — EMPLOYMENT DATA

Employment at this establishment--Report all permanent, temporary, or part-time employees including apprentices and on-the-job trainees unless specifically excluded as set forth in the instructions. Enter the appropriate figures on all lines and in all columns. Blank spaces will be considered as zeros.

JOB CATEGORIES	NUMBER OF EMPLOYEES										
	OVERALL TOTALS (SUM OF COL B THRU K)	MALE					FEMALE				
	A	WHITE (NOT OF HISPANIC ORIGIN) B	BLACK (NOT OF HISPANIC ORIGIN) C	HISPANIC D	ASIAN OR PACIFIC ISLANDER E	AMERICAN INDIAN OR ALASKAN NATIVE F	WHITE (NOT OF HISPANIC ORIGIN) G	BLACK (NOT OF HISPANIC ORIGIN) H	HISPANIC I	ASIAN OR PACIFIC ISLANDER J	AMERICAN INDIAN OR ALASKAN NATIVE K
Officials and Managers											
Professionals											
Technicians											
Sales Workers											
Office and Clerical											
Craft Workers (Skilled)											
Operatives (Semi-Skilled)											
Laborers (Unskilled)											
Service Workers											
TOTAL											
Total employment reported in previous EEO-1 report											

(The trainees below should also be included in the figures for the appropriate occupational categories above)

Formal On-the-job trainees												
	White collar											
	Production											

1. NOTE: On consolidated report, skip questions 2-5 and Section E.
2. How was information as to race or ethnic group in Section D obtained?
   1 ☐ Visual Survey   3 ☐ Other — Specify ....
   2 ☐ Employment Record   ....
3. Dates of payroll period used –

4. Pay period of last report submitted for this establishment

5. Does this establishment employ apprentices?
   This year? 1 ☐ Yes 2 ☐ No
   Last year? 1 ☐ Yes 2 ☐ No

Section E — ESTABLISHMENT INFORMATION

1. Is the location of the establishment the same as that reported last year?
   1 ☐ Yes 2 ☐ No 3 ☐ Did not report last year 4 ☐ Reported on combined basis

2. Is the major business activity at this establishment the same as that reported last year?
   1 ☐ Yes 2 ☐ No 3 ☐ No report last year 4 ☐ Reported on combined basis

OFFICE USE ONLY

3. What is the major activity of this establishment? (Be specific, i.e., manufacturing steel castings, retail grocer, wholesale plumbing supplies, title insurance, etc. Include the specific type of product or type of service provided, as well as the principal business or industrial activity.)

e.

Section F — REMARKS

Use this item to give any identification data appearing on last report which differs from that given above, explain major changes in composition or reporting units, and other pertinent information.

Section G — CERTIFICATION (See Instructions G)

Check one
1. ☐ All reports are accurate and were prepared in accordance with the instructions (check on consolidated only)
2. ☐ This report is accurate and was prepared in accordance with the instructions.

Name of Certifying Official	Title	Signature		Date
Name of person to contact regarding this report (Type or print)	Address (Number and street)			
Title	City and State	ZIP code	Telephone Area Code	Number	Extension

All reports and information obtained from individual reports will be kept confidential as required by Section 709 (e) of Title VII financial institutions in which government funds are held or savings bonds are issued must file the annual report. The annual report must be filed by March 31 for the preceding year. The form requires employment data by job category, classified according to various protected groups.

APPLICATION FLOW DATA.   Under EEO laws and regulations, employers may be required to show that they do not discriminate in the recruiting and selection of protected groups. For instance, the number of women who applied and the number hired may be compared with the selection rate for men to determine if adverse impact exists. The fact that protected group identification is not available on company records is not considered a valid excuse for failure to provide the data required.

Because racial data are not permitted on application blanks or other preemployment records, the EEOC allows a "visual" survey or a separate "applicant information form" that is not used in the selection process. An example of such a form is shown in Figure 6–2. Notice that this form is filled out voluntarily by the applicant and that the data must be maintained separately from all selection-related materials.

The importance of good record-keeping is seen in the case of a small manufacturing firm in the southwestern United States with 40 employees that did not have any EEO-related records. Because it was located in a small town, the owner of the company, Mr. Ryan (not his real name), felt that keeping such records was a waste of time and governmental imposition. Subsequently, a woman who applied for a manufacturing job was not hired. She then filed a discrimination complaint with the state EEO agency. Because there appeared to be adverse impact, the burden of proof shifted to the employer. When the investigator checked on the complaint, he asked Ryan how many women worked in the company the previous three years, what jobs they held, and the number of women who applied for plant jobs in those three years. Without any records, Ryan had difficulty refuting the charge. The result was a substantial penalty imposed on Ryan and his firm in the form of back pay and penalties. In addition, he had to give the complainant a job with retroactive seniority. Without adequate records on past practices, Ryan and his firm were subjected to even greater pressures and penalties than they might otherwise have had.

EEO Compliance Investigation

When a discrimination complaint is received by the EEOC or a similar agency, it must be processed. The process outlined here is the one used by the EEOC beginning in 1986–87.

In a typical situation, a complaint goes through several stages before the compliance process has been completed.[2] First, the charges are filed by an individual, a group of individuals, or their representative. A charge must be filed within 180 days of when the alleged discriminatory action occurred. Then the regulatory commission staff reviews the specifics of the charges to determine if it has jurisdiction, which means that the agency is authorized to investigate that type of charge. If jurisdiction exists, a notice of the charge must be served on the employer within ten days after the filing, and the employer is asked to respond. Following the charge notification, the EEOC's major thrust turns to gathering information on the specifics.

The next stage involves conciliation efforts by the agency and the employer if the charge is found to be valid. If the employer agrees that discrimination has

Figure 6–2
Applicant Flow Data Form

THE C COMPANY

THE FOLLOWING STATISTICAL INFORMATION IS REQUIRED FOR COMPLIANCE WITH FEDERAL LAWS ASSURING EQUAL EMPLOYMENT OPPORTUNITY WITHOUT REGARD TO RACE, COLOR, SEX, NATIONAL ORIGIN, RELIGION, AGE OR HANDICAP AS WELL AS THE VIETNAM ERA READJUSTMENT ACT. THE INFORMATION REQUESTED IS VOLUNTARY AND WILL REMAIN SEPARATE FROM YOUR APPLICATION FOR EMPLOYMENT.

A   MONTH   DAY   YEAR   APPLICATION DATE
    1   6

B   [ ] — [ ] — [ ] A   APPLICANT SOCIAL SECURITY NUMBER
    7   16

C   [ ] FIRST INITIAL   D   [ ] MIDDLE INITIAL
    17   18

E   LAST NAME
    19   32

F   STREET   ADDRESS
    33   58

G   CITY   STATE (first 2 letters)   ZIP
    59   71   72 73   74   78

H   [ ] 1/ EEO CODES   EEO CODES 1/
    A—White Male   F—Hispanic Female (Spanish Origin)
    B—White Female   G—American Indian/Alaskan Native Male
    C—Black Male   H—American Indian/Alaskan Native Female
    D—Black Female   I—Asian or Pacific Islander Male
    E—Hispanic Male   J—Asian or Pacific Islander Female
    (Spanish Origin)

I   MONTH   DAY   YEAR   BIRTH DATE
    80 81   82 83   84 85

J   [ ] ARE YOU HANDICAPPED—Impairment which substantially limits one   NO —LEAVE BLANK
    86   or more of a person's life activities   YES—ENTER 'Y' Ask for Form 2

K   [ ] ARE YOU A DISABLED VETERAN—   30% V.A. Compensation or   NO —LEAVE BLANK
    87   discharged because of disability   YES—ENTER 'Y'
                                       incurred in line of duty   Ask for Form 2

L   [ ] ARE YOU A VIETNAM ERA VETERAN—   180 days Active Duty between   NO —LEAVE BLANK
    88   Aug. 15, 1964 & May 7, 1975   YES—ENTER 'Y'
                                                                         Ask for Form 2

JOB YOU HAVE APPLIED FOR (see reverse side) _____

LOCATION APPLICATION IS MADE FOR _____
                                (City or Town)   State

TO BE COMPLETED BY OFFICE ACCEPTING
APPLICATION

[ ] DIVISION

DEPT. APPLICATION IS MADE FOR

_____

EEO STAFF USE ONLY

    90   99

M   [ ] REFERRAL SOURCE
    89
    A—Walk in/Write in
    B—Ad Response
    C—State Employment Agency
    D—College Placement Office
    E—Minority Referral Agency
    F—CETA Referral
    G—Private Employment Agency

_____
Applicant's Signature

occurred and the employer accepts the proposed settlement, then the employer posts a notice of relief within the company and takes the agreed-on actions. This notice indicates that the employer has reached a conciliation agreement on a discrimination charge, and reiterates the employer's commitment to avoid future discriminatory actions.

However, if the employer objects to the charge and rejects conciliation, the agency can file suit or issue a "right-to-sue" letter to the complainant. Likewise, if no charge is brought against the employer by the agency, a right-to-sue letter is issued or the complainant can appeal to the full EEOC in Washington, D.C., or the appropriate state or local body.

INDIVIDUAL RIGHT TO SUE.   If the enforcement agency decides that it will not bring suit on behalf of the complainant, the individual has the right to bring suit. He or she can request a **right-to-sue letter** from the EEOC which, when issued, notifies the person that he or she has ninety days in which to file a personal suit in federal court. The suit usually is brought in the U.S. District Court having jurisdiction in the area.

> **A RIGHT-TO-SUE LETTER** is issued by the EEOC and notifies the person that he/she has ninety days in which to file a personal suit in federal court.

LITIGATION.   In the court litigation stage, a legal trial takes place in the appropriate state or federal court. At that point both sides retain lawyers and rely on the court to render a decision. If either party disagrees with the court ruling, either can file appeals with a higher court. The U.S. Supreme Court becomes the ultimate adjudication body.

INTERNAL EMPLOYER INVESTIGATION.   Many problems and expenses associated with EEO complaints can be controlled by employers who vigorously investigate their employees' discrimination complaints before they are taken to outside agencies. An internal employee complaint system and prompt, thorough responses to problem situations are essential tools in reducing EEO charges and in remedying illegal discriminatory actions. More on protecting employee rights is contained in Chapter 17.

Another way in which employers and regulatory agencies try to reduce the potential for discrimination is through *affirmative action*. This effort requires continuing commitment by an employer to improve its EEO posture, rather than to comply with certain standards or to resolve an individual charge with a one-time effort.

■ ■ AFFIRMATIVE ACTION

> **AFFIRMATIVE ACTION** requires employers to identify problem areas in the employment of protected group members and set goals and take steps to overcome those problems.

As described in Chapter 5, **affirmative action** means that an employer sets goals and takes positive steps to guarantee equal employment opportunities for protected group members. Affirmative action focuses on the hiring, training, and promoting of protected groups where there are deficiencies. An affirmative action plan (AAP) is a formal document available for review by employees and enforcement officers.

Who Must Have an AAP?

Affirmative action requirements are enforced by the OFCCP. Only employers who meet OFCCP regulations must have a formally prepared AAP. The requirements primarily come from Executive Orders 11246, 11357, and 11478.

I. Purpose
II. Policy Statement
III. Dissemination of Policy
IV. Responsibility for Implementation
V. Work Force Analysis
  a) Facility Organization Chart
  b) Work Force Analysis
  c) Job Group Analysis
VI. Availability Analysis
VII. Goals and Timetables
VIII. Identification of Problem Areas
IX. Development, Execution, and Support of Action-oriented Programs
X. Internal Audit and Reporting
XI. Consideration of Minorities and Women not Currently in the Work Force
XII. Compliance with Religion and National Origin Guidelines
XIII. Analysis of Previous Year Goal Accomplishment
XIV. Lines of Progression
XV. Compliance with Sex Discrimination Guidelines
XVI. EEO-1 Reports
XVII. New Hires and Terminations
XVIII. Transfers and Promotions
Appendix I Handicapped and the Vietnam Era/Disabled Veteran

Figure 6–3
Sample Table of Contents for an Affirmative Action Plan

Generally, an employer with 50 employees and over $50,000 in government contracts must have a formal, written affirmative action plan. A government contractor with fewer employers who has contracts totaling more than $50,000 can be required to have an AAP if it has been found guilty of discrimination by the EEOC or other agencies. The contract size can vary depending on the protected group and the different laws on which the regulations rest.

Courts have noted that any employer that is not a government contractor may have a *voluntary* AAP, although the employer must have such a plan if it wishes to be a government contractor. A *required* AAP means that a court has ordered an employer to have an AAP as a result of past discriminatory practices and violations of laws.

Contents of the AAP

The contents of an AAP and the policies flowing from it must be available for review by managers and supervisors within the organization. Plans vary in length; some can be long and require extensive staff time to prepare. The table of contents of a plan for a small employer is shown in Figure 6–3. One of the major sections of an AAP is the utilization analysis.

UTILIZATION ANALYSIS. An AAP **utilization analysis** identifies the number of protected group members employed and the types of jobs they hold. According to Executive Order 11246, employers who are government contractors meeting the requirements for contract size and number of employees levels must provide data on protected groups. The data can be classified according to the job categories outlined in EEO-1 form, section D (see Figure 6–1).

UTILIZATION ANALYSIS
identifies the number of protected group members employed and the types of jobs held in an organization.

AVAILABILITY ANALYSIS. As part of the utilization analysis, an availability analysis also must be conducted. An **availability analysis** identifies the number of protected

AVAILABILITY ANALYSIS
identifies the number of protected group members available to work in the appropriate labor market.

group members available to work in the appropriate labor market in a given job. This analysis, which can be developed with data from a state labor department, the U.S. Census Bureau, and other sources, serves as a basis for determining if *underutilization* exists within an organization. The census data also must be matched to job title and job groups used in the utilization analysis.[3]

UNDERUTILIZATION.   As discussed in Chapter 5, the 4/5ths rule is a guide to underutilization of protected group members. To calculate underutilization, the employer considers the following:[4]

- Protected group members in the surrounding area population
- Protected group members in surrounding area work force compared with total work force in the organization
- Amount of unemployed members of protected groups in the surrounding area
- General availability of protected group members having requisite skills in the immediate area and in an area in which an employer reasonably could recruit
- Availability of promotable and transferable protected group members within the organization
- Existence of training institutions that can train individuals in the requisite skills
- Realistic amount of training an employer can do to make all job classes available to protected group members

Fortunately for many employers, much of the data on the population and work force in the surrounding area is available in computerized form, so availability analysis and underutilization calculations can be done more easily. However, an employer still must maintain an accurate profile of the internal work force. Also, the employer can determine the protected group status of applicants by reviewing applicant flow data. These analyses may be useful in showing that the reason why an employer has underutilization of a protected group is because of an inadequate applicant flow of protected group members, in spite of special efforts to recruit them.[5] As discussed in Chapter 21, having an integrated human resource information system (HRIS) can reduce the time and effort required to do these analyses.

Development of an Affirmative Action Plan

The development of an AAP must be built on a commitment to affirmative action. The commitment must begin at the top of the organization, as the research study on AAPs indicates (see the accompanying P/HR: Research). The crucial factor is the appointment of an affirmative action officer to monitor the plan and ensure that the commitment is implemented. A survey of 114 employers indicated that primary responsibilities of such an administrator are to: (1) ensure EEO compliance, (2) listen to employee complaints, (3) conduct EEO investigations, (4) review hiring decisions, and (5) set hiring goals.[7]

Once a plan is developed, it should be distributed and explained to all managers and supervisors. It is particularly important that everyone involved in the selection process review the plan and receive training on its content.[8] Periodic reviews and update briefings also should be done, because the AAP plan must be updated and reviewed each year to reflect changes in the utilization and availability of protected group members.

P/HR: Practice *and* Research	Effective Affirmative Action Programs

To identify the criteria associated with effective affirmative action programs, Michael Hitt and Barbara Keats contacted members of an association of affirmative action officers working for colleges and universities in one state. These officers worked with, and had responsibility for, the affirmative action programs in their institutions.

As reported in the *Journal of Applied Behavioral Science*, Hitt and Keats prepared 30 case studies, each describing an affirmation action program in 13 different areas. Each case study has some variations on the different areas. Each member of the association received a set of all cases, instructions, and a questionnaire.

The questionnaire required respondents to rate the effectiveness of each simulated program on a seven-point scale, ranging from very effective to very ineffective. Thirty-one of the 55 association members returned the questionnaires.

Analysis of the returned questionnaires revealed that the officers viewed four areas as having the most impact on the effectiveness of affirmative action program. These four are (in order):

1. Commitment from higher administration
2. Receptive attitude by key staff members
3. Credibility of affirmative action programs and officers
4. Formal and/or information grievance procedures

Although not surprising, the results emphasize the importance of support for affirmative action by top executives and key staff members. By their commitment, these individuals enhance the credibility and commitment of the institution to affirmative action. If affirmative action officers are credible and appropriate grievance procedures exist, individuals who believe they have been treated unfairly initially can address their problems internally in the organization rather than externally to enforcement agencies [6]

■■ ■■ EQUAL EMPLOYMENT AND MANAGEMENT PRACTICES

A wide variety of managerial practices have been affected by equal employment and affirmative action regulations. Some management practices have been upheld and some have been found to be illegal. It is sometimes difficult to draw general conclusions from court decisions because each court approaches each situation with a legal analysis of that particular situation, rather than trying to establish broad principles. At times, different courts have reached different conclusions when viewing similar situations. As a result, inconsistencies exist.

Title VII of the 1964 Civil Rights Act specifically states that employers may discriminate on the basis of sex, religion, or national origin if the characteristic can be justified as a "*bona fide* occupational qualification reasonably necessary to the normal operation of the particular business or enterprise."[9]

Bona Fide Occupational Qualification (BFOQ)

A **bona fide occupational qualification (BFOQ)** is a legitimate reason why an employer can exclude persons on otherwise illegal bases of consideration.

A BONA FIDE OCCUPATIONAL QUALIFICATION (BFOQ) is a legitimate reason why an employer can exclude persons on otherwise illegal bases of consideration.

What constitutes a BFOQ has been subject to different interpretations in various courts across the country. Some of the examples are obvious, such as being able to advertise for males as models for clothing ads, or females as actresses for theatrical productions, or youthful-looking actors for film roles. Other decisions in which a BFOQ was at issue include the following:

- Women could be excluded from jobs as prison guards in an all-male, maximum security prison because of the assault possibilities and the security risks posed for other guards and inmates.[10]
- Loyola University of Chicago could use a Jesuit-only policy for selecting individuals for certain teaching positions in the university's philosophy department.[11]
- Age was not a legal BFOQ in a case in which an age limit was placed on construction workers because individuals above an age limit vary in their physical capabilities.[12]

Business Necessity and Job-Relatedness

A BUSINESS NECESSITY
is a business practice necessary for safe and efficient organizational operations.

The view of what is a "business necessity" has been subject to numerous court decisions. A **business necessity** is a business practice necessary for safe and efficient organizational operations.

Education requirements often are based on business necessity. In one case, the requirement by a hotel of English language proficiency by its employees was ruled to be a justifiable business necessity.[13] Most employers have identified minimum education requirements for some jobs. An employer who requires a minimum level of education, such as a high school diploma, must be able to defend the requirement as essential to the performance of each job. For instance, equating a degree or diploma with the possession of math or reading abilities is considered questionable. Having a global requirement of a degree cannot always be justified on the basis of the need for a certain level of ability.[14] However, a requirement by United Airlines to require a college degree and 500 hours of flight time for flight officer candidates was upheld.[15]

In summary, employers can use educational requirements as selection criteria, but should use them only in situations in which the educational requirements are necessary for job performance. Thus, it is not illegal for an employer to inquire about the education an applicant has attained, provided that "automatic cutoffs" in education level that may be used by an employer are determined to be specifically related to the job being sought by the applicant.

Employment Inquiries and Retaliation

Although many different questions are asked in interviews and on application blanks, not all of them may be permitted under existing equal employment regulations. Managers must take care to avoid the appearance, as well as the actual act, of discrimination. Employers are prohibited by the various EEO laws from retaliating against individuals who file discrimination charges with government agencies. For example, an employer was ruled to have engaged in retaliation when an employee who filed a discrimination charge was assigned undesirable hours and his work schedule was changed frequently.[16]

After-Hire Inquiries

Once an employer tells an applicant he or she is hired (the "point of hire"), inquiries that were prohibited earlier may be made. After hiring, medical examination forms, group insurance, and other enrollment cards containing inquiries related directly or indirectly to sex, age, or other bases may be requested. Photographs or evidence of race, religion, or national origin also may be requested after hire for legal and necessary purposes, but not before. Such data should be maintained in a separate personnel records system in order to avoid their use when making appraisals, discipline, termination, or promotion decisions.

It should be emphasized that employers still can obtain needed information about applicants as long as the information cannot be used for discriminatory purposes. Each case regarding discrimination is considered on its own merit. Although precedents such as those discussed earlier certainly do apply, they are not guarantees that an employer will or will not be charged and found guilty of discrimination. Employers must be aware of precedents and of the intent and interpretation of the law by the EEOC and other enforcement agencies. As additional court decisions are made, employers should keep informed of changes that occur.

Figure 6–4 contains a list of pre employment inquiries that may or not be discriminatory. All those pre-employment inquiries labeled in the figure as "may be discriminatory" have been so designated because of findings in a variety of court cases. Likewise, those labeled as "may not be discriminatory" are practices that are legal, but only if they reflect a "business necessity" or are job-related for the specific job under review.

■■ ■ SEX DISCRIMINATION

Title VII of the Civil Rights Act prohibits discrimination in employment on the basis of sex. As with racial discrimination, it has taken a series of court decisions and EEOC rulings to determine exactly how broad that prohibition is.

Discrimination in Selection and Job Conditions

The composition of the work force in the United States has changed as a growing number of women have entered. One result of this change is the movement of women into jobs traditionally held by men. More women are obtaining jobs such as welders, railroad engineers, utility repair specialists, farm equipment sales representatives, sheet metal workers, truck drivers, and carpenters. Yet, many kinds of discrimination in the assignment of women to jobs still exist.

SEXUAL STEREOTYPING. The selection or promotion criteria that employers use can discriminate unfairly against women. In the *Price Waterhouse v. Hopkins* case mentioned in Chapter 5, the U.S. Supreme Court addressed the "sexual stereotyping" done by the firm. Several partners in the accounting firm described Hopkins as "overly aggressive" and "displaying a masculine attitude." One partner advised her to "walk more femininely, talk more femininely, wear makeup, have her hair styled, and wear jewelry." The court ruled that gender stereotyping played a role in the decision to deny Hopkins promotion to partner, which was a violation of Title VII of the Civil Rights Act.[17]

Figure 6–4
Guidelines to Lawful and Unlawful Pre-employment Inquiries

SUBJECT OF INQUIRY	IT MAY NOT BE DISCRIMINATORY TO INQUIRE ABOUT:	IT MAY BE DISCRIMINATORY TO INQUIRE ABOUT:
1. Name	a. Whether applicant had ever worked under a different name	a. The original name of an applicant whose name had been legally changed b. The ethnic association of applicant's name
2. Age	a. If applicant is over the age of 18 b. If applicant is under the age of 18, or 21 if job-related (i.e. selling liquor in retail store)	a. Date of birth b. Date of high school graduation
3. Residence	a. Applicant's place of residence, length of applicant's resident in state and/or city where employer is located	a. Previous addresses b. Birthplace of applicant or applicant's parents
4. Race or Color	a. General distinguishing characteristics such as scars, etc.	a. Applicant's race or color of applicant's skin
5. National Origin & Ancestry		a. Applicant's lineage, ancestry, national origin, descendants, parentage, or nationality b. Nationality of applicant's parents or spouse
6. Sex & Family Composition		a. Sex of applicant b. Dependents of applicant c. Marital status d. Childcare arrangements
7. Creed or Religion		a. Applicant's religious affiliation b. Church, parish or holidays observed
8. Citizenship	a. Whether the applicant is a citizen of the U.S. b. Whether the applicant is in the country on a visa, which permits him to work or is a citizen	a. Whether applicant is a citizen of a country other than the United States
9. Language	a. Language applicant speaks and/or writes fluently, only if job-related	a. Applicant's native tongue, language commonly used at home
10. References	a. Names of persons willing to provide professional and/or character references for applicant	a. Name of applicant's pastor or religious leader
11. Relatives	a. Names of relatives already employed by the company	a. Name and/or address of any relative of applicant b. Who to contact in case of emergency
12. Organizations	a. Applicant's membership in any union, professional, service, or trade organization	a. All clubs or social organizations to which applicant belongs
13. Arrest Record & Convictions	a. Convictions, if related to job performance (Disclaimer should accompany)	a. Number and kinds arrests b. Convictions unless related to job performance
14. Photographs		a. Photographs with application, resume, or before hiring
15. Height & Weight		a. Any inquiry into height and weight of applicant except where a BFOQ
16. Physical limitations	a. Whether applicant has the ability to perform job-related functions	a. Whether an applicant is handicapped or the nature or severity of a handicap b. Whether applicant has ever filed worker's compensation claim c. Any recent or past operations or surgery and dates

Figure 6–4, Continued

SUBJECT OF INQUIRY	IT MAY NOT BE DISCRIMINATORY TO INQUIRE ABOUT:	IT MAY BE DISCRIMINATORY TO INQUIRE ABOUT:
17. Education	a. Training applicant has received if related the job applied for b. Highest level of education attained, if validated that having certain educational background (i.e. high school diploma or college degree) is necessary to perform the specific job	
18. Military	a. What branch of the military served in b. Type of education or training received in military c. Rank at discharge	a. Type of military discharge
19. Financial Status		a. An applicant's debts or assets b. Garnishments

SOURCE: Employee Relations-Management Services, Inc., 12220 Westover Rd.; Omaha, NE 68154. May not be used without permission.

Other cases have found that women were not allowed to enter certain jobs or job fields because of sexual stereotyping. Particularly problematic is the use of marital or family status as a basis for not selecting women. The P/HR: Practice on ethical issues in interviewing women identifies some of the ways discrimination selection can occur.

NEPOTISM.   Many employers have antinepotism policies that prohibit any relatives from working for the same employer. The policies most frequently cover brothers, sisters, mothers, father, sons, daughters, and spouses. However, in some cases, antinepotism policies have been ruled to discriminate against women more than men because women tend to be denied employment more often or leave employers more often if two employees get married. For example, in one insurance firm a man and women in the same department started dating and ultimately got married. Upon their marriage, the couple was told that one of them would have to quit or the company would terminate one. Because the man's job was a higher-level one, the woman was forced to quit and find other employment. Other firms only require that relatives cannot work directly for or with each other or be placed in a position where potential collusion or conflicts could occur. Such policies have been upheld in court.[18]

In a related area, inquiries about previous names (not maiden name) under which any applicant may have previously worked may be necessary in order to check reference information with former employers, educational institutions, or employers' own files, in the case of former employees. This kind of inquiry is not illegal.

HEIGHT/WEIGHT RESTRICTIONS.   Many cases involving discriminatory use of height/weight restrictions were actually sex or race discrimination cases and illustrate adverse impact against women. Employers had used them to keep out women or members of minority groups. For example, the state of Alabama violated Title VII in setting height and weight restrictions for correctional counselors. The restrictions (5 feet 2 inches and 120 pounds) would exclude 41.14 percent of the female

P/HR: Practice *and* Research

Ethical Issues in Interviewing Women

A faculty member at Memphis State University, Arthur Eliot Berkeley, wrote the following observations of the behavior and questioning techniques used in job interviews for the *Wall Street Journal.* He obtained his information from numerous conversations with personnel specialists, interviewers, and employees. What he said raises some ethical issues with equal employment implications.

"It's the law: Interviews for such employment-related decisions as hiring, transfer, and promotion are supposed to be conducted in an objective fashion with no personal inquiries that aren't clearly job-related. For example, an interviewer should not ask a young woman about her marital status, birth control, or plans for childbearing.

If a position involves extensive travel with frequent overnights away from home, an interviewer might legitimately ask whether any situation in the candidate's life would serve as a bar to travel. Otherwise, for a typical officebound job involving regular business hours, no such inquiry would be permissible.

All personnel administrators and most, if not all, managers know the law. Yet what actually occurs in an interview frequently deviates dramatically from the legally permissible. For years the actual substance of interviews has been a dirty little secret with no one willing to own up to the sorts of illegal inquiries frequently made of candidates.

Most impermissible areas of inquiry appear to be directed at women. Most typically, the concern of the interviewer is a young woman's childbearing plans and child-care situation. Given managers' great curiosity about such matters, how is the information—unlawful if not clearly job-related—obtained?

* *Sneaky Stratagems:* One large

manufacturing firm (and a huge federal contractor) uses the simple expedient of having a low-level personnel clerk ask the candidate about her choice of health insurance plans. An executive from the firm says: "During a lull in between interviews, I have a clerk ask whether the applicant wants individual, husband-and-wife, or family coverage, and in choosing an option, the candidate will usually tell the clerk everything we need to know."

Another effective technique is used by a large financial-service firm, which takes the job candidate to lunch at a nice restaurant. Given the informal atmosphere, the applicant is more easily caught off-guard by a personal inquiry. Typically the prospective supervisor and his assistant eat lunch with the candidate and begin to discuss their children.

One of the firm's supervisors says: "I'll say something like: 'Our car-pool arrangements got messed up this morning and I was almost late for work.' Then I ask the applicant if anything like that ever happens to her. And almost always, the information I want will just come pouring out. The candidate will say something like no, she has no children, isn't even married, or doesn't want children. Or she'll tell me how she's a single mother with two little girls and is always having a problem with car pools and sisters. This tells me what I need to know."

* *The Direct Approach:* Most starkly, some employers—often in an informal or cocktail setting—will ask flat out about a woman's family situation, putting the candidate in an extremely delicate position. If the female applicant refuses to answer the question, citing its illegality, she runs a very real risk of alienating the interviewer and wrecking her chances of being hired. If she answers to the question truthfully, the information may prove fatal to her candidacy.

* *Sneaky Responses:* In what was the most startling revelation in this area, I learned that many women respond falsely to these illegal inquiries, rationalizing that since the questions are unlawful, they are morally entitled to offer untrue responses. Said one woman, the divorced mother of two children, one of whom is severely handicapped: "Even though I'm a very reliable worker, I knew if I told the truth, I wouldn't get the job, and I needed this job badly. So I said I wasn't married—which was true—and I had no intention of having children—which is sort of true because certainly I don't plan to have any more children . . . I got the job. I figured that my kids were none of their business, so it didn't matter what I told them. Once I was hired, what could they do?"

* *The Implications:* When disobedience of any law becomes as widespread as it apparently has here, it seems clear that a new approach is necessary. Increased enforcement of the law with stiffer penalties is one approach, but this is almost bound to fail. Both interviewer and candidate probably would become even more skilled at evading the law—to everyone's detriment.

The best approach is to encourage discussion and education on the subject. If both interviewer and candidate can get beyond the gamesmanship and focus in on the optimum fit between the job and the person, everyone will benefit.

Interviewers should learn not merely the techniques for a lawful employment interview, but, even more important, the reasons for the restrictions. They need to be made to question and confront their underlying prejudicial assumptions and then to change them. Only then can candidates trust the interview process and end this unethical cycle."[19]

population of the country but less than 1 percent of the men. The Supreme Court found that the state's attempt to justify the requirements as essential for job-related strength failed for lack of evidence. The Court suggested that if strength was the quality sought, the state would have adopted a strength requirement.[20]

RESTRICTIVE STATE LAWS.   In the past, many states had laws to "protect" women by requiring that they be restricted to a certain number of working hours a week or by specifying the maximum weight a woman was allowed to lift at work. The EEOC has disputed these laws in court, and in most cases, the restrictions have been ruled invalid because they conflict with federal law and are not reasonable grounds for denying jobs to women. For example, women were excluded from certain jobs in a firm because of some strenuous physical demands and hours of work. The company's defense was a state law that prohibited women workers from repeated lifting of more than 25 pounds. The decision in the case was that such requirements were unnecessarily restrictive and hence were illegal discrimination.[21]

JOB CONDITIONS.   Having different job conditions for men and women also can be discriminatory. In one case, an EEO violation occurred when a retail firm allowed male sales clerks to wear slacks, shirts and ties, but required women sales clerks to wear smocks.[22] Another retailer paid over $2,500 in back pay for firing a full-figured female employee because, according to the owner, her figure was too distracting, especially when she wore sweaters.[23]

Sexual Harassment

The EEOC has issued guidelines designed to curtail sexual harassment. A variety of definitions of sexual harassment exist, but generally **sexual harassment** refers to actions that are sexually directed, unwanted, and subject the worker to adverse employment conditions. The EEOC guidelines indicate that unwelcome sexual advances, requests for sexual favors, or verbal or physical acts of a sexual nature that affect decisions about employment conditions, promotions, and pay raises

SEXUAL HARASSMENT
refers to actions that are sexually directed, unwanted, and subject the worker to adverse employment conditions.

Reprinted with special permission of King Features Syndicate, Inc.

constitute sexual harassment.[24] Sexual harassment can occur between a boss and subordinate, among co-workers, and among nonemployees who have business contracts with employees. A few sexual harassment cases also have been filed involving a manager and an employee of the same sex. However, according to EEOC statistics, well over 90 percent of the situations have been harassment of women by men.

TYPES OF SEXUAL HARASSMENT.   The EEOC guidelines and court cases have identified two types of sexual harassment:

- *Quid pro quo* occurs when an employer or supervisor links specific employment outcomes to the individual's granting sexual favors.
- *Hostile Environment* occurs when the sexual harassment has the effect of unreasonably interfering with employee work performance or when an intimidating or offensive working condition is created.

The first type (*quid pro quo*) occurs when supervisors or managers demand sexual favors in exchange for the employee receiving a raise or promotion, access to training, a favorable performance appraisal rating, or not being fired. This type of harassment has been labeled "sexual extortion."[25]

Harassment by supervisors and managers who expect sexual favors as a condition for a raise or promotion is totally inappropriate behavior in a work environment. This view has been supported in a wide variety of cases, including one in which a woman U.S. Army officer was punished for sexually harassing an enlisted man. In another case, the court ruled in favor of a female who brought suit against a bank because she had been fired for refusing her male supervisor's demand for sexual favors.[26] Also, granting special treatment or favoring an employee who has an affair with a supervisor discriminates against other employees who do not receive favored treatment. In one case, a Veterans Administration supervisor promoted an employee with whom the supervisor was having an affair. Another employee filed a discrimination charge for being denied the promotion. The court ruled in favor of the second employee.[27]

The second type of sexual harassment involves the creation of a hostile work environment. A landmark case decided by the U.S. Supreme Court, *Meritor Savings Bank v. Vinson*, ruled that creation of a hostile work environment due to sexual harassment is illegal, even if the complainant suffered no earnings or job loss. The case was brought by a former female employee who charged that a vice president of the bank sexually harassed her.[28] A California nurse filed sexual harassment charges against a hospital because her supervising doctor made obscene gestures and grabbed other nurses while they were trying to work.[29] The court ruled that even though the nurse who brought suit had not been fondled and touched, a hostile work environment had been created. However, an employer won a case when a female mechanic charged sexual harassment, because the only specific example of offensive behavior was a senior mechanic's request to join him at a restaurant after work.[30]

What all of these cases illustrate is that what may be seen as harmless joking, teasing, or fun by some may be seen as offensive and hostile by others. Comments on dress or appearance, telling jokes that are suggestive or sexual in nature, allowing centerfold posters to be on display, or making continual requests for getting together after work all can lead to the creation of a hostile work environment.

PREVENTING SEXUAL HARASSMENT.   To protect themselves from sexual harassment charges, employers must take affirmative action to avoid such charges. Some actions suggested by the EEOC guidelines include:

- Developing a policy on sexual harassment and distributing a copy of the policy to all employees
- Identifying ways in which individuals who feel they have been harassed can report the incidents without fear of retaliation, and creating procedures to ensure that complaints are satisfactorily investigated and appropriate action is taken
- Communicating to all employees, especially to supervisors and managers, concerns and regulations regarding sexual harassment and the importance of creating and maintaining a work environment free of sexual harassment
- Disciplining offenders by using organizational sanctions up to and including firing the offenders
- Training all employees, especially supervisors and managers, about what constitutes sexual harassment, and alerting employees to the issues and behaviors involved

All these actions aim at prevention. Court cases make it clear that employers have a duty to do more than publish a policy. For example, in the *Bundy v. Johnson* case, a female vocational rehabilitation specialist (Bundy) suffered from sexual propositions and sexual intimidation, and was passed over for a promotion. She filed a complaint within the department, but no organizational investigation followed. The court decision favored Bundy and found that a violation of Title VII occurred "where an employer created or condoned a substantially discriminatory work environment, regardless of whether the complaining employee lost any tangible job benefits."[31]

In summary, employers generally are held responsible for sexual harassment unless the employers take appropriate action once an employee complains of harassment. Employers also are responsible for sexual harassment of an employee by a fellow employee if the employer knew (or should have known) of the conduct. This policy holds unless the employer can show that immediate and appropriate corrective action was taken.

Pregnancy Discrimination

Before the passage of the Pregnancy Discrimination Act (PDA) of 1978, many employers had policies that effectively denied the right of women who took maternity leave to return to work at their employers. The major effect of the act has been that an employer no longer may have a policy for maternity leaves different from the policy used for other personal leaves or medical disabilities. Also, an employee who takes such a leave is assured a job, provided that she returns in the agreed-on time frame, though the job to which she returns does not have to be the same job at the same rate of pay. It is also a violation of the act to refuse to hire a woman who is pregnant.

In 1987, the U.S. Supreme Court issued a major decision concerning a California state law that required employers to grant up to four months' unpaid leave for pregnancy and the same or similar job on an employee's return to work, even if the employer does not allow other disability leaves. The Supreme Court decision did not require all employers to provide pregnancy leaves, but it did allow states to pass such laws.[32] As a result, a number of other states have passed similar laws. At the federal level, Congress has considered bills to require employers to offer such leaves, as well as paternity leaves, in either birth or adoption situations, but as of the writing of this text, no federal law had been passed.

In addition, a U.S. Supreme Court decision in a case involving a shipbuilding worker extended the PDA provisions to the wives of male employees. The decision in that case required that an employer's medical insurance plan provide the same pregnancy coverage and benefits to spouses of workers as given to married female employees.[33]

Another facet of pregnancy discrimination concerns women who quit their jobs because of pregnancy. A 1987 decision by the U.S. Supreme Court allows states to deny unemployment benefits to women if they quit their jobs because of pregnancy, as long as the employer follows a consistently applied leave policy.[34]

Compensation Issues and Sex Discrimination

A number of concerns have been raised about employer compensation practices that discriminate on the basis of sex. At issue in several compensation practices is the extent to which men and women are treated differently, with women most frequently receiving less compensation or benefits. Equal pay, comparable worth, and unisex pensions are three prominent issues.

EQUAL PAY.   The Equal Pay Act enacted in 1963 forbids employers to pay lower wage rates to employees of one sex for equal work performed under similar working conditions. Tasks performed only intermittently or infrequently do not make jobs different enough to justify significantly different wages. According to the act, differences in pay may be allowed because of: (1) differences in seniority, (2) differences in performance, (3) differences in quality and/or quantity of production, and (4) factors other than sex.

COMPARABLE WORTH
requires that jobs with comparable knowledge, skills, and abilities be paid similarly.

COMPARABLE WORTH.   The **comparable worth** idea extends the concept of equal pay to require that employers provide similar pay for jobs that require comparable knowledge, skills, and abilities.

A major reason for the development of the comparable worth idea is the continuous gap between the earnings of women and men. According to Bureau of Labor Statistics data, the income of full-time working women is about 70 percent of men's earnings. In addition, the market rates for many jobs held primarily by women are lower than rates for jobs dominated by men.[35]

Employers traditionally have tied pay for their jobs to what other employers pay for similar jobs. Advocates of comparable worth assert that using market rates perpetuates the gap in earnings between men and women working full time, even though they are employed in distinctly different jobs.

Those favoring comparable worth also maintain that employees who perform comparable jobs should be paid relatively the same, even though they may have significantly different duties. But the grounds for determining comparability of jobs is subject to dispute. For instance, some nurses in Denver filed suit because their salaries were less than the salaries of tree trimmers and painters. In this case, the court decided that comparing jobs of entirely different skills was beyond the scope of existing laws.[36]

The U.S. Supreme Court denied support to the concept of comparable worth. In a case brought against the state of Washington, the U.S. Supreme Court decided to reverse the decision by a lower court. In that case the union representing state employees filed suit claiming that approximately 15,000 women employees were paid significantly less for performing work of comparable value to that performed by men. Before the filing of the suit, the state had a consulting study done, which revealed that female-dominated jobs were paid about 20 percent less than male-dominated jobs requiring comparable knowledge, skills, and abilities. However, the Washington State legislature initially did not approve the legislation to implement the study recommendations. The U.S. Ninth Circuit Court of Appeals said: "The law does not permit the federal courts to interfere in the market-based system for the compensation of Washington employees." Also, that decision stated that an employer does not have to implement changes even though a study indicated what might have been more equitable. The U.S. Supreme Court upheld the decision against comparable worth by a lower court. A suit against the state of Michigan in 1989 by women employees resulted in a similar rejection of comparable worth.[37]

Even though court support for comparable worth has been lacking, a number of state and local government employers have mandated "pay equity" for public-sector employees through legislation. The state of Washington negotiated a settlement, funding for which was approved by the state legislature. According to the settlement, the state had to spend $41.4 million on pay equity adjustment from April 1986 to June 1987. Thereafter, every July through 1992, additional funds of $10 million cumulatively were to be allocated for pay equity adjustments. The total cost of the settlement ultimately will be about $482 million to such employees as nurses, word-processing operators, library technicians, and clerk typists.[38]

In Ontario, Canada, comparable worth legislation has been passed that applies to both public- and private-sector employers. Similar legislation has not been enacted in the United States.

BENEFIT COVERAGE.   A final area of sex-based differences in compensation relates to benefit coverage. One concern has been labeled "unisex" pension coverage. The *Arizona Governing Committee v. Norris* decision held that an employer's deferred compensation plan violated Title VII because female employees received lower monthly benefit payments than men upon retirement, despite the fact that women contributed equally to the plan. Although the difference in benefit payments was due to sex-segregated actuarial tables, which reflected that women, as a group, live longer than men, the court rejected the employer's defense that sex may be used to predict longevity.[39]

The impact of the decision was that many pension plans had to be revised. Regardless of longevity differences, men and women who contribute equally to pension plans must receive equal monthly payments.

■■ ■ AGE DISCRIMINATION

The Age Discrimination in Employment Act (ADEA) of 1967, amended in 1978 and 1986, applies to all individuals over 40 years of age. For many years, race and sex discrimination cases overshadowed age discrimination cases. However, starting with the 1978 amendments to the ADEA, a dramatic increase in age discrimination suits occurred. Over the eight-year period more than 100,000 age discrimination complaints were filed with the EEOC. A majority of the charges were based on employee terminations or involuntary retirements.[40]

Forced Retirement and Terminations

As highlighted in Chapter 3, early retirement programs and organizational downsizing have been used by many employers to reduce their employment costs. Illegal age discrimination may result when an employer wishes to reduce a work force. By eliminating older workers, an employer also may be reducing the most costly portion of the employment budget because older workers tend to have higher salaries due to greater length of service and experience. However, these reductions must be based on job-related criteria. Otherwise, age discrimination may be found if those over forty are adversely impacted.

Westinghouse Electric Corporation found the cost of age discrimination was $35 million for 4,000 older employees who were denied severance pay after their jobs were eliminated through plant closings. Even though the employees were eligible for pensions, the company attempted to force each employee to choose between a pension and severance pay.[41] In another case, Pan American World Airways was permitted to eliminate eleven supervisory positions at Kennedy Airport in New York City. The employees identified for termination were selected through a systematic peer review process done by supervisors. The results of that peer review were forwarded to the P/HR department for summarization, and the supervisors were terminated. When the airline was sued, a U.S. District Court ruled that Pan Am used nondiscriminatory business-related bases for its decision, and illegal age discrimination had not occurred.[42]

There are a number of industries in which mandatory retirement ages of 55 or 60 have been used by employers. In some situations the requirements have been due to federal restrictions. For example, the Federal Aviation Administration has regulations requiring that commercial airline and corporate pilots must retire at age 60. But several airlines lost suits in which they required pilots to retire, instead of offering them transfers to flight engineer positions, which are not primary flying positions. In these and other situations, age was being used as a BFOQ. A successful use of a BFOQ was made by Hughes Helicopter, which won a case in which experimental test pilots were required to retire at age 55.[43]

Ensuring that age discrimination does not affect employment decisions requires a number of practices. These practices are not exclusively for age discrimination situations; they should be used in all circumstances. Documentation of performance must be completed by supervisors and managers. Care must be taken that references to age ("good old Fred" or "need younger blood") in conversations with older employees are not used.

Terminations must be handled carefully and must be job-related and performance-based. When a retail collection manager over age 40 was terminated by Sears, Roebuck after receiving five negative performance appraisal ratings from five different supervisors, the termination was ruled to be performance-based, not age discrimination.[44]

Age-Based Hiring and Promoting

Age discrimination also occurs when an individual over the age of 40 is denied employment or promotion because the employer feels that the applicant is "too old" or "not young enough." Only if employers have established age as a BFOQ have age limitations been upheld by courts.[45]

◼◼ ◼ DISCRIMINATION AGAINST THE DISABLED

As mentioned in Chapter 5, federal legislation prohibits discrimination in employment against disabled persons and requires affirmative action by employers with federal contracts over $2,500. In addition, federal contractors with more than 50 employees and over $50,000 in contracts must have written affirmative action plans, as stated earlier in this chapter.

Who Is Covered?

A disabled person is someone who has a "physical or mental impairment that substantially limits that person in some major life activities, has a record of, or is regarded as having, such an impairment."[46] Persons who qualify for protection under the act are those who have obvious disabilities such as the absence of a limb or sight as well as others with actual physical or mental impairments. But regulations limit the extent to which employers must accommodate current users of illegal drugs, homosexuals, people with sexual disorders, and compulsive gamblers.

Some court decisions and laws have protected individuals who may be perceived as impaired to a degree that their employment is affected, Thus, even individuals with facial disfigurements or those who may be considered "unattractive" could qualify as disabled.[47]

Other court decisions have found individuals who have high blood pressure, epilepsy, allergies, obesity, and color blindness to be disabled. A color-blind man filed a discrimination charge after being denied a promotion to a railroad engineer position because he failed a color-blindness test in which he was shown plates of colored dots that had numbers imbedded in them. The railroad company felt the test necessary because engineers must recognize red, green, amber, blue, and white traffic signals. The Oregon Court of Appeals ruled against the railroad company because the test was not uniformly given to all applicants, and the individual could identify red and green on a color chart, although not during the color-dot test.[48]

Contagious Diseases and AIDS

In recent years, the types of disabilities that are protected against discrimination by the various local, state, and federal acts have expanded. For example, a U.S. Supreme Court case held that an employer cannot discriminate against an individual whom the employer feels may have a contagious disease. The case involved an individual who had a relapse of tuberculosis and was discharged from her job as a school teacher because her employer feared she might be contagious.[49]

The most feared contagious disease is acquired immune deficiency syndrome (AIDS). The disease was almost unknown in 1980; but by 1990 estimates were that approximately one million people in the United States either had AIDS or were carrying the AIDS virus but would not contract the disease themselves. As increasing numbers of AIDS victims are diagnosed, more employers are facing lawsuits on employment-related discrimination from those afflicted with the disease.

Because there is no known cure for AIDS, it is a fatal illness in virtually all situations. Only a person's life span is in doubt. Consequently, employers and other employees often react with fear of hysteria about working with an AIDS victim. For example, in Broward County, Florida, Todd Shuttleworth found out that he had AIDS. Because his supervisors were concerned about his infecting other workers through regular contact at work, he was fired from his $18,000 a year job as a budget analyst. In this case, the Florida Commission on Human Relations ruled that Shuttleworth was a victim of unlawful handicap discrimination, and Shuttleworth agreed to a settlement of $196,000. He died a few years later.[50]

More than twenty states have passed laws specifically declaring discrimination against AIDS victims illegal. In at least 15 other states court decisions have extended disability protection to AIDS victims. Most of these laws and decisions make it clear that just the fear of contracting the disease is not sufficient justification for terminating someone. Instead, the burden is placed on employers to seek sound medical justification for their actions against AIDS victims.

If an employer does have an employee with AIDS, educating other employees is more appropriate than terminating the victim's employment. A medical leave of absence (without pay if that is the general policy) can be used to assist the AIDS-afflicted employee during medical treatments. Employees who indicate they will not work with an AIDS victim should be told that their refusal to work is not protected by law and they could be subjected to disciplinary action up to and including discharge.

In summary, if AIDS is the Black Plague of today, it represents a challenge to employers, as well as to other segments of society. Enlightened employer actions are required to avoid discriminating against those afflicted with AIDS.

"Reasonable Accommodation" for Disabled Individuals

Employers are required to provide "reasonable accommodation" for disabled individuals to ensure that illegal discrimination does not occur. Reasonable accommodation includes actions that do not place an "undue hardship" on an employer.[51] In determining undue hardship, factors such as costs, employer size, and type of facilities all can be considered.

There are several areas of reasonable accommodation. First, disabled individuals must have *access to work areas*. Steps, extremely narrow corridors, and/or absence of elevators, may prevent an otherwise qualified person from applying for employment because of his or her inability to get to the employment office. Accessibility to restrooms and equipment within them also are required so that architectural barriers do not result in discrimination.

A second area of reasonable accommodation is the assignment of work tasks. This requirement may mean modifying jobs, work schedules, equipment, or work area layouts. Some examples include teaching sign language to a supervisor so that a deaf person can be employed; modifying work schedules to assist disabled workers; buying special amplifiers for hearing-impaired employees; or having another worker perform minor duties. For example, one firm made reasonable accommodation for an employee in a wheelchair by moving some furniture to widen an aisle and having another employee file the correspondence typed by the physically impaired employee. Under the ADA of 1990, employers even may have to hire readers, interpreters, or personal attendants to assist disabled individuals during the workday. However, there are few specific rules on which an employer can rely because every situation is considered on its own merits by the courts.

▦ ▇ OTHER BASES OF DISCRIMINATION

The original purpose underlying the passage of the Civil Rights Act of 1964 was to address race discrimination. These concerns continue to be important today, and employers must be aware of potential discriminating practices on the basis of race. Also, the requirements of the EEOC and the affirmative action requirements of the OFCCP specifically designate race as an area for investigation and reporting. Race is often a factor in discrimination on the basis of national origin. This topic is examined next, followed by a discussion of religious discrimination and other types of discrimination.

Discrimination on National Origin and Citizenship

The passage of the Immigration Reform and Control Act (IRCA) in 1986 clarified an issue that had confronted politicians, labor leaders, and employers for many years: What rights do people from other countries, especially those illegally in the United States, have concerning employment and equality? Illegal aliens often are called *undocumented workers* because they do not have the appropriate permits and documents from the Immigration and Naturalization Service. The IRCA requires that employers who knowingly hire illegal aliens be penalized. Employers must verify that prospective employees are eligible to work in the United States. As discussed in detail in Chapter 9, employers must ask for proof of identity, such as driver's license with a picture, Social Security card, birth certificate, immigration permit, or other documents.

The IRCA also makes it illegal for an employer to discriminate based on an individual's national origin or citizenship. However, because of the anxiety over complying with IRCA, some employers have adopted the illegal approach of not hiring individuals who are "foreign looking." Hispanic leaders have voiced concern about employers refusing to hire Hispanics, a particular hardship for the growing number of Hispanic men and women who are U.S. citizens. Cases brought by the EEOC also have sought to extend Title VII protection against race discrimination to undocumented workers who are illegally working in the United States. Lower court decisions have been inconsistent, with some courts ruling one way and some the opposite.[52] Until the U.S. Supreme Court makes a ruling, this issue likely will remain unresolved.

FOREIGN LANGUAGE REQUIREMENTS.   Questions about an applicant's language skills should be limited to those situations in which workers will have job-related reasons for using the language. For example, a government agency that is hiring a social worker to assist in neighborhoods in which Spanish is the predominant language could legitimately inquire about an applicant's ability to speak Spanish fluently and/or give a Spanish language test to the applicant. However, a retailer in Houston who inquired about languages spoken or written by *all* applicants might be accused of using the inquiries to discriminate against Hispanic individuals even though specific job-related justification is identified in some jobs.

The court decisions in this area generally have rejected attempts by employers to ban employees from speaking foreign languages at all times in work areas. However, some court decisions have supported the idea that some business operations require communications in a single language. For instance, a Honolulu court ruled that denying employment to a person because he could not communicate clearly due to a hard-to-understand accent was acceptable because the job he applied for required him to communicate with up to 300 individuals per day.[53]

Some states have recently passed laws making English the official language of the state. Therefore, employers should monitor developments at both the federal and state levels.

Religious Discrimination

Title VII of the Civil Rights Act also identifies discrimination on the basis of religion as illegal. However, religious schools and institutions can use religion as a BFOQ for employment practices on a limited scale. A major guide in this area was established by the U.S. Supreme Court in two cases.

TWA V. HARDISON.[54]   Hardison worked for TWA in Kansas City and was a member of the Worldwide Church of God, which forbids working on Saturday. Under the terms of a union contract, however, workers with low seniority, such as Hardison, could be called to work special assignments on Saturdays. TWA offered to change the work assignment, but the union objected. Then TWA tried other alternatives, but none were acceptable to Hardison and the union. Ultimately, Hardison refused to work on Saturday, was discharged, and filed suit. The ruling by the Supreme Court was that an employer is required to make *reasonable accommodations* of an employee's religious beliefs. Because TWA had done so, the ruling denied Hardison discrimination charges.

ANSONIA BOARD OF EDUCATION V. PHILBROOK.[55]   In this case, a high school teacher and a member of the Worldwide Church of God said that the school board's policy on leaves from work did not give him enough time off to observe required religious holy days; consequently, his salary should not have been docked for missing those additional days. The U.S. Supreme Court ruled against Philbrook by an eight-to-one vote. The court decision said that an employer must provide some reasonable accommodation, but it need not be the accommodation preferred by the employee.

"REASONABLE ACCOMMODATION."   Offering alternative work schedules, making use of compensatory time off, or otherwise adjusting to employees' religious beliefs are recommended to employers.[56] But once "reasonable" accommodation efforts (a somewhat vague standard) have been made, the employer is considered to have abided by the law.[57]

Other Types of Discrimination

Discrimination can occur on many bases, some not as visible as race, sex, or age. The sections that follow illustrate how some more indirect indicators of protected group status have been used by employers and viewed by courts.

DISCRIMINATION AND APPEARANCE.   Several cases have been brought to court in which appearance factors have figured. Court decisions consistently have allowed employers to have dress codes as long as they are applied uniformly. But requiring women to dress differently from men, such as having a dress code for women but not for men, has been ruled to be discriminatory,. Most of the dress standards contested required workers to dress in a conservative manner.[58]

Other individuals have brought cases of employment discrimination based on obesity or on unattractive appearance. A woman weighing over 300 pounds was rejected for employment as a clerical worker for an electric utility. In another case, an airline fired a woman flight attendant for being unattractive and overweight. Employers lost in both cases because of their inability to prove any direct job-related value in their requirements.

Cases also have addressed the issue of beards, mustaches, and hair length and style. For example, courts generally have rejected charges brought by minority-group individuals that policies prohibiting beards or long sideburns are racially discriminatory.[59]

CONVICTION AND ARREST RECORDS.   Generally courts have held that conviction records may be used in determining employability if the offense was considered job-related in nature. For example, a bank could use an applicant's conviction for forgery as a valid basis for rejection. However, some courts have held that only job-related convictions occurring within the most recent five to seven years are allowed.[60] Consequently, employers inquiring about convictions often add a phrase such as "indication of a conviction will not be an absolute bar to employment."

A telephone company had the policy of not hiring individuals who had criminal convictions. In response to a suit by members of a racial minority group, a U.S. appeals court ruled that the company's policy was a legitimate business necessity because its insurance policy excluded coverage for theft losses if the company had knowledge of an employee with a dishonest conduct record.[61]

Use of arrest records, as opposed to conviction records, generally has been viewed with suspicion by courts in employment discrimination cases. An arrest does not require guilt, but a conviction reflects that guilt has been decided. Statistics indicate that in some geographic areas, a greater number of racial minority group members are arrested than nonminorities. Consequently, using arrests, not convictions, may have an adverse impact on some groups protected by Title VII.

SENIORITY AND DISCRIMINATION.   Conflict between EEO regulations and company practices that give preference to employees on the basis of seniority represent another problem area. Employers, especially those with union contracts, frequently make layoff, promotion, or internal transfer decisions by giving employees with longer service first consideration. However, the use of seniority often means that there is an adverse impact on protected group members, who may have been the most recent workers hired. The result of this system is that protected group members who have gotten jobs through an affirmative action program are at a disadvantage because of their low levels of seniority. They may find themselves "last hired, first fired" or "last hired, last promoted."

Numerous conflicting and contradictory court decisions have been made in cases that deal with seniority and discrimination. Support for a bona fide seniority system was given by the U.S. Supreme Court in the Memphis fire fighters case. The decision in that case said, "Mere membership in the disadvantaged class is insufficient to warrant a seniority award."[62] Further support was given in the *Wygant v. Jackson Board of Education* case, in which the Supreme Court ruled that layoff provisions that protected racial minority individuals violated the rights of nonminority individuals under a valid seniority plan.[63]

These cases illustrate a continuing tension between providing equal opportunity for groups that have suffered past discrimination and protecting the rights of white or male employees. Underlying all these seniority-oriented decisions is the issue of reverse discrimination, discussed in Chapter 5.

SEXUAL PREFERENCE AND GAY RIGHTS.   Several cases and laws in some states and cities have addressed discrimination against individuals with nonheterosexual preferences. In Massachusetts, Wisconsin, and some cities it is illegal to discriminate against gay individuals.[64] At the federal level support for gay rights in employment has been limited. In one case the court decided that an individual's sexual preference or orientation had not qualified him for disability status under the Rehabilitation Act.

Whether homosexual individuals have rights under the equal protection amendment to the U.S. Constitution has not been decided by the U.S. Supreme Court.[65] Regarding transsexuals, who are individuals who have had sex-change surgery, court cases and the EEOC have ruled that sex discrimination under Title VII refers to a person's gender at birth, not to those who have had gender-altering operations.[66] Also, the courts have not given consistent answers to the question of whether transsexuals can be classified as disabled or handicapped.

SUMMARY

- Implemention of EEO requires a number of actions. One is to comply with the appropriate record-keeping requirements, such as completing the annual report (EEO-1) and keeping applicant flow data.
- Many employers must develop affirmative action plans (AAPs) that identify problem areas in the employment of protected group members and initiate goals and steps to overcome those problems.
- Employers must be able to defend their management practices based on bona-fide occupational qualifications (BFOQ), as a business necessity, or as job-related.
- Managers should become knowledgeable about employment inquiries that are acceptable and those that may be illegal.
- Sex discrimination exists when the following occurs: unequal job assignments, sexual harassment, pregnancy discrimination, and unequal compensation for similar jobs.
- Age discrimination, especially in the form of forced retirements and terminations, is a problem area that must be addressed by employers.
- Sexual harassment occurs under two conditions: (a) quid pro quo and (b) hostile environment.
- The definition of who is disabled has been expanding in recent years.
- Reasonable accommodation is a strategy that can be used to deal with discrimination on the bases of religion and disabled status.
- Discrimination on the basis of national origin still is illegal, but the Immigration Reform and Control Act has affected how employers inquire about and verify citizenship.

REVIEW AND DISCUSSION QUESTIONS

1. Discuss: "How can I report race to the EEOC when I cannot ask about it on my application blank?"
2. What is affirmative action? Why is it important?
3. Evaluate the following statement by the president of a small company: "I can hire or promote whomever I please, as long as I get someone who can do the job."
4. Based on your past experiences, identify examples of sex discrimination in job conditions, sexual stereotyping, and pregnancy discrimination.
5. Give example of the two types of sexual harassment that you have observed in employment situations.
6. Why are age discrimination issues growing in importance?
7. Give two examples of reasonable accommodation that would apply to discrimination based on religion or disabled status.
8. Respond to the following comment made by the president of a company: "It's getting so you can't ask anybody anything personal, even their name, before you hire them."

CASE	Affirmative Action is Good Business

Many employers have discovered that equal employment opportunity (EEO) is good business and results in using the talents of a wide range of employees. Although examples can be cited in many areas, the experiences some companies have had with women executives are illustrative.

At Gannett Co., parent company of USA Today and numerous other newspapers throughout the United States, the top P/HR executive is Madelyn Jennings. The publisher of USA Today is Cathleen Black, who says people outside the company seem surprised that she "runs the whole show" at the national daily newspaper. At other newspapers owned by Gannett, 19 of the 74 publishers are women. Says Jennings, "We mean to reflect the communities we serve. That means hiring women and minorities." In addition, Gannett ensures that EEO is a high priority by tying managerial bonuses to achieving EEO goals.

Merck and Company, a large pharmaceutical manufacturer with 61 plants and over 15,000 employees, has taken affirmative action seriously, especially the requirement to implement programs and to train employees in the impact of discrimination and the importance of affirmative action. Affirmative action training is done through a program entitled Phase III, which is a structured, one-day group discussion. The typical group contains 10 to 15 employees and is led by one of the 1,000 specially training Merck managers. Using videotaped situations that depict typical discrimination problems such as sexual harassment, reverse discrimination, and subtle forms of discrimination, participants discuss their feelings and attitudes about affirmative action and race and sex bias. Nearly every employee has participated in a session, and post-session feedback from attendees has been overwhelmingly positive.

Merck's efforts illustrate the firm's commitment to equal employment affirmative action. In addition to reinforcing the company's compliance with externally-imposed requirements, Merck reveals its desire to enhance work relationships between and among employees with widely differing backgrounds.

Similar efforts have been carried out in the Celanese Fibers Group. Over 1,400 persons participated in workshops entitled "Improving the Quality of Work Life." The workshops used a confrontational approach and included male/female and minority/nonminority confrontation situations.

During the workshops, mixed sex and race groups are asked to discuss problems such as sexual harassment, patronizing behavior by whites, and other common work situations. By having employees express their feelings and their attitudes about such situations, the participants are forced to evaluate the accuracy or inaccuracy of their own biases and prejudices. The ultimate goal of the Celanese workshops appears to have been reached: to get workers to discover that their interests are similar to those of others. From that discovery, better working relationships can develop.[67]

QUESTIONS

1. Why is having bonuses tied to EEO goals an important part of EEO and affirmative action compliance?
2. How does the Merck case illustrate the broad efforts necessary under an affirmative action program?

NOTES

1. Adapted from Brian S. Moskal, "Sexual Harassment," *Industry Week*, July 3, 1989, 22–27; "Training Helps Fight Sexual Harassment," *Omaha World-Herald*, August 28, 1988, 8G; "Sex Harassment in U.S. Jobs Still 42%," *Denver Post*, June 30, 1988, A8.

2. For more details on the process, see Michael D. Levin-Epstein, *Primer of Equal Employment*, 4th ed. (Washington, D.C.: Bureau of National Affairs, 1987), 120–123.

3. Dawn S. Keene, "A Headache-Free Affirmative Action Plan," *Journal of Staffing and Recruitment*, Fall 1989, 36–46.

4. Adapted from Donald W. Myers, *Human Resources Management: Principles and Practices* (New York: Commerce Clearing House, 1986), 83–84.

5. Susan Schenkel-Savitt and Steven P. Seltzer, "Recruitment as a Successful Means of Affirmative Action," *Employee Relations Law Journal 13* (1988): 465–479.

6. Adapted from Michael A. Hitt and Barbara W. Keats, "Empirical Identification of the Criteria for Effective Affirmative Action Programs," *Journal of Applied Behavioral Science 20* (1984): 203–222.

7. *EEO Policies and Programs*, PPF Survey No. 141 (Washington D.C.: Bureau of National Affairs, May 1986), 66.

8. Eric Matusewitch, "Pitfalls of Informal Affirmative Action," *Personnel Journal*, January 1990, 84–90.

9. Civil Rights Act of 1964, Title VII, Sec. 703e.

10. *Dothard v. Rawlinson*, 433 US 321 (1977).

11. *Prime v. Loyola University of Chicago* 42 FEP Cases 1 (1986).

12. Levin–Epstein, op. cit., 64–65.

13. *Mejia v. New York Sheraton Hotel*, 18 FEP 602 (1978).

14. *U.S. v. Georgia Power Company*, 5 FEP No. 588 (1973).

15. *Spurlock v. United Airlines*, 475 F2d 216 (1972).

16. EEOC Decision, #72-0455, 4 FEP Cases 306.

17. "Supreme Court Rules on Gender Stereotypes Under Title VII," *Personnel Journal*, July 1989, 12.

18. For example, see *Fitzpatrick v. Duquesne Light Co.*, 85–3101 (1986).

19. Adapted from Arthur Eliot Berkeley, "Job Interviewers' Dirty Little Secret," *Wall Street Journal*, March 20, 1989, A13. Reprinted with permission of Arthur E. Berkley, Memphis, TN; and The Wall Street Journal © 1989 Dow Jones & Company, Inc. All rights reserved.

20. *Dothard v. Rawlinson*, 433 U.S. 321 (1977).

21. *Rosenfeld v. Southern Pacific Co.*, 444 F.2d 1219, (1971).

22. *Donald v. Burlington Coat Factory*, No. C-1-86-0069 (S.D.Ohio 1987).

23. *Omaha World-Herald*, September 29, 1986, 3B.

24. U.S. Code 24 CFR 1604.11.

25. Sheryl A. Greene, "Reevaluation of Title VII Abusive Environment Claims Based on Sexual Harassment after *Mentor Savings Bank v. Vinson*," T. *Marshal Law Review*, Spring 1987–1988, 29–65.

26. *Miller v. Bank of America*, 600 F.2d 211 (1979).

27. *Toscano v. Ninno*, DDE, No. 82-315-WKS (August 31, 1983).

28. *Meritor Savings Bank (FBS) v. Vinson*, 106 S.Ct. 57 aff. and remanded 106 S.Ct. 2399 (1986).

29. Wade Lambert and Martha Brannigan, "Harassment Law is Broadened in California," *Wall Street Journal*, January 24, 1990, B6.

30. *Scott v. Sears, Roebuck & Co.*, 798 f.2d 210 (1986).

31. *Bundy v. Johnson*, 641 F.2d 934 (D.C.Dir.1981).

32. *California Federal Savings and Loan Association v. Guerra*, 107, S.C. 683 (1987).

33. *Newport News Ship Building and Dry Dock Co. v. EEOC*, U.S., 77 L.Ed.2d 89, (1983).

34. Stephen Wermiel, "Justices Decide States Can Deny Benefits to Women Leaving Jobs for Pregnancy," *Wall Street Journal*, January 22, 1987, 58.

35. Elaine Sorensen, "Measuring the Pay Disparity Between Typically Female Occupations and Other Jobs: A Bivariate Selectivity Approach," *Industrial and Labor Relations Review* 42 (1989): 624–639.

36. *Lemons v. Denver*, 17 FEP Cases 906 (D.C.-R.I., 1982).

37. *United Auto Workers v. Michigan*, ——— F.2d. ——— (1989).

38. *American Federation of State, County, and Municipal Employees v. State of Washington*, 700 F.2d 1401 (Ninth Circuit, 1985) as adapted from Reichenberg, "Pay Equity in Review," *Public Personnel Management* 15 (1986): 220–221.

39. *Arizona Governing Committee v. Norris*, 103 S.Ct. 3492 (1983).

40. "Age-Bias Suits on Rise," *The Rotarian*, February 1988, 13.

41. *EEOC v. Westinghouse*, 48 FEP 734; "Westinghouse Settles Age Suit," *Omaha World-Herald*, August 19, 1988. A43.

42. *Personnel Journal*, January 1987, 17–18.

43. *Williams v. Hughes Helicopter*, 42 EPD 36, 768 (1986).

44. *Sherrod v. Sears, Roebuck & Co.*, 36 EPD 36, 073 (1986).

45. Durwood Ruegger, "A Twenty-Year History and Review of the ADEA," *Labor Law Journal* 40 (1989): 31–36.

46. The Consortium for Citizens with Disabilities, "Americans with Disabilities Act," Personnel Journal, August 1990, 84–86.

47. Ronald A. Lindsay, "Discrimination Against the Disabled: The Impact of the New Federal Legislation," *Employee Relations Law Journal* 15 (Winter 1989–90): 333–345.

48. *Quinn v. Southern Pacific Transportation Co.*, No. CA–A28468 (Oregon Ct.App. 1985).

49. *School Board on Nassau County, Florida v. Arline*, 107 S.C. 1123 (1987).

50. *U.S. News & World Report*, March 16, 1987, 10–11.

51. Gerber DeJong and Raymond Litchery, "Physical Disability and Public Policy," *Scientific American*, June 1983, 40–49.

52. Charles E. Mitchell, "Illegal Aliens, Employment Discrimination, and the 1986 Immigration Reform and Control Act," *Labor Law Journal* 40 (1989): 177–182.

53. *Fragante v. Honolulu*, 87–2921, 9th Cir. (1989).

54. *Trans World Airlines v. Hardison*, 432 U.S. 63 (1977).

55. *Ansonia Board of Education v. Philbrook*, 107 S.Ct. 367 (1986).

56. Stephen J. Pullum, "Some Principles Concerning Religious Discrimination in the Workplace," *SAM Advanced Management Journal*, Winter 1988, 33–38.

57. Robert M. Preer, Jr., "Reasonable Accommodation of Religious Practices: The Conflict Between the Courts and the EEOC," *Employee Relations Law Journal* 15 (1989): 67–99.

58. Eric Matusewitch, "Tailor Your Dress Code," *Personnel Journal*, February 1989, 86–91.

59. For example, see *Brown v. D.C. Transit* 523 F.2d 725 (1975).

60. Eric Matusewitch, "Employment Rights of Ex-Offenders," *Personnel Journal* 61 (1983): 951–954.

61. *U.S. News & World Report*, November 21, 1983, 78.

62. *Memphis Firefighters, Local 1784 v. Stotts*, 467 U.S. 561 (1984).

63. *Wygant v. Jackson Board of Education*, 106 S.Ct. 1842 (1986).

64. "Two States Outlaw Job Bias Against Gays," *HR News*, February 1990, A11.

65. Sabrina M. Wrenn, "Gay Rights and Workplace Discrimination," *Personnel Journal*, October 1988, 91–102.

66. Eric Matusewitch, "The Legal Status of Transsexuals in the Workplace," *Personnel Journal*, August, 1988, 74–78.

67. Adapted from *Business Week*, June 23, 1986, 75–77; *Resource*, September 1982, 2; Charles M. Kelly, "How to Reduce Bias on the Job—and Increase Productivity," *Management Review*, February 1983, 14–18.

Analyzing and Staffing Jobs

The first phase of staffing any organization is understanding the jobs to be done. What do people do in a given job? Is there a better way to do it? What specific qualities must a candidate have to be able to do the job? When a person is hired, both management and the employee must have a clear understanding of the job to be performed. A job is the basic organizational unit of work.

Chapter 7 considers job analysis—the process of getting information about jobs performed in the organization. Various job analysis techniques are described, and the effect of jobs on human behavior is considered.

Chapter 8 examines the process involving organizational recruiting of a pool of possible employees. They may come from internal or external sources. College recruiting and executive search are two special means discussed. Recruiting has taken on a special significance for many organizations because of the tight labor market in many areas. The goal of a good recruiting program is to generate a large choice in the pool of applicants.

Once a pool of applicants has been accumulated, the actual selection for employment takes place. A variety of data sources can be used for selection decisions. Application blanks, interviews, tests, physical examinations, references, and assessment centers all can be used. However, regardless of the methods chosen, the goal is to choose the person most likely to do a good job for the organization. Finally, the method of offering employment to an applicant is examined. Chapter 9 presents information on the selection process.

Job Analysis

After you have read this chapter, you should be able to:

1. Define job analysis, job descriptions, and job specifications
2. Identify how job analysis information is used in at least five other P/HR activities
3. List and explain four job analysis methods
4. Discuss how behavioral and legal considerations affect job analysis
5. Identify the five steps in conducting a job analysis
6. Describe why job descriptions and job specifications are interrelated

P/HR: Today *and* Tomorrow   Old Jobs, New Jobs

Change is a constant, and change in jobs is no exception. Jobs and occupations change today at a rapid rate as organizations adjust to a changing business environment. But this change is not just a modern phenomenon. In fact, jobs have changed from the beginning of time. Long ago, food gathering was done by women, while men did the hunting. Then came a period where most people engaged in subsistence farming. Jobs changed from hunting and gathering to plowing, planting, and harvesting.

In the Middle Ages, the newly emerging jobs were those done by crafts workers and artisans. During the Renaissance, business, trade, and manufacturing were the "hot" job classifications. Next, the Industrial Revolution pulled many people off the farms and put them into factories.

In the twentieth century, new jobs and careers emerged, died, and were replaced. Elevator operators, bowling pinsetters, linotype operators, milkmen, and hundreds of other job categories have passed or are passing away.

Today, we are in what is called the *post-industrial* period. Predictions are that by the year 2000, 80 percent of the work force will be engaged in the "information" industry. Professional workers such as lawyers, accountants, teachers, professors, engineers, reporters, and librarians always have been information workers. The application of computer technology has given impetus to job proliferation in the information industry.

Not all traditional jobs will die off, of course. The U.S. Bureau or Labor Statistics estimates that there were 600,000 jobs for janitors in 1990 compared with 200,000 for computer systems analysts, 800,000 jobs for fast-food workers and 88,000 jobs for computer operators. But new jobs are emerging so fast that such information as the education or training needed, working conditions, and typical earnings cannot be developed fast enough for either employers or job seekers.

Recently, the industries that have shown the greatest growth in jobs have been construction (although it suffers in recessions), services, and retail trade. Jobs in services have been relatively insulated from recessions.[1] Occupations that will account for the greatest increase in the number of jobs through the year 2000 are predicted to be managerial, engineering, computer science, sales, teachers, and health professionals.[2] Among those occupations expected to decline the fastest between now and the year 2000 are assemblers, railroad workers, petroleum plant operators, chemical plant operators, and certain telephone company jobs.[3]

Generally, jobs which require more education will grow faster. Jobs will continue to be available for those with only high school education, but it will be even more difficult to find a job with good pay and advancement opportunities.[4]

Within these category changes, old jobs die out (it is hard to find a buggywhip braider anymore), and new jobs are born. Consider, for example, a relatively new job, that of industrial hygienist. This new specialty consists of people who evaluate and control health hazards where people work. Industrial hygienists can head off worker compensation claims and spot potential hazards that most people do not notice. When one group of computer-room employees was experiencing headaches and nausea on a regular basis, an industrial hygienist discovered that someone had blocked a vent and that the gas water heater burner was not taking in enough air, thereby creating carbon monoxide in the office and making people sick.

Another case concerned tennis ball testers who commonly suffered a tendon disorder in their wrists. The solution was to change the work routine so that they squeezed a ball only when their wrists were not bent. Even "clean" industries can cause problems, such as the hazard of lead poisoning among those who do soldering work in electronics plants. As other new jobs develop, analyzing them and deciding how people should be trained to do them will present new challenges.

"The British created a civil-service job in 1803 calling for a man to stand on the cliffs of Dover with a spyglass. He was supposed to ring a bell if he saw Napoleon coming. The job was abolished in 1945."

Robert Sobel

Job analysis is the most basic (if least glamorous) building block of sound P/HR practices. **Job analysis** is a systematic way to gather and analyze information about the content of jobs, human requirements, and the context in which jobs are performed.

The results of the job analysis process are used to design (or redesign) jobs, and place them in relation to other jobs in the organization. More specifically, job analysis can be used to provide legal protection for the employer, develop selection and training programs, classify jobs, aid in paying employees equitably, and improve performance appraisals.

Most methods of job analysis require that a knowledgeable person describe what goes on in the job or make a series of judgments about specific activities required to do the job. Such information can be provided by the employee doing the job, the supervisor, and/or a trained job analyst. Each source is useful, but each has drawbacks. The supervisor seems to be the best source of information on what *should be* done, but the employee knows most about what actually *is* done. However, both may lack the skills needed to use a job analysis questionnaire and write up the results. Thus, job analysis requires a high degree of coordination and cooperation between the P/HR unit and operating managers.

The responsibility for job analysis depends on who can best perform various aspects of the process. Figure 7–1 is a typical division of job analysis responsibilities in organizations that have a P/HR unit. In small organizations, managers have to perform all the work activities in Figure 7–1. In larger companies, the P/HR unit supervises the process to maintain its integrity, and writes the job descriptions and specifications for uniformity. The managers review the efforts of the P/HR unit to ensure accuracy and completeness. They also may request analysis or reanalysis when jobs change significantly.

JOB ANALYSIS
is a systematic way to gather and analyze information about the content of jobs, human requirements, and the context in which jobs are performed.

■■ ■ NATURE OF JOB ANALYSIS

Job analysis is the most basic P/HR activity because it identifies what people do in their jobs and what they need in order to do the job satisfactorily. It is a systematic

P/HR UNIT	MANAGERS
■ Prepares and coordinates job analysis procedures	■ Complete or assists in completing job analysis
■ Writes job descriptions and job specifications for review by managers	■ Review and maintain continuing accuracy of job descriptions and job specifications
■ Revises and periodically reviews job descriptions and job specifications	■ May request job analysis or reanalysis
■ Checks on managers' inputs to make sure they are properly done	■ Develop performance standards with assistance from specialists
■ May seek outside experts in difficult or unusual analyses	

Figure 7–1
Job Analysis Responsibilities

investigation of the tasks, duties, and responsibilities required in a job and of the necessary skills, knowledge, and abilities someone needs to perform the job adequately.

Before discussing job analysis further, some clarification of terms is useful. A **job** is an organizational unit of work composed of tasks, duties, and responsibilities. Although the terms **job** and **position** often are used interchangeably, there is a difference in meaning. A **position** is a collection of tasks, duties, and responsibilities performed by one person. Thus, if a food store has seven individuals working as cashiers, there are seven positions associated with the one job of cashier.

Job analysis usually involves collecting information on the characteristics of a job that differentiate it from other jobs. Information that can be helpful in making the distinction includes:

JOB
is a grouping of similar positions having common tasks, duties, and responsibilities.

POSITION
is a collection of tasks, duties, and responsibilities performed by one person.

- Work activities
- Behaviors required
- Working conditions
- Interaction with others
- Performance expected
- Machines and equipment used
- Personnel requirements
- Supervision given and received

Conventional job analysis looks at the demands the job makes on an employee. When completed, it provides a description of acceptable performance and helps to identify the kind of person that should fill the job.

■■ ■ USES OF JOB ANALYSIS

Job analysis is a process used to identify the components of a job, which then can be communicated to employees so they know exactly what to do. Figure 7–2 shows that job analysis serves as the basis from which job descriptions and job specifications are prepared.

Job Descriptions

JOB DESCRIPTION
specifies in written form the tasks, duties, and responsibilities of a job.

Basically, a job description indicates what is done, why it is done, where it is done, and briefly, how it is done. As such, a **job description** identifies the tasks, duties, and responsibilities in a job. *Performance standards* should flow directly from a job description, telling what the job accomplishes and what performance is considered satisfactory in each area of the job description. The reason is clear. If employees know what is expected and what constitutes good or poor performance, they have a much better chance of performing satisfactorily. Unfortunately, performance standards often are omitted from job descriptions.

Job Specifications

JOB SPECIFICATIONS
list the knowledge, skills, and abilities an individual needs to do the job satisfactorily.

The job description describes activities and responsibilities in the job, whereas **job specifications** list the knowledge, skills, and abilities an individual needs to perform the job satisfactorily. An example of a job specification for a clerk-typist might be: "Types 50 words per minute with no more than two errors; successful completion of one year of high school English or passing of an English proficiency test." It is

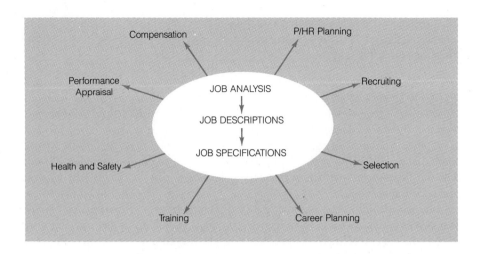

Figure 7-2
Job Analysis and P/HR Activities

important to note that accurate job specifications are what a person needs to do the job, not necessarily what qualifications the current employee possesses.

Job Analysis and P/HR Activities

Effective P/HR management requires that both employees and managers have a clear understanding of the duties and responsibilities to be performed on jobs. Job analysis helps them develop this understanding.

LEGAL COMPLIANCE.   Job analysis is especially critical for legal compliance with EEO and other governmental regulations. As emphasized in Chapter 6, only by tying P/HR requirements to specific job factors can an employer defend P/HR practices as job-related and business necessity. Likewise, whether individuals must be paid overtime rates depends on their meeting specific conditions about the type, nature, and frequency of the tasks they perform. Job analysis is beneficial in other P/HR activities as well, as Figure 7-2 illustrates.

COMPENSATION.   Job analysis information is very useful in determining compensation. In a survey of employers, over three-fourths use job analysis results in establishing the compensation for jobs.[5] Although people are paid for the work they do, individuals should be paid more for doing more difficult jobs. Information from job analysis can be used to give more weight, and therefore more pay, to jobs with more difficult tasks, duties, and responsibilities. Much of the "comparable worth" controversy has revolved around the degree to which jobs traditionally held by men (for example, those that require extensive physical skills) are equal/not equal to clerical and other jobs traditionally held by women.

HUMAN RESOURCE PLANNING.   A key part of HR planning is auditing of current jobs. A current job description provides the basic details necessary for this internal assessment, including such items as what jobs exist, what are the reporting relationships of jobs, and how many positions and jobs are currently present.

RECRUITMENT.   Job analysis is used to identify job specifications in order to plan how and where to obtain employees for anticipated job openings. An understanding of the skills needed and the types of jobs that may be open in the near future enables managers to achieve better continuity and plan the staffing of their organizations more effectively.

EMPLOYEE SELECTION.   Selecting a qualified person to fill a job requires thorough knowledge of the work to be done and the qualifications needed for someone to perform the work adequately. Without a clear and precise understanding of what a job entails, a manager cannot select effectively someone to do the job. If a retail store manager has not clearly identified what a clerk is to do, the manager will not know if the person hired should be able to lift boxes, run a cash register, or keep the accounting books.

Internal selection decisions made through promotions and transfers of current employees to new jobs also must be based on required qualifications. For example, a job analysis in a small manufacturer of electric equipment showed that the Accountant II job, which traditionally had required a college-trained person, really could be handled by someone with high school training in bookkeeping and several years of experience. As a result, the company could select from within and promote a current accounting clerk. In addition to saving on recruiting costs, promotion can have a positive impact on employee commitment and career-planning efforts.

CAREER PLANNING AND DEVELOPMENT.   Job description information can be helpful in career planning by showing an employee what *will be* expected in jobs he or she may choose to move to in the future. Job specification information also can point out areas in which an employee might need to develop to further a career.

TRAINING AND ORIENTATION.   By providing a definition of what activities comprise a job, the supervisor can easily explain to a new employee the specific things he or she must learn to do the job well. It is difficult for employees to perform well if they are confused about what the job is and what they are supposed to do.

PERFORMANCE APPRAISAL.   By comparing what an employee is supposed to be doing to what the person actually has done, a supervisor can determine the level of the employee's performance and competency. One objective for many organizations is to pay people for performance. To do this fairly, it is necessary to base this kind of comparison on performance standards. Because performance standards list what is satisfactory performance in each area of the job, the employee receives a clear idea of what is expected. The development of clear and realistic performance standards can prevent communication problems that often arise when an employee's performance is appraised. For example, a performance standard for one duty of an accounting manager might be "Invoicing to be completed within two work days of receipt of orders."

SAFETY AND HEALTH.   Job analysis information is useful in identifying possible job hazards and working conditions associated with jobs.[6] From the information gathered, managers and P/HR specialists can work together to identify health and safety equipment needed, specify work methods, and train workers on safety and health practices.

P/HR: Practice *and* Research	Job Analysis in the Coast Guard

The U.S. Coast Guard used an innovative method of job analysis to gather data on the job of machinery technician (MT), which is the largest and most complex job in the organization. The methodology revolved around a panel of experts who identified and reviewed the tasks in the MT's job. "Clean air filter", "change lube oil" and "operate multimeter" were three of the tasks identified.

The panel was composed of nine experienced MT's. This group ultimately identified over 1,500 tasks, which were placed into four categories: operating, maintaining, troubleshooting, repairing.

These categories were used to develop a questionnaire that listed each task, asked if the job incumbent ever did that task, and if so, how much time was spent doing the task. The questionnaire was mailed to 3,000 MT's who completed questionnaires that were returned to job analysts who analyzed, interpreted, and summarized the information. What emerged from the process was a profile of the major and minor tasks, necessary training, and advancement qualifications for the job of machinery technician in the U.S. Coast Guard.[7]

■■ ■ JOB ANALYSIS METHODS

Job analysis does not have to be a complicated process. However, the systematic investigation of jobs content should be done in a practical, logical manner. The process of collecting and using information about a job is aimed at determining what work is done, how it is done, and what skills and abilities are needed by someone to do it. (See the P/HR Practice on job analysis in the Coast Guard for a discussion of one approach to job analysis.)

Information about jobs can be gathered in several ways. Four common methods are: (1) observation, (2) interviewing, (3) questionnaires, and (4) structured analysis. Combinations of these approaches frequently are used depending on the situation and the organization.

Observation

Observation may be continuous or based on sampling. A manager, job analyst, or industrial engineer observes the individual performing the job and takes notes to describe the tasks and duties performed.

Use of the observation method is limited because many jobs do not have complete and easily observed job cycles. For example, complete analysis of a pharmaceutical sales representative's job would demand that the observer follow the sales representative around for several days. Furthermore, many managers may not be skilled enough to know what to observe and how to analyze what they see. Thus, observation may be more useful in repetitive jobs and in conjunction with other methods. Managers or job analysts using other methods may watch parts of a job being performed to gain a general familiarity with the job and the conditions under which it is performed. Multiple observations on several occasions also will help them better use some of the other job analysis methods.

WORK SAMPLING.   Work sampling differs from observation in that it does not require attention to each detailed action throughout an entire work cycle. Instead, a manager can determine the content and pace of a typical workday through statistical sampling of certain actions rather than through observation and timing of all actions. Work sampling is particularly useful for clerical jobs.

However, work sampling is not always well received. For example, the Idaho Department of Health and Welfare instituted work sampling to increase efficiency. Seven randomly selected times a day, a whistle blew. The thirty workers were required to fill out forms describing what they were doing at the moment the whistle went off. Data were collected then and analyzed to determine better ways to design the jobs.

The worker's reactions were highly negative. The process, they felt, was insulting, degrading, and disruptive. One secretary fumed, "It is insulting to my intelligence the way they go about these things." Another noted, "Yesterday morning there wasn't a single whistle. They all blew in the afternoon and everyone was sitting on pins and needles afraid to take a break or go to the bathroom." Another said the study did not bother her but the focus on secretaries did. "I think everyone should be a part of it, not just the clerical staff." Because of such reactions, the study was ultimately dropped. It should be noted that work sampling methods can include random observations without using whistles or bells.

Interviewing

The interview method of gathering information requires that the manager or P/HR specialist visit each job site and talk with the employees performing each job. A structured interview form is used most often to record the information. Frequently, the employee and the employee's supervisor must be interviewed to obtain a complete understanding of the job. During the job analysis interview, the manager or P/HR specialist must make judgments about the information to be included and its degree of importance.

Although research has shown that incumbents know their jobs best, their perceptions of their jobs can be affected by their most recent activities. If an incumbent is asked to describe his or her job at two different times during the year, the incumbent may use different words and focus on different duties. Further, the incumbent is very much aware that it may be beneficial to inflate the results because the analysis results may be used in making pay decisions.[8]

Group interviews also can be used. Members of the group are usually experienced job incumbents and/or supervisors. The method is expensive because of the number of people involved, and it usually requires the presence of a representative from the P/HR department as a mediator. However, it does bring together a large body of experience concerning a particular job in one place at one time. For certain difficult-to-define jobs, group interviews are probably most appropriate.

The interview method can be quite time-consuming. If a firm has thirty different jobs and the job analysis interviewer spends thirty to forty-five minutes on each interview, the time needed for interviewing and obtaining the analysis information is fifteen to twenty hours. The time problem will be compounded if the interviewer talks with two or three employees doing the same job. Furthermore, professional and managerial jobs are more complicated to analyze and usually require a longer interview.

For these reasons, combining the interview with one of the other methods is suggested. For example, if a job analyst has observed an employee perform a job, a check on observation data can be made by also interviewing the employee.

Likewise, the interview is frequently used as a follow-up to the questionnaire method.

Questionnaire

The questionnaire, such as the one in Figure 7–3, is a widely used method of gathering data on jobs. A survey instrument consisting of open-ended questions is developed and given to employees and managers to complete. Sometimes it is beneficial for the employee and supervisor to complete the questionnaire independently. Discrepancies can be highlighted and explored during interviews. At least one employee per job should complete the questionnaire, which is then returned to the supervisor or manager for review before being used in preparing job descriptions.

The major advantage of the questionnaire method is that information on a large number of jobs can be collected inexpensively in a relatively short period of time. However, follow-up observation and discussion are often necessary to clarify questions arising from inadequately completed questionnaires and to deal with other interpretation problems.

The questionnaire method assumes that employees can accurately analyze and communicate information about their jobs. That may not be a valid assumption in all cases. Research shows that job analysis outcomes are affected by the employees selected to fill out the questionnaire. Different employees produce different job analysis outcomes.[9] Employees may vary in their perceptions of the job, and even in their *literacy*. The ability to read and write accurately could affect how employees use the questionnaire to describe their jobs. For these reasons, the questionnaire method is usually combined with interviews and observations to clarify and verify the questionnaire information. In one survey, about two-thirds of all firms made use of both interviews and questionnaires.[10]

One type of questionnaire sometimes used is a *checklist*. Differing from the open-ended questionnaire, the checklist offers a simplified way for employees to give information. An obvious difficulty with the checklist is its construction, which can be a complicated and detailed process.

Structured Methods

Several job analysis methods are built on the checklist approach. The two most prominent of these structured methods are the position analysis questionnaire (PAQ) and functional job analysis (FJA).

Position Analysis Questionnaire (PAQ). The PAQ is a specialized questionnaire method incorporating checklist methods. Each job is analyzed in terms of 187 "elements" of a job. A sample page is illustrated in Figure 7–4. The PAQ is divided into six divisions, each division containing numerous job elements. The divisions include:

- Information input: Where and how does the worker get information to perform the job?
  - *Mental process:* What levels of reasoning are necessary on the job?
  - *Work output:* What physical activities are performed?
  - *Relationships with others:* What relationships are required to perform the job?
  - *Job context:* What working conditions and social contexts are involved?
  - *Other:* What else is relevant to the job?[11]

Figure 7–3
Job Analysis Questionnaire

I. PERSONAL INFORMATION

1. Name (Last, First, Middle)	8. Department
2. Social Security Number	9. Board, Commission, Bureau, Institution (Where applicable)
3. Official Title of Position	10. Division, Section, Unit
4. Work Title of Position Part time ____ Permanent ____ Full time ____ Temporary ____ Seasonal ____	11. Work Address (Mailing Address)
5. Years in Present Position	12. Regular Schedule of Hours and Shift Rotation (If Any)
6. Name and Class of Immediate Supervisor	DATE ANALYST
7. Name and Class of Next Higher Level Supervisor	CLASSIFICATION TITLE

II. DIFFICULTY OF WORK

Percent of Time	TASK STATEMENTS 13. Performs what action? To whom or what? To produce what? Using what tools, equipment, work aids, processes?

14. What *KNOWLEDGE*, procedures, practices, policies, and other guidelines do you use in the performance of the duties you listed? (Include any subject areas, technical knowledge, or specialized knowledge. Qualify the knowledges as *much, some, general, extensive*.)

15. What *ABILITIES/SKILLS* are required for the position? (Explain the abilities and/or skills required to perform the job, such as the ability to write reports, to train new employees, to type, to operate a bulldozer.)

16. What minimum level of education/training and experience is needed for successful performance of the duties and responsibilities of the position? (Include licenses and/or certificates, special courses, etc.)

17. How much time did it take you to reach a satisfactory level of efficiency in the position and what kind of training did you receive to reach this level?

III. RESPONSIBILITY

18a. List name and class titles of employees under your *immediate supervision*. (If more than ten, list only class titles and number in each class.)

18b. Extent of Supervision:
- ____ Assign work
- ____ Oversee and review work
- ____ Approve work
- ____ Train workers
- ____ Performance rating
- ____ Recommend hiring, firing, promotion
- ____ Discipline
- ____ Plan methods, procedures, work flow
- ____ Others (explain)

19. What guidelines are used in completing your tasks? (Include reference works, manuals, precedents, oral and written instructions, textbooks, standard methods, procedures, etc.)

20. *Who* reviews or checks your work? *How* is it reviewed? *When* is it reviewed?

21. What happens when an error is found? How would it be found? How soon would it be found? Give specific examples.

22. Does this position require unusual physical demands such as standing, stooping, pulling, climbing, lifting or any special physical requirements such as eye-hand coordination, keen hearing, etc.?

23. In what working conditions is this position performed? Are there any hazards? Is work done in extreme weather conditions?

24. Does this position entail responsibility for the safety of other employees or the public?

25. Describe any contact (in person, by telephone, or by letter) with people other than your supervisors or subordinates you make as a regular part of your work. Describe how often, with whom, and why you have these contacts.

26. Does this position involve travel? Describe.

Figure 7–4
**Sample PAQ Item Mental
Processes**

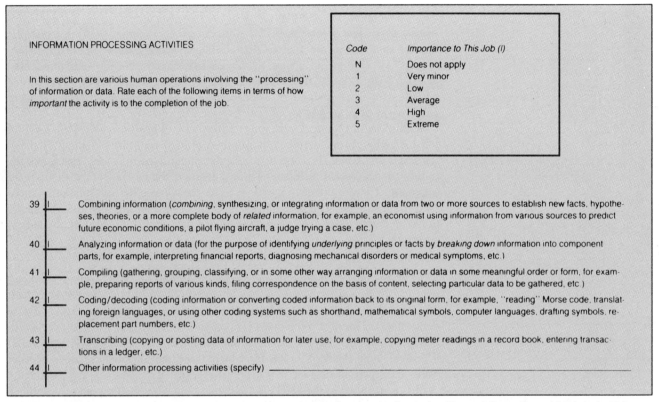

SOURCE: E. J. McCormick, P. R. Jeanneret, and R. C. Mecham, *Postion Analysis Questionnaire,* Occupational Research Center, Dept. of Psychological Sciences, Purdue University, West Lafayette, IN 47907. Copyright 1969 by Purdue Research Foundation.

The PAQ focuses on "worker-oriented" elements that describe behaviors necessary to do the job, rather than on "job-oriented" elements that describe the technical aspects of the work. The assumption made in the PAQ is that comparing worker behaviors across jobs is more valid than trying to compare the technological similarities of different jobs in different work fields.

The PAQ can be completed by job analysts who interview workers and observe work as it is being done. It also can be completed by the worker. However, the reading level of the PAQ is estimated to be at least college-graduate level, so unless the employee's reading ability is at that level, a job analyst should fill in the questionnaire.[12]

The PAQ is used primarily to develop job evaluation systems and compensation programs. Recent studies on the cost and amount of information necessary to use a PAQ effectively suggest that there are no shortcuts through the process and that the amount of information an analyst obtains about the job affects validity.[13] But the benefits are considerable. They way in which the PAQ structures job elements makes it possible for specialists to analyze almost any type of job. The PAQ has been found to be relatively stable even when someone attempts to manipulate information and interest levels of employees vary.[14] It also has been used successfully to classify positions into job families based on analysis of job description narratives, which are readily available in most companies.[15]

Although its complexity may deter many potential users, the PAQ is easily quantified and can be used to conduct validity studies on selection tests.[16] The PAQ may find its best use in compensation activities to ensure internal pay fairness because it considers the varying demands of different jobs.

FUNCTIONAL JOB ANALYSIS (FJA).   Functional job analysis (FJA) is a comprehensive approach to job analysis that considers (1) the goals of the organization, (2) what a worker does to achieve those goals in his job, (3) the level and orientation of what workers do, (4) performance standards, (5) training content. A functional definition of what is done in a job can be generated by examining the three components of *data, people,* and *things.* (see Figure 7–5).

Within each of these classifications a hierarchy of functions exists; the levels of this hierarchy can be identified by numbers of increasing size. Figure 7–5 shows the levels and numbers associated with the dimensions of a job. The lower the number under Data, People, and Things, the more the job has complexity in those functions. These numbers, as well as those providing other information, can be used to identify and compare important elements of jobs given in the *Dictionary of Occupational Titles* (DOT), a standardized data source provided by the federal government.

USE OF THE DOT.   In Figure 7–6, the identification code for Director of Athletics (090.117–022) can be used to give a brief description of how the DOT is used. The first three digits (090) indicate the occupational code, title, and industry designations. The next three digits (117) represent the degree to which a director of athletics *typically* has responsibility and judgment over *data, people,* and *things.* The final three digits (022) are used to indicate the alphabetical order of titles within the occupational group having the same degree of responsibility and judgment.

FJA, as captured in the DOT, is a valuable source of job information, regardless of the job analysis method used. The DOT describes a wide range of jobs (as shown in Figure 7–6). A manager or P/HR specialist confronted with preparing a large number of job descriptions can use the DOT as a starting point. The job description from the DOT then can be modified to fit the particular organizational situation. The importance of the DOT is demonstrated by the fact that job descriptions based on it are considered satisfactory by federal employment enforcement agencies. However, some people feel that the DOT system underrepresents service industry jobs and is too manufacturing-oriented.[17]

Figure 7–5
Work Functions from *Dictionary of Occupational Titles*

DATA (4th Digit)	PEOPLE (5th Digit)	THINGS (6th Digit)
0 Synthesizing	0 Mentoring	0 Setting Up
1 Coordinating	1 Negotiating	1 Precision Working
2 Analyzing	2 Instructing	2 Operating-Controlling
3 Compiling	3 Supervising	3 Driving-Operating
4 Computing	4 Diverting	4 Manipulating
5 Copying	5 Persuading	5 Tending
6 Comparing	6 Speaking-Signalling	6 Feeding-Offbearing
	7 Serving	7 Handling
	8 Taking Instructions-Helping	

SOURCE: U.S. Department of Labor, *Dictionary of Occupational Titles,* 4th ed. (Washington, D.C.: Government Printing Office, 1977), xviii.

Functional job analysis, with the help of the the DOT, can help managers who are not P/HR specialists in developing occupational "career ladders" by identifying jobs requiring progressively more skill or responsibilities. This identification can clarify promotion practices. Because FJA is standardized, statistical data can be

---

090.117-022 DIRECTOR, ATHLETICS (EDUCATION)

Plans, administers, and directs intercollegiate athletic activities in college or university. Interprets and participates in formulating extramural athletic policies. Employs and discharges coaching staff and other department employees on own initiative or at direction of board in charge of athletics. Directs preparation and dissemination of publicity to promote athletic events. Plans and coordinates activities of coaching staff. Prepares budget and authorizes department expenditures. Plans and schedules sports events, and oversees ticket sales activities. Certifies reports of income produced from ticket sales. May direct programs for students of physical education.

151.047-010 DANCER (AMUSE. & REC.)

Dances alone, with partner, or in group to entertain audience: Performs classical, modern, or acrobatic dances, coordinating body movement to musical accompaniment. Rehearses dance movements developed by CHOREOGRAPHER (amuse. & rec.). May choreograph own dance. May sing and provide other forms of entertainment. May specialize in particular style of dancing and be designated according to specialty as ACROBATIC DANCER (amuse. & rec.); BALLET DANCER (amuse. & rec.); BALLROOM DANCER (amuse. & rec.); BELLY DANCER (amuse. & rec.); CHORUS DANCER (amuse. & rec.); INTERPRETATIVE DANCER (amuse. & rec.); STRIP-TEASE DANCER (amuse. & rec.); TAP DANCER (amuse. & rec.).

160.162-010 ACCOUNTANT, TAX (PROFESS. & KIN.)

Prepares Federal, state, or local tax returns of individual, business establishment, or other organization: Examines accounts and records and computes tax returns according to prescribed rates, laws, and regulations. Advises management regarding effects of business, internal programs and activities, and other transactions upon taxes and represents principal before various governmental taxing bodies. May devise and install tax record systems. May specialize in particular phase of tax accounting, such as income, property, real estate, or Social Security taxes.

166.117-018 MANAGER, PERSONNEL. (PROFESS. & KIN.)

Plans and carries out policies relating to all phases of personnel activity. Recruits, interviews, and selects employees to fill vacant positions. Plans and conducts new employee orientation to foster positive attitude toward company goals. Keeps record of insurance coverage, pension plan, and personnel transactions, such as hires, promotions, transfers, and terminations. Investigates accidents and prepares reports for insurance carrier. Conducts wage survey within labor market to determine competitive wage rate. Prepares budge of personnel operations. Meets with shop stewards and supervisors to resolve grievances. Writes separation notices for employees separating with cause and conducts exit interviews to determine reasons behind separations. Prepares reports and recommends procedures to reduce absenteeism and turnover. Contracts with outside suppliers to provide employee services, such as canteen, transportation, or relocation service. May keep records of hired employee characteristics for governmental reporting purposes. May negotiate collective bargaining agreement with BUSINESS REPRESENTATIVE LABOR UNION (profess. & kin.)

709.684-026 BIRD—CAGE ASSEMBLER (WIREWORK)

Fabricates wire birdcages, using handtools and drill press: Cuts wire to specified length, using wirecutter. Positions metal plate in jib, and drills holes around circumference of plate, using drill press. Fits ends of wires into holes in plate, and fastens upper ends of wire together to form cage.

Figure 7–6

Sample Job Titles and Descriptions from *Dictionary of Occupational Titles*

SOURCE: U.S. Department of Labor, *Dictionary of Occupational Titles,* 4th ed. (Washington, DC: Government Printing Office, 1977), 66, 86, 91, 98, 665.

Evaluation of Job Analysis Methods

With all the different methods of job analysis available, questions about the effectiveness and validity of each have been raised. As reported in the *Academy of Management Journal*, Levine, Ash, Hall, and Sistrunk studied seven job analysis methods.

A questionnaire was sent to experienced job analysts. Ninety-three responses were received from participants in a wide variety of organizations. The first part of the questionnaire contained descriptions of seven very specialized job analysis methods: critical incident technique, position analysis questionnaire, job elements method, ability requirements scales, functional job analysis, task inventory, and threshold traits analysis.

The second part of the questionnaire asked respondents to rate the methods on practicality, costs, and other factors. Demographic information and details on the degree of familiarity with the methods were gathered in the third section of the questionnaire.

Analysis of the responses revealed that the experienced job analysts viewed some methods as better for some purposes than others. For example, the FJA and PAQ were rated higher for job evaluation (compensation) usage, where as the critical incident technique (which identifies incidents illustrating behaviors that were especially effective or ineffective in doing a job) was rated lower than all other methods for job classification. Regarding practicality, the PAQ was rated among the highest in terms of standardization, ease of use, and reliability.[19]

developed for P/HR decision making, such as for test validation in which statistical percentages can be assigned to each of the three dimensions (data, people, things). FJA may not give enough information for wage classification or job evaluation, but it can be used with (another method) for those purposes. Some criticize the method for requiring too much time.

Combination Methods

There are indeed a number of different ways to obtain and analyze information about a job. Each has strengths and weaknesses and a combination of methods generally is preferred over one method alone, as demonstrated in the P/HR: Research on evaluation on job analysis methods. Also, new methods continue to be developed.[18]

■■ ■■ BEHAVIORAL AND LEGAL ASPECTS OF JOB ANALYSIS

When systematically analyzing jobs, managers must be aware of two general concerns. One is the reaction of employees and managers to this intensive look at their jobs. The other concern is the impact of governmental constraints, especially from EEO guidelines, on job analysis and its outcomes. First consider the impact of human behavior on the job analysis process.

Behavioral Aspects of Job Analysis

A detailed examination of jobs, while necessary, can be a demanding and threatening experience for both managers and employees, depending on the situation.

In one printing firm, two employees having different jobs in the production planning department refused to complete questionnaires. Through interviews it was learned that they were doing parts of each other's jobs, and they were concerned that management might discipline them or force them to change back to the way that the jobs had been designed by management.

EMPLOYEE FEARS.   As the example indicates, some employees fear that management's analysis of their jobs will put a "straitjacket" on them. They feel that creativity and flexibility may be limited by formalizing the duties, responsibilities, and qualifications. However, it does not necessarily follow that analyzing a job will limit job scope or depth.

Another fear that some employees have concerns the *purposes* of a detailed job investigation. The attitude that "as long as someone doesn't know precisely what I am supposed to be doing, I am safe" may generate attempts to hide the uniqueness of a job. The employee's concern is that someone must feel they did something wrong if such a searching look is being taken. Consequently, management should explain the job analysis process and why it is being done.

RESISTANCE TO CHANGE.   As jobs change, there is a continued need to update and revise job descriptions and job specifications. Because people become used to working within defined boundaries, any attempt to change those "job fences" generates fear, resistance, and insecurity. Suggesting it is time to revise job descriptions provokes anxiety because the employees' safe and secure job worlds are threatened. Their jobs may be changed and they may have to take on new and difficult responsibilities. Further, there is always the fear that change could have a negative impact on pay.

Because resistance to change is a natural reaction, managers should expect it and be prepared to deal with it. Perhaps the most effective way to handle this resistance is to involve employees in the revision process. Complicating the process is the fact that as work changes and becomes more complex, especially at managerial and administrative levels, it is more difficult to analyze and determine exactly what constitutes a job.

OVEREMPHASIS ON CURRENT EMPLOYEES.   A good analysis and the resulting job description and specifications *should not describe just what the person currently doing the job does and what his or her qualifications are.* The person may have unique capabilities and the ability to expand the scope of the job to assume more responsibilities. The company would have difficulty finding someone exactly like that individual if he or she left.

INFLATED JOB SIGNIFICANCE.   Employees and managers also have some tendencies to inflate the importance and significance of their jobs. Because job analysis information is used for compensation purposes, they hope that by puffing up their jobs, higher pay levels will result. As the P/HR: Practice indicates, titles often get inflated also.

MANAGERIAL STRAITJACKET.   Through the information developed in a job analysis, the job description is supposed to capture the scope of a job. However, some employees' may use job descriptions to limit managerial flexibility, putting a straitjacket on a manager.

P/HR: Practice *and* Research   Title Inflation

We have all heard of monetary inflation and grade inflation, but another problem we *don't* hear much about is *title inflation*. Thomas Amory, Chairman of William H. Clark Associates, says "In good times companies tend to confer titles to employees. I've seen plenty of instances where if a guy wants a *vice-president* title, top management will make him a VP—as long as it doesn't imablance the salary scale."

A big-sounding title may impress your mother, but if it lacks power, it may be a joke around the office. And, in some instances titles have little to do with actual job duties. At New York's Citibank, for example, Dr. C. G. Weiman became one of the Corporation's Senior Vice Presidents. But his duties remained the same: he is the company physician! Dr. Weiman believes his title was granted to show outsiders that Citibank "believes in health."

Conferring titles seem harmless enough, but some note that it can lead people outside the company to think that someone they are dealing with has more power and authority than he or she does. Digital Equipment Corporation has another perspective—it doesn't get too concerned about conferring titles because, a company spokesperson says, "We don't want people thinking rigidly about their jobs—we want them to think creatively about their jobs." Titles may channel thinking, and good ideas may get lost because "that isn't in my job description."[20]

One example of using job descriptions to restrict work occurred when air traffic controllers "followed the book," which caused havoc with airplane departures and landings at major airports. The attitude "It's not in my job description" can become burdensome for management involved in changing an organization, its technology, and jobs in response to changing economic or social conditions.

Consequently, some nonunion employers refuse to show job descriptions to their employees. This refusal makes it difficult for an employee to say, "I don't have to do that because it is not in my job description." In some organizations with a unionized work force, very restrictive job descriptions exist. Therefore, the final statement in many job descriptions is often the *miscellaneous clause*, which consists of a phrase similar to "Performs other duties as needed upon request by immediate supervisor." This statement covers the abnormal and unusual situations that may occur in an employee's job and is an attempt to prevent an employee from saying, "It's not covered in my job description."

Legal Aspects of Job Analysis

In addition to behavioral concerns, managers must also be aware of the legal impact of job analysis. The earlier equal employment discussion in Chapters 5 and 6 made reference to the need for "job-relatedness" in staffing activities. A job analysis provides the basis for job-relatedness through the development of job descriptions and job specifications. In a sense, it is the foundation for many P/HR activities. The interest in job analysis by those outside the P/HR area results from the importance assigned to the activity by the federal courts. The acceptability of selection procedures and pay issues often hinges on job analysis..

No specific job analysis method has received the stamp of approval from the various courts in all situations. Therefore, when dealing with issues that may end

- ■ The job analysis must be performed on the exact job for which the selection device is to be used.
- ■ It must be in written form, such as in a job description.
- ■ The analyst must be able to describe the procedure.
- ■ Data must come from *several* up-to-date sources.
- ■ The data should be collected by an expert job analyst.
- ■ Tasks, duties, and activities must be identified.
- ■ The amount of competency for entry level must be specified.
- ■ Knowledge, skills, and abilities should be identified.[21]

Figure 7–7
Legal Standards for Job Analysis When Validating Selection Instruments

up in court, such as comparable worth or layoffs, care must be taken to make certain the method (or methods) match the context.

Comparable worth is a difficult issue that job analysis does not fully address. How do you compare the physical danger of underground coal mining with the burnout-producing mental and emotional demands of nursing or teaching? The comparability of jobs also may determine who is included in the pool of those to be laid off in bad times.

Federal EEO enforcement guidelines clearly indicate that a sound and comprehensive job analysis is required to validate selection criteria. Without a systematic investigation of a job, an employer may be using requirements that are not specifically job-related. For example, if a trucking firm requires a high school diploma for a dispatcher's job, the firm must be able to indicate how such an educational requirement matches up to the tasks, duties, and responsibilities of a dispatcher. The only way the firm might be able to justify the requirement would be to identify the knowledge, skills, and abilities needed by the dispatcher and to show that they only could be obtained through formal education.

In one case, the court ruled that the employee's job description, not the tasks actually performed, should be used to determine job qualifications related to possible handicapped discrimination.[22] In summary, it is extremely difficult for an employer to have a legal staffing system without performing job analysis. Job analysis is the most basic P/HR activity, primarily because it focuses on the jobs employees perform. A careful review of the criteria used by the courts in their assessment of job analysis shows that certain standards are expected. These standards, exhibited in Figure 7–7, also provide a view of a professional job analysis process.

■■ ■ CONDUCTING A JOB ANALYSIS

Conducting a job analysis requires use of a logical multistep process. The process outlined in this section is a typical one; however, some variations will occur if different methods are used and as the number of jobs changes.

I. Identify Jobs and Review Existing Documentation

The first step is to identify the jobs under review. For example, are the jobs to be analyzed hourly jobs, clerical jobs, all jobs in one division, or all jobs in the entire organization?

Part of the identification phase is to review existing documentation, such as existing job descriptions, organization charts, previous job analysis information, and relevant DOT statements. In this phase, who will be involved in conducting the job analysis, and what methods the analyst will use are identified, as well as how current incumbents and managers will participate in the process and how many employees' jobs will be analyzed.

II. Explain the Process to Managers and Employees

A crucial step is to explain the process to managers, affected employees, and other concerned people such as union stewards. The communications, memos, and explanations should address the concerns and anxieties mentioned earlier in this chapter. Items to be covered often include the purpose of the job analysis, the steps and time schedule, how managers and employees will participate, who is doing the analysis, and whom to contact as questions arise.[23]

III. Conduct the Job Analysis

The next step is actually gathering the job analysis information. Questionnaires might be distributed, interviews conducted, observations made. Depending on the methods used, this phase often requires follow-up contacts to remind managers and employees to return questionnaires or to reschedule interviews. As the job analysis information is received, analysts review it to ensure its completeness. Additional clarifying information can be gathered, usually in the form of interviews.

IV. Prepare Job Descriptions and Specifications

All job analysis information must be sorted, sifted, and used in the drafting of job descriptions and specifications for each job. Usually, the drafts are prepared by members of the P/HR department, then sent to appropriate managers and employees for their review. Following the review, all necessary changes are made and the final job descriptions and specifications are prepared.

Once job descriptions and specifications are prepared, the manager should provide feedback to the current job holders, especially to those who assisted in the job analysis. One feedback technique is to give employees a copy of their own job descriptions and specifications for review. Giving the current employees the opportunity to make corrections, ask for clarification, and discuss their job duties with the appropriate manager or supervisor enhances manager–employee communications. Questions may arise about how work is done, why it is done that way, and how it can be changed. When employees are represented by a union, it is essential that union representatives be included in reviewing the job descriptions and specifications to lessen the possibility of future conflicts.

V. Maintain and Update Job Descriptions and Specifications

Once job descriptions and specifications are completed and reviewed with all appropriate individuals, a system must be developed to keep them current. Otherwise the entire process, beginning with a job analysis, may have to be repeated in several years. Because organizations are dynamic and evolving entities, rarely do all jobs stay the same for years.

Someone in the P/HR department usually has responsibility for assuring that job descriptions and specifications stay current. Managers play a crucial role because they are the ones closest to the jobs and know when changes occur. One effective way to ensure that appropriate reviews occur is when job descriptions and job specifications are used in other P/HR activities. Each time a vacancy occurs, the job description and specifications should be reviewed and revised as appropriate *before* recruiting and selection efforts begin. Likewise, in some organizations managers review the job description during each performance appraisal interview. This review enables the job holder and the supervisor to discuss whether the job description still describes the actual job adequately or whether it need to be revised. In addition, a comprehensive and systematic review may be done during P/HR planning efforts. For many organizations, a complete review is made once every three years, and more frequently when major organizational changes are made.

JOB DESCRIPTIONS AND JOB SPECIFICATIONS

The output from analysis of a job is usually job descriptions and job specifications. Both are compiled and prepared to summarize concisely the job analysis information for each job. Job descriptions and job specifications should be accurate, readable, understandable, and usable.

Two events tend to generate changes in job description and job specification activity. One is change in the organization (growth, restructuring, downsizing). The other is routine periodic review of jobs.

More than 100 major management uses of job descriptions have been documented.[24] But perhaps no benefits are any greater than the fact that individual employees get documentation from management that identifies their jobs. In return, the organization gets a timely set of definitions that permits defensible assignment of jobs and pay levels.[25]

Job Description Components

The typical job description, such as the one in Figure 7–8, contains three major parts. The nature of each part is discussed next.

IDENTIFICATION.   The first part is the identification section in which the employee's job title, department, and reporting relationship are presented. Additional information such as the date of analysis, a job number, the number of employees holding the job, and the current pay scale of the job occupants can also be included.

GENERAL SUMMARY.   The second part, the general summary, is a concise summation of the general responsibilities and components that make the job different from others. One P/HR specialist has characterized the general summary statement as follows: "In thirty words or less, describe the essence of the job."

SPECIFIC DUTIES.   The third part of the typical job description, the specific duties section, contains clear and precise statements on the major tasks, duties, and responsibilities performed. The most time-consuming aspect of writing job descriptions is this listing of specific duties.

Writing Job Descriptions

In writing job descriptions, it is important to use precise action verbs that accurately describe the employee's tasks, duties, and responsibilities. (For example, avoid the

Figure 7–8
Job Description and Specifications

JOB TITLE: Compensation Manager

INCUMBENT:

SUPERVISOR'S TITLE: Senior Vice President—Human Resources

NO. _____

GRADE _____

STATUS Exempt

CLASS O/M

GENERAL SUMMARY: Responsible for the design and administration of all cash compensation programs. Insures proper consideration of the relationship of salary to performance of each employee and provides consultation on salary administration to Managers and Supervisors.

PRINCIPAL DUTIES & RESPONSIBILITIES:

1. Insures the preparation and maintenance of job descriptions for each present and proposed position. Prepares all job descriptions, authorizing final drafts. Coordinates periodic review of all job descriptions making revisions as necessary; educates employees and supervisors on job description use and their intent by participation in formal training programs and by responding to questions from employees and supervisors; maintains accurate file of all current job descriptions, distributing revised job descriptions to appropriate individuals.

2. Insures the proper evaluation of job descriptions. Serves as chair of Job Evaluation Committee, coordinating its activities. Resolves disputes over proper evaluation of jobs; assigns jobs to pay ranges; re-evaluates jobs periodically through the Committee process; conducts initial evaluation of new positions prior to hiring; insures integrity of job evaluation process.

3. Insures that Company compensation rates are in accordance with the Company philosophy. Maintains current information concerning applicable salary movements taking place in comparable organizations; obtains or conducts salary surveys as necessary; conducts analysis of salary movements among competitors and presents recommendations on salary movements on an annual basis.

4. Insures proper consideration of the relationship of salary to the performance of each employee. Reviews all performance appraisals and salary reviews, authorizing all pay adjustments.

5. Develops and administers the performance appraisal program. Develops and updates performance appraisal instruments; assists in the development of training programs designed to educate supervisors on appropriate use of performance appraisal—may assist in its delivery; monitors the use of the performance appraisal instruments to insure the integrity of the system and its proper use.

6. Assists in the development and oversees the administration of all bonus payments up through the Officer level.

7. Researches and provides recommendations on executive compensation issues.

8. Coordinates the development of an integrated Human Resource information system. Assists in identifying needs; interfaces with the Management Information Systems Department to achieve departmental goals for information needs.

9. Performs related duties as assigned or as the situation dictates.

REQUIRED KNOWLEDGE, SKILLS & ABILITIES:

1. Knowledge of compensation and personnel management practices and principles.

2. Knowledge of effective job analysis procedures.

3. Knowledge of survey development and interpretation practices and principles.

4. Knowledge of modern principles and practices of performance appraisal design and administration.

5. Skill in conducting job analysis interviews.

6. Skill in writing job descriptions, memorandums, letters and proposals.

7. Skill in making presentations to groups, in conducting job analysis interviews, and in explaining divisional policies and practices to employees and supervisors.

8. Skill in performing statistical computations including regression, correlation, and basic descriptive statistics.

9. Ability to conduct effective meetings.

10. Ability to plan and prioritize work.

EDUCATION & EXPERIENCE:

This position requires the equivalent of a college degree in Business Administration, Psychology or a related degree plus 3–5 years experience in Personnel Administration, 2-3 of which should include compensation administration experience. An advanced degree in Industrial Psychology, Business Administration, or Personnel Management is preferred, but not required.

COMMENTS:

This position may require up to 15% travel.

Used with Permission

Figure 7–9
Job Description Duty Statements

	Action Verb	To What Applies?	Using What?	Why/How/How Often?
Payroll Clerk	Prepares	Payroll reports	From timecards	On a biweekly basis
Benefits Manager	Conducts and analyzes	Benefits surveys		In order to maintain competitiveness with area employers

use of vague words, such as processes, maintains or handles. Specific duties should be grouped and arranged in some logical pattern. If a job requires an accounting supervisor to prepare several reports, among other functions, statements relating to the preparation of reports should be grouped together.

The general format for the specific duty statements is shown in Figure 7–9. There is a real art to writing job descriptions that are sufficiently descriptive without being overly detailed. When writing a duty statement, the writer preparing the job description should use precise and clear language but should not fall into the trap of writing a motion analysis. The statement, "Walks to filing cabinet, opens drawer, pulls folder out, and inserts material in correct folders," is an extreme example of a motion statement. The specific duty statement, "Files correspondence and memoranda to maintain accurate customer policy records," is sufficiently descriptive without being overly detailed. The *miscellaneous clause* mentioned earlier is typically included to assure some managerial flexibility.

Some job descriptions contain sections about materials or machines used, working conditions, or special tools used. This information is often included in the specific duty statements or in comment sections.[26]

Writing job descriptions of executive and upper management jobs is challenging. Because of the wide range of duties and responsibilities, those job descriptions often are written in more general terms than descriptions of jobs at lower levels in the organization.

Writing Job Specifications

Job specifications, a logical outgrowth of a job description, attempt to describe the key qualifications someone needs to perform the job satisfactorily. Specific factors identified often can be grouped into three categories: knowledge, skills, and abilities (KSAs). Factors within these categories include education, experience, work skill requirements, personal requirements, mental and physical requirements, and working conditions and hazards. A job specification for a remote visual display terminal operator might include a required education level, a certain number of months of experience, a typing ability of 60 wpm, a high degree of visual concentration, and ability to work under time pressure. Notice that the KSA statements in Figure 7–8 are the job specifications for the compensation manager.

The analyst can write a job specification by talking with the current holder of the job about the qualifications needed to perform the job satisfactorily. However, caution is needed because the characteristics of the current job occupant should not be the sole basis for the job specification statements. The current incumbent's job qualifications often exceed the *minimum* KSAs required of someone to perform the job satisfactorily. The analyst often uses opinions of supervisors in determining qualifications. Checking the job requirements of other organizations with similar jobs is another means of obtaining information for job specifications.

CRITICAL KSA(S).   In writing job specifications, it is important to list specifically those KSAs essential for satisfactory job performance. Only job-related items that are nondiscriminatory should be included. For example, a high school diploma should not be required for a job unless the manager can demonstrate that an individual with less education cannot perform the job as well. Because of this concern, some specification statements, read, "High school diploma or equivalent acceptable experience."

SUMMARY

- Job analysis is a systematic investigation of the tasks, duties, and responsibilities required in a job, and the skills, knowledge, and abilities necessary to do the job.
- The end products of job analysis are job descriptions, which identify the tasks, duties, and responsibilities in jobs; and job specifications, which list the knowledge, skills, and abilities needed to perform a job satisfactorily.
- Job analysis information is useful in many other P/HR activities: human resource planning, recruiting, selection, career planning, training, performance appraisal, health and safety, thus making it a basic P/HR activity.
- The four general methods of gathering job analysis information are observation, interviews, questionnaires, and standardized methods. In practice, a combination of methods is often used.
- The position analysis questionnaire (PAQ), a structured questionnaire, is widely used to analyze jobs.
- The functional job analysis (FJA) uses standardized task statements and job descriptions to examine data, people, and things. The *Dictionary of Occupational Titles* (DOT) can be used with FJA to analyze jobs.
- Job analysis, while seemingly straightforward, has several behavioral implications that managers should consider: employees' fear of the process and resistance to change, management's tendency to overemphasize the current job holder's qualifications, and the danger of job descriptions putting a straitjacket on managerial flexibility.
- Legally, job analysis must conform to ideas of the courts about what good job analysis is. This is especially true if the information is used in validating tests or in other EEO-related decisions.
- The process of conducting a job analysis is as follows:
    I. Identify the target jobs and review existing documentation on them
   II. Explain the process to managers and employees
  III. Conduct the job analyses
   IV. Prepare job descriptions and job specifications
    V. Maintain and update job descriptions and specifications
- Writing job descriptions and job specifications, especially for executive jobs, can be tricky. But once prepared, the two tools provide good feedback to job holders.

REVIEW AND DISCUSSION QUESTIONS

1. Clearly define and differentiate among job analysis, job descriptions, and job specifications.
2. Job analysis is the most basic P/HR activity. Discuss why.
3. Describe the four general methods of analyzing jobs, devoting two sentences to each method.
4. How do human behavior and governmental considerations affect the job analysis process?
5. Explain how you would conduct a job analysis in a company that never had job descriptions.
6. Discuss how you would train someone to write a job description and job specifications for a small bank.

CASE	How Pamida Used Job Analysis

Pamida is an Omaha-based retail chain that serves the upper Midwest with more than 160 stores in 12 states. Its outlets, which are predominantly in rural communities, provide a wide variety of merchandise, from automotive and sporting goods to clothing. Pamida employs approximately 5,500 people.

In its first 20 years, Pamida had no formal wage and salary system, nor did it have a program to develop and maintain job descriptions. Development of a complete wage and salary system meant creating job descriptions for all jobs in the company.

The process began with the employees in store operations, because that area had the greatest number of people. Job analysis questionnaires were sent to selected employees throughout the company. In some stores, all employees completed questionnaires; in other stores, only one category of employees was sampled; and in another group of stores, supervisors completed questionnaires on the employees supervised. Over 300 questionnaires were returned to the newly hired compensation manager. After analysis, distinct jobs were defined and job descriptions were written, after which they were reviewed for accuracy by store operations management.

The analysis and resulting job descriptions resolved several thorny organizational issues for store operations. Title usage throughout the company became standardized. Whereas one job had been variously referred to as bookkeeper, office manager, and secretary, the job title now became office clerk. Different levels of store managers and assistant managers, were established according to the store size and responsibilities. The job of area leader consolidated the activities previously performed by individual department heads and gave store managers greater flexibility in assigning work to employees. An organization chart was developed for each store, based on store size and sales volume.

Job descriptions were also written for hourly and salaried positions at the home office. Questionnaires were used to obtain information and where necessary, personal interviews were used to clarify details. Draft descriptions were reviewed by the supervisor, the employee, and the respective vice presidents.

Today, to keep job descriptions current, supervisors review employees' job descriptions at each performance appraisal and notify the Human Resource Department when any significant change occurs in jobs so that the descriptions can be revised. All changes are coordinated through the compensation manager.

QUESTIONS

1. How does the process described in the case compare to the steps mentioned in the chapter?
2. Identify why managerial and employee communications and participation in the case are so critical.
3. What potential weaknesses in the process do you see?

NOTES

1. W. J. Howe and W. Parks II, "Labor Market Completes Sixty Years of Expansion," *Monthly Labor Review*, February 1989, 8.
2. G. Silvetri and J. Lukasiewicz, "Projections 2000," *Monthly Labor Review*, September 1987, 61.
3. Ibid., 61.
4. R. Kutscher, "Overview and Implications of the Projections to 2000," *Monthly Labor Review*, September 1989, 8.
5. Maryellen LoBosco, "Consensus on Job Analysis, Job Evaluation, and Job Classification," *Personnel*, May 1985, 70–74.
6. D. W. Meyers, *Human Resource Management* (New York: Commerce Clearing House, 1986), 105.
7. Adapted from J. Markowitz, "Managing the Job Analysis Process," *Training and Development Journal*, August 1987, 64–66.
8. H. Risher, "Job Evaluation: Validity and Reliability," *Compensation and Benefits Review*, January–February 1989, 24.
9. W. Mullins and W. Kimbrough, "Group Composition as a Determinant of Job Analysis Outcomes," *Journal of Applied Psychology* 73, (1988): 657–664.
10. LoBosco, op. cit., 71.
11. Ernest J. McCormick et al., *PAQ: Job Analysis Manual* (Logan, Utah: PAQ Services, 1977).
12. S. Bemis, et al., *Job Analysis* (Washington, D.C.: Bureau of National Affairs, 1987), 31.
13. S. Bulton and R. Harvey, "A Comparison of Holistic vs. Decomposed Ratings of PAQ Work Dimensions," *Personnel Psychology* 41, (1988): 761; R. Harvey, S. Lozada-Larsen, "Influence of Amount of Job Descriptive Information on Job Analysis Rating Accuracy," *Journal of Applied Psychology* 7, (1988): 457–461; J. S. Parrow, "The Utility of PAQ In Relating Job Behavior to Traits," *Journal of Occupational Psychology* 62, (1989): 151–162.
14. R. D. Arvey et al., "Narrative Job Descriptions as Potential Sources of Job Analysis Ratings," *Personnel Psychology* 35 (1982): 618–629.
15. A. P. Jones et al., "Potential Sources of Bias in Job Analytic Procedures," *Academy of Management Journal* 35 (1982): 813–828.
16. M. Campion, "Ability Requirement Implications of Job Design: An Interdisciplinary Perspective," *Personnel Psychology* 42 (1989): 9.
17. Steven P. Galante, "Service Concerns Feel Slighted by Federal Classification Code," *Wall Street Journal*, March 17, 1985, 19.
18. M. H. Banks et al., "The Job Component Inventory and the Analysis of Jobs Requiring Limited Skill," *Personnel Psychology* 36 (1983): 57–66.
19. Adapted from E. L. Levine et al., "Evaluation of Job Analysis Methods by Experienced Job Analysts," *Academy of Management Journal* 26 (1983): 339–348.
20. Adapted from B. A. Jacobs, "Title Wave Engulfs Corporate America," *Industry Week*, April 19, 1982, 111–112.
21. Adapted from D. E. Thompson and T. A. Thompson, "Court Standards for Job Analysis in Test Validation," *Personnel Psychology* 35 (1982): 865–874.
22. *Guinn v. Bolger* 36 FEP Cases 506 (D.D.C. 1984).
23. Frederick S. Hills, *Compensation Decision Making* (Chicago: Dryden Press, 1987), 146.
24. P. Grant, "What Use Is a Job Description?" *Personnel Journal*, February 1988, 45.
25. W. Kennedy, "Train Managers to Write Winning Job Descriptions," *Training and Development Journal*, April 1987, 62.
26. For a guide on preparing and writing job descriptions, see R. I. Henderson, *Compensation Management*, 5th ed. (Reston, Va: Reston Publishing, 1988), 201–229.

Recruiting

Chapter 8

After your read this chapter, you should be able to:

1. Define recruiting and outline a typical recruiting process
2. Explain the basic recruiting concepts of labor force population, applicant population, and applicant pool
3. Compare internal and external sources of candidates
4. Identify three internal sources of candidates
5. List and briefly discuss five external recruiting sources
6. Discuss why the evaluation of recruiting efforts is important

P/HR: Today *and* Tomorrow	Computerized Recruiting

An increasing number of employers are utilizing computers to assist in their efforts to recruit employees. Computerized aids for recruiters include:

- Databases of resumes that are kept and accessed to identify potential candidates as openings arise
- "Personalized" letters that are computer-generated to respond to applicants
- Computerized matching services available through some employment agencies and search firms

Some of the external computer database systems available are offered by employment search firms. One system is Electronic Job Matching (EJM), available from Human Resource Management Center, a Tampa, Florida firm. Employers who contact the firm and provide details about openings receive information on potential candidates from the EJM database. Specific biographical data on the candidates referred by EJM allow employers to identify whom they wish to hire. Another is available from Corporate Organizing and Research Service (CORS), which has assisted over 4000 corporations in locating qualified applicants in its database. Databases offered by other firms are specialized by such occupational fields as engineering, banking, and health care industries.

Internally, employers can purchase software to aid their efforts also. One internal system is called Roscoe the Recruiter. This system allows an employer to organize data on current employees, as well as on applicants. Data on the individual's work history, education, salary history, and skills are entered from application blanks, resumes, and employee personal records. When an opening becomes available, the details of the opening are entered, and candidates whose backgrounds and skills appear to be a match are identified.

Another system is the Restrac Resume Reader available from Micro Trac systems. This software allows employers to enter resumes and then sort the resumes by occupational fields, skills, areas of interests, and previous work histories. For instance, if a firm has an opening for someone with an MBA and marketing experience, the key words *MBA* and *marketing* can be entered and all resumes containing these two items will be identified.

The advantages of all of these products and services is that they allow recruiters to identify potential candidates more easily, instead of recruiters having to sort through numerous stacks and files of resumes. Employers who have used both the internal and external systems indicate that they reduce recruiting costs associated with advertising expenditures, search firm fees, and internal processing and record retention expenses.[1]

"If you can't staff your store, you can't operate your store."

Richard Pires

The objective of the recruiting process is to provide a sufficiently large group of qualified candidates so that satisfactory employees can be selected. **Recruiting** is the process of generating a pool of qualified applicants for organizational jobs. If the number of available candidates only equals the number of people to be hired, there is no selection—the choice has already been made. The organization must either leave some openings unfilled or take all the candidates.

RECRUITING
is the process of generating a pool of qualified applicants for organizational jobs.

■ ■ ■ THE RECRUITING PROCESS

The steps in a typical recruiting process are identified in Figure 8–1. Recruiting efforts translate human resource plans into action and also fill openings when unexpected vacancies occur. Even during periods of reduced hiring, implementation of long-range plans means keeping in contact with outside recruiting sources to maintain visibility and maintaining employee recruiting channels in the organization. These activities are essential when management must step up recruiting activity on short notice.

In larger organizations, a manager notifies someone in the P/HR unit that an opening needs to be filled. Submission of a *requisition* to the P/HR unit, much as a supply requisition is submitted to the purchasing department, is a common way to trigger recruiting efforts. The P/HR representative and the manager must *review the job description and specifications* so that both have clear and up-to-date information on the job duties and the specific desired qualifications. For example, whether a job is for a computer programmer or for a systems analyst would significantly affect the screening of applicants and the content of a recruiting advertisement. Familiarity with the job makes it easier to identify the minimum qualifications someone needs to perform the job satisfactorily.

Following this review, the actual recruiting effort begins. *Internal sources* of available recruits through transfers, promotions, and job posting usually are checked first. Then *external resources* are contacted as required, and all applicants are screened through the selection process. *Follow-up* is necessary to evaluate the effectiveness of the recruiting efforts and to tie those efforts back into the human resource plan and ongoing recruiting activities.

Recruiting during the 1990s will increase in importance as companies search through a shrinking supply of appropriately trained persons to find good employees.[2] Additionally, recruiting is expensive. Estimates are that it costs one-third of a new hire's first year's salary to recruit him or her. Training and learning costs add another 50 percent or more.[3]

Recruiting Responsibilities

In most large organizations, human resource planning and recruiting activities are coordinated through the P/HR department, which maintains and analyzes human resource plans as part of a perpetual recruiting effort. Often other managers help recruiting efforts by determining the skills and qualifications that individuals need to fill vacancies in their areas. Figure 8–2 shows a typical distribution of recruiting responsibilities between the P/HR department and managers. In small organiza-

Figure 8–1
The Recruiting Process

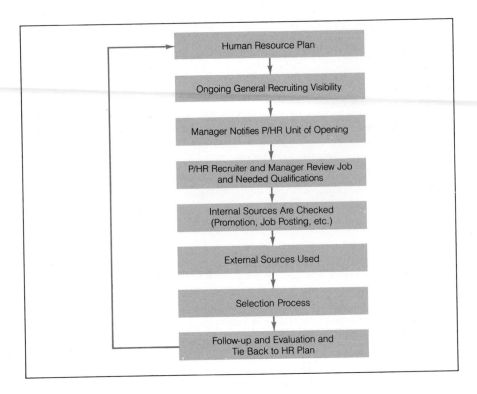

tions, and even in some divisions of large organizations, several different managers may work on recruiting.

Basic Recruiting Concepts

Recruiting and selection are closely related. Recruiting determines the types of applicants from which selection will be made. Selection involves the actual choosing of a new employee based on predictive information obtained from that applicant.

To understand the environment in which recruiting takes place, three different groups are conceptually important. Those three groups are labor force population, applicant population, and applicant pool.

LABOR FORCE POPULATION. The labor force population includes all individuals who are available for selection if all possible recruitment strategies are used. The labor force population offers a vast array of possible applicants who must be reached in very different ways. Different recruiting methods, for example newspaper ads versus college recruiting, will reach different segments of the population.

APPLICANT POPULATION. The applicant population is a subset of the labor force population that is available for selection using a particular recruiting approach. For example, an organization might limit its recruiting for management trainees to M.B.A. graduates from the top ten business schools. This recruiting method will result in a very different group of applicants from those who would have applied had the employer chosen to advertise openings for management trainees on a local radio station.

P/HR UNIT	MANAGERS
■ Forecasts recruiting needs ■ Prepares copy for recruiting ads and campaigns ■ Plans and conducts recruiting efforts ■ Audits and evaluates recruiting activities	■ Determine qualifications and anticipate needs ■ Assist in recruiting effort ■ Provide management review of recruiting efforts

Figure 8–2
Recruiting Responsibilities

At least four recruiting decisions affect the nature of the applicant population:

1. *Recruiting method* (advertising medium chosen, use of employment agencies)
2. *Recruiting message* (what is said about the job, salary, duties, opportunities, and *how* it is said)
3. *Applicant qualifications required* (education level, amount of experience necessary, training opportunities)
4. *Administrative procedures* (time of year recruiting is done, follow-ups with applicants, use of previous applicant files)

APPLICANT POOL.   The applicant pool consists of all persons who are actually evaluated for selection. Many factors can affect the size of the applicant pool. For example, the organization mentioned previously is likely to interview only a small percentage of the M.B.A. graduates at the top ten business schools. Because not all graduates will want to interview, the applicant population at this step is greatly reduced. The reputation of the organization and industry as a place to work, the screening efforts of the organization, and the information available to the applicant population are three such factors. Assuming a suitable candidate is found, the final selection is made from the applicant pool.

Realistic Job Previews

Generally, job seekers appear to have little information about the organizations to which they apply for jobs. Yet attributes of the job and the organization, even though not well understood initially, are given considerable weight when people actually apply for a job. Pay, nature of the work, geographic location, and opportunity for promotion are important to professionals. Job security is important to blue-collar applicants. Some employers oversell their jobs and choose to make them appear better than they are in recruiting advertisements. Some research suggests that *realistic job previews* better allow people to select whether a particular job is suited to their needs. From the employer's standpoint, realistic job previews have been linked to reduced turnover, but they also may lead to an increase in candidates who refuse job offers. Ethically, realistic presentation of the job is preferable to misrepresentation, regardless of the impact on the recruiting effort.[4]

Recruiting: Continuous versus Intensive Efforts

Recruiting efforts may be viewed as either *continuous* or *intensive*. Continuous efforts to recruit have the advantage of keeping the employer in the recruiting market. For example, with college recruiting, it appears to be advantageous for some organizations to have a recruiter on a given campus each year. Those

Tough Recruiting at Retail

Retail stores in certain parts of the country are encountering a challenge in finding and keeping good store-level employees. The problem is especially pronounced in certain parts of the country with high per capita income or low unemployment. Discounters usually pay a lower hourly wage and are at an even greater disadvantage for obtaining hourly employees. Traditional methods, such as running ads in the local newspaper, have failed, and some chains are turning to other, more flexible methods—ones that also are more costly.

In one community with a 2.3 percent unemployment rate, a retail chain responded with these recruiting innovations:

- Provided a bonus for employees who recruit others
- Placed recruiting flyers in stores circulars
- Recruited in depressed parts of the country and paid some moving expenses
- Used a night crew for stocking to attract moonlighters

Other organizations have done the following:

- Placed hiring booths in problem stores to speed up hiring
- Provided vans to take employees to and from central-city areas where they live
- Experimented with flexible work schedules
- Experimented with hiring more part-timers and senior citizens[5]

All of these approaches have been successful, to some degree. But as more retailers adapt such innovative recruiting methods, the competition for retail workers likely will become even more intense.

---

employers that visit a campus only occasionally are less likely to build a following in that school over time.

Intensive recruiting may take the form of a vigorous recruiting campaign aimed at hiring a given number of employees, usually within a short period of time. Such efforts may be the result of failure in the P/HR planning system to identify needs in advance or to recognize drastic changes in work force needs due to unexpected work loads.

Special Recruiting Problems

Special problems sometimes surface in recruiting efforts. Certain firms such as those in the fast-foods and retailing industries, have had continuing difficulties in recruiting sufficient employees for lower-paying jobs (see the P/HR: Practice on recruiting at retail). These industries have traditionally relied on younger employees in the 18 to 24 age group, which as a group, will continue to diminish in number through 1995. But jobs in those industries will continue to increase rapidly for the next ten years.

Small employers may have difficulties recruiting against larger ones because smaller organizations often cannot offer extensive training programs and may not offer as many benefits. Consequently, creative approaches may be needed. One small firm in California has successfully recruited salespeople from unusual sources. During earlier years the firm found that disenchanted schoolteachers were excellent prospects. More recently, newer college graduates working in well-managed restaurants have been a good source. After a year or two, they were ready for greater opportunity, adapted quickly, and showed good customer skills.[6]

■■ ■ INTERNAL VERSUS EXTERNAL RECRUITING SOURCES: A COMPARISON

The organization may use both inside and outside sources. Pros and cons are associated with both promotion from within (internal source for recruitment) and hiring outside the organization (external recruitment) to fill openings. Figure 8–3 summarizes some most commonly cited advantages and disadvantages of each type of source.

Promoting from within, generally, is thought to be a positive force in rewarding good work. However, if followed exclusively, it has the major disadvantage of perpetuating old ways of operating. Recruiting externally for professionals, such as accountants or computer programmers, may be cheaper than training them. It also infuses the organization with new ideas. But recruiting from outside the organization for any but entry-level positions presents the problem of adjustment time for the new persons. A serious drawback to external recruiting is the negative impact that often results from selecting an outsider instead of promoting a current employee.

Most organizations combine the use of internal and external methods. Organizations that operate in rapidly changing environments and competitive conditions may need to place a heavier emphasis on external sources. However, for those organizations existing in environments that change slowly, promotion from within may be more suitable. A look at both internal and external sources of employees for jobs follows.

■■ ■ INTERNAL RECRUITING SOURCES

Among internal recruiting sources are present employees, friends and employees, former employees, and previous applicants. Promotions, demotions, and transfers also can provide additional people for an organizational unit, if not for the entire organization.

Using internal recruiting sources has some advantages over external sources. First, it allows management to observe an employee over a period of time and to evaluate that person's potential and specific job performance. Second, an organi-

ADVANTAGES	DISADVANTAGES
Internal	
■ Morale of promotee	■ Inbreeding
■ Better assessment of abilities	■ Possible morale problems of those not promoted
■ Lower cost for some jobs	■ "Political" infighting for promotions
■ Motivator for good performance	■ Need strong management development program
■ Causes a succession of promotions	
■ Have to hire only at entry level	
External	
■ "New blood," new perspectives	■ May not select someone who will "fit"
■ Cheaper than training a professional	■ May cause morale problems for those internal candidates
■ No group of political supporters in organization already	■ Longer "adjustment" or orientation time
■ May bring industry insights	

Figure 8–3
Internal versus External Sources

zation that promotes its own employees to fill job openings may give its employees added motivation to do a good job. Employees may see little reason to do more than just what the current job requires if management's policy is to hire externally. This concern is the main reason why an organization generally considers internal sources of qualified applicants first.

Job Posting and Bidding

One procedure for recruiting employees for other jobs within the organization is a *job-posting and bidding* system. Employees can be notified of all job vacancies by posting notices, circulating publications, or in some other way inviting employees to apply for jobs. In a unionized organization, job posting and bidding can be quite formal; the procedure often is spelled out in the labor agreement. Seniority lists may be used by organizations that make promotions based strictly on seniority.

A job-posting system gives each employee an opportunity to move to a better job within the organization. Without some sort of job posting and bidding, it is difficult to find out what jobs are open elsewhere in the organization. The most common method employers use to notify current employees of openings is to post notices on bulletin boards in locations such as employee lounges, cafeterias, and near elevators.

Job-posting and bidding systems can be ineffective if handled improperly. Jobs should be posted *before* any external recruiting is done. The organization must allow a reasonable period of time for present employees to check notices of available jobs before it considers external applicants. When employees' bids are turned down, they should be informed of the reasons.

Answers to many potential questions must be anticipated: What happens if there are no qualified candidates on the payroll to fill new openings? Is it necessary for employees to inform their supervisors that they are bidding for another job? How much notice should an employee be required to give before transferring to a new department? When should job notices not be posted?

An example of how a job-posting system works at a large manufacturing firm is discussed next. At that firm, employees can only bid for jobs at their own location, although employees may move to other locations through promotion. The posting procedure begins with dissemination of a job-posting announcement based on a supervisory requisition. With the exception of the two lowest entry-level job grades, no external recruitment is done until internal sources, such as job posting, are used. An employee interested in a posted job files an application that is screened by a P/HR representative and the supervisor of the posted job. Only after screening is completed and a qualified applicant is chosen to be interviewed is the employee's current supervisor notified. Interviews are then conducted. Unsuccessful applicants are notified by the P/HR representative, who may discuss career interests and training needs with the rejected employee. If an employee is successful, a job offer is made to the employee after the current supervisor is notified of the intended offer.

Internal Recruiting Data Base

As the chapter opening discussion illustrates, computerized talent banks or "skills inventories" can furnish a listing of the talents, abilities, and skills available for organizations. Traveler's Corporation, the insurance giant, was probably the first

| P/HR: Practice *and* Research | A Global "Internal" Data Base |

When Janet Berry went looking for a job, she was not pleased with her first forays into the job market. A private employment agency wanted too much money, and the locations in the want ads were tough to find for the new resident of Omaha, Nebraska.

Mrs. Berry had moved to Omaha with her husband, a military em-ployee at Offutt Air Force Base. After two weeks she hit upon the job bank offered by the Air Force's Family Support Center. The bank is used to match civilian spouses with pro-spective employers in the Omaha area. Janet found her job.

The job bank is expanding beyond the limits of one air base. It is linked by computer to similar banks at other air bases. Eventually, plans are for a network linking 123 bases around the world. That change could mean that people like Janet Berry could start hunting for a new job *before* moving to a new city. Services such as this are designed to help with the job dis-locations that are associated with military careers.[10]

to use such a listing for retirees willing to work part-time, but Wells Fargo Bank in California also has used the idea.[7] Retirees are but one possible source of input to the data base. Current employees' skills are an obvious source as well. A listing of current employees lends itself to many other useful applications for the information.[8]

Completely external skills and job banks exist and may grow in popularity also.[9] However, recruiting data bases that combine internal and external sources are operational in large organizations now, as the P/HR Practice on a global "internal" data base illustrates.

Recruiting Through Current Employees

A reliable source of people to fill vacancies can be reached through current em-ployees who may know of good prospects among their families and friends. The employees can acquaint potential applicants with the advantages of a job with the company, furnish letters of introduction, and encourage them to apply.

This source is usually one of the most effective methods of recruiting because many qualified people can be reached at a low cost. In an organization with a large number of employees, this approach can develop quite a large pool of potential employees. Most employees know from their own experiences about the require-ments of the jobs and for what sort of person the company is looking. Often employees have friends or acquaintances who meet these requirements.

Fidelity Investments developed a program to recruit data-processing employees that offered employee spouses $2,000 for each person they recruited who remained on the payroll over a year. The program brought in seventy-three workers in one year at a cost of $97,000—a fraction of the fees employment agencies would have charged.[11]

However, a word of caution is appropriate. When the organization has an un-derrepresentation of a particular minority group, word-of-mouth referral has been considered a violation of Title VII of the Civil Rights Act. An organization composed primarily of nonprotected-class individuals presumably would prefer more of the same for consideration as employees.

Promotions and Transfers

Most companies choose to fill vacancies through promotions or transfers from within, if possible. Although most often successful, promotions from within have some drawbacks as well. The person's performance on one job may not be a good predictor of performance on another, as different skills may be required on the new job. For example, the successful employee may not make a good supervisor because in most supervisory jobs an ability to accomplish the work through others requires skills with people that may not have been a factor in previous jobs.

A study of promotions across five decades showed remarkable stability. Change in jobs or "job evolution" accounted for more vacancies than did turnover.[12] It is clear that pyramidal organizations do not always have pyramidal chances for promotion. However, promotions may not speed the movement of minorities and women throughout the organization.[13]

Recruiting Former Employees and Applicants

Former employees are also a good internal source of applicants. Some retired employees may be willing to come back to work on a part-time basis or may recommend someone who would be interested in working for the company. Sometimes people who have left the company to raise a family or complete a college education are willing to come back to work. Individuals who left for other jobs might be willing to return for a higher rate of pay. Job sharing and flextime programs may be useful with retirees or others who previously worked for the organization. The main advantage in hiring former employees is that their performance is known. As mentioned earlier, Travelers Insurance started a retirees' job bank to bring Travelers' retirees back to work on a part-time basis. A media campaign targeted at Travelers' retirees netted between 200 and 250 people ranging from typists to accountants (see Figure 8–4).[14]

In a study of 6,600 job changes over 20 years, one researcher found that only 5 percent of the managers were willing to take back an employee.[15] But a more competitive business climate seems to be changing managers' attitudes toward a high-performing former employee. It depends on why the employee left in the first place. If there were problems with the boss or company, it is unlikely that matters have improved with the employee's absence. But if someone goes off to fulfill a dream, the employee's reason for leaving seems more legitimate. Concerns that employers have in rehiring former employees include trade-secret infringements, vindictiveness, and fear of morale problems among those who stayed.

PREVIOUS APPLICANTS.   Another source of applicants can be found in the organizational files. Although not truly an internal source, those who have previously applied for jobs can be recontacted by mail, a quick and inexpensive way to fill an unexpected opening. Although "walk-ins" are likely to be more suitable for filling unskilled and semiskilled jobs, some professional openings can be filled by applicants for previous jobs. One firm that needed two cost accountants immediately contacted qualified previous applicants and was able to hire two individuals who were disenchanted with their current jobs.

SOURCE: *Hartford Courant,* No. 31 The Travelers Companies, advertiser; Hirsch Elliot, Inc., advertising agency.

Figure 8–4
Retiree Recruiting Advertisement

■■■ ■ EXTERNAL RECRUITING SOURCES

If internal sources do not produce an acceptable candidate, several external sources are available. These sources include schools, colleges and universities, employment agencies, temporary help firms, labor unions, media sources, and trade and competitive sources.

School Recruiting

High schools or vocational/technical schools may be a good source of new employees for many organizations. A successful recruiting program with these institutions is the result of careful analysis, thorough training and planning, and continuous contact with the individual schools.

Major considerations for such a recruiting program are:

■ School counselors and other faculty members concerned with job opportunities and business careers for their students should be contacted regularly.
■ Good relations should be maintained with faculty and officials at all times, even when there is little or no need for new employees.
■ Recruiting programs can serve these schools in ways other than the placement of students. For instance, the organization might supply educational films, provide speakers, or arrange for demonstrations and exhibits.

- Many organizations compete for their share of capable graduates. Continuing contact and good relations provide a better opportunity to secure the best graduates.
- The extent and scope of this recruiting program will depend on needs. However, a long-range view of recruiting is more desirable than a campaign approach.
- Some larger schools have a centralized guidance/placement office. Contact can be established and maintained with the supervisors of these offices; they are in a good position to help plan and conduct recruiting activities.

School counselors generally are interested in the employer's policies and working conditions and will cooperate with an organization that treats its employees fairly. Promotional brochures that acquaint students with starting jobs and career opportunities can be distributed to counselors, librarians, or others. Participating in career days and giving tours of the company to school groups are other ways of maintaining good contact with school sources. Cooperative programs in which students work part-time and receive some school credits also may be useful in generating qualified applicants for full-time positions.

College Recruiting

At the college or university level, the recruitment of graduating students is a large-scale operation for many organizations. Most colleges and universities maintain placement offices in which employers and applicants can meet. However, college recruiting presents some interesting and unique problems.

The major determinants that affect the selection of colleges at which an employer interviews are:

- Current position requirements
- Past experience with placement offices and previous graduates
- Organizational budget constraints
- Cost of available talent
- Market competition

College recruiting can be expensive; therefore, an organization should determine if the positions it is trying to fill really require a college degree. A great many positions do not; yet many employers insist on filling them with college graduates. The result may be employees who must be paid more and who are likely to leave if the jobs are not sufficiently challenging.

There is a great deal of competition for the top students in a college and much less competition for those farther down the ladder. Attributes that recruiters seem to value most highly in college graduates—poise, oral communication skills, personality, appearance, and written communication skills—all typically are mentioned ahead of grade point average (GPA).

Research has shown that a candidate's impression of an organization often is based on his or her encounter with the recruiter.[16] Successful recruiters are those who are enthusiastic and informed, show an interest in the applicant, use interview time well, and avoid overly personal or deliberately stressful questions.

College grads often fail to meet organizational expectations of performance and commitment. For their part, recruiters tend to misperceive the importance of various job rewards to college graduates. The recruiter overestimates the importance of intrinsic rewards (such as challenge, responsibility, advancement) while underestimating extrinsic rewards (such as pay, benefits, and security.) Students purposely communicate preferences for instrinsic rewards in order to portray attitudes they feel interviewers wish to see. Such miscommunication may contribute to poor placement decisions and subsequent performance problems and turnover. Recruiting efforts and materials that are targeted appropriately can help address these problems.[17]

Labor Unions

Labor unions are a source of certain types of workers. In some industries, such as construction, unions have traditionally supplied workers to employers. A labor pool is generally available through a union, and workers can be dispatched to particular jobs to meet the needs of the employers. The hiring hall is usually the contact point.

In some instances, the union can control or influence recruiting and staffing needs. An organization with a strong union may have less flexibility than a non-union company in deciding who will be hired and where he or she will be placed. Unions also can work to an employer's advantage through cooperative staffing programs, as they do in the building, and printing industries. Such cooperation has not been the case in manufacturing. There, union shops have given management a free hand in hiring, while unions have insisted on strong seniority provisions for promotions.

Trade and Competitive Sources

Other sources for recruiting are *professional and trade associations*, *trade publications*, and *competitors*. Many professional societies and trade associations publish a newsletter or magazine containing job ads. Such publications may be a good source for specialized professionals needed within an industry. Ads in other specialized publications or listings at professional meetings also can be good sources of publicity about professional openings.

An employer may meet possible applicants who are currently employed by a competitor at professional associations and industry meetings. Some employers directly contact individuals working for competitors. Employees recruited from these sources spend less time in training because they already know the industry.

Temporary Help

Perhaps the most accessible and immediate source of certain types of help is the temporary-help agency. These agencies typically supply secretarial, clerical, or semiskilled labor on a day-rate basis. As Figure 8–5 indicates, temporary employees are used for a variety of reasons. The use of temporary help may make sense for an organization if its work is subject to seasonal or other fluctuations. Hiring temporary help may be more efficient than hiring permanent employees to meet peak employment needs, in which case the employer either has to find some tasks to keep employees busy during less active periods or must resort to layoffs.

More recently, "temp" opportunities are opening up for professional and executive-level jobs, such as chefs, accountants, nurses, and managers.[18] Downsizing has taken layers of management out of many firms, so companies may be hesitant to begin adding them back for projects that may be temporary. The same downsizing has made available "temporary executives" with experience that would not have been available in years past. Others have taken early retirement but want to continue working on a part-time basis.

Figure 8–5
Use of Office Temporary Help

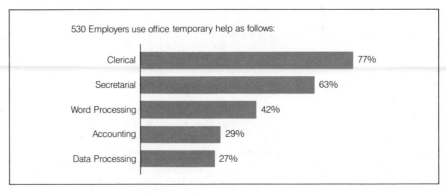

SOURCE: Adapted from *Modern Office Technology*, November 1989, 63–64.

Temporary workers can and often do accept regular staff positions. In effect, this "try before you buy" approach is potentially beneficial to both employer and employee. However, some temporary-help services bill the client company a "liquidated damages charge," which is imposed if a temporary worker is hired full-time by the client company within a time period—usually 90 days.[19]

EMPLOYEE OR INDEPENDENT CONTRACTOR?   Changes in the work force have led to more flexible work hours, part-time work, or working at home for many people. This trend and the use of temporary workers gives rise to some interesting legal questions as to whether someone is an employee or not. Independent contractors, leased employees, and temporaries are categories that may cause confusion (and legal questions). Basically, there is only one meaningful legal distinction— employee or independent contractor. If someone is *not* an employee, he or she is either an independent contractor or works for an independent contractor (as with leased or temporary employees).

It would be reasonable to assume that lawyers, courts, and administrative agencies at all levels have a way to tell the two groups apart. However, this assumption is not the case. Definitions vary greatly from state to state and agency to agency.

Employment Agencies

Every state in the United States has a *state* employment agency. These agencies operate branch offices in many cities throughout the state and do not charge fees to applicants or employers.

Private employment agencies also are found in most cities. For a fee collected from either the employee or the employer, these agencies will do some preliminary screening for an organization and put the organization in touch with applicants. These agencies differ considerably in terms of level of service, costs, policies, and types of applicants they provide. Employers can reduce the range of possible problems with these sources by giving an employment service a good definition of the position to be filled, including such details as job title, skills needed, experience and education required, and pay ranges available.

Executive Search Firms

Some employment agencies focus their efforts on executive, managerial, and professional positions. These *search firms* may work on either a retainer basis or a fee

P/HR: Practice *and* Research

Ethical Issues In Recruiting

Recruiting is an area with the potential for *many* ethical concerns. The ethical dilemma of an executive search firm recruiting employees from client firms is certainly one such concern. Another with which most people can identify closely is looking for another job while presently employed. Looking for another job is, in the eyes of many management groups, an act of disloyalty. The question "May we contact your present employer?" causes anxiety for many employees. Employees are often tempted to keep the whole affair very secret until a decision has been made to go. Sometimes this decision may involve untruth by omission, if not outright falsehoods, to maintain the deception.

No company can satisfy the career goals of all its employees. Indeed, some turnover is beneficial for any organization. Further, good employees *will* be contacted by other firms and owe it to themselves to investigate such opportunities. There are few logical reasons for companies to force employees to sneak around while looking for another job. They are not disloyal. They are doing what all people do from time to time— look for ways to stretch themselves and improve their lot.

Job search is a fact of life, and organizations may in fact come out ahead by a more enlightened approach, because the employees who do choose to leave can do so with a better feeling about their former employers. The individuals who are looking to leave also are not put in the ethically unhappy position of having to cover up their actions.

based on the pay level of the hired employee. Those fees may range as high as 33 percent of the employee's first-year salary. Most employers pay the fee, but there are some circumstances in which the employee will pay the fee. For placing a high-level executive job, a search firm may receive $300,000 or more, counting travel expenses, the fee, and other compensation. The size of the fees and the aggressiveness with which some search firms pursue candidates for openings have led to the firms being called *headhunters*.

Although many organizations prefer to fill top and upper-middle management jobs from within, when outside search for an executive is necessary, personal contact (the "old boy" or "old girl" network) is most often used. However, executive search firms may be used if other methods do not turn up a successful candidate.

From a poll of over 1,700 senior managers from *Fortune* 500 companies, Korn/Ferry International developed a composite profile of the successful executive. This composite executive is a 53-year-old white Protestant male, son of a white-collar worker. He is married, and has never been divorced, does not smoke or use drugs, and drinks only moderately. He earns about $200,000 in base salary a year in today's dollars and is a registered Republican. He comes from a city of about 100,000 inhabitants, where he attended public school, and is college educated. If he holds a graduate degree, it is likely to be an M.B.A.[20]

The executive search field is split into two groups: (1) contingency firms that charge a fee only after a candidate has been hired by a client company, and (2) retainer firms that charge a client a set fee whether or not the contracted search is successful. Most of the larger firms work on a retainer basis.

Search firms are ethically bound not to approach employees of client companies in their search efforts for another client. As search firms are retained by more corporations, an increasing number of potential candidates become off-limits. At some point, the large search firms feel they may lose their effectiveness, because they will have to shun the best candidates for some jobs because of conflict-of-interest concerns (See Ethical Issues in Recruiting.)

Although a firm may conduct an external search to fill its executive opening, it may also have within its own corporate structure an individual to fill the vacant slot. Often, long before vacancies in top executive spots occur, the firm has asked "Who will rise in the organization and who will be left behind?" No question is of greater importance in management development and corporate strategy in the long run. Executive search should *always* have one paramount purpose: to assist the organization in filling open positions with qualified people who produce.[21]

Media Sources

Media sources—newspapers, magazines, television, radio and billboards—are widely used and familiar to many people looking for jobs. Almost all newspapers carry "help wanted" sections and these frequently provide applicants for many organizations. For example, the *Wall Street Journal* is a major source used to recruit managerial and professional employees.

Newspapers are convenient because there is a short lead time—usually two or three days at most—for placing an ad. For positions that must be filled quickly, newspapers may be a good source. However, there can be a great deal of "wasted circulation" with newspaper advertising because most newspapers do not aim to reach any specialized employee markets. Often applicants are only marginally suitable, primarily because employers do not describe the jobs and the necessary qualifications very well. Many employers have found that it is not cost-efficient to schedule newspaper ads on days other than Sunday.

When using recruitment advertisements, employers should ask five key questions:

1. What do we want to accomplish?
2. Who are the people we want to reach?
3. What should the advertising message convey?
4. How should the message be presented?
5. In which medium should it run?

Other media sources include general magazines, television and radio, and billboards. These sources are usually not suitable for frequent use, but may be used for one-time campaigns aimed at quickly finding specially skilled workers. General Electric once used a billboard at a major plant to advertise its openings for welders. Radio ads also have been tried by some employers.[22]

Recruitment advertising is a form of direct response marketing. That is, employers are placing ads to generate direct, measurable responses. The more ads they place and track, the better they will become at projecting what responses to expect. To track responses, an employer first must code the ads. The easiest way to do this is to use different contact names and addresses (for example, specify a department number).

Then, the employer must be sure to note the source each time a response is received. It is best to have one person responsible for opening and coding mailing responses. More people may be needed to respond to call-ins, so they should have some easy and convenient method to record the original source. If one or two people are responsible for screening phone calls, they should ask applicants where they saw the ad. If there are several people regularly taking call-in messages, an organization might consider having a special memo pad just for such inquiries, with a "source" section indicated right on the form.

Judging the success of an ad by the total number of responses is a mistake. For example, it is better to have 10 responses, with 2 qualified applicants than thirty responses with only two qualified applicants.

◼◼ ■ EVALUATING RECRUITING EFFORTS AND SOURCES

Evaluating the success of recruiting efforts is important because evaluation helps to identify whether or not the time and money spent in recruiting is paying back in kind. General areas for proper evaluation of recruiting include:

- ■ *Quantity of Applicants.* Because the goal of a good recruiting program is to generate a large pool of applicants from which to choose, quantity is a natural place to begin evaluation. Are the job vacancies being filled?
- ■ *Quality of Applicants.* In addition to quantity, there is the issue of whether the applicant pool is appropriately qualified for the job openings. Do the applicants meet job specifications and can they perform the jobs?
- ■ *Cost Per Applicant Hired.* Cost varies depending on the position being filled, but knowing how much it costs to fill an empty position puts turnover and salary in perspective. The greatest single expense in recruiting is the cost of having a recruiting staff. The average cost (according to one source) is about $6,000 per employee.[23] Is the cost for employees from this recruiting source excessive?
- ■ *EEO/AA Goals Met.* Especially when a company is engaged in affirmative action to meet required goals for hiring protected-class individuals, the recruiting program is the key activity used to meet those goals. Is recruiting providing qualified applicants with an appropriate mix of protected-class individuals?

Specific Recruiting Evaluation Methods

Although the quantity, quality, cost, and meeting EEO goals are important general measures of the success of a recruiting program, there are some more specific evaluations that often are useful as well. Several of them are discussed next.

SELECTION RATES.   The selection rate is the percentage hired from a given group of applicants; for example, 3/10 (or 30 percent) equals the number of hired divided by the number of applicants. The numerator goes down as unemployment rates in the job market go down. The selection rate also is affected by the sophistication of the selection process. A relatively unsophisticated selection program might pick 8 out of 10 applicants for the job. Four of those might turn out to be good employees. A more valid selection process might pick 5 out of 10 applicants and only have one mediocre employee in the five.

BASE RATE.   In the example above, the base rate of good employees in the population is 4 out of 10. That is to say, if 10 people were hired at random, one would expect four of them to be good employees. A good recruiting program should be aimed at attracting the four in ten who are capable of doing well on this particular job. Realistically, no recruiting program will attract *only* the 4 in 10 who will succeed. However, efforts to make the recruiting program attract the largest proportion of those in the base rate group can make recruiting efforts more effective.

YIELD RATIOS.   Yield ratios can be calculated for each step of the recruiting/selection process, and the result is a tool for approximating the necessary size of the initial applicant pool. Figure 8–6 shows that to end up with 25 hires for the job in question, the company must begin with 300 applicants in the pool, as long as yield ratios remain the same at each step.

TIME ELAPSED.   Hiring needs occur in a time frame. If an organization needs a vice president/marketing *right now*, having to wait 4 months to find the right one presents a problem. Generally speaking, it is useful to calculate the average amount of time it takes from contact to hire for each source of applicants because some sources may be faster than others for a particular employer.[24]

LONG-RUN MEASURES.   Certain long-term measures of recruiting effectiveness are quite useful. Information on job performance, absenteeism, cost of training, and turnover by recruiting source helps to adjust future recruiting. For example, some companies find that recruiting at certain colleges or universities furnishes stable, high performers, whereas other schools provide employees who are more prone to turnover.

Recruiting Sources: Costs and Benefits

P/HR managers correctly regard recruiting as an important activity. Inability to generate enough or the appropriate type of applicants for jobs can be costly. When recruiting fails to bring in enough applicants, a common response is to raise starting salaries. This action initially may help recruiting, but often at the expense of others already in the organization. Also, the overall compensation posture in the organization may be comprised.

Cost/benefit information on each recruiting source should be calculated. Comparing the length of time applicants from each source stay in the organization with the cost of hiring from that source offers a useful perspective. Further, yield ratios from each source can help determine which sources generate the most employees.

When making a cost/benefit analysis, costs may include both *direct costs* (advertising, recruiters' salaries, travel, agency fees, telephone) and *indirect costs*

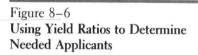

Figure 8–6
Using Yield Ratios to Determine Needed Applicants

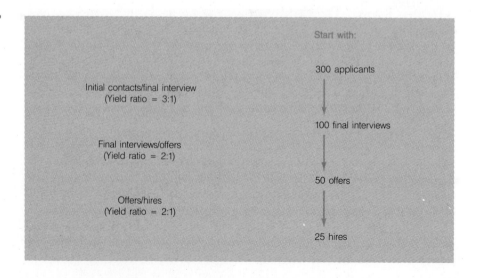

Start with:

300 applicants

Initial contacts/final interview
(Yield ratio = 3:1)

100 final interviews

Final interviews/offers
(Yield ratio = 2:1)

50 offers

Offers/hires
(Yield ratio = 2:1)

25 hires

P/HR: Practice *and* Research

Recruiting Source and Performance

Jean Kirnon and two colleagues looked at both an applicant pool and its resulting class to new hires in an effort to clarify questions about the effectiveness of recruiting sources. The job for which the applicants applied was that of insurance agent in a large insurance company. The pool was over 5,000 applicants.

As reported in *Personnel Psychology*, demographic variables, self-reported in a background questionnaire, were used to place the applicants in ethnic, age, and sex groups. The main part of the questionnaire was a validated biographical inventory used to establish the proba-

bility that a given applicant would be successful. Applicants were asked how they learned about the job: agent referral, newspaper ad, employment agency, etc. For those who were hired, productivity and longevity data were available.

When the data were analyzed, some interesting results were apparent. Referrals by agents, managers, and those who had come in on their own scored the highest on the biographical inventory measure of applicant "quality."

Both female and black applicants were more likely to have applied as a result of a newspaper ad than by re-

ferral from someone else. "Informal" sources of recruitment (referred by someone or a self-initiated visit) had higher selection rates than "formal" sources of newspaper ads, employment agencies, and school placement. However, once hired there was little difference among sources in turnover and no difference in performance on the job.

The study revealed that the greatest variation in people's ability to do the job occurs in the original applicant pool. The variability decreases as the more homogeneous group finally is chosen for employment.[25]

(involvement of operating managers, public relations, image). Benefits to consider include the following:

- Length of time from contact to hire
- Total size of applicant pool
- Proportion of acceptances to offers
- Percentage of qualified applicants in the pool

In summary, the effectiveness of various recruiting sources will vary depending on the nature of the job being filled and the time available to fill it. But unless calculated, the effectiveness may not be entirely obvious. The P/HR Research: Recruiting Sources and Performance describes one study that considered two sources of applicants.

SUMMARY

- Recruiting is the process of generating a pool of qualified applicants for organizational jobs through a series of activities.
- The applicant population is affected by recruiting method, message, applicant qualification, and administrative procedures.
- The decision to use internal or external sources should be based on the advantages and disadvantages associated with each.
- Two general groups of recruiting sources exist: internal sources and external sources. An organization must decide whether it will look primarily within

the organization or outside for new employees, or use some combination of each source.

■ Current employees, former employees, and previous applicants are the most common internal sources available.

■ External recruiting sources include schools, colleges and universities, employment agencies, temporary-help firms, labor unions, professional or trade, and media sources.

■ The costs and benefits of recruiting efforts should be audited to assess how well HR planning and recruiting responsibilities are being performed by the P/HR unit and operating managers.

REVIEW AND DISCUSSION QUESTIONS

1. Design a recruiting process for a sales representative's job.
2. How does applicant pool follow from labor force population and applicant population?
3. List two pros and cons for internal sources and for external sources of recruits.
4. Which internal sources are least likely to present an EEO problem?
5. Why do organizations use college recruiting and executive search firms?
6. Discuss three ways to evaluate recruiting efforts.

CASE   Employee Leasing

Run a business without employees? Impossible! Yet today, there are an increasing number of professionals and small businesses that do just that through employee leasing.

Although not designed only as a substitute for recruiting, employee leasing is a concept that has grown rapidly in recent years. Introduced in 1972, it is a means of solving P/HR problems, including paperwork, recruiting, and turnover for small-to medium-sized companies. The process is simple: a business signs an agreement with an employee leasing company, after which the existing staff is hired by the leasing firm and leased back to the company. The leasing firm then handles all paperwork, recruiting, and tax liabilities.

By pooling employees from many small businesses, the leasing company can usually get big company benefits for its "employees," which are not available to employees of smaller firms. There is strength in large numbers. For example, when Wayne Mohle started his three-person accounting firm in Chico, California, he used employee leasing. As a small company, he could not get insurance for one employee whose son had diabetes, or dental insurance for the others. The leasing company provides both for the employees. In addition, offices with fewer than six employees can only get maternity coverage with a large deductible; some smaller offices can't get any coverage. Many business owners originally used employee leasing because it was good for their pensions. Internal Revenue Service regulations require that pension plans be the same for all employees. The leasing company took care of pensions for employees, leaving employers free to set up more generous plans for themselves. However, tax law changes now require organizations that lease more than 20 percent of their employees to treat them as their own employees in setting up a pension plan.

The new law has forced the 300-plus leasing companies in the country to sell employers on the other services they can provide. For a fee, a small business owner or operator turns his or her staff over to the leasing company, which then writes the paychecks, pays the taxes, prepares and implements P/HR policies, and keeps all the required records.

All this service comes at a high cost. Leasing companies often charge between 4 and 6 percent of a monthly salary for their services. While leasing may save employers money on benefits, it can also increase payroll costs. For some organizations, it is well worth it. At Bartex, a Dallas construction company, the leasing company takes care of all matters—no small task in the boom-and-bust construction business. Employees receive better benefits than they would have otherwise received and are generally satisfied with "being leased." In a Small Business Administration study of twenty-one companies leasing employees, all were found to be pleased with leasing. Their workers had more benefits and paperwork had been reduced. Twelve of the twenty-one firms felt spending less time on P/HR matters was an advantage.[26]

QUESTIONS

1. What are potential disadvantages of employee leasing?
2. What evaluation techniques discussed in the chapter could be used to assess the effectiveness of employee leasing?

NOTES

1. Adapted from Christopher J. Bachler, "High-Tech Head Hunting," *Human Resource Executive*, May 1990, 49–54.
2. J. R. Redeker, "Recruitment in the '90's: Welcome to Hard Times," *Journal of Staffing and Recruitment*, Summer 1989, 47–50.
3. M. Taylor and T. Bergmann, "Organizational Recruitment Activities and the Applicants' Reactions at Different Stages of the Recruitment Process," *Personnel Psychology* 40 (1987): 261–262.
4. J. P. Wanous, "Installing a Realistic Job Preview: Ten Tough Choices," *Personnel Psychology* 42 (1989): 117–132.
5. A. S. Bagerstock, "Recruiting Options that Work," *Personnel Administrator*, March 1989, 52–55.
6. T. Hammond, "The Small Company's Secret Weapon," *INC*, December 1989, 132.
7. "Firms Draw on Job Banks When Resources Are Low," *New York Times*, January 12, 1990, 10.
8. L. M. Herren, "The Right Recruitment Technology for the 1990's," *Personnel Administrator*, April 1989, 48–52.
9. "Recruiting Data Bases," *Wall Street Journal*, December 5, 1989, 1.
10. Adapted from J. Gaugh, "Air Force Jobs Will Get Global Touch," *Omaha World Herald*, September 24, 1987, 1G.
11. "Recruiting—Hitting the Jackpot," *INC.*, March 1987, 88.
12. S. Stewman, "Demographic Models of Internal Labor Markets," *Administrative Science Quarterly* 31 (1986): 212–247.
13. "Promotions for Females," *Wall Street Journal*, October 28, 1986, 1.
14. A. Banks, "We Want You Back," *Journal of Staffing and Recruiting*, Summer 1989, 10–12.
15. B. Brophy, "Welcoming Alumni Back to the Fold," *U.S. News & World Report*, February 24, 1986, 58.
16. M. Harris and L. Fink, "A Field Study of Applicant Reactions to Employment Opportunities," *Personnel Psychology* 40 (1987): 765–783.
17. S. Lawrence, "College Recruitment: The Best Gets the Brightest," *Recruitment Today*, August 1988, 33–39.

18. M. J. McCarthy, "Temp Jobs Are Hot," *Wall Street Journal*, June 1, 1988; 25, "Professionals, Execs Join Ranks of 'Temp' Workers," *Denver Post*, September 18, 1989, 1E.

19. N. Molloy and W. Lewis, "How to Get the Most Out of Temporary Help," *Journal of Staffing and Recruitment*, Summer 1989, 40–44.

20. L. B. Korn, "Executive Change and Changing Executives," *Management Review*, August 1985, 30–33.

21. H. Ogilvie, "Getting Your Money's Worth from Executive Recruiters," *Journal of Staffing and Recruitment*, Summer 1989, 57–60.

22. J. Koch, "Applicants Tune In to Radio," *Recruitment Today*, Fall 1989, 7–12, T. Chauran, "Prime Time for Televised Recruitment," *Recruitment Today*, May/June 1989, 53, B. Hodes, "But Advertising Doesn't Work for Me," *Journal of Staffing and Recruitment*, Summer 1989, 51.

23. "A Higher Cost Per Hire," *Recruitment Today*, Fall 1989, 27.

24. T. Chauran, "Get High Mileage from Your Advertising Dollar," *Recruitment Today*, February/March 1989, 48.

25. Adapted from Jean Kirnon et. al., "The Relationship Between Recruiting Sources, Applicant Quality, and Hire Performance: An Analysis by Sex, Ethnicity, and Age," *Personnel Psychology* 42 (1989): 293–307.

26. T. Ulrich and C. Hollon, "A Guide to Employee Leasing," *Business*, October/December 1988, 44–47; S. Woolley, "Give Your Employees a Break—By Leasing Them," *Business Week*, August 14, 1989, 135; R. Schnapp, "Differentiate Between Employees and Independent Contractors," *Recruitment Today*, Fall 1989, 25.

Selecting
Human Resources

Chapter 9

After you read this chapter, you should be able to:

1. Define selection and explain several reasons for having a specialized employment unit
2. Diagram a typical selection process in sequential order
3. Discuss the reception and application form phases of the selection process
4. Identify two general and three controversial test types
5. Discuss three types of interviews and six key considerations or problems in the selection interview
6. Construct a guide for conducting a selection interview
7. Explain how legal concerns affect background investigations of applicants
8. Determine why medical examinations, including drug testing, may be useful in selection

P/HR: Today *and* Tomorrow

Selecting at Sears Telecatalog

The Sears Telecatalog Center in Fort Wayne, Indiana, is one of ten regional centers taking orders from customers who call an 800 number. Employment at each Center ranges from 1,500 to 2,500 employees, virtually all of whom work part-time as customer consultants taking orders from catalog shoppers. At each of the Telecatalog Centers, the selection process includes a mini-application blank, telephone screening interview, clerical test, math test, personal computer (PC) interview, realistic job preview, and personal in-depth interview.

Assume you are an applicant at Fort Wayne. When you stop at the center to ask about employment, you first complete a mini-application. When you give it to the receptionist, you are told that you will be contacted by phone about any part-time openings that may fit your available times.

Later, you receive a call from Steve Stephenson, personnel manager or another staff member. The personnel staff member then conducts a structured telephone screening interview. Because catalog consultants talk on the telephone constantly, your voice clarity, pace, and grammar will be evaluated during the phone interview.

Assuming you are still seen as a viable candidate, you will be scheduled for testing and further interviews. When you arrive at your scheduled time, you will fill out a more detailed application.

The next stage in the selection process is testing. Because most jobs in the center require attention to detail and make use of numbers, a math test will assess your arithmetical skills while a clerical test will identify speed and accuracy in performing routine clerical tasks.

Next is a two-part interview. First, there is a computer-assisted interview, which addresses very simple computer skills such as entering personal information and selecting responses to multiple-choice questions. This PC interview can reveal concerns you may have about working with computers, which is important because nearly all positions at telecatalog centers require computer use. Also, it has been found that applicants sometimes are more open with a computer-assisted interview because they are not attempting to impress or outguess an interviewer. Developed specifically for Sears Telecatalog, the content of the PC-interview identifies answers you give that are not consistent with telecatalog attendance, customer service, or dress policies and those that may be a problem for the specific position for which you are applying. A printout of the computer-assisted interview includes all questions and answers given, highlights inconsistent answers, and identifies interview questions for areas of follow-up or special interest to be covered in the personal interview. All applicants completing the PC interview also receive a personal interview, so the selection or rejection decisions are not made by the computer.

While waiting for the face-to-face interview, you get a realistic job preview through a video showing the center and people performing as customer consultants. After thoroughly reviewing the PC interview printout application and screening form, a supervisor or manager will greet you and give you a tour of the call floor so you can see the work setting. You then have a 30-minute interview with a supervisor or manager where greater use is made of open-end rather than closed-end questions, but there is a core group of questions asked of all applicants.

You are thanked for coming and told you will be contacted later. If you match the job requirements, you will be contacted by telephone to discuss your work schedule, pay, and benefits. If you do not match the job requirements, you will receive that notification by letter.

Gael Hanauer, center manager in Fort Wayne says, "Our selection process is designed to allow for the most efficient use of time and resources for both applicants and Sears. If people are treated with respect and see a well-organized, friendly selection process, then it communicates the kind of employer we are."[1]

"Selecting qualified employees is like putting money in the bank."

John Boudreau

The systematic efforts taken by the Sears Telecatalog Centers to select employees emphasize the importance of P/HR selection. More than anything else, personnel selection should be seen as a *matching process*. How well an employee is matched to a job affects the amount and quality of the employee's work. This matching also directly affects training and operating costs. Workers who are unable to produce the expected amount and quality of work can cost an organization a great deal of money, time, and trouble.

Proper matching also is important to the individual applying for a job. The wrong choice of a vocation or improper job placement can result in wasted time for the employee, who could be getting useful experience in a more suitable field. In addition, poor placement can result in an unhappy individual or even in dismissal if the employee simply cannot do the job.

The financial impact of selection on an organization is much more than most people realize. A study of the validity of the selection devices used by the federal government for white-collar jobs showed that if the government's selection devices were improved, increases in output of $600 million a year could be realized. Or, if productivity at the present level was acceptable, then hiring could be reduced by 20,044 persons per year.[2] By changing a selection system that relies on education and experience for one based on valid measures of cognitive ability, the federal government and many other organizations could save money and boost productivity.

■■ ■ NATURE OF SELECTION

Selection is the process of choosing individuals who have relevant qualifications to fill jobs in an organization. The selection process begins when a manager or supervisor requests an employee to fill a certain vacancy. The request is sent to the employment office or a P/HR staff member. A job description, based on job analysis, identifies the vacancy. A job specification, which may also accompany the request, describes the kind of person needed to fill the vacancy. Employment or P/HR specialists use the job description and specifications to begin the recruiting process. From the pool of applicants generated by recruiting activities, one person is selected to fill the job.

The process for selecting managers is a bit different. Managers selected from outside the organization often are chosen by upper management on the basis of reference checks, intuition, and interviews. The difficulty of specifying *exactly* the behaviors needed to be a successful manager makes management selection more difficult than selection of a good typist.[3] Middle- and upper-level management selection may be handled outside the customary selection responsibilities detailed in the following section.

Selection Responsibilities

The selection portion of the staffing process is shown in Figure 9–1. In different organizations, these activities are done to a greater or lesser degree by P/HR specialists or managers.

SELECTION
is the process of choosing individuals who have relevant qualifications to fill jobs in an organization.

Figure 9–1
Selection Responsibilities

P/HR UNIT	*MANAGERS*
■ Provides initial employment reception ■ Conducts initial screening interview ■ Administers appropriate employment tests ■ Obtains background and reference information ■ Refers top candidates to managers for final selection ■ Arranges for the employment physical examination, if used ■ Evaluates success of selection process	■ Requisition employees with specific qualifications to fill jobs ■ Participate in selection process as appropriate ■ Interview final candidates ■ Make final selection decision, subject to advice of P/HR specialists ■ Provide follow-up information on the suitability of selected individuals'

Until the impact of EEO regulations became widespread, the basic selection process was performed in a rather unplanned manner in many organizations. In some, each department screened and hired its own employees. Many managers insisted on selecting their own people because they were sure no one else could choose employees for them as well as they could. This practice still prevails in some organizations, especially in smaller ones. But the fairness and validity of these approaches often are questionable.

Other organizations maintain the traditional practice that the P/HR unit does the initial screening of the candidates, while the appropriate managers or supervisors make the final selection. As a rule, the higher the position within the organization, the greater the likelihood that the ultimate hiring decisions will be made by operating managers rather than by P/HR specialists.

The Employment Office

Selection activities may be centralized into a specialized organizational unit that is part of a P/HR department. This specialization often depends on the size of the organization. In smaller organizations, especially in those with less than 100 employees, a full-time P/HR specialist or unit may be impractical.

The employment division of the P/HR unit is generally concerned with the following operations: (1) receiving applicants, (2) interviewing applicants, (3) administering tests to applicants, (4) conducting background investigations, (5) arranging for physical examinations, (6) placing and assigning new employees, (7) coordinating follow-up of these employees, (8) termination interviewing, and (9) maintaining adequate records and reports.

Some important reasons for coordinating the employment function within such a unit are:

■ It is easier for the applicant because there is only one place to apply for a job.
■ It helps coordinate contact with outside applicant sources because issues pertaining to employment can be cleared through one central location.
■ It frees operating managers to concentrate on their operating responsibilities. This release is especially helpful during peak periods.
■ It can provide for better selection because it is done by a specialist trained in staffing.
■ The applicant is assured of more consideration for a greater variety of jobs.

| P/HR: | Practice *and* Research | Fire the Personnel Office
by Andy Rooney |

Looking for work is one of the worst things to have to do. There's nothing good about it. You don't really know how to get started, you feel like a jerk, and it's demeaning every step of the way. You'd rather no one knew you were doing it.

There aren't many of us who haven't looked for work at some time in our lives. There are 10 million Americans doing it right now, today, and I feel terrible for them.

Considering that just about everyone has looked for work, it's amazing how lousy the people with jobs are to the people without them. You'd think they'd never looked for jobs themselves. You'd think they were born with jobs.

Once a person gets to be in the position of hiring or firing someone, he or she seems to forget what it's like to be unemployed. Why is that?

The person who interviews you always acts as if he or she was president of the company. You know darn well it's just a flunky's job but you don't dare let on you know that because your application could end up in the wastebasket. When he turns away from you and walks to a desk or a file cabinet, you feel like giving him a swift kick in his smug tail.

I remember the first time I looked for work. There were hundreds of classified ads in the paper under the Help Wanted heading and I figured it was going to be easy.

Well, it didn't take me long to find out that the number of Help Wanted pages in the classified section of the newspaper has very little to do with getting a job.

First, you count out all the ads looking for nuclear physicists, registered nurses, animal trainers and, if you don't know anything about computers, you count out the ads looking for computer programmers.

As soon as you get some experience looking in the classified section, you get discouraged. You begin to read the classifieds the way you read the phone book when you're looking for one number. You know all those hundreds of listings don't mean anything. You get to spot the ones looking for door-to-door salesmen to work on commission only. There's usually one or two categories that mean anything to you. If anything is listed there, you're probably too late.

Unemployment is as much of a mystery as a cancer and almost as bad. I've never understood why there should be any real unemployment. Do we mean there isn't any work to be done anywhere in the country? Do we mean people have everything they want to eat? Everything they need by way of housing?

What we need is a president who can figure out a way to match up those 10 million unemployed with the 10 million Help Wanted ads. And when that's done, I hope everyone fires those people in the personnel office.[4]

- Selection costs may be cut because duplication of effort is avoided.
- With increased government regulations affecting the selection process, it is important that people who know about these rules handle a major part of the selection process.

Selection and Employer Image

In addition to matching qualified people to jobs, the selection process has an important public relations dimension. Discriminatory hiring practices, impolite interviewers, unnecessarily long waits, inappropriate testing procedures, and lack of follow-up letters can produce unfavorable impressions of an employer. Writer and TV commentator Andy Rooney addresses some of the image problems caused by poor P/HR office behavior in the P/HR: Practice.

Disparate Treatment

One factor that should not differ during the selection process is the treatment of the individual applicants. If some applicants are required to pass through more phases of the selection process than others, the possibility of disparate treatment exists. **Disparate treatment** occurs when employees who are members of a protected group are treated differently from other employees. For example, one small manufacturing firm required all female applicants to take a mechanical aptitude test, but male applicants were not required to take the test. Another firm checked credit references on all minority applicants but did not check these references on white applicants.

▪▪ ▪ THE SELECTION PROCESS

Most organizations take certain common steps to process applicants for jobs. Variations on this basic process depend on organizational size, nature of the jobs to be filled, number of people to be selected, and pressure of outside forces such as EEO considerations.

This process can take place in a day or over a much longer period of time. If the applicant is processed in one day, the employer usually checks references after selection. Often one or more phases of the process are omitted or the order changed, depending on the employer.

The selection process shown in Figure 9–2 is typical. The applicant, say, a young woman, comes to the organization, is directed to the employment office, and received by a receptionist. Some firms conduct a very brief interview to determine if an applicant is or is not qualified before being given an application form. In this case, the receptionist gives the woman an application form to complete. The completed application form serves as the basis for an initial screening interview. After the interview, the applicant may be told that she does not fit any position the company has available.

But if the applicant is thought to have the minimum necessary qualifications, she may go on to an in-depth interview or to testing, depending on the job sought and the cost of testing. If the person is applying for a job that requires typing, she may be given a typing test before the in-depth interview. However, if the person is applying for a job as a lab technician, she probably will have the in-depth interview before any tests are given. If the individual does not meet the minimum validated test scores or is deemed unsuitable through the in-depth interview, she likely will be rejected.

Assuming everything is satisfactory to this point, the applicant's references and background may be investigated. If the responses are favorable, the applicant may be asked to take a physical examination. Based on the results of the physical exam, the young woman will have a job or be rejected. Some organizations wait to give a physical until after the individual has accepted the job, especially if the job has no specific physical requirements.

Reception

The importance of making a favorable impression at the reception stage cannot be overemphasized. The person's attitudes about the organization, and even about the products or services it offers, can be influenced at this encounter. Whoever meets

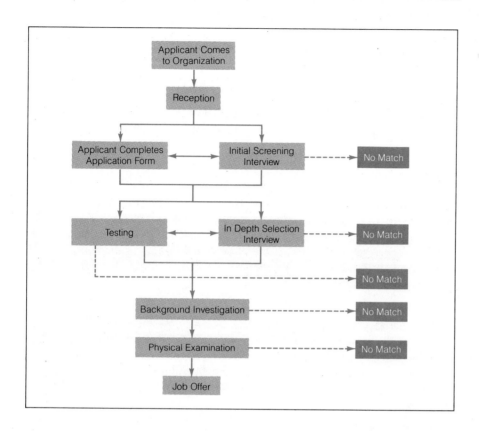

Figure 9–2
A Typical Selection Process

the applicant initially should be tactful and able to offer assistance in a courteous, friendly manner. If no jobs are available, applicants can be informed at this point. Employment possibilities must be presented honestly and clearly. At the Sears Telecatalog Center in Fort Wayne, the reception process helps to create a favorable image of the company.

Initial Screening Interview

In some cases, before the applicant has filled out the application blank for an available job, it is appropriate to have a brief interview, called an *initial screening interview*, to see if the applicant is likely to match any jobs available in the organization. Sears Telecatalog uses the telephone interview in this manner. In most organizations, this initial screening is done by the employment office or someone in the P/HR department. In other situations, the applicant may complete an application form before the short interview.

At the screening interview, the interviewer can ask questions to determine if the applicant is likely to have the ability to perform available jobs. Typical questions might concern job interests, location desired, pay expectations, and availability for work. One firm that hires security guards and armored car drivers uses the screening interview to verify if an applicant meets the minimum qualifications for the job. These questions ask if the applicant has a valid driver's license, has been free of any criminal conviction in the past five years, and has used a pistol. Because these items and others are required minimum standards, any applicant who cannot answer them according to the requirements is not given an application form to complete.

COMPUTER AND ELECTRONIC INTERVIEWS.   A number of firms are using computerized or other electronic interviewing techniques to conduct the initial screening interview. The PC interview used by Sears Telecatalog is one example. Another example comes from a major hotel chain at which applicants for hotel front-desk jobs view a videotape of certain customers service situations, and then indicate how they believe each situation should be handled. Based on those responses, the applicants are evaluated to determine if they are acceptable candidates for employment.

Application Forms

Application forms are a widely used selection device. Properly prepared, like the one in Figure 9–3, the application form serves four purposes: (1) It is a record of the applicant's desire to obtain a position. (2) It provides the interviewer with a profile of the applicant that can be used in the interview. (3) It is a basic personnel record for applicants who become employees. (4) It can be used for research on the effectiveness of the selection process.

EEO CONSIDERATIONS AND APPLICATION FORMS.   Although application forms may not usually be thought of as "tests," the Uniform Guidelines and court decisions define them as employment tests. Consequently, the data requested on application forms must conform to EEO guidelines and be valid predictors of job-related behaviors.[5] Questions of doubtful legality that typically are found on application forms are:[6]

- Marital status
- Height/weight
- Number and ages of dependents
- Information on spouse
- Date of high school graduation
- Who to contact in case of emergency and relationship to employee

The reason for concern about such questions is that they can have adverse impact on some protected groups. For example, the question about dependents can be used to pinpoint women with small children who may not be hired because of a manger's perception that they will not be as dependable as those without small children. Or, the high school graduation date gives a close identification of a person's age, which could be used to discriminate against individuals over age 40.

One interesting point to remember is that many employers must collect data on the race and sex of those who apply to fulfill requirements for reporting to EEOC, but the application blank cannot contain these items. As discussed in Chapter 6, the solution picked by a growing number of employers is one in which the applicant provides EEOC reporting data on a separate form. This form is then filed separately and not used in any other P/HR selection activities.

USING APPLICATION FORMS.   Many employers use only one application form, but this practice may not target the application form to specific occupational groups. For example, a hospital might need one form for nurses and medical technicians, another for clerical and office employees, another for managers and supervisors, and one for support persons in housekeeping and food service areas.

The information received on application forms or resumes may not always be completely accurate. This problem is discussed in greater detail later but an

Figure 9–3
Sample Application Form

THE C COMPANY

AN EQUAL OPPORTUNITY EMPLOYER

PLEASE PRINT ALL INFORMATION

Name

Present Address (Number, Street, City, State and ZIP Code)	Telephone Number	Alternate Phone Number

Relatives working for The C Company (Name, relationship and department in which they work)

Type of work preferred	Are you willing to work:		
		YES NO	Work skills you possess
Work location preferred	Over 40 hours per week?	☐ ☐	
	Irregular shifts?	☐ ☐	Typing ___ WPM
	Nights?	☐ ☐	Shorthand ___ WPM
	Saturdays or Sundays?	☐ ☐	Keypunch ___ SPH
Would you accept any other positions?	Holidays?	☐ ☐	License(s) _____
☐ YES ☐ NO	Travel?	☐ ☐	Other _____
Date Available for Employment			_____

ADDITIONAL WORK SKILLS

Circle highest grade completed:

High School _____   9   10   11   12   Graduated? ☐ YES ☐ NO
College _____   13   14   15   16   Degree Received ____ Major ____
Graduate School _____   Other schools (Vocational, Military, etc.) _____

Have you ever been employed by The C Company before?	☐ YES ☐ NO

If Yes, Position	From	To	Reason for Leaving
Department	Supervisor Name & Title		Location

IF YOU ARE NOT A U.S. CITIZEN, DOES YOUR VISA OR IMMIGRATION STATUS PERMIT LAWFUL EMPLOYMENT? ☐ YES ☐ NO ☐ N/A	IF EMPLOYED, CAN PROOF OF CITIZENSHIP, VISA OR ALIENT REGISTRATION NUMBER BE PROVIDED? ☐ YES ☐ NO ☐ N/A

List current and previous employers: (List most current first, next most current second, etc.)
May we contact your current employer? ☐ YES ☐ NO

Position	Employer	Location	
Supervisor	Telephone Number	Dates Worked From To	Pay Rate $

Position	Employer	Location	
Supervisor	Telephone Number	Dates Worked From To	Pay Rate $

Position	Employer	Location	
Supervisor	Telephone Number	Dates Worked From To	Pay Rate $

Have you been convicted of a crime within the last seven years or have you been imprisoned for the conviction of a crime within the last seven years?   ☐ YES ☐ NO   The existence of a record of convictions for criminal offenses is not considered an automatic bar to employment.

Date of conviction _____ Describe Circumstances _____

Military service? ☐ YES ☐ NO	If Yes, From To	Branch of Service	MOS/Duties
Highest Rank Obtained	Reserve status ☐ NATIONAL GUARD ☐ ACTIVE RESERVE ☐ NONE		

important point must be made here. In an attempt to correct inaccuracies, many application forms carry a statement that the applicant is required to sign, at the bottom of the form. In effect, the statement reads: "I realize that falsification of this record is grounds for dismissal if I am hired." Whether this phrase reduces inaccurate information on the application form is not known. However, "misrepresentation" of facts has been used by employers to terminate someone who has been hired.

Application forms traditionally have asked for references and requested that the applicant give permission to contact them. Rather than asking for personal or general references, it may be more useful to request the names of previous supervisors on the application form.

WEIGHTED APPLICATION FORMS.   One way employers can make the application form more job-related is by developing a weighted application blank. A job analysis is used to determine ability, skills, and behavioral characteristics needed for the job. Then weights, or numeric values, are placed on different responses to application blank items, and the responses of an applicant are scored and totalled.[7]

There are several problems associated with weighted application forms. One difficulty is the time and effort required to develop such a form. For many small employers and for jobs that do not require numerous employees, the cost of developing the weights can be prohibitive. Also, the blank must be updated every few years to ensure that the factors previously identified are still valid predictors of job success. Finally, many items identified by earlier studies as good predictors of success cannot be asked now because of EEO restrictions. For example, asking about family responsibilities (marital status, number of children) and age is likely to cause difficulty because the job-relatedness of those inquiries is doubtful. Consequently, relatively few employers use weighted application blanks. It appears that weighted application blanks are more attractive in theory than in practice.

RESUMES.   One of the most common methods applicants use to provide background information is the resume. Resumes, also called vitae (or *curriculum vitae*) by some, vary in style and length. Technically, a resume used in place of an application form must be treated by an employer as if it were an application form for EEO purposes. Consequently, even though an applicant may furnish some "illegal information" voluntarily on a resume, the employer should not use that information during the selection process. Because resumes contain only information applicants want to present, some employers require that all who submit resumes complete an application form as well, so similar information will be available on all applicants. Individuals who mail in resumes are sent thank-you letters and blank applications forms to be completed and returned. Appendix D "Starting A Career" contains some suggestions on resume preparation and other areas.

Immigration Requirements

In 1986, Congress passed the Immigration Reform and Control Act (IRCA) requiring that within 24 hours of hiring, an employer must determine whether a job applicant is a U.S. citizen, registered alien, or illegal alien. Figure 9–4 shows the I-9 form that employers must use to identify the status of potential employees. Many employers have applicants complete the I-9 form during the application process. Others have individuals submit the documents on their first day of em-

Figure 9–4
Employment Eligibility Verification Form I-9

EMPLOYMENT ELIGIBILITY VERIFICATION (Form I-9)

1 **EMPLOYEE INFORMATION AND VERIFICATION:** (To be completed and signed by employee.)

Name: (Print or Type) Last	First	Middle	Birth Name
Address: Street Name and Number	City	State	ZIP Code
Date of Birth (Month/Day/Year)		Social Security Number	

I attest, under penalty of perjury, that I am (check a box):

☐ 1. A citizen or national of the United States.

☐ 2. An alien lawfully admitted for permanent residence (Alien Number A _____) .

☐ 3. An alien authorized by the Immigration and Naturalization Service to work in the United States (Alien Number A _____ .
or Admission Number _____ ,   expiration of employment authorization, if any _____) .

I attest, under penalty of perjury, the documents that I have presented as evidence of identity and employment eligibility are genuine and relate to me. I am aware that federal law provides for imprisonment and/or fine for any false statements or use of false documents in connection with this certificate.

Signature	Date (Month/Day/Year)

PREPARER/TRANSLATOR CERTIFICATION (To be completed if prepared by person other than the employee). I attest, under penalty of perjury, that the above was prepared by me at the request of the named individual and is based on all information of which I have any knowledge.

Signature	Name (Print or Type)		
Address (Street Name and Number)	City	State	Zip Code

2 **EMPLOYER REVIEW AND VERIFICATION:** (To be completed and signed by employer.)

Instructions:

Examine one document from List A and check the appropriate box, **OR** examine one document from List B **and** one from List C and check the appropriate boxes. Provide the **Document Identification Number** and **Expiration Date** for the document checked.

List A Documents that Establish Identity and Employment Eligibility	List B Documents that Establish Identity	**and**	List C Documents that Establish Employment Eligibility
☐ 1. United States Passport	☐ 1. A State-issued driver's license or a State-issued I.D. card with a photograph, or information, including name, sex, date of birth, height, weight, and color of eyes. (Specify State)_____)		☐ 1. Original Social Security Number Card (other than a card stating it is not valid for employment)
☐ 2. Certificate of United States Citizenship			☐ 2. A birth certificate issued by State, county, or municipal authority bearing a seal or other certification
☐ 3. Certificate of Naturalization	☐ 2. U.S. Military Card		
☐ 4. Unexpired foreign passport with attached Employment Authorization	☐ 3. Other (Specify document and issuing authority) _____		☐ 3. Unexpired INS Employment Authorization Specify form # _____
☐ 5. Alien Registration Card with photograph			
Document Identification # _____	**Document Identification** # _____		**Document Identification** # _____
Expiration Date (if any) _____	**Expiration Date (if any)** _____		**Expiration Date (if any)** _____

CERTIFICATION: I attest, under penalty of perjury, that I have examined the documents presented by the above individual, that they appear to be genuine and to relate to the individual named, and that the individual, to the best of my knowledge, is eligible to work in the United States.

Signature	Name (Print or Type)	Title
Employer Name	Address	Date

Form I-9 (05/07/87)
OMB No. 1115-0136

U.S. Department of Justice
Immigration and Naturalization Service

ployment. Employers *do* have a responsibility to make sure that the documents noted on the bottom of the I-9 form, such as U.S. passport, birth certificate, original Social Security cards, driver's license, or others that are submitted by new employees, "reasonably appear on their face to be genuine."[8]

■ ■ SELECTION TESTING

Many people claim that formal tests can be of great benefit in the selection process when properly used and administered. Considerable evidence supports this claim. Because of EEO concerns, many employers reduced or eliminated the use of tests beginning in the early 1970s. A survey done in the early 1980s revealed that 112 of 437 organizations surveyed had discontinued or changed their selection process in the preceding five years.[9] But test usage appears to be increasing again. A 1988 survey of 167 firms found that 84 percent of the responding employers used tests.[10]

Choosing and Using Selection Tests

The most important factor to consider when choosing and using any employment test is the *validity* of the test. As emphasized in Chapters 5 and 6 on EEO regulations, unless the test measures what it is supposed to measure (validity) on a consistent basis (reliability), it should not be used. Recently, the growth in testing has focused on the need for properly done validity studies, if tests are to be used as part of a selection process. The complexity of designing a validity study includes issues such as choosing predictive or concurrent validity, as we have already seen. No specific design is considered appropriate for all purposes.[11]

Interpreting test results is not always straightforward either, even beginning with a valid test. Individuals trained in testing and test interpretation should be involved in establishing and maintaining a testing system. Finally, the role of tests in the overall selection process must be kept in perspective. Tests represent only one possible data source.

According to the Uniform Guidelines, any employment requirement is a "test." The focus in this section is on formal tests. As Figure 9–5 shows, a variety of types of tests are used. Notice that most of them focus on specific job-related aptitudes and skills. Some are paper-and-pencil tests (such as a math test), others are motor skill tests, and still others use machines (polygraphs, for instance). Some employers purchase prepared tests, whereas others develop their own. The following discussion highlights several types of formal tests that may be used for selection purposes.

Ability and Aptitude Tests

Ability tests assess the skills that individuals have already learned. *Aptitude tests* are used to measure general ability to learn or acquire a skill. The typing tests given at many firms to secretarial applicants are examples of a commonly used abilities test. Other widely used tests include ones testing mechanical abilities and manual dexterity.

Another type of abilities test used at many organizations simulates job tasks. These *work sample tests*, which require an applicant to perform part of the job being applied for, are especially useful. The 40-yard dashes and blocking drills used in pro football training camps are examples. Requiring a person applying for a truck driver's job to back a truck to a loading dock is another. If you have ever

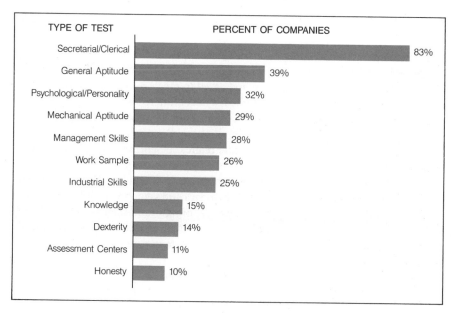

TYPE OF TEST	PERCENT OF COMPANIES	
Secretarial/Clerical		83%
General Aptitude		39%
Psychological/Personality		32%
Mechanical Aptitude		29%
Management Skills		28%
Work Sample		26%
Industrial Skills		25%
Knowledge		15%
Dexterity		14%
Assessment Centers		11%
Honesty		10%

Figure 9–5
Tests used for Selection (1988)

SOURCE: "Most Employers Test New Job Candidates, ASPA Survey Shows," *Resource*, June 1988, 2.

rented a trailer and tried to back your car and trailer into a driveway, you can understand why such proficiency would be important to test.

Mental ability and aptitude tests measure reasoning capabilities of applicants. Some of the abilities tested include spatial orientation, comprehension and retention span, and general and conceptual reasoning, among others. The General Aptitude Test Battery (GATB) discussed in Chapter 5 is a widely used test of this type. The math test used at the Sears Telecatalog Centers is another example.

General intelligence tests measure general knowledge and reasoning aptitudes and abilities. These intelligence tests were more widely used before the *Griggs v. Duke Power* decision in 1971 (see Chapter 5). However, some firms still use general intelligence tests, such as the 12-minute *Wonderlic Personnel Test* or the *Wechsler Adult Intelligence Scale*. It is essential that these tests be validated as job-related to the specific jobs for which individuals are being selected.

ASSESSMENT CENTERS AND SELECTION.   An assessment center is not necessarily a place, but a selection and development device composed of a series of evaluative exercises and tests. In one assessment center, candidates go through a comprehensive interview, pencil-and-paper test, individual and group simulation, and work exercises. The candidates' performances are then evaluated by a panel of trained raters. It is crucial to any assessment center that the tests and exercises reflect the job content and type of problems faced on the jobs for which individuals are being screened.[12]

A number of state and local governments use the assessment center when selecting department or division heads, because potential charges of political favoritism could be leveled if they used a less comprehensive selection process. One major city has used the assessment center to select its director of public works, fire chief, city engineer, and employee relations administrator.

Assessment centers are especially useful in determining promotable employees and in helping to develop them. These issues are discussed in Chapter 11.

General Personality and Psychological Tests

Some tests attempt to measure personality characteristics. The legendary Rorschach "inkblot" test and the Thematic Apperception Test (TAT) are examples. In the TAT, an applicant is shown a picture and asked to create a story about the picture. A picture might show an executive sitting at a desk cluttered with papers, apparently gazing at a photograph of family members on the desk. Some of the most well-known personality tests include the Minnesota Multiphasic Personality Inventory (MMPI), the Predictive Index, the Edwards Personal Preference Schedule, and the California Personality Inventory.

The most frequently used personality test in America and probably the world, the MMPI has been translated into 100 languages and taken by millions of people. Here and abroad it figures heavily in hiring and promotion of policemen, firemen, airline pilots, and those who work in sensitive areas of nuclear power plants. A revised version of the MMPI was developed in 1989 to update the test and eliminate obsolete language.[13]

Some of the questions asked on the MMPI include the following:[14]

- Have you ever indulged in unusual sex practices?
- Does life give you a raw deal?
- Do you like to go to parties and other affairs where there is lots of loud fun?
- Do you get all the sympathy you should?

Such tests are difficult to validate as job-related for many jobs. They are the least-preferred tests from a legal standpoint in many situations.[15] Due to their nebulous definitions of personality and the difficulties of tying specific personality characteristics to specific job requirements, general psychological and personality tests represent the shakiest type of tests used for selection purposes. After all, being an extrovert or an introvert may have little to do with successful performance of individuals who become internal accountants, welders, or shipping room clerks. Therefore, employers should use personality tests only when validated as useful in identifying specific job-related factors.

Controversial Psychological Tests

Several types of tests that are used by employers for pre-employment screening have generated controversy. Two of those, drug testing and genetic testing, are explored later in the chapter. The three tests discussed next are polygraphs, honesty tests, and graphoanalysis.

POLYGRAPH.   The polygraph, more generally and incorrectly referred to as the "lie detector," is a mechanical device that measures a person's galvanic skin response, heart rate, and breathing rate. The theory behind the polygraph is detection through the body's physiological response to questions. If a person answers incorrectly, the body will "reveal" the falsification through the polygraph's recording mechanisms.

Before 1989, thousands of employers used polygraph results to screen potential employees. The biggest users were in service industries such as retail, fast food, and health care. The purpose of polygraph use was to reduce employee theft. Individuals whose answers revealed a potential pattern of dishonesty were eliminated from employment consideration. However, serious questions were raised about polygraph use in employment settings, especially about its constitutionality and the invasion of the privacy of those tested.

As a result of those concerns, Congress passed the Employee Polygraph Protection Act of 1988. Effective in 1989, the act bars polygraph use for pre-employment screening purposes by most employers. However, federal, state, and local governmental agencies are exempt from the act. Also exempted from the law are certain private-sector employers such as security companies and pharmaceutical companies. The act does allow employers to continue to use polygraphs as part of an internal investigation for theft or losses. But the polygraph must be administered voluntarily and the employee can end the test at any time. More on the use of polygraphs for internal investigations is contained in Chapter 17.

HONESTY TESTS.   Another type of controversial test is one that purports to measure employee honesty. The Reid Report and the Stanton Survey are the two most widely used of these pencil-and-paper tests. Individuals who take honesty tests answer yes or no to a list of questions. Sample questions include:[16]

■ Would you tell your boss if you know of another employee stealing from the company?
■ Is it all right to borrow company equipment to use at home if the property is always returned?
■ Have you ever told a lie?
■ Have you ever wished you were physically more attractive?

Firms use honesty tests to help reduce losses due to employee theft. With pre-employment polygraph testing no longer allowed, a growing number of firms have turned to such tests. In addition to being able to screen out potentially dishonest individuals, these firms believe that giving honesty tests sends a message to applicants and employees alike that dishonesty will not be tolerated.[17]

Concerns about the validity of honesty tests continue to be raised, and many firms using them do not do validation studies on their experiences.[18] Instead, they rely on the general validation results given by the test developers, even though that practice is not consistent with the Uniform Selection Guidelines. A review of research on the validity of honesty tests by independent researchers found that honesty tests may be useful as a broad screening device for organizations, but the tests may not be as good at predicting that a single individual will steal.[19] Also, the use of these tests can have a negative public relations impact on applicants. A final concern is the invasion of individual privacy through the type of questions asked.

GRAPHOANALYSIS (HANDWRITING ANALYSIS).   A third controversial type of test is the use of *graphology*, which is an analysis of an individual's handwriting in order to identify personality characteristics. Such items as how people dot an "i," cross a "t," or write with a left or right slant, and the size and boldness of the letters they form supposedly tell graphologists about individuals' personalities and their suitability for employment.

GRAPHOLOGY is an analysis of an individual's handwriting in order to identify personality characteristics.

With the restrictions on polygraph tests, a number of companies, including some large corporations, are turning to graphoanalysis to screen employees. One graphoanalysis firm has over 200 corporate clients, including Renault USA. The cost of an analysis ranges from $175 to $500, and includes an examination of about 300 personality traits.[20]

The major problem with such a test is that so much depends on the graphologist who interprets the results. Also, as with many personality tests, an employer might have difficulty identifying the relationship between a series of personality traits and job performance. Formal scientific evaluations of graphology are not easily found. It is an accepted criminal investigation tool, but its value as a personality predictor is much more controversial. In fact, many graphologists recommend that graphoanalysis results should be used as an additional source of information about applicants, not as a screening device by itself.[21]

SELECTION INTERVIEWING

A general selection interview is designed to probe areas of interest to the interviewer in order to determine how well the applicant will match the needs of the organization. This in-depth interview is designed to integrate all the information from application forms, tests, and reference checks so that a selection decision can be made. Because of the integration required and the desirability of face-to-face contact, the interview is the most important phase of the selection process in many situations. Conflicting information may have emerged from the tests, application forms, or references. As a result, the interviewer must obtain as much pertinent information about the applicant as possible during the limited interview time, evaluate this information against job standards, and make a decision.

The interview is not an especially valid predictor of job performance, but it has high "face validity"; that is, employers like it and it seems to be valid to them. Virtually no employers are likely to hire individuals without interviewing them.

Validity and Reliability of the Interview

Research on employment interviewing indicates that the procedure has low to moderate validity. If the interview is unstructured, as many interviews are, then the interview seems to have low validity. If the interview has a consistent set of questions asked of all applicants, then the validity increases.[22] One research review of a number of studies found that the interview does have some validity in being able to predict the job performance of those interviewed.[23]

Some interviewers may be better than others at selecting individuals who will perform better. Studies have found that there is very high *intra*rater (the same interviewer) reliability but only moderate-to-low *inter*rater (different interviewers) reliability.[24] Many factors affect the accuracy of the interview, from stereotypes carried by interviewers to the order in which interviewees are seen. The important

FRANK AND ERNEST® by Bob Thaves

point to remember is that the validity of the interview depends on the type of interview used and the capabilities of the individual interviewers.

Equal Employment and Interviewing

The interview, like a pencil-and-paper test and an application form, is a type of predictor and must meet the standards of job-relatedness and nondiscrimination. Some court decisions and EEOC rulings have attacked the interviewing practices of some organizations as discriminatory.

An interviewer making hiring recommendations must be able to identify the factors that shaped the decision. If that decision is challenged, the organization must be able to show justification. Everything written or said can be probed for evidence in a lawsuit. Lawyers recommend the following to minimize EEO concerns with interviewing.[25]

- Identify objective criteria related to the job to be looked for in the interview.
- Put criteria in writing.
- Provide multiple levels of review for difficult or controversial decisions.

The interview that most meets these recommendations is the structured interview, one of the major types of interviews.

Types of Interviews

There are three special types of interviews: *structured interviews*, *nondirective interviews*, and *stress interviews*. Each type is discussed next.

STRUCTURED INTERVIEW. The purpose of the **structured interview** is to generate data on applicants through the use of some standardized questions. In contrast, if an interviewer asks one applicant a question and does not ask the same question of another applicant, the interviewer has no similar basis for evaluating each of the applicants.

This type of interview also allows an interviewer to prepare job-related questions in advance, and then complete a standardized interviewee evaluation form. Completion of such a form provides documentation if anyone, including an EEO enforcement body, should question why one applicant was selected over another.[26] Sample questions that might be asked of an applicant for a production maintenance management opening are:

- Tell me about how you trained workers for their job.
- How can you tell how much work you and the maintenance crew will have to do during a day?
- What effect does the production schedule of the plant have on what a mechanic ought to repair first?
- How do you know what the needs of the plant are at any given time and what mechanics ought to be doing?
- How did you or would you go about planning a preventive maintenance program in the plant.[27]

As you can see, the structured interview is almost like an oral questionnaire and offers greater consistency and accuracy than some other kinds of interviews. The structured interview is especially useful in the initial screening because of the large

STRUCTURED INTERVIEW
uses a set of standardized questions that are asked all job applicants.

number of applicants in this step of the selection process. Obviously, it is less flexible than more traditional interview formats, and therefore may be less appropriate for second or later interviews.

Even though a series of patterned questions are asked, the structured interview does not have to be rigid. The predetermined questions should be asked in a logical manner, but the interviewer can avoid reading the questions word for word down the list. The applicant should be allowed adequate opportunity to explain answers clearly. The interviewer should probe until he or she fully understand the applicant's response.

Research on interviews consistently has found the structured interview to be more reliable and valid than other approaches.[28] The format for the interview ensures that the same interviewer has similar information on each candidate, so there is higher intrarater reliability. Also, the fact that several interviewers ask the same base of questions of applicants has led to better interrater reliability.[29]

NONDIRECTIVE INTERVIEW
uses general questions, from which other questions are developed.

NONDIRECTIVE INTERVIEW.   The **nondirective interview** is used mainly in psychological counseling, but it is also widely used in selection. The interviewer asks general questions designed to prompt the applicant to discuss herself or himself. The interviewer then picks up on an idea in the applicant's response to one question to shape the next question. For example, if the applicant says, "One aspect that I enjoyed in my last job was my supervisor," the interviewer might ask, "What type of supervisor do you most enjoy working with?"

Difficulties with a nondirective interview include keeping it job-related and obtaining comparable data on each applicant. Many nondirective interviews are only semiorganized; the result is a combination of general and specific questions that are asked in no set order.

Some managers may indicate a preference for the nondirective interview as a way to hide a lack of preparation for the interview. Also, not having the same data from each applicant, a manager may hire one applicant instead of another because of "general attractiveness" or "good vibes." Not restricted to physical appearance, the idea of "general attractiveness" is often a result of an interviewer's subjective perceptions and biases, which may not bear any direct relationship to an applicant's ability to perform the job. Although these biases can enter into a structured interview also, they are more likely to appear in the nondirective interview.

STRESS INTERVIEW
is used to create pressure and stress on an applicant to see how the person responds.

STRESS INTERVIEW.   The **stress interview** is a special type of interview designed to create anxiety and put pressure on the applicant to see how the person responds. In the stress interview, the interviewer assumes an extremely aggressive and insulting posture. Those who use this approach often justify its use with individuals who will encounter high degrees of stress on the job, such as a consumer complaint clerk in a department store or an air traffic controller.

The stress interview is a "high-risk" approach. The typical applicant is already somewhat anxious in any interview. The stress interview can easily generate a very poor image of the interviewer and the employer and create resistance by applicants who might be offered jobs.

Interviewing Basics

Many people think the ability to interview is an innate talent, but this contention is difficult to support. Just because someone is personable and likes to talk, there is no guarantee that the person will be a good interviewer. Interviewing skills are developed through training and through following some of the outlined suggestions.

PLANNING THE INTERVIEW.   Effective interviews do not just happen; they are planned. Preinterview planning is essential to a well-conducted in-depth selection interview. This planning begins with selecting the time and place for the interview.[30] Sufficient time should be allotted so that neither the interviewer nor interviewee feel rushed. Also, a private location is important so that both parties can concentrate on the interview content. The interviewer should review the application form and order data for completeness and accuracy before beginning the interview, and also should make notes to identify specific areas for questioning the applicant about during the interview.

CONTROL.   An important aspect of the interview is control. If the interviewer does not control the interview, the applicant usually will. Control includes knowing in advance what information must be collected, systematically collecting it, and stopping when everything needed is collected.

Having control of the interview does not mean doing a lot of talking. The interviewer should talk no more than about 25 percent of the time in an in-depth interview. If the interviewer talks more than that, the interviewer is being interviewed.

REALISTIC JOB PREVIEW.   Although the interviewer should limit the amount of time he or she spends talking, a key part of the interview is to offer information about the job for which the interviewee is applying. One approach that has been widely researched is the ***realistic job preview (RJP).*** An RJP is the process through which an interviewer provides a job applicant with an accurate picture of a job.

The purpose of an RJP is to inform job candidates of the "organizational realities" of a job so that they can more accurately evaluate their own job expectations. By presenting applicants with a clear picture of the job, the organization hopes to reduce employee disenchantment or unrealistic expectations, and thereby to experience less turnover and employee dissatisfaction. A review of research on RJPs found that they tend to result in applicants having lower job expectations.[31] If an RJP is to be used, care must be taken when it is developed and implemented into the selection process.[32]

> A REALISTIC JOB PREVIEW (RJP) is the process through which an interviewer provides a job applicant with an accurate picture of a job.

Questioning Techniques

The questioning techniques an interviewer uses can and do significantly affect the type and quality of the information obtained. Some specific suggestions follow.

GOOD QUESTIONS.   Many questions an interviewer asks assume that the past is the best predictor of the future, and it usually is. An interviewer is less likely to have difficulty when questioning the applicant's demonstrated past performance than when asking vague questions about the future.

Some types of questions provide more meaningful answers than others. Good interviewing technique depends on the use of open-ended questions directed toward a particular goal. An open-ended question is one that cannot be answered yes or no. *Who, what, when, why, tell me, how, which* are all good ways to begin questions that will produce longer and more informative answers. "What was your attendance record on your last job?" is a better question than "Did you have good attendance on your last job?" because the latter question can be answered simply, "Yes."

POOR QUESTIONS.   Certain kinds of questions should be avoided:

1. *Questions that rarely produce a true answer:* An example is "How did you get along with your co-workers?" This question is almost inevitably going to be answered, "Just fine."
2. *Leading questions:* A leading question is one in which the answer is obvious from the way in which the question is asked. For example, "You do like to talk to people, don't you?" Answer: "Of course."
3. *Illegal questions:* Questions that involve race, creed, sex, national origin, marital status, number of children, and so on are illegal. They are also just as inappropriate in the interview as they are on the application form.
4. *Obvious questions:* An obvious question is one for which the interviewer already has the answer, and the applicant knows it. Questions already answered on the application blank should be probed, not reasked. If an interviewer asks, "What high school did you attend?" Joyce Sauer is likely to answer, "As I wrote on my application form, South High School in Caveton." Instead, ask questions that probe the information given: "What were your favorite subjects at South High, and why?"
5. *Questions that are not job-related:* All questions asked should be directly related to the job for which the applicant has applied. Some people believe discussion about the weather, sports, or politics helps a candidate relax and become at ease. However, those questions consume interview time that could be more appropriately used in other ways. Also, many times the interviewee does not relax and the interviewer may not listen to the responses because he or she is using the "chit-chat" time to review the candidate's application form or to otherwise make up for the interviewer's lack of planning and preparation.

There are certain question areas that an interviewer probably should minimize. These areas can be referred to as the "egad" factors, which are questions the interviewer asks about the applicant's expectations, goals, aspirations, and desires. Although the answers to an egad question may be meaningful, usually the applicant will respond with a prepared "pat" answer. For example, in answer to the question, "What are your aspirations?" the college graduate will often respond that he or she wants to become a company vice president. The person settles for vice president instead of president in order not to appear egotistical. Yet it is considered culturally desirable in our society to demonstrate a certain amount of ambition, and the vice presidential level appears to be appropriate.

LISTENING RESPONSES.   The good interview avoids listening responses such as nodding, pausing, casual remarks, echoing, and mirroring. Listening responses are an essential part of everyday, normal conversation. Although they are necessary to maintain rapport, these responses may unintentionally provide feedback to the applicant. Applicants may try to please the interviewer and look to the interviewer's listening responses for cues. Even though the listening responses may be subtle, they do provide information to the applicant.

Problems in the Interview

There are a number of pitfalls that interviewers should avoid. Operating managers and supervisors most often use poor interviewing techniques because they do not

| P/HR: Practice *and* Research | The Effects of Pre-interview Impressions by Interviewers |

The degree to which an interviewer's pre-interview impressions of an applicant affect how the subsequent interview is conducted and how the applicant is evaluated was the subject of a research study conducted by Amanda Phillips and Robert Dipboye. As reported in the *Journal of Applied Psychology*, the researchers were able to conduct their study in nineteen branch offices of a large financial services company. Data were gather on 34 interviewers and 164 applicants. The applicants were candidates for employment as account executives at the financial firm, a job in which various financial products such as stocks, bonds, and mutual funds are sold to retail clients.

To conduct the study, each of the interviewers was given three questionnaires related to each applicant. Two of the questionnaires were to be filled out by the interviewers, one before and one after the interview, and one questionnaire by each of the applicants after the interview. The first questionnaire completed by interviewers was a pre-interview impression survey, which required interviewers to evaluate applicants based on the application blank data submitted by each applicant. On this instrument interviewers were asked to rate the following:

1. The applicant's qualifications for the job.
2. How well the applicant would perform on exercises that simulated tasks performed by account executives.
3. How confident the interviewer was about whether the applicant would be hired.

Following the interview, each interviewer and applicant filled out a post-interview instrument. The interviewers were asked to evaluate the applicants' interview performances, how well the performances truly reflected his/her qualifications, and how confident they were about whether the applicant ultimately would be hired. The applicants were asked to answer questions about how the interviewer would evaluate their job qualifications, the skills the interviewer exhibited during the interview, how appealing the account executive job and the company were, and how the interviewer conducted the interview.

The researchers analyzed the questionnaire responses from 118 applicants and all 34 interviewers. Some of the results revealed the following:

- The more favorable the interviewers' premature impressions, the more time during the interviews was spent trying to recruit the applicant for the company.
- The more favorable the interviewers' views of applicant's qualifications before the interview, the greater the likelihood that the applicant was seen as answering interviewer questions well.
- The more favorable the interviewers' pre-interview impressions of the applicant, the more positive their post-interview evaluations of the applicants were.

Phillips and Dipboye concluded that the pre-interview impressions of interviewers can and do predict the subsequent conduct and evaluation of selection interviewees. In discussing the results of their study, they urged that in order to improve the selection interview process, it is important that interviewers be given tools and training on how to evaluate applicants, so that their pre-interview impressions can be based on more solid and objective factors.[33]

interview often and have not been trained to interview. Some common problems encountered in the interview are highlighted next.

SNAP JUDGMENTS. Ideally, the interviewer should collect *all* the information possible on an applicant before making a judgment. Reserving judgment is much easier to recommend than to do because it is difficult not to form an early impression. Too often, interviewers form an early impression and spend the balance of the interview looking for evidence to support it. This impression may be based on a review of an individual's application blank or on more subjective factors such as dress or appearance. Consequently, many interviewers make a decision within the first four or five minutes on the job suitability of applicants. The P/HR Research discusses a study on the effects of pre-interview judgements on interviewing.

NEGATIVE EMPHASIS.   Research studies show that unfavorable information about an applicant is the biggest factor considered in interviewers' decisions about overall suitability. Unfavorable information is given roughly twice the weight of favorable information. It has been found that a single negative characteristic may bar an individual from being accepted, whereas no amount of positive characteristics will guarantee a candidate's acceptance.

HALO EFFECT.   Interviewers should try to avoid the "halo effect," which occurs when an interviewer allows a prominent characteristic to overshadow other evidence. The halo effect is present if an interviewer lets a candidate's accomplishments in athletics overshadow other aspects, which leads the interviewer to hire the applicant because "athletes make good salespeople." "Devil's horns" (a reverse halo effect), such as an unattractive physical appearance or a low grade point average, may affect an interviewer as well.

BIASES.   An interviewer must be able to recognize his/her personal biases. For example, studies on the interview process indicate that women are rated lower by both female and male interviewers.[35] Other studies have found that interviewers tend to favor or select people who are perceived to be similar to the interviewer. This similarity can be on age, race, sex, previous work experiences, personal background, or other factors. As the work force demographics shift and become more diverse, interviewers will have to be even more aware of this "similarity bias."

The selection of an applicant who falls below standards or the rejection of an applicant who meets standards is an indication that personal bias has influenced a selection decision. An interviewer should be honest and write down the reasons for selecting a particular applicant. The solution to the problem of bias lies not in claiming that a person has no biases, but in demonstrating that they can be controlled.

CULTURAL NOISE.   The interviewer must learn to recognize and handle "cultural noise"—responses the applicant believes are socially acceptable rather than facts. Applicants want a job; to get it they know they have to get by the interviewer. They may feel that if they divulge any unacceptable facts about themselves, they may not get the job. Consequently, applicants may by reluctant to tell an interviewer all about themselves. Instead, they may try to give the interviewer responses that are socially acceptable but not very revealing.

An interviewer can handle cultural noise by not encouraging it. If the interviewer supports cultural noise, the applicant will take the cue and continue those kinds of answers. Instead, the applicant can be made aware that the interviewer is not being taken in. An interviewer can say, "The fact that you are the best pitcher on your softball team is interesting, but tell me about your performance on your last job."

What Interviewers Evaluate

Overall, interviewers look for evidence that an applicant is well-rounded, competent, and successful. One study found that a number of factors were considered during an interview. Figure 9–6 shows them in order of importance. Notice that work experience is rated eighth and grade-point average and outside activities were

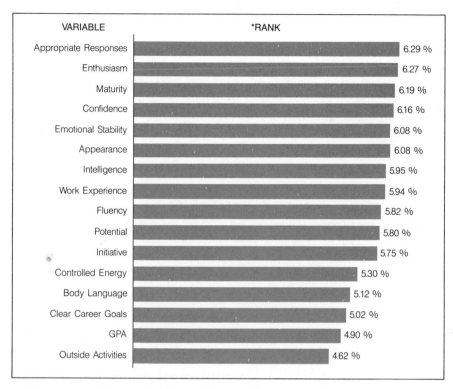

VARIABLE	*RANK
Appropriate Responses	6.29 %
Enthusiasm	6.27 %
Maturity	6.19 %
Confidence	6.16 %
Emotional Stability	6.08 %
Appearance	6.08 %
Intelligence	5.95 %
Work Experience	5.94 %
Fluency	5.82 %
Potential	5.80 %
Initiative	5.75 %
Controlled Energy	5.30 %
Body Language	5.12 %
Clear Career Goals	5.02 %
GPA	4.90 %
Outside Activities	4.62 %

Figure 9–6
Employment Variables Considered During an In-House Interview

SOURCE: Joe A. Cox et al., "A Look Behind Corporate Doors," *Personnel Administrator,* March 1989, 58. Used with permission.

rated last. Other studies have shown attractiveness, dress, and perceived age of applicants to affect such decisions. [36]

BACKGROUND INVESTIGATION

Background investigation may take place either before or after the in-depth interview. Checking a person's background may require investing some time and money, but it is generally well worth the effort. It may be a shock to many people's basic beliefs about the goodness and honesty of others, but many employers have found that applicants frequently misrepresent their qualifications and background.

Many universities report that inquiries on graduates and former students often reveal that the individual never graduated or may never have attended the university! Another type of credential fraud uses the mail-order "degree mill." To enhance their chances of employment, individuals purchase degrees from organizations that grant unaccredited degrees for a fee. One school advertising in major publications claims that a person can receive a degree with "no exams, no studying, no classes." Anyone can see advertisements for these "opportunities" by reading the classified ads in many national magazines and publications.

Estimates are that about 30 percent of all resumes contain at least one lie or "factual misstatement." The only way for employers to protect themselves from resume fraud and false credentials is to request verification or proof from applicants either before or after hire. If hired, the employee may be terminated for falsifying employment information. Therefore, it is unwise for employers to ignore the problem or continue to assume that "someone else had already checked."

Types of References

Background references can be obtained from several sources. Some of the following references may be more useful and relevant than others, depending on the jobs for which applicants are being considered. Major reference catagories include:

- Academic references
- Prior work references
- Financial references
- Law enforcement records
- Personal references

Personal references often are of little value; they probably should not even be required. No applicant will ask somebody to write a recommendation who is going to give a negative response. Therefore, personal references from relatives, ministers, or family friends are likely to be a weak source of selection information. Instead, greater reliance should be placed on work-related references from previous employers and supervisors.

Legal Constraints on Background Investigations

Various federal and state laws have been passed to protect the rights of individuals whose backgrounds may be investigated during pre-employment screening. Depending on the state, employers may be able to request information from law enforcement agencies on any applicant, or they may be prohibited from getting certain credit information. Many of the state laws that have been passed to protect the privacy of individuals also place restrictions on the actions of employers.

IMPACT OF PRIVACY LEGISLATION.   A variety of federal and state laws has been passed to protect the privacy of personal information. The most important is the Federal Privacy Act of 1974, which applies primarily to government agencies and units. However, bills to extend the provisions of the privacy act to other employers have been introduced in Congress at various times. Under the 1974 act, a governmental entity must have a signed written release from a person before information can be given to someone else. As an example, many colleges will not release a person's grade and/or transcripts unless the individual gives written authorization. Under some legislation proposed in the past, either a copy or the obtained information would be given to the individual or the person would be given the right to inspect the personnel file. Other privacy provisions that would affect personnel files and records are discussed in Chapter 17. The P/HR: Practice on the ethics of using credit information without notification to applicants illustrates why privacy concerns have affected reference-checking practices.

DEFAMATION AND SLANDER.   In a number of court cases individuals have sued their former employers for slander, libel, or defamation of character as a result of what the employer said to other potential employers that prevented the individuals from obtaining jobs.

P/HR: Practice *and* Research	Ethical Issues in Selection

The use of an individual's credit history during the employment selection process raises some ethical issues. Some firms that use credit histories as a part of their reference-checking process do so for job-related purposes. For example, an individual's financial history may be very relevant to a bank hiring loan officers. However, other firms may not be justified in asking for such information, and they deliberately may be violating the federal Fair Credit Reporting Act (FCRA).

That act requires that an employer reveal to the applicant that a consumer credit report will be obtained and used during the selection process. Also, the FCRA requires that whenever employment is denied because of credit information obtained from a credit-reporting firm, the employer must advise the applicant the reason for the denial and give him or her the name of the credit-reporting agency. Finally, the FCRA requires that if an "investigative consumer report" is requested by an employer, the individual must be notified within three days. An investigative consumer report is one in which a person's character, mode of living, or personal characteristics are investigated through interviews with neighbors, friends, previous employers, or others.

In spite of the act, many employers often check credit histories on applicants without notification or approval by the individuals being investigated. Such actions are particularly prevalent in the retail and financial industries, to check individual credit histories for credit or purchasing approvals. However, numerous firms do not notify credit agencies that their inquiries are employment-related. Some examples of misuse by both employers and credit-reporting agencies include:

- A medium-sized retailer checks credit histories on every applicant after the screening interview in order to decide who to invite back for second interviews.
- A financial firm always checks credit histories on all racial minority applicants, but only checks credit records of white applicants for certain jobs.
- A reporter told a credit bureau that he would be hiring one or two employees and needed credit reports on applicants. He then gave the name, address, and So-

cial Security numbers of two of his fellow reporters (with their permissions) to two credit-reported firms. One firm charged $20 per report and the other a $500 sign-up fee and $15 per report. The reporter obtained almost complete financial information on his two colleagues.

- Just to test accessibility of credit records, the same reporter requested a credit history on Vice President Dan Quayle. He received a complete listing, including the fact that Quayle had a big mortgage and more charges at Sears than at some luxury men's stores.

As would be expected, the credit-reporting firms say that the blame for misuse of credit records should be placed on those requesting the information, not the credit bureaus. Yet the easy access to those records raises disturbing privacy concerns. As our society becomes more computerized and information-intensive, the ethics of credit reference checking during employment will continue to be an issue.[37]

Some examples illustrate why employers should be careful when giving reference information.[38]

- An executive at one firm remarked that a former employee was a "sociopath." The former employee sued and won $1.9 million in a judgment against the employer and the executive.
- Over $500,000 was paid by both Pan Am World Airways and Equitable Life to settle lawsuits on references given on former employees.

Figure 9–7

Guidelines for Defensible References

1. Don't volunteer information. Respond only to specific company or institutional inquiries and requests. Before responding, telephone the inquirer to check on the validity of the request.
2. Direct all communication only to persons who have a specific interest in that information.
3. State in the message that the information you are providing is confidential and should be treated as such. Use qualifying statements such as "providing information that was requested"; "relating this information only because it was requested"; or "providing information that is to be used for professional purposes only."
4. Provide only reference data that relates and pertains to the job and job performance in question.
5. Avoid vague statements such as: "He was an average student"; "She was careless at times"; "He displayed an inability to work with others."
6. Document all released information. Use specific statements such as: "Mr. _____ received a grade of C—an average grade"; "Ms. _____ made an average of two bookkeeping errors each week"; or "This spring, four members of the work team wrote letters asking not to be placed on the shift with Mr. _____."
7. Clearly label all subjective statements based on personal opinions and feelings. Say "I believe . . ." whenever making a statement that is not a fact.
8. When providing a negative or potentially negative statement, add the reason or reasons why, or specify the incidents that led you to this opinion.
9. Do not answer trap questions such as "Would you rehire this person?"
10. Avoid answering questions that are asked "off the record."

SOURCE: "Employment References: Do You Know the Law?" by James D. Bell, James Castagnera, and Jane Patterson Young, copyright February 1984. Reprinted with the permission of *Personnel Journal*, Costa Mesa, California, all rights reserved.

Consequently, many organizations have adopted policies restricting the release of reference information.[39] Figure 9–7 lists some specific suggestions that employers should follow for releasing such information.

NEGLIGENT HIRING.   The costs of a failure to check references may be high. A number of organizations have found themselves targets of lawsuits that charge negligence in hiring workers who commit violent acts on the job. For example, B & L Trucking in Chicago hired a male driver who had been arrested for sexual assault. He picked up a teenage hitchhiker and raped her, for which he was sentenced to 50 years in jail. The hitchhiker sued B & L, arguing that the company had a "general duty to hire competent employees." This duty included a responsibility to check criminal records.[40]

In another case, a female tenant in an apartment complex was assaulted by the resident manager, who used his passkey to enter her apartment. The tenant sued and won $90,000 when she showed that the only check made before the manager was hired was to contact the applicant's mother and sister.[41] Other cases of negligence have been brought against truck firms for hiring people whose driving records were poor and who later caused major accidents.

Lawyers say that an employer's liability hinges on how well it investigates an applicant's fitness. Prior convictions and frequent moves or gaps in employment should be a cue for further inquiry. Yet lawyers also advise organizations who are asked about former employers to give out only name, employment date, and title. This restriction places employers in the position of needing information on those it may hire, but being unwilling to give out information in return.

Details on the application form provided by the applicant should be investigated to the extent possible, so the employer can show that due diligence efforts were undertaken. Also, applicants should be asked to sign releases authorizing the employer to check references, and those releases should contain a statement releasing the reference givers from any future liability actions.[42]

Reference-Checking Methods

Several methods of obtaining reference information are available to an employer. Telephoning a reference is the most-used method, although many firms prefer written responses.

TELEPHONE REFERENCE CHECKING.   Many experts recommend using a structured telephone reference check form.[43] Typically, questions asked on such a form focus on factual verification of information given by the applicant, such as employment dates, salary history, type of job responsibilities, and attendance record. Other questions often include reasons for leaving the previous job, the individual's manner of working with supervisors and other employees, and other less factual information. Naturally, many firms will only provide the factual information. But the use of the form can provide evidence that a diligent effort was made.

WRITTEN METHODS OF REFERENCE CHECKING.   Some organizations have preprinted reference forms that they send to individuals who are giving references for applicants. These forms often contain a release statement signed by the applicant, so that those giving references can see that they have been released from liability on the information they furnish. Specific or general letters of reference also are requested by some employers or provided by applicants.

Medical Examinations

A medical examination may be given to all applicants who otherwise meet hiring requirements. Often this examination is one of the last steps in the employment process. A medical examination is usually given in a company medical office or by a physician approved and paid by the organization. The purpose of a medical examination is to obtain information on the health status of an applicant. Medical information is useful in:

- Assigning workers to jobs for which they must be physically and emotionally fit and capable of performing in a sustained and effective manner
- Providing data about an individual as a basis for future health guidance
- Safeguarding the health of present employees through the detection of contagious diseases
- Protecting applicants who have had health defects from undertaking work that could be detrimental to themselves or endanger the employer's property
- Protecting the employer from workers' compensation claims that are not valid because the injuries/illnesses existed when the employee was hired.

Physical standards for jobs should be realistic, justifiable, and geared to the job requirements.[44] Disabled workers can perform satisfactorily in many jobs. However, in many places, they are rejected because of their handicaps, rather than being carefully screened and placed in appropriate jobs.

Some organizations ask applicants to complete a pre-employment health checklist. Then, depending on the responses given, a physical examination may be scheduled with a physician. With the cost of a simple physical examination being $75 or more per person, it is easy to see the potential savings in using a questionnaire.

DRUG TESTING.   Drug testing also may be a part of the physical exam, or it may be done separately if a medical examination is not a part of the selection process. As a part of the selection process, drug testing has increased in the past few years, not without controversy. Over a six-year period, the percentage of Fortune 500 companies using drug testing to screen applicants and current employees for drug use grew from about 5 percent to over 40 percent.[45] With the passage of the Drug-Free Workplace Act in 1989, drug testing was established as an accepted part of the selection process for private-sector employers doing business with the federal government.[46]

To use drug testing as a part of the selection process, employers should recognize that drugs tests are not infallible—for a variety of reasons. Consequently, the type of tests used must be scientifically sound. As discussed in more detail in Chapter 17, the accuracy of drug tests varies according to the type of test used, the item tested, and the quality of the laboratory where the test samples are sent. If an individual tests positive for drug use, then a second, more detailed analysis should be administered by an independent medical laboratory. Because of the potential impact of prescription drugs on test results, applicants should complete a detailed questionnaire before the drug test. Whether urine, blood, or hair samples are used, the process of obtaining, labeling, and transferring the sample to the testing lab should be outlined clearly and definite policies and procedures established.

As discussed in Chapters 5 and 6, drug testing also has legal implications. In a number of cases, courts have ruled that individuals with previous drug addiction problems are handicapped. Also, pre-employment drug testing must be administered in a nondiscriminatory manner, instead of being used selectively with certain groups. The results of the drug tests also must be used in a consistent manner, so that all individuals testing positive are treated uniformly. If a production worker applicant tests positive, he should be rejected for employment, just as an applicant to be vice president of marketing should be if she tests positive.

Undoubtedly, during the 1990s drug testing will continue to be a growing area of employer—and legal—interest. The laws and practices affecting drug testing as part of the selection process will continue to evolve.

GENETIC TESTING.   Another controversial area of medical testing is genetic testing. One survey of large companies revealed that a few firms were using genetic tests, but many more of them were considering their use in the future.[47]

Employers that use genetic screening tests do so for several reasons. The tests may link workplace health hazards and individuals with certain genetic characteristics. Also, genetic testing may be used to make workers aware of genetic problems that may occur in certain work situations. The third use is the most controversial: to exclude individuals from certain jobs if they have genetic conditions that increase their health risks. Because someone cannot change his or her genes, the potential for racial, sex, or some other type of discrimination is very real. For example, sickle-cell anemia is a condition found only in blacks. If chemicals in a particular work environment can cause health problems for individuals with sickle-cell anemia, blacks can be screened out. At one time DuPont Corporation required genetic testing for blacks (to determine those who have the potential for sickle-cell anemia.) DuPont received criticism for this program and, as a result, made it voluntary. Blacks could be tested if they chose, so that the individuals could decide if they wanted to accept the health risks of certain jobs.[48]

At this point, genetic testing for employment-related purposes is limited. Congressional hearings on the topic have examined many of the issues involved, but no specific laws dealing with genetic testing have been passed and relatively few employers are using genetic tests for employment screening. Nevertheless, in the future, more applicants may be tested to determine how their chromosomes and genes match up with jobs and job hazards.

SUMMARY

- Selection is a process that matches individuals and their qualifications to jobs in an organization.
- Because of governmental regulations and the need for better coordination between the P/HR unit and other managers, many organizations have established a centralized employment office as part of the P/HR department.
- From the reception of an applicant, through the application and initial screening process, testing, in-depth selection interview, and background investigation, to the physical examination, the entire process must be handled by trained, knowledgeable individuals.
- Application forms must meet EEO guidelines and ask only for job-related information.
- Selection testing, which appears to be growing in use, requires that all tests used be valid and reliable.
- Selection tests include: (1) ability and aptitude tests, (2) general personality and psychological tests, and (3) assessment centers. Tests should relate directly to the jobs for which individuals apply.
- Controversial general psychological tests used to select employees are polygraphs, honesty tests, and graphoanalysis.
- From the standpoint of effectiveness and equal employment compliance, the most useful interview is the structured interview, although nondirective and stress interviews also are used.
- Sound interviewing requires planning and control. Applicants must be provided a realistic picture of the jobs for which they are applying. Good questioning techniques can reduce problems.
- Background investigations can be conducted in a variety of areas, but concerns about individual privacy must be addressed.
- Care must be taken when either getting or giving reference information to avoid the potential legal problems of defamation, libel, slander and negligent hiring.
- Medical examinations may be an appropriate part of the selection process for some employers.
- Drug testing has grown in use as a pre-employment screening device, in spite of some problems and concerns associated with its accuracy and potential for discrimination on the part of employers.

REVIEW AND DISCUSSION QUESTIONS

1. Why do many employers have a specialized employment office?
2. You are starting a new manufacturing company. What phases would you go through to select your employees?

3. Agree or disagree with the following statement: "A good application form is fundamental to a good selection process." Explain your conclusion.
4. Discuss the following statement: "We stopped giving tests altogether and rely exclusively on the interview for hiring."
5. Make two lists. On one list indicate what information you would want to obtain from the screening interview; on the other indicate what information you would want to obtain from the in-depth interview.
6. Develop a structured interview guide for a 20-minute interview with a retail sales clerk applicant. Include specific questions you would ask.
7. How would you go about investigating a new college graduate's background? Why would this information be useful in making a selection decision?
8. List the advantages and disadvantages of having a complete medical examination given to all potential employees.

CASE | Selection for Temporary Employees

Manpower, Inc., a Milwaukee-based worldwide supplier of temporary help, identified a need for a better system of selecting clerical employees for today's automated office. Manpower employees are assigned on a temporary basis to companies throughout the world. They fill in for permanent employees who are absent or on vacation, and help companies get through unusually heavy workloads or special projects. Clerical workers supplied by Manpower include word-processing operators, data-entry operators, mini- and microcomputer operators, typists, stenographers, transcriptionists, accounting clerks, and others.

In a typical year, Manpower employs 700,000 people worldwide. Like any business that hires and places its workers, Manpower needed effective selection tools and training techniques. As a firm in an industry with a fluid work force, it was essential that Manpower's selection and training systems be highly accurate, as well as time- and cost-effective. Further, those systems needed to be flexible enough to expand along with new developments in office automation.

The company developed solutions on two fronts: selection and training. Tests were developed specifically for the selection of temporary workers for automated offices. Ultraskill, a hands-on exercise, measures accuracy, speed, and diagnoses an applicant's strengths and weaknesses in the clerical skills most important for automated workstation operators. In an exercise that reflects the real business world, Ultraskill requires the applicant to create a document from a handwritten rough draft or dictation, edit it, and print a final copy. In addition, a series of paper-and-pencil recognition and proficiency tests assess knowledge of a specific word-processing system. Manpower's two-pronged approach, using one set of tests for knowledge and another for skills, results in a more complete evaluation of workers for the automated office.

All of Manpower's tests are professionally developed and validated in accordance with EEOC standards and American Psychological Association guidelines. Test validation is not only important for the purpose of meeting EEO requirements, but also to ensure that the test measures the skills and abilities most relevant to the job being filled.

The basis of Manpower's entire selection system, called the predictable performance system, is job analysis. Thorough analysis of clerical positions was the first step in the development of the tools that enable Manpower to make the best possible match of its employees to temporary assignments. Additional elements of Manpower's selection system include a structured interview that draws information about an applicant's experience, abilities and interests. Information on customer needs and preferences is obtained through detailed assignment orders, surveys of customers' work environments, and temporary worker performance appraisals. The same sophisticated personnel tools and procedures apply to the selection of workers for light industrial assignments.

The development of Manpower's predictable performance system warranted a major investment of research, time and money. However, all those involved in the process, benefit, including Manpower's managers, employees, and customers.[49]

QUESTIONS

1. What are the components of the selection process that are used by Manpower?
2. Discuss how the testing process and types of test used are tailored to be job-related.
3. Compare the sophistication of Manpower's selection process with that you have experienced when applying for jobs.

NOTES

1. Adapted from personal interviews in February 1990. Used with permission. No further reproduction rights may be granted.
2. F. L. Schmidt, et al., "The Economic Impact of Job Selection Methods on Size, Productivity, and Payroll Costs of the Federal Workforce: An Empirically Based Demonstration," *Personnel Psychology* 39 (1986): 1–27.
3. Saul W. Gellerman, "The Art of Management Selection," *Recruitment Today*, Summer 1989, 41–51.
4. Andy Rooney, "Fire the Personnel Office," *Chicago Tribune Syndicate*. Reprinted by permission: Tribune Media Services.
5. Bill Leonard, "Right Questions on Applications Avoid Trouble," *HR News*, February 1990, B9, 15.
6. James P. Jolly and James G. Frierson, "Playing It Safe," *Personnel Administrator*, June 1989, 44–50.
7. To learn more about the construction of a weighted application blank, see Robert D. Gatewood and Hubert S. Feild, *Human Resource Selection*, 2nd ed. (Chicago: Dryden Press, 1990), 421–459.
8. David Gold and Beth Unger, "One Dual-Purpose Document Enough for IRCA," *Resource*, December 1989, 4.
9. "Employee Selection Procedures," *Bulletin to Management*, ASPA-BNA Survey #45, May 5, 1983, 2.
10. "Most Employers Test New Job Candidates, ASPA Survey Shows," *Resource*, June 1988, 2.
11. M. Sussmann and D. Robertson, "The Validity of Validity: An Analysis of Validation Study Designs," *Journal of Applied Psychology* 71 (1986): 461–468.
12. Jeffrey S. Schippmann, Garry L. Hughes, and Erich P. Prien, "Raise Assessment Standards," *Personnel Journal*, July 1988, 68–79.
13. "Use of Personality Tests Extends to Work," *Omaha World-Herald*, November 5, 1989, 11G.
14. Adapted from B. Staples, "Personality Tests under Scrutiny," *Chicago Sun Times*, March 27, 1984, 29.
15. G. Stephen Taylor and Thomas W. Zimmerer, "Personality Tests for Potential Employees: More Harm than Good," *Personnel Journal*, January 1988, 60–64.
16. "Saint or Sinner? Score Yourself Honestly," *Omaha World-Herald*, October 18, 1981, 7A.
17. John W. Jones and William Terris, "After the Polygraph Ban," *Recruitment Today*, May/June 1989, 25–31.
18. Robin Inwald, "How to Evaluate Psychological/Honesty Tests," *Personnel Journal*, May 1988, 42–46.
19. Paul R. Sackett, Laura R. Burris, and Christine Callahan, "Integrity Testing for Personnel Selection: An Update," *Personnel Psychology* 42 (1989): 491–529.
20. "Graphology Company Puts New Slant on Hiring," *USA Today*, December 8, 1989, 4B.
21. M. Susan Taylor and Kathryn K. Sackheim, "Graphology," *Personnel Administrator*, May 1988, 71–76.

22. W. H. Wiesner and S. F. Cronshaw, "A Meta-Analytic Investigation of the Impact of Interview Format and Degree of Structure on the Validity of the Employment Interview," *Journal of Occupational Psychology* 61 (1988): 275–290.

23. Michael M. Harris, "Reconsidering the Employment Interview: A Review of Recent Literature and Suggestions for Future Research," *Personnel Psychology* 42 (1989): 691–726.

24. R. D. Arvey and J. E. Campion, "The Employment Interview: A Summary of Recent Research," *Personnel Psychology* 35 (1986): 570–578.

25. M. K. Denis, "Subjective Decision Making: Does It Have a Place in the Employment Process?" *Employee Relations Law Journal* 11 (1986): 269–290.

26. Michael A. Campion, Elliott D. Pursell, and Barbara K. Brown, "Structured Interviewing: Raising the Psychometric Properties of the Employment Interview," *Personnel Psychology* 41 (1988): 25–42.

27. Robert Bloom and Erich P. Prien, "A Guide to Job-Related Employment Interviewing," *Personnel Administrator*, October 1983, 81–86ff.

28. Patrick M. Wright, Philip A. Lichtenfels, and Elliot D. Pursell, "The Structured Interview: Additional Studies and a Meta-Analysis," *Journal of Occupational Psychology* 62 (1989): 191–199.

29. Harris, op. cit.

30. Bruce Coorpender, "Interviews that Work," *Recruitment Today*, Fall 1989, 16–19.

31. Steven L. Premack and John P. Wanous, "A Metal-Analysis of Realistic Job Preview Experiments," *Journal of Applied Psychology*, 70 (1985): 706–719.

32. John P. Wanous, "Installing a Realistic Job Preview: Ten Tough Choices," *Personnel Psychology* 42 (1989): 117–134.

33. Adapted from Amanda Peek Phillips and Robert L. Dipboye, "Correlational Tests of Prediction from a Process Model of the Interview," *Journal of Applied Psychology* 74 (1989): 41–52.

34. T. W. Dobmeyer and M. D. Dunnette, "Relative Importance of Three Content Dimensions in Overall Suitability Ratings of Job Applicant Resumes," *Journal of Applied Psychology* 54 (1970): 69.

35. Judy D. Olian, Donald P. Schwab, and Yitchak Haberfeld, "The Impact of Applicant Gender Compared to Qualifications on Hiring Recommendations," *Organizational Behavior and Human Decision Processes* 41 (1988): 180–195.

36. M. E. Heilman and M. H. Stopeck, "Attractiveness and Corporate Success: Different Causal Attributions for Males and Females," *Journal of Applied Psychology* 70 (1985): 379–388; S. Forsythe et al., "Influence of Applicant's Dress on Interviewer's Selection Decisions," *Journal of Applied Psychology* 70 (1985): 374–378; R. Gorden and R. D. Arvey, "Perceived and Actual Ages of Workers," *Journal of Vocational Behavior* 28 (1986): 21–28.

37. Developed based on information in John R. Erickson, "Defamatory Employment References and the Fair Credit Reporting Act," *Labor Law Journal* (1989), 150–157; "Is Nothing Private?" *Business Week*, September 4, 1989, 74–83.

38. Donald F. Dvorak, "References, Resumes, and Other Lies," *Industry Week*, October 17, 1988, 14.

39. Charles W. Langdon and William P. Galle, Jr., ". . . And What Was the Reason for Departure?" *Personnel Administrator*, August 1989, 62–70.

40. L. W. Sherman, "Make Sure Job Seekers are not Career Criminals," *Wall Street Journal*, October 6, 1986, 24.

41. Jane Easter Bahls, "Your Worker's Crime May Make You Pay," *Nation's Business*, December 1988, 38–39.

42. Donald J. Peterson and Douglas Messengill, "The Negligent Hiring Doctrine—A Growing Dilemma for Employers," *Employee Relations Law Journal* 15 (1989): 419–432.

43. Erwin S. Stanton, "Fast-and-Easy Reference Checking by Telephone," *Personnel Journal*, November 1988, 123–130.

44. Edwin A. Fleishman, "Some New Frontiers in Personnel Selection Research," *Personnel Psychology* (1988), 679–699.

45. Stephen J. Vodanovich and Milano Reyna, "Alternatives to Workplace Testing," *Personnel Administrator*, May 1988, 78–84.

46. Stanley Mazaroff and Jeffrey P. Ayres, "Controlling Drug Abuse in the Workplace: The Legal Groundrules," *Legal Report*, American Society for Personnel Administration, Spring 1989, 1–8.

47. "The Genetic Age," *Business Week*, May 28, 1990, 68–84.

48. William Pat Patterson, "Genetic Testing," *Industry Week*, June 1, 1987, 45–49.

49. Used with permission of Manpower, Inc. July 1987.

Training and Developing Human Resources

In any organization, employees must receive some training to perform in their jobs, and to grow in their abilities. Training provides employees with opportunities to learn new skills. The organization thus develops its internal talent for the future.

Training and orientation are the topics of Chapter 10. Orientation is the first organizational training an employee receives. Before a person can perform well on the job, he or she must be properly introduced, or oriented, to the organization. Determining training needs and evaluating the effectiveness of training are two important aspects of P/HR management, but two that are seldom done well. Training is most effective when it is specifically aimed at the individual needs of employees. An ideal training evaluation consists of checking to see if a newly-trained employee can now do something he or she could not do before training.

Chapter 11 examines on-the-job and off-the-job methods to develop employees. Development is broad, long-range training. By developing employees, especially managers, an organization prepares itself for the future. Career planning is an important aspect of employee development.

Once an employee has been trained to perform a job, a manager must review performance. This review is a vital part of ongoing development because it provides feedback on what an employee is doing well and on what areas need improvement.

Appraisal is the process of examining employee performance. Appraisals are useful in solving some performance problems, but they can create other problems. Chapter 12 examines behavioral reactions to appraisals, common mistakes made in appraising performance, and other components of the appraisal process.

Orientation and Training

After you have read this chapter, you should be able to:

1. Define training and discuss its legal aspects
2. Describe five characteristics of an effective orientation system
3. Discuss at least four learning principles that relate to training
4. Discuss the major phases of a training system
5. Identify three ways to determine training needs
6. List and discuss at least four training methods
7. Give an example of each of the levels of training evaluation
8. Identify three designs used in evaluating training

P/HR: Today *and* Tomorrow   Remedial Training

U.S. employers face a major challenge in the 1990s if they are to compete effectively in the global economy. That challenge is the lack of basic educational capabilities of a large and growing segment of the population.

Some sobering statistics are as follows:[1]

- More than 20 million Americans cannot read, write, figure, or communicate well enough to perform most jobs.
- Approximately one of every four ninth graders will not complete high school; for Hispanics and Blacks the percentage who drop out approaches 50 percent.
- About 40 percent of all new jobs added to the U.S. work force between 1990 and 2000 will require at least one year of college

Employers must find enough qualified workers, especially in light of changing U.S. demographics. Already, some organizations are addressing the problem. One survey of 613 firms found that 26 percent of them currently are providing remedial training, and about three-fourths of the respondents anticipate increasing their remedial training programs in the next five years. The basic skills deficiencies identified included the following: writing, math, reading, communication, reasoning, and English as a second language.[2]

Consider the remedial training offered by Spring Industries, a South Carolina textile manufacturing company, for the 25,000 employees in its 25 plants. Beginning in 1988, the firm began teaching basic literacy, reading, and basic technical skills classes for employees. Assistance in developing and conducting the classes has been obtained through York Technical College located in Rock Hill, South Carolina.

When the program was presented, about 1,800 people indicated interest in participating, and about 1,400 followed through and enrolled. Participation is voluntary; the role of supervisors and managers is to encourage and support workers who express interest. On completion of classes, employees get a personal letter from the chairman of the board of the company. Employees who complete their high school equivalency degree (GED) receive a personal letter from the governor of the state.

The program has been evaluated since its inception. For instance, based on feedback from the attendees, it became apparent that the technical skills training program was presented at too difficult a level for participants, so the program was revised. Other changes may be made also as the program managers gain more experience. One possibility that has been discussed is some type of incentive system to reward individuals who complete classes successfully.

The value of this remedial training program is summarized by Tommy Myers, director of programs for Spring Industries:

"We want to help upgrade the educational skills of our work force, but this goes far beyond the company. Yes, it's going to have long-term benefits for us as a company, but it benefits the individuals. It enriches their lives, [and] helps them to be better parents and citizens."[3]

"Learning is either a continual thing or it is nothing at all."

Frank Tyger

Training has both current and future implications for the success of organizations. As the opening discussion indicates, the training or retraining of individuals for the jobs of the future may determine the future success of many U.S. firms. Remedial training is a major issue confronting employers for the 1990s.

Another major issue is the retraining of existing workers whose knowledge and skills have become obsolete. A 1989 survey of about 400 firms found that 75 percent anticipated increasing their retraining activities over the following 3 to 5 years. The survey identified employees in technical and sales/customer service occupation as having the greatest retraining needs.[4]

Effective training is an investment in the human resources of an organization, with both immediate and long-range returns. As the remedial training program at Spring Industries indicates, training not only can lead to better jobs for employees, but it has many advantages for the organization as well. Training can contribute to higher production, fewer mistakes, greater job satisfaction, and lower turnover. Also, it can enable employees to cope with organizational, social, and technological change.

Organizations in the United States recognize the importance of training, if the expenditures made on training are indicators. One study estimated that employers spent $5.3 billion on training and development of human resources in a recent year.[5] Another estimate is that training expenditures represent about 1 or 2 percent of payroll expenses in the average organization. That same study found that employers provide 69 percent of the formal training of employees, and 31 percent of the formal training is done by outside providers.[6]

Training programs sometimes have unanticipated consequences. Training is a cost, and some employers have gone to court to try and require individuals who leave the firms to repay such costs. For instance, Electronic Data System (EDS) sued a worker who signed a "promissory note" to repay the firm $9,000 if he left the firm voluntarily or was fired for cause within 24 months of starting a special training program. The employee contested the suit by saying that he did not learn anything he did not already know; thus he received no benefits from the training.[7]

■■ ■ NATURE OF TRAINING

Training is a learning process whereby people acquire skills or knowledge to aid in the achievement of goals. Because learning processes are harnessed to a variety of organizational purposes, training can be viewed either narrowly or broadly. In a limited sense, training provides employees with specific identifiable knowledge and skills for use on their present jobs. Sometimes a distinction is drawn between *training* and *development,* with development being broader in scope and focusing on individuals gaining *new* knowledge and skills useful for present and future jobs.[8] However, attempting to classify learning experiences as either training or development is difficult.

TRAINING
is a learning process whereby people acquire skills or knowledge to aid in the achievement of goals.

Legal Aspects of Training

Because training has both current and future consequences for job success, it is affected by equal employment and other laws and regulations. One area of concern is the practice used to select individuals for inclusion in training programs. The criteria used must be job-related and not unfairly restrict protected-group individuals from participating in training programs. Another concern is having pay differences based on training to which protected-group members have not had equal access. A third area is the use of training as a criterion for selecting individuals for promotions.[9] In summary, fair employment laws and regulations definitely do apply to training, and employers must be aware of them.

Training Responsibilities

One division of training responsibilities is shown in Figure 10–1. The P/HR unit serves as a source of expert training assistance and coordination. The unit often has a more long-range view of employee careers and development of the entire organization than do individual operating managers. This difference is especially true at lower levels in the organization.

On the other hand, managers are likely to be the best source of technical information used in skilled training. They also are in a better position to decide when employees need training or retraining. Because of the close and continual interaction they have with their employees, managers determine and discuss employee career potentials and plans.

Many types of training exist. Job skill training, supervisory training, and management development are a few. Job skill training is discussed later in this chapter, and employee development is covered in the next chapter.

Orientation is another type of training. Unlike training that is more skill-oriented, orientation is a special kind of training designed to provide the basic information an employee needs to function in the company.[10] The discussion in the following section centers on orientation.

■■ ■ ORIENTATION

ORIENTATION
is the planned introduction of employees to their jobs, co-workers, and the organization.

During **orientation** new employees receive an introduction to their job, co-workers, and the organization. However, orientation should not be a mechanical process. Because all employees are different, a sensitive awareness to anxieties, uncertainties, and needs is important.

Purposes of Orientation

The orientation process has several important purposes. But the overall goal is to help new employees learn about their new work environments. This goal is met in several ways.

CREATE AN INITIAL FAVORABLE IMPRESSION.   A good orientation program creates a favorable impression of the organization and its work. Just as your favorable first impression of a person helps you to form a good relationship, a good initial impression of the company, co-workers, and supervisor can help a new employee adjust. This impression begins even before the new employees report to work. Providing sufficient information about when and where to report the first day, getting all relevant paperwork handled efficiently, and having personable and efficient people to assist the new hire all contribute to creating a more favorable impression.[11]

P/HR UNIT	MANAGERS
■ Prepares skill training materials ■ Coordinates training efforts ■ Conducts or arranges for off-the-job training ■ Coordinates career plans and personnel development efforts ■ Provides input and expertise for organizational development	■ Provide technical information ■ Monitor training needs ■ Conduct the on-the-job training ■ Continually discuss employees' future potential and monitor employees' growth ■ Participate in organizational change efforts

Figure 10–1
Training Responsibilities

ENHANCE INTERPERSONAL ACCEPTANCE.   Another purpose of orientation is to ease the employee's entry into the work group. New employees often are concerned about meeting the people in their work units. They may be thinking, "How will I get along with these people?" "Will they be friendly?"

While new employees must be "socialized", or introduced to what the work group expects of them, the expectations of a group of employees may not always parallel management's formal orientation. However, if a manager does not have a well-planned formal orientation, the new employee may be oriented *only* by the group.

Many organizations use a "buddy" system whereby an existing employee is paired with a new employee as part of the orientation process. One research study found that the socialization of newcomers is higher when both newcomers and insiders interact.[12]

INCREASE INDIVIDUAL AND ORGANIZATIONAL PERFORMANCE.   An effective orientation program will reduce the adjustment problems of new employees by creating a sense of security, confidence, and belonging. Thus, employees can perform better because they will learn faster. By getting employees started in the organization properly, the organization receives a number of benefits also. Corning, Inc. found that individuals who had been through more orientation seminars had a 69 percent lower turnover rate over a two-year period of time. Texas Instruments found that annual turnover rates decreased 40 percent, and much of the decline was attributed to more effective orientation of new employees.[13]

Some other benefits of better employee orientation are:

■ Stronger loyalty through greater commitment to values and goals
■ Lower absenteeism
■ Higher job satisfaction

Orientation Responsibilities

Orientation requires cooperation between individuals in the P/HR unit and other managers and supervisors. In a small organization without a P/HR department, such as a machine shop, the new employee's supervisor or manager has the total orientation responsibility. In large organizations with P/HR departments, managers and supervisors, as well as the P/HR department, should work as a team in employee orientation.

Figure 10–2 illustrates a common division of orientation responsibilities in which managers work with P/HR specialists to orient a new employee. Together they must

Figure 10–2
Orientation Responsibilities

P/HR UNIT	MANAGERS
■ Places employee on payroll ■ Designs formal orientation program ■ Explains benefits and company organization ■ Develops orientation checklist ■ Evaluates orientation activities	■ Prepare co-workers for new employee ■ Introduce new employee to co-workers ■ Provide overview of job setting and work rules

develop an orientation process that will communicate what the employee needs to learn.

Certain types of information probably can be presented best by the immediate supervisor, while other orientation information can be explained better by the P/HR unit. A supervisor may not know all the details about health insurance or benefit options, but he or she usually can present information on safety rules, allowing the P/HR department to explain benefits.

■■ ■ ESTABLISHING AN EFFECTIVE ORIENTATION SYSTEM

A systematic approach to orientation requires attention to attitudes, behaviors, and information that new employees need. Unfortunately, orientation often is conducted rather haphazardly. The general ideas that follow highlight some components of an effective orientation system.

Prepare for New Employees

New employees must feel that they belong and are important. Both the supervisor and the P/HR unit should be prepared to receive the new employee. Supervisors should receive some training on how to perform their orientation responsibilities.[14] It is very uncomfortable for an employee to arrive at work and have a manager say, "Oh, I didn't realize you were coming to work today" or "Who are you?" This depersonalization obviously does not create an atmosphere of acceptance and trust.

Further, co-workers should be informed about a new employee's arrival. This is especially important if the new employee will be assuming certain duties that might threaten a current employee's job status and security. The manager or supervisor should prepare the current employees by discussing the purpose for hiring the new worker.

Some organizations use co-workers or peers to conduct part of the new employee orientation. It is particularly useful to involve more experienced and higher-performing individuals who can serve as role models for new employees.[15] However, choosing the wrong role model may lead to misorientation. One study found that the influence of information sources tended to change as the employee gained experience. Co-workers increased in importance as information sources over time.[16]

Provide New Employees Needed Information

The guiding question in the establishment of an orientation system is, "What does the new employee need to know *now*?" Often new employees receive a large amount of information they do not immediately need, and they fail to get the information they really need the first day of a new job.

Some organizations systematize this process by developing an orientation check-list. Figure 10–3 indicates the items to be covered by the P/HR department representative and/or the new employee's supervisor. Using a checklist, the manager and the P/HR representative can ensure that all necessary items have been covered at some point, perhaps during the first week. Many employers have employees sign the checklist to verify that the employees have been told of pertinent rules and procedures.

Three types of information usually are included in the orientation process. The information ranges from the nature of the organization and its culture to the specifics of a normal workday.

NATURE OF ORGANIZATION AND ITS CULTURE.   One type of information is a general organizational orientation. This overview might include a brief review of the organization; its history; its structure; who the key executives are; what its purpose is; its products and/or services; how the employee's job fits into the big picture; and any other general information. If the employer prepares an annual report, giving an employee a copy helps provide a general overview of an organization and its components.

To understand the organization fully, new employees also should be oriented to the culture of the organization. As discussed in Chapter 3, organizational culture is the shared values and beliefs guiding the actions of members of the organization. Giving informal information on such factors as typical dress habits, lunch practices, and what executives are called will aid the adjustment of new employees.

ORGANIZATIONAL POLICIES, RULES, AND BENEFITS.   Another important type of initial information is the policies, work rules, and benefits for employees. Typically, this information is presented by both the P/HR unit and the supervisor. Employee policies about sick leave, tardiness, absenteeism, vacations, benefits, hospitalization, parking, and safety rules are important facts that every new employee should know.

NORMAL WORKDAY.   The immediate supervisor or manager probably is better prepared to outline a normal day for the employee. The manager or supervisor should devote some time during the first morning solely to covering daily routine information with the new employee.[17] This information includes such essentials as introducing the new employee to other employees, showing the employee the work area, letting the new employee know when and where to take coffee breaks and lunch, indicating what time work begins and ends, identifying where to park, and indicating where the restrooms are.

Determine How to Present the Information

Managers and P/HR representatives should determine the most appropriate ways to present orientation information. For example, rather than telling an employee about them verbally, information on company sick leave and vacation policies may be presented on the first day in an employee handbook. The manager or P/HR representative can review this information a few days later to answer any of the employee's questions.

Figure 10–3
Orientation Checklist

Name of Employee _____
Starting Date _____
Department _____

P/HR DEPARTMENT
Prior to Orientation
____ Complete Form A and give or mail
     to new employee
____ Complete Form B
____ Attach Form B to "Orientation
     Checklist-Supervisor" and give to
     the supervisor
Employee's First Day
*Organization and Personnel Policies
     and Procedures*
____ History of XYZ Inc.
____ Organization chart
____ Purpose of the company
____ Employee classifications
Insurance Benefits
____ Group health plan
____ Disability insurance
____ Life Insurance
____ Worker's Compensation
Other Benefits
____ Holidays
____ Vacation
____ Jury and election duty
____ Funeral leave
____ Health services
____ Professional discounts
____ Child Care
End of Orientation—First Day
____ Make appointment for second day
____ Introduce employee to supervisor
Other Items
____ Job Posting
____ Bulletin board—location and use
____ Safety
____ No drinking
____ Where to get supplies
____ Employee's records—updating

Employee Signature _____

Date

Name of Employee _____
Starting Date _____
Department _____
Position _____
SUPERVISOR
Employee's First Day
____ Introduction to Co-workers
____ Tour of department
____ Tour of company
Location of
____ Coat closet
____ Rest room
____ Telephone for personal use and
     rules concerning it
Working Hours
____ Starting and leaving
____ Lunch
____ Breaks
____ Overtime
____ Early departures
____ Time clock
Pay Policy
____ Pay period
____ Deposit system
Other Items
____ Parking
____ Dress
Employee's Second Day
____ Pension retirement plan
____ Sick leave
____ Personal leave
____ Job posting
____ Confidentiality
____ Complaints and concerns
____ Termination
____ Equal Employment Opportunity
During Employee's First Two Weeks
Emergencies
____ Medical
____ Power failure
____ Fire

At the end of the employee's first two
weeks, the supervisor will ask if the
employee has any questions concerning
any items. After all questions have been
satisfied, both the employee and the
supervisor will sign and date this form
and return it to the P/HR Department.

Orientation Conducted By

INFORMATION OVERLOAD.   One common failing of many orientation programs is *information overload*. When so many facts are presented to new employees, they may ignore important details or inaccurately recall much of the information. By being given an employee handbook, the new employee can refer to information when needed. Often, employees are asked to sign a form indicating that they have received the handbook and have read it. This requirement gives legal protection for employers who may have to enforce policies and rules later. By having signed forms, employees cannot deny that they were informed about policies and rules.

Employees will retain more of the orientation information if it is presented in a manner that encourages them to learn. Orientation materials, such as handbooks and information leaflets, should be made available and be reviewed periodically for updates and corrections. Some organizations have successfully used film strips, movies, slides, charts, and teaching machines. However, even if such aids are used, the emphasis should be on presenting information, not on "entertaining" the new employee.

Evaluation and Follow-Up

A systematic orientation program should have an evaluation and follow-up. Too often, typical orientation efforts assume that, once oriented, employees are familiar with everything they need to know about the organization forever.

A P/HR representative or a manager can evaluate the effectiveness of the orientation by follow-up interviews with new employees a few weeks or months after the orientation. Employee questionnaires also can be used. Some organizations even give new employees a written test on the company handbook two weeks after orientation.

REORIENTATION.   A reorientation program in which all employees periodically are given a refresher "introduction" should be part of follow-up. Reorientation is an opportunity to reinforce policies and procedures, and it is especially important in preparing employees for organizational changes.[18] For example, if one company is purchased by another, a reorientation for employees from both firms may be necessary because of changes in operating relationships and policies caused by the merger.

Orientation is a never-ending process of introducing both old and new employees to the current state of the organization. To be assets to their organizations, employees must know organizational policies and procedures. But learning does not stop after this initial introduction. Working in organizations is a continual learning process, and learning is at the heart of all training activities.

■■ ■ LEARNING PRINCIPLES: THE PSYCHOLOGY OF LEARNING

There are different learning approaches and theories used by researchers, some of which do not produce consistent results.[19] Learning is a complex psychological process that is not fully understood by practitioners or research psychologists.

Often, trainers or supervisors present information and assume that it has been learned. But learning takes place only when information is received, understood, and internalized, so that some change or conscious effort has been made to use the information. Managers can use the research on learning to make their training efforts more effective. Some major learning principles that guide training efforts are presented next.

Intention to Learn

People learn at different rates and are able to apply what they learn differently. *Ability* to learn must be accompanied by motivation or *intention* to learn.[20] Motivation to learn is determined by the answers to questions like "How important is my job to me?" "How important is it that I learn that information?" "Will learning this help me in any way?" "What's in it for me?"

People are more willing to learn when the material is important to them. Some of the following goals may encourage intention to learn in certain people:

- Achievement
- Advancement
- Authority
- Co-workers' influence
- Comprehension
- Creativity

- Curiosity
- Fear of failure
- Recognition
- Responsibility
- Status
- Variety

Whole Learning

It is usually better to give an overall view of what a trainee will be doing than to deal immediately with the specifics. This concept is referred to as *whole learning* or *Gestalt learning*.

Job training instructions should be broken down into small elements *after* employees have had an opportunity to see how all the elements fit together. For example, in a plastics manufacturing operation, it would be desirable to explain to trainees how the raw chemical material comes to the plant and what is done with the plastic moldings after they are used in the manufacturing process. The information is explained as an entire logical process, so that trainees can see how the various actions fit together into the big picture. After a supervisor explains the entire operation, he or she can break the information into the specifics with which the trainee must deal.

Reinforcement

The notion of reinforcement is based on the *law of effect*, which states that people tend to repeat response patterns that give them some type of positive reward and avoid actions associated with negative consequences. The rewards (reinforcements) an individual receives can be either external or internal. For example, a registered nurse receives an external reward for learning how to use a new electrocardiogram machine by receiving a certificate of completion.

An internal reward appeals to the trainee's internal needs. Consider a machinist who learned to use a new lathe in the machine shop. At first he made many mistakes. With time and practice he began to do better and better. One day he knew he had mastered the lathe; he was very pleased with himself. This feeling of accomplishment is a type of internal reward.

Many training situations provide both internal and external rewards. If a new salesclerk answers her supervisor's question correctly and is complimented for giving the correct answer, she may receive both an external reward (the compliment) and an internal reward (a feeling of pride).

Behavior Modification

A comprehensive approach to training has been developed based on the concept of reinforcement. This approach is known as *behavior modification*. Using the theories of psychologist B. F. Skinner, behavior modification has become increasingly popular. Skinner states that "learning is not doing; it is changing what we do."[21]

INTERVENTION STRATEGIES.   Behavior modification makes use of four means of changing behavior, labeled *intervention strategies*. The four strategies are positive reinforcement, negative reinforcement, punishment, and extinction.

A person who receives a desired reward receives **positive reinforcement**. If an employee is on time every day during a week and, as a result, receives extra pay equivalent to one hour of normal work, the employee has received positive reinforcement of his or her good attendance by receiving a desired reward.

Negative reinforcement occurs when an individual works to avoid an undesirable "reward." An employee who arrives at work on time every day may do so to avoid a supervisor's criticism. Thus, the potential for criticism leads to the employee taking the desired action.

Action taken to prevent a person from repeating undesirable action is **punishment**. A grocery manager may punish a stock clerk for leaving the stockroom dirty by forcing him or her to stay after work and clean it up.

Behavior can also be modified through a technique known as **extinction**. Extinction refers to a situation in which an individual receives no response. Assume that an employee dresses in a new style to attract the attention of her superior. The supervisor just ignores the new type of dress. There is no reinforcement, positive or negative, and no punishment given. With no reinforcement of any kind, it is likely that the employee will quit dressing in that fashion. The hope is that unreinforced behavior will not be repeated.

All four strategies can work to change behavior. In fact, combinations may be called for in certain situations. But research suggests that for most training situations, positive reinforcement of the desired behavior is most effective.

Immediate Confirmation

Another learning concept closely related to reinforcement is **immediate confirmation**. This concept calls for feedback as soon as possible after training. To illustrate, a corporate purchasing department has developed a new system for reporting inventory information. The new system is much more complex than the old one and requires the use of a new form that is longer and more difficult to complete. However, it does give computerized information much more quickly and helps eliminate errors in the recording process, which delay the total inventory report. The purchasing manager who trains inventory processors may not have the trainees fill out the entire inventory form when teaching them the new procedure. Instead, the manager may explain the total process, then break it into smaller segments and have each trainee complete the form a section at a time. By checking each individual's form for errors as each section is completed, the purchasing manager can give immediate feedback or confirmation before the trainees fill out the next section. This immediate confirmation corrects errors that, if made throughout the whole form, might establish a pattern to be unlearned.

POSITIVE REINFORCEMENT occurs when a person receives a desired reward.

NEGATIVE REINFORCEMENT occurs when an individual works to avoid an undesirable reward.

PUNISHMENT is action taken to repel the person from the undesired action.

EXTINCTION is the absence of a response to a situation.

IMMEDIATE CONFIRMATION indicates that people learn best if reinforcement is given as soon as possible after training.

Practice

Learning new skills requires practice. Research and experience show that the following considerations must be addressed when designing training practice applications: active practice, reality of the practice, spaced versus massed practice.

Active practice is more effective than simply reading or passively listening. Once some basic instructions have been given, active practice should be built into every learning situation. It is one of the advantages of good on-the-job training. Assume a person is being trained as a customer service representative. After being given some basic selling instructions and product details, the trainee should be allowed to call on a customer to use the knowledge received.

SPACED PRACTICE
occurs when several practice sessions are spaced over a period of hours or days.

MASSED PRACTICE
occurs when a person does all of the practice at once.

SPACED VERSUS MASSED PRACTICE.   Active practice can be structured in two ways. The first one, **spaced practice**, works better for some kinds of learning, whereas massed practice is better for others. If the trainee is learning physical skills (like learning to ski), several practice sessions spaced over a period of hours or days result in greater learning than the same amount of practice in one long period. Training cashiers to operate a new machine could be alternated with having the individuals do a task they already know how to do. Thus, the training is distributed instead of being concentrated into one period. For this reason, some organizations spread their orientation of new employees over an entire week by devoting an hour or two daily to orientation, instead of covering it all in one day. This incremental approach to skill acquisition minimizes the physical fatigue that deters learning.

For memorizing tasks, **massed practice** is usually more effective. In massed practice a person does all of the practice at once. Can you imagine trying to memorize the list of model options for a dishwasher as an appliance distribution salesperson one model per day for 20 days? By the time you learned the last option you would have forgotten the first one.

Learning Curves

People learn in different patterns in different training situations. In the *decreasing returns* pattern, the amount of learning and/or the skill level increases rapidly at first, then the *rate* of improvement slows. For example, when an employee first learns to operate a stamping machine, the rate of production increases rapidly at first, then slows as the normal rate is approached. Learning to perform most routine jobs follows such a curve.

The *increasing returns* pattern is much less common. It occurs most often when a person is learning a completely unfamiliar task. Starting a completely new job with little formal orientation or training might require a slow beginning while the important vocabulary and relationships are learned. Then the learner begins to pick up expertise quickly.

A third pattern, the *S-shaped curve*, is a combination of the decreasing return and increasing return curves. S-curves usually result when a person tries to learn an unfamiliar, difficult task that also requires insight into the basics of the job. In this pattern, learning occurs slowly at first, then increases rapidly for a while, and then flattens out. Learning to debug computer systems is one example, especially if the learner has had little previous contact with computers.

The *plateau curve* indicates that as knowledge, skills, or speed is being acquired, the learner often reaches a point when there is no apparent progress. At this point, trainees should be encouraged and advised that these plateaus are expected, common, understandable, and usually are followed by new surges in learning.[22] Encouragement prevents despair or a desire to give up. The plateau curve is very common.

Behavior Modeling

Behavior modeling is the most elementary way in which people learn—yet it can be among the best. Modeling is copying someone else's behavior. Modeling also can work to keep people from making mistakes they see others make. The use of behavior modeling is particularly appropriate for skill training in which the trainees must use both knowledge and practice.[23] In such training situations, individuals must learn specific information and then apply it. For example, a workshop that trains managers how to conduct job interviews might include presenting information on equal employment regulations and the types of questions to ask and not ask. Next, the trainees can be shown a videotape of an interview in which the interviewers use the information previously presented. Then the trainees can apply their knowledge to interviews in role-playing situations. By videotaping the role-play interview, the managers can receive feedback and reinforce their performance, and then apply it in practice situations.

Most training programs are not structured adequately to take advantage of modeling. Passive classroom training whereby individuals listen to lectures allows little modeling, while videotapes of people showing the desired behavior allows much more. (The importance of such modeling is seen in the P/HR: Research on training methods for acquiring computer skills.) When modeling is used, it is important to select a model who can and will exhibit the desired behaviors. An informal group leader who shares management's values often is a good choice. Likewise, a longer-service employee can become a younger one's mentor by using modeling and other psychological processes.

Transfer of Training

The purpose of conducting training is for the employees to use the training on their jobs or to transfer the training from the class to the job. For effective transfer of training to occur, two conditions must be met:[25]

1. The trainees must be able to take the material learned in training and apply it to the job context in which they work.
2. Use of the learned material must be maintained over time on the job.

To aid transfer of training to the job situations, the training should be as much like the jobs as possible. In the training situation, trainees should be able to picture the types of situations they can expect on the job. For example, training managers to be better interviewers should include role-playing with "applicants" who can respond in the same way that real applicants would.

SYSTEMS APPROACH TO TRAINING

The success of any training can be gauged by the amount of learning that occurs and is transferred to the job. Too often, unplanned, uncoordinated, and haphazard training efforts significantly reduce the learning that can be expected. Training and learning will take place, especially through informal work groups, whether an

BEHAVIOR MODELING
is copying someone else's behavior.

P/HR: **Practice *and* Research**   Training Methods for Acquiring Computer Skills

An increasing number of jobs require workers to have computer knowledge and skills. At the same time, work force changes mean that employers will have to train or retrain all workers in computer knowledge and skills. To do this training, a variety of methods can be used. As described in *Personnel Psychology*, Gist, Rosen, and Schwoerer conducted a study to examine the impact of training methods and trainee age on teaching computer software skills.[24]

The study was conducted with individuals recruited through newsletters who volunteered to receive three hours of training on using a computer software spreadsheet program. The 146 individuals who volunteered for the program averaged 40 years of age, with almost half below and half above age 40. The three-hour program consisted of an introduction to microcomputing, the skills needed to use a spreadsheet program, and an

applications problem requiring use of spreadsheets. Before the training, the participants filled out a questionnaire giving demographic information and previous computer experience.

The class was divided into two groups, with each group having both younger and older workers. Each group was taught by a different training method. Trainers in one group used a tutorial approach, in which step-by-step instructions were given on computer diskettes. The trainees paced themselves, and if they gave incorrect responses at any step, they had to correct their mistakes before proceeding. The other group was taught by a modeling approach. The trainee first viewed a videotape that showed someone using the spreadsheet software; at each step the result was shown on the videotape. The videotape was stopped after each demonstration and the trainees did

the procedure just shown. If mistakes were made, the trainees had to correct them before proceeding further.

Following the training, the trainees were asked to perform 25 specific tasks using the spreadsheet software, and their performance results were scored as correct or incorrect.

The authors found that the trainees using the modeling approach scored somewhat better than those using the tutorial approach. However, the older trainees scored significantly lower in both groups. Results indicated that the modeling method of training appears to be a superior approach when teaching computer software skills, although more research is needed in other settings. But the other finding about older individuals having more difficulty acquiring computer skills has important implications as employers train and retrain older individuals.

organization has a coordinated training effort or not. Employees learn from other employees, but without a well-designed systematic approach to training, what is learned may not be what is best for the organization. Figure 10–4 shows the components of the three major phases in a training system: (1) the assessment phase, (2) the implementation phase, and (3) the evaluation phase.[26]

In the *assessment* phase, planners determine the need for training and specify the objectives of the training effort. Looking at the performance of clerks in a billing department, a manager might find that their data-entry and keyboard capabilities are weak and that they would profit by having specific instruction. An objective of increasing the clerks' keyboard entry speed to 60 words per minute without errors might be established. The number of words per minute without errors is the criterion against which training success can be measured and represents the way in which the objective is made specific. To make the bridge between assessment and implementation, the clerks would be given a keyboard data-entry test.

Using these results, *implementation* then can begin. For instance, the billing supervisor and a P/HR training specialist could work together to determine how to

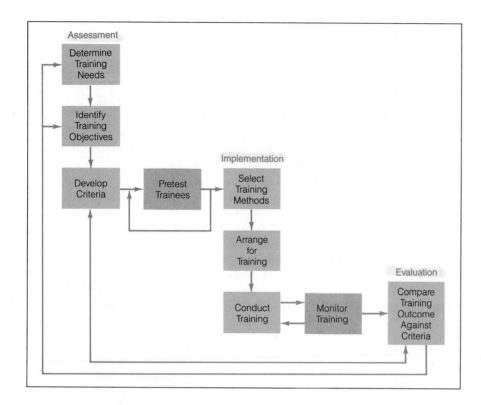

Figure 10–4
Model of Training System

train the clerks to increase their speed. Arrangements for instructors, classrooms, materials, and so on are made at this point. A programmed instruction manual might be used in conjunction with a special data-entry class set up at the company. Then training is actually conducted.

The *evaluation* phase is crucial and focuses on measuring how well the training accomplished what its orginators expected. Monitoring the training serves as a bridge between the implementation and evaluation phases.

■■ ■ TRAINING NEEDS ASSESSMENT

Training is designed to help the organization accomplish its objectives. Determining organizational training needs is the diagnostic phase of setting training objectives. Just as a patient must be examined before a physician can prescribe medication to deal with the ailment, an organization or an individual employee must be studied before a course of action can be planned to make the "patient" function better. Managers can identify training needs through three types of analyses:

■ Organizational analyses
■ Task analyses
■ Individual analyses

Organizational Analyses of Training Needs

The first way of diagnosing training needs is through organizational analysis. Organizational analysis considers the organization as a system. As part of the corporate strategic human resource planning, it is important to identify the knowledge, skills, and abilities that will be needed by employees in the future as both jobs and the organization change. For example, as part of a 5-year business plan, a manufacturer of mechanical equipment identifies the need to shift production to computer-based electronic equipment. As the organization implements its plans, current employees will need to be retrained so that they can do electronic instead of mechanical assembly work.

Both internal and external forces that will impact the training of workers must be considered. As the chapter-opening discussion of remedial training illustrates, technical obsolescence of current employees and an insufficiently educated labor pool from which to draw new workers should be confronted before those training needs become critical. One study of adult literacy programs found that most were established to address business needs, such as work force and technology issues.[27]

Organizational analyses also can be done using various operational measures of organizational performance. On a continuing basis, detailed analysis of P/HR data can show training weaknesses. Departments or areas with high turnover, high absenteeism, low performance, or other deficiencies can be pinpointed. After such problems are analyzed, training objectives can be developed. Specific sources of information for an organizational-level needs analysis may include:

- Grievances
- Accident records
- Observations
- Exit interviews

- Complaints from customers
- Equipment utilization figures
- Training committee observations
- Waste/scrap/quality control data

Task Analyses

The second way to diagnose training needs is through analyses of the tasks performed in the organization. To do this, it is necessary to know what the job requirements in the organization are. Job descriptions and job specifications provide information on the performance expected and skills necessary for employees to accomplish the required work. By comparing the requirements of the job with the knowledge, skills, and abilities of employees, training needs can be identified.[28]

Texas Instruments used task analyses to identify the tasks to be performed by engineers who were to be trained as instructors to train other employees. By listing the tasks required of a technical instructor, management established a program to teach the specific skills needed by the engineers to become successful instructors.[29]

Individual Analyses

The third means of diagnosing training needs focuses on individuals and how they perform their jobs. The use of performance appraisal data in analyzing training program needs is the most common approach. To assess training needs through the performance appraisal process, an employee's performance inadequacies first must be determined in a formal review. Then some type of training is designed to help the employee overcome the weakness. Figure 10–5 shows how analyses of the job and the person mesh to identify training needs.

Another way to assess individual training needs is by asking employees. Both managerial and nonmanagerial employees can be surveyed, interviewed, and/or tested.[30] The result can give managers insight into what employees believe their problems are and what actions they recommend. In one such survey, 110 city/county

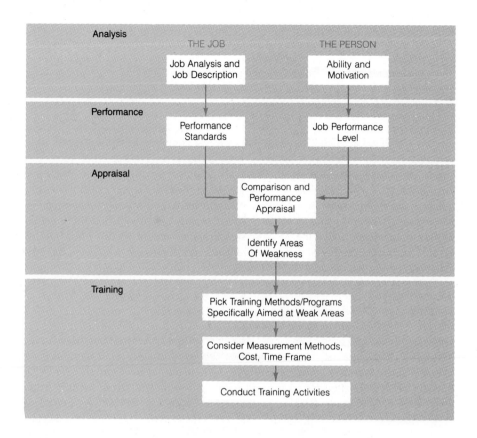

Figure 10–5
Using Job Performance to Analyze Training Needs

public administrators were questioned to see what training they felt they needed. The survey revealed that the administrators' top needs were learning how to make effective decisions, how to use their time better, and how to set goals properly.[31]

A survey can take the form of questionnaires or interviews with supervisors and employees on an individual or group basis. The purpose is to gather information on problems, as perceived by the individuals involved. Sources include:

- Questionnaires
- Job knowledge tools
- Skill tests
- Attitude surveys
- Records of critical incidents
- Data from assessment centers
- Role-playing results

DEMOGRAPHIC ANALYSES.   A useful approach that combines individual and organizational analyses examines the training needs of individuals by demographic factors such as age, education level, or gender.[32] For example, one study found that individuals in their 40's wanted management training, those in their 50's wanted technological training, but those in their 60's wanted little training of any kind.[33]

Determining Training Priorities

Because training seldom is an unlimited budget item and there are multiple training needs in the organization, it is necessary to prioritize needs. Ideally, training needs are ranked in importance on the basis of organizational objectives, with the training most needed to improve the health of the organization done first. However, other considerations may enter into the decision:

- Upper management choices
- Time
- Trainers' abilities and motivations
- Money
- Likelihood of tangible results

An example of successful needs analysis was undertaken by a middle-sized wholesaler in Denver, Colorado. The company was experiencing a high error rate in its shipping records, which were prepared by a group of 23 clerical employees. The needs assessment consisted of checking all shipping records for one week and tabulating errors for each clerk. Five people accounted for 90 percent of the errors. These 5 then were observed for four hours each until a clear pattern emerged and the source of the error was identified. The company discovered that these people did not understand four of the 25 basic shipping transactions. A two-hour training session for those employees then was prepared and presented, which reduced the error rate by 95 percent.

Setting Training Objectives

Once training needs are determined, objectives should be set to meet these needs. As Figure 10–6 suggests, training objectives can be of three types. The most basic type is *regular training* which is ongoing. Orientation is an example of regular training because it attempts to provide learning for all employees as they begin work in the organization. *Problem solving* is the second type of training. Emphasis is on solving a particular problem instead of on presenting general information concerning problem areas. The final type is *innovative training*, or change making, which has a longer-range focus.

■■ ■ TRAINING METHODS

Objectives have been determined, and now the actual training effort begins. Regardless of whether the training is job-related or developmental in nature, a particular training method must be chosen. The following overview of common training methods and techniques classifies methods into several major groups. Other methods that are used more frequently for management development are discussed in the next chapter.

Figure 10–6
Types of Training Objectives

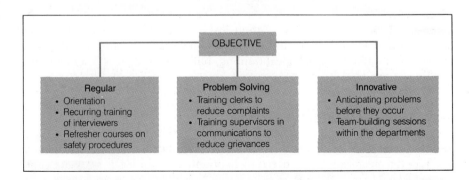

Regular	Problem Solving	Innovative
• Orientation	• Training clerks to reduce complaints	• Anticipating problems before they occur
• Recurring training of interviewers	• Training supervisors in communications to reduce grievances	• Team-building sessions within the departments
• Refresher courses on safety procedures		

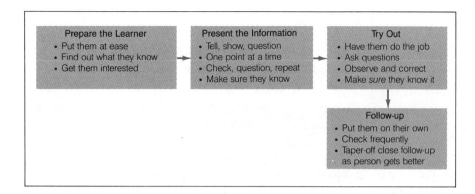

Figure 10–7
**Job Instruction Training (JIT)
Process**

On-the-Job Training

The most common type of training at all levels in an organization is on-the-job training (OJT). Whether or not the training is planned, people do learn from their job experiences, particularly if these experiences change over time. On-the-job training usually is done by the manager and/or other employees. A manager or supervisor who trains an employee must be able to teach, as well as show, the employee. The problem with OJT is that it often is haphazardly done. Trainers may have no experience in training, no time to do it, and no desire to participate. Under such conditions, learners essentially are on their own and training likely will not be effective.

A special, guided form of on-the-job training is job instructional training (JIT). Developed during World War II, JIT was used to prepare civilians with little experience for jobs in the industrial sector producing military equipment. Because of its success, JIT is still used. Figure 10–7 shows the steps in the JIT process.[34]

On-the-job training is by far the most commonly used form of training because it is flexible and relevant to what the employee is doing. However, OJT has some problems as well. It can disrupt regular work, and the person doing the training may not be an effective trainer. Unfortunately, OJT can amount to no training in some circumstances, especially if the trainee simply is abandoned to learn the job alone.

SIMULATION TRAINING.   Simulation training uses a duplicate work operation that is set up independently of the work site. In this setting, trainees can learn under realistic conditions but away from the pressures of the production schedule. Having a receptionist practice on a switchboard in a simulated setting before taking over as a telephone receptionist allows the person to learn the job more easily and without stress. Consequently, there may be fewer mistakes in handling actual incoming calls. Airlines use simulators to train pilots and cabin attendants, astronauts train in mock-up space capsules, and nuclear power plant operators use model operations control rooms and consoles.

One caution about simulated training is that it must be realistic. The equipment should be similar to the type the trainee actually will use so transfer of learning can be made easily.

Cooperative Training

There are two widely used cooperative training methods: internships and apprentice training. Both mix classroom training and on-the-job experiences.

INTERNSHIP.   An internship is a form of on-the-job training that usually combines job training with classroom instruction in trade schools, high schools, colleges, or universities. According to one study, over 200,000 college students per year worked full- or part-time in cooperative programs and internships. Many fields were represented, including accounting, engineering, newspaper reporting, and P/HR management.[35]

APPRENTICE TRAINING.   Another form of cooperative training that is used by employers, trade unions, and government agencies is apprentice training. An apprenticeship program provides an employee with on-the-job experience under the guidance of a skilled and certified worker. Certain requirements for training, equipment, time length, and proficiency levels may be monitored by a unit of the U.S. Department of Labor. According to governmental sources, in a recent year approximately 280,000 apprentices were in training, and there were about 44,000 apprentice programs in operation.[36] Apprentice training is used most often to train people for jobs in skilled crafts, such as carpentry, plumbing, photoengraving, typesetting, and welding. Apprenticeships usually last two to five years, depending on the occupation. During this time the apprentice receives lower wages than the certified individual.

Behaviorally-Experienced Training

Some training efforts focus on emotional and behavioral learning. Employees can learn about behavior by *role playing*, in which individuals assume an identity in a certain situation and act it out. *Business games*, *case studies*, other cases called *incidents*, and short work assignments called *in-baskets* are other behaviorally-experienced learning methods. *Sensitivity training* or *laboratory training* is an example of a method used for emotional learning.

The critical issue in any situation using these methods is the purpose of the exercise. Employees may perceive role playing as fun or annoying, but they should understand clearly what the exercise is attempting to teach. Also, they must be able to transfer the learning back to their jobs. In addition, some behavioral methods are controversial and raise ethical issues (see P/HR: Practice on "New Age" training).

Classroom and Conference Training

Training seminars, courses, and presentations can be used in both job-related and developmental training. Lectures and discussions are a major part of this training. The numerous management development courses offered by trade associations and educational institutions are examples of conference training.

Company-conducted short courses, lectures, and meetings usually consist of classroom training, while company sales meetings are a common type of conference training. This type of training frequently makes use of training techniques such as case discussions, films, and tapes to enhance the learning experience.

P/HR:	Practice *and* Research	Ethical Issues in Training

One of the more controversial training methods that some firms have used is "New Age" (NA) training. This training was developed by Werner Erhard, also known for founding the *est* human potential movement. During the NA sessions, trainees are required to reveal intimate and personal episodes in their lives. The training uses meditation, yoga, self-hypnosis, and other behavioral techniques to change employee attitudes, values, and beliefs. According to some critics, trainees are pressured to make total commitment to their employers and to believe that people create their own realities and determine what their world will be.

Some employers that have required workers to participate in NA training include car dealerships,

farmers cooperatives, and others. Some individuals who refused to participate in NA training or who objected to the training methods used and values espoused during training have been fired. Several have filed lawsuits charging their employers and the NA training firms with violating their personal privacy and requiring them to change their religious beliefs. For example, the sales manager of a car dealership in Pierce County, Washington, said he was fired because his Christian beliefs were not consistent with the NA training materials and content. In another case, a group of employees for a produce market cooperative in Atlanta, Georgia, filed suit saying that the NA training used hypnosis to try to

change their religious beliefs and to make them discuss intimate details of their relationships with spouses and parents.

As would be expected, the NA training firm of Transformational Technologies (Greenbrae, California) and its affiliate Consulting Technologies (Miami, Florida) disputes the accusations of assaults on religious beliefs and invasion of privacy. Nevertheless, the use of NA training raises profound and disturbing ethical issues about what the rights of employees and employers are when individuals are requested to participate in training by their employers, particularly when changes in values, beliefs, and behaviors are the focus of the training.[37]

Training methods of this kind are familiar to trainees because they have seen them in school. However, they are essentially one-way communications. Although they may be good for knowledge enhancement, they probably are not appropriate for motor-skill acquisition without some practice also being included.

■ ■ TRAINING MEDIA

Several aids are available to the trainer presenting training information. Some aids can be used in many settings and with a variety of training methods. The most common ones are programmed instruction, computer-assisted instruction, and audiovisual aids.

Programmed Instruction

Programmed instruction is a method of guided self-learning that provides step-by-step learning and immediate confirmation to trainees. The information to be learned is divided into modules. Using either a "teaching machine" or a book, small segments of information of progressively greater difficulty are presented. Trainees respond to each segment by answering a question or by responding on a machine. They receive an answer or look it up. Correct responses allow trainees to proceed to other material. If incorrect responses are given, trainees are guided back to previous material for review.

Examination of the effectiveness of programmed instruction reveals that it reduces average training time, but it does not appear to be more or less effective in increasing retention than conventional training. The logical conclusion is that managers or trainers should not expect programmed instruction to do their training better, only faster.

Computer-Assisted Instruction

Computer-assisted instruction (CAI) allows trainees to learn by interacting with a computer. Application of CAI technology is driven by the need to improve the efficiency or effectiveness of a training situation and to enhance the transfer of learning to improve job performance.[38] Computers lend themselves well to instruction, testing, drill and practice, and application through simulation. All the advantages are based on the capability for interaction that a computer possesses.

However, computer-assisted instruction presents some problems. Large time expenditures for programming and debugging lead to high development costs. A second class of problems is that the nature of the interaction can be too limited or too simplistic. At present, most CAI systems are restricted to input from a keyboard or some other form of touch. Perhaps CAI will fulfill its real potential when trainees can converse in their normal language with a machine that "understands" *why* a learner has made a particular mistake.

Audiovisual Aids

Other technical training aids are audio and visual in nature, including audio and video tapes, films, closed-circuit television, and interactive video teleconferencing. Interactive video capability simply adds audio and video capability to CAI, but uses a touch-screen input instead of typing on a keyboard. These aids can be tied into satellite communications systems to convey the same information, such as new product details to sales personnel in several states.

But trainers must avoid becoming dazzled with the machine gadgetry and remember that the real emphasis is on learning and training. The effectiveness of the technologies and media need to be examined as a part of the evaluation. All but interactive video are one-way communications. They may allow presentation of information that cannot be recreated in a classroom. Demonstrations of machines, experiments, and examinations of behavior are examples.

■■ ■ EVALUATION OF TRAINING

Evaluation of training compares the post-training results to the objectives expected by managers, trainers, and trainees. Too often, training is done without any thought of measuring and evaluating how well the training worked. Because training is both time consuming and costly, evaluation of the results should be built into any training effort. Unfortunately, because of the perceived difficulties and the inability to identify specific outcomes as a result of training, post-training evaluation and follow-up often are ignored.[39]

One way to evaluate training is to examine the costs associated with the training and the benefits received through **cost/benefit analysis.** Comparing costs and ben-

COST/BENEFIT ANALYSIS is comparing what efforts will cost with the benefits received to see which is greater.

COSTS	BENEFITS
■ Trainer's salary	■ Increase in production
■ Materials for training	■ Reduction in errors
■ Living expenses for trainer and trainees	■ Reduction in turnover
■ Cost of facilities	■ Less supervision necessary
■ Equipment	■ Ability to advance
■ Transportation	■ New skills lead to ability to do more jobs
■ Trainee's salary	■ Attitude changes
■ Lost production (opportunity cost)	
■ Preparation time	

Figure 10–8
Costs and Benefits of Training Evaluation

efits is easy until one has to assign an actual dollar value to some of the benefits. The best way is to measure the value of the output before and after training. Any increase represents the benefit resulting from training. Careful measurement of both the costs and benefits may be difficult in some cases. Figure 10–8 shows some costs and benefits that may result. Some benefits (such as attitude change) also are hard to quantify. However, a cost–benefit comparison remains the best way to determine if training is cost-effective. For example, General Electric, on evaluating a traditional safety training program, found the program did not lead to a reduction in accidents. Therefore, the program was redesigned so that better safety practices resulted.[40]

Levels of Evaluation

It is best to consider how training is to be evaluated *before* it begins. Kirkpatrick identified four levels at which training can be evaluated.[41] According to him, training becomes more rigorous and specific as the levels advance. Later research has examined this schematic and raised questions about how independent each level is from the others,[42] but the four levels described here (also see Figure 10–9) are widely used to focus the efforts of P/HR professionals on the importance of evaluating training.

REACTION.   Organizations evaluate the reaction level of trainees by conducting interviews or by administering questionnaires to the trainees. However, the immediate reaction may measure only how the people liked the training, rather than how it benefitted them.

1. **Reaction**	How well did the trainees like the training?
2. **Learning**	To what extent did the trainees learn the facts, principles, and approaches that were included in the training?
3. **Behavior**	To what extent did their job behavior change because of the program?
4. **Results**	What final results were achieved (reduction in cost, reduction in turnover, improvement in production, etc.)?

Figure 10–9
Levels of Training Evaluation

SOURCE: Ralph F. Catalnello and Donald L. Kirkpatrick, "Evaluating Training Programs—The State of the Art," *Training and Development Journal*, May 1968, 2–3. Reproduced by special permission from the May 1968 *Training and Development Journal*. Copyright 1968 by the American Society for Training and Development, Inc.

LEARNING.   Organizations evaluate learning levels by measuring how well trainees have learned facts, ideas, concepts, theories, and attitudes. Tests on the training material are commonly used for evaluating learning and can be given both before and after training to compare scores. In evaluating training courses at IBM, test results are used to determine how well the courses have provided employees the desired content. If test scores indicate learning problems, then instructors get feedback and the courses are redesigned so that the content can be delivered more effectively.[43] Of course, learning enough to pass a test does not guarantee that the trainee can *do* anything with what was learned.

BEHAVIOR.   Evaluating training at the behavioral level measures the effect of training on job performance through interviews of trainees and their co-workers and observation of job performance. But behavior is more difficult to measure than reaction and learning. Even if behaviors do change, the results that management desires may not occur.

RESULTS.   Employers evaluate results by measuring the effect of training on the achievement of organizational objectives. Because results such as productivity, turnover, quality, time, sales, and costs are more concrete, this type of evaluation can be done by comparing records before and after training.

The difficulty with this measurement is pinpointing whether training caused the changes in results. Other factors may have had a major impact as well. Correlation does not imply causation. For example, a department manager for a shoe manufacturer has completed a supervisory training program. By comparing turnover in the department before and after the training, the company can obtain some measure of training effectiveness. But turnover is also dependent on the current economic situation, the demand for shoes, and the quality of employees being hired. Therefore, when evaluating results, managers should be aware of all issues involved in determining the exact effect of the training.

Evaluation Designs

There are many ways to design and evaluate training programs to determine their effects. The three most common are shown in Figure 10–10. The level of rigor of the designs increases with each.

POST-MEASURE.   The most obvious way to evaluate training effectiveness is to determine after the training whether the individuals can perform the way management wants them to perform after they have received training. Assume that you, as a manager, have 20 typists whom you feel could improve their typing speed. They are given a one-day training session and then given a typing test to measure their speed. If the typists can all type the required speed after training, was the training good? It is difficult to say; perhaps they could have done as well before training. You cannot know whether the typing speed is a result of the training or could have been achieved without training.

PRE-POST-MEASURE.   By designing the evaluation differently, the issue of pre-test skill levels could have been considered. If you had measured the typing speed before

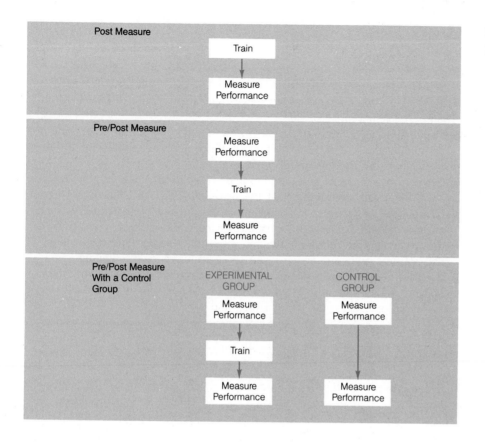

Figure 10–10
Training Evaluation Designs

and after training, you could have gotten a better idea of whether the training made any difference. However, a question remains. If there was a change in typing speed, was the training responsible for the change, or did these people simply type faster because they knew they were being tested? People often perform better when they know they are being tested on the results.

PRE-POST-MEASURE WITH CONTROL GROUP.   Another evaluation design can address this problem. In addition to the 20 typists who will be trained, you can test another group of typists who will not be trained to see if they do as well as those who are to be trained. This second group is called a *control group*. If, after training, the trained typists can type significantly faster than those who were not trained, you can be reasonably sure that the training was effective. The final portion of Figure 10–10 shows the sequence for a pre-post-measure design with a control group.

Other designs also can be used, but these three are the most common. When possible, the pre-post-measure or pre-post-measure with control group designs should be used because they provide much stronger measurement than the post-measurement alone.

SUMMARY

- Remedial training and retraining existing workers are the major challenges facing employers in the 1990s.
- Training is a learning process whereby people acquire skills or knowledge to aid in the achievement of goals.
- Training has legal implications, such as who is selected for training, the criteria used for the selection, pay differences based on training, and use of training when making promotion decisions.
- Orientation is a special kind of training designed to help new employees learn about their work environment.
- Components of an effective orientation system include preparing for new employees; determining what information is needed and when it is needed by the employees; presenting information about the workday, the organization, and policies, rules, and benefits; and doing evaluation and follow-up.
- Basic learning principles that guide training efforts are concerned with intention, whole learning, reinforcement, behavior modification, immediate confirmation, practice, patterns, modeling, and transfer.
- A training system should include assessment, implementation, and evaluation phases.
- Of the many training methods, on-the-job training (OJT) is the most often used (and abused) method.
- Training media such as programmed instruction, computer-assisted instruction, and other audiovisual aids each have advantages and disadvantages. They should be matched with training situations where they best apply because they will not all work in all situations.
- Evaluation of training success is important because if the training does not return as much in benefits as it costs, there is no reason to train. Training can be evaluated at four levels: reaction, learning, behavior, and results.
- A pre-post-measure with control group design is the most rigorous training evaluation design described here.

REVIEW AND DISCUSSION QUESTIONS

1. Why must employers be concerned about complying with equal employment requirements when selecting people for training?
2. Discuss the importance of orientation and tell how you would orient a new management trainee.
3. Describe how you would use some of the learning concepts discussed in the chapter to train someone to operate a fax machine.
4. What are the three major phases in a training system? Identify the processes within each phase.
5. Assume that you want to identify the training needs of a group of sales employees in a luxury-oriented jewelry store. How would you go about this task?
6. You are training someone to use a computer word-processing software program. What training methods would you use?
7. You want to evaluate the training received by some data input operators:
   (a) Give examples of how to evaluate the training at four different levels.
   (b) What type of training design would you use, and why?

CASE	Retraining Obsolete Workers

Times change, and as they do, organizations must change to stay competitive. They may have to adopt new production processes, cut costs (perhaps by cutting labor), or simply develop new ways of doing work within the old framework. Employees are affected by these changes in several ways. They may find themselves having to learn new methods, completely retrain for a new job in the same organization, or lose a job altogether as an old industry dies.

People react in different ways to starting over. Many fear the new and unknown. They may approach retraining only under duress. Others may gladly move toward retraining. For example, Wanda Horn found herself at age 33 in a dead-end clerical job paying $13,300 per year. She had heard of the opportunities in word processing and quit the dead-end job to retrain herself. Today she holds a responsible job paying $25,000 per year. Wanda is just one example of people who find themselves in dead-end jobs, or jobs that are becoming obsolete, and do something about it.

Many people who were laid off (often permanently) from the steel mills and auto plants during economic recessions faced similar problems. For those who were younger, the transition was often less difficult. Many actually ended up with better jobs than they had. But others sat and waited for a recall that never came. Blue-collar layoffs traditionally were viewed as temporary, but times have changed.

Retraining efforts at many companies have met with mixed success. Some programs retrained people for jobs that did not exist in certain geographic areas—and many people are unwilling to move. Other programs have been successful at placing employees in other jobs, but at pay rates considerably below their previous levels. One reason for the latter problem is that the great majority of laid-off workers are semiskilled and have no formal education beyond high school.

For years, IBM has had a policy that tries to minimize layoffs, although some layoffs have occurred. Nevertheless, the key to the success of such a policy is retraining employees in obsolete jobs for new jobs in the company.

For professionals, retraining may take many forms. For example, learning to work with microcomputers in their classes has meant a major retraining effort for faculty members at many universities. One finance professor gave his students a tough pencil-and-paper problem as a homework assignment. Some of the students knew how to work with the microcomputers and were able to arrive at a set of solutions within minutes. Other students who had not used the computer came close to rioting after spending an average of ten hours on the problem without finding an answer. The professor, realizing that the computer was far superior to other methods, finally learned to use the machine and integrated it into other classes.[44]

QUESTIONS

1. How would you as a manager justify to top management the training costs associated with a training program?
2. Discuss how the training examples in the case could be evaluated.

NOTES

1. Kirkland Ropp, "A Reform Movement for Education," *Personnel Administrator*, August 1989, 39–41; "Needed: Human Capital," *Business Week*, September 19, 1988, 100–144.

2. *1989 SHRM Training/Retraining Survey*, (Alexandria, Va: Society for Human Resource Management, 1989), 18–21.

3. Adapted from Lynn F. McGee, "Teaching Basic Skills to Workers," *Personnel Administrator*, August 1989, 42–47.

4. *1989 SHRM Training/Retraining Survey*, 12–15.

5. Morton E. Grossman, "The $5.3 Billion Tab for Training," *Personnel Journal*, July 1989, 54–56.

6. Anthony P. Carnevale, "The Learning Enterprise," *Training and Development Journal*, February 1989, 26–33.

7. "Making Employees Repay Training Costs Called Trend," *Omaha World-Herald*, November 12, 1989, 1G.

8. David E. Bartz, David R. Schwandt, and Larry W. Hillman, "Differences Between T' and D'," *Personnel Administrator*, June 1989, 164–170.

9. James S. Russell, "A Review of Fair Employment Cases in the Field of Training," *Personnel Psychology* 37 (1984): 261–276.

10. Stephen B. Wehrenberg, "Skill and Motivation Divide Training and Orientation," *Personnel Journal*, May 1989, 111–113.

11. Gene Germoel, "A Good Start for New Hires," *Nation's Business*, January 1989, 21–24.

12. Arnon E. Reichers, "An Interactionist Perspective on Newcomer Socialization Rates," *Academy of Management Review* 12 (1987): 278–787.

13. Madeline E. Cohen, "Orientation—The First Step in Team Building," *Training and Development Journal*, January 1988, 20–23.

14. Claudia Reinhardt, "Training Supervisors in First–Day Orientation Techniques," *Personnel*, June 1988, 24–28.

15. Debra R. Comer, "Peers as Providers," *Personnel Administrator*, May 1989, 84–86.

16. J. G. Thomas, "Sources of Social Information: A Longitudinal Analysis," *Human Relations* 39 (1986): 885–870.

17. Joseph F. McKenna, "Welcome Aboard," *Industry Week*, November 6, 1989, 31–38.

18. Thomas N. Martin and Joy Van Eck Peluchette, "Employee Orientation," *Personnel Administrator*, March 1989, 60–64.

19. For a review, see Robert Glaser and Miriam Bassok, "Learning Theory and the Study of Instruction," in *Annual Review of Psychology*: 40 (1989), 631–666.

20. R. Noe and N. Schmitt, "The Influence of Trainee Attitudes on Training Effectiveness: Test of a Model," *Personnel Psychology* 39 (1986), 497–529.

21. B. F. Skinner, "The Origins of Cognitive Thought," *American Psychologist* 44 (1989): 13–18.

22. Jerry Melnick, "Resilience Training: Reaping Success From Failure," *Personnel*, March 1989, 74–77.

23. William M. Fox, "Getting the Most from Behavior Modeling Training," *National Productivity Review* 17 (1988), 238–245.

24. Adapted from Marilyn Gist, Benson Rosen, and Catherine Schwoerer, "The Influence of Training Method and Trainee Age on the Acquisition of Computer Skills," *Personnel Psychology* 41 (1988): 225–265.

25. Timothy T. Baldwin and J. Kevin Ford, "Tranfer of Training: A Review and Directions for Future Research," *Personnel Psychology* 41 (1988): 63–105.

26. Adapted from I. L. Goldstein, *Training in Organizations* (Monterey Calif.: Brooks-Cole, 1986).

27. Richard G. Zalman, *Paradigms for Literacy and Learning*, an unpublished Master's Thesis, Massachusetts Institute of Technology, 1989.

28. Michael J. Gent and Gregory Dell'Omo, "The Needs Assessment Solution," *Personnel Administrator*, July 1989, 82–84.

29. Jerry L. Wircenski, Richard L. Sullivan, and Polly Moore, "Assessing Training Needs at Texas Instruments," *Training and Development Journal*, April 1989, 61–63.

30. R. A. Noe and J. K. Ford, "Self-Assessed Training Needs: The Effects of Attitudes towards Training, Managerial Level, and Function," *Personnel Psychology* 40 (1987): 39–53.

31. F. W. Swierczek and L. Carmichael, "Assessing Training Needs: A Skills Approach," *Public Personnel Management* 14 (1985): 259–274.

32. Gary P. Latham, "Human Resource Training and Development," *Annual Review of Psychology* 39 (1988): 545–582.

33. F. D. Tucker, "A Study of the Training of Older Workers," *Public Personnel Management*, Spring 1985, 85–95.

34. War Manpower Commission, *The Training within Industry Report* (Washington, D.C.: Bureau of Training, War Manpower Commission, 1945), 195.

35. "Co-op Programs Goal: Earn While You Learn," *Omaha World-Herald*, November 6, 1988, 16G.

36. William H. Miller, "New Life for an Old Idea," *Industry Week*, October 2, 1989, 78.

37. Adapted from "Workers Challenging 'New Age' Training," *Omaha World-Herald*, April 2, 1989, 1G.

38. Ralph E. Ganger, "Computer-Based Training Improves Job Performance," *Personnel Journal*, June 1989, 116–123.

39. T. V. Rao and E. Abraham, "Human Resource Development," *Management Labour Studies* 2 (1986): 73–85.

40. M. A. Vojtecky and M. F. Schmitz, "Program Evaluation and Health and Safety Training," *Journal of Safety Research* 17 (1986): 57–63.

41. D. L. Kirkpatrick, "Four Steps to Measuring Training Effectiveness," *Personnel Administrator*, November 1983, 19–25.

42. George M. Alliger and Elizabeth Janak, "Kirkpatrick's Levels of Training Criteria: Thirty Years Later," *Personnel Psychology* 42 (1989): 331–342.

43. Ursula F. Fairbairn, "Lessons in Education at IBM," *Personnel*, April 1989, 12–18.

44. Adapted from "Retraining for What?" *Industry Week*, December 8, 1986, 68–70; F. D. Tucker, "A Study of the Training of Older Workers; Implications for HRD Planning," *Public Personnel Management*, Spring 1985, 85–95; J. M. Schlesinger, "Struggling Back," *Wall Street Journal*, January 16, 1987, 1; S. Barber, "Faculty Training on the PC: Compute or Perish?" *Newsline* (AACSB) February 1984, 15–19.

Employee Development and Careers

Chapter *11*

After you have read this chapter, you should be able to:

1. Define human resource development and identify two conditions for its success
2. List and describe at least four on-the-job and off-the-job development methods
3. Discuss specific benefits and problems associated with assessment centers
4. Differentiate between organization-centered and individual-centered career planning
5. Explain how life stages and career stages parallel each other

P/HR: Today *and* Tomorrow	Careers And Families : Mommy Track And Superdad?

Statistic: In one-fourth of the sixty-four million American families, both parents work and children are fourteen years or younger.

Statistic: Women with children under twelve missed 11.7 work days per year. Men with children under twelve missed 9.4 days per year. Women with no children missed 9.6 days, and men without children missed 7.4 days

Statistic: Of women of childbearing age, 69 percent are employed.[1]

The competing demands of family and career have come into sharper focus as the number of families with two wage earners has dramatically increased. Felice Schwartz suggested recently in a *Harvard Business Review* article that there are two basic kinds of working women, "career-primary" and "career and family," and that employers should set up different tracks to accommodate their different goals. The "career and family" path became labeled the "mommy track" to reflect women who choose to forgo promotions or career moves because of their desire to incorporate family concerns with career *decisions*. However, the concept of the two types created a firestorm of reaction. One survey found that 63 percent of female executives think it is a *bad* idea to have two "tracks".[2]

Whether it is a bad idea or not for a woman's career to take a less-demanding path to accommodate the needs of young children is an open question. But what *is* clear is that many men, women, *and* their employers are all having to face the issue.

NCNB, a large bank-holding company in the Southeast, came to grips with the problem; it had to.[3] Seventy percent of the company's employees are women, and more than one in four had a child in childcare. More than 33 percent were interested in working less than full-time to better care for their families. The company responded with a two-track plan.

Initially, the bank's "select time" two-track project ran into problems. The first participants found themselves filling out time cards, paying more for health care, and losing pension seniority. When those issues were resolved, there was still the prejudice of full-time workers who tended to believe: Time equals dedication; accessibility must be in person; and the "select-timers" were "playing" when with their kids. Although the organization has tried to address these issues, the question remains about the long-term prospects for those who choose to go part-time with their careers for a period of time.

Still other companies have discovered that career versus family is not only a woman's problem. Du Pont surveyed over 4,000 of its employees and found that family obligations are playing a greater role for men as well. There, it appears that Superdad joins Supermom in trying to combine careers and parenthood. Du Pont is 65 percent male.[4] In an earlier survey, 18 percent of the men said they were interested in less than full-time work to care for family, but three years later 33 percent were interested.

Further, a significant part of the work force, male *and* female, indicated that they avoided jobs involving travel and relocation. In one study, 25 percent of the men and 50 percent of the women said they have considered finding another job which might offer more flexibility in family matters.[5] Other studies show that up to one-third of all relocation "opportunities" are being turned down because of family considerations—perhaps more so by women than by men.[6]

The conflict between family and work is not new for the 1990s. But only recently has it reached such proportions, with two working parents in many families and an impending shortage of certain high-demand workers. Employers may find the interplay of careers and family responsibilities the most pressing issue of the 1990s.

"A career is really a state of mind. A person's identity becomes tied up with a career."

David Friedland

Development occurs from the experiences people encounter as they mature and is different from simple training. It is possible to train most people to ride a bicycle, drive a truck, operate a computer, or assemble a radio. Those skills can be developed with technical training. But how can someone be trained to demonstrate judgment, responsibility, compassion, or empathy in dealing with people? Such factors may or may not develop over time with experiences that may occur accidentally, as part of a planned program, or not at all. Managers particularly need a variety of experiences to enhance their development; but a planned system of developmental experiences for employees can help expand the overall level of abilities in an organization and increase its potential and flexibility.

■■ ■ HUMAN RESOURCE DEVELOPMENT

The purpose of **human resource development** is to enhance an employee's capacity to handle greater responsibilities successfully. Development usually is concerned with improvement in the intellectual or emotional abilities needed to do a better job. This improvement may be accomplished through formal and informal means.

Some current trends in employee development include:

- Shared responsibility for development between employee and company
- More emphasis on horizontal movement to provide breadth
- Increased use of mentors
- Continued training
- Emphasizing the manager as "developer"[7]

Employee development is a multifaceted and long-term process. There is not one best way to develop managers. Success depends on the variety of potential activities, factors within the individual, and jobs and policies within the organization. Employee development is often viewed as the key to combating today's economic ills. Yet evaluating the various methods and making a prudent choice is no easy task.

Within the organization, both the P/HR department and the operating managers have some responsibilities for employee and management development. As shown in Figure 11–1, P/HR specialists typically take a guided and coordinated approach to development. However, managers at all levels must be deeply involved for development to succeed.

HUMAN RESOURCE DEVELOPMENT focuses on increasing capabilities of employees for continuing growth and advancement in the organization.

Conditions for Successful Employee Development

It has been emphasized that employee development is much more than just acquiring a specific skill, such as learning to type. Development might include such diverse aims as: (1) changing attitudes about the involvement of employees, (2) improving abilities to communicate, or (3) using better judgment on innovative decisions. Regardless of the objective, two conditions are critical for successful employee development: top management support and understanding the interrelated nature of development.

Figure 11–1
Human Resource Development Responsibilities

P/HR UNIT	MANAGERS
■ Develops and coordinates employee and management development efforts ■ Maintains management replacement charts ■ Evaluates employee development efforts for the organization ■ Administers details of development programs ■ Keeps abreast of new advances in development techniques	■ Participate in management development programs ■ Identify employees' development needs ■ Assign employees tasks designed to "stretch" them ■ Plan for their own development ■ Evaluate subordinates' development

TOP MANAGEMENT SUPPORT. Top management must believe strongly in the importance of HR development. Without commitment to development—especially management development—the process often becomes only a staff function made up of externally-presented courses and seminars. Top management must be willing to delegate some decision-making authority to lower-level staff members in the organization in order to develop young managers. These efforts must be made even if some of them fail. If top management is afraid or unwilling to relinquish control and authority to a younger manager for learning purposes, little management development is likely to result.

RELATIONSHIP OF DEVELOPMENT TO OTHER P/HR ACTIVITIES. Important relationships exist between human resource development efforts and selection, placement, compensation, and appraisal activities. Development is no substitute for good selection. If a person chosen for a job does not have the capacity to do the work, no amount of development will change that. Likewise, improper placement of a person within the organization can seldom be rectified by development. Expecting one set of behaviors from an employee but rewarding that person through pay raises for another set of behaviors also will not lead to the desired development. Here is an example: Managers in one firm are expected to meet quarterly with each employee in their departments to discuss performance issues. However, one manager consistently has refused to do so. In spite of his refusal, the manager has continued to receive excellent ratings and above-average salary increases. Consequently, the manager continues to ignore his developmental responsibilities.

Development Planning

Planning for career paths and the development needed to move people along those paths must begin with the overall strategic plan of the organization. The demand for specific specialties depends on the overall strategy and technology to be used. However, to make planning for human resource development effective, the following must be included:

■ Performance appraisals of key players to identify the areas in which they need development
■ Evaluation of the capabilities that the organization needs for its future
■ Succession planning to identify replacements and provide management continuity
■ Career management programs to reflect the future needs of the organization

Standard career paths include a range of possible moves from any position, laterally across departments, vertically within a department, etc. But each possible path represents *actual* positions, the experience needed to fill the positions, and the relationship of positions to each other.

Replacement charts (similar to depth charts used by football teams that show the backup players at each position) give a simple model of the process. The purpose of replacement charts is to ensure that the right individual is available at the right time and has had sufficient experience to handle the job. In Figure 11–2, a replacement chart for the APLO Manufacturing Company is shown.

Replacement charts can be part of the development planning process. Note that the chart specifies the kind of development each individual needs for promotion. Ms. Wilson needs exposure to manufacturing to be promotable to superintendent. Her job as office manager has not given her much exposure to the production side of the company. Ms. Paul needs exposure to plant operations and personnel. Mr. French needs to learn how to handle young, aggressive managers. However, Mr. French's appraiser felt French would not be promotable to superintendent, even with additional training. Such information can be used of identify "career paths" and "promotion ladders" for people.

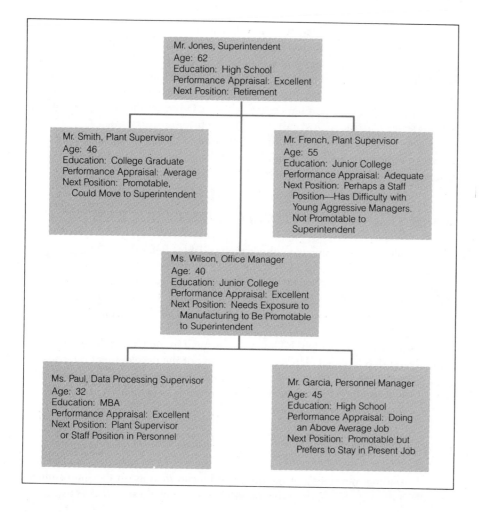

Figure 11–2
Replacement Chart for APLO Manufacturing Company

Succession planning can be especially important in small- and medium-sized firms, but studies show that firms of this size compose the group that has done the least in this area. Only 24 percent of firms with reported earnings from $2 million to $100 million have formal succession plans.[8]

Problems With Development Efforts

Development efforts are subject to certain common mistakes and problems. Most of the problems result from inadequate planning and narrow thinking about co-ordinated employee development efforts.

The most common problems include the following:

- Inadequate needs analysis
- Trying out fad programs or training methods
- Abdicating responsibility for development to staff
- Trying to substitute training for selection
- Lack of training among those who lead the development activities
- Using only "courses" as the road to development
- Encapsulated development

Management development as a whole has been found to be moderately effective. However, not all development efforts lead to improvements.[9]

ENCAPSULATED DEVELOPMENT occurs when an individual learns new methods and ideas in a development course and returns to a work unit that is still bound by old attitudes and methods.

ENCAPSULATED DEVELOPMENT.   The last item on the list may require some explanation. **Encapsulated development** occurs when an individual learns new methods and ideas in a development course and returns to a work unit that is still bound by old attitudes and methods. The reward system and the working conditions have not changed. Although the trainee has learned new ways to handle certain situations, these methods cannot be applied because of resistance from those having an investment in the status quo and the unchanged work situation. The new knowledge remains encapsulated in the classroom setting. Encapsulated development is an obvious waste of time and money. It can be avoided if training received is reinforced by the trainee's supervisor.

■ ■ CHOOSING A DEVELOPMENT PROGRAM

Many employee development methods are available. Before describing several of these, it is important to identify some criteria for their use. The goals of the development effort can be: (1) people-oriented, (2) job-specific (technical), or (3) oriented toward planning and conceptual learning. Different techniques serve these different goals. Figure 11-3 shows the extent to which each method is suited to each goal.

It is estimated that over $40 billion a year is spent in the United States on formal training and development. Unfortunately, many of the development efforts suffer because programs are often very broad based and not developed with specific individuals in mind.[10] Individual development needs always should be considered in designing development programs.

On-the-Job Methods

As with training, development methods can be classified as on the job or off the job. On-the-job methods generally are directly job-related, so that effective devel-

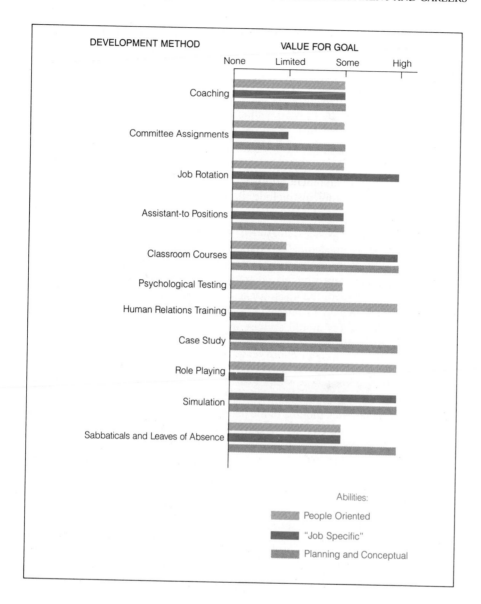

Figure 11–3
Matching Development Goals and Methods

opment can be tailored to fit each trainee's background, attitudes, needs, expectations, goals, and future assignments. However, off-the-job methods usually cannot be tailored as well to the exact needs of each trainee. Also, the employee's development is influenced to a large extent by the immediate supervisor, and the trainee is likely to accept the superior's expectations in an on the job situation.

The major difficulty with on the job methods is that often too many unplanned activities are grouped under the heading of development. It is imperative that managers plan and coordinate development efforts so that the desired learning actually occurs.

COACHING.   The oldest on-the-job development technique is that of coaching, which is the daily instruction given to employees by their immediate supervisors. It is a continual process of learning by doing. For effective coaching, a healthy and open relationship must exist between employees and their supervisors or managers. Also, managers and supervisors should have some training to be effective as coaches. One company, a major insurance firm in the Midwest, conducts formal training courses to improve managerial coaching skills.

Unfortunately, as with other on-the-job methods, coaching can be too easy to implement without any planning at all. If someone has been good at a job or a particular part of a job, there is no guarantee that he or she will be able to coach someone else to do it well. It is often too easy to fall short in guiding the learner systematically, even if the "coach" knows which systematic experiences are best. Sometimes doing a full day's work gets priority over learning and coaching. Also, many skills have an intellectual component that might be better learned from a book or lecture before coaching occurs.

COMMITTEE ASSIGNMENTS.   Assignment of a promising employee to important committees can be a broadening experience. Employees who serve on committees that made important decisions and plans may gain a real grasp of personalities, issues, and processes governing an organization. Assigning employees to a safety committee may give them the safety background they need to become supervisors. Also, they may experience the problems involved with maintaining employee safety awareness. But managers should exercise caution because committee assignments often become time-wasting activities.

JOB ROTATION

is shifting an employee from one position to another.

JOB ROTATION.   **Job rotation,** shifting an employee from one position to another, is widely used as a development technique. For example, a promising young manager may spend three months in the plant, three months in corporate planning, and three months in purchasing. When properly handled, rotation encourages a deeper and more general view of the organization. The General Electric Company uses job rotation during a fifteen-month sales training program. Trainees work in at least three areas . Included are assignments in contractor sales, retail sales, credit, advertising, and product training.

In some organizations, job rotation is unplanned, whereas other organizations have elaborate charts and schedules precisely planning the program for each employee. Managers should recognize that job rotation can be expensive. A substantial amount of managerial time is lost when the trainee changes positions because he or she must become reacquainted with different people and techniques in each new unit.

"ASSISTANT-TO" POSITIONS.   The assistant-to position is a staff position immediately under a manager. Through this job, trainees can work with outstanding managers they may not otherwise meet. Some organizations have "junior boards of directors" or "management cabinets" to which trainees may be appointed. Assignments such as these are useful if trainees have the opportunity to deal with challenging or interesting assignments.

Off-the-Job Techniques

Off-the-job development techniques can be effective because an individual has an opportunity to get away from the job and concentrate solely on what is to be learned. Meeting with other people who are concerned with somewhat different problems and different organizations may provide an employee with new perspectives on old problems. A variety of methods may be used.

CLASSROOM COURSES AND DEGREES.   Many off-the-job development programs include some classroom instruction. The advantage of classroom training is that it is widely accepted because most people are familiar with it. Specialists, either organization employees or outside experts, can conduct such training.

A disadvantage of classroom instruction is the lecture system, which encourages passive listening and lack of participation. Sometimes trainees have little opportunity to question, clarify, and discuss the lecture material. Classroom effectiveness depend on the size of the group, the ability of the instructor, and the subject matter.

Many organizations encourage continuing education by paying for employees to take college courses. A total of 91 percent of the organizations in one survey indicated that they would reimburse employees for school tuition (see Figure 10–4). Some employers encourage employees to study for advanced degrees, such as an M.B.A., in the same manner. Employees often earn these degrees at night school, after their regular workday ends.

Organizations also may send employees to externally sponsored seminars or short courses. In one recent year, U.S. organizations spent $8 billion to send eight million employees to professional seminars of one type or another.[11] These programs are offered by many colleges and universities and by professional associations such as the American Management Association.

Some larger organizations have established training centers exclusively for their own employees. For example, the federal government has created executive seminar centers in Kingspoint, New York, and in Berkeley, California. Trainees in the courses offered are exposed to a variety of problems and learning materials.

Many universities and their business schools are more than willing to accommodate corporate customers also. Of the forty-six leading graduate business programs, more than half have jumped on the "custom program" bandwagon.[12] The Kellogg Graduate School of Management at Northwestern University's Evanston Illinois, campus is a good example.

There are several common complaints about external classroom programs. Too many times, a high percentage of the participants simply are not ready for the

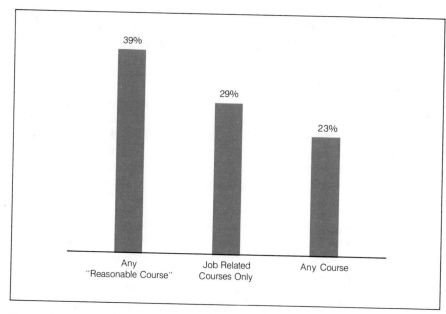

Figure 11–4
Type of Course Reimbursed by Employer

SOURCE: Adapted from "Back to School," *Wall Street Journal*, October 7, 1986, 35.

courses they take. Some individuals attend at the wrong time in their careers, others may be near retirement. Many participants sent by their employers have not had the preliminary training in management that the programs assume. However, these problems can be overcome with some planning.

Interestingly, more education does *not* always lead to a better worker. One study showed that white male workers with substantially more schooling than others in the same occupation "often earn less than their adequately educated and under-educated counterparts."[13] However, more education clearly does pay when it qualifies people for more sophisticated jobs.

PSYCHOLOGICAL TESTING.   Psychological pencil-and-paper tests have been used for several years to determine an employee's developmental potential. Intelligence tests, verbal and mathematical reasoning tests, and personality tests are often used. Such testing can furnish useful information to employees about such factors as motivation, reasoning difficulties, leadership styles, interpersonal response traits, and job preferences. It is then up to the employee to take steps to address each area.

The biggest problem with psychological testing lies in interpreting the results. An untrained manager, supervisor, or worker usually cannot accurately interpret test results. After a professional reports scores to someone in the organization, the interpretation is left essentially to untrained employees who may attach their own meanings to the results. It also should be recognized that some psychological tests are of limited validity and desirable responses can be faked easily by the test taker. Thus psychological testing is appropriate only when closely supervised by a qualified professional throughout the testing and feedback process.

HUMAN RELATIONS TRAINING.   Human relations training originated in the well-known Hawthorne studies. Initially, the purpose of the training was to prepare supervisors for "people problems" brought to them by their employees. This type of training focuses on the development of human relations skills a person needs to work well with others. Many human relations training programs are aimed at new or relatively inexperienced first-line supervisors and middle managers. Human relations programs typically have sessions on motivation, leadership, communication, and humanizing and workplace. The programs often emphasize participation and carefully examine the prerequisites of high employee morale.

No one questions the importance of human relations skills in successful management. In fact, again and again they are cited as the major difference between successful and unsuccessful management. The problem with such programs is the difficulty in measuring their effectiveness. The development of human relations skills is a long-range goal; tangible results are hard to identify over the span of several years. Consequently, such programs often are measured only by participants' reactions to them. As mentioned in the previous chapter, reaction-level measurement is the weakest form of evaluating the effectiveness of training.

CASE STUDY.   The case study is a classroom-oriented development technique that has been widely used. Cases provide a medium through which the trainee can study the application of management or behavioral concepts. The emphasis is on application and analysis, not mere memorization of concepts.

One common complaint is that cases sometimes cannot be made sufficiently realistic to be useful. Also, cases may contain information inappropriate to the kinds of decisions that trainees would make in a real situation.

ROLE PLAYING.   Role playing is a development technique requiring the trainee to assume a role in a given situation and act out behavior associated with that role. Participants gain an appreciation of the many behavioral factors influencing on-the-job situations. For instance, a labor relations director, may be asked to play a role of the union vice president in a negotiating situation to give the director insight into the constraints and problems facing union bargaining representatives. Role playing is a useful tool in some situations, but a word of caution applies: Trainees are often uncomfortable in role-playing situations, and the trainer must introduce the situation with care so that learning can occur.

SIMULATION (BUSINESS GAMES).   Several business games or simulations are available commercially. Some are computer-interactive games in which individuals or teams draw up a set of marketing plans for an organization to determine such factors as the amount of resources to allocate for advertising, product design, selling, and sales for effort.[14] The participants make a decision, then the computer tells them how well they did in relation to competing individuals or teams.

Simulations have been used to diagnose organizational problems as well.[15] When properly done, a simulation can be a useful management development tool. However, simulation receives the same criticism as role-playing: realism is sometimes lacking and the learning experience is diminished. Learning must be the focus, not just "playing the game."[16]

SABBATICALS AND LEAVES OF ABSENCE.   Sabbatical leaves are a useful development tool. Sabbaticals have been popular for many years in the academic world, where professors take a leave to sharpen their skills and advance their education or research. Similar sorts of plants have been adopted in the business community. For example, Xerox Corporation gives some of its employees six months or more off with pay to work on "socially desirable" projects. Projects include training people in urban ghettos or providing technical assistance to overseas countries. According to U.S. Labor Department Statistics, 13 percent of U.S. corporations offer sabbaticals.[17]

Paid sabbaticals can be an expensive proposition, however. Also, the nature of the learning experience is not within the control of the organization and is left somewhat to chance. (Some organizations believe that a wilderness experience will develop their managers' abilities; see P/HR: Practice).

Assessment Centers

Assessment centers are not places as much as they are a collection of instruments and exercises designed to diagnose a person's development needs. They also are useful for selecting managers. Typically in an assessment center experience, a potential manager spends two or three days away from the job performing many activities. These activities may include role playing, pencil-and-paper tests, cases, leaderless group discussions, management games, in-basket exercises where the trainee handles typical problems coming across a manager's desk, and peer evaluations. Police and fire departments, as well as many large organizations, are using assessment centers. A study of fire departments in major cities revealed that the most commonly used exercises are in-baskets. (90.6 percent), leaderless groups (84.4 percent), structured interviews (71.9 percent), problem solving (68.8 percent), written assignments (68.8 percent), and fire-scene incident command situations (59.4 percent).[19]

| P/HR: | Practice *and* Research | Employee Development in the Wilderness |

More and more organizations are packing executives off to ordeals in the wilderness for their own good! From Maine to California, a week in the wilderness is gaining favor as a development tool. General Foods, Xerox, GE, Honeywell, Burger King, AMEX, and other organizations have participated.

The idea for these wilderness excursions is as follows: For individuals, such experiences can increase self-confidence and help them reevaluate personal goals and efforts. For work units, a shared risk outside the office environment can create a sense of teamwork. The challenges may include rock climbing in the California desert, white-water rafting on the Rogue River, backpacking in the Rocky Mountains, or handling a longboat off the cost of Maine.

John Temple of Touche Ross's New Jersey operation took several other partners in the consulting practice on an eight-day compass expedition in the Adirondacks and still sees results six months later. "Our meetings go much smoother now," he says. "It has made a dramatic difference."

There are perils, however, as some who participate in Outward Bound Experiences have not been able to handle the physical and emotional challenges associated with rappeling down a cliff or climbing a 40 foot tower. The survival-type management development course may have more impact then many other management seminars. However, the Japanese version of unusual and rigorous development programs, called "Hell Camp" by some, did not go over well in the United States. The samurai management training, which has been likened to Marine boot camp, had no American signees in its first offering in Malibu, California.[18]

Assessment centers are praised because they are thought to overcome the biases inherent with interview situations, supervisor ratings, and written tests. Experience has shown that such key variables as leadership, initiative, and supervisory skills are almost impossible to measure with paper-and-pencil tests. Another advantage of assessment centers is that they help identify potentially talented employees in a large organization. Supervisors may nominate people for the assessment center or employees may volunteer. The volunteering process especially helps people who may not be recognized by their supervisors.

OPERATION OF CENTER.   During the exercises, the participants are observed by several specially trained judges. For the most part, the exercises are samples of managerial situations that require the use of managerial skills and behaviors.

One major company has made large-scale use of assessment centers. Trained observers watch the candidates' behaviors in detail and record impressions. Each assessor writes a report on each candidate and gives it to the candidate's superior to use in selection and promotion decisions. The reports often identify guidelines for further development of the assessed employee.

PROBLEMS.   Assessment centers are an excellent means for determining management potential. However, some managers may use the assessment center as a way to avoid difficult promotion decisions. Suppose a plant supervisor has personally decided that an employee is not a qualified candidate for promotion. Rather than stick by the decision and tell the employee, the supervisor may send the employee to the assessment center, hoping that the report will show that the employee is not qualified for promotion. Problems between the employee and the supervisor will be worse if the employee receives a positive report. But if the report is negative, the supervisor's views are validated. Using the assessment center in this way is not recommended. Two other problems often encountered are: (1) making sure the exercises in the assessment center are valid predictors of management performance, and (2) properly selecting and training the assessors.

Finally, assessment centers are expensive. The actual cost varies from organization to organization, but it ranges from $600 to $6,000 for each candidate who goes through a center. However, the cost of making a mistake in management selection is great, too. Some estimates far exceed $20,000 worth of legal, salary, and benefit payments to terminate a department head. Many major firms that have created assessment centers, including General Electric, Union Carbide, AT&T, and IBM, have decided they are worth the cost.

VALIDITY OF CENTERS.   The validity of assessment centers for selection has been the subject of many studies. These studies generally have suggested that assessment centers predict management success much better than other methods. However, some researchers have been concerned with the very positive statistical results in these studies. They question whether the use of salary growth and advancement is appropriate to measure the success of assessment centers. It can be argued that these items may not be related to competence, effectiveness, or superior performance.

Recently, some researchers have argued that performance ratings at assessment centers are influenced by the way assessors deal with the information derived from the assessment center and by the methods used.[20] Further, there is the difficulty in defining the effective manager. Managerial jobs are broadly defined, yet tests to pick managers must be precisely defined.[21] This dilemma reduces the generalizability of any battery of exercises and suggests that assessment center exercises should be validated for each organization.

■■ ■ MANAGEMENT DEVELOPMENT: AN OVERVIEW

The manager's job has become much more complicated than it used to be. In the minds of some, a manager today needs to be "part John Wayne and part Yoda."[22] But many are skeptical about the chances of learning problem solving, creativity, and decision making in a seminar.[23] Still, seminars are popular. Although no evidence exists, the perception is widely held that not having available management development in the form of seminars and tuition reimbursement can measurably hurt recruiting of managers.[24]

A study of management development practices in U.S. companies offers a good overview of the field.[25] One thousand U.S. companies were contacted and the following picture emerged from an analysis of the data. Less than one-third of U.S. companies conduct a needs assessment to determine the specific development needs of their managers. Larger companies are more likely to do so. Most larger companies (over 1,000 employees) have formal management development. Long-term university programs are used primarily for upper-level managers. Programs usually are chosen to provide a specific skill—*not* for general education. There is limited evidence that the companies systematically evaluate the effectiveness of the development activities. However, the study indicated that the largest increases in management development in the near future are likely to be in company-specific programs, reflecting the trend that U.S. companies are increasingly becoming their own educational providers. Most respondents listed the following content areas as needing more attention in the future: *strategic planning, managing people, marketing, ethics, finance,* and *computers.*

■ ■ MANAGERIAL MODELING AND MENTORING

There is an old adage in management development that says managers tend to manage as they were managed. Another way of saying this is that managers learn by *modeling* the behavior of other managers. This is not surprising because a great deal of human behavior is learned by modeling others. Children learn by modeling parents and older children; they are quite comfortable with the process by the time they grow up.

BEHAVIOR MODELING
is copying someone else's behavior.

Behavior modeling, which is copying someone else's behavior, has been used successfully in industry in several ways.[26] Over 2,700 first-line supervisors at General Electric have been trained in the use of modeling to help ease the hard-core unemployed into the work world. As a supervisory development method, modeling has been used by firms such as Quaker Oats, Ford Motor Company, Xerox, Lukens Steel, Gulf Oil, and American Cyanamid.

Modeling is a natural way for managers to develop because it probably will occur regardless of design, intent, or desire. Management development efforts can take advantage of natural human behavior by matching young or developing managers with appropriate models and then reinforcing the desirable behaviors exhibited.

Modeling is less a straightforward imitation or copying process than is commonly believed. Research on modeling reveals that the process itself is considerably more complex.[27] But regardless of the complexity, modeling *does work*, and exposure to both positive and negative models can be beneficial to a new manager.

MENTORING
is a relationship between a manager at midpoint in his or her career and a young adult in the first stage of a career.

Mentoring is a relationship between a manager at midpoint in his or her career and a young adult in the first stage of a career. Such a relationship aids the younger person in developing technical, interpersonal, and political skills. Senior adults may feel challenged and creative in being a mentor with wisdom to share.[28]

One study identified four stages in most successful mentor–learning relationships.[29] These are shown in Figure 11–5.

■ ■ CAREERS

In the past, career guidance was considered a service for high school or college students. Today, as the employee work role becomes more complex, more employers are providing career counseling. Exxon Corporation is just one of many employers that use career planning for their managers.

Figure 11–5
Stages in Mentor-Learner Relationships

1. **Initiation:** The initiation stage lasts six to twelve months. The young adult admires the senior manager's competence and recognizes the capacity to be a source of support and guidance. The older manager realizes the younger manager is someone with potential and is "coachable."

2. **Cultivation:** This stage lasts from two to five years. The senior manager provides challenging work, coaching, visibility, protection, and sponsorship. The young manager gains self-confidence, new attitudes, values, and styles of operation.

3. **Separation:** The third phase is marked by some turmoil, anxiety, and feeling of loss. The young manager experiences independence and autonomy, while the senior manager can demonstrate his or her success at developing management talent as they move apart.

4. **Redefinition:** The relationship becomes a friendship. The senior manager continues to be a supporter and takes pride in the younger manager's accomplishments. The younger manager responds with gratitude for the early years, but is not dependent.

Certain common career concerns are frequently expressed by employees in all organizations. These concerns include the following:

- What do I really want to do?
- What do I know how to do?
- What career opportunities can I expect to be available?
- Where do I want to go?
- What do I need to do to get there?
- How can I tell how well I am doing?

Usually, in-house career planning and guidance is limited to what the organization has to offer. However, these internal opportunities may not reflect adequately all possibilities, especially those in other organizations.

Organization-Centered versus Individual-Centered Career Planning

The nature of career planning can be somewhat confusing because two different types exist. Career planning can be *organization-centered* and/or *individual-centered*.

Organization-centered career planning focuses on jobs and on constructing career paths that provide for the logical progression of people between jobs. These paths represent ladders that each individual can climb to advance in certain organizational units. For example, a person might enter the sales department as a sales counselor, then be promoted to account director, to sales manager, and finally to vice president of sales.

Individual career planning, on the other hand, focuses on individuals rather than jobs. People's goals and skills are the focus of the analysis. Such analyses might consider situations both within and outside the organization that can expand an employee's capabilities. The individual perspective has been the major thrust in career research to date.[30] The points of focus for organization- and individual-oriented career planning are compared in Figure 11–6.

Human resource planning forms the base for successful organizational career planning. Only by forecasting the demand for people needed in various future jobs and assessing the current internal supply of people and their potentials can analysts put together a career system for the organization.

If careful matching of organizational needs and personal goals takes place, human resource planning will cover both the organizational and individual perspectives. Unfortunately, many organizations often compile recruiting plans, career ladders, or both without considering how current employees fit into those plans. Research

ORGANIZATIONAL CAREER PERSPECTIVE	INDIVIDUAL CAREER PERSPECTIVE
■ Identify future organizational staffing needs ■ Plan career ladders ■ Assess individual potential and training needs ■ Match organizational needs with individual abilities ■ Audit and develop a career system for the organization	■ Identify personal abilities and interests ■ Plan life and work goals ■ Assess alternative career paths inside and outside the organization ■ Note changes in interests and goals as career and life stage change

Figure 11–6
Organizational and Individual Career Planing Perspectives

suggests that it is the match between individual and organizational career plans that mainly determines employee satisfaction and how long an employee stays with an organization. It is much more important than having career assistance programs in the company.[31]

How Do People Choose Careers?

Four general individual characteristics affect how people make career choices.

1. *Interests:* People tend to pursue careers that they believe match their interests.
2. *Self-identity:* A career is an extension of a person's self-image, as well as a molder of it.
3. *Personality:* This factor includes an employee's personal orientation (whether the employee is realistic, enterprising, artistic, etc.) and personal needs (including affiliation, power, and achievement needs).
4. *Social backgrounds:* Socioeconomic status and the education and occupation level of a person's parents are a few factors included in this category.

Less is known about how and why people choose specific organizations. One factor is the opportunity and availability for a job when the person is looking for work. The amount of information available about alternatives is an important factor as well. Beyond these issues, people seem to pick organizations on the basis of a "fit" between the climate of an organization as they perceive it and their own personal characteristics.

Career/Life Stages

A CAREER
is the sequence of work-related positions occupied throughout a person's life.

A **career** usually includes many positions, stages, and transitions, just as a person's life does. Progression from childhood through adulthood follows a pattern. Although it is not exactly the same for everyone, there is a similar pattern for careers, especially for those who do not have interruptions in their careers. Women may follow different life and career stages, depending on family and childrearing concerns. Research suggests that people's psychological needs differ during the career stages. Also, job performance and attitudes both can vary according to career stage.[32] Figure 11–7 diagrams the combination of life stages and career stages.

EXPLORATION.   From approximately late adolescence to age twenty-five, individuals feel a need to break with their parents and establish themselves. The career searching during this time goes through a testing period and an educational process, and individual self-esteem plays a major role.[33] Experiences in college or trade school, socialization, and "reality testing" are important parts of this stage. Studies show that more exploration leads to better career choices for the individuals.[34]

TRIAL AND AUTONOMY.   As a person establishes autonomy, the principal concern becomes proving competence. Toward the end of the period, the emphasis shifts to children and the person begins asking, "What is life all about?" Career growth is rapid.

QUESTIONING.   From the early 40s, an individual's questioning becomes more intense. There is an increasing awareness of a time squeeze. People may wonder, "Have I made the right choice and is there still time to change?" The infamous

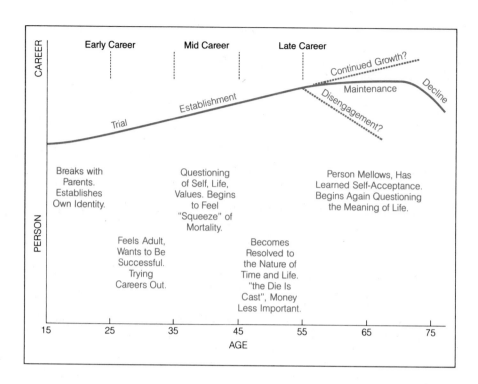

Figure 11–7
Career/Life Stages

"midlife crisis" hits and the person must resolve these difficult issues. One psychiatrist says: "The first 20 years are a blissful fantasy that life won't 'catch' us. Then somewhere along in the next 10 or 15 years, something makes us catch a glance at the end of the room.[35]"

MATURITY.   This period is one of resolution. The individual typically is comfortable in a career, money is less of an issue, and the troubling issues of the 40s have been resolved. Life settles down to become more even.

LATE CAREER.   During this period, a person's attention may turn to personal health. Managers may concern themselves with the next generation of managers. The individual's focus is much more personally-oriented, and less organizationally-oriented.

Retirement

Whether retirement comes at 55 or 70, it can be a major shock for some people. Of course, from the standpoint of the organization, retirement is an orderly way to move people out at the end of their careers. Some organizations are experimenting with "phased retirement" through gradually reduced workweeks or increased vacation time. The purpose of such programs is to make the break in work life more gradual for the retiree.

Some common emotional adjustments faced by the retiree include:

■ *Self-Management:* The person must adjust to being totally self-directed after retirement. There is no longer any supervisor or work agenda dictating what to do.

- *Need to Belong:* When a person retires he or she is no longer a member of the work group that took so much time and formed an important social structure for so many years. What will take its place?
- *Pride in Achievement:* Achievement reinforces self-esteem and is often centered around work. In retirement, past achievements quickly wear thin as a source of self-esteem.
- *Territoriality:* Personal "turf," in the form of office, company, and title, are lost in retirement. They must be replaced with other sources to satisfy a person's territoriality needs.
- *Goals:* Organizations provide many of a person's goals. That may leave some people unprepared to set their own goals when they retire.

Pre-retirement and post-retirement programs aimed at these problems can help employees make the transition to a useful retirement. The phenomenon of "forced" early retirement that began in the 1980s has forced thousands of managers and professionals to come to grips with what is important to them while they are still young and healthy. Because of economic factors, many organizations have used early retirement to reduce their work forces. In one year, 17 percent of men and 7 percent of women between 55 and 61 received pensions, which is double the figures of the preceding ten years.[36] Some of these young retirees "go fishing," but many begin second careers.

Effective Individual Career Planning

Good career planning at the individual level first requires that a person accurately know himself or herself. A person must face issues such as: How hard am I really willing to work? What factors are most important to me? What trade-off between work and family or leisure am I willing to make? These questions and others must be confronted honestly before personal goals and objectives can be realistically set. Professional counseling sometimes may be needed to help individuals make these decisions.

Supervisors and managers can help a person determine what skills and talents are necessary for success at each organizational level. Other information on occupations or careers outside the employee's current organization often must be gathered by the employee. Once this material is gathered, decisions can be made.[37]

Individual career goal setting is an important first step. Once goals have been set, plans must be formulated for their achievement. This planning consists of a series of actions that will lead to the goals. Research has been done on the type of person most likely to explore and set goals in planning a career. A study of managers found that those with highly demanding jobs, those who wanted different positions, and those low in anxiety were most likely to set goals for their careers and explore other jobs. There were no differences between men and women in this regard.[38]

Changing jobs and careers has become an accepted practice in recent years, and it can be financially rewarding; estimates are that individuals average around a 10 percent increase in salary on a new job.[39] However, "job-hopping" (changing jobs very frequently) can cause problems in retirement, vacation, seniority, and other benefits.[40] Perhaps more important is the perception that job-hopping is a sign of instability, especially in more mature managers.[41]

Career Path Development

To develop career paths, the organization logically should map out steps that employees might follow over time. One method is to gather information on historical patterns of movement in the organization. Unfortunately, this information shows what patterns have been developed in the past, not necessarily what they should be.

A better method is to select groups of appropriate jobs, or "job families," at lower levels that will prepare an employee for a job at a higher level. Career paths developed from such an analysis may emphasize upward mobility within a single area or occupation, such as that shown in Figure 11–8.

However, career paths do not have to be linear, nor do they always have to move up the organizational structure. Lateral movement within levels should be a possibility as well.

THE DUAL-CAREER LADDER. Professional and technical people, such as engineers and scientists, are a difficult challenge for the organization in developing career paths. Those who want to stay in their labs or at their drawing boards rather than move into management face a dilemma. Advancement frequently requires a move into management. Most of these people like the idea of the responsibility and opportunity associated with advancement, but they do not want to leave the technical puzzles and problems at which they excel.

The dual-career ladder is an attempt to solve this problem. A person can advance up either the management ladder or a corresponding ladder on the technical side. Unfortunately, the technical ladder sometimes is viewed as leading to "second-class citizenship" within the organization.[42] Figure 11–9 shows a dual-career path.

Middle Management Woes

The large pockets of unemployment in certain industries are well-documented. Technology, foreign competition, and the "factory of the future" all have taken their toll. But an entirely different group of employees recently has fallen on hard times as well—middle management.

In the last several years, 500,000 able and seasoned managers have been dumped from the payrolls of America's largest corporations. Takeovers, belt tightening, deregulation, restructuring, and downsizing have led to managerial layoffs at firms from AT&T to Xerox.

Surveys show that middle managers' optimism about opportunity for advancement has declined. But middle managers are not a disappearing breed. In small-

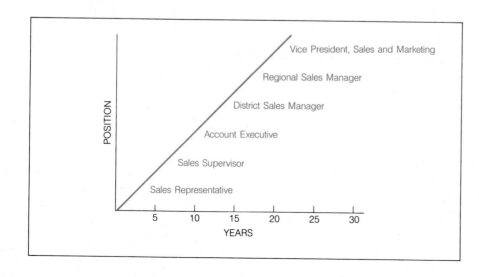

Figure 11–8
Career Path within a Single Area

Figure 11–9
A Dual-Career Path

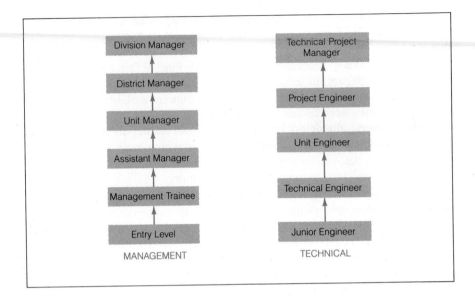

and middle-sized organizations across the country, the ranks of middle managers actually are growing. However, large industrial organizations which became bloated with managers are *not* the source of these jobs. Such organizations finally have been forced to deal with the problem of overstaffing. For those managers left behind, the game has changed. They will have additional responsibility and more influence in the decision-making process. The result for the large firm is a leaner, more competitive organization. The result for the small- and middle-sized firms to which the displaced managers go is a bonanza of talent and experience.[43] The effect of "breaks" or "gaps" in employment of the displaced manager is examined in the P/HR Research.

Dual-Career Marriages

The increasing number of women in the work force, particularly in professional careers, has greatly increased the number of dual-career families. The U.S. Bureau of Labor Statistics reported that 54 percent of all couples are dual-career couples. Leading areas of growth in the number of dual-career couples are the West Coast, Denver, Chicago, New York, and the Washington D.C.-Baltimore area.

The situation in which both mates are managers, professionals, or technicians has doubled since 1970 with the expansion of two-income families. Professional couples traditionally have been subject to transfers as part of the path upward in organizations. However, the two-professional family is much less mobile because transfer interfers with a spouse's career.

RECRUITMENT.   The reality of dual-career issues begins for employing organizations with the recruitment of a member of a dual-career couple. Increasingly, the best job candidate must have an equally attractive job for his/her spouse at the new location. Dual-career couples have more to lose when relocating, and as a result often exhibit higher expectations and requests for help and money to make

| P/HR: Practice *and* Research | Effect of "Gaps" in Employment on Careers |

Schneer and Reitman examined the effect that breaks in employment had on the subsequent careers of MBA's. As reported in the *Academy of Management Journal*, they surveyed 925 MBA's that had graduated 10 to 15 years previously. Average age was 38; 88 percent were currently employed full time, and the returns were almost equaly divided between men and women.

Twenty-four percent of the women and 12 percent of the men had experienced an employment gap. The reason for the gap cited most frequently by men was organizational restructuring. Child-rearing was most frequently cited by women. MBA's with employment gaps earned 14 percent less than those who had been continuously employed. Women were more likely to experience gaps *but* career satisfaction was more likely to be reduced for men than for women as a result of those gaps in employment.

The researchers speculate that gender-related career path stereotypes (men must work straight through a career, but it is acceptable for women to take time out to raise children) affect society's perceptions and therefore what men and women expect in their careers.[44]

a change that affect both careers. Employers also are concerned about turnover induced by transfer of a spouse.

DEALING WITH DUAL CAREERS.   It is important that career development problems of dual-career couples be recognized as early as possible, especially if they involve transfer, so that realistic alternatives can be explored. Early planning by employees and their supervisors can prevent crisis. Whenever possible, having both spouses involved, even when one is not employed by the company, has been found to enhance the success of such efforts.[45]

For dual-career couples with children, the family may take precedence. Thus, one spouse may be more willing to be flexible in the type of job taken for the sake of the family. During early childrearing years, flexible working arrangements such as part-time work, flex-time, and work-at-home arrangements may be job-sharing solutions.

RELOCATION.   Dual-career couples, besides having invested in two careers, have established support networks of friends and neighbors to cope with their transportation and dependent-care needs. These needs, in a single-career couple, would normally be met by the other spouse. Relocation of one spouse in a dual-career couple means upsetting this carefully constructed network or creating a "commuting" relationship.

If a company has no spouse-assistance program, an employee may be hesitant to request such services and may turn down the relocation. The dual-career family has not been the norm for very long and traditional role expectations remain. Male employees still fear they will appear "unmanly" should a wife refuse to become a trailing spouse in support of her husband's career, while female employees may feel guilty about violating the traditional concept of male career dominance.

When relocation is the only way to handle a staffing situation, employers increasingly have support services to help the couple adapt to the new location. Some companies go so far as to hire the spouse at the new location or find the spouse a job with another company. At times, companies have agreed to pay part of the salary or benefits when another company hires the spouse and to reciprocate at some future time. When such arrangements cannot be made, professional job-search counseling can be obtained for the spouse. It makes sense to take into account the dual-career social trend when revising P/HR policies on employee relocation assistance.[46] Some approaches that could be considered are:

1. Payment of employment agency fees for the relocating spouse.
2. Pay for a designated number of trips for the spouse to look for a job in the proposed new location.
3. Help the spouse find a job within the same company or in another division or subsidiary of the company.
4. Develop computerized job banks on spouses who are available for job openings to share with other companies in the area.
5. Form a consortium of companies in a particular geographic area that could share resumes of spouses of relocated employees—either formally or informally.

Moonlighting

Moonlighting traditionally was formally defined as work outside a person's regular employment that took twelve or more additional hours per week. More recently, the concept of moonlighting has been expanded to include such activities as self-employment, investments, hobbies, and other employee interests for which additional remuneration is received. The perception that moonlighting is a fixed outside commitment is no longer sufficiently broad since the forms that it may take are varied and sometimes difficult to identify. Figure 11–10 shows how multiple job holding has grown.

A growing number of managers are dividing their work efforts by moonlighting as consultants or self-employed entrepreneurs. Consulting not only increases income but it provides new experiences and diversity to managerial lives as well. Moonlighting is no longer just a second job for the underpaid blue-collar worker but also a career development strategy for some professionals.

Many individuals also view such activities as extra security, especially in these times of layoffs among middle managers. Most of these managers cannot afford to

Figure 11–10
Multiple Job Holders, by Sex

Data Source: Bureau of Labor Statistics (Thousands of persons aged 16 or over) U.S. Dept. of Labor

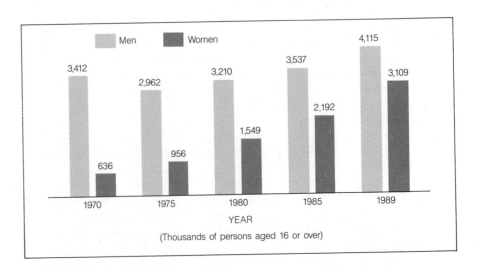

walk away from their corporate salaries, but they are looking elsewhere for fulfillment. A P/HR manager at a TV network sneaks off to work for a training firm she and a friend set up. An advertising executive at a cosmetics company accepts freelance assignments from his employer's clients. A computer software expert secretly develops a home computer program to market on his own. If someone is working for a company and freelancing in the same area, questions about whose ideas and time is involved are bound to arise.

Some organizations threaten to fire employees who are caught moonlighting, mainly to keep them from becoming competitors. But it does not seem to stop the activities. Other organizations permit freelance work so long as it is not directly competitive. Many believe their staff members should be free to develop their own special interests.

There is evidence that some multiple job holders work a second job in preparation for a career change. More than 8 percent of the men and 6 percent of the women in one study reported working two jobs in order to gain the necessary experience to meet the skill requirements of another job.[47] Whether or not a career change is sought, the concept is "job insurance." Moonlighting can be viewed in the same context as auto, car, home, or life insurance. The second job could serve as a backup in the event the primary job is lost.

Moonlighting is not without its problems. The main argument against moonlighting has been that energy is being used on a second job that should be used on the primary job. This could lead to poor performance, absenteeism, and reduced job commitment. However, these arguments are less valid with ever-shorter average workweeks.

The key for the employer in dealing with moonlighting employees is to devise and communicate a policy on the subject. Such a policy should focus on defining those areas where the employer limits employee activities because of business reasons.

SUMMARY

- Development is different from training because it focuses on less tangible aspects of performance such as attitudes and values.
- Successful development requires top management support and an understanding of its relationship to other P/HR activities.
- Replacement charts are like football depth charts. From them, decisions can be made about developing people internally or going outside for new talent.
- On-the-job development methods include coaching, special projects, committee assignments, job rotation, and assistant-to positions.
- Off-the-job development methods include classroom courses, special programs, psychological testing, human relations training, case study, role playing, simulation, and sabbatical leaves.
- Assessment centers provide valid methods of assessing management talent and development needs.
- Mentoring and modeling are two natural ways for younger managers to acquire the skills and know-how necessary to be successful. Mentoring follows a four-stage progression in most cases.
- Career planning may focus on organizational needs or individual needs (or both).
- A person chooses a career based on interests, self-image, personality, and social background.

■ A person's life follows a pattern, as does his or her career. Putting the two together offers a perspective that can be useful in understanding employee problems.

■ Retirement often requires one or more common emotional adjustments.

■ Development of career paths may be done by charting ways of moving up in the organization or by identifying job families that will provide the desired experience to move up.

■ Dual-career ladders are used with scientific or technical employees.

■ Dual-career marriages increasingly are becoming a consideration when relocating employees. Organizations are having to reconsider career moves in this context.

REVIEW AND DISCUSSION QUESTIONS

1. What is P/HR development and why is top management support so important to it?
2. You are the head of a government agency. What two methods of on-the-job development would you use with a promising supervisor? What two off-the-job methods would you use? Why?
3. Why do you believe that many large organizations have started assessment centers?
4. "Women managers should be treated like men when it comes to development activities. Neither group should receive special treatment or have unique activities planned for them." Discuss.
5. Discuss whether you would prefer organization-centered or individual-centered career planning.
6. Identify your anticipated career stages in conjunction with the life stages discussed in the chapter.

CASE   Fast-Track Kids: New Generation of Corporate Climbers

Although many of them are the sons and daughters of the "organization men" who built corporate America, the new fast-track generations bears little resemblance to their predecessors. The new breed is better educated, willing to challenge the status quo, and more self-confident. So says a *Business Week* study in which over 100 interviews with business schools, executive recruiters, and executives were conducted to establish a profile of the 35-year-old-and-under group of emerging business leaders. The study also notes a dark side. These fast-risers are impatient for raw authority, have little loyalty to employers, and seem to lack sensitivity and people skills.

To develop this raw talent, many organizations strive to strike a balance between polishing the rough edges and retraining the young executives' ambition. Organizations want to help these young managers develop strategic vision and skills in different functions. Some try to emphasize "soft" skills, such as how to motivate employees, that usually are not taught in M.B.A. programs.

The case of one fast-tracker illustrates the careers of many of this breed. Barrie G. Christman, 35, was promoted to chief executive of Mellon Banks (MD). She commands a business with $220 million in assets after only 12 years with the company. Her career took off after she began as a credit analyst and loan officer and was later picked to head a pilot program to market lending to midsized companies. Then a move to headquarters preceded her promotion to the Maryland operation. Christman got where she is by demonstrating unusual drive and initiative. For example, she got her M.B.A. while working, and she has continued by routinely racking up 12 hour days in completing her responsibilities.

However, Christman has made big sacrifices, such as moving five times in 12 years. She has had to give up hobbies and she held off marriage until age 32. In her comments, there is a wisp of regret at not having had time yet to have children. Her husband has followed her on the last two moves and even changed careers to accommodate her moves.

Ms. Christman does not doubt that her success has been worth the trouble. In fact, she is impatient to get ahead. Her philosophy: "Get the biggest breadth of experience at a fairly rapid pace."[47]

QUESTIONS

1. What kind of changes could be expected from these fast-trackers when they hit middle age, according to the life-cycle information presented in this chapter?
2. What kind of management development efforts are most likely to be effective in overcoming the problems noted with the fast-trackers?

NOTES

1. M. L. Sher and G. Brown, "What to Do with Jenny?" *Personnel Administrator*, April 1989, 31–41.

2. C. Trost, "Mommy Track Debate," *Wall Street Journal*, May 23, 1989, 1.

3. C. Trost, "How One Bank Handled a 'Two–Track' Career Plan," *Wall Street Journal*, March 3, 1989, B1.

4. "Survey: Family Bigger Influence on Career," *Omaha Herald*, January 22, 1989, 9G.

5. Ibid.

6. C. Trost, "Labor Letter," *Wall Street Journal*, May 23, 1989, 1; "Families Pay Emotional Cost of Relocating," *Omaha Herald*, February 19, 1989, 1G.

7. J. L. Wein, "The Right Way to Read a Resumé," Recruitment Today, Spring 1990, Vol. 3, No. 2, p. 8.

8. "Odds and Ends," *Wall Street Journal*, November 21, 1989, B1.

9. Adapted from M. Bourke and R. Day, "A Cumulative Study of the Effectiveness of Management Training," *Journal of Applied Psychology* 71 (1986): 232–245.

10. R. McAfee and P. J. Champagne, "Employee Development: Discovering Who Needs What," *Personnel Administrator*, February 1988, 92.

11. "Swelling Seminars," *Wall Street Journal*, October 21, 1986, 1.

12. L. Baum, "Where You Can Study Postal Management 101," *Business Week*, April 11, 1988.

13. "Learning More," *Wall Street Journal*, January 2, 1990, 1.

14. J. Solomon, "Now Simulators for Piloting Companies," *Wall Street Journal*, July 31, 1989, B1.

15. R. E. Kaplan et al., "A Mirror for Managers: Using Simulation to Develop Management Teams," *Journal of Applied Behavioral Science* 21 (1985): 241–253.

16. N. Boudette, "High Risk Actions—With No Real Risk," *Industry Week*, September 18, 1989, 59–61; T. Welter, "Simulation," *Industry Week*, March 6, 1989, 40–43.

17. "Work Dropouts Seek New Perspectives with Sabbaticals," *Omaha World Herald*, February 5, 1989, 1G.

18. W. G. Symonds, "A School of Hard Rocks," *Business Week*, March 3, 1986; "Executives Test Their Leadership Skills in Outdoor Programs," *Wall Street Journal*, April 29, 1986, 1; R. Phalon, "Hell Camp, Malibu-Style," *Forbes*, December 28, 1987, 110.

19. S. J. Yeager, "Use of Assessment Centers by Metropolitan Fire Departments in North America," *Public Personnel Management* 15 (1986): 55.

20. W. H. Silverman et al., "Influence of Assessment Center Methods on Assessor's Ratings," *Personnel Psychology* 39 (1986): 565.
21. D. F. Olshfski and R. D. Cunningham, "Establishing Assessment Center Validity," *Public Personnel Management* 15 (1986): 85–98.
22. A Carnevale, "Management Training—Today and Tomorrow," *Training and Development Journal*, December 1988, 8.
23. W. G. Thomas, "Training and Development *Do* Make Better Managers," *Personnel*, January 1988, 52.
24. J. Buttimer and J. Fisher, "The Importance of Comprehensive Management Development," *Human Resources Professional*, May/June 1989, 53.
25. L. M. Saari, et al., "A Survey of Management Training and Education Practices in U.S. Companies," *Personnel Psychology* 41 (1988): 731–743.
26. P. J. Decker, "The Enhancement of Behavior Modeling Training of Supervisory Skills by the Inclusion of Retention processes," *Personnel Psychology* 29 (1982): 323–333.
27. C. C. Manz and H. P. Sims, Jr., "Beyond Imitation: Complex Behavior and Affective Linkages Resulting from Exposure to Leadership Training Models," *Journal of Applied Psychology* 71 (1986): 571–578.
28. J. Johnson, "With a Little Help from Her Friends," *Nation's Business*, January 1989, 28.
29. K. E. Kram, "Phases of the Mentor Relationship," *Academy of Management Journal* 26 (1983): 608–625.
30. M. B. Arthur et al., *Handbook of Career Theory* (Cambridge: Cambridge University Press), 1989.
31. D. Hall and J. Richter "Career Gridlock: Baby Boomers Hit the Wall," *The Executive*, Aug. 1990, 7–23.
32. W. L. Cron and J. W. Slocum, Jr., "The Influence of Career Stages on Salespeople's Job Attitudes, Work Perceptions, and Performance," *Journal of Marketing Research* 23 (1986): 119–129.
33. R. A. Ellis and M. S. Taylor, "Role of Self-Esteem within the Job Search Process," *Journal of Applied Psychology* 68 (1983): 632–639.
34. H. D. Grotevant and C. R. Cooper, "Exploration as a Predictor of Congruence in Adolescent's Career Choices," *Journal of Vocational Behavior* 29 (1986): 201–215; D. Blustein and J. Phillips, "Individual and Contextual Factors in Career Exploration," *Journal of Vocational Behaviors* 33 (1988): 203–216.
35. J. Beondi, "The Middle Ages," *Valley Magazine*, July 1990, 33.
36. S. Feinstein, "Early Retirement," *Wall Street Journal*, January 9, 1987, 1.
37. S. K. Stout et al., "Dynamics of the Career Plateauing Process," *Journal of Vocational Behavior* 32 (1988): 74–91.
38. T. D. Sugalski and J. H. Greenhaus, "Career Exploration and Goal Setting among Managerial Employees," *Journal of Vocational Behavior* 29 (1986): 102–114.
39. "The Right Report," Right Associates—Management Consultants 5 no. 1 (1988).
40. P. Strassels, "It's Your Money," *Nation's Business*, January 1989, 70.
41. M. Kastre, "The Two Year Itch," *National Business Employment Weekly*, June 19, 1988, 12.
42. M. Goldstein, "Dual-Career Ladders," *Industry Week*, January 14, 1988, 57–60.
43. R. Gerevas, "Keeping Good Managers Happy on a Slower Track," *Business Month*, May 1989, 79; C. Hymowitz, "More Executives Finding Changes in Traditional Corporate Ladders," *Wall Street Journal*, November 14, 1986, 23; adapted from M. L. Goldstein, "What Future for Middle Managers?" *Industry Week*, December 8, 1986, 45–62; B. Jacobs, "Surviving a Takeover," *Industry Week*, December 8, 1986, 64; and E. Gottschalk, Jr., "More Ex-Managers Seek to Turn Hobbies into Full-Time Businesses," *Wall Street Journal*, December 23, 1986, 23.
44. J. A. Schneer and F. Reitman, "Effects of Employment Gaps on Careers of MBAs. . .," *Academy of Management Journal*, 33(1990): 391–406.
45. A. H. Cook, "Public Policies to Help Dual-Earner Families Meet the Demands of the Work World," *Industrial and Labor Relations Review*, 42(1989): 201–215.
46. R. Half, "Managing Your Career," *Management Accounting*, August 1986, 16.
47. Adapted from T. Cason and J. A. Byrne, "Fast-Track Kids;" and Matt Rothman, "Breathing New Life into a Failed S & L," *Business Week*, November 10, 1986, 90–94.

Chapter 12

Appraisal of Human Resources

After you have read this chapter, you should be able to:

1. Identify the major uses of appraisals
2. Discuss three different categories of raters
3. Give examples of three general types of appraisal methods
4. Explain several rater errors
5. Describe how to construct behaviorally-anchored rating scales (BARS)
6. Identify the management by objectives (MBO) process
7. Discuss several concerns about appraisal feedback interview
8. List the characteristics of a legal appraisal system
9. Describe at least two characteristics of an effective appraisal system

P/HR: Today *and* Tomorrow

An Unresolved Appraisal Issue: Grading Teachers

Concern with the quality of American public education has focused in recent years on the performance of classroom teachers. Government officials and others have argued that a performance appraisal system for teachers could help identify those who are not performing up to standards. After all, the performance appraisal system has been used in business and industry for years. A report card for the teachers might be another step in improving instruction in public schools.

Teaching, however, presents some special problems for appraisal. Performance standards obviously should be set either in terms of changes in the pupils' abilities or in terms of teacher behaviors that can be clearly linked by research to learning. Emphasizing such items as how well the teacher gets along with students or how the room appears is beside the point. In fact, the idea that there is a single best method of teaching may prevent an unbiased evaluation of just how good a teacher may be.

When (or if) proper criteria for teacher evaluation are identified and used, they will become targets for teaching activity. Yet discovering those criteria is not easy. Witness one study of 60 teachers. Trained observers visited their classes for two years and reported on how well the teachers did on 25 abilities often measured in teacher competency tests. When the results were formulated, it became clear that not much was clear. About half the measures had no relationship to either student achievement scores or student self-esteem (the dependent variables used in the study.) Skills such as using praise, responding to student questions, and giving students a voice in decision-making actually were negatively related to academic achievement. Use of supportive classroom techniques also was negatively related to self-esteem. This is only one study; but the mixed or negative support given to factors thought to be related to good teaching suggests that those who wish to formulate teaching appraisal standards should proceed with caution.

Teacher evaluation had never been much of an issue in another school district. In fact, the teachers themselves helped to draw up the system that was in operation. But now they are afraid of the new system because it could be misused by new administrators. Teachers who should *not* be among the first to go in a cutback could be laid off. They feel that if an administrator wants to dump somebody, all the administrator would have to do is rig the performance appraisal system to rank the teacher low and he or she would be gone.

Clearly, teacher evaluation at any level is neither easy nor noncontroversial. For performance appraisal to be properly applied to this kind of endeavor will require a major advancement in the technology of appraisal, as well as common sense in the use of any resulting "measuring stick."[1]

"Let's face reality, sloppy management is easy. That's why we have so much of it."

Jan Muezyk

After an employee has been selected for a job, has been trained to do it, and has worked on it for a period of time, his or her performance should be reviewed. **Performance appraisal,** the process of evaluating how well employees do their jobs, also has been called employee rating, employee evaluation, performance review, performance evaluation, and results appraisal.

That sounds simple enough. Research shows that performance appraisal (PA) is widely used for wage/salary administration, performance feedback, and identification of individual employee strengths and weaknesses.[2] Certainly performance appraisal is a common P/HR activity. Well over 80 percent of U.S. companies have PA systems for office, professional, technical, supervisory, middle managers and nonunion production workers.[3]

Yet performance appraisal is widely found to be management's most *disliked* activity.[4] There may be good reasons for that feeling. Not all performance appraisals are positive, and for that reason the task may be unpleasant. It may be difficult to differentiate among employees if good performance data are not available. Further, some supervisors are uncomfortable with the role of "playing God" with employees' raises and careers, which they feel performance appraisal requires.

> **PERFORMANCE APPRAISAL**
> is the process of determining how well employees do their jobs compared with a set of standards and communicating that information to the employees.

■■ ■ USES OF PERFORMANCE APPRAISAL

These difficulties and others are examined as this exploration of PA unfolds. Perhaps the best way to begin is to look at the three major uses of PA, as shown in Figure 12–1.

Compensation Administration

A performance appraisal system is the link between the reward an employee hopes to receive and his/her productivity. The linkage can be thought of as **productivity → performance appraisal → rewards.** If any link fails, more productive employees do not receive more rewards. This approach to compensation is at the heart of the idea that raises should be given for merit rather than for seniority. Under merit systems, employees receive raises based on performance. The manager's role is as evaluator of a subordinate's performance, and the focus is usually a comparison of performance levels among individuals.

Yet few American workers see much linkage between the level of their efforts and the size of their paychecks—according to a survey of 5,000 American employees only 28 percent saw a link. Further, only about one-third of the sample rated their

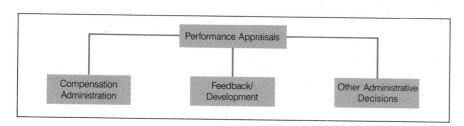

Figure 12–1
Uses Of Performance Appraisal

supervisor as good at giving performance feedback.[5] However, most research indicates that salary administration usage of performance appraisal is very common.

Performance Feedback

Performance appraisal, even if it is not linked to wage/salary treatment, is a primary source of information for employees on areas in which they are doing well and where improvement is possible. So performance appraisal information has a *training* use. It identifies the weaknesses, potentials, and training needs of employees. Performance appraisal can inform employees about their progress and tell them what skills they need to develop to become eligible for promotions, transfers, etc.

The manager's role in such a situation is like that of a coach. The "coach's" job is to reward good performance with recognition, explain what improvement is necessary in some areas, and show the employee *how* to improve. People do not always know where they could improve and management really cannot expect improvement if it is unwilling to explain where and how improvement can occur.[6] The purpose of PA feedback is to change or reinforce individual behavior rather than to compare individuals.

Other Administrative Decisions

Several other uses of performance appraisal results can be classified as "organizational maintenance decisions." Retention, termination, layoff, and transfers to other assignments often require meeting the basic legal requirement that if such actions are taken on the basis of performance, then performance must be measured formally. The focus for such activities is both among individuals and comparison with a standard. The manager is back in role of judge once again.

■■ ■ JOB CRITERIA AND PERFORMANCE STANDARDS

JOB CRITERIA
are the elements of a job to be
evaluated during performance
appraisal.

STANDARD
is an expected level of performance.

Job analysis helps identify the most important duties and tasks of each job. **Job criteria** are the elements of the job to be evaluated during performance, and they should be specified. For example, a criterion for a typist's job might be typing speed; another might be typing accuracy.

The various job criteria should be compared with a **standard,** which is the expected level of performance. For the typist's job, the standard might be fifty words per minute and no more than two errors. The various criteria for a given job also should be *weighted.* Weighting the various parts of the job means deciding the relative importance of criterias. For example, the typist's job speed might be twice as important as accuracy, and accuracy might be as important as getting to work on time and being there every day. Thus, the weighting might look like this:

Criterion	Weight
Typing speed	2
Accuracy	1
Attendance	1
Tardiness	1

Performance is almost never one-dimensional. For example, university professors are evaluated by students on one dimension of their performance: *teaching,* and teaching is multi-dimensional as well. But for most professors, there are at least two other important dimensions that students often do not see: *research* and *service.*

In some universities, teaching might carry more weight than research. At other institutions, the reverse may be true depending on the mission of the university. Some students probably have encountered a professor or two who has a national reputation as a researcher but who could not teach effectively. Likewise, in baseball the leading home-run hitter may not be the best fielder or hit for the highest average. In summary, there always are several dimensions to job performance.

Performance appraisal data even can be translated into economic terms to indicate what payoff improved performance has had for the organization.[7] Performance standards are the yardstick measures against which dimensions of performance are assessed. Standards measure results, which are the degree to which specific, well-defined work activities are accomplished. Standards often are established for:

- Quantity of output
- Quality of output
- Timeliness of results
- Manner of performance
- Effectiveness in use of resources

Realistic, measurable, clearly understood performance standards benefit both the organization and the employee. It is important to establish standards *before* the work is performed so that all involved will understand the level of accomplishment expected.

Finally, there is some advantage in defining the level of performance associated with each term used to describe performance. For example: How great is "outstanding"? What does "poor" mean? What is "average"? An identification of these terms is useful but it may be difficult. Figure 12–2 shows one attempt to define terms used in one organization.

■■ ■ INFORMAL VERSUS SYSTEMATIC APPRAISAL

Performance appraisal may occur in two ways, informally or systematically. An *informal appraisal* is conducted whenever the supervisor feels it is necessary. The day-to-day working relationship of a manager and an employee offers an opportunity

---

Outstanding: The person is so successful at this job criterion that special note should be made. Compared with the usual standards and the rest of the department, this performance ranks in the top 10 percent.

Very Good: Performance at this level is one of *better* performance in the unit, given the common standards and unit results; clearly, better-than average performance.

Satisfactory: Performance is at or above the minimum standards. This level of performance is what one would expect from most experienced, competent employees.

Marginal: Performance is somewhat below the minimum-level standard on this job dimension. However, there appears to be potential to improve the rating within a reasonable time frame.

Unsatisfactory: Performance on this item in the job is well below standard and there is serious question as to whether the person can improve to meet minimum standards.

Figure 12–2
Terms Used In Rating Performance

Figure 12–3
Appraisal Responsibilities

P/HR UNIT	MANAGERS
■ Designs and maintains formal system ■ Establishes formal report system ■ Makes sure reports are on time ■ Trains raters	■ Actually rate performance of employees ■ Make formal reports ■ Review appraisals with employees

for the employee's performance to be judged. This judgment is communicated through conversation on the job, over coffee, or by on-the-spot examination of a particular piece of work. Informal appraisal is especially appropriate when time is an issue. Studies show that the longer feedback is delayed, the less likely it is to motivate behavior change.[8]

A *systematic appraisal* is used when the contact between manager and employee is formalized and a system is established to report supervisor impressions and observations on employee performance. When a formalized or systematic appraisal is used, the interface between the P/HR unit and the appraising manager becomes more important. A P/HR specialist can assist the manager in seeing that the appraisal is done effectively.

Appraisal Responsibilities

The appraisal process can be quite beneficial to the organization and to the individuals involved if done properly. It also can be the source of a great deal of discontent. In situations in which an employer must deal with a strong union, performance appraisals may be conducted only on salaried, nonunion employees. The union's emphasis on seniority over merit is the major cause of union resistance to appraisals.

Figure 12–3 shows that the P/HR unit typically designs a systematic appraisal system. The manager does the actual appraising of the employee, using the procedures developed by the personnel unit. As the formal system is being developed, the manager usually offers input on how the final system will work. Only rarely does a P/HR specialist actually rate a manager's employees.

Timing of Appraisals

Timing of appraisals is important. Appraisals should be done on a regular basis, and in the opinion of many, they should be separated from the merit discussion by a period of time. Systematic appraisals typically are conducted once or twice a year. One study of 244 organizations showed that appraisals most often were conducted once a year, usually near the employee's anniversary date.[9]

This regular time interval is a feature of formal or systematic appraisals and distinguishes them from informal appraisals. Both employees and managers are aware that performance will be reviewed on a regular basis, and they can plan for necessary adjustments. Nevertheless, an informal appraisal should be conducted whenever a manager feels it is desirable.

The timing of performance reviews and salary discussions should be different because:

■ Pay decisions may include factors other than performance. For example, a good performer may get the same raise as a poor employee because raises are granted "across-the-board" that year.

- Performance appraisal can be reinforcing by itself, especially if there are not raises in a given year. The reinforcement value can be lost if pay is brought in at that point.
- People may focus more on the pay treatment than on what they have done well or need to improve.
- Sometimes managers may manipulate performance appraisal ratings to justify the desired pay treatment for a given individual.

Just because performance appraisal and pay are discussed separately does not guarantee that problems will not occur, but separate sessions can help minimize them.

WHO DOES THE APPRAISING?

Performance appraisal can be done by:

- Supervisors who rate their employees
- Employees who rate their superiors
- Peers who rate each other
- Some combination of raters
- Self
- Outside sources

The first method is the most common. The immediate superior has the sole responsibility for appraisal in most organizations, although it is common practice to have the appraisal reviewed and approved by the supervisor's boss. Combinations of these methods are possible, too.

Supervisor Rating of Subordinates

Rating of employees by supervisors is based on the assumption that the manager is the most qualified person to evaluate the employee's performance realistically, objectively, and fairly. The "unity of command" notion—that every subordinate should have only one superior—underlies this approach.

As with any rating system, the supervisor's judgment should be objective and based on actual performance. Toward this end, some managers keep logs of what employees have done. These logs provide examples when rating time arrives. They also serve to jog the memory, because managers cannot be expected to remember every detail of performance over a six-month or one-year period. A manager's appraisal typically is reviewed by the manager's superior to make sure that the manager has done a proper job of appraisal and, if the review and merit discussion is not separated, that the recommended pay increase is justified. (Figure 12–4 shows this review process.)

One recent study has shown that managers and employees evaluate performance appraisal systems on different bases. Managers tend to evaluate the system on how well it helps them communicate employee performance to employees. Employees rate the fairness of a performance appraisal on how:

- Salary treatment is based on rating.
- Ratings are based on actual performance.
- Standards are consistently applied.
- Input is solicited and used *before* rating.
- Two-way communication is allowed during the interview.[10]

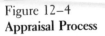

Figure 12–4
Appraisal Process

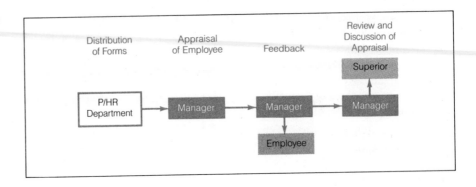

COMMITTEE OF SUPERIORS.   If rating is done by a committee of superiors, more useful information may be available because more people have had a chance to know and observe the individual being rated. With more information, an organization can better pinpoint employees for promotions or future job assignments.

As with any P/HR technique, however, there are some disadvantages. Having more information does not necessarily mean better information. Without objective data to make appraisals, committees may simply be pooling their collective ignorance.

MULTIPLE RATING SYSTEM.   The multiple rating system is simple. It merely requires that several superiors separately fill out rating forms on the same employee. The results are then tabulated. For instance, a young loan officer in a bank who is responsible for loan judgments may have her performance reviewed by a group of superiors comprising the bank's loan committee. This method preserves the role of judge for the superiors involved in the rating process.

Employee Rating of Superiors

The concept of having superiors rated by employees is being used in a number of organizations today (see the P/HR: Practice on performance appraisal in reverse). A prime example of this type of rating takes place in colleges and universities where students evaluate a professor's performance in the classroom. Industry also has used employee ratings for developmental purposes—to help superiors improve themselves or to help organizations assess managerial leadership potential.

Research suggests that subordinate appraisals do serve a useful purpose in P/HR decision-making. But a combination of subordinate appraisals *and* assessment center data proved superior to either method used independently to improve management performance.[12]

ADVANTAGES.   The advantages of having employees rate superiors are at least two. First, in situations where superior-employee relationships are critical, employee ratings can be quite useful in identifying competent superiors. The rating of leaders by combat soldiers is an example. Second, this type of rating program can help make the superior more responsive to employees, though this advantage can quickly become a disadvantage if it leads to the superior trying to be "nice" rather than trying to manage the workers. Nice people without other qualifications may not be good managers in many situations.

P/HR: Practice and Research

Performance Appraisal in Reverse

At Photocircuits, a New York company that manufactures printed circuit boards, managers and supervisors get regular reviews by their workers. Employees fill out questionnaires on supervisory attitudes that ask:

- Does your manager show interest in you as a person?
- Does he or she accept suggestions easily?
- Does he or she give criticism in a fair and considerate manner?

Employees summarize strong and weak points, then discuss the appraisal with their boss.

At first, employees had trouble being critical of the boss. Initial appraisals were uncritical, even "glowing." However, company president John Endee encouraged honest appraisal. "This sort of program doesn't work in a climate of fear," he said. He was told by one employee that he was "too aggressive" and "frightened people."

Fear can work on managers too. Some were afraid of being evaluated by employees. But criticism of management occurs all the time. Employees constantly criticize their boss behind his back. The manager who has a problem—who needs to improve his behavior or attitude—will be made aware of this by the very people who can help him most.[11]

DISADVANTAGES.   A major disadvantage is the negative reaction many superiors have to being evaluated by employees. Fear of reprisal may be too great for employees to give realistic ratings. The principles of "proper" superior–employee relations may be violated by having workers rate superiors. They may resist rating their bosses because they do not perceive it as an appropriate part of their job. If the situation is the case, workers may rate the superior only on the way the superior treats them, and not on critical job requirements.

The problems associated with employees rating superiors seem to limit the usefulness of this appraisal approach to certain situations, such as in a university or an engineering research department. The traditional nature of most organizations appears to restrict the applicability of employee rating except for self-improvement purposes.[13]

Peer Ratings

The use of peer groups as raters in a third type of appraisal system. The peer technique seldom is used in open committee form. If a group of salespersons met as a committee to talk about one another's ratings, future work relationships might be impaired. Therefore, the peer rating approach is best done if individual ratings are summarized. A notable exception is ODS Corporation in Tokyo where employees bargain each year with their peers and the president for pay raises.[14] Most of the research on peer ratings has been done on military personnel at the management or pre-management level (officers or officer candidates) rather than on employees in business organizations.

There are several likely reasons for the scarcity of peer ratings in industry. Members of peer groups in industry may not be as closely knit as peer groups in military training settings. Also, peer ratings may be most useful when done by and for managers to identify leadership potential.

Levi Strauss & Company used peer ratings to make a different type of decision. As part of a work force reduction of 3,600, approximately 2,000 executive, sales, and other professional employees rated fellow employees. These ratings, along with ratings from supervisors, were used to identify candidates who would lose their jobs.[15]

Self-Ratings

Self-appraisal works in certain situations. Essentially, it is a self-development tool that forces employees to think about their strengths and weaknesses and set goals for improvement.[16] If an employee is working in isolation or possesses a unique skill, the employee may be the only one qualified to rate his or her own behavior. but employees may not rate themselves as supervisors would rate them; therefore, it is difficult to evaluate self-ratings because people may be rating themselves on quite different standards. Nonetheless, research suggests the performing individual can be a valuable and credible source of performance information.[17] Self-generated feedback may be especially helpful in building a person's belief in his/her ability to perform a given task.[18]

Outside Raters

Rating also may be done by outsiders. Outside experts may be called in to review the work of a college president, for example, or professional assessors at an assessment center might evaluate a person's potential for advancement in an organization. Outsiders may furnish managers with professional assistance in making appraisals, but there are obvious disadvantages. The outsider may not know all the important contingencies within the organization. In addition, outsider appraisals are time-consuming and expensive.

The customers or clients of an organization are an obvious source of outside appraisals. For salespeople and other service jobs customers may provide the only really clear view of certain behaviors. Xerox Corporation uses measures of customer satisfaction with service as a portion of the input for top company marketing executives' bonuses.[19]

■■ ■■ METHODS FOR APPRAISING PERFORMANCE

Appraisals can be conducted by a number of methods. In Figure 12–5 the various methods are categorized into four major groups.

Category Rating Methods

The simplest methods for appraising performance are those that require a manager to mark an employee's level of performance on a specific form. The graphic rating scale and checklist, are common category rating methods.

GRAPHIC RATING SCALE.   The graphic rating scale is the most frequently used method. Figure 12–6 shows a graphic rating scale form used by managers to rate office employees. The rater checks the appropriate place on the scale for each duty

P/HR: Practice *and* Research

Multiple Use of Performance Appraisal

Research at Colorado State University studied the uses to which performance appraisal data is put in American organizations. As reported in the *Journal of Applied Psychology*, 106 different organizations responded. Salary administration, and performance feedback, as one would expect, were cited as areas upon which PA had the greatest impact.

Performance appraisal, however, was typically found to be used for a variety of purposes and those purposes were sometimes incompatible (such as feedback and salary administration). When using PA as a tool to assist in deciding who will get a promotion or for salary determination, raters may be forced to focus on comparisons between individuals. Alternatively, when using performance appraisal for determining training needs, factors within that one individual should be the focus. If PA data is collected with one of these two purposes in mind it is unlikely to be as effective when used for the other purpose.

Organizations that consist of few departments that work closely together tend to use PA to identify "within individual" needs such as training and development as opposed to using it to determine differences between individuals.

The research suggested that performance appraisal data is used not only for making determinations within and between individuals, but also for documenting personnel decisions and maintaining the management system.[29]

listed. More detail can be added in the space for comments following each factor rated.

There are some obvious drawbacks to the graphic rating scale. Often separate traits or factors are grouped together and the rater is given only one box to check. Another drawback is that the descriptive words sometimes used in such scales may have different meanings to different raters. Factors such as *initiative* and *cooperation* are subject to many interpretations, especially in conjunction with words such as *outstanding, average,* or *poor.*

Graphic rating scales in many forms are used widely because they are easy to develop. But for the same reason, they encourage errors on the part of the raters.[20] Because graphic rating scale information forms the basis for many performance appraisals, a major concern is that these scales encourage errors on the part of the raters. But, as the P/HR: Research indicates, multiple use of appraisal information occurs.

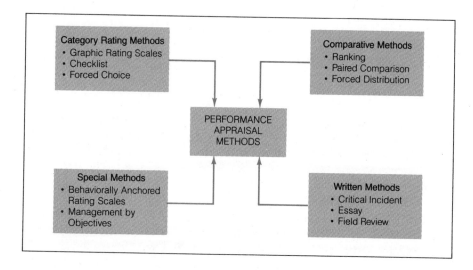

Figure 12–5
Performance Appraisal Methods

Figure 12–6
Sample Performance Appraisal Form (Simplified)

Date Sent	**4/19/90**	Return by	**5/10/90**
Name	**Jane Doe**	Job Title	**Receiving Clerk**
Department	**Receiving**	Supervisor	**Fred Smith**

Full-time _____ / _____   Part-time _____   Date of Hire   **10/12/88**

Period _____   From _____   To _____

Reason for appraisal (check one): Discharge _____

Regular interval _____ / _____   Probationary _____   Counseling only _____

Major job duties
  Job duty 1: _____ **Inventory receipt and checking** _____

Lowest		Satisfactory		Highest
1	2	3	4	5

Explanation _____

  Job duty 2: _____ **Accuracy of records kept** _____

Lowest		Satisfactory		Highest
1	2	3	4	5

Explanation _____

  Job duty 3: _____ **Maintain good vendor relations** _____

Lowest		Satisfactory		Highest
1	2	3	4	5

Explanation _____

OVERALL:
Consider a general view of the employee's job performance during the rating period:

Lowest		Satisfactory		Highest
1	2	3	4	5

Explanation _____

CHECKLIST. The checklist is a simple rating method in which the manager is given a list of statements or words and asked to check those representing the characteristics and performance of the employee. The checklist can be modified so that varying weights are assigned to the statements or words. The results can then be quantified. Usually, the weights are not known by the rating supervisor and are tabulated by someone else, such as a member of the P/HR unit.

There are several difficulties with the checklist: (1) As with the graphic rating scale, the words or statements may have different meanings to different raters; (2) The rater cannot readily discern the rating results if a weighted checklist is used;

(3) The rater does not assign the weights to each factor. These difficulties limit the use of the information when a rater discusses the checklist with the employee, placing a barrier to effective developmental counseling.

The following are typical checklist statements:

————— can be expected to finish work on time
————— seldom agrees to work overtime
————— is cooperative and helpful
————— accepts criticism
————— strives for self-improvement

Comparative Methods

Comparative methods require that managers directly compare the performances of their employees against one another. For example, a data entry operator's performance would be compared with that of other data entry operators by the computing supervisor. This group of comparative techniques includes *ranking, paired comparisons,* and *forced distribution.*

RANKING.   The ranking method is relatively simple. Using it, the rater lists all employees from highest to lowest.

The primary drawback of the ranking method is that the size of the difference among individuals is not well defined. For example, there may be little difference in performance between individuals ranked second and third, but a big difference in performance between those ranked third and fourth. This drawback can be overcome to some extent by assigning points to indicate the size of the gaps existing among employees.

Ranking also means that someone must be last. It is possible that the last-ranked individual in one group would be the top employee in a different group. Further, ranking may be affected by rater bias or varying performance standards.

Exxon uses ranking as a part of its performance appraisal system. The ranking is done by the immediate supervisor *and* the next level of managers. This approach is an attempt to eliminate situations in which a manager rates all employees as top performers or all as equally good.

PAIRED COMPARISONS.   The rater using the paired comparison method formally compares each employee with every other employee in the rating group one at a time. The number of comparisons can be calculated using the formula $\frac{n(n-1)}{2}$ where n is the number of people rated. For example, a manager with fifteen employees would compare one person's performance with those of the other fourteen employees. Each employee, in turn, would be compared in similar fashion. The manager doing the ratings would have to make 105 different comparisons on each rating factor. Use of the paired comparison method gives more information about individual employees than the straight ranking method does. Obviously, the large number of comparisons that must be made is the major drawback of this method. Figure 12–7 illustrates the paired comparison method with three individuals.

FORCED DISTRIBUTION.   The forced distribution method is also a comparative technique but without the drawback of the large number of comparisons in the

Figure 12–7
Paired Comparisons

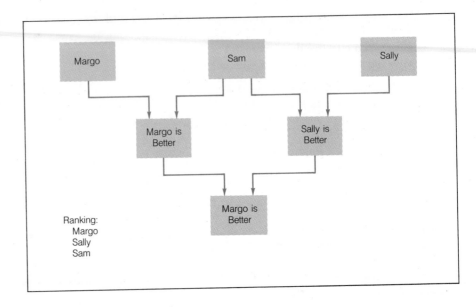

paired comparison method. By using the forced distribution method, a head nurse can rank nursing personnel along a scale, placing a certain percentage of employees at various performance levels. This method assumes that the widely known "bell-shaped curve" of performance exists in a given group. Figure 12–8 shows a scale used with a forced distribution.

A drawback of forced distribution is that a supervisor may resist placing any individual in the lowest (or the highest) group. Difficulties can arise when the rater must explain to the employee why he or she was placed in one grouping and others were placed in higher groupings. Further, with small groups, there may be no reason to assume that bell-shaped distribution of performance really exists. Finally, in some cases the manager may feel forced to make distinctions among employees that may not exist.

Narrative Methods

Some managers or P/HR specialists are required to provide written narrative appraisal information. Documentation and description are the essence of the *critical incident*, the *essay*, and the *field review* methods. These records indicate an employee's actions rather than an actual rating.

CRITICAL INCIDENT.   In the critical incident method the manager keeps a written record of the highly favorable and unfavorable actions in an employee's performance. When something happens (a critical incident involving an employee), the manager writes it down. A list of critical incidents is kept during the entire rating period for each employee. The critical incident method can be used with other methods to document the reasons why an employee was rated in a certain way.

The critical incident method also has its unfavorable aspects. First, what constitutes a critical incident is not defined in the same way by all supervisors. Next, producing daily or weekly written remarks about each employee's performance can take considerable time. Further, employees may become overly concerned about what the superior writes and begin to fear the manager's "black book."

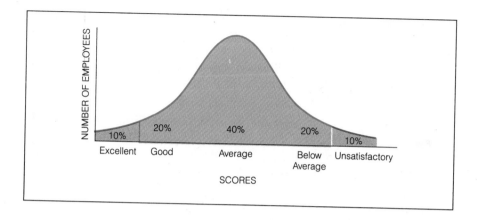

Figure 12–8
Forced Distribution on a Bell-shaped Curve

ESSAY. The essay, or free-form appraisal, method requires the manager to write a short essay describing each employee's performance during the rating period. The rater usually is given a few general headings under which to categorize comments. The intent is to allow the rater more flexibility than other methods do. Research shows that raters are able to impose order on unorganized performance information on their own.[21]

One drawback to the essay method is that some supervisors communicate in writing better than others do, so the quality of the ratings depends on the writing ability of the raters. Also, the method can be time-consuming, and it is difficult to quantify or express numerically for administrative purposes.

FIELD REVIEW. Under the field review method, the P/HR unit becomes an active partner in the rating process. A member of the unit interviews the manager about each employee's performance. The P/HR representative then compiles the notes of each interview into a rating for each employee. Then the rating is reviewed by the supervisor for needed changes. This method assumes that the representative of the personnel unit knows enough about the job setting to help supervisors give more accurate and thorough appraisals.

The major limitation of the field review method is that the P/HR representative has a large amount of control over the rating. Although this control may be desirable from one viewpoint, supervisors may see it as a challenge to their managerial authority. In addition, the field review method can be time-consuming, particularly if a supervisor has to rate a large number of employees.

▬▬ ■ SPECIAL APPRAISAL SYSTEMS: BARS AND MBO

Two special appraisal systems that attempt to overcome some of the difficulties of the methods just described are behaviorally-anchored rating scales (BARS) and management by objectives (MBO). Behaviorally-anchored rating scales seem to hold promise for situations in which many people are doing the same job, whereas MBO is useful for management appraisals.

Behaviorally-Anchored Rating Scales (BARS)

A BARS system [occasionally called a behavioral expectation scale (BES) and slightly different in degree from a behavioral observation scale (BOS)[22]] describes examples of good or bad behavior. These examples are "anchored," or measured, against a scale of performance levels. Figure 12–9 shows a BARS that rates a college professor's attitude toward students. What constitutes various levels of performance is clearly defined in the figure. Spelling out the behavior associated with each level of performance helps minimize some of the problems noted earlier.

CONSTRUCTING BARS.   Construction of a BARS begins with identification of important *job dimensions*. The dimensions are the most important performance factors in an employee's description. To continue with the college professor example, assume the major job dimensions associated with teaching are:

1. Course organization
2. Attitude toward students
3. Fair treatment
4. Competence in subject area

Short statements, similar to critical incidents, that describe both desirable and undesirable behaviors (anchors) are developed. Then they are "retranslated" or assigned to one of the job dimensions. This task is usually a group project, and assignment to a dimension usually requires the agreement of 60 to 70 percent of the group. The group, consisting of people familiar with the job, then assigns each "anchor" a number, which represents how good or bad the behavior is. When numbered, these anchors are fitted to a scale. Figure 12–10 shows a flow diagram of the BARS construction process.

Behaviorally-anchored rating scales require extensive time and effort to develop and maintain. Several appraisal forms also are necessary to accommodate different types of jobs in an organization. In a hospital, nurses, dieticians, and admission clerks all have different jobs; separate BARS forms would need to be developed for each discrete job.

Figure 12–9
Behaviorally Anchored Rating Scale for Professor's Attitude Toward Students

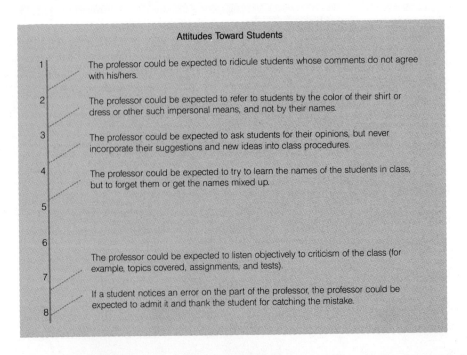

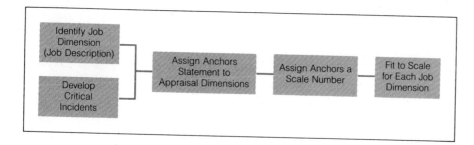

Figure 12–10
Flow Diagram of BARS Construction

Behaviorally-anchored rating scales, BESs, and BOSs represent an emerging area of research and application. However, BARS may not represent the ultimate objective, job-related appraisal system.[23]

Management By Objectives (MBO)

A system of "guided self-appraisal" called management by objectives (MBO) is useful in appraising managers' performances. Although not limited to the appraisal of managers, MBO is most often used for this purpose. Disenchantment with previously discussed approaches has increased the popularity of MBO. Other names for MBO include *appraisal by results, targeting-coaching, work planning and review, performance objectives,* and *mutual goal setting.*

Management by objectives specifies the performance goals an individual hopes to attain within an appropriate length of time. The objectives each manager sets are derived from the overall goals and objectives of the organization, although MBO should not be a disguised means for a superior to dictate the objectives of individual managers or employees.

KEY MBO IDEAS.   Three key assumptions underlie an MBO appraisal system. First, if an employee is involved in planning and setting the objectives and determining the measure, a higher level of commitment and performance may result.

Second, if what an employee is to accomplish is clearly and precisely defined, the employee will do a better job of achieving the desired results. Ambiguity and confusion—and therefore less effective performance—may result when a superior determines the objectives for an individual. By having the employee set objectives, the individual gains an accurate understanding of what is expected.

Third, performance objectives should be measurable and should define results. Vague generalities, such as "initiative" or "cooperation," which are common in many superior-based appraisals, should be avoided. Objectives are composed of specific actions to be taken or work to be accomplished. Sample objectives might include:

- Submit completed regional sales report no later than the third working day of every month.
- Obtain orders from at least five new customers per month.
- Maintain payroll costs at 10 percent of sales volume.
- Have scrap loss less than 5 percent.
- Fill all organizational vacancies within thirty days after openings occur.

Figure 12–11
MBO Process

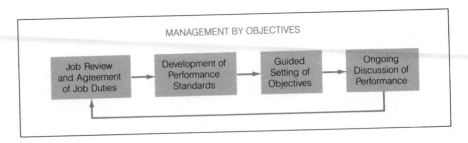

THE MBO PROCESS.   Implementing a guided self-appraisal system using MBO is a four-stage process. These phases are shown in Figure 12–11 and discussed next.

1. *Job Review and Agreement.* The employee and the superior review the job description and the key activities that comprise the employee's job. The idea is to agree on the exact makeup of the employee's job.
2. *Development of Performance Standards.* Specific standards of performance must be mutually developed. This phase specifies a satisfactory level of performance that is specific and measurable. For example, a salespersons's quota of selling five cars per month may be an appropriate performance standard because selling that number of cars can be measured and considered as a satisfactory level of performance.
3. *Guided Objective Setting.* Objectives are established by the employee in conjunction with, and guided by, the superior. For the automobile salesperson, an objective might be to improve performance; the salesperson might set a new objective of selling six cars per month. Notice that the objective set may be different from the performance standard. Objectives should be realistically attainable.
4. *Ongoing Performance Discussions.* The employee and the superior use the objectives as bases for continuing discussions about the employee's performance. Although a formal review session may be scheduled, the employee and the manager do not necessarily wait until the appointed time for performance discussion. Objectives are modified mutually and progress is discussed during the period.

MBO CRITIQUE.   No management tool is perfect, and certainly MBO is not appropriate for all employees or all organizations. Jobs with little or no flexibility are not compatible with MBO. An assembly-line worker usually has so little job flexibility that performance standards and objectives are already determined. The MBO process seems to be most useful with managerial personnel and employees who have a fairly wide range of flexibility and self-control over their jobs. When imposed on a rigid and autocratic management system, MBO may fail. Extreme emphasis on penalties for not meeting objectives defeats the development and participative nature of MBO. Figure 12–12 summarizes the previous discussion by showing PA methods and raters in combination.

■ ■ RATER ERRORS

There are many possible sources of error in the performance appraisal process. One of the major sources is mistakes made by the rater. There is no simple way to eliminate these errors, but making raters aware of them is helpful.

METHODS				
	Category Rating Methods	Comparative Methods	Narrative Methods	BARS	MBO
RATER					
Supervisor Rating Subordinates	✓	✓	✓	✓	✓
Employees Rating Superiors	✓		✓	✓	
Peers Rating Each Other	✓	✓	✓	✓	
Combination	✓	✓	✓	✓	✓
Self-Rating	✓	✓	✓		
Outside Sources	✓	✓	✓		

Figure 12–12
PA Methods And Who Uses Them

Problems of Varying Standards

When appraising employees, a manager should avoid using different standards and expectations for individual employees performing similar jobs, which is certain to incur the anger of employees. The problem is likely to exist when ambiguous criteria and subjective weightings by supervisors are used.

Even if an employee actually has been appraised on the same basis as other employees, the employee's perception is critical, If a student felt a professor had graded his exam harder than another student's exam, he might ask the professor for an explanation. The student's opinion might not be changed by the professor's claim that she had "graded fairly." So it is with performance appraisals in a work situation. If performance appraisal information is to be helpful, the rater must use the same standards and weights for every employee and be able to defend the appraisal.

Recency Problem

A rater should not give greater weight to recent occurrences when appraising an employee's performance than to the person's earlier performance. However, research shows this effect does indeed occur.[25] Giving a student a course grade based only on performance in the last week of class or giving a drill press operator a high rating even though he/she made the quota only in the last two weeks of the rating period are examples.

The recency problem is an understandable rater error because it is difficult to remember performance that may be seven or eight months old. Employees also become more concerned about their performance and behavior as formal appraisal time approaches. Some employees may attempt to take advantage of the recency factor by currying favor with their boss shortly before their appraisals. The problem

P/HR: Practice *and* Research   Dwindling Complaints

Several years ago, University Research Corporation of Chevy Chase, Maryland, surveyed its employees to find out what they thought of the firm's appraisal system. The complaints were voluminous. Employees described the system as arbitrary and capricious.

"When I became president," recalls Gary F. Jonas, "the number one management issue facing our corporate leadership was an unfair performance appraisal system." In revamping its approach, the company emphasized flexibility and self-evaluation. The work planning/performance review system is a form of MBO, Mr. Jonas notes, "because we recognized that jobs change, tasks end, and performance expectations are often modified. The

system had to accommodate our dynamic and changing work environment."

When a task is completed, or University Research is at the end of a review period, an employee completes a performance appraisal form which assesses how well he or she did in meeting preset goals. The form includes a "work plan" outlining key subtasks and deadlines. Once the employee has written this brief self-assessment, the supervisor adds a brief critique and selects one of five "grades"—from "did not meet any performance expectations" to "exceeded all performance expectations." After the form is filled out, the supervisor and the staff member discuss the evaluation and develop work plans for the next review period.

Employees' complaints about performance appraisal unfairness have been virtually eliminated at University Research. "While they may not agree with the judgments of the supervisor, they do feel that the system gives them a fair shake," says Mr. Jonas. "The old system was haphazard—and worse, it was demoralizing and undermined employee performance."

The new system has done more than improve morale, he adds. It has improved the entire process of corporate planning: "The need to define responsibilities helps our managers plan for their whole division. It helps them delegate better, determine staffing needs, and be surer of their evaluations."[24]

can be minimized by using critical-incident recording, or some other method of documenting both positive and negative performance occurrences.

Rater Bias

Another error occurs when a rater's values or prejudices distort the rating. If a manager of a machine section in a tool plant has a strong dislike of certain ethnic groups, this bias is likely to result in distorted appraisal information for some people. Age, religion, seniority, sex, appearance, or other arbitrary classifications may be reflected in appraisals if the appraisal process is not properly designed. Having a supervisor's ratings checked by his or her superior should uncover this problem if it exists.

Rater bias is difficult to overcome, especially if a manager is not aware of the bias or will not admit that such bias is affecting appraisals. Examination of ratings by higher-level managers may help correct this problem.

Rater Patterns

Student are well aware that some professors tend to grade easier or harder than others. Likewise, a manager may develop a "rating pattern." When appraisers rate all employees within a narrow range, this is called a **central tendency error**. For example, Dolores Bressler, office manager, tends to rate all her employees as average. Even the poor performers receive an average rating from Dolores. Jane Carr, the billing supervisor, believes that if employees are poor performers, they should be rated below average. An employee of Jane's who is rated average may well be a better performer than one rated average by Dolores.

Leniency errors often are the result of a superior's reluctance to give a low appraisal. The opposite side of the coin is often called a *strictness* error. Appraisers generally find it difficult to evaluate others, especially if negative evaluations must be given. The leniency error (or any rater error for that matter) can render an appraisal system useless. If everyone is judged *excellent* or *outstanding*, the system has done little to differentiate among employees.

Making an appraiser aware that he or she has fallen into a pattern is one way to deal with the problem. Including precise and explicit definitions of categories on the rating form and allowing for considerable rating spread on each item are other ways to reduce the effect of rater patterns.

HALO EFFECT.   The **halo effect** occurs when a manager rates an employee high or low on all items because of one characteristic. For example, if a worker has few absences, her supervisor might give her a high rating in all other areas of work, including quantity and quality of output, because of her dependability. The manager may not really think about the employee's other characteristics separately.

An appraisal that shows the same rating on all characteristics may be evidence of the halo effect. Clearly specifying the categories to be rated, rating all employees on one characteristic at a time, and training raters to recognize the problem are some means of reducing the halo effect.[26]

Contrast Error

Rating should be done on the basis of standards that are established before the rating. The **contrast error** is the tendency to rate people relative to other people rather than to performance standards. For example, individuals have been in situations in which they were the poorest performer in a good group, or the best performer in a poor group.

If everyone else in a group is doing a mediocre job, a person performing somewhat better may be rated as excellent because of the contrast effect. But in a group performing well, the same person might have received only a poor rating. Although it may be appropriate to compare people at times, the rating should reflect performance against job requirements, not against other people.

■■ ■ THE APPRAISAL FEEDBACK INTERVIEW

Once appraisals have been made, it is important to communicate them. The results should be discussed with employees so they have a clear understanding of how they stand in the eyes of their immediate superiors and the organization. The appraisal feedback interview can clear up misunderstandings on both sides. In this interview, the manager should emphasize counseling and development, not solely tell the employee, "Here is how you rate and why." Focusing on development gives both parties an opportunity to consider the employee's performance and its potential for improvement.

CENTRAL TENDENCY ERROR is rating persons in a narrow band in the middle of the rating scale.

HALO EFFECT is rating a person high or low on all items because of one characteristic.

CONTRAST ERROR is the tendency to rate people relative to other people rather than to performance standards.

Common Concern

The appraisal interview presents both an opportunity and a danger. It is an emotional experience for the manager and the employee because the manager must communicate both praise and constructive criticism. A major concern is how to emphasize the positive aspects of the employee's performance while still discussing ways to make needed improvements. If the interview is handled poorly, the employee may feel resentment and conflict may result, which probably will be reflected in future work.

Employees usually approach an appraisal interview with some concern. They often feel that discussions about performance are very personal and important to their continued job success. At the same time, they want to know how the manager feels they have been doing.

It is fairly common for organizations to require that managers discuss appraisals with employees.[27] Figure 12–13 summarizes hints for an effective interview.[28]

Reactions to Performance Appraisals

The reaction of students to grades and tests (which are both forms of performance appraisal) illustrates the emotional and behavioral nature of appraisal. Students typically are concerned about the equity of the grading process and the criteria on which they will be evaluated. Like students, employees are concerned about the fairness, consistency, and usefulness of appraisals. Managers also have these concerns.

REACTIONS OF MANAGERS.   Managers and supervisors who must complete appraisals on their employees often resist the appraisal process. The manager may feel he or she is put in the position of "playing God." A major part of the manager's role is to assist, encourage, coach, and counsel employees to improve their performance. However, being a judge on the one hand and a coach and counselor on the other causes internal conflict and confusion for the manager.

The fact that appraisals may affect an employee's future career may cause raters to alter or bias their rating. This bias is even more likely when managers know that they will have to communicate and defend their ratings to the employees, their bosses, or P/HR specialists. From the manager's viewpoint, providing negative feedback to an employee in an appraisal interview easily can be avoided by making the employee's ratings positive.

Reactions such as these are attempts to avoid unpleasantness in an interpersonal situation. In the end, this avoidance helps no one. A manager owes an employee a well-considered appraisal.

Figure 12–13
Hints for the Appraisal Interview

DO	DON'T
■ Prepare in advance	■ Lecture the employee
■ Focus on performance and development	■ Mix performance appraisal and salary or promotion issues
■ Be specific about reasons for ratings	■ Concentrate only on the negative
■ Decide on specific steps to be taken for improvement	■ Do all the talking
■ Consider your role in the subordinate's performance	■ Be overly critical or "harp on" a failing
■ Reinforce the behavior you want	■ Feel it is necessary that both of you agree on all areas
■ Focus on the future performance	■ Compare the employee with others

P/HR: Practice *and* Research — Ethics In Performance Appraisals

"We should never have kept him in that job so long. It was a mistake and now we have to bite the bullet." "We were wrong. Fred should have been told years ago that his performance was marginal." "We should have fired Fred ten years ago."

So went the comments just before the decision was made to dismiss Fred Johnson, a supervisor and twenty-year-employee at a large firm in the telecommunications industry. Fred did not represent what, in the view of management, today's supervisors should be. His performance had consistently been rated "satisfactory"—three on a five-point scale. No one had ever said anything to him that would cause him to be concerned about his future. There were certainly no rave reviews, but no condemning comments either and he had received "merit" pay increases over his twenty years with the company. But the ground rules had changed, and suddenly he was out.

If management wants to make employment changes, it clearly has the right to do so. However, is it ethically proper to disregard years of "satisfactory" (by management's own rating) performance? Or, should Fred's boss identify the specific goals to be met and a timetable for meeting them, knowing full well that Fred is likely to fail?

Dentists allegedly extract their mistakes; physicians are said to bury theirs. What is the ethical course of action a company should take when changes must be made, but years of past performance appraisals do not indicate that anything is wrong with an individual's performance?

REACTIONS OF THE APPRAISED EMPLOYEE.   A common reaction by employees is to view appraising as a zero-sum game (in which there must be a winner and a loser). Employees may well see the appraisal process as a threat and feel that the only way to get a higher rating is for someone else to receive a low rating. This win–lose perception is encouraged by comparative methods of rating.

Appraisals can be both zero-sum and non-zero-sum (in which both parties win and no one loses) in nature. Emphasis on the developmental and self-improvement aspects of appraisal appears to be the most effective means to reduce some zero–sum reactions from those participating in the appraisal process.

Another common employee reaction is similar to students' reactions to tests. Because a professor prepares a test he or she feels is fair, it does not necessarily follow that the students will feel the test is fair. They simply may see it differently. Likewise, employees being appraised will not necessarily agree with the manager doing the actual appraising. In most cases, however, employees will view appraisals done well for what they are meant to be—constructive feedback.

■■ ■ PERFORMANCE APPRAISAL AND THE LAW

A growing number of court decisions have focused on performance appraisals, particularly in relation to equal employment opportunity (EEO) concerns. In addition, there are ethical issues that have legal consequences associated with them. The Uniform Guidelines issued by the Equal Employment Opportunity Commission (EEOC) and other federal enforcement agencies make it clear that performance appraisals must be job-related and nondiscriminatory. A review of court cases filed on age discrimination charges showed that employers using only "informal" methods of performance appraisal lost those cases more than half the time.

Court Cases and Appraisals

It may seem somewhat odd to emphasize that performance appraisals must be job-related because appraisals are supposed to measure how well employees are doing their jobs. Yet in numerous cases, courts have ruled that performance appraisals were discriminatory and not job-related.[30]

A recent case is an important illustration. Fort Worth Bank and Trust is a relatively small bank with eighty employees. It hired Clara Watson as a proof operator. Two years later she was promoted to teller. Eight years after going to work for the bank she was promoted to commercial teller. She then applied over the next year and a half for four different promotions. In each case, a white employee was selected over Watson, who is a minority. The bank admitted it had no precise and formal criteria to evaluate good performance for the positions for which Watson had applied. It relied instead on the subjective judgment of supervisors. Watson resigned, sued, and won. In *Watson v. Fort Worth Bank and Trust*, the U.S. Supreme Court ruled a violation of Title VII of the Civil Rights Act occurred when an employer's *subjective* promotion criteria resulted in disproportionately fewer minority employees receiving promotions. The court noted that an "undisciplined system of subjective decision making" could have the same negative consequences as a process that was intended to discriminate. Performance appraisal systems without formal criteria and standards appear to qualify as subjective.[31]

Elements of a Legal Performance Appraisal System

The elements of a performance appraisal system that can survive court tests can be determined if existing case law is investigated. These elements are:

- Absence of adverse impact evidence or presence of validity evidence
- Formal evaluation criteria that limit a manager's absolute discretion in the appraisal process
- A formal rating instrument
- Personal knowledge and contact with the individual whose work is being rated
- Training of supervisors in using instrument properly
- A review process that prevents one manager acting alone from controlling an employee's career
- Counseling or guidance for helping poor performers improve performance

It is clear that the courts are interested in fair and nondiscriminatory performance appraisals. Employers must decide how to design their appraisal systems to satisfy the courts, enforcement agencies, and their employees.[32]

▄▄ ▄ AN EFFECTIVE PERFORMANCE APPRAISAL SYSTEM

Regardless of which performance appraisal method is used, an understanding of what an appraisal is supposed to do makes or breaks the system. When performance appraisal is used to develop the employee as a resource, it usually works. When management uses it as a whip or fails to understand its limitations, it fails. The key is not which form or which method of performance appraisal to use but managers who understand its purposes. In its simplest form, performance appraisal is a manager's statement: "Here are your strengths and weaknesses, and here is a way to shore up the weak areas." It can lead to higher employee motivation and satisfaction as well.

Training Appraisers

Appraiser training is valuable. Offering managers and supervisors insights and ideas on rating, documenting appraisals, and conducting appraisal interviews increases the value and acceptance of an appraisal program.[33] In many organizations, managers and supervisors have had little appraisal training. Training appraisers gives them confidence in their ability to make appraisals and handle appraisal interviews. Familiarity with common rating errors can improve rater performance as well.[34]

Beware "The Number"

There is a nagging tendency to distill the performance appraisal system to a single number that can be used to support pay raises. Systems based on this concept reduce the complexity of each individual's contribution in order to satisfy compensation system requirements rather than to give employees feedback or pinpoint training and development needs. In fact, a single rating often is a barrier to useful performance discussions because what is emphasized is attaching a label to a person's performance and defending or attacking that label. Effective performance appraisal systems recognize that human behaviors and capabilities cannot be meaningfully collapsed into a single score[35]

SUMMARY

- Appraising employee performance is useful for compensation, feedback, and administrative purposes.
- Performance appraisal can be done either informally or systematically. If done systematically, appraisals usually are done annually.
- Appraisals can be done by superiors, employees, peers, or a combination of raters.
- Superiors' ratings of employees are most frequently used.
- Four types of appraisal methods are available: category ratings, comparative ratings, written appraisals, and special rating methods.
- Category rating methods, especially graphic rating scales, are the most widely used methods.
- Ranking, paired comparison, and forced distribution are all comparative methods.
- Written methods of appraisal include the critical incident technique, the essay approach, and the field review.
- Behaviorally-anchored ratings scales (BARS) and management by objectives (MBO) are two special methods of appraisal.
- Construction of a BARS requires a detailed job analysis; the rating criteria and anchors must be job-specific.
- Management by objectives is an approach that requires joint goal setting between a superior and an employee.
- Several performance appraisal problems are varying standards, rater bias, rater patterns, leniency, and halo effect.
- The appraisal feedback interview is a vital part of any appraisal system.
- Both managers and employees may react to appraisals by exhibiting signs of resistance.
- Federal employment guidelines and numerous court decisions have scrutinized performance appraisals. Subjectivity and the absence of specific job-relatedness can create legal problems.

■ Training of appraisers and guarding against "number magic" are important in an effective appraisal system.

REVIEW AND DISCUSSION QUESTIONS

1. What are the three major uses of performance appraisals?
2. Identify the advantages and disadvantages of using different rater approaches.
3. What are the three methods of appraisal? Which method would you prefer as an employee? As a manager? Why?
4. Suppose you are a supervisor. What errors might you make when doing an employee's performance appraisal?
5. Describe how to prepare a BARS for a payroll clerk.
6. Identify MBO and some problems associated with it.
7. Construct a plan for a post appraisal interview with an employee who has performed poorly.
8. Discuss the following statement: "Most performance appraisal systems in use today would not pass legal scrutiny."
9. Why is training of appraisers so vital to an effective performance appraisal system?

| CASE | **Performance Appraisal at Xerox** |

Xerox's Reprographic Business Group (RBG), develops, designs, engineers, and manufactures the corporation's main copier. Reprographic Business Group *had* a performance appraisal system in place that had been used for annual appraisals for more than 20 years: managers rated employees' performance and assigned a number to that performance. In short, the system was typical of what is usually done by most employers in the United States.

Atypical, however, was Xerox's willingness to listen to employee and manager complaints about the system and then undertake to make it more useful for all concerned. One major complaint was that 95 percent of the ratings were 3s or 4s (on a 5-point scale). Merit increase amounts (tied to the appraisals) were within 1 to 2 percent of one another. In addition, appraisal discussions had become unpleasant situations for managers and employees alike.

Xerox set up a task force to design a new performance appraisal system. The task force used surveys of the work force and then developed the new system they labeled PF + D (performance feedback and development). Key features of the system are:

■ Objectives are set between manager and employee.
■ A six-month review of progress takes place.
■ A final written appraisal is done at year end.
■ No numerical summary rating is used.
■ Merit increase discussions are separated by two months from the performance appraisal discussions.
■ The focus is on coaching and development.

Videotapes of behavioral modeling were used to teach managers how to conduct appraisals. Further, managers and employees were surveyed during the first-year operation of the new system to see how it was working and what changes, if any, were needed.

The results of the surveys were encouraging. Of those surveyed, 81 percent felt they better understood what their work group was trying to accomplish; 84 percent felt their appraisal was fair; 70 percent met their objectives; and 72 percent said they understood how merit pay figures were determined. Survey results were slightly more favorable for salaried employees than for hourly ones.

In summary, Xerox feels that these results, combined with the redefinition of the managers as a coach and developer, will help improve teamwork, a strategic part of RBG's approach to innovation and productivity.[36]

QUESTIONS

1. What are the pertinent elements in the success of Xerox's approach?
2. What potential problems can you identify?

NOTES

1. M. G. Derven, "The Paradox of Performance Appraisals," *Personnel Journal*, February 1990, 107–111.

2. J. Cleveland, K. Murphy, and R. Williams, "Multiple Uses of Performance Appraisal Prevalence and Correlates," *Journal of Applied Psychology* 74 (1989): 130–135.

3. D. J. Mitchell, *Human Resources Management: An Economic Approach* (Boston: PWS-Kent Publishing, 1989), 76.

4. W. Einstein and J. LeMere-LaBonte, "Performance Appraisal: Dilemma or Design?" *SAM Advanced Management Journal*, Spring 1989, 26.

5. C. Kleiman, "How Well You Work May Not Matter," *Chicago Tribune*, June 19, 1988, 8.

6. L. Sadler, "Two-Sided Performance Reviews," *Personnel Journal*, January 1990, 75–78.

7. W. F. Cascio and R. A. Ramos, "Development and Application of a New Method for Assessing Job Performance in Behavioral/Economic Terms," *Journal of Applied Psychology* 71 (1986): 20–28.

8. S. L. Bordman and Gerald Melnick, "Keep Productivity Ratings Timely," *Personnel Journal*, March 1990, 50.

9. "HRM Update," *Personnel Administrator*, June 1989, 16.

10. J. Greenberg, "Determinants of Perceived Fairness of Performance Evaluations," *Journal of Applied Psychology* 71 (1986): 340–342.

11. Adapted from L. Reibstein, "Firms Ask Workers to Rate Their Bosses," *Wall Street Journal*, June 13, 1988, 1; and "Reversing Performance Reviews," *Psychology Today*, March 1984, 80.

12. H. Bernardin, et al., "Can Subordinate Appraisals Enhance Managerial Productivity?" *Sloan Management Review*, Summer 1987, 68.

13. G. McEvoy, "Evaluating The Boss," *Personnel Administrator*, September 1988, 115–120.

14. M. Berger, "Now the Japanese Bring Democracy to Salary Review," *International Management*, October 1986, 58–60.

15. J. Pilch, "Setting Goals for Management Performance," *Modern Office Technology*, November 1988, 90.

16. Charles Lee, "Smoothing Out Appraisal Systems," *HR Magazine*, March 1990, 72–76.

17. J. Farh, "An Empirical Investigation of Self-Appraisal-Based Performance Evaluation," *Personnel Psychology* 41, (1988): 141–156.

18. M. Gist, "Self-Efficacy: Implications for OB and HRM," *Academy of Management Review* 12 (1987): 472–485.

19. J. Nelson-Horchler, "Performance Appraisals," *Industry Week*, September 19, 1988, 61.

20. R. Jacobs and S. Kozlowski, "A Closer Look at Halo Error in Performance Ratings," *Academy of Management Journal*, 28 (1985): 201–212.

21. A. DeNisi, et al., "Organization of Information Used for Performance Appraisals: Role of Diary Keeping," *Journal of Applied Psychology* 74 (1989): 124–129.

22. S. J. Carroll and C. E. Schneier, *Performance Appraisal and Review Systems* (Glenview, Ill.: Scott Foresman, 1982), 114.

23. K. Martin, "Dual-Objective Performance Measurement," *Human Resources Professional*, May/June 1989, 47–50.

24. Adapted from B. S. Moskal, "Employee Ratings: Objective or Objectional?" *Industry Week*, February 8, 1983, 51.

25. D. Steiner and J. Rain, "Immediate and Delayed Primary and Recency Effects in Performance Evaluation," *Journal of Applied Psychology* 74 (1989): 136–142.

26. A. Henik and J. Tzelgov, "Control of Halo Effort: A Multiple Regression Approach," *Journal of Applied Psychology* 70 (1985): 577–580.

27. H. Klein et al., " Systems Model of the Performance Appraisal Interview Process," *Industrial Relations* 26, (1987) 267–278.

28. J. Prince, "Does Salary Discussion Hurt the Developmental Performance Appraisal?" *Organizational Behavior and Human Decision Process* 27 (1989) 357–375.

29. J. M. Cleveland, et al., "Multiple Uses of Performance Appraisal . . .," *Journal of Applied Psychology* 74, 1989): 130–135.

30. *Brito v. Zia Company*, 478 F.2d 1200 (1973); *Albermarle Paper Co. v. Moody*, 74–389 (1975); *U.S. v. City of Chicago*, 549 F.2d 415 (1977) *Cert. denied* 434 U.S. 875 (1977).

31. G. Mertens, "*Watson v. Fort Worth Bank and Trust*: Unanswered Questions," *Employee Relations Law Journal 14* (Autumn 1988): 163–173.

32. G. Barrett and M. Kernan, "Performance Appraisal and Termination: A Review of Court Cases Since *Brito v. Zia* with Implications for Personnel Practices," *Personnel Psychology*, 40 (1987): 489–501.

33. John Lawrie, "Prepare for a Performance Appraisal," *Personnel Journal*, April 1990, 132–136.

34. R. Heneman et al., "Performance-Rating Accuracy: A Critical Review," *Journal of Business Research 15* (1987): 431–445.

35. W. Fox, "Improving Performance Appraisal Systems," *National Productivity Review*, Winter 1987–88, 20–27.

36. Adapted from N. R. Deets and D. T. Typler, "How Xerox Improved Its Performance Appraisals," *Personnel Journal*, April 1986, 50–52.

Compensating Human Resources

One reason for appraising employee performance is to reward more work with more compensation. Most people "sell" their services to organizations for money, but pay usually means more to people than just legal tender. Compensation is both a reward for effort and a status symbol. People want to be compensated fairly and are concerned about equitable treatment in pay. However, fairness is complicated since what may seem fair to a manager may *not* seem fair to the employee.

Equitable pay can be determined in a number of ways. Well-designed P/HR systems are built on job evaluation and pay surveys to insure that employees are paid fairly. Chapter 13 also discusses legal constraints that influence compensation practices.

People are paid not only in money. Incentives and executive "perks" are also forms of compensation. Different incentive plans can be designed to achieve a variety of results. Some incentive systems and executive compensation plans are discussed in Chapter 14.

Chapter 15 discusses a major expense item for organizations— employee benefits. A wide variety of benefits can be offered ranging from the company-sponsored bowling teams to retirement and health insurance plans. Health-care cost containment has become a major concern for most employers. Flexible benefits allow employees more benefits for dollars spent. Now that benefits average about 37 percent of the payroll dollar, both employees and managers want well-designed plans that distribute benefits equitably.

Compensation Administration

After you have read this chapter, you should be able to:

1. Explain the role of labor markets in compensation
2. Discuss the three bases of compensation
3. Identify the basic provisions of the Fair Labor Standards Act
4. Briefly explain three federal laws that can affect compensation practices
5. Define job evaluation and discuss four methods of performing it
6. Outline the process of building a wage and salary administration system

P/HR: Today *and* Tomorrow

Pay For Performance, Skill, Knowledge, Or Competency?

Many employers have had "merit" pay programs that, in theory, rewarded employees for performance: Employees whose performance was better than others merited better pay increases. But in many organizations the system became so distorted that virtually everyone became "meritorious," and most people received basically the same percentage of pay increases. One survey of managers from a variety of organizations found that three-fourths of them felt that their companies did not give true merit increases, or if they did, the performance appraisals and rewards tied to them were inadequate.[1] As an example, over 98 percent of all U.S. Postal Service employees received merit raises in a recent year. Similar distortions have occurred in many private sector organizations also.

To restore credibility and reward performance, a growing number of employers have relabeled their programs as "pay-for-performance." For example, Chrysler Corporation's pay-for-performance system eliminated cost-of-living adjustments for 14,000 non-union white-collar workers and replaced them with pay increases tied to employees' job performance as determined by annual performance appraisal by their supervisors. In the first year of the system, employees whose performance was satisfactory received at least 3 percent pay increases. Those performing better received increases as high as 15 percent. Employees whose performance was not satisfactory received no pay increases.

Another alternative to the problems of merit pay systems is variously called skill-, knowledge-, or competency-based pay.[2] With KBP (or SBP or CBP), the assumption is that rewards should be given for acquired skills, not necessarily the performance of those skills. The KBP worker is paid at a rate based on the knowledge or skill that he or she has. Raises are given when the worker learns to do other jobs and is therefore more valuable to the company. For example, a printing firm has two-color, four-color, and six-color presses. The more colors, the more skill is required. Consequently, as press operators learn how to operate the more complex presses, they have higher base pay rates, even though they may be running only two-color jobs.

There is little research on the effects of KBP systems because they are very new in U.S. firms. However, from the limited information available it appears that:

- KBP systems are more flexible.
- Employees like KBP systems.
- Direct wage costs are higher.
- Training costs are higher.
- Employees are more satisfied with their pay.
- Pay is seen as more fair.

These new approaches to pay reflect employers' unhappiness with the results of traditional pay schemes. Time will tell if they are successful.

"Money is power, freedom, a cushion, the root of all evil, the sum of blessings."

Carl Sandburg

Establishing and maintaining a pay system that supports organizational objectives and strategies is an underlying theme for compensation. To activate a pay-for-performance system (described in P/HR: Today and Tomorrow) or any other pay system, specialized planning is needed to ensure that payroll expenditures are made in a sound and effective manner. For the organization, compensation is really about balancing labor costs with fairness to employees and the ability to attract and keep employees.

BASIC COMPENSATION CONSIDERATIONS

Economists explain that labor services are purchased as inputs to the production process from which the employer's profits flow. So, what the employer wants is not just a person's *presence* at work, but effort and productive activity at a "reasonable" cost.

The most common means of payment based on time is *hourly* pay; employees paid hourly are said to receive **wages** which are payments directly calculated on the amount of time worked.

Salary is another means of paying people for the time worked. Being salaried typically has carried higher status for employees than being paid wages. Salary is payment that is consistent from period to period and is not directly related to the number of hours an individual works.

Compensation serves the function of allocating people among firms based on the attractiveness of the job and pay package. Firms must be reasonably competitive in pay rates to hire and keep the people they need.

WAGES
are payments directly calculated on the amount of time worked.

SALARY
is payment that is consistent from period to period.

Labor Markets and Compensation

Occasionally, employers complain that they cannot get employees for particular occupations. One view is that if a labor shortage exists for that occupation, employers simply should raise the wage paid for that occupation until enough workers are attracted. Such adjustment does take place in a labor market but it is slow.

Employers may increase overtime for existing employees, use less qualified persons, or train the people they need before raising wages. Two reasons employers may be hesitant to raise wages immediately are that other employees may be discontented as a result of raising compensation for the group in short supply, and unions may be hesitant to see traditional pay schedules disturbed.

Labor shortages are a problem for the employer, but the other extreme, unemployment, is a problem for individuals in the labor force. Unemployment represents an excess supply of workers, either in the labor market as a whole, or more frequently in a particular occupation. At the height of the Great Depression of the 1930s, in the United States one out of every four workers was unemployed, a figure not approached since. But unemployment still occasionally has become a problem in the economy. Just as prolonged shortages of labor will eventually raise wages, so prolonged surpluses will have the opposite effect. Large-scale unemployment slows the rate of wage increases and can even lead to wage cuts. The oil "bust" in several Southwestern U.S. States in the mid 1980's is illustrative of this occurrence.

Meaning of Compensation of Employees

The compensation employees receive is often a prime reason for working. However, compensation usually has several meanings to employees.

ECONOMIC.   The economic meaning is the most obvious because pay serves as a way of obtaining the necessities and luxuries people need and want. For most people, employment in an organization is the way to obtain economic resources that can be exchanged for such items as food, rent or house payments, a car, clothes, furniture, vacations, and countless other goods and services. A study by the Bureau of Labor Statistics revealed that most people did not want to work fewer hours if it meant earning less money.[3] The economic allure of compensation is summed up in the following statement from an anonymous employee: "Some people are rich and some are poor—rich is better!"

PSYCHOSOCIAL.   Compensation's meaning also can be psychosocial in nature. Pay and other types of compensation offer a symbolic means of "keeping score" and a sense of achievement. If a cost accountant receives a raise, he may see his change in compensation as recognition of his efforts and he may derive a sense of achievement from his work. This internal satisfaction may mean more to him than what he can buy with the additional money. Conversely, the absence of adequate compensation may cause him to become discouraged or dissatisfied.

Psychosocial factors are based on the equity perceptions of individuals For example, a division manager might compare her pay, and therefore status in the organization, with that of other division managers. She may be satisfied with her pay, or she may become dissatisfied because other division managers have higher pay and higher status. The results of the research on perceptions of pay at a light manufacturing firm discussed in the P/HR: Research indicate that equity perceptions by individuals are based on comparisons.

People compare their base pay to determine how they rank in the social structure. As a measure of **status,** the social ranking of a person in relation to others, compensation gives highly rewarded individuals high social standing and importance. Because compensation can symbolize status, pay and other forms of compensation often remain important even though the basic material needs of an employee are satisfied. For example, an executive who is provided a luxury company car, such as a Mercedes Benz or a Cadillac, may see it as a status symbol, even though a less expensive car of a different make would fulfill the executive's basic transportation needs.

GROWTH.   Compensation also is a means to measure how well employees have grown in their performance and capabilities. Based on expectancy theory, increased compensation can serve as a goal for which people will strive if they see that greater effort brings more compensation. However, the amount and type of compensation that serves to motivate one employee to produce more may not motivate another employee.[5]

STATUS
social ranking of a person in relation to others.

| P/HR: Practice *and* Research | International Preferences for Compensation Allocations |

A very interesting study reported in the *Academy of Management Journal* compared preferences for allocating rewards across the United States, Japan, and Korea. 132 Americans, 117 Japanese, and 140 Korean college students received written scenarios describing contributions of individuals to a work group. The students evaluated the contributions and then responded to a scale asking them to estimate the likelihood of giving rewards and how they would be allocated to the individuals in the description.

Results showed that the United States students were most generous with monetary rewards and the Japanese least generous. Korean students were most generous with social rewards. However, for all three countries and for both monetary and social rewards, more rewards were allocated to high levels of performance than to low levels of performance.

Apparently the "equity norm" is active in all three countries. The idea of equity, of course, suggests that rewards will be allocated to group members according to their contribution.[4]

Forms of Compensation

The three specific forms of compensation are pay, incentives, and benefits. **Pay** refers to the base wages or salaries employees receive. Compensation such as bonuses, commissions, and profit-sharing plans are **incentives** designed to reward employees for results produced beyond normal expectations. Health insurance, vacation pay, or retirement pensions are examples of **benefits,** which are more indirect rewards given for organizational membership.

PAY
is the basic compensation an employee receives, usually as a wage or salary.

INCENTIVE
is compensation that rewards an employee for efforts beyond normal performance expectations.

BENEFIT
is additional compensation to an employee or group of employees as a part of organizational membership.

Bases for Compensation

There are three bases for compensation: *time, productivity,* or a *combination* of time and productivity.

TIME.   Employees may be paid for the amount of time they are on the job. The two pay classes in many organizations are identified according to the way pay is distributed and the nature of the jobs. The classifications are: (1) *hourly* and (2) *salaried.*

Several organizations have switched to an all-salaried approach with their manufacturing and clerical employees in order to create a great sense of loyalty and organizational commitment.[6] The results in Figure 13–1 indicate that salaried workers view their jobs differently from hourly workers.

PRODUCTIVITY.   Another general basis for compensation is to tie pay to productivity. Commissions set as a percentage of sales are a common example of pay based on productivity. Another productivity-based means is a **piece-rate system.** An employee who works in an electronics plant packaging radios is paid on the basis of how many he or she packages. If the employee is paid 50 cents for each radio packaged and is expected to package eighty radios a day, a person will earn

A PIECE-RATE SYSTEM
is one in which an employee is paid for each unit of production.

Figure 13–1
Hourly vs. Salaried Workers: How They View Their Jobs

A survey of hourly and salaried workers revealed the following:
■ 52% of hourly workers didn't see a clear link between good performance and pay increases, vs 38% of salaried workers.
■ 45% of hourly workers were satisfied with their pay, vs. 53% of salaried workers.
■ 54% of hourly workers were satisfied with their benefits, vs. 64% of salaried workers.
■ 35% of hourly workers felt secure in their jobs, vs. 46% of salaried workers.
■ 47% of hourly workers would recommend their company as a place to work, vs. 58% of salaried workers.
■ 54% of hourly workers rated their work environments positively, vs. 65% of salaried workers.

SOURCE: Adapted from the Wall Street Journal, May 9, 1989, B1.

$40 per day. Employees who want to earn more can produce more units by working at a faster pace.

A productivity-based pay system should be developed with caution so that quality, as well as quantity, is encouraged. For example, paying the radio packager only on the basis of quantity might lead the worker to pack radios carelessly, thus sacrificing quality. Another possible drawback to a piece-rate system is that a productivity compensation rate must be determined for each specific job. Time and motion studies are used for this purpose.

Other methods of piece-rate pay have been used at various times. "Modified" piece-rate plans offer workers the opportunity to receive higher pay for units produced above a quota. For example, if the radio packager's standard is to package eighty radios per day, the employee might be paid extra for each additional radio packaged.

COMBINATION METHODS.   Employees also can be paid according to a combination of time and productivity. The base pay–commission arrangements for sales representatives are familiar combinations used by many organizations.

One study of 750 companies revealed that salaried-only representatives earned one-fourth the amount per year of those paid on a commission-only basis. The average for commission-only representatives was $185,600 per year, whereas salary-only representatives average $47,700 per year.[7] Executive-level managers typically receive a salary plus some type of bonus based on profitability. These combination systems are examined in more detail in Chapter 14.

Whatever the methods used, it is important that the task be matched with the type of compensation appropriate for it. Individuals paid on an hourly basis, such as producing or clerical workers, typically have more routine and shorter job cycles than white-collar professionals do. If the task is such that individual productivity can be determined, a piece-rate or incentive type of system may be appropriate.

■■ ■ COMPENSATION AND ORGANIZATIONAL STRATEGY

Because compensation is such a key activity, compensation philosophies and objectives must reflect the overall culture, life-cycle stages, and strategic plans of the organization. As Figure 13–2 shows, the compensation practices appropriate for a new organization may be different from those for a mature, bureaucratic organization.[8] For example, if a firm wishes to create an innovative, entrepreneurial culture, the firm may offer stock equity programs so that employees can participate in the growth and success of the company. However, for a large stable organization, highly structured pay and benefit programs may be more appropriate.[9]

For virtually every kind of organization, the *objectives* of a sound pay system are:

- To minimize turnover, grievances, and perceptions of inequity as a result of dissatisfaction with the compensation package
- To control labor costs with carefully designed programs that identify a job's value and an employee's value to the organization
- To identify the appropriate frequency and size of raises, and restrain individual manager's ability to give unwarranted raises
- To induce and reward higher levels of performance
- To identify prevailing market wages and salaries
- To administer pay within legal constraints

Compensation Responsibilities

Compensation costs are significant expenditures in most organizations. At one large hotel, employee payroll and benefits expenditures comprise about 50 percent of all business costs. Although compensation costs are relatively easy to calculate, the value derived by employers and employees is much more difficult to identify. To administer these expenditures wisely, P/HR specialists and other managers must work together.

A typical division of compensation responsibilities is illustrated in Figure 13–3. Personnel/human resource specialists usually guide the overall development and administration of an organizational compensation system by conducting job evaluations and wage surveys. Also, because of the technical complexity involved, P/HR specialists typically are the ones who develop the wage and salary structures, and policies. On the other hand, operating managers try to match employees'

Figure 13–2
Compensation And Life Cycle

COMPENSATION	INTRODUCTORY	GROWTH	MATURITY	DECLINE
Pay	Competitive, but conservative wages/ salaries	Moderate wages/salaries	Above market wages/salaries	High wages and salaries with pressure for reductions
Incentives	Stock/equity possibilities	Bonuses tied to objectives; stock options	Bonuses, incentive plans, stock options	Reduced bonuses; cost-saving incentive plans
Benefits	Core benefits; very basic	Complete benefits at moderate level; limited executive perks	Comprehensive benefits; expanded executive perks	Cost-consciousness to limit benefit costs; "frozen" executive perks

Figure 13–3
Compensation Responsibilities

P/HR UNIT	*MANAGERS*
■ Develops and administers compensation system ■ Conducts job evaluation and wage survey ■ Develops wage/salary structures and policies	■ Attempt to match performance and rewards ■ Recommend pay rates and pay increases, based upon guidelines from P/HR unit ■ Monitor attendance and productivity for compensation purposes

efforts with rewards by using guidelines provided by the P/HR unit when recommending pay rates and pay increases. Much managerial activity goes into monitoring employee attendance and productivity. Because time and/or productivity are the bases for compensation, this monitoring is a vital part of any manager's job.

Unions and Compensation

A major variable affecting the compensation systems used by an employer is whether any employees are represented by a labor union. In nonunion organizations, employers have significantly more flexibility in determining pay levels and policies. Unionized employees usually have their pay set according to the terms of a collective bargaining contract between their employers and the unions that represent them. Because pay is a visible issue, it is a primary concern for workers, and it is natural for unions to emphasize pay levels.

According to U.S. Bureau of Labor Statistics data, employers having unionized employees generally have higher wage levels than nonunion employers. The strength and extent of unionization in an industry and in an organization also affect wage levels. Firms in heavily unionized industries with highly unionized work forces generally have higher wage levels.

■■ ■ LEGAL CONSTRAINTS ON PAY SYSTEMS

Good pay systems are legal pay systems. There is a myriad of government constraints on pay practices. Minimum wage standards and hours of work are two important areas that are addressed by the laws.

Fair Labor Standards Act

The major law affecting compensation is the Fair Labor Standards Act (FLSA). The act has three major objectives: (1) to establish a minimum wage floor, (2) to encourage limits on the number of weekly hours employees work through overtime provisions, and (3) (to discourage oppressive use of child labor.) The first two objectives are the most relevant in this chapter. First passed in 1938, the FLSA has been amended several times in order to raise the minimum wage rates and expand the employers covered.

EMPLOYERS COVERED.   Unless otherwise noted in the discussion that follows, both private and public sector employers are affected by the act. Generally, private sector employers engaged in interstate commerce and retail service firms with two or more employees and gross sales of at least $500,000 per year are covered by the act. Very small, family-owned and operated entities and family farms generally are excluded from coverage. Most federal, state, and local government employers are subject to the provisions of the act also, except for military personnel, volunteer workers, and a few other limited groups. Covered employers must keep accurate time records on all employees subject to the act, and the government can request access to those records. [10]

EXEMPT AND NONEXEMPT STATUS.   Under the FLSA, employees are classified as exempt or nonexempt. **Exempt employees** are those who hold positions identified as *executive, administrative, professional,* or *outside sales,* for whom employers are not required to pay overtime. [12]

> EXEMPT EMPLOYEES
> are those who are not required to be paid overtime under the Fair Labor Standards Act.

Three major factors are considered in determining whether an individual holds an exempt position. Figure 13–4 shows the impact of these factors on each type of exemption. They are:

- Discretionary authority for independent action
- Percentage of time spent performing routine, manual, or clerical work
- Earnings level

Under provisions of the FLSA, jobs can be categorized in three groupings:

- Hourly
- Salaried-nonexempt
- Salaried-exempt

Hourly jobs are those that require employers to pay overtime and comply with the FLSA. Each salaried position must be identified as *salaried-exempt* or *salaried-nonexempt.* Employees in positions classified as salaried-nonexempt are covered by the overtime provisions of the FLSA, and therefore must be paid overtime. Salaried-nonexempt positions would include secretarial, clerical, or salaried blue-collar positions.

MINIMUM WAGE.   The FLSA sets a minimum wage to be paid to the broad spectrum of covered employees. The actual minimum wage must be changed by congressional action. The lower minimum-wage level is set for "tipped" employees who work in restaurants, but their payment must at least equal the minimum wage when "average" tips are included. Under the most recent legislation, minimum wage was set at $4.25 per hour as of April 1, 1991. Further, a "training wage" of $3.35 per hour for up to ninety days for some employees was made available for employers to use through March 31, 1993.

OVERTIME POSITIONS.   The FLSA also contains overtime pay requirements. Still in effect under the 1938 version are provisions setting overtime pay at one and a half times the regular pay rate for all hours in excess of 40 per week, except for employees who are not covered by the law.

The work week is defined as a consecutive period of 168 hours (24 hours × 7 days) and does not have to be a calendar week. Hospitals are allowed to use a 14-day period instead of a 7-day week as long as overtime is paid for hours worked beyond 8 in a day or 80 in a 14-day period. Overtime provisions do not apply to farm workers, who also have a lower minimum wage schedule. No daily number of hours requiring overtime is set, except for special provisions relating to hospitals

Figure 13–4
Wage–Hour Status Under Fair Labor Standards Act

EXEMPTION CATEGORY	A DISCRETIONARY AUTHORITY	B % OF TIME	C EARNINGS LEVELS
Executive	1. Primary duty is managing 2. Regularly directs work of at least two others 3. Authority to hire/fire or recommend these	1. Must spend 20% or less time doing clerical, manual, routine work (less than 40% retail or service establishments)	1. Paid salary at $155/wk or 250
Administrative	1. Responsible nonmanual or office work related to management policies 2. Regularly exercises discretion and independent judgment and makes important decisions 3. Regularly assists executives and works under general supervision	1. Must spend 20% or less time doing clerical, manual, routine work (less than 40% retail or service establishments)	1. Paid salary at $155/wk or 250
Professional	1. Performs work requiring knowledge of an advanced field *or* creative and original artistic work *or* works as teacher in educational system 2. Must do work that is predominantly intellectual and varied.	1. Must spend less than 20% of time doing nonprofessional work	1. Paid salary at least $170/wk or $250/wk if meets A1
Outside Sales	1. Customarily works away from employer site *and* 2. Sells tangible or intangible items *or* 3. Obtains order or contracts for services	1. Must spend 20% or less time doing work other than outside selling	1. No salary test

NOTE: For more details see *Executive, Administrative, Professional, and Outside Sales Exemptions Under the Fair Labor Standards Act,* WH Publication no. 1363 (Washington, DC: U.S. Department of Labor, Employment Standards Administration, Wage and Hour Division).

and other specially-designated organizations. Thus, if a manufacturing firm has a 4-day/10-hour schedule, no overtime pay is required by the act.

COMPENSATORY TIME-OFF.   The only major exception to those provisions are for public sector employees such as fire and police employees, and a limited number of other workers. Because they often are on 24-hour duty, these individuals may receive compensatory time. Often called "comp time," **compensatory time** is given off in lieu of payment for time worked.

COMPENSATORY TIME-OFF
is time-off given in lieu of payment for time worked.

Police and fire officers can accumulate up to 480 hours; all other covered public sector employees can accumulate up to 240 hours of comp time. When those hours are used, the employees must be paid their normal rates of pay, and the comp time hours used *do not* count as hours worked in the paid week. For most employers, especially those in the private sector, comp time *is not* a legal means of paying overtime to workers unless it is done in the same pay period and at a rate of one and a half for all hours worked over 40 in a week.

ENFORCEMENT.   Compliance with the provisions of the FLSA is enforced by the Wage and Hour Division of the U.S. Department of Labor. To meet its requirements, employers must keep accurate time records and maintain these records for several years. Inspectors from the Wage and Hour Division investigate complaints filed by individuals who believe they have not received the overtime payments due them. Also, certain industries which historically have had a large number of wage and hour violations can be targeted, and firms in those industries can be investigated.

Penalties for wage and hour violations often include awards of back pay for affected current and former employees up to two years. The experience of Hudson Oil shows that violations can be very costly. Kansas City–based Hudson Oil and its subsidiaries had to make a large back-pay settlement as a result of violations of federal wage and hour laws. The firm violated the FLSA by not keeping adequate records of the hours employees worked, nor had it paid employees minimum wages and overtime as required. Over 30,000 employees who worked for Hudson Oil split approximately $9 to $10 million back pay.[12]

Public Contracts Act (Walsh–Healey)

Many provisions of the Walsh–Healey Public Contracts Act of 1936 were incorporated into the FLSA passed two years later. The Walsh–Healey Act requires companies with *federal supply contracts* exceeding $10,000 to pay a prevailing minimum wage. This act applies only to those working directly on the contract or who substantially affect its performance. For example, if a company has a contract to supply shoes to the army, those employees directly involved in making and supplying the shoes have to paid a minimum wage. Executive, administrative, and maintenance employees are not covered by the act.

Davis–Bacon Act of 1931

Still in force with many of the original dollar levels intact, the Davis–Bacon Act of 1931 affects compensation paid by firms engaged in federal construction projects valued in excess of $2,000. It deals only with federal construction projects and requires that the "prevailing wage" rate be paid on all federal construction projects. States also have had their own versions of the Davis–Bacon provisions, but many of them are being dropped.

Equal Pay Act of 1963

Another piece of legislation that was passed as a major amendment to the FLSA in 1963 is the Equal Pay Act. The original act and subsequent amendments focus on wage discrimination on the basis of sex. The act applies to both men and women and prohibits paying different wage scales to men and women performing substantially the same jobs. Except for differences justifiable on the basis of merit (better performance) or seniority (longer service), similar pay must be given for jobs requiring equal skills, equal effort, equal responsibility, or for jobs done under similar working conditions.

Most of the equal pay cases decided in court have been situations in which women were paid less than men for doing similar work, even though different job titles were used. For example, equal pay violations have been found in health-care institutions in which male physicians assistants were paid significantly more than females with equal experience and qualifications who were called "nurse practitioners."

State Laws

Modified versions of federal compensation laws have been enacted by many states and municipal government bodies. These laws tend to cover workers included in intrastate commerce not covered by federal law. If a state has a higher minimum wage than that set under the Fair Labor Standards Act, the higher figure becomes the required minimum wage.

Many states once had laws that limited the number of hours women could work. However, these laws generally have been held to be discriminatory in a variety of court cases. Consequently, most states have dropped such laws.

Garnishment Laws

GARNISHMENT
is a court action in which a portion of an employee's wages is set aside to pay a debt owed a creditor.

Garnishment of an employee's wages occurs when a creditor obtains a court order that directs an employer to submit a part of the employee's pay to the creditor for debts owed by the employee. Regulations passed as a part of the Consumer Credit Protection Act established limitations on the amount of wages that can be garnished and restricted the right of employers to discharge employees whose pay is subjected to a single garnishment order. All 50 states have laws that apply to wage garnishments.

■■ ■ WAGE AND SALARY ADMINISTRATION

The development, implementation, and ongoing maintenance of a base pay system usually is described as **wage and salary administration.** The purpose of wage and salary administration is to provide pay that is both competitive and equitable. Underlying the activities administered are pay policies that set the overall direction of pay within the organization.

Pay Policies

WAGE AND SALARY ADMINISTRATION
is the activity involved in the development, implementation, and maintenance of a base pay system.

Organizations must develop policies as general guidelines to govern pay systems. Uniform policies are needed for coordination, consistency, and fairness in compensating employees. One specific organizational policy decision defines the relationship between pay expenditures and such factors as productivity, sales, or number of customers. In the retail industry, it is common to have a policy of maintaining payroll expenditures about 10 percent of gross sales volume. These policies reflect a major consideration in management decision making: how much can an organization afford to pay employees.[13]

MARKET COMPETITIVENESS.   A major policy decision must be made about the comparative level of pay the organization wants to maintain. Specifically, an employer must identify how competitive it is and wishes to be in the market for employees. Organizations usually want to "pay market," that is, to *match* the "going rates" paid employees by competitive organizations.

Some organizations choose to *lead* the market by paying above market. This policy aids in attracting and retaining employees. One transportation firm that pays about 10 to 15 percent above local market medians for clerical employees consistently has a waiting list for qualified word-processing and other office workers. By paying above market, the firm feels that it deters efforts to unionize its office workers.

On the other hand, some employers may deliberately choose to *lag* the market by paying below market. If there is an excess of qualified workers in the area, an adequate number of people are willing to work for lower pay. Also, an organization may not be able to afford to pay going rates because of financial pressures. Some governmental entities that have only a certain amount of tax revenues are in this situation, and raising taxes is not possible politically. Organizations in declining industries and some small businesses may face affordability problems also. However, the impact of pay rates below market can result in higher turnover or in having to hire less-qualified employees.

PAY SECRECY.   Another policy decision concerns the degree of openness or secrecy that the organizations allow regarding their pay systems. Pay information kept secret in "closed" systems includes how much others make, what raises others have received, and even pay grades and ranges in the organization. One reason for secret or closed pay systems is the fear that open pay systems will encourage petty complaints and create discontent and tensions. If an accountant knows for sure that he is paid less than another accountant, he may become dissatisfied at receiving "inequitable" treatment. Also, with a closed pay system, managers do not have to explain and justify pay differences.

OPEN PAY SYSTEMS.   Because comparison is such a critical part of how employees view compensation, some theorists advocate the need to "open up" pay systems by providing more pay information to employees. A growing number of organizations are opening up their pay systems to some degree. Information that some firms supply to employees includes compensation policies, a general description of the basis for the compensation system, and where an individual's pay is within a salary grade. By being given pay information, employees have the necessary information to make more accurate equity comparisons. It is crucial in an open pay system that managers be able to explain satisfactorily any pay differences that exist.

Policies that prohibit discussion of individual pay are likely to be violated anyway. Co-workers do share pay information, and an open pay system recognizes this fact. By having the pay system explained, employers can avoid distortions and other misinformation carried by the grapevine.

Development of a Pay System

Once pay policies have been determined, the actual development of a pay system begins. As Figure 13–5 shows, the development of a wage and salary system assumes that accurate job descriptions are available. The job descriptions then are used in two activities: *job evaluation* and *wage/salary surveys*. These activities are designed

Figure 13–5
Compensation Administration Process

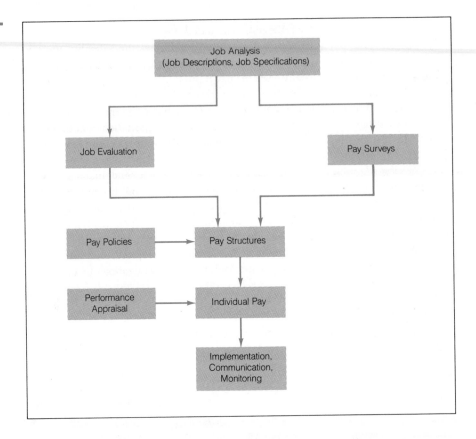

to ensure that the pay system is both internally equitable and externally competitive. The data compiled in those two activities are used to design *pay structures*, including *pay grades* and minimum-to-maximum *pay ranges*. After the pay structures have been developed, individual jobs must be placed in the appropriate pay grades and employees' pay adjust based upon length of service and performance. Finally, the pay system must be monitored and updated.

To aid in understanding the development of a wage and salary system, a continuous example is followed through all the stages. Danbo Manufacturing Company is a firm with a nonunion work force located in Arkansas. It has approximately 300 employees, including 30 clerical/office employees and 20 supervisory and management personnel. More details on Danbo are developed through examples in each section.

▬▬ ▬ JOB EVALUATION

Job evaluation flows from the job analysis process and is based on job descriptions. In a job evaluation, the job description of every job within an organization is examined by comparing:

JOB EVALUATION
is the systematic determination of the relative worth of jobs within an organization.

■ Relative importance of the job
■ Relative skills needed to perform the job
■ Difficulty of one job compared with other jobs

Job evaluation provides a basis for determining the relative worth of jobs. To produce a pay system that ensures *internal equity* for jobs is the main focus. It is crucial for an employer to pay employees so that they perceive that their pay is appropriate in relation to the jobs performed by others. If the secretary in the marketing department at Danbo does secretarial work for three sales representatives and has numerous other duties, that person may expect to be paid more than the manufacturing department secretary who spends most of the time completing production reports. Thus, internal equity is achieved through job evaluation when employees are paid in relation to the internal value and importance of each job.

Systematic evaluation of jobs attempts to reduce favoritism and ultimately leads to "job pricing." Although the approach is systematic, job evaluation can never be totally objective.[14] Subjective judgments cannot be avoided, and managers and P/HR specialists should not overemphasize the objectivity of the job evaluation system. Using a job evaluation committee in which several evaluators rate jobs can help improve the reliability of the evaluation. However, unions generally distrust job evaluations and view them as being manipulated for the benefit of management.

For these reasons, firms often bring in outside consultants to perform the job evaluation. In one study, one-third of the firms surveyed used outside consultants to establish pay structures for management people and one-fourth used them for nonmanagement positions.[15]

There are several methods used to determine internal job worth through job evaluation. All methods have the same general objective, but each differs in its complexity and means of measurement. Regardless of the method used, the intent is to develop a usable, measurable, and realistic system to determine compensation in an organization.

The American Compensation Association (ACA) conducted a survey of its members in the United States and 1,845 members responded. The results were:[16]

- Job evaluation point plans are the most popular.
- Market pricing is next in popularity and most usually used for executive jobs.
- Job evaluation is most often performed by a compensation analyst (37 percent), next most often by a committee (20 percent).

Market Pricing

Some employers do not use a special job evaluation method. Instead, they assume that the pay set by other employers is an accurate reflection of a job's worth, so they set their pay rates at the market rate or **market price** of jobs. One difficulty with this approach is the assumption that jobs are the same in another organization, which is not necessarily the case. Direct market pricing also does not adequately consider the impact of economic conditions, employer size, and other variables. Consequently, more complex methods have been developed.

MARKET PRICE
is the prevailing wage rate paid a job in the immediate job market.

Ranking Method

The ranking method is one of the simplest methods of job evaluation. It places jobs in order, ranging from highest to lowest in value to the organization. The entire job is considered rather than the individual components. Several different methods of ranking are available, but several problems exist.

Ranking methods are extremely subjective, and managers may have difficulty explaining why one job is ranked higher than another to employees whose pay is affected by these rankings. When there are a large number of jobs, the ranking method also can be awkward and unwieldy. Consider a P/HR specialist in Danbo who must rank all eighty-five jobs, from file clerk to president. This method would be almost impossible to use in a way that could be justified. Therefore, the job ranking method is more appropriate to a small organization having relatively few jobs.

Classification Method

The classification method of job evaluation was developed under the old U.S. Civil Service system and was widely copied by state and local government entities. A number of classes, or GS grades, are defined. Then the various jobs in the organization are put into grades according to common factors found in jobs, such as degree of responsibility, abilities or skills, knowledge, duties, volume or work, and experience needed. The grades are then ranked into an overall system.

One major reason for the popularity of the job classification method is that it is a system employees and managers can understand. Also, it has some flexibility when classifying a wide variety of jobs.

The major difficulty with the classification method is the subjective judgments needed to develop the grade descriptions and to place jobs accurately in them. With a wide variety of jobs and generally written grade descriptions, some jobs may appear to fall into two or three different grades.

Another problem with the classification method is that it relies heavily on job titles and duties and assumes that they are similar from one organization to another. For these reasons many federal, state, and local government entities have shifted to point systems.

Point Method

The point method is the most widely used job evaluation method. It breaks down jobs into various identifiable components and places weights or points on these components. By identifying factors that are common to the jobs under study, P/HR specialists develop these components from a job analysis. Then the relative weights, or points, are assigned to each degree of the component.

The point method is more sophisticated than the ranking and classification methods. Because the different job components carry different weights, each is assigned a numerical value. The values of the various components then are added for each job and compared with other jobs.

The individual using the point chart in Figure 13–6 looks at a job description and identifies the degree to which each element is necessary to perform the job satisfactorily. For example, the points assigned for a payroll clerk might be as follows: Education (42 points, 3rd degree); Responsibility for Trust Imposed (50 points, 4th degree); and Work Environment (25 points, 2nd degree). To reduce subjectivity, such determinations often are made by a group of people familiar with the jobs. Once point totals have been determined for all jobs, the jobs are grouped together into pay grades.

A special type of point method is used by a consulting firm. Hay and Associates, has received widespread application, although it is most often used with exempt employees. The Hay plan uses three factors: *know-how, problem solving*, and *accountability*, and numerically measures the degree to which each of these three elements is required in each job.

The point method has grown in popularity because it is a relatively simple system to use. It considers the components of a job rather than the total job, and is a much more comprehensive system than either the ranking or classification method. Once points have been determined and a job evaluation point manual has been

Figure 13–6
Point Method Chart

CLERICAL GROUP					
SKILL	1ST DEGREE	2ND DEGREE	3RD DEGREE	4TH DEGREE	5TH DEGREE
1. Education	14	28	42	56	
2. Experience	22	44	66	88	110
3. Initiative & ingenuity	14	28	42	56	
4. Contacts with others	14	28	42	56	
Responsibility					
5. Supervision received	10	20	35	50	
6. Latitude & depth	20	40	70	100	
7. Work of others	5	10	15	20	
8. Trust imposed	10	20	35	50	70
9. Performance	7	14	21	28	35
Other					
10. Work environment	10	25	45		
11. Mental or visual demand	10	20	35		
12. Physical effort	28				

The specific degrees and points for Education, Trust Imposed, and Work Environment are as follows:

Education is the basic *prerequisite* knowledge that is essential to satisfactorily perform the job. This knowledge may have been acquired through formal schooling such as grammer school, high school, college, night school, correspondence courses, company education programs, or through equivalent experience in allied fields. Analyze the minimum *requirements of the job and not the formal education of individuals performing it.*

1st Degree—Requires knowledge usually equivalent to a two-year high school education. Requires ability to read, write, and follow simple written or oral instructions; use simple arithmetic processes involving counting, adding, subtracting, dividing and multiplying whole numbers. May require basic typing ability.

2nd Degree—Requires knowledge equivalent to a four-year high school education in order to perform work requiring advanced arithmetic processes involving adding, subtracting, dividing, and multiplying or decimals and fractions; maintain or prepare routine correspondence, records, and reports. May require knowledge of advanced typing and/or basic knowledge of shorthand, bookkeeping, drafting, etc.

3rd Degree—Requires knowledge equivalent to four-year high school education plus some specialized knowledge in a particular field such as advanced stenographic, secretarial or business training, elementary accounting, or a general knowledge of blueprint reading or engineering practices.

4th Degree—Requires knowledge equivalent to two years of college education in order to understand and perform work requiring general engineering or accounting theory. Must be able to originate and compile statistics and interpretive reports, and prepare correspondence of a difficult or technical nature.

Responsibility for Trust Imposed This factor appraises the extent to which the job requires responsibility for safeguarding confidential information and the effect of such disclosure on the Company's relations with employees, customers or competitors.

1st Degree—Negligible. Little or no confidential data involved.

2nd Degree—Some access to confidential information but where responsibility is limited or where the full import is not apparent.

3rd Degree—Occasional access to confidential information where the full import is apparent and where disclosure may have an adverse effect on the Company's external or internal affairs.

4th Degree—Regularly works with and has access to confidential data, which if disclosed could seriously affect the Company's internal or external affairs or undermine its competitive position.

5th Degree—Full and complete access to reports, policies, records, and plans of Company-wide programs, including financial cost and engineering data. Requires the utmost discretion and integrity to safeguard the Company's interests.

Work Environment This factor appraises the physical surroundings and the degree to which noise is present at the work location. Consider the extent of distraction and commotion caused by the sounds.

1st Degree—Normal office conditions. Noise limited to the usual sounds of typewriters and other equipment.

2nd Degree—More than average noise due to the intermittent operation by several employees of adding machines, calculators, typewriters, or duplicating machines.

3rd Degree—Considerable noise generated by constant machine operation such as is present in the Data Processing section.

SOURCE: *Wage and Salary Administration: A Guide to Current Policies and Practices* (Chicago: Dartnell Corp.), pp. 135–141. Used with permission. Revision published every three years.

developed, the method can be used easily by people who are not specialists. The system can be understood by managers and employees, which gives it a definite advantage.

Another reason for the widespread use of the point method is that it evaluates the components of a job and determines total points before the current pay structure is considered. In this way, an assessment of relative worth can be made instead of relying on past patterns of worth.

One major drawback to the point method is the time needed to develop a system. For this reason, manuals and systems developed by management consultants or other organizations often are used by employers. Although not perfect, research studies have found that the point method of job evaluation generally is reliable and valid.[17] Because it quantifies jobs elements, it is probably better than the two previous systems discussed.

FACTOR COMPARISON. The factor comparison method, which is very quantitative and complex, involves determining the key jobs, called benchmark jobs, in an organization. A **benchmark job** is one performed by several individuals with similar duties that are relatively stable, requiring similar KSAs, and found in many other organizations. For example, a benchmark job in Danbo Manufacturing might be that of assembly worker.

The factor comparison method actually is a combination of the ranking and point methods. To understand this method, refer to the example in Figure 13–7. First, key (benchmark) jobs are identified and the compensable factors selected. In the example, the factors are levels of responsibility, physical demands, skills required, knowledge demands, and working conditions. Second, all benchmark jobs are ranked factor by factor. For example, the production supervisor is ranked highest and the custodian lowest on the responsibility factor. Similar rankings are made on all other factors.

In the third step, the jobs are compared with existing market rates for the benchmark jobs, and monetary values are assigned to each factor. For example, in Figure 13–7 the market value for a clerk–typist is $5.20. Fractions of the total amount

A BENCHMARK JOB
is one performed by several individuals with similar duties that are relatively stable, requiring similar KSAs, and found in many other organizations.

Figure 13–7
Factor Comparison Chart, Danbo Manufacturing Corporation

BENCHMARK JOBS	RESPONSIBILITY		PHYSICAL DEMANDS		SKILLS REQUIRED		KNOWLEDGE REQUIRED		WORKING CONDITIONS		MARKET PAY/HOUR
Clerk-Typist	8	($.50)	5	(1.00)	1	(3.00)	8	(.30)	6	(.40)	$5.20
Secretary	7	( )	8	( )	4	( )	7	( )	8	( )	$6.00
Payroll Clerk	6	( )	6	( )	7	( )	5	( )	7	( )	$6.15
Design Engineer	2	( )	9	( )	9	( )	19	( )	10	( )	$12.70
Computer Operator	4	( )	10	( )	6	( )	4	( )	9	( )	$5.80
Supervisor	1	( )	7	( )	5	( )	2	( )	5	( )	$9.30
Warehouse Worker	9	( )	1	( )	10	( )	10	( )	3	( )	$6.50
Custodian	10	( )	4	( )	8	( )	9	( )	4	( )	$4.50
Assembly Worker	5	( )	2	( )	3	( )	6	( )	1	( )	$7.10
Machine Operator	3	( )	3	( )	2	( )	3	( )	2	( )	$6.90

NOTE: Rank of 1 is highest.

($5.20) must be allocated to each factor. With skills required being the most important factor for the clerk–typist, it is assigned a value of $3.00. Because the clerk–typist was ranked highest of all jobs on skills required, all other jobs must be given values less than $3.00 on the skills-required factor. The fourth step is to evaluate all other jobs in the organization by comparing them with the benchmark jobs.

One of the major advantages of the factor comparison method is that it is tied specifically to one organization. Each organization must develop its own key jobs and its own factors. For this reason, buying a packaged system may not be appropriate. The factor comparision method does establish quantitative weights, as the point method does, but it requires the evaluator to make a specific comparative identification of the weights assigned. Finally, factor comparision not only tells which jobs are worth more, it also indicates how much more, so factor values can be more easily converted to monetary wages.

The major disadvantages of the factor comparison method are its difficulty and complexity. To see the complexity of this method try to complete the chart. It is not an easy system to explain to employees and it is time consuming to establish and develop. Also, a factor comparison system may not be appropriate for an organization with many similar types of jobs. Managers attempting to use the method should consult a specialist or one of the more detailed compensation books or manuals that discuss the factor comparison method.

Job Evaluation and Comparable Worth

Employers usually view evaluating jobs to determine rates of pay as a separate issue from selecting individuals for those jobs. However, this nation has had a long history of classifying jobs, at least implicitly, as "male" or "female." Although that is changing, there are still more nurses, elementary school teachers, and secretaries who are female than are male.

As noted previously, **comparable worth** is the concept that all jobs requiring comparable knowledge, skills, and abilities be paid similarly regardless of labor market considerations. Growing concerns about comparable worth have been translated into laws. These laws and agreements all focus on public sector jobs, especially those in state governments. In one study, ten states had established comparable worth policies: Hawaii, Iowa, Maine, Michigan, Minnesota, Montana, Ohio, Oregon, Washington, and Wisconsin. Also, more than twenty other states had conducted pay equity–comparable worth studies.[18]

Comparable-worth advocates have attacked typical job evaluations as gender-biased. Many jobs traditionally held by women are clerical and service, whereas many jobs dominated by men are craft and manual. Critics have charged that traditional job evaluation programs weigh knowledge, skills, and working conditions used in many female-dominated jobs less that the same factors in male-dominated jobs. For example, according to one writer, "Working conditions are usually defined in terms of heat, dirt, noise, and the like. Seldom are they defined in terms of tedium, boredom, or inability to move from the work station. Under such constraints female-dominated jobs invariably come out more poorly paid."[19] Research supporting this view indicates that different job evaluation methods may produce differing results and different pay structures.[20]

One review of 68 court cases revealed that evidence on the fairness of job evaluation plans had little impact on the case decisions.[21] Many employers base their pay rates heavily on *external equity* comparisons in the labor market, which

COMPARABLE WORTH
requires that jobs with comparable knowledge, skills, and abilities be paid similarly.

is their major defense for adopting the pay systems they have. Undoubtedly, with additional court decisions, governmental actions, and research, job evaluation activities will face more pressures to address the comparable worth.

The Canadian province of Ontario was the first major governmental jurisdiction anywhere to make private businesses adopt an "equal pay for equal work" plan. Under the law, if "women's jobs" pay less than "men's jobs" of equal value, the women must get raises. (Men holding those jobs get them, too.) In reevaluating its jobs to comply with the law, one publishing company rated librarians (female job) the same as truck loaders (male job), giving the librarians a $3,000 raise.[22] The critieria were as follows:

Criteria	Female Job Class: Newspaper Librarian	Male Job Class: Truck Loader
Skill	570	430
Effort	580	590
Responsibility	470	390
Working Conditions	450	660
Total	2,070	2,070

But determining the "worth" of dissimilar jobs has proved to be so difficult for most employers that the provincial government itself failed to meet its deadline for posting a plan. Private employers face even bigger problems.

■ ■ BUILDING A PAY SYSTEM

Determining internal equity through job evaluation is a key part of building a total pay system. Another part of the process is to survey the pay other organizations provide for similar jobs.

Pay Survey

PAY SURVEY
a collection of data on existing compensation rates for workers performing similar jobs in organizations.

A **pay survey** is a collection of data on compensation rates for workers performing similar jobs in organizations. An employer may use wage–salary surveys conducted by other organizations or may decide to conduct its own survey.[23]

USING PREPARED PAY SURVEYS.   Many different surveys are available from a variety of sources. National surveys on many jobs and industries are available through the U.S. Department of Labor, the Bureau of Labor Statistics, or through national trade associations. In many communities, employers participate in a wage survey sponsored by the Chamber of Commerce to provide information to new employers interested in locating in the community.

When using surveys from other sources, it is important to use them properly. Some questions that should be addressed are:

1. Is the survey a realistic sample of those employers with whom the organization competes for employees?
2. Is the survey "balanced" so that organizations of varying sizes, industries, locales, etc. are included?
3. How current is the data and when was the survey conducted?

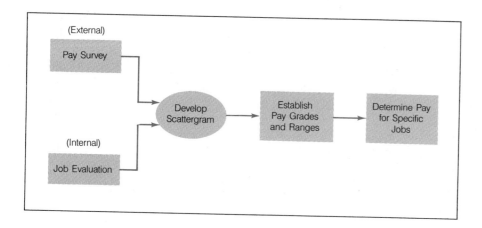

Figure 13–8
Establishing A Pay Structure

4. How established is the survey and how qualified are those who conducted it?
5. Does it contain job summaries so that appropriate match-ups can be made?

DEVELOPING A PAY SURVEY.   If needed pay information is not already available, the employer can undertake its own pay survey. Employers with comparable positions should be selected. Also, employers considered to be "representative" should be surveyed.[24] If the employer conducting the survey is not unionized, the pay survey probably should examine unionized as well as nonunionized organizations. Developing pay competitive with union wages may deter employees from joining a union.

The positions to be surveyed also must be decided. Not all jobs in all organizations can be surveyed, and not all jobs in all organizations will be the same. An accounting clerk in a city government office might perform a different job from an accounting clerk in a credit billing firm. Therefore, managers should select jobs that can be easily compared, have common job elements, and represent a broad range of jobs. Key or benchmark jobs are especially important ones to include. Also, it is advisable to provide brief job descriptions for jobs surveyed in order to ensure more accurate matches.

The next phase of the pay survey is for managers to decide what compensation information is needed for various jobs. Information such as starting pay, base pay, overtime rate, vacation and holiday pay and policies, and bonuses all can be included in a survey. However, requesting too much information may discourage survey returns.

The results of the pay survey usually are made available to those participating in the survey in order to gain their cooperation. Most surveys specify confidentiality, and data are summarized to assure anonymity. Different job levels often are included and the pay rates are presented both in overall terms and on a city-by-city basis to reflect regional differences in pay.

Pay Structure

Once survey data are gathered, the pay structure for the organization can be developed. One means of tying pay survey information to job evaluation data is to plot a *"wage curve"* or *"scattergram."* This plotting is done by first making a graph that charts job evaluation points to pay survey rates for all surveyed jobs.

Figure 13–9
Pay Scattergram

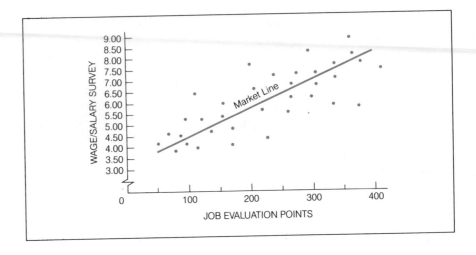

Use of survey data puts more emphasis on external market conditions. In this way the distribution of pay for surveyed jobs can be shown and a trend line using the "least squares regression method" can be drawn to plot a "market line." This line shows the relationship between job value, or points, and wage salary survey rates. (For details on this method see any basic statistics text.) An example is shown in Figure 13–9.

PAY GRADES
are used to group together individual jobs having approximately the same job worth.

ESTABLISHING PAY GRADES.   **Pay grades** are used to group together individual jobs having approximately the same job worth. While there are no set rules to be used when establishing pay grades, some overall suggestions have been made. Generally, eleven to seventeen grades are used in small companies such as Danbo Manufacturing.

By using pay grades, management can develop a coordinated pay system, without having to determine a separate pay rate for each job in the organization. An employer using a point method of job evaluation would group jobs having about the same number of points into one pay grade. As discussed previously, the factor comparison method uses monetary values. An employer using that method can easily establish and price pay grades. A vital part of the classification method is developing grades, and the ranking method can be converted to pay grades by grouping several ranks together.

CALCULATING PAY RANGES.   Using the market line as a starting point (see Figure 13–10), maximum and minimum pay levels for each pay grade can be determined by making the market line the midpoint line of the firm's new pay structure. By calculating values that are the same percentage above and below the midpoint value, the minimums and maximums can be determined. For example, if the market line (midpoint line) at a point is $5, going up and down 10 percent establishes a minimum and maximum of $4.50 to $5.50.

A smaller minimum-to-maximum range should be used for lower-level jobs than for higher-level jobs, primarily because employees in lower-level jobs tend to stay in them for shorter periods of time and have greater promotion possibilities. At Danbo Manufacturing, a clerical-typist might advance to the position of secretary or word processing operator. However, a design engineer likely would have fewer possibilities for future upward movement in the organization. At the lower end of a pay structure, the pay range may be 20 percent (minimum to maximum), whereas

GRADE	POINT RANGE	HOURLY PAY RANGE
1	101–135	$4.11–$5.13
2	136–170	$4.73–$5.91
3	171–205	$5.44–$6.80
4	206–240	$6.26–$7.82
5	241–275	$7.20–$9.00
6	276–310	$8.28–$10.35
7	311–345	$9.52–$11.90
8	over 345	$10.97–$13.71

*NOTE: 15% between grade minimums, with a 25% grade spread.

Figure 13–10
Example of Priced Labor Grades

upper-level ranges may be as high as 100 percent (minimum to maximum). The same percentage range used at all levels can make administration of a pay system easier in small firms such as Danbo.

Experts recommend having overlap between grades, such as those in Figure 13–10, allows an experienced employee in a lower grade to be paid more than a less experienced employee in a job in the next pay grade. Overlap between three adjacent grades, but no more than three is advised. Figure 13–10 shows the pay grades determined through a typical point system.

■■ ■ INDIVIDUAL PAY

Once managers determine rate ranges for pay ranges, they can set the specific pay for individuals. Each of the dots in Figure 13–11 represents an individual employee's current pay in relation to the pay ranges that have been developed. Setting a range for each pay grade gives flexibility by allowing individuals to progress within a grade instead of having to be moved to a new grade each time they receive a raise. Also, a pay range allows managers to reward the better-performing employees, while maintaining the integrity of the pay system.

Rates Out of Range

A job whose pay rate is above the range is identified as a **red-circle job.** A red-circle job is noted on the graph in Figure 13–11. For example, assume an employee's current pay is $7.18 per hour, but the pay grade of that job is between $5.44 and $6.80. The person would be red-circled and attempts would be made over a period of time to bring the employee's rate into grade.

Several approaches can be used to bring a red-circled person's pay into line.[25] Although the fastest way would be to cut the employee's pay, that approach is not recommended and is seldom used. Instead, the employee's pay may be frozen until the pay range can be adjusted upward to get the employee's pay rate back into the grade. The employee also can be transferred to a job with a higher grade or have responsibilities added to the red-circled job, which would result in greater job evaluation worth, thus justifying its being upgraded. Another approach is to give the employee a small lump-sum payment but not adjust the pay rate when others are given raises.

An individual whose pay is below the range is in a **green-circle job.** Generally, it is recommended that the green-circled individual receive pay increases to get to

RED-CIRCLE JOB
occurs when the incumbent is paid above the range set for the job.

GREEN–CIRCLE JOB
is one in which the incumbent is paid below the range set for the job.

Figure 13–11
**Pay Structure Depicted
Graphically**

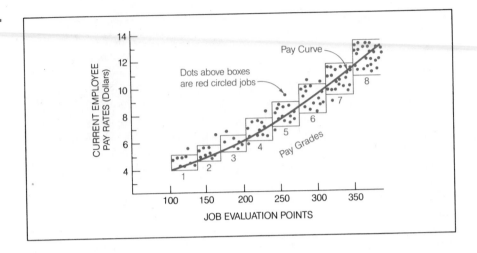

the pay grade minimum fairly rapidly. More frequent increases can be given if the increase to minimum would be large (15 percent or more).

Occasionally, managers may have to deviate from the priced grades to hire scarce skills to respond to competitive market shortages of particular job skills. If skilled people such as welders are in short supply, the worth of a welder's job may be evaluated to be $6 to $10 an hour, but the going rate for welders in the community may be $12 an hour. To fill the position, the firm must pay $12 an hour.

"All I did was tell him his starting salary."

Pay Compression

One major problem many employers face is **pay compression,** which occurs when a small range of pay differences exists among individuals. Pay compression occurs for a number of reasons, but the major one is that labor market pay levels increase more rapidly than an employer's pay adjustments. An increase in the federal minimum wage can cause compression pressures also. To illustrate, because of a shortage in the labor market, Danbo Manufacturing was forced to hire new machine operators at $7.00 per hour, although several operators who have been with the firm for five years are making only $7.10 per hour.

Pay compression is a difficult problem. The major ways to deal with it are through wider pay grades and more grade overlaps. Another strategy is to have a policy of maintaining a percentage differential, for example 15 to 20 percent, if the compression occurs between supervisors' pay and the pay of those supervised. Compression between first-line supervisors and those they supervise is a common problem, especially when few first-line supervisors receive overtime pay but their employees do.

PAY COMPRESSION
occurs when pay differences among individuals become small.

Pay Increases

Once pay ranges have been developed and individuals' placement within the range have been identified, managers must look at adjustment to individual pay. Decisions about pay increases often are some of the more critical ones that affect relationships among employees, their managers, and the organization. Individuals have expectations about their pay and about how much increase is "fair," especially in comparison to the increases received by other employees. There are several ways to determine pay increases.

SENIORITY.   Seniority, or time within the organization or on a particular job, is one approach to increasing pay rates. Many employers have policies that require persons to be employed for a certain length of time before they are eligible for pay increases. Pay adjustments based on seniority often are set as automatic steps once a person is employed the required length of time, although performance must be at least satisfactory in many nonunion systems.

MATURITY CURVES.   A closely related approach uses maturity curves. **A maturity curve** depicts the relationship between experience and pay rates. Pay rises as an employee's experience increases, which is especially useful for professionals and skilled craft employees. Unlike a true seniority system in which a pay raise occurs once someone has put in the required time, maturity curves are built on the assumption that as experience increases, proficiency and performance increases, so pay raises are appropriate. If proficiency does not increase, theoretically pay adjustments are reduced, although that seldom happens in practice.

A MATURITY CURVE
depicts the relationship between experience and pay rates.

COST-OF-LIVING ADJUSTMENTS (COLA).   One common pay raise practice is the use of a *standard raise* or *cost-of-living raise.* Giving employees a standard percentage increase enables them to maintain the same real wages in a period of economic inflation. Often these adjustments are tied to changes in the Consumer Price Index (CPI) or some other general economic measure. Unfortunately, some employers give across-the-board raises and call them *merit raises.* If all employees get a pay increase, the cost-of-living adjustment frequently is viewed as having little to do with merit and good performance. For this reason, employers giving a basic percentage increase to all employees should avoid using the term *merit* in awarding it. The merit or performance part should be identified as that amount above the standard raise.

PAY-FOR-PERFORMANCE.   As the discussion at the beginning of this chapter indicates, pay-for-performance is becoming a very popular way to change the way pay increases have been distributed in many organizations.

In a true performance-oriented system, no pay raises are given except for increases in performance. Giving pay increases to people because they have 10 to 15 years' experience, even though they are medicore employees, defeats the approach. Also, unless the performance-based portion of a pay increase is fairly significant, employees may feel it is not worth the extra effort.[26] Giving an outstanding industrial designer making $40,000 a year the "standard raise" of 6 percent plus 1 percent for merit means only $400 for merit versus $2,400 for "hanging around another year."

Many employers profess to have a pay system based on performance, as indicated by performance appraisal ratings.[27] But reliance on performance appraisal information for making pay adjustments assumes that the appraisals are done well, especially for employees whose work cannot be measured easily. Consequently, some system for integrating appraisals and pay changes must be developed and applied equally. Often this integration is done through the use of a *pay adjustment matrix* or *salary guide chart* (see Figure 13–12). Such charts base adjustments off of a person's **compa-ratio,** which is a pay level divided by the midpoint of the pay range.

Such charts reflect a person's upward movement in an organization. Upward movement depends on the person's performance, as rated on an appraisal, and on where the person is within the pay range, which has some relation to experience also. A person rated as exceeding standards (4) whose compa-ratio was 94 would be eligible for a raise of 7 to 9 percent according to the chart in Figure 13–12.

COMPA-RATIO
is a pay level divided by the midpoint of the pay range.

Figure 13–12
Pay Adjustment Matrix

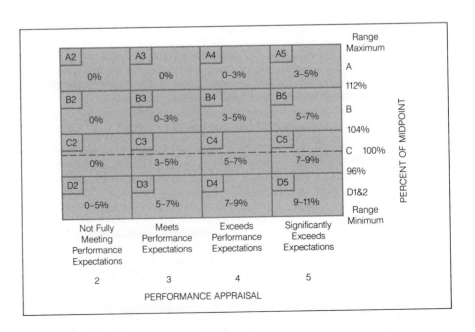

Notice that as a person moves up the pay range, the employee must exhibit a higher performance to obtain the same raise as someone lower in the range performing at the "meets performance expectations" (3) level. Charts can be constructed to reflect the specific pay-for-performance policy and philosophy in an organization. Another way to pay-for-performance is by a lump-sum increase.

Most employees who receive pay increases, either for merit or seniority, first have their base pay adjusted and then receive an increase in the amount of their regular monthly or weekly paycheck. For example, an employee who made $1,200 per month, and received a 6 percent increase, would get a paycheck for $1,272 per month. However, some employers have adopted a different approach—lump-sum increases (LSI).

LUMP-SUM PAY INCREASES.   In an LSI plan, an employee receives a one-time payment of the yearly pay increase. In our example, the employee would receive a check for $864 (before taxes are deducted) which is $72/mo. × 12 months. Some organizations place a limit on how much of a merit increase can be taken as a lump-sum payment. Other organizations split the lump sum into two checks, each representing one-half the year's pay raise. Organizations that use the LSI often limit eligibility for the plan to employees with longer service who are not in high turnover groups. Also, some employers treat the lump-sum payment as an advance, which must be repaid if the employee leaves the firm before the year is finished.

As with any plan, there are advantages and disadvantages. The major advantage of an LSI plan is that it heightens employees' awareness of what their performance "merited." A lump-sum check also gives employees some flexibility in their spending patterns so that they can buy big-ticket items without having to take out a loan. In addition, the firm can slow down the increase of base pay, so that the compounding effect of succeeding raises is reduced. Unionized employers, such as Boeing and Ford, have negotiated LSI plans as a way to hold down base wages, which also holds down the rates paid for overtime work. Pension costs and some other benefits, often tied to base wages, can be reduced some also.

One disadvantage is administrative tracking, including a system to handle income tax and Social Security deductions from the lump-sum check. Also, workers who take a lump-sum payment may become discouraged because their base pay has not changed. Unions generally resist LSI programs because of this and because of the impact on pensions and benefits.[28] To some extent, this problem can be reduced some if the merit increase is split to include some in the base pay and some in the lump-sum payment.

SUMMARY

- Compensation provided by an organization can come through pay (base wages and salaries), incentives (performance-based rewards), and benefits (indirect compensation).
- Compensation responsibilities of both P/HR specialists and managers must be performed well because compensation practices are closely related to organizational strategies, life cycles, and culture.
- Determination of compensation can be based on time, productivity, or a combination of the two, and should be matched to the tasks performed.
- A variety of forces external to the organization, including unions and economic factors, affect the types and amount of compensation given employees.

■ The Fair Labor Standards Act, as amended, is the law that affects pay systems most. It requires most organizations to pay a minimum wage and to meet the overtime provisions of the act, including appropriately classifying employees as exempt or nonexempt.

■ Other laws have been passed that place restrictions on employers who have federal supply contracts, federal construction contracts, or who garnish employees' pay.

■ Regardless of whether compensation is seen by employees principally in terms of economic, psychosocial, or growth factors, managers should be concerned with offering adequate rewards in exchange for employees' inputs.

■ Differing degrees of pay secrecy or pay openness can be practiced.

■ Administration of a wage/salary system requires the development of pay policies that take into account the pay offered by other employers.

■ To ensure internal equity, job evaluation is necessary. Job evaluation is concerned with determining the relative worth of jobs. It can be done through the use of market pricing, ranking, classification, point, or factor comparison methods.

■ Once the job evaluation process has been completed, wage/salary survey data must be collected and pay structure developed. To have an effective pay system, changes will have to be made on a continual basis.

■ Individual pay treatment must take into account an employee's placement within pay grades and their ranges. Problems of rates above or below range and pay compression must be addressed.

■ Pay increases can be based on seniority, cost-of-living adjustments, performance, or a combination of those approaches.

REVIEW AND DISCUSSION QUESTIONS

Why must the types of compensation used be related to the strategy and life-cycle stage of the organization?

Give an example of the basic approaches for determining compensation and how each might be affected by external factors.

What factors whould be considered to determine if an employee who worked over 40 hours in a week would be due overtime?

What is the focus of the following laws:

a. Walsh-Healey Act

b. Davis-Bacon Act

c. Equal Pay Act

Considering all methods, why do you believe the point method is the most widely used job evaluation method?

You have been named compensation manager for a hospital. How would you establish a pay system?

| CASE | **Equitable Compensation** |

A financial institution headquartered in a town of approximately 25,000 people had assets of approximately $250 million and 85 employees. It also had branches in some smaller farming communities around the headquarters community.

Until several years ago, the firm had been operating with a compensation system that had been devised by its accounting firm several years earlier. However, because of growth and changes within the firm, the P/HR manager, felt it was time for a complete review of the firm's base compensation program. The review became even more important as the firm like many other savings and loans, faced earnings declines and losses because of economic and interest rate factors, deregulation of the industry, and declining agricultural economic conditions.

To begin the project the P/HR manager contacted a professional acquaintance with expertise in compensation who had assisted other financial institutions in similar projects as a consultant. After an initial meeting with the consultant, a detailed review of all of the firm's job descriptions was done. Some changes were identified in the loan operations area and revised descriptions were written.

The next stage of the project was a comparison of the firm's existing pay structure to that of other employers in the area and in the industry. A job evaluation committee, composed of several executives, a supervisor in the accounting area, the P/HR manager, and the consultant, was formed. Using a job evaluation point system, the committee individually assigned points to all jobs in the organization on such factors as *knowledge required, experience required, supervision given and received, interpersonal contacts,* and *working conditions.* Then the committee met several times, compared points assigned for each job, discussed each job, and reached a point total consensus for each job.

Using all this data, the consultant constructed a recommended pay structure containing about 20 separate pay grades and the minimum and maximum pay for each range. Based on the job evaluation points assigned, all jobs were placed into the appropriate grades. Then the pay for all employees was reviewed to determine to what extent employees were being paid below, within, or above the recommended pay ranges. With only a few exceptions, all employees' pay fell within the new ranges. The committee decided to address those situations at the time of the next pay raises.

From that point on, all managers and supervisors completed performance appraisals on their employees on their anniversary dates. With the appraisal information, employees were given pay adjustments in line with the overall budgetary parameters determined to be realistic at the time. Although the P/HR manager has since retired, the firm has continued to administer its base compensation program in a fair and effective manner during the succeeding years.

NOTES

1. Therse R. Welter, "Compensation System Called Unfair," *Industry Week,* January 26, 1987, 17–18.

2. R. L. Bunning, "Skill-Based Pay," *Personnel Administrator,* June 1989, 65; N. Crandall and P. Schindler, "Why Competency-based Pay," *Perspectives,* 1990, 7; H. Tosi and L. Tosi, "What Managers Need to Know about Knowledge-based Pay," *Organizational Dynamics,"* Winter 1986, 52–64; B. Tesfay, "Compensation," *Personnel Journal,* January 1990, 81.

3. Cathy Trost, "All Work and No Play? New Study Shows How Americans View Jobs," *Wall Street Journal,* December 30, 1986, 23.

4. K. I. Kim, *et al.,* "Reward Attractions in the US, Japan, and Korea," *Academy of Management Journal,* 33 (1990): 188–198.

5. For an expanded discussion, see Frederick S. Hills, *Compensation Decision Making* (Chicago: Dryden Press, 1987), 29–39, and Richard Henderson, *Compensation Administration,* 5th ed. (Englewood Cliffs, N.J.: Prentice–Hall, 1989.)

6. S. Jordan, "No One Punches Clock at Paper Mill," *Omaha World-Herald,* March 10, 1990, 26.

7. *Wall Street Journal,* September 16, 1986, 1.

8. Adapted from Kathryn McKee, First Interstate Bancorp, 1986; A. C. Hax, "A New Competitive Lesson: The Human Resource Strategy," *Training and Development Journal*, May 1985, 76–82; and T. A. Barocci and T. A. Kochan, *Human Resource Management and Industrial Relations* (Boston: Little, Brown, 1985), 101–109.

9. J. Tibbetts and E. Donovan, "Compensation and Benefits for Startup Companies," *Harvard Business Review*, January/February 1989, 140–147.

10. For more specifics, see Employment Standards Administration, Wage and Hour Division, *Handy Reference Guide to the Fair Labor Standards Act*, WH Publication 1282 (Washington, D.C.: U.S. Department of Labor).

11. For more details, see Employment Standards Administration, Wage and Hour Division, *Executive, Administrative, Professional and Outside Sales Exemptions Under the Fair Labor Standards Act*, WH Publication 1363 (Washington, D.C.: U.S. Department of Labor).

12. *Donovan v. Hudson Stations Inc.*, 25 HW 795.

13. R. Meehan and G. V. Lemesis, "Compensation Plan Analysis," *HR Magazine*, February 1990, 69–72.

14. G. Meng, "Link Pay to Job Evaluation," *Personnel Journal*, March 1990, 98–104.

15. D. J. Mitchell, *Human Resource Management: An Economic Approach*, (Boston: PWS-Kent Publishing), 1989, 184.

16. "Survey of Job Evaluation Practices," *American Compensation Association*, August 1989, 1–12.

17. H. Risher, "Job Evaluation: Validity and Reliability," *Compensation and Benefit Review*, January/February 1989, 22–36.

18. *Pay Equity: Status of State Activities*, No. GAO/GGD-86-141 BR (Washington, D.C.: U.S. General Accounting Office, 1986)

19. Hills, op. cit., 312.

20. Robert M. Madigan and David J. Hoover, "Effects of Alternative Job Evaluation Methods on Decision Involving Pay Equity," *Academy of Management Journal* 29 (1986): 84–100.

21. Marsha Katz, Helen LaVan, and Maura S. Molloy, "Comparable Work: Analysis of Cases and Implications for HR Management," *Compensation and Benefits Review*, May/June 1986, 26–38.

22. L. Kilpatrick, "In Ontario 'Equal Pay for Equal Work' Becomes a Reality . . .," *Wall Street Journal*, March 9, 1990, B1.

23. Margaret Dyckman, "Take the Mystery Out of Salary Surveys," *Personnel Journal*, June 1990, 104–106.

24. Gregory A. Syer, "The Exempt Salary Survey, Part I: Collecting Information," *Personnel*, June 1986, 45–49.

25. Paul R. Reed and Mark J. Kroll, "Red-Circle Employee: A Wage Scale Dilemma," *Personnel Journal*, February 1987, 92–95.

26. Edward G. Wertheim, "Merit Pay Programs," *Business Report from Northeastern University*, n.d., 1–3.

27. B. Wisdom, "Before Implementing a Merit System . . .," *Personnel Administrator*, October 1989, 46–49.

28. S. Ward, "Lump-Sum Plans Become Labor's Latest Battleground," *USA Today*, November 7, 1989, A1, 2.

Incentives and Executive Compensation

After you have read this chapter, you should be able to:

1. Define an incentive and list four guidelines for an incentive program
2. Discuss three types of individual incentives and some problems with them
3. Describe the nature of a Scanlon plan and an employee stock ownership plan (ESOP)
4. Identify three components of executive compensation

P/HR: Today *and* Tomorrow

Here Come Riskier Pay Plans!

Wage earners get paid by the hour, salaried employees are paid by the year, and only executives get bonuses. Right? Wrong! Or rather, that's the way things used to be, but things have changed. The changes have occurred because the old system hasn't worked very well recently. Employers were unhappy with the level of effort elicited by traditional pay systems and felt the need to tie pay more closely to performance, making pay an incentive to work harder.

The American Productivity and Quality Center reports that 75 percent of employers now use at least one form of "nontraditional" pay plan, and most of those have been adopted in the last five years. These plans link pay to performance *and* they put more of each employee's pay "at risk." Cynics suggest that CEOs have some nerve adopting such plans for employees when their own often huge salaries are not tied to performance. But that too is changing slowly.

The need for new ways of paying people to increase their productivity has resulted in many different approaches, plans, and ideas. But experts say that about half of the pay-for-performance plans they see *don't work!* Poor design and poor administration are the culprits.

Employers flock to see the classic example of incentive pay at Lincoln Electric Company in Cleveland. (See the case on Lincoln Electric at the end of the chapter for more detail.) Lincoln pays its factory employees on a piece rate. Workers average bonuses of 97.6% of their regular earnings. Lincoln, can boast of 54 years without a losing quarter, 40 years with no layoffs, and employees who are about three times as productive as workers in similar settings.

Many elements must be present for incentive plans to work, but two of the most important ones sometimes are also the most difficult. Management must be willing to *share* and *listen*. Sharing the increased fruits of increased efforts in an equitable fashion is obviously a key—yet management may have difficulty sharing enough. Listening to employee ideas, concerns, and providing information on the budget, business conditions, and the economy are critical as well.

Money *can* motivate. The hard part is using it to motivate the kind of behavior desired by management. Designing an incentive program is far from easy, but the efforts can be well worth the cost. While incentive plans are risky, not having one might be riskier.[1]

"Incentive is the driving force which can improve one's fated course."
                                                                    A. L. Romanoff

P/HR professionals are under more pressure to design and install variable pay systems because the feeling is that they provide more incentive, greater reward, and lower fixed labor costs.[2] Some employers use performance-based pay systems to encourage individual effort, teamwork, and better organizational results. Federated Department Stores is even using incentive bonuses to encourage managers to stay with the company as it tries to fight its way back from bankruptcy.[3]

But linking pay to performance is not *always* successful or even appropriate. For example, if the output cannot be objectively measured, how can management reward the higher performers with more pay? Managers even may not be able to identify accurately the higher performers. Requirements for successful incentive plans are developed in this chapter.

▬▬ ▬ INCENTIVES

The main purpose of incentives is to tie employees' rewards closely to their output. An **incentive** provides compensation that is related directly to output performance. Whether an individual will strive for increased productivity and receive the rewards that follow better performance depends on the individual. Also, some well-paid people may prefer some extra time off for higher productivity rather than more money.

AN INCENTIVE
is compensation that rewards an employee for efforts beyond normal performance expectations.

Incentive System Guidelines

Incentive systems can be complex and take many forms. Managers should consider the following general guidelines when establishing and maintaining such systems.

REWARD WHAT IS IMPORTANT.   Since people tend to produce what is measured and rewarded, it is important to make sure that what is being rewarded is *really* what is needed and something important is not being left out. For example, assume a hotel reservation center sets incentives for its employees to lower their time spent per call. That reduction may occur, but customer service and the number of reservations made might drop as employees rush callers to reduce talk time.

TIE INCENTIVES TO PERFORMANCE.   Incentive systems should be tied as much as possible to performance. If an incentive is actually to spur increased performance and effort, employees must see a direct relationship between their efforts and their rewards. Further, both workers and managers must see the rewards as equitable and desirable. If a *group* incentive system is to be used, it clearly should reflect employees' efforts as a group of individuals.

RECOGNIZE INDIVIDUAL DIFFERENCES.   Incentive plans should provide for individual differences. People are complex, and a variety of incentive systems may have to be developed to appeal to various organizational groups and individuals. Not everybody will want the same type of incentive rewards. Further, not every job will be appropriate for incentives. Focus on those jobs with a high discretionary content where employees can really make a difference in output.

RECOGNIZE ORGANIZATIONAL FACTORS.   The incentive system chosen should be consistent with the climate and constraints of an organization. For example, it is inconsistent to devise an incentive plan requiring a high degree of employee participation if the organization adheres to traditional procedures and rules and does not allow participation. The incentive plan also should be compatible with organizational resources and be developed with the firm's financial officers to determine how much incentive compensation an organization can afford.

SEPARATE PLAN PAYMENTS FROM BASE PAY.   Successful incentive plans separate the incentive payment from base salary. That separation makes a clear connection between performance and pay. It also reinforces the notion that one part of the employee's pay must be "re-earned" in the next performance period.

CONTINUE TO MONITOR.   An incentive system should consistently reflect current technological and organizational conditions. Offering an incentive for sales clerks to sell outdated merchandise in order to clear it out of stock would be more appropriate than offering them incentives to sell only current fashion items that are already in high demand.

Incentive systems should be reviewed continually to determine whether they are operating as designed. Follow-up, through an attitude survey or other means, will determine if the incentive system is actually encouraging employees to perform better. If it is not, then managers should seriously consider changing the system.

Types of Incentives

Organizations often use a combination of incentive systems. As Figure 14–1 shows, incentive plans can be *individual, group,* or *organizational.* The latter category includes both profit-sharing and employee ownership plans. A discussion of each type follows.

The use of organizational-level incentives can give quite different results from individual-level incentives. As Figure 14–2 shows, individual plans work well to tie pay to performance when productivity is being directly measured, but they do not encourage people to cooperate with one another. Either group or organizational plans work better if cooperation or acceptance is important.

■■ ■ INDIVIDUAL INCENTIVES

Though there are different types of individual incentive systems (see the P/HR: Practice), they all attempt to relate individual effort to pay. For a sales clerk who works on a base pay-plus-commission system, the commission portion represents the individual incentive compensation.

Individual incentive systems may have to be tailored to individual desires; thus, if a worker wants additional time-off instead of additional take-home pay, an effective incentive system will have to provide that option. Expectancy theory indicates that incentives are most effective when employees clearly can see that their extra work leads to increased rewards.

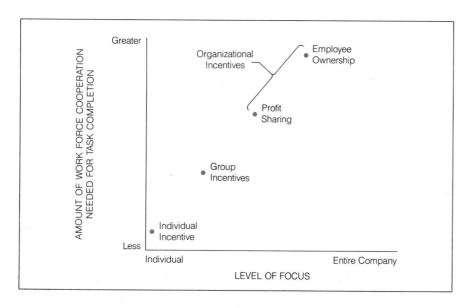

Figure 14–1
Incentive Plans: Focus and Cooperation Requirements

Requirements for Successful Individual Incentives

Although individual incentives are most frequently used in for-profit organizations, they also can be developed for use in not-for-profit organizations as well.[5] The following requirements are necessary, but perhaps not sufficient, for a successful individual incentive system.

- An employee must *want* higher pay.
- More effort can produce more production.
- Costs can be controlled by employee effort.
- Quality standards can be measured and maintained.
- Delays in the flow of work can be controlled.
- Changes in tasks are infrequent.

Figure 14–2
Advantages and Disadvantages of Incentive Plans

TYPE OF INCENTIVE PLAN	HOW IS PERFORMANCE MEASURED?	HOW MUCH DOES IT TIE PAY TO PERFORMANCE	HOW MANY NEGATIVE SIDE EFFECTS ARE REPRODUCED?	HOW MUCH COOPERATION IS ENCOURAGED?	HOW HIGH IS EMPLOYEE ACCEPTANCE OF THE PLAN?
Individual plans	Productivity	5	3	1	2
	Cost effectiveness	4	2	1	2
	Superiors' rating	4	2	1	2
Group plans	Productivity	4	1	3	3
	Cost effectiveness	3	1	3	3
	Superiors' rating	3	1	3	3
Organizational plans	Productivity	3	1	3	4
	Cost effectiveness	3	1	3	4
	Profit	2	1	3	3
(Scale: 1 = Low, 5 = High)					

SOURCE: Adapted from work by Edward E. Lawler, III.

P/HR: Practice *and* Research	A Variety of Incentives

Many different incentive programs have been developed. The ones described below illustrate the variety and creativity that can be used.

James Balkcom, chief executive officer (CEO) of Tecksonic Industries, found his plant flooded with orders and a backlog that would not shrink despite double shifts, fifteen-hour workdays, and six-day work weeks. He began to worry about fatigue among his work force, many of whom were working mothers. "We were so far behind that the lost production time didn't really matter," he said as he gave everyone a crisp $100 bill and a day off. Was it worth it? "It really fired people up," he said. The firm soon plowed through the backlog.

In Arlington County, Virginia, the police department devised a scheme to reward top performing officers. A felony arrest was worth 50 points, a traffic ticket 1 point, driving while intoxicated, 10 points, and so on. Officers scoring more than 35 points a day (which was above average) are given priority in picking work and neighborhood assignments. As a result, productivity has risen.

Boston Gas Company employees who did not have an accident were eligible for lottery drawings. Winners got $25 catalog certificates. The company said that the first year of the incentive-for-safety program was its safest ever.[4]

Piece-Rate Systems

The most basic individual incentive system is the piece-rate system. Under the straight piecework system, organizations determine wages by multiplying the number of units produced (such as garments sewn or customers contacted) by the piece-rate for one unit. The rate for each piece does not change regardless of the number of pieces produced. Because the cost is the same for each unit, the wage for each employee is easy to figure, and labor costs may be accurately predicted.

At Union National Bank in Little Rock, Arkansas, piece-rate incentives were first used in the proof department. The proof department employees encode machine readable numbers on the bottoms of checks so they can be computer processed. Before the incentive program began, production was 1,065 items per person per hour, about average for most banks. When operators were given feedback on how many items they had produced and paid a bonus on their daily output, production increased to 2,800 items per hour, the maximum rate for which incentive money was paid. When the maximum was lifted altogether, performance went to 3,500 per hour, with individuals occasionally producing as high as 4,460 items per hour.

The proof department program has been in effect for six years, and proof operators earn from 50 to 70 percent over their base salary in incentives. Turnover has dropped from 110 percent to virtually zero. Absenteeism has gone from 4.24 percent to 2.23 percent. Staffing was reduced from eleven to three full-time employees. Overtime dropped from 475 hours per year to 13 per year and savings from processing the checks faster is about $100,000 per year.[6] This piece-rate system clearly works very well.

DIFFERENTIAL PIECE-RATE.   A *differential piece-rate* system pays employees one piece-rate wage if they produce less than a standard output, and a higher piece-rate wage if they produce more than the standard. Developed by Frederick W. Taylor in the late 1800s, this system is designed to stimulate employees to achieve or exceed established standards of production. Managers often determine the quotas or standards by using time and motion studies. For example, assume that the standard quota for a worker is set at 300 units per day and the standard rate is 14¢ per unit. For all units over the standard, however, the employee receives 20¢ per unit. Under this system, the worker who produces 400 units in one day would get $62 in wages (300 × 14¢) + (100 × 20¢). There are many other possible combinations of straight and differential piece-rate systems. The specific system used by a firm depends on many situational factors.

Despite their incentive value, piecework systems are difficult to use because standards for many types of jobs are difficult and costly to determine. In some instances, the cost of determining and maintaining the standards may be greater than the benefits derived from piecework. Jobs in which individuals have little control over output or in which high standards of quality are necessary also may be unsuited to piecework. Though the system still is widely used in certain industries, such as the garment industry, it is seldom used in white-collar, office, and clerical jobs, in which an individual employee's performance often is affected by factors beyond the employee's control. For example, paying a bank teller on a piece-rate basis for each customer transaction would be inappropriate. The teller does not control whether the customer chooses one line or another, and probably is not responsible for that customer choosing to make a deposit or withdrawal. However, tellers might be given incentives for new accounts opened or number of transactions handled.

Commissions

An individual incentive system widely used in sales jobs is the **commission**. A commission is compensation computed as a percentage of sales in units or dollars. Commissions are integrated into the pay given to sales workers in two common ways: straight commission and bonuses.

A COMMISSION
is compensation computed as a percentage of sales in units or dollars.

STRAIGHT COMMISSION.   In the straight commission system, a sales representative receives a percentage of the value of the sales made. Consider a sales representative working for a consumer products company. She receives no compensation if no sales are made, but for all sales made in her territory she receives a percentage of the total amount. The advantage of this system is that the sales representative must sell to earn. The disadvantage is that it offers no security for the sales staff, even though the product or service sold might be one that requires a long lead time before purchasing decisions are made. One sales representative with a telecommunications firm spent five months working with a large corporation to sell a $1 million phone and communication system, for which the representative received a sizable commission. But during the five months, he received no income; he was paid only when the sale was closed and the equipment installed.

For that reason, some employers use a **draw** system, in which the sales representative can draw advance payments against future commissions. The amount drawn then is deducted from future commission checks. From the employer's side, one of the risks in a draw system is that future commissions may not be large enough to repay the draw, especially for a new or marginally successful salesperson.

A DRAW
is an amount advanced to an employee and repaid from future commissions earned by the employee.

In addition, arrangements must be made for repayment of drawn amounts if an individual leaves the organization before earning the draw in commission.

According to a national survey, about 20 percent of all sales representatives are paid through commissions only. The most frequently used form of sales compensation is the *salary-plus-commission* approach.[7]

SALARY-PLUS-COMMISSION.   The salary-plus-commission method of compensation combines the stability of a salary with the performance aspect of a commission. A common split is 80 percent salary to 20 percent commission, although that split varies by industry and with other factors.

Consultants criticize many sales commission plans as being too complex to motivate sales representatives. Others are too simple, focusing only on the salesperson's pay, not on organizational objectives. Although a majority of companies use overall sales growth as the only performance measure, performance would be much better if these organizations used a variety of criteria, including new accounts and product mix that reflect marketing plans.[8]

SPECIAL INCENTIVE PROGRAMS.   Although special incentive programs can be developed for groups and for entire organizations, they focus on rewarding only high-performing individuals. Giving the salesperson who sells the most new cars a trip to Las Vegas is one example of a special incentive program. Sales contests, productivity contests, and other incentive schemes can be conducted so that individual employees receive extra compensation. The discussion in the P/HR: Practice illustrates how employees of one company struck it rich.

Special incentive programs are used widely in sales-related jobs. Cash, merchandise, travel, and combinations of those are the most frequently used rewards. The main reasons for using awards are to achieve immediate sales gains and to focus attention on specific products.[10]

Bonuses

Individual incentive compensation in the form of bonuses often is used at the executive or upper management levels of an organization, although it is increasingly used at lower levels, too. Employers want to get away from the idea of regular raises, which are not always possible in hard times, or wise even in good times. At a large forest products company in Seattle, 1,000 employees earning $75,000 or more per year were eligible for bonuses in one year. In the next year, 5,000 employees with salaries as low as $35,000 were eligible. Bonuses generally ranged from 10 to 12 percent of salary. Because they were not paid to everyone and one year's bonus did not guarantee next year's bonus, the chain of lock-step wage increases was broken.[11]

E.T.C. Carpet Mills Ltd. in Santa Ana, California, wanted the firm to be more competitive by giving waiting customers faster service. It was not unusual for customers to wait one-and-a-half hours for an order at competing firms; E.T.C. decided to try for a ten-minute or less waiting period. A bonus fund was set up in the shipping department. When an order was finished within ten minutes, the company put $1 in the fund. Every three months the balance was divided among the department's ten employees. As a result, employees got bonuses of $600 each, and the department developed a reputation for quick customer service.[12]

P/HR: Practice and Research — Strike It Rich

National Linen Service, based in Atlanta, has 64 plants in the Sunbelt region from Florida to California, providing linens and uniforms to a wide range of businesses. Each day the 1,250 National Linen route drivers pick up soiled linens and uniforms and replace them with clean ones. However, the route drivers, called *route sales representatives*, also are encouraged to look for new business and possible customers while making their route deliveries.

In the past, National Linen had used short sales contests to generate additional sales. During the contests, commissions were raised and new business generated; but then the route sales representatives stopped selling until a new contest was announced.

To overcome these problems, the company developed a ten-month incentive program using a bowling theme called "Strike It Rich." During the program, drivers received their normal commissions for new accounts. In addition, each month sales representatives were awarded points for making new sales. Depending on the average weekly dollar amount of new account sales, a driver received a Spare (2,236 points), a Strike (4,472 points), or a Super-Strike (6,708 points). Those who held on to new accounts also generated additional superstrikes, strikes, and spares. Sales managers and route supervisors accumulated points based on the results of their sales representatives.

All points earned could be converted into a gift certificate that could be used to purchase items from a merchandise award catalog. Each Super-Strike earned allowed a driver to enter a Grand Slam drawing for a new car or ten consolation certificates valued at $1,000 each.

From the company standpoint, the most important result of the program was that sales increased by 35 percent—even more than management expected. Also, sales held fairly steady at the new level after the program ended and the route sales representatives were more aware of their selling responsibilities. In sum, the company and its route sales representatives did "strike it rich" through the use of a special incentive program.[9]

Lump-sum payments or bonuses are less costly than general wage increases,[13] since bonuses do not become part of the general wage scale. Bonuses give companies more flexibility in dealing with business cycles. Almost half of U.S. workers covered by major labor agreements have had some sort of bonus payment built into their compensation.[14]

One method of determining an employee's annual bonus is to compute it as a percentage of the individual's base salary. Often such programs pay bonuses only if specific departmental or organizational objectives are achieved. Though technically this type of bonus is individual, it comes close to being a group or organization incentive system. Because it is based on the profits of the division, management must consider the total performance of the division and its employees.

Problems With Individual Incentives

There are many problems with incentives at all three levels. Although the benefits of an effective incentive program are obvious, acknowledging potential problems is an important part of properly designing an incentive program:[15]

- Putting a price on a job may reduce the intrinsic attractiveness of the job.
- It is difficult to make fine distinctions accurately among the performances of many employees.

Figure 14–3
Relationship between Trust and Objectivity in Individual Incentive Systems

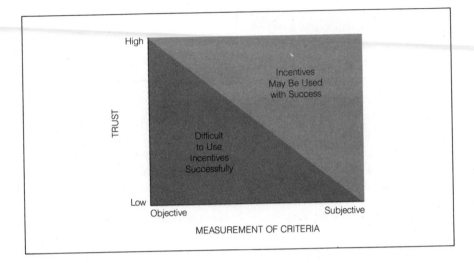

- Many employees prefer the security of automatic increases in pay based upon length of service in the organization even though they may complain about their size, instead of having incentives paid based on performance as judged by their immediate supervisors.
- The system *must* be kept current. For example, a bonus payment to a sales clerk on the dollar value of sales may require changes to compensate for inflation or changes in the product line.
- *Employee competition* for incentives may produce undesirable results. Paying sales clerks in a retail store a commission may encourage "fighting" over customers. Some sales clerks may be reluctant to work in departments that sell low-cost items if their commissions are figured on the basis of total sales. For example, clerks in a department store may concentrate on selling major appliances without giving adequate attention to the small household appliances.
- As illogical as it may seem, informal group pressure and sanctions commonly are used to restrict the amount that individuals produce. Those who seek to maximize their earnings by exceeding group–imposed limits are labeled "rate busters" or something even more graphic. Rate restrictors often feel they are being made to suffer by comparison with the higher producers.
- Any incentive system requires a *climate of trust and cooperation* between employees and manager. Figure 14–3 illustrates how the factors of trust and objectivity are related. As the amount of trust between employees and managers increases, the criteria used for determining rewards tied to performance may become less objective. In some situations, trust may be so low that even use of highly objective measures may be unwise. However, if workers have a high level of trust and good working relationships with their superiors, they may accept more subjective performance measures.
- An incentive system can sometimes lead to overemphasis on one dimension of a job. A department store manager who is rewarded only for keeping costs down may not make some necessary expenditures for store maintenance. Also, increased productivity may be purchased at the expense of quality. Or an employee in a mattress factory who receives incentive compensation based on the number of units produced may turn out many mattresses, but they may be of lower quality than they would have been without the incentive system.

■ Finally, unions may resist individual incentive systems. Many unions are built on the concepts of security, seniority, and group solidarity instead of individual productivity. Incentive systems may favor only the most highly motivated, competent workers and may actually depress the average workers' earnings. For this and other reasons, employers often use group or organizational incentive systems.

■■ ■ GROUP AND ORGANIZATIONAL INCENTIVE SYSTEMS

Group and organizational incentive systems provide rewards to all employees in a work unit, department, division, or organization. These incentives are designed to promote cooperation and a coordinated effort within the group or organization.

Group Incentives

A group incentive system may be useful in overcoming some problems associated with individual incentives, such as employee competition. But the size of the group is critical. If it becomes too large, employees may feel their individual efforts will have little or no effect on the total performance of the group and the resulting rewards.

Incentive plans for small groups are a direct result of the growing number of complex jobs requiring interdependent effort. Small-group plans may encourage teamwork in groups where interdependence is high.[16] They have been used in many service-oriented industries because of a high degree of contact with customers that may require teamwork. When there are no customers, employees are idle. With a team approach, idle employees can perform other tasks until customers arrive. Such flexibility reduces costs.

Flexibility in using employees can be a benefit of the team approach in nonservice industries as well. Consider the maintenance department in a manufacturing plant which consisted of five employees responsible for keeping the machinery running. Management used a team incentive based on "loss due to machine downtime," which meant that the team, rather than just one individual, could be sent to repair critical machinery. For instance, during one week, the group performed 205 hours of work, and the dollar loss due to machine downtime was $8,500. Using historical figures on the cost of downtime, the employer calculated the team's incentive payment for the week at 33.9 percent of their base pay.[17]

In summary, group incentives seem to work best when: (1) tasks require significant individual coordination and (2) group size is kept small (perhaps less than ten). If these conditions cannot be met, then either individual or organizational incentives may be best.[18]

PROBLEMS WITH GROUP PLANS.   Groups, like individuals, may restrict output, resist revision of standards, and seek to gain at the expense of other groups. Compensating different employee groups with separate incentives may cause them to overemphasize certain efforts to the detriment of the overall organizational good. For example, conflict often arises between the marketing and production functions of organizations because marketing's incentive compensation is based on what is sold, while production's incentive compensation is based on keeping unit production costs as low as possible. Marketing representatives may want to tailor products to customers' needs to increase their sales, but production managers want long production runs to lower costs. The overall company good, therefore, may be sidetracked. To deal with problems such as these, organizational incentive systems have been developed.

Organizational Incentives

An organizational incentive system compensates all employees in the organization based on how well the organization as a whole does during the year. The basic concept behind organizational incentive plans is that overall efficiency depends on organizational or plantwide cooperation. The purpose of these plans is to produce teamwork. For example, the conflict between marketing and production can be overcome if management uses an incentive that emphasizes organizational profit and productivity. To be effective, an incentive program should include everyone from nonexempt employees to managers and executives.[19] Common organizational incentive systems include gain sharing and profit sharing.

Gain Sharing

GAIN SHARING
sharing with employees of greater-than-expected gains in profits and/or productivity.

Gain sharing is the sharing with employees of greater-than-expected gains in profits and/or productivity. Gain sharing attempts to increase "discretionary effort," that is, the difference between the maximum amount of effort a person can exert and the minimum amount of effort necessary to keep from being fired. One study by Daniel Yankelovich concludes that discretionary effort in the American workplace is low. Forty-four percent of American job holders say they do not put much effort into their jobs over and above what is required to keep the job. Seventy-five percent say they could be significantly more effective on their jobs than they are now.[20]

It can be argued that workers currently are not paid for discretionary effort in most organizations. They are paid to meet the minimum acceptable level of effort required. However, when workers *do* exercise discretionary effort, the organization can afford to pay them more than the going rate because the extra effort produces financial gains over and above the returns of minimal effort. Figure 14–5 compares group incentives, gainsharing, and profit sharing.

IMPROSHARE.   Improshare stands for Improved Productivity Through Sharing, and it was created by Mitchell Fein, an industrial engineer. It is similar to a piecework plan except it rewards all workers in the organization. Input is measured in hours and output in physical units. A standard is calculated and a bonus is paid weekly based on the extent to which the standard is exceeded.

For example, if an organization produces an average of 1,000 units per week with 4,000 hours of labor (direct and indirect), each unit requires four hours to produce. If on a given week 4,000 hours are used to produce 1,200 units, a savings of 800 hours has occurred (4 × 1,200 = 4,800 hours usually required; 4,800 − 4,000 = 800 hours). The company split the gains 50:50 with its employees, so a bonus is given for 400 hours (.50 × 800). Four hundred hours is 10 percent of the 4,000 hours actually worked, so each employee gets a 10 percent bonus in his or her paycheck. The employees have done their part to improve productivity per worker-hour and are rewarded for it.

Figure 14–4

Gain Sharing, Group Incentives, and Profit Sharing

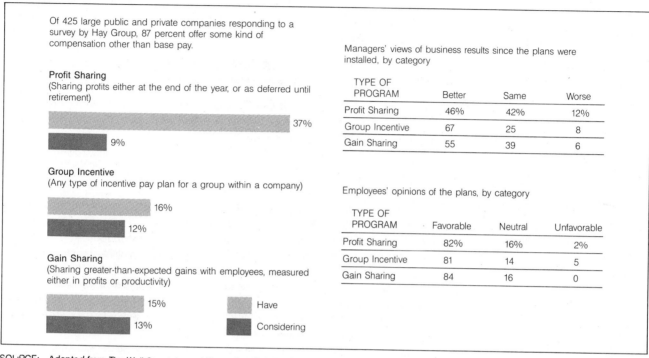

Of 425 large public and private companies responding to a survey by Hay Group, 87 percent offer some kind of compensation other than base pay.

Profit Sharing
(Sharing profits either at the end of the year, or as deferred until retirement)

37%

9%

Group Incentive
(Any type of incentive pay plan for a group within a company)

16%

12%

Gain Sharing
(Sharing greater-than-expected gains with employees, measured either in profits or productivity)

15%   ☐ Have

13%   ☐ Considering

Managers' views of business results since the plans were installed, by category

TYPE OF PROGRAM	Better	Same	Worse
Profit Sharing	46%	42%	12%
Group Incentive	67	25	8
Gain Sharing	55	39	6

Employees' opinions of the plans, by category

TYPE OF PROGRAM	Favorable	Neutral	Unfavorable
Profit Sharing	82%	16%	2%
Group Incentive	81	14	5
Gain Sharing	84	16	0

SOURCE: Adapted from *The Wall Street Journal*, December 5, 1988, B1.

SCANLON PLAN.   Since its development in 1927, the Scanlon plan has been implemented in many organizations, especially in smaller unionized industrial firms. The basic concept underlying the Scanlon plan is that efficiency depends on teamwork and plantwide cooperation. The plan has two main features: (1) a system of departmental committees and a plant-screening committee to evaluate all cost-saving suggestions, and (2) a direct incentive to all employees to improve efficiency.

The system is activated through departmental employee committees that receive and review cost-saving ideas. Suggestions beyond the level of authority of departmental committees are passed to the plant-screening committee for review. Savings that result from suggestions are passed on to all members of the organization.

Incentive rewards are paid to employees on the basis of improvements in pre-established ratios. Ratios of "labor costs to total sales value" or "total production" or "total hours to total production" most commonly are used. Savings due to differences between actual and expected ratios are placed in a bonus fund. A predetermined percentage of this fund is then split between employees and the organization.

The Scanlon plan is not a true profit-sharing plan because employees receive incentive compensation for reducing labor costs, regardless of whether the organization ultimately makes a profit. Organizations that have implemented the Scanlon plan have experienced an increase in productivity and a decrease in labor costs. Also, employee attitudes have become more favorable, and cooperation between management and workers has increased.

RUCKER PLAN. The Rucker plan, almost as old as the Scanlon plan, was developed in the 1930s by economist Allan W. Rucker. The Scanlon formula measures performance against a standard of personnel costs in ratio to the dollar value of productions, whereas the Rucker formula introduces a third variable: the dollar value of all materials, supplies, and services that the organization uses to make its product. The Rucker formula is:

$$\frac{\$Value\ of\ Personnel\ Costs}{\$\ Value\ of\ Production - \$\ Value\ of\ Materials,\ Supplies,\ Services}$$

The result is what economists call the "value added" to a product by the organization. The use of value added rather than the dollar value of production builds in an incentive to save on other inputs.

Profit Sharing

PROFIT SHARING
distributes a portion of the profits of the organization to employees.

As its name implies, a **profit-sharing** program distributes a portion of organizational profits to the employees. Typically, the percentage of the profits distributed to employees is agreed on by the end of the year, before distribution.

The major objectives of profit-sharing plans are to make employees more profit-conscious, to encourage cooperation and teamwork, and to involve employees in the success and growth of the organization. In some profit-sharing plans, employees receive their portion of the profits at the end of the year; in others, the profits are deferred, placed in a fund, and made available to employees on retirement or on their leaving the organization.

Unions used to be skeptical of profit-sharing plans, because the system only works when there are profits to be shared. Often the level of profits is influenced by factors not under the employee's control. However, in recent years, organized labor has supported profit-sharing plans in which employees' pay increases are tied to improved company performance.

When used in the lower echelons of the organization, profit sharing has three potential drawbacks. First, the definition of profit depends on the accounting system used. It can therefore be redefined depending on management's motives. Second, profits may vary a great deal from year to year—resulting in windfalls and losses beyond the employees' control. Third, the payoff may be seen as too far removed from employees' efforts to serve as a strong link between better performance and higher rewards.[21]

Employee Stock Ownership Plan (ESOP)

AN EMPLOYEE STOCK OWNERSHIP PLAN (ESOP)
is a stock bonus plan whereby employees gain ownership in the organization for which they work.

A common type of profit sharing is the **employee stock ownership plan (ESOP)**. An ESOP is designed to give employees some ownership of the organization for which they work, thereby increasing their commitment, loyalty, and effort. Employees stock ownership plans also have been used by employees to buy out firms that might otherwise have been closed. Also, organizations that promote employee ownership through grants of stock receive favorable income tax treatment.

ESTABLISHING AN ESOP. An organization establishes an ESOP by using its stock as collateral to borrow capital from a financial institution. Once the loan repayment begins through the use of company profits, a certain amount of stock is released and allocated to an Employee Stock Ownership Trust (ESOT). Employees are

P/HR: Practice *and* Research	Ethical Issues With ESOPs

Employee ownership has proved effective in motivating employees to work harder. Further, almost everyone loves the concept of employee ownership as a kind of "people's capitalism." But the downside of ESOPs is worthy of note. Employees should carefully consider the motives of management in deciding whether an ESOP is an ethical as well as safe alternative to profit sharing and employee benefits.

A company that borrows money to create an ESOP has a tax-subsidized, low-cost way to provide employee benefits. Employee stock ownership increases workers' exposure to risk in the fluctuations of the fortunes of their company. This concentration is even riskier for retirees because the value of pension fund assets also depends on how well the company does.

ESOPs too often have become a management tool to fend off unfriendly takeover attempts. Holders of employee-owned stock often align with management to turn down bids that would benefit outside stockholders but would replace management and restructure operations. Surely, ESOPs were not created to entrench inefficient management.

assigned shares of company stock, kept in the trust, based on their length of service and pay levels. On retirement, death, or separation from the organization, employees or their beneficiaries can sell the stock back to the trust or on the open market, if the stock is publicly traded.[22]

ADVANTAGES AND DISADVANTAGES.   There are several advantages to an ESOP. The major one is that the firm receives highly favorable tax treatment of the earnings that are earmarked for use in the ESOP. Second, an ESOP gives employees a "piece of the action" so that they can share in the growth and profitability of their employer. One study concluded that ESOPs have met the goal of widening employee ownership of stock in their organizations.[23]

However, the sharing also can be a disadvantage because employees have "all their eggs in one basket" (see Ethical Issues with: ESOPs). Both their base wages or salaries and their retirement benefits are dependent on the performance of the organization. If the stock has not increased in value because the organization has not prospered, the employee may become disenchanted with this form of compensation. In particular, setting up an ESOP to save an organization that would have otherwise gone bankrupt does not guarantee organizational survival. But in spite of these disadvantages, ESOPs have grown in popularity.[24]

Employee stock ownership plans are subject to changes in the tax law. Generally, the employers who have treated all employees alike are affected the least. Those who provide different levels of benefits for different groups of employees are affected the most.[25]

◼◼ ◼ EXECUTIVE COMPENSATION

Many organizations, especially large ones, administer executive compensation somewhat differently than compensation for lower-level employees. Such admin-

Sibson and Company, management compensation specialists, surveyed 345 executive compensation committees of the largest U.S. companies. Their sample included members of the board of directors and P/HR executives. The survey asked what factors were considered in assessing the performance of the company's chief executive officer (CEO). As reported in *Directors and Boards*, the results showed that both quantitative and qualitative factors were considered.[26]

Measure	Percent Citing the Measure
Qualitative	
Establishing Strategic Direction	86%
Building Management Team	84
Leadership Qualities	79
Providing for Succession	75
Implementing Strategy	64
Employee/Labor Relations	34
Technology Leadership	21
Board Relations	13
Investor Relations	10
Community/Gov't Relations	9
Quantitative	
Earnings per Share over 2 to 5 Years	66
Total Return to Shareholders	56
Return on Invested Capital	41
Return Measure Trends	40
Return on Stockholder's Equity	33
Cash Flow	32
Yearly/Quarterly EPS	13
Stock Price Performance	9
Book Value Performance	6
Dividend Payout Record	6

*Percent reflects compensation committee member ranking of measure as critical/very important.

istration often includes incentives, as well as others forms of compensation. An executive typically is someone in the top two levels of an organization, such as president or corporate vice president. Two objectives influence executive compensation: (1) tying the overall performance of the organization over a period of time to the compensation paid executives and (2) ensuring that the total compensation given key executives is competitive with the compensation packages in other firms that might employ them.[27]

Pay for performance plans for lower-level employees are more volatile than those for higher-level executives. A *Wall Street Journal* study of executive pay discovered that in the study year when corporate profits fell 4.2 percent, CEO cash compensation (salaries and bonuses) *rose* by 8 percent.[28]

Another study suggested that size of the organization had more to do with executive pay than performance.[29] However, the inconsistency across companies raises questions about executive compensation and the equity when compared to that given to middle managers.[30] Research shows that performance levels is only one of the criteria used in assigning such pay raises.[31]

At the heart of most executive compensation plans is the idea that executives should be rewarded if the organization grows in profitability and value over a period of years. Because many executives are in high tax brackets, their compensation often is provided in ways that offer significant tax savings. Therefore, their total compensation package is more significant than their base pay.

Executive Compensation Components

Executive base pay is similar in concept to the compensation given other employees. However, the other two components, incentives and benefits, accentuate the idea of executive compensation as a package.

Performance-based supplemental compensation in the form of executive bonuses and stock options attempt to tie executive compensation to the long-term growth and success of the organization. As would be expected, this supplemental compensation is prevalent in the private sector, but rarely used in the public sector and other nonprofit organizations. The final component of an executive compensation package is composed of a wide range of special benefits and amenities known as *perquisites*, often referred to as "perks." As shown in Figure 14–5, the average top executive's compensation package during the 1980s was 46 percent salary, 26 percent annual bonus, and 28 percent long-term incentives.

The trend is toward increasingly long-term incentives, possibly in response to criticisms that American executives pay too much attention to current earnings

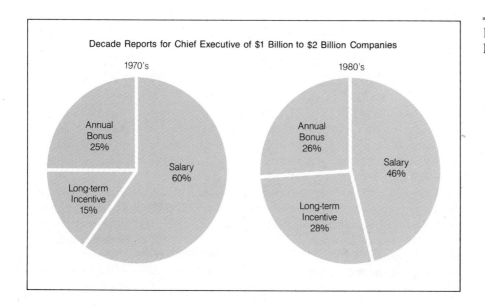

Decade Reports for Chief Executive of $1 Billion to $2 Billion Companies

1970's

Annual Bonus 25%

Salary 60%

Long-term Incentive 15%

1980's

Annual Bonus 26%

Salary 46%

Long-term Incentive 28%

Figure 14–5
Executive Compensation Plans

and not enough to longer-term issues.[32] Executive salaries, bonuses, and long-term incentives are discussed in this chapter, but first it is important to indicate how executive compensation is determined. The president of a family-owned company told a consultant, "My compensation will be whatever I want it to be that the company can afford." That approach may be widespread in private companies, but in publicly-owned firms (those that trade their stock on the open market) executive compensation oversight and review responsibilities commonly are handled by a compensation committee.

COMPENSATION COMMITTEE usually is a subgroup of the board of directors composed of outside directors.

COMPENSATION COMMITTEE.   A **compensation committee** usually is a subgroup of the board of directors composed of directors who are not officers of the firm. Compensation committees generally make recommendations to the board of directors on overall pay policies, salaries for top officers, supplemental compensation such as stock options and bonuses, and additional perquisites for executives. A survey of 122 companies revealed that about 40 percent of the compensation committees also become involved in top management succession planning. More than two-thirds of America's public companies have compensation committees.[33]

Executive Pay

Salaries of executives vary by type of job, size of organization, region, and industry. Top executives in the New York City area and in California have higher average cash compensation than executives in the southeastern and southwestern United States. On average, salaries make up about half of top executives' total compensation. One study of executive cash compensation (which includes salary and cash bonuses) revealed that what an executive earns depends more on the company's ability to pay and on the complexity of the job held than on the executive's experience and education.[34]

Bonuses, long-term performance awards, and stock options have different time frames, focuses, and measures, as Figure 14–6 shows. The mix chosen should be tailored to the particular need of an organization.

Performance-Based Supplemental Compensation

Executive compensation usually is tied to performance of the organization as a whole or to the performance of a unit for which an executive has responsibility. The most common supplemental methods are bonuses and stock options.

EXECUTIVE BONUS PLANS.   Because executive performance may be difficult to determine, bonus compensation must reflect some kind of performance measure if it is to be meaningful. As an example, a retail chain with over 250 stores ties annual bonuses for managers to store profitability. The bonuses have amounted to as much as 35 percent of a store manager's base salary.

Bonuses for executives can be determined in several ways. A discretionary system whereby bonuses are awarded based on the judgments of the chief executive officer and the board of directors is a simple way. However, the absence of formal, measurable targets is a major drawback of this approach. Also, bonuses can be tied to specific measures, such as to return on investment, earnings per share, or net profits before taxes. More complex systems create bonus pools and thresholds above which bonuses are computed. Whatever method is used, it is important to describe

	ANNUAL BONUS	LONG-TERM PERFORMANCE AWARDS	STOCK OPTIONS
TIME FRAME	1 Year	3 to 5 Years	Up to 10 Years
FOCUS	Securing and Sustaining Competitive Advantage	Economic Value	Total Return to Shareholders
MEASURES	■ Performance Against Strategic Goals ■ Financial	■ Return ■ Growth	■ Stock Prices ■ Dividends

Figure 14–6
Components of an Executive Compensation Plan

SOURCE: *Wall Street Journal,* April 10, 1987, p. 29. Used with permission.

it so that executives trying to earn bonuses understand the plan; otherwise the incentive effect will be diminished.

STOCK OPTIONS.   Another way to furnish incentive compensation to executives is through stock options. A **stock option** gives an employee the right to buy stock in a company, usually at an advantageous price. Different types of stock options have been used depending on the tax laws in effect.[35]

Stock options increased in use as a component of executive compensation during the 1980s. According to one report, 89 percent of the 500 largest industrial companies offered stock options, compared with only 52 percent in the 1970s.[36] Employers may use a variety of very specialized and technical approaches to stock options,[37] which are beyond the scope of this discussion.

"GOLDEN AND SILVER PARACHUTES."   One special type of benefit available to some executives is known as a "golden parachute." A golden parachute provides protection and security to executives who may be affected if their firms are acquired by another firm. Typically, employment contracts are written to give special compensation to executives if they are negatively affected in an acquisition or merger. For example, the chief executive officer of Federal-Mortgage Corporation is guaranteed five years of salary if termination occurs for any reason besides retirement, death, disability, or resignation within 12 months after demotion. Essex Chemical Corporation offers golden parachute protection for the top five officers and Phillips Petroleum Company provides protection for the top six officers.

Parachutes are now the norm. One survey revealed that 54 percent of the large organizations queried have them. The chairman of Revlon owns the biggest parachute; he gets $35 million if the company is taken over.

A related phenomenon has been labeled the "silver parachute." Herman Miller, a Zeeland, Michigan, manufacturer of office furniture, has designed a generous severance pay and benefits plan that goes into effect if a hostile takeover threatens

A STOCK OPTION
gives an employee the right to buy stock in a company, usually at a fixed price for a period of time.

any of the 3,500 employee's jobs. All employees with at least two years' service would be protected. They would get at least one full year's salary if they are fired within two years for other than just cause.

Miller says the idea is to protect the employees. Of course, the plan should also serve to deter takeover artists. Whether golden or silver, the parachute phenomenon is a clear response to the takeover strategy that many organizations have followed.[37]

CRITICISM OF PERFORMANCE-BASED SUPPLEMENTS.   The major criticism of executive compensation is the disparity between total compensation received and corporate performance. Although supplements such as bonuses and stock options are supposed to be tied to the performance of the organization, several studies have found that this is not the case.[39]

Another criticism is that executive compensation does not offer long-term rewards. Instead, performance within a given year leads to large rewards even though corporate performance over time may be mediocre. This difference is especially apparent if the yearly measures are carefully chosen. Executives can even manipulate earnings per share by selling assets, liquidating inventories, or reducing re-

Figure 14–7
Executive Perks

	PERCENTAGE OF COMPANIES OFFERING PERK	PERCENTAGE OF EMPLOYEES ELIGIBLE*
Airline VIP club membership	34	1.2
Chauffeur service	40	0.1
Communications equipment (such as car phone)	22	0.2
Company car	68	1.1
Company plane	63	0.3
Company WATS line (home use)	11	0.3
Country club membership	55	0.5
Estate planning	52	0.6
Executive dining room	30	1.3
Financial counseling	64	0.6
Financial seminars	11	2.8
First-class air travel	62	0.7
Health club membership	19	0.7
Home security system	25	0.2
Income-tax preparation	63	0.7
Legal counseling	6	0.6
Loans (low interest or interest-free)	9	3.2
Luncheon club membership	55	0.8
Personal liability insurance	50	1.0
Physical exam	91	6.5
Reserved parking	32	1.0
Spouse travel	47	1.0

*Percentage of salaried employees at surveyed companies offering perk.

SOURCE: Adapted from Hewitt Associates, 1990

search and development expenditures. All these actions may make organizational performance look better, thus giving executives bigger bonuses, but they may impair the long-term growth of the organization.[39] Reaction to the large bonuses received by General Motors and Ford executives illustrates some of the problems with large supplements. For these reasons, stock options provide a better tie to performance over time than do bonuses.

Executive Benefits and Perquisites

In addition to the regular benefits received by other employees, executives often have other special benefits and perquisites available to them. **Perquisites** ("perks") are special executive benefits that are usually noncash items. Figure 14–7 on the previous page lists some that are available.

Perks and special executive benefits are useful in tying executives to organizations and in demonstrating their importance to the company. It is the "status enhancement" value of perks that is important to many executives. Visible symbols of status allow executives to be seen as "very important people (VIPs)" inside and outside their companies. In addition, perks can offer substantial tax savings because many perks may not be taxed as income.

PERQUISITES
("perks") are special benefits for executives that are usually noncash items.

SUMMARY

- An incentive is additional compensation related to performance
- An effective incentive program should tie incentives to performance, recognize individual differences, recognize organizational factors, and be monitored continually.
- There are three types of incentive systems: individual, group, and organizationwide.
- Individual incentives include piece-rate systems, commissions, special incentive programs, and bonuses.
- To overcome some problems associated with individual incentives, group and organizational incentive systems are used.
- One organizational incentive system is the Scanlon plan. The Scanlon plan provides rewards to employees based on cost savings. It emphasizes cooperation and participation.
- Profit-sharing plans set aside a portion of the profits earned by organizations for distribution to employees.
- An employee stock ownership plan (ESOP) is a stock bonus in which employees gain ownership in the firm for which they work.
- Executive compensation must be viewed as a total package composed of pay, performance-based supplemental compensation, and special benefits or perquisites.
- A compensation committee, which is a subgroup of the board of directors, has authority to review executive compensation plans.
- Performance-based supplemental compensation plans often represent a significant portion of an executive's compensation package. Executive bonus plans and stock options are the two most common plans. An incentive option is a special type of stock option that has wide usage.
- Many different special benefits and perks, all of which provide additional noncash compensation, are available to executives.

REVIEW AND DISCUSSION QUESTIONS

1. Identify what an incentive is and list some key guidelines that should be followed when an incentive system is established.
2. Give several examples of individual incentives that you have received or that have been used in an organization in which you were employed. What problems did you observe with them?
3. Why do you think that increased emphasis on productivity in the United States has led to greater interest in Scanlon plans and ESOPs?
4. Why are performance-based supplements and special benefits and perks important in an executive compensation package?

CASE   **Incentive Management at Lincoln Electric**

A company 90 years old, still using an incentive system it started in 1907, may serve as an example of the future. Cleveland-based Lincoln Electric Company has been using incentive compensation effectively, with its employees, most of whom are production workers manufacturing the firm's major products, arc welding equipment and induction motors. The incentive plan remains in effect today.

The management practices used with the 2,500 employees at Lincoln are unique. Most workers are paid on a piece-rate basis, which means that there is no base pay. If a worker is sick, he or she receives no pay, and if a defective machine is produced, the worker must fix it on his or her own time. Turnover averages a low 6 percent a year. There have been no layoffs since 1951, and employees with at least two years' service are guaranteed at least 30 hours per week of work. Employees have averaged as much as $45,000 yearly, which includes a year-end bonus that often doubles employees' base pay. The bonuses are given for teamwork and reliability, and employees who make productivity-improving suggestions receive bonus points. Overtime is mandatory when orders back up. Further, employees own over 70 percent of the company's stock, which they must sell back at book value when they leave.

At the heart of the management system at Lincoln is employee self-motivation. There is no seniority system at Lincoln, and all employees compete on merit for the few jobs that are not paid by piecework. Richard Sabo, a Lincoln electric employee, recalls a brief period where he was paid nothing for his work. He was assigned to produce a part but after working for two days, he discovered that all his output was defective. At any other company, Sabo would have been paid for his time spent in making the defective parts. But at Lincoln Electric he is paid only for his usable output; if he produces nothing usable, he is paid nothing. Sabo, who is now Lincoln Electric's manager of educational services, says that even when it happened he felt the treatment was fair. After all, if the company had not made anything from his two days, why should they pay for wasted work?

Some people have not been able to handle the productivity pressure. One disgusted ex-employee referred to Lincoln as a "sweatshop," and another said that it was both physically and mentally tough on workers. The environment is intensely competitive also. Nevertheless, Lincoln Electric has continued to grow and prosper using its "incentive management system."[41]

QUESTIONS

1. Why does this system work for Lincoln Electric?
2. Would it work for a state government agency? Why?
3. What elements of an effective incentive plan can you infer from this description of Lincoln Electric's operation?

NOTES

1. Adapted from N. Perry, "Here Come Richer, Riskier Pay Plans," *Fortune*, December 19, 1988, 51–58.

2. C. Cumming and D. Neceda, "Rewards or Incentives: Is There a Difference?" *Perspectives* 1, no. 2, 4.

3. E. Pollock, "Troubled Firms Offer Lures to Keep Staff," *Wall Street Journal*, March 20, 1990, B1.

4. Adapted from "Managing People," *INC*, October 1986, 127; "Police Score Points," *Wall Street Journal*, December 30, 1986, 1; and "Incentive Plans," *Wall Street Journal*, January 27, 1987, 1.

5. G. S. Crystal and S. J. Silverman, "Not-for-Profit Organizations Need Incentive Compensation," *Personnel*, April 1986, 7–12,; D. Lehman, "Improving Employee Productivity through Incentives," *Journal of Systems Management*, March 1986, 14–20.

6. W. Dierks and K. A. McNally, "Incentives You Can Bank On," *Personnel Administrator*, March 1987, 61–62.

7. R. Ricklefs, "Wither the Payoff on Sales Commissions?" *Wall Street Journal*, March 6, 1990, B1.

8. A. Dunkin, "Now Salespeople Really Must Sell for their Supper," *Business Week*, July 31, 1988, 50–52.

9. Adapted from R. Manhood, "National Linen Drives Home a Message," *Sales and Marketing Management*, April 2, 1984, 107–110.

10. "Nontraditional Rewards Catch On," *Industry Week*, February 1, 1988, 5.

11. "Bonuses for the Masses," *Forbes*, July 28, 1986, 10.

12. "Motivation," *INC*, December 1986, 120.

13. B. G. Posner, "If at First You Don't Succeed," *INC*, May 1989, 132–134.

14. J. Leib, "Employee Bonuses Popular Option in the 80s," *Denver Post*, December 24, 1989, 61.

15. Some of the problems noted below were identified in T. Rollins, "Pay for Performance: Is It Worth the Trouble?" *Personnel Administrator*, May 1988, 43–46.

16. J. R. Laatsch, "Pay for Performance in Action: A Case Study," *Personnel*, June 1989, 11.

17. S. Globerson, *Performance Criteria and Incentive Systems* (Amsterdam: Elsevier, 1985), 168–170.

18. T. Rollins, "Productivity-based Group Incentive Plans: Powerful, but Use with Caution," *Compensation and Benefits Review*, May/June 1989, 39–50.

19. G. Florkowski, "Analyzing Group Incentive Plans," *HRM Magazine*, January 1990, 36–38.

20. E. Ost, "Gainsharing's Potential," *Personnel Administrator*, July 1989, 92–96.

21. G. Florkowski, "The Organizational Impact of Profit Sharing," *Academy of Management Review* 12 (1987): 622–636.

22. R. Maturi, "ESOPs for the Millions," *Industry Week*, October 2, 1989, 87.

23. C. Farrell, "Staffing Nest Eggs with ESOPs," *Business Week*, April 24, 1989, 124.

24. C. Farrell, "Suddenly Blue Chips Are Red-Hot for ESOPs," *Business Week*, March 20, 1989, 144.

25. D. Kirkpatrick, "How the Workers Run Avis Better," *Fortune*, December 5, 1988, 103–114.

26. Adapted from "What Directors Say . . .," *Directors and Boards*, Summer 1986, 38.

27. G. Crystal, "Executive Compensation," *Personnel*, January 1988, 33.

28. A Bennett, "Pay for Performance," *Wall Street Journal*, April 18, 1990, R7.

29. J. Gilder, "Executive Pay: In Search of the Missing Link," *Human-Resource Executive*, May 1989, 28.

30. M. Verespej, "Merit Raises: A Joke," *Industry Week*, February 19, 1990, 73; J. Nelson-Horchler, "The $550 Million Question," *Industry Week*, June 19, 1989, 85; M. Mazer, "Executive Compensation: Are the Huge Salaries Devensible?" *Journal of Staffing and Recruitment*, Summer 1989, 61.

31. P. Sherer, et al., "Managerial Salary-Raise Decisions: A Policy Capturing Approach," *Personnel Psychology* 40 (1987): 27.

32. G. S. Crystal and M. R. Hurwich, "The Case for Divisional Long-Term Incentives," *California Management Review*, Fall 1986, 60.

33. J. W. Fischer, Jr., "Crafting Policy for Performance and Rewards," *Directors and Boards*, Winter 1986, 26.

34. N. C. Agarwal, "Determinants of Executive Compensation," *Industrial Relations* 20 (1981): 36–45.

35. S. Woolley, "Smart Money," *Business Week*, August 29, 1988, 86.

36. J. Goodson et al., "Stock Options," *Personnel Administrator*, August 1988, 71.

37. G. Paulin, "The Use and Misuse of Restructured Stock," *Compensation and Benefits Review*, May/June 1989, 51–59.

38. "New Regulations for Golden Parachutes," *Perspectives* n.d. *1*, and "Silver Parachute Protects Work Force," *Resource*, January 1987, 3.

39. L. Gomez-Mejia, "Managerial Control Performance, and Exec Compensation," *Academy of Management Journal* 30 (1987): 51–70, and T. J. Bergmann, *et al.*, "Rewards Tied to Long-Term Success," *HR Magazine*, May 1990, 67–72.

40. J. Kerr and R. Bettis, "Boards of Directors, Top Management Compensation and Shareholder Returns," *Academy of Management Journal* 30, (1987): 645–664.

41. Adapted from Gene Epstein, "Inspire Your Team," *Success*, October 1989, 12; Bruce G. Posner, "Right from the Start," *INC.*, August 1988, 95–96; William Baldwin, "This Is The Answer," *Forbes*, July 5, 1982, 50–52; and Mary Ann Mrowea, "Ohio Firm Relies on Incentive Pay System to Motivate Workers and Maintain Profits," *Wall Street Journal*, August 12, 1983, 19.

Employee Benefits

After you have read this chapter, you should be able to:

1. Define a benefit and discuss three benefit challenges for the 1990s
2. Identify some strategic benefits issues and approximate average benefit costs
3. Explain two security benefits
4. List and define at least eight pension-related terms
5. Explain why health-care cost management has become important and list some methods of achieving it
6. Identify several types of financial and other benefits
7. Concisely describe several benefits related to time-off
8. Discuss benefits communication and flexible benefits as benefits administration considerations

P/HR: Today *and* Tomorrow — Flexible Benefits at United Hospitals

All employers, including health-care providers, are concerned about the escalating costs of employee benefits, especially health-care costs. For hospitals, the need to have benefits tailored to varied work forces of part-timers, full-timers, medical/nursing professionals, and support staff, with all their individual differences, presents special problems. To address these problems, United Hospitals, Inc. (UHI) decided to implement a flexible benefit program, called Flex, for its 3,500 individual employees in its four-hospital system.

A flexible benefit program permits employees to decide which benefits they will receive and how much of them they wish, within some broad limitations placed by the employer on costs and types of benefits offered. To implement Flex at UHI, a task force from the finance, P/HR, and management information systems departments received plans and proposals from consultants, insurance providers, and computer software vendors. The task force decided to develop the Flex plan themselves instead of having it done for them by outsiders.

The implementation of Flex included developing a suitable design, an administrative system that interfaced with existing systems, and a communications program that enabled employees to get the most value from the program. The task force worked for almost a year to produce a program that would meet corporate goals and the budget and time constraints set by top management. The key to success seemed to lie in the great amount of advanced planning done in all areas.

A significant effort was made to communicate with employees about why changes were necessary. The purpose was to help employees accustomed to receiving the traditional benefits programs offered by insurance carriers adjust to the new reality. Based on intensive feedback from a group of employees selected from throughout UHI, the task force members proceeded to fashion a benefits program.

As a result of all of the input, UHI ended up using a core-plus-options approach. Employees selected a core set of benefits, including ones such as single health and life insurance equal to their annual salaries. Then each full-time employee was allocated a monthly base amount of dollars for use in "purchasing" benefits. Flex contained three base allowance programs. Each base allowance had different parameters to it which allowed employees to purchase their current benefit package, trade in some benefits for others, trade vacation time for additional benefit coverage, lower employee contributions, or others.

UHI managers engaged in extensive communication efforts. All employees received a personalized enrollment form along with a workbook containing instructions and a sample form. In addition, employee meetings were held in which a slide-and-tape presentation was followed by a question-and-answer session. The audiovisual program urged employees to think through their decisions, and individual consultations were scheduled at employees' requests.

The result of Flex in just one year indicated that its implementation achieved the primary goal of controlling the escalation in benefit costs. Benefit costs in the first year increased only 3 percent, resulting in a savings of over $2.5 million when compared with projections under the old benefits program. Also, the Flex plan contributed to the defeat of a unionization effort among 450 employees at one UHI hospital, so it appears that UHI did "Flex for success."[1]

"We used to call them 'fringe benefits,' but we quit using the word 'fringe' when we saw the magnitude of that figure."

James Morris

Efforts such as those by United Hospitals Inc. to limit benefits costs illustrate the practices used to manage employee benefit programs. A **benefit** is additional compensation given to employees as a reward for organizational membership. The benefits given to employees by an employer represent *indirect compensation*, that is, tangible rewards in a form other than money.

BENEFIT
is additional compensation given to employees as a reward for organizational membership.

■■ ■ BENEFITS CHALLENGES OF THE 1990s

During the 1990s, employers will have to anticipate and respond to several challenges in the area of employee benefits. In addition to continuing to administer the traditional benefits programs common in many organizations, employers face concerns:

- Mandated benefits
- Health-care cost containment
- Family-related issues

Mandated Benefits

One developing trend is **mandated benefits,** which means that employers are required by law to provide certain benefits previously offered voluntarily. The concept of mandated employee benefits is not new. Examples of benefits that have been required at federal and state levels include Social Security, workers' compensation, and unemployment insurance.

MANDATED BENEFITS
means that employers are required by law to provide certain benefits previously offered voluntarily.

Before 1984, employers were required to give few benefits, except for those listed above. However, beginning with the Consolidated Omnibus Budget Resolution Act (COBRA) of 1984, federal regulations requiring employers to provide certain benefits began to proliferate. Numerous bills requiring employers to offer benefits in a variety of areas continue to be introduced in the U.S. Congress. Some areas include:

- Universal health-care benefits provided to all workers
- Child-care assistance
- Parental/medical leave for either parent at birth or on adoption
- Pension plan coverage for more workers
- Core benefits for part-time employees working at least 500 hours per year

Several states have leapfrogged the federal government by requiring employers in those states to provide some of the benefits just listed. For example, Massachusetts requires all but the smallest employers to provide health-care benefits or pay into a state fund. Other states have mandated child-care assistance or parental leave for new parents.

There are several reasons why employers face increasing pressure to provide benefits. A major one is that federal and state governments want to shift many of the social costs for health care and other expenditures to employers. This shift would relieve some of the budgetary pressures facing legislators to raise taxes and cut governmental spending.

Figure 15–1
Increases in Employers' Average Health-Care Costs

	AVERAGE PREMIUM	PERCENTAGE OF PAYROLL
1980	$710	4.9
1981	824	5.3
1982	1,009	6.0
1983	1,211	6.9
1984	1,453	7.9
1985	1,671	8.7
1986	1,880	9.4
1987	2,159	10.4
1988	2,555	11.7
1989	3,117	13.6

SOURCE: *Industry Week*, December 4, 1989, 89.

Also, demographic changes in the United States mean that more workers will need child care and older citizens will require more health care. By mandating benefit coverage, employers will be forced to help fund more of these benefit costs.

Employer reactions to efforts to mandate benefits have been swift and vehement. Employers emphasize that small businesses are more heavily burdened because they have a smaller staff to handle the increased work of benefit administration. Fears about the costs of providing the mandated benefits also trigger the reaction. One study estimated that labor costs for businesses would increase at least $40 billion per year if all of the mandated benefits being proposed were enacted.[2] As the U.S. work force ages and becomes more diverse, other benefit issues will arise in which mandatory benefit coverage may be attempted or may occur.[3] Undoubtedly, employers also will continue to resist and lobby against efforts to mandate more benefits.

Health-Care Costs

Cost for health care in the United States have risen dramatically in the past three decades. In 1960, about $26 billion was spent on health care, representing 5.4 percent of the nation's gross national product (GNP).[4] By the year 2000, health-care costs are expected to triple to $1.5 trillion.[5]

Employers have felt the increase in costs also. As shown in Figure 15–1, the average premiums and percentage of payroll expended by employers both rose during the 1980s. Some examples illustrate the impact on employers:[6]

- Over a three-year period, NYNEX saw health-care costs increase at least 20 percent per year.
- Allied-Signal Corporation experienced a 39 percent rise in health-care benefit costs in one year.
- In a recent year, a St. Louis employer with 45 workers had health benefit costs of $67,000, up 7 percent over the previous year, even though benefits were cut.
- Ben and Jerry's Homemade, Inc., a Vermont-based ice-cream company, received a health insurance premium notice from an insurer raising rates 75 percent in one year, resulting in the firm changing its insurance carrier and raising employee deductibles.
- The costs for health benefits add over $700 to the cost of every car manufactured by Chrysler, Ford, and General Motors.

Employers have reacted in a variety of ways. Some with a unionized work force have used collective bargaining sessions to demand that workers pay more of the health-benefit costs. As a result, several companies experienced strikes by workers who refused to give up health benefits totally paid by their employers. Other employers have required their nonunion employees to pay higher deductibles, obtain second-opinions before elective surgery, use designated preferred providers, pay higher rates, or other changes.

Some employers even are talking about a solution that previously was rejected as too radical: national health insurance managed by the federal government.[7] Companies and unions endorsing such an approach have included Bethlehem Steel, the United Steelworkers union, AT&T, the Communications Workers of America, and Chrysler Corporation.[8] More on health-care cost management approaches appears later in this chapter.

Family-Related Issues

A third benefits area that has received increasing attention as a result of work force and social changes of the 1980s is family-related issues. The three most prominent concerns are parental/medical leave, child care, and elder care.

PARENTAL LEAVE.   In the past ten years, many employer policies regarding parental leave have become more flexible. As a result of the Pregnancy Discrimination Act of 1978, *maternity leave* must be treated in the same manner as any other medical condition or disability that would require a leave. Therefore, pregnant women may work as long as their physicians allow, in most situations, just as an employee with a heart condition would be allowed to do. Except in five states, employers are not required to provide parental leave to employees, either male or female.

At the federal level, bills have been introduced to require all employers to provide family leave, parental leave (mother or father), adoption leave, and leave to care for an ill parent. The Family and Medical Leave bill, which was first introduced in 1986 but had not passed into law at the time that this text was written, would require employers to give up to eighteen weeks of unpaid parental leave and up to twenty-six weeks of unpaid medical leave, while continuing the employee's health benefits. Employers also would have to provide a job with equivalent pay, benefits, and seniority. These requirements would apply to all employers with 50 or more employees. Needless to say, employers vehemently have opposed these laws because of the costs and restrictions. Parental leave laws have been passed in several states, including Minnesota, Tennessee, Oregon, Connecticut, and Rhode Island.[9] Employers will continue to receive pressure to provide child-care-related leaves.

CHILD CARE.   More than seven out of ten women between the ages of twenty-five and fifty-four are now in the labor force. With more women working instead of staying home to care for children, there are more dual-career households. According to the U.S. Census Bureau estimates, about 54 percent of all married mothers having children under the age of six are working, and that figure is estimated to jump to 65 percent by 1995. For single mothers, child care is also a pressing need.[10] Yet there are not enough child-care facilities, and when they are available, many workers cannot afford them.[11] One survey of 762 employees in a Virginia company found that over half of all workers experienced difficulty in obtaining quality child care, felt infant-care expenses were too high, and saw the locations and hours for child-caregivers as inconvenient.[12]

Employers are addressing the child-care issue in several ways. About 700 organizations, most of which are hospitals, have established on-site day-care facilities.[13] Costs and concerns about liability and attracting sufficient employee use are major reasons that few on-site facilities have been established. Other options offered by employers include:[14]

- Providing referral services to aid parents in locating child-care providers
- Establishing discounts at day-care centers, that may be subsidized by the employer
- Arranging with local hospitals to offer sick-child programs that are partially paid for by employers
- Developing after-school programs for older school-age children, often in conjunction with local public and private school systems

As mentioned earlier, the federal government has not mandated that employers provide child-care assistance. But legislation has been proposed to allow tax breaks to employees for child-care expenses, provide federal funds to establish child-care facilities near worksites, give direct aid to low-income families for child care, and other provisions. This legislation, known as the Act for Better Child-Care services, was introduced in 1989.

ELDER CARE.   Another family-related issue of growing importance is caring for elderly relatives. Different organizations have surveyed their employees and found that as many as 30 percent of their employees have had to miss work to care for an aging relative. The responsibilities associated with caring for elderly family members has resulted in reduced work performance, increased absenteeism, and more personal stress for the affected employees. The results of a survey of personnel executives on elder care showed that about two-thirds believed that elder care is an issue that should be addressed by their companies; however, only three of the executives said that they had established elder-care benefits.[15] Many more employers will have to respond to this issue in the 1990s as the U.S. population continues to age.

■■ ■ BENEFITS OVERVIEW

Benefits are an important component of effective P/HR management. The management of employee benefits is very complex, requiring significant time and effort spent. The operational and technical facets often take precedence over strategic considerations in daily management, but strategy considerations must be examined also. Some of the strategic issues to be addressed concerning employee benefits are:[16]

- How much total compensation, including benefits, should be provided?
- What part should benefits be of the total compensation of individuals?
- What are the purposes for offering each type of benefit?
- What expense levels are acceptable for each benefit offered?
- Which employees should be given or offered which benefits?

By answering these questions, P/HR managers and top executives obtain both strategic and operational perspectives on employee benefits programs.

Benefit Costs

Benefits represent significant expenditures from an employer's point of view. The U.S. Chamber of Commerce surveys a large number of industries on a regular basis to determine the extent of benefit payments. In a recent survey, benefits represented an average of 37 percent of organizational total payroll. As a result, the average employee received $10,750 worth of benefits per year. However, the amount of benefits varied significantly in different fields. For example, an employee in the department store industry averaged 34.5 percent of salary in benefits, while an employee in the petroleum industry averaged 46.1 percent of salary in benefits.[17]

Figure 15–2 shows some details from the Chamber of Commerce survey. The greatest cost increases have been those associated with health care. Health-related benefits were up 16 percent in one year, with the average employee receiving $2,538 per year. The increase in 1988 was the largest increase in the ten-year history of the U.S. Chamber of Commerce survey.

Benefits and Taxation

Benefit expenditures have grown because employees get the *value* of the money spent without actually receiving money. That is why benefits generally are not taxed as income to employees, in spite of repeated attempts by the U.S. Internal Revenue Service to do so. For this reason, benefits represent a somewhat more valuable reward to employees than an equivalent cash payment. For example, assume that employee Henry Schmidt is in a 25 percent tax bracket. If Henry earned $400, he would have to pay $100 in taxes. Then if he had to pay $300 for tuition for some graduate classes at a local university, he would have to earn $400 in order to have the $300 for tuition. But if the employer provides a tuition plan that meets IRS regulations and pays the $300, Henry does not claim that amount as income, and therefore doesn't have to pay taxes on it. So benefits are a desirable form of compensation to employees, and more benefits are more desirable. That is a primary reason why the growth in employer benefits costs has been greater than the growth in base pay costs.

Types of Benefits

Employees are given many different benefits, as shown in Figure 15–3. They are grouped into several types, each of which is discussed in this chapter:

- Security benefits
- Retirement benefits
- Health-care benefits
- Financial and other insurance benefits
- Social, recreational, and other benefits
- Time-off benefits

▪▪ SECURITY BENEFITS

Several benefits offer protection and/or security to employees. Some are required by federal and state laws. Others are given voluntarily by management or are made

Figure 15–2
Average Individual Employee
Benefit Costs

TYPE OF BENEFIT	TOTAL, ALL COMPANIES
Total employee benefits as percent of payroll	37.0
1. Legally required payments (employers' share only)	8.9
a. Old-Age, Survivors, Disability, and Health Insurance (employer FICA taxes) and Railroad Retirement Tax	6.9
b. Unemployment compensation	0.8
c. Workers' compensation (including estimated cost of self-insured)	1.1
d. State sickness benefits insurance	....
2. Retirement and saving (employers' share only)	5.0
a. Defined benefit pension plan contributions	2.0
b. Defined contribution play payments	0.9
c. Profit sharing	0.7
d. Stock bonus and employee stock ownership plans (ESOP)	0.2
e. Pension plan premiums (net) under insurance and annuity contracts (insured and trusted)	0.5
f. Administrative and other costs	0.7
3. Life insurance and death benefits (employers' share only)	0.6
4. Medical and medically-related benefit payments (employers' share only)	8.7
a. Hospital, surgical, medical, and major medical insurance premiums (net)	6.5
b. Retiree (payments for retired employees) hospital, surgical, medical, and major medical insurance premiums (net)	0.8
c. Short-term disability, sickness or accident insurance (company plan or insured plan)	0.4
d. Long-term disability or wage continuation (insured, self-administered, or trust)	0.2
e. Dental insurance premiums	0.6
f. Other (vision care, physical and mental fitness, benefits for former employees)	0.3
5. Paid rest periods, coffee breaks, lunch periods, wash-up time, travel time, clothes-change time, get ready time, etc.	2.3
6. Payments for time not worked	10.6
a. Payments for or in lieu of vacations	5.5
b. Payment for or in lieu of holidays	3.3
c. Sick leave pay	1.3
d. Parental leave (maternity and paternity leave payments)	....
e. Other	0.4
7. Miscellaneous benefit payments	0.9
a. Discounts on goods and services purchased from company by employees	0.2
b. Employee meals furnished by company	0.1
c. Employee education expenditures	0.2
d. Child care	....
e. Other	0.5
Total employee benefits as cents per hour	519.8
Total employee benefits as dollars per year per employee	$10,750

. . . Less than 0.05%

SOURCE: Adapted from data contained in *Employee Benefits, 1989 Edition* (Washington D.C.: Chamber of Commerce of the United States, 1989).

Figure 15–3

Benefits Classified by Type

SECURITY	RETIREMENT	HEALTH-CARE	INSURANCE	FINANCIAL	SOCIAL & RECREATIONAL	TIME-OFF
Workers' compensation	Social Security (retirement)	Medical	Survivor benefits	Credit union	Tennis courts	Lunch/rest breaks
Unemployment compensation	Pension fund	Dental	Life insurance	Cash profit sharing	Bowling league	Vacation time
Social Security	Early retirement	HMO Fees	Accidental dismemberment insurance	Company-provided car or housing	Company newsletter	Company-subsidized travel
Old age, survivors, & disability insurance	Pre-retirement counseling	Vision care	Disability insurance	Purchase discounts	Professional memberships	Holidays
State disability insurance	Retirement gratuity	Prescription drugs	Travel accident insurance	Stock plans	Counseling	Personal days
Medicare hospital benefits	Retirement annuity		Legal prepaid	Child care	Company-sponsored events	Sick pay
Severance pay	Disability retirement benefits		Auto insurance	Financial counseling	Cafeteria	Military reserve time-off
Supplemental unemployment insurance				Moving expenses	Service award jewelry	Election day
Leave of absence				Educational assistance		Social-service sabbatical
				Relocation mortgage differential		

available through provisions in labor–management contracts. *Workers' compensation, unemployment compensation,* and *Social Security* are the most important of the security benefits.

Workers' Compensation

Workers' compensation provides benefits to a person injured on the job. Starting with the Federal Employees' Compensation Act of 1908 and laws enacted by California, New Jersey, Washington, and Wisconsin in 1911, workers' compensation laws to aid injured employees have spread to all the remaining states. Federal employees are covered under the Federal Employees' Liability Act administered by the Department of labor.

Workers' compensation requires employers to give cash benefits, medical care, and rehabilitation services to employees for injuries or illnesses occurring within the scope of employment. Employees are entitled to quick and certain payment from the workers' compensation system without proving that the employer is at fault. In exchange, employees give up the right of tort actions and awards. The employer enjoys limited liability for occupational illnesses and injury.

WORKERS' COMPENSATION provides benefits to a person injured on the job.

Employers provide workers' compensation coverage by purchasing insurance from a private carrier or state insurance fund or by providing self-insurance. Only six states have state-required workers' compensation systems.[18] Employers that self-insure are required to post a bond or deposit securities with the state industrial commission. State laws usually require that employers have a specific number of employees before they are permitted to use self-insurance. Group self-insurance is permitted in some states.

CRITICISM OF WORKERS' COMPENSATION LAWS.   Because workers' compensation costs are borne by employers, the types of injuries covered include more than on-the-job physical injuries. Coverage has been expanded in many areas to include emotional impairment that may have resulted from a physical injury, job-related strain, stress, anxiety, or pressure.

Costs of these programs have increased dramatically, and numerous examples of abuse have been found. For example, in a recent year, workers' compensation premiums paid by employers increased 12.1 percent, primarily because of increased litigation and higher medical costs.[19] Another even more dramatic example is the situation faced by railroads covered by the Federal Employees' Liability Act. The fifteen member railroads in 1989 paid about $1 million in worker compensation injuries, which represented over 40 percent of the railroads' annual profits.[20]

Employers with high workers' compensation costs attempt to reduce their impact in several ways.[21] One obvious way is to improve employee safety through extensive safety training and accident investigation procedures. Another is to try to have injured workers return to work earlier, possibly on lighter-duty jobs. However, employers must be cautious about requiring workers to return to work too early or they may face additional litigation.[22]

Unemployment Compensation

Another benefit required by law is unemployment compensation, which was established as part of the Social Security Act of 1935. Each state operates its own unemployment compensation system, and provisions differ significantly from state to state.[23]

Employers finance this benefit by paying a tax on the first $7,000 (or more, in 37 states) annual earnings of each employee. The tax is paid to state and federal unemployment compensation funds. The payment percentages for employers are based upon "experience rates," which reflect the number of claims filed by workers who leave. If an employee is out of work and is actively looking for employment, he or she normally receives up to 26 weeks of pay, at the rate of 50 to 80 percent of normal pay.

Most employees are eligible. However, workers fired for misconduct or those who are not actively seeking employment are generally ineligible.

CRITICISM OF UNEMPLOYMENT INSURANCE.   Proposed changes in unemployment insurance laws have been introduced in bills at both state and federal levels for two reasons: (1) Abuses are estimated to cost millions each year. (2) State unemployment funds are exhausted during economic slowdowns. A major revision to standardize the laws has been suggested. Many states allow union workers who are on strike to collect unemployment benefits, a provision bitterly opposed by many employers.

SUPPLEMENTAL UNEMPLOYMENT BENEFITS. Supplemental unemployment benefits (SUB) are closely related to unemployment compensation, but they are not required by law. First obtained by the United Steelworkers in 1955, a SUB program is a benefit provision negotiated by a union with an employer as part of the collective bargaining process. The provision requires organizations to contribute to a fund that supplements the unemployment compensation available to employees from federal and/or state sources, or both.

SEVERANCE PAY. Severance pay is a security benefit voluntarily offered by employers. Employees who lose their jobs permanently may receive a lump-sum payment if they are terminated by the employer. For example, if a plant closes because it is outmoded and no longer economically profitable to operate, the employees who lose their jobs may receive a lump-sum payment based on their years of service. Severance pay provisions often appear in union–management agreements and usually provide larger payments for employees with longer service. Many firms also provide *outplacement* assistance in the form of resume writing, interviewing skills workshops, and career counseling.

The Worker Adjustment and Retraining Notification Act of 1988 requires that many employers give sixty-days' notice if a mass layoff or facility closing is to occur. The act does not require employers to give severance pay.[24]

Social Security

The Social Security Act of 1935, with its later amendments, established a system providing *old age, survivor's, disability,* and *retirement benefits.* Administered by the federal government through the Social Security Administration, this program provides benefits to previously employed individuals. Both employees and employers share in the cost of Social Security by paying a tax on the employee's wages or salaries. As Figure 15–4 shows, both the percentage tax paid and the earnings levels covered have increased over time.

COVERAGE. To receive benefits under Social Security, an individual must have engaged in some form of employment covered by the act. Most private enterprises, most types of self-employment including farming, active military service, some nonprofit organizations, and most government agencies must provide Social Security benefits. Amendments to the Social Security Act in 1984 brought coverage to all federal government employees hired starting in 1984. A phased-in limitation was placed on "double dippers," individuals who receive both federal civil service pensions and other pensions.

SOCIAL SECURITY CHANGES. Because the Social Security system affects a large number of individuals and is government operated, it is a politically sensitive program. Social Security increases are often voted by Congress, and Social Security payments have been tied to the cost of living (through the consumer price index). This action, plus the increasing number of persons covered by the Social Security system, has raised concerns about the availability of future funds from which to pay benefits. An aging population due to increased longevity also may place severe strains on the system. By increasing the payment percentage and the earnings levels against which those percentages apply, congressional representatives hoped to avoid

Figure 15–4
Social Security Wage Base and Tax Rates for Employees & Employers

CALENDAR YEAR	Wage Base	Total Rate
1974	$13,200	5.85%
1975	14,100	5.85
1976	15,300	5.85
1977	16,500	5.85
1978	17,700	6.05
1979	22,900	6.13
1980	25,900	6.13
1981	29,700	6.65
1982	32,400	6.70
1983	35,700	6.70
1984	37,800	7.00
1985	39,600	7.05
1986	42,000	7.15
1987	43,800	7.15
1988	45,000	7.51
1989	48,000	7.51
1990	51,300	7.65

SOURCE: Social Security Administration, U.S. Government, 1989.

future funding problems. Yet critics believe that future changes will be needed to ensure the viability of the Social Security system after the year 2000.

■ ■ RETIREMENT-RELATED BENEFITS

A widespread package of benefits offered by most employers attempts to provide income for employees when they retire. Few people have independent reserves to use when they retire. However, financial resources represent only one facet of the broader issue of retirement policies.

Retirement Policies

As a result of a 1986 amendment to the Age Discrimination in Employment Act, most employees can no longer be forced to retire at any age. Employers have developed different policies to comply with these regulations. "Normal retirement" is the age at which employees can retire and collect full pension benefits. Employers must decide whether or not individuals who continue work past age 65 should receive the full benefit package, especially pension credits. As changes in Social Security increase the age for full benefits past 65, these policies likely will be modified.

Despite removing mandatory retirement provisions, the age at which individuals retire has continued to decline in the United States. In 1990, the average retirement age was sixty-two, and it is projected by the U.S. Bureau of Labor Statistics to drop to fifty-nine by the year 2000.

EARLY RETIREMENT.   Provisions for early retirement currently are included in many pension plans. Early retirement gives people an opportunity to get away from a long-term job. Individuals who have spent twenty-five or thirty years working for the same employer may wish to use their talents in other areas. One survey of executives found that 31 percent wanted to retire before age sixty, and another 50 percent wanted to retire between ages sixty and sixty-five.

Some employers can use early retirement buy-out programs to cut back a work force and reduce costs. Care must be taken to make the early retirement programs truly voluntary. Forcing workers to take advantage of an early retirement buy-out program has led to age discrimination suits by employees who do not wish to retire early.[26]

Phased-in and part-time retirements are other approaches. According to the U.S. Social Security Administration, about 22 percent of the workers between ages sixty and sixty-four have part-time jobs.[27] Some organizations, such as Travelers Corp., offer older employees part-time work with reduced hours and pay.

Awareness of the special needs and anxieties of employees as they approach retirement is vital. These problems may be addressed through a pre-retirement counseling program.

Pre-Retirement Counseling

Pre-retirement counseling is aimed at easing employees' anxieties and preparing them for retirement and the benefits associated with it. The biological changes of aging may be a concern, but suddenly having no job can cause even more anxiety and stress.

Pre-retirement counseling should not begin just before retirement; it should be a systematic process of gradual preparation. A survey of 235 organizations indicated that about three-fourths begin pre-retirement programs when employees are about age fifty-six. About 60 percent invite employees and their spouses to attend personalized meetings and seminars, with two-hour sessions being the most common length. Topics most frequently covered are health, housing, Social Security, legal, and financial considerations, and use of leisure time."[28]

Health-Care Benefits for Retirees

As people age, their health problems may intensify. Prolonged hospital stays can be extremely costly, and many older persons worry about having sufficient resources to sustain them through serious illnesses—and after.

The federal government provides some medical assistance to all elderly who are covered by Social Security through Medicare, beginning at age 65. During the 1988–89 period, congressional efforts to expand medicare to cover catastrophic health-care costs were met with howls of outrage from more affluent elderly who were required to pay a surtax for increased benefits. Consequently, the catastrophic provisions were repealed.

The cost of retiree health-care benefits has been growing. According to one estimate, the average retiree medical plan cost to employers was almost $2,400 per retiree under age 65, which is 11 percent higher than the medical plan costs for all plan participants, active and retired.[29] For companies with aging work forces and many retirees, health-care benefits for retirees will continue to increase. For example, at Bethlehem Steel, there are 70,000 retired employees and spouses, but only 33,000 active employees.[30]

To deal with the increasing costs, many employers are cutting back on retiree benefits. One survey found that 41 percent of the surveyed employers had made some changes and reduced some benefits in order to reduce costs.[31] These cutbacks

P/HR: Practice *and* Research

Ethical Issues In Employee Benefits

For many retirees the pension and health-care benefits provided by their former employers are the core of their retirement security, both financial and emotional. At the same time, pension benefits and retiree health-care costs represent major expenses and/or a source for additional savings for employers. but there is another dimension to this issue: *How ethical is it for a firm to cap or cut the pensions and health-care benefits offered to retired former employees?*

Several examples illustrate the problem. In 1984, Bethlehem Steel attempted to raise the deductibles paid by employees and retirees for health insurance. However, the retirees sued and the resulting out-of-court settlement reduced the financial impact of deductibles on retirees, but not on current employees. In 1986, LTV Corporation filed for bankruptcy and attempted to classify retiree health and life insurance benefits as creditor debts that could be cancelled by bankruptcy. As a result, employees at one LTV plant went on strike and threatened a lawsuit, so LTV backed down and restructured the benefits. At Commonwealth Edison in Chicago, health benefits for retirees under age sixty-five cost about 60 percent more than for current workers of all ages. Once Medicare takes effect at age sixty-five, the company's costs decline.

Employers have tried to combat rising costs by trying such strategies as:

- Cancelling retiree health-care benefits, especially if the retiree takes another job, even part-time, offering some benefit coverage
- Restricting retirement benefits for current retirees by raising deductibles, cutting coverage, or reducing employer contributions
- Lobbying for tax law changes to allow employers to tap excess pension benefits to fund retiree health-care costs, resulting in lower pension payments to retirees

All of these approaches raise troubling ethical issues. Many of the retirees worked for their employers for twenty, thirty, forty years or more.[32] Yet the reward for long and loyal service increasingly is a reduction in the health-care benefits for those retirees.

raise both ethical and accounting issues. The ethical issues are addressed in the P/HR: Practice.

The accounting issues have arisen because the Financial Accounting Standards Board (FASB) has stated that firms should be required to establish accounting reserves for funding retiree health-care benefits. Most firms do not set aside funds for these benefits, and they face greater pressures on future earnings because they will have to pay those costs out of current yearly income. The FASB proposal would affect many firms because they would have to reflect the liability on financial statements and reduce their current earnings each year to fund the retiree health-care benefits. One firm with 20,000 employees has to pay retiree health costs of $1.5 million per year. But that firm would have to recognize an expense of $21 million in one year if it considered the accrued future benefits costs.[33] Naturally, such an impact has been resisted by employers.

Pensions

A second group of retirement benefits is provided through private pension plans established and funded by employers and employees. Organizations are not required to offer pensions plans to employees. As a result, only 46 percent of all full-time U.S. workers are covered by pension plans.[34] Smaller firms offer pensions less often; a survey of 822 small employers found that only about 19 percent of them had pension coverage.[35]

The major reasons why firms do not offer pension plans are the costs and administrative burdens imposed by governmental legislation if pension plans are given. Also, many firms do not offer benefits to employees who work part-time as long as they work fewer than 1,000 hours in a calendar year, which is a requirement of the Employee Retirement Income Security Act.

EMPLOYEE RETIREMENT INCOME SECURITY ACT.   Because most pensions are so complex, employees often do not bother to learn about the provisions and advantages of various plans. Widespread criticism of pension plans led to the passage of the Employee Retirement Income Security Act (ERISA) in 1974. The purpose of this law and subsequent amendments to it is to regulate private pension plans in order to assure that employees who put money into pensions plans or depend on a pension for retirement funds actually will receive the money when they retire.

PENSION CONTRIBUTIONS.   Pension plans can be either contributory or noncontributory. In a **contributory plan,** money for pension benefits is paid in by both employees and employers. An employer provides all the funds in a **noncontributory plan.** As would be expected, the noncontributory plan is preferred by employees and labor unions.

> In a CONTRIBUTORY PLAN
> the money for pension benefits is paid in by both employees and employers.
>
> In a NONCONTRIBUTORY PLAN
> all the funds for pension benefits are provided by the employer.

PENSION BENEFITS.   Pension plans can pay benefits based on one of two types of plans. A **defined-contribution plan** is one in which the employer makes an annual payment to an employee's pension account. The key to this plan is the *contribution rate*; employee retirement benefits depend on fixed contributions and employee earnings levels. Profit-sharing plans, employee stock ownership plans (ESOPs), and thrift plans often are defined-contribution plans. Because these plans hinge on the investment returns of the previous contributions, which can vary according to profitability or other factors, employees' retirement benefits are less secure and predictable. But because of their structure, they are preferred by younger, shorter-service employees.

> A DEFINED-CONTRIBUTION PLAN
> is one in which the employer makes an annual payment to an employee's pension account.

A **defined-benefit plan** is one in which an employee is promised a pension amount based on age and service. In this plan the employer's contributions are determined by actuarial calculations that focus on the *benefits* to be received by employees after retirement and the *methods* used to determine such benefits. The amount of an individual employee's benefits is determined by the person's length of service with the organization and the person's average earnings over a five-year or longer period. A defined-benefit plan gives the employee greater assurance of benefits and greater predictability in the amount of benefits that will be available at retirement. Therefore, it generally is more preferred by older workers.

> A DEFINED-BENEFIT PLAN
> is one in which an employee is promised a pension amount based on age and service.

PORTABILITY.   Another feature of some employee pensions is **portability**. In a portable plan, employees can move their pension benefits from one employer to another. A commonly used portable pension system in colleges and universities is the Teacher Insurance Annuity Association (TIAA) system. Under this system, any faculty or staff member who accumulates pension benefits at one university can transfer these benefits to another university within the TIAA system.

> PORTABILITY
> is a pension plan feature that allows employees to move their pension benefits from one employer to another.

If individuals are not in a portable system, they must take a *lump-sum settlement* of money that they contributed to the plan plus accumulated interest on their contributions when they leave. Unless their pensions are vested, they do not receive the employer's contribution. But they can roll the lump sum over into an individual retirement account (IRA) or other retirement plan.

VESTING
is the right of employees to receive
benefits from their pension plans.

VESTING RIGHTS.   Certain rights are attached to employee pension plans. **Vesting** is the right of employees to receive benefits from their pension plans. Typically, vesting assures employees of a certain pension, provided they have worked a minimum number of years. If employees resign or are terminated before they are vested (that is, before they have been employed for the required time), no pension rights accrue to them except the funds that they have contributed. If employees stay the allotted time, they retain their pension rights and receive benefits from the funds contributed by both the employer and themselves.

Discrimination in Pension Plans

The pension area is like many others in the P/HR management area—it is constantly changing. The more recent changes highlighted in this section are concerned with making pension plans nondiscriminatory. The term *nondiscriminatory* has two different meanings here. They are discussed next.

DISCRIMINATION FAVORING HIGHLY COMPENSATED INDIVIDUALS.   The Tax Reform Act of 1986 contained a provision, referred to as Section 89, to ensure that qualified retirement plans did not unreasonably benefit highly compensated individuals. The section required that at least 70 percent of the non-highly compensated employees be covered by the pension plan if one existed. Other stipulations also were included.

The proposed rules were extremely complex and would have required significant administrative costs for employers to comply with them. As a result of the number of complaints, Congress repealed Section 89 in November 1989. However, it is likely that simpler regulations will be drafted in order to ensure that pension plans are set up to benefit all employees, not just highly paid individuals.

DISCRIMINATION AGAINST WOMEN.   Statistics have shown that women generally live longer than men. As a result, before 1983, women received lower benefits. However, this kind of discrimination was declared illegal by a U.S. Supreme Court decision against pension plans that required women to contribute greater amounts because they live longer, as a group. The *Arizona Governing Committee v. Norris* ruling forced pension plan administrators to use "unisex" mortality tables that do not reflect the gender differential in mortality.[36] To bring legislation in line with this decision, the Retirement Equity Act was passed in 1984 as an amendment to ERISA and the Internal Revenue Code. It liberalized pension regulations that affect women, guaranteed access to benefits, prohibited pension-related penalties during absences from work, such as maternity leave, and lowered the vesting age.

Pension Plan Terminations and Asset Use

ERISA has provided increased security to employees who contributed to a pension plan because they can have more confidence that they will receive their benefits on retirement. A significant number of firms, especially smaller companies, have terminated their pension plans. The Employee Retirement Income Security Act also probably has had the effect of limiting the number of new plans introduced because compliance is seen as too costly. The greatest difficulty in complying with ERISA seems to be the voluminous paperwork required in record keeping and reporting.

A fairly recent and potentially dangerous use of pension funds is as a source of financing for companies acquiring other firms. For example, when a West German company bought Great Atlantic & Pacific Tea (A&P), it borrowed a large amount of the money for the purchase. Once the purchase was completed, the German firm used $200 million in excess A&P pension funds to pay much of the debt of the acquisition. Other corporate raiders also have terminated pension plans and used the excess assets to pay down the debt used to acquire the firm. For retirees, use of pension assets puts their pension benefits at greater risk and may lead to reduced benefits. It is likely that legislative efforts to restrict practices such as these will be proposed in the future.

Individual Retirement Benefit Options

The availability of retirement benefit options makes the pension area more complex. Three options are individual retirement accounts (IRAs), 401(k) plans, and Keogh plans.

INDIVIDUAL RETIREMENT ACCOUNT.   An **individual retirement account (IRA)** allows an employee to set aside funds that are tax deferred until the employee retires. The major advantages of an IRA are the ability to accumulate extra retirement funds and the shifting of taxable income to later years, when total income, and therefore taxable income is likely to be lower. Until 1987, many workers took advantage of IRAs offered by financial institutions, insurance companies, and brokerage firms. However, with the passage of the Tax Reform Act of 1986, IRA use became more limited.

> An INDIVIDUAL RETIREMENT ACCOUNT (IRA)
> allows an employee to set aside funds in a special account which are tax-deferred until the employee retires.

401(K) PLAN.   The 401(k) plan gets its name from Section 401(k) of the federal tax code. A **401(k) plan** allows employees to choose whether to receive cash or have employer contributions from profit-sharing and stock-bonus plans placed into tax-deferred accounts. Because of the deferral feature, 401(k) plans also are called *salary reduction plans.* In these plans employees can elect to have their current pay reduced by a certain percentage and that amount paid into a 401(k) plan.

> A 401(k) PLAN
> allows employees to receive cash or to have employer contributions from profit-sharing and stock-bonus plans placed into a tax-deferred account.

KEOGH PLAN.   A **Keogh plan,** also called an H.R. 10 plan, is a special type of retirement plan that allows self-employed persons to establish individualized pension plans. These individuals can set aside a percentage of their income into a pension account. Keogh plans can either be defined contributions or defined benefits in nature. Because of the complexity and special regulations covering Keogh plans, it is not unusual that advice from tax specialists must be obtained by self-employed individuals.

> A KEOGH PLAN (H.R. 10 PLAN)
> allows self-employed individuals to establish an individualized pension plan.

■ ■ HEALTH-CARE BENEFITS

Employers provide a variety of health-care and medical benefits. The most common ones are employees and dependent medical, dental, prescription drug, and vision-care coverage. Basic health-care insurance to cover both normal and major medical expenses is highly desired by employees. Likewise, dental insurance is highly desired by a growing number of employees. A study found that 86 percent of the companies offered dental benefits. Many dental plans also have orthodontic coverage, which is usually more costly. The same survey found that about one-third of the employers provided vision-care coverage.[37] Some employer medical insurance plans also offer psychiatric counseling, prescription drug coverage, and other medically related coverage. But, as discussed earlier, the rapidly escalating costs of health-care benefits are a major concern for employers.

Health Insurance

The traditional approach for providing employees health-care benefits has been through health insurance. This insurance typically is purchased from insurance carriers such as Mutual of Omaha, Aetna, or Blue Cross and Blue Shield. Until employer health-care expenses started rising so rapidly, many employers offered what is called *first-dollar coverage*. In this type of coverage, all expenses, from the first dollar of health-care costs, are paid by the employee's insurance, with the exception of costs associated with hospitalized illness covered by major medical plans. Commonly, a small deductible amount is paid by employees for illnesses covered under major medical plans, but most basic coverage plans have not had an employee-paid deductible. Experts say that by having first-dollar coverage in the basic plan, employees may see a doctor for every slight illness, which results in an escalation of the costs of the benefits.

Consequently, employers increasingly are providing health-care insurance that is comprehensive, which means that employees pay a deductible on all medical care costs. Many employers also are raising the deductible from $50 to $200 or more. Others now require co-payment.

CO-PAYMENT
requires employees to pay part of insurance premium costs.

CO-PAYMENT.   As health insurance costs have risen, employers have attempted to shift some of those costs to employees. **Co-payment** requires employees to pay a monthly amount as part of insurance premium costs. A survey of over 200 manufacturers found that only about 56 percent paid the entire cost of premiums for employees, and 32 percent paid all the costs of dependent coverage.[38]

Attempts by employers to shift some costs to employees have been met with fierce resistance by unions. One poll of fifty labor union leaders found that limiting health-care sharing was their top priority in labor contract negotiations.[39]

COBRA PROVISIONS.   Legal requirements passed in the Consolidated Omnibus Budget Reconciliation Act (COBRA) in 1986, increased employer health-care costs. Provisions within the law required that most employers (except churches and the federal government) with twenty or more employees offer *extended health-care coverage* to the following groups:

■ Employees who voluntarily or involuntarily quit, except those terminated for "gross misconduct"
■ Widowed or divorced spouses and dependent children of former or current employees
■ Retirees and their spouses whose health-care coverage ends

Employers must notify appropriate employees and/or their spouses within 60 days after the employees quit, die, get divorced, etc. The extended coverage must be offered for 18 to 36 months, depending on the qualifying circumstances. The employer may charge no more than 102 percent of the premium costs to insure a similarly covered employee, but the individual not employed by the organization must pay the premiums.

For most employers, the COBRA requirements mean additional paperwork and related costs. For example, firms must not only track the former employees but also notify their qualified dependents. The 2 percent premium addition generally does not cover all relevant costs, which often run several percentage points more. As an example, since 1987, Marriott Corporation has paid over $3 million in claims submitted by individuals eligible under COBRA. Also, the notification costs have run over $40,000 per year, well above the 2 percent addition.[40] Consequently, additional management efforts to reduce overall health benefits costs become even more important.

Health-Care Cost Management

Faced with spiraling costs for health-care benefits, many employers have begun aggressive efforts to manage and control such costs. Instead of offering health insurance to employees and paying all or most of the premiums, employers are using a variety of strategies to contain costs. These strategies are often referred to as *managed care*.[41] All the approaches require employers to be aggressive in managing their health-care costs. Some common methods used to reduce employer health-care expenses, discussed next, are:

- Self-funding
- Preferred provider organizations (PPOs)
- Health maintenance organizations (HMOs)
- Utilization review
- Others

SELF-FUNDING.   **Self-funding** occurs when an employer sets aside funds to pay health claims in lieu of insurance coverage. Basically, the employer earmarks a certain amount (for example, $800,000) to cover normal medical insurance benefits. The exact figure is based on an analysis of previous health benefit use patterns. Instead of buying health insurance plans from a firm such as Blue Cross and Blue Shield or Aetna, the employer sets aside funds and also buys an *excess policy*. The employer agrees to pay up to the normal amount ($800,000 in the example) of employees' health-care costs. These plans also are called *stop-loss* plans because the company expenses stop at the set level. The excess policy then provides coverage for all expenses beyond that level. Just as the premium for your care insurance is much lower if you choose a $1,000 deductible rather than a $100 deductible, the employer pays significantly less for the excess coverage than it would for a total coverage package.

Furthermore, the employer earns interest on the funds that are set aside because these funds are paid out during the year as employees use their health benefits, rather than at the beginning of the year to pay an insurance premium. Employers can either process the claims themselves or contract with an outside service to administer them. Some large insurance firms even provide this claims administration service for a percentage fee of the value of the claims. Many other special options also are available.

PREFERRED PROVIDER ORGANIZATION (PPO).   Another cost containment strategy is the establishment of a preferred provider organization (PPO). A Preferred

SELF-FUNDING
occurs when an employer sets aside funds to pay health claims in excess of the amount provided by funding in lieu of insurance coverage.

A PREFERRED PROVIDER ORGANIZATION (PPO) is a health-care provider that contracts with an employer or an employer group to provide health-care services to employees at a competitive rate.

Provider Organization (PPO) is a health-care provider that contracts with an employer or an employer group to provide health-care services to employees at a competitive rate.

By encouraging employees to use lower-cost providers, employers can reduce their benefit outlays. Hospital-based PPOs and groups of physicians have the assurance of a continuing source of patients, even though employees have the freedom to go to other providers if they want to pay the difference in costs.

HEALTH MAINTENANCE ORGANIZATION (HMO).   A unique form of health care is available through a **health maintenance organization (HMO),** which provides services for a fixed period on a prepaid basis. Unlike other health-care benefits, the HMO emphasizes prevention as well as correction. An employer contracts with an HMO, which has doctors and medical personnel on its staff, to furnish complete medical care, except for hospitalization. The employer pays a flat rate per enrolled employee or per family. The covered individuals may then go to the HMO for health care as often as they need. Supplemental policies for hospitalization also are used.

A HEALTH MAINTENANCE ORGANIZATION (HMO) is a form of health care that provides services for a fixed period on a prepaid basis.

The HMO Act of 1973 requires that employers with twenty-five or more employees offer an HMO as an option to their employees if one is available in the local area. As a result, HMOs have grown in popularity.

UTILIZATION REVIEWS.   Many employers are finding that some of the health care provided by doctors and hospitals is unnecessary, incorrectly billed, and deliberately overcharged. Consequently, the employers and insurance firms are requiring that the work and charges be audited and reviewed through a **utilization review**. The utilization review process includes the following:[42]

UTILIZATION REVIEW is an auditing of the services and costs billed by health-care providers.

- *Pre-certification review:* Approval of a second medical opinion is required before employees receive certain elective medical treatments. Such reviews encourage use of outpatient surgery and reduce hospital use.
- *Concurrent review:* At the same time that health-care treatment and/or hospitalization begin, the appropriateness of the medical procedures used are reviewed by nurses and doctors hired by the review firm.
- *Case management:* Independent medical professionals monitor the treatments given to employees with catastrophic health problems to ensure that they are necessary and that less-costly options are considered.
- *Post-treatment bill review:* An independent firm reviews bills submitted by health-care providers to ensure that all charges are appropriate and realistic.

OTHER COST MANAGEMENT EFFORTS.   Other means used to contain health-care costs include preventive health and physical *"wellness" programs* and *communications efforts* to make employees more knowledgeable about health-care costs. Wellness programs try to encourage employees to have more healthy lifestyles. Included in wellness programs are activities such as smoking cessation classes, diet and nutrition counseling, exercise and physical fitness centers and programs, and health education. Wellness programs are discussed in more detail in the next chapter.

Employers also are educating employees about health-care costs and how to reduce them. Newsletters, formal classes, and many other approaches are used, all of which are designed to make employees more aware about why health-care costs are increasing and what employees can do to control them.

■■ ■ FINANCIAL AND OTHER BENEFITS

Employers have offered workers a wide range of special benefits. From the point of view of the employer, such benefits can be useful in attracting and retaining employees. Workers like receiving special benefits because they are not taxed as income. To give a perspective on the variety of benefits offered, *financial, educational, social and recreational,* and *miscellaneous* benefits are highlighted next.

Financial Benefits

Financial benefits can include a wide variety of items. A *credit union* provides savings and lending services for employees. *Purchase discounts* allow employees to buy goods or services from their employers at reduced rates. For example, a furniture manufacturer may allow employees to buy furniture at wholesale cost plus 10 percent. Or a bank may offer the use of a safety deposit box and free checking to its employees.

Employee *thrift, saving,* or *stock investment plans* may be made available. Some employers match a portion of the employee's contribution. These plans are especially attractive to executive and managerial personnel. To illustrate, in a stock purchase plan the corporation provides matching funds equal to the amount invested by the employee to purchase stock. In this way, employees can benefit from the future growth of the corporation. Also, it is hoped that employees will develop a greater loyalty and interest in the organization and its success.

Financial planning and counseling is especially valuable to executives. They may need information on investments, tax shelters, and comprehensive financial counseling because of their higher compensation. One survey of firms with over $400 million in revenues found that 48 percent offered financial counseling to executives.[43] Other employees benefit from financial planning and counseling as well. These financial planning benefits likely will grow as a greater percentage of workers approach retirement age.

Numerous other financial-related benefits may be offered, such as the use of a company car, company expense accounts, and help in buying or selling a house when an employee is transferred.

Other Insurance Benefits

In addition to health-related insurance, some employers also provide other types of insurance. These benefits have major advantages for employees because many employers pay some or all of the costs. In addition, cheaper insurance rates are available through group programs.

LIFE INSURANCE. It is common for employers to provide *life insurance* for employees. Life insurance is bought as a group policy, and the employer pays the premiums, but the level of coverage is usually low and is tied to an employee's base pay. A typical level of coverage is 1½ or two times an employee's annual salary. Some executives may get more as part of an executive compensation package. One survey found that 97 percent of the 227 employers surveyed offer company-sponsored life insurance for salaried employees, and 49 percent of the firms provide such coverage for hourly employees. About three-fourths of the firms do not require any employee contributions.[44]

DISABILITY INSURANCE.   Other insurance benefits frequently tied to employee pay levels are *short-term* or *long-term disability insurance*. This type of insurance provides continuing income protection for employees if they become disabled and unable to work. Long-term disability insurance is much more common because many employers cover short-term disability situations by allowing employees to acrue the sick leave granted annually.

LEGAL INSURANCE.   As society becomes more complex, more people need legal assistance. However, attorney fees have increased to the point that many who need such assistance with wills, contracts, divorces, and other situations cannot afford legal advice. An insurance plan that pays a portion of legal fees saves the employees money because the fees are paid with pretax dollars, not out of the employees' take-home pay.

Educational Benefits

Another benefit used by employees comes in the form of *educational assistance* to pay for some or all costs associated with formal education courses and degree programs, including the costs of books and laboratory materials. Some employers pay for schooling on a proportional schedule, depending on the grade received by employees; other simply require a passing grade of C or above.

Such programs have been used by fast-food chains and other firms in order to attract and retain part-time workers in tight labor markets. At Burger King, employees can qualify for up to $2,000 of tuition-aid credits over a two-year period. Au Bon Pain, based in New England, offers employees with at least 750 hours of service a choice of a $1,000 scholarship or a cash bonus of $500.[45]

TAX STATUS OF EDUCATIONAL BENEFITS.   Unless the education paid for by the employer meets certain conditions, the cost of the education aid must be counted as taxable income by employees. To qualify as nontaxable income under Section 127 of the Internal Revenue Code, the education must be:[46]

■ *Job-related*, such that it is used to maintain or improve a person's skills for the current job
■ *Expressly required*, either to meet specific current job requirements or for the person to maintain required professional standing (such as licenses, continuing education, etc.)
■ *Above minimum standards*, meaning that it is not education that is necessary for the person to qualify for a job initially

Because of U.S. federal budget deficits, repeated attempts have been made to include all educational benefits as taxable income to employees, thereby raising the taxes to be paid by employees using those benefits. Some proposals have attempted to narrow the criteria for deciding if education is job-related and expressly required. As of the writing of this text, those efforts have been unsuccessful, so that many of the employer-paid courses under tuition-aid plans remain nontaxable to employees.

Child Care as a Benefit

As mentioned earlier, child-care assistance is being offered by a growing number of employers. For organizations considering child care as a benefit, it is clear that the needs assessment is important. The number of employees eligible to use the service and the number willing to use it is not the same. Some employer-sponsored child-care centers have been closed, and one of the major reasons is that too few employees were using them so the centers could not meet their costs. Nevertheless, many employers probably will consider adding this benefit or using one of the options discussed earlier.

Social and Recreational Benefits

Some benefits and services are social and recreational in nature, such as bowling leagues, picnics, parties, employer-sponsored athletic teams, organizationally owned recreational lodges, and other sponsored activities and interest groups. Dances, dinners, and other social events give employees an opportunity to become better acquainted and strengthen interpersonal relationships. The employer should retain control of all events associated with the organization because of possible legal responsibility.

The idea behind social and recreation programs is to promote employee happiness and team spirit. Employees *may* appreciate this type of benefit, but managers should not necessarily expect increased job productivity or job satisfaction as a result.

Other Benefits

Other benefits too numerous to detail here are made available by various employers. Food services, counseling services such as employee assistance plans, paid professional memberships, and organizationally provided uniforms are just a few. Some unusual benefits now being offered by companies include vacations at company-owned properties and free tickets to basketball games or first-run films.[47]

■ ■ TIME-OFF BENEFITS

Employers give employees paid time-off for a variety of circumstances. Paid lunch breaks and rest periods, holidays, and vacations are the most well known. But leaves are given for a number of other purposes as well. Some more common time-off benefits are discussed next.

Holiday Pay

Most, if not all, employers provide pay for such established holidays as Labor Day, Memorial Day, Christmas, New Year's Day, and the Fourth of July. Other holidays are offered to some employees through selected laws or union contracts. According to one survey, the average number of holidays given is nine days per year. About two-thirds of the employers surveyed had "floating holidays" which can be selected by employees at their discretion or selected by management or management/union agreements.[48]

As an abuse control measure, employers commonly require employees to work the last scheduled day before the holiday and the first scheduled workday after a holiday to be eligible for holiday pay. Also, some employers pay time and a half to hourly employees who must work holidays. Exempt employees can take "comp time" (compensatory time-off) and have a different day off with their manager's agreement.

Vacation Pay

Paid vacations are a common benefit. As Figure 15–5 shows, employees often have graduated vacation-time scales based on length of service. Some organizations also allow employees to accumulate unused vacation. As with holiday pay, employees are required to work the day before and the day after vacations to prevent abuse.

One issue that has received legal attention is the right of employees to unused vacation time if they voluntarily or involuntarily quit their jobs. Most states have not regulated this area, but some states have laws that require employers to pay former workers for vacation pay owed at the time the individuals quit or are terminated. Employers have challenged those laws in both state and federal courts, and the rulings have been inconsistent. Until the U.S. Supreme Court accepts a case on this issue and makes a ruling, employers doing business in several states may face different regulations.

Leaves of Absence

Leaves are given for a variety of reasons. All of the leaves discussed next add to employer costs.

Figure 15–5
Weeks of Paid Vacation

SOURCES: Adapted from "Weeks of Paid Vacation," *Omaha World-Herald*, July 16, 1989, 1G; and "How Long Are Your Vacations?" *Industry Week*, July 3, 1989, 8.

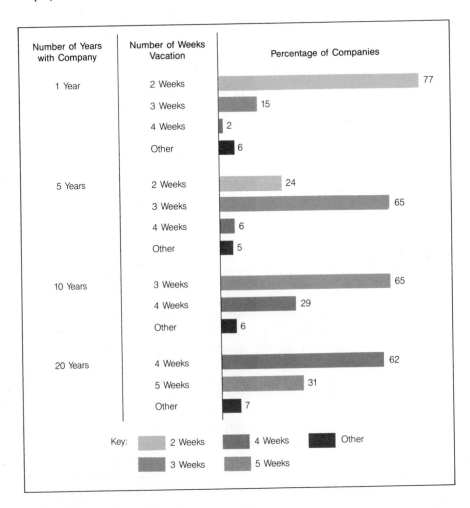

MEDICAL LEAVE.   Several situations may qualify an employee for medical leave. As mentioned earlier, one of the most volatile issues is the right of women to return to work after they have taken leave to give birth. Under the Pregnancy Discrimination Act, an employer is not required to guarantee that a woman will get her same job back if she is on maternity leave. However, an employer must offer a woman a job, not necessarily at the same rate of pay, if similar policies are used for workers who have other reasons for medical leave.

Some organizations offer *paternity leave* for male workers, often through paid annual leave, paid sick leave, or unpaid paternity leave. But few employers offer specifically designated paid paternity leave and where it is offered, relatively low percentage of men take it. The primary reason for the low usage is a perception that it is not as socially acceptable for men to stay home for child-related reasons. That view likely will change as a result of there being more dual-career couples in the work force.[49]

SICK LEAVE.   Closely related to medical leave is sick leave. Many employers allow their employees to miss a limited number of days because of illness without losing pay. Some employers allow employees to accumulate unused sick leave, which may be used in case of catastrophic illnesses. Others pay employees for unused sick leave.

Some organizations have shifted emphasis to reward people who do not use sick leave by giving them *well-pay*. Well-pay rewards employees who stay well, unlike sick pay, which pays people who are sick.

Other employers have made use of the *earned-time* concept. One organization found that when it stopped designating a specific number of sick-leave days and implemented a plan that combined sick leave, vacations, and holidays into a total of days that employees could take off with pay, absenteeism dropped, time-off was better scheduled, and employee acceptance of the sick-leave policy improved.

OTHER LEAVES.   Other types of leaves are given for a variety of purposes. Some, such as *military leave, election leave,* and *jury leave,* are required by various state and federal laws, although employers commonly pay on the difference between the employee's regular pay and the military, election, or jury pay. Some firms grant employees time off and give them regular pay while the employees also receive military pay. Federal law prohibits taking discriminatory action against military reservists by requiring them to take vacation time in order to attend summer camp or other training sessions. However, the leave request must be reasonable and truly required by the military.[50]

Funeral or bereavement leaves is another common leave offered. This leave is usually up to three days for immediate family members, as specifically defined in many employer's policy manuals and employee handbooks. Some policies also give unpaid time off for the death of more distant relatives or friends.

■ ■ BENEFITS ADMINISTRATION

With the myriad of benefits and regulations, it is easy to see why many organizations must have coordinated efforts to administer benefit program. Figure 15–6 shows how benefits administration responsibilities can be split between P/HR specialists and other managers. Notice that the greatest role is played by P/HR specialists, but managers are responsible for the communication aspects of benefits administration.

Figure 15–6
Benefit Responsibilities

P/HR UNIT	MANAGERS
■ Develops and administers benefit systems	■ Answers simple questions on benefits
■ Answers employees' technical questions on benefits	■ Maintain liaison with personnel specialists on benefits
■ Assists employees in claiming benefits	■ Maintain good communications with employees near retirement
■ Coordinates special preretirement programs	

Benefits Communication

Employees generally are rather ignorant about the values and costs associated with benefits they receive from employers. Yet, as the P/HR: Research indicates, benefits communication and benefits satisfaction are linked. Many employers have instituted special benefit communication systems to inform employees about the value of the benefits provided. [52] Explaining benefits during new employee orientation programs, holding periodic meetings, preparing special literature, and using in-house employee publications to heighten awareness of benefits are among the methods used. For example, when Wang Laboratories, the Massachusetts-based computer firm, introduced its "Next Generation" flexible benefits program, its communication efforts ranged from seminars and newsletters to interactive ideas and telephone hotlines. [53]

Many employers also give employees an annual "personal statement of benefits" that translates benefits into dollar amounts. Federal regulations under ERISA require that employees receive an annual pension-reporting statement, which also can be included in personal statements. By having a personalized statement, each employee can see how much his or her own benefits are worth. Employers are hopeful that by educating employees on benefits costs, costs can be managed better and the employees will have a higher appreciation for the employer expenditures.

Flexible Benefits Systems

FLEXIBLE BENEFITS SYSTEM allows employees to select the benefits they prefer from groups of benefits established by the employer.

A **flexible benefits**, or "cafeteria-style," approach allows employees to select the benefits they prefer from groups of benefits established by the employer. The description of United Hospital's Flex plan at the beginning of the chapter illustrates how such systems can be used. By making a variety of "dishes," or benefits, available, the organization allows each employee to select an individual combination of benefits within some overall limits. These systems recognize that individual employee situations differ because of age, family status, and lifestyles. For instance, individuals in dual-career marriages may not want the same benefits from two different employers. Under a flex plan, one of them can forego some benefits available in the spouse's plan and take other benefits instead. Some of the most common areas of choice are shown in Figure 15–7.

As a result of the changing composition of the work force, flexible plans have grown in popularity. One survey found that the number of companies offering flex plans increased 22 percent in a recent year. By 1990, over one-third of all employers having benefit plans offered flex plans. [54]

P/HR:	Practice *and* Research	Benefits Communication

Researchers have examined the link between benefits communication and how employees view their benefits. As described in *Personnel Psychology*, Dreker, Ash, and Bretz examined how benefit coverage and employee cost sharing affect employees' satisfaction with their total compensation. To conduct the research they examined pay and benefit practices at eight different state highway patrol departments. Before surveying employee satisfaction, the researchers interviewed personnel specialists at each organization and reviewed relevant policy and procedure documentation.

Following this internal review, a cover letter and survey were sent to 2,925 persons, of whom 1,433 returned surveys (a 49 percent response). First, the survey asked for basic demographic data such as state, gender, age, years of service, education level, etc. This was followed by eighteen questions on pay satisfaction, in which respondents chose answers on (a five-part scale.) Finally, participants were asked to compare their benefits with those provided by similar law enforcement agencies by rating each type of benefit on (a five-point scale.)

The results offered some interesting insights. As would be expected, respondents generally indicated that benefit satisfaction increased with improved benefit coverage and decreased when higher costs were born by the individuals. Also, the more accurate the information about actual coverage levels that individuals had, the greater their benefit satisfaction. Little consistent relationship was found between pay level satisfaction and benefit satisfaction.

The authors conclude that improving benefit satisfaction, (even when providing additional benefit coverage,) is directly linked to the quality and extent of the benefit communication efforts made by employers. As more and more organizations contemplate cost shifting to employees, they must give greater attention to better benefits communications programs.[51]

FLEXIBLE SPENDING ACCOUNTS.   Under current tax laws, (Section 125 of the Tax Code administered by the Internal Revenue Service) employees can divert some of their income before taxes into accounts to fund some benefits. A **flexible spending account** allows employees to contribute pre-tax dollars to buy additional benefits. An example helps to illustrate the advantage of these accounts to employees. Assume an employee earns $3,000 per month. Further, he has $100 per month deducted to put into flexible spending accounts. That $100 does not count as gross income for tax purposes, thus reducing his amount of taxable income. Then the employee uses the money in his account to purchase additional benefits.

Under tax law at the time of this writing, the funds in the account can be used only to purchase the following: (1) additional health care (including offsetting deductibles), life, or disability insurance; or (2) child-care benefits. However, tax regulations require that if the employees do not spend all of the money in their accounts by the end of the year, they must take the remaining balance as cash and pay income tax on it or forfeit it. Therefore, it is important that employees estimate very closely the additional benefits they will use.

These plans have grown in popularity as more flexible benefit plans have been adopted by more employers. Of course, such plans and their tax advantages can be changed as Congress passes future tax-related legislation.

ADVANTAGES OF FLEXIBLE BENEFIT PLANS.   The flexible benefits approach has several advantages. First, this scheme takes into consideration the complexity of

FLEXIBLE SPENDING ACCOUNT allows employees to contribute pre-tax dollars to buy additional benefits.

Figure 15–7
Flexible Benefits Program Choices (percentages of flexible plans offering each benefit)

SOURCE: *Journal of Accountancy*, January 1989, 93. Used with permission.

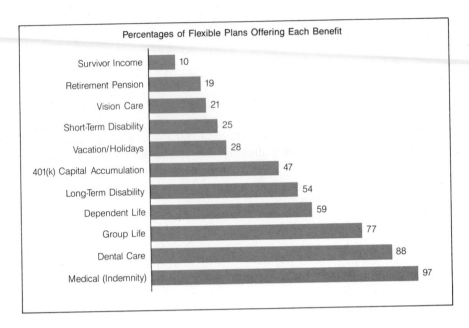

Percentages of Flexible Plans Offering Each Benefit

Benefit	Percentage
Survivor Income	10
Retirement Pension	19
Vision Care	21
Short-Term Disability	25
Vacation/Holidays	28
401(k) Capital Accumulation	47
Long-Term Disability	54
Dependent Life	59
Group Life	77
Dental Care	88
Medical (Indemnity)	97

people and situations. Because employees in an organization have different desires and needs, they can *tailor benefit packages* to fit their individual life situations.

The second advantage, and certainly an important one to most employers, is that flex plans can aid in *benefit cost-control efforts*. The impact of flex plans is seen in a study done over several years that compared flex plans with the more fixed types. The study found that employers without flex plans had medical-care costs rise 41.1 percent, while employers with flex plans experienced an increase of 22.7 percent.[55] Although employers without flex plans could take some cost-containment steps, the decision by employers to reduce benefits or increase required employee's co-payments is made easier and is more palatable to employees by integrating these measures into flex plans.

Another advantage of the flexible benefit approach is heightened *employee awareness* of the cost and the value of the benefits. By having to determine the benefits they will receive, employees know what the trade-offs are.

The fourth advantage is that employers with flexible benefit plans can recruit, hire, or retain employees more easily because of the *attractiveness* of flexible plans. By being able to tailor benefits to their needs, employees may not be as interested in shifting to other employers with fixed benefits plans.

DISADVANTAGES OF FLEXIBLE BENEFIT PLANS.   The flexible approach to benefits is not without some drawbacks. The major problem is the *complexity* of keeping track of what each individual chooses, especially if there are a large number of employees. Sophisticated computer software is now available to manage these complexities. Another difficulty is the *increase in benefits communications costs*. As more benefits are made available, employees may not be able to understand the options because the benefits structure and its provisions often become quite complicated.

Another problem is that an *inappropriate benefit package* may be chosen by employees. A young construction worker might not choose disability benefits; however, if he or she is injured, the family may suffer financial hardship. Part of this problem can be overcome by requiring employees to select a core set of benefits (life, health, and disability insurance) and by offering options on other benefits. Also, because many insurance plans are based on a group rate, the employer may face higher rates if insufficient numbers of employees select an insurance option or if only the higher-risk employees select and use certain benefits.[56]

Despite these disadvantages, it is likely that flex plans will continue to grow in popularity. The ability to match benefits to differing employee needs, while also controlling some costs, is so attractive that employers will try to find ways to overcome the disadvantages while attuning their benefit plans to the 1990s.

SUMMARY

- Benefits provided additional compensation to employees as a reward for organizational membership.
- Employers in the 1990s face major benefits issues. Three prominent ones are mandated benefits, health-care cost containment, and family-related issues.
- Mandatory benefits means that employers are required by law to provide certain benefits previously offered voluntarily.
- The rapid escalation of health-care benefit costs has prompted employers to use different means to slow down their cost increases.
- Family-related challenges for the 1990s include parental leaves, child care, and elder-care assistance.
- Benefits should be viewed strategically, not just operationally.
- Because benefits generally are not taxed, they are highly desired by employees. As a result, the average employee now receives an amount equal to about 37 percent of his/her pay in benefit compensation.
- The Tax Reform Act of 1986 made significant changes in tax laws that affect some employee benefits.
- The general types of benefits include those for security, retirement, health care, financial, social and recreational, and time off.
- Workers' compensation, unemployment compensation, and Social Security are three prominent security-oriented benefits.
- Organizations that provide retirement-related benefits should develop policies on early retirement, offer pre-retirement counseling, and plan how to integrate Social Security benefits into employees' benefit plans.
- The pension area is a complex area governed by the Employee Retirement Income Security Act (ERISA). There are a number of key terms that must be learned in order to understand ERISA.
- Retiree health-care costs represent an area of increasing concern for employers.
- Individual Retirement Accounts, 401(k) plans, and Keogh plans are important individual options available for supplementing retirement benefits.
- Health-care benefits are the most costly insurance-related benefits. Employers have become more aggressive in managing their health-care costs through self-funding, preferred provider organizations, and health maintenance organizations.
- Various types of insurance, financial planning, tuition aid, and other benefits that employers may offer enhance the appeal of benefits to employees.
- Holiday pay, vacation pay, and various leaves of absence are means of providing time-off-related benefits to employees.

- Because of the variety of benefit options available and the costs involved, employers need to develop a system to communicate these options and costs to their employees.
- Flexible benefit systems, which can be tailored to individual needs and situations, have grown in popularity.

REVIEW AND DISCUSSION QUESTIONS

1. Discuss the following statement: "The solution to the three benefit challenges is to have more mandatory benefits."
2. Why have benefits grown in strategic importance to employers?
3. Why are workers' compensation, unemployment compensation, and Social Security appropriately classified as security-oriented benefits?
4. Take a position on the following statement and explain your reasoning: "Early retirement probably will be considered the normal idea by the year 2000."
5. Define the following terms: (a) contributory plan, (b) define benefit plan, (c) portability, and (d) vesting
6. Discuss the following statement: "Health-care costs are out of control in the United States and it is up to employers to put pressure on the medical system to reduce costs."
7. What types of financial and other benefits would you most prefer? Why?
8. Some experts have forecast that time-off-related benefits will expand in the future. Why?
9. Why are benefits communications and flexible benefit systems so intertwined?

| CASE | **Health-Care Cost Management** |

Lindberg Corporation, a Chicago-based firm, manufactures commercial heat-treating equipment and employs about 1,100 people in twenty-six locations around the United States. Because of a desire to reduce benefit costs for health care, Lindberg embarked on an ambitious health-care cost management program.

Through a variety of efforts, the firm received a return of $14 for every dollar spent, while making few changes in the coverage available to employees. Total claims paid were reduced by 16 percent, for a savings of $188,000. These impressive results were obtained through a cooperative effort with Parkside Medical Services, which provides medical intervention and control services.

The program operates in this way. Patient service coordinators at Parkside (who are specially trained registered nurses) offer counseling and guidance on health-care services to employees through toll-free telephone lines. Employees can choose their own physician and hospital, but it is mandatory for them to contact Parkside before being treated, except for emergency admissions or urgent situations. Parkside professionals contact the appropriate medical providers and discuss possible alternative treatments and ways to reduce costly hospital stays. The patient services coordinators also discuss the available options with employees, and the employees decide what medical services they will use.

Lindberg gives some examples of how the program works:

"An employee in a rural area was scheduled for a knee operation which would have incapacitated him for a period of three to four months. Through a second opinion consultation in a nearby metropolitan area, a less invasive procedure was recommended and the employee returned to work in less than two weeks."

"A woman planning to have her gallbladder removed contacted patient services for the required second opinion. A test performed as part of the consultation indicated a normal gallbladder. The patient's significant weight loss was attributed to anorexia, and the patient services coordinator provided support in identifying treatment resources in a nearby city. Unnecessary surgery was avoided."

To introduce the program, corporate P/HR professionals and Parkside managers developed an educational program that was conducted at all company plants. Also, union representatives were briefed on the program in the twelve unionized plants. As union contracts expired, the new health-care cost strategies became topics of collective bargaining. The unions representing the employees in eight plants agreed to put the changes into the existing contracts without reopening the contract.[57]

QUESTIONS

1. Identify how the success of Lindberg's effort relied on employee communication.
2. What other health-care cost management approaches might be appropriate?

NOTES

1. Adapted from M. Michael Markowich, "United Hospitals Makes Flex Fly," *Personnel Journal*, December 1989, 40–47.

2. "How Costly Are Mandated Benefits?" *Nation's Business*, April 1988, 12–14.

3. Carson E. Beadle, "The Future of Employee Benefits: More Mandates Ahead," *Compensation and Benefits Review*, November/December 1988, 36–44.

4. "OUCH: The Squeeze on Your Health Benefits," *Business Week*, November 20, 1989, 110–116.

5. Michael A. Verespej, "Rx for Costs Elusive," *Industry Week*, December 4, 1989, 88–91.

6. Adapted from Calvin Lawrence Jr., "Health-Care Costs Hang Up More than Phone Firms," *USA Today*, August 9, 1989, B1; "OUCH," 110–116; Kevin Maney, "Employers Battle Price 'Hemorrhage,'" *USA Today*, September 19, 1989, 1A–2A.

7. Joani Nelson-Horchler, "U.S. 'Catching' Socialism," *Industry Week*, August 21, 1989, 45–47.

8. "National Health Plans, *Wall Street Journal*, May 16, 1989, 1.

9. James A. Burnstein and Jeri A. Lindahl, "Parental-Medical Leave: A New Trend in Labor Legislation," *Employee Relations Law Journal* 14 (1988): 299–305.

10. U.S. Department of Labor, *Child Care: A Work Force Issue* (Washington, D.C.: Government Printing Office, April 1988).

11. Stanley D. Nollen, "The Work-Family Dilemma: How HR Managers Can Help," *Personnel*, May 1989, 25–30.

12. Cathy Trost, "Toddling Trend: Child Care Near the Office," *Wall Street Journal*, October 6, 1986, 31.

13. *Child Care: The Facts* (New York: Child Care Action Campaign, 1988).

14. Lisa R. Cole, "Child Care and Business," *Business and Economic Review*, January–March 1989, 4–9.

15. Margaret Magnus, "Eldercare: Corporate Awareness But Little Action," *Personnel Journal*, June 1988, 19–23.

16. David Bowen and Christopher A. Wadley, "Designing a Strategic Benefits Program," *Compensation and Benefits Review*, September/October 1989, 44–57.

17. *Employee Benefits, 1989 Edition* (Washington D.C.: U.S. Chamber of Commerce, 1989), 11–14.

18. G. Czech, "Private Plans Go the Distance," *Best's Review*, July 1989, 50–52, 92–94.

19. L. J. Stern, "Workers Compensation and General Liability," *Best's Review*, October 1989, 12.

20. Ron Stodghill, "Is This Liability Law a Gravy Train?" *Business Week*, November 6, 1989, 93.

21. William D. Bolton, "Workers' Comp: A Disabled System" *Industry Week*, January 22, 1990, 34.

22. John C. Coleman III, "Caution Is Key When Injured Workers Return," *Personnel Journal*, February 1989, 54–63.

23. Roger Thompson, "Unemployment: Cutting the Cost," *Nation's Business*, November 1989, 71–73.

24. "Plant Closing Notification Rules: A WARN Compliance Guide," *Bulletin to Management*, May 18, 1989, 1–15.

25. "Desire to Retire," *Wall Street Journal*, December 8, 1989, R6.

26. Paul Salvatore, "Age Discrimination and Differentiated Early Retirement Incentives," *ILR Report*, Spring 1988, 15–17.

27. "Phased Retirement Finds Fans," *Omaha World-Herald*, November 19, 1989, IG.

28. Patrick J. Montana, "Pre-Retirement Planning: How Corporations Help," *Personnel Administrator*, June 1986, 121–126.

29. "Rising Health Benefits: Retiree Costs," *Journal of Accountancy*, July 1989, 23.

30. Amanda Bennett, "Firms Stunned by Retiree Health Costs," *Wall Street Journal*, May 24, 1988, 37.

31. Ibid.

32. Susan B. Garland, "The Retiring Kind Are Getting Militant About Benefits," *Business Week*, May 28, 1990, 29.

33. Joseph F. McKenna, "Accounting For a Land Mine," *Industry Week*, July 17, 1989, 48–50.

34. "U.S. Private-Pension Coverage Falls to 46%," *Denver Post*, November 2, 1989, 5.

35. *Compensation and Benefits Review*, March/April 1989, 3–13.

36. *Arizona Governing Committee v. Norris*, 103 S.Ct. 3492, 32 FEP Cases 233 (1983).

37. Morton E. Grossman and Margaret Magnus, "The Boom in Benefits," *Personnel Journal*, November 1988, 50–55.

38. *Survey: More Firms Using Cost-Sharing for Insurance*, *Omaha World-Herald*, May 28, 1989, 8G.

39. Albert R. Karr and Mary Lu Carnevale, "Facing Off Over Health-Care Benefits," *Wall Street Journal*, August 11, 1989, B1.

40. Donald Westerfield and Paul Wilson, Jr., "COBRA Strikes Business in the Jugular," *Management Accounting*, January 1989, 73.

41. Frederic R. Curtiss, "Managed Health Care: Managed Costs?" *Personnel Journal*, June 1989, 72–85.

42. "When You Think Hospital Bills Are Too High: Utilization Review," *Inc.*, December 1989, 147–148.

43. "A Popular Perk among Large Companies," *Compensation and Benefits Review*, July/August 1989, 5.

44. Len Strazewski, "Employers Reevaluate Life and Disability," *Human Resource Executive*, May 1989, 30–33.

45. Sal D. Rinella and Robert J. Kopecky. "Burger King Hooks Employees with Educational Incentives," *Personnel Journal*, October 1989, 90–07.

46. "When the Deduction Is for Employee Education," *CPA Client Bulletin*, November 1989, 3.

47. Lisa Birnbach, "Going Beyond Free Donuts and Coffee," *Personnel Administrator*, November 1988, 72–75.

48. *Paid Holidays and Vacation Policies*, Personnel Policies Forum No. 142 (Washington D.C.: Bureau of National Affairs, November 1986).

49. "More New Dads Expect to Take Time Off," *Omaha World-Herald*, July 16, 1989, 19G.

50. *Eidukonis v. Southeastern Pennsylvania Transportation Authority*, (3rd Cir, 88–1506, 1989).

51. Adapted from George F. Dreker, Ronald A. Ash, and Robert D. Bretz, "Benefit Coverage and Employee Cost: Critical Factors in Explaining Compensation Satisfaction," *Personnel Psychology* 41 (1988): 237–254.

52. Charles J. Whitaker, "The Value of Benefits," *HR Magazine*, April 1990, 83–85.

53. Tim Chauran, "Benefits Communication that Goes the Distance," *Personnel Journal*, January 1989, 70–71.

54. "Flexible Benefits: A Wave of the Future?" *Compensation and Benefits Review*, September/October 1989, 8.

55. J. Geisel, "Increases Smaller for Flex Plans," *Business Insurance*, January 1989, 26–27.

56. "Tough Choices: Extra Vacation or a Free Trip to the Dentist," *Finance Executive*, May 1989, 6–7.

57. Adapted from Lawrence J. Hicks and Jo Ann T. Fritsch, "A Win/Win Approach to Health-Care Cost Management," *Personnel Administrator*, April 1986, 109–116.

Employee and Labor Relations

A part of P/HR management is to provide employees with safe working environments and to acquire help for those with health problems. Healthy and safe employees are likely to be more productive than those affected by illness or unsafe working conditions. Every year organizations lose money because of illness, accidents, and injuries on the job. Suggestions for dealing with employee health and safety and some details of the Occupational Safety and Health Act are included in Chapter 16.

Employee rights and employer responsibilities have received increasing attention. Chapter 17 outlines the major issues in this area including such aspects as employment-at-will, employee handbooks as contracts, just cause, and employee privacy. P/HR policies, procedures, and rules are examined also.

Some organizations interact formally with their employees through unions. Chapter 18 provides a synopsis of the evolution of unionism and labor legislation in the United States. Even though union membership in the U.S. has declined, the process of unionization in an organization should be understood by all managers and P/HR staff members.

If an organization is unionized, a labor contract outlines the relationship between an employer and a union. In Chapter 19 the process of reaching a contract agreement, known as collective bargaining, and typical issues in collective bargaining are discussed. Included in all labor contracts is a grievance procedure that identifies how employee-employer problems are to be resolved.

Health and Safety

After you have read this chapter, you should be able to:

1. Define health and safety and explain their importance in an organization
2. Discuss three factors that affect health and safety in organizations
3. Explain the impact of four health problems in organizations
4. Identify how organizations can respond to employee alcoholism, drug abuse, and other health problems
5. Identify basic provisions of the Occupational Safety and Health Act of 1970
6. Describe OSHA record-keeping and inspection requirement, and five types of OSHA citations
7. Discuss both positive and negative problems with OSHA
8. Identify and briefly explain the basic components of a systems approach to safety

P/HR: Today *and* Tomorrow

Puff or Put Out That Cigarette?

The social acceptability of smoking had *increased* over the 50 years preceding the U.S. Surgeon General's first warning, issued in 1970, that smoking was a hazard to health. But the picture is changing. The last decade especially has seen a spate of published reports and advertisements by public service organizations about the health effects of smoking. Another major report by the Surgeon General has been issued on the effects of secondhand smoke. Today, a more militant nonsmoking population faces an increasingly defensive smoking population.

Arguments and rebuttals characterize the smoke-at-work controversy. Statistics are rampant. On the one hand, scientific studies (over 33,000 at last count) and health organizations contend that one-third of all cancer deaths, one-fourth of all heart disease, and 80 percent of all emphysema are attributable to smoking. Further, 50 percent of all cancer deaths among males in their working years are smoking related. Tobacco companies, on the other hand, still argue that scientific evidence does not support a link between smoking and cancer or heart disease. R. J. Reynolds Tobacco Company contends that the media are responsible for alarm "being translated into heightened social strife and unfair smoking legislation."

A multitude of state and local laws have been passed that deal with smoking in the workplace and public places. Passage of these laws have been viewed by many employers positively, as they relieve employers of the responsibility for making decisions on smoking issues.

The courts have been hesitant to address the smoking-at-work issue. They clearly prefer to let employers and employees work it out rather than prohibiting or supporting smoking. Although many smoking employees *do* complain initially when a smoking ban is instituted, there seems to be relatively little difficulty after a few weeks.

Perhaps some larger issues related to smoking still remain in the workplace since the best educated and most privileged are giving it up, while the less privileged continue to take it up. Some people argue that the potential for discrimination in both hiring and firing practices is hidden in this issue. Further, if employers have the right to hire only nonsmokers in order to cut their insurance and health-care costs, would they then also have the right to hire only those with no hereditary risk of cancer or heart disease?

Over 85 percent of all companies have "no smoking" areas and a majority of large firms have smoking policies to address employee health concerns. These policies vary a great deal. One example of an extreme policy is Baker Hughes Inc. of Houston, Texas, where smokers pay $10 a month to the company. The company's position is that employees who are smokers cost the employer the most for health care and should pay for it. Indeed, the estimated cost to employers has been estimated between $600 and $4,600 per smoker annually. Smokers have higher absenteeism rates, twice as many work-related accidents, and are 50 percent more likely to be hospitalized.

But Eleanor Wood, a 3 pack-a-day smoker who works for the Houston firm says: "Charge me, but charge the people who drink and have insurance claims as a result of alcoholism, people who are on other kinds of drugs, or anyone whose lifestyle isn't 100 percent pure and clean."[1]

"If only it weren't for the people always getting tangled up with the machinery . . . Earth would be an engineer's paradise."

Kurt Vonnegut

Employers are obligated to provide employees with a safe and healthy environment. Requiring them to work with unsafe equipment or in areas where hazards are not controlled is a highly questionable practice that has led to the passage of workplace safety laws. Managers also must ensure that employees are safety conscious and maintain good health. Both managers and P/HR specialists have responsibilities for health and safety in an organization. This chapter identifies ways in which organizations can maintain safe working environments for employees.

■■ ■ HEALTH AND SAFETY DEFINED

The terms *health* and *safety* are closely related. Although they are often used in the same context, a distinction should be made.

Health is a broader and somewhat more nebulous term than safety. A healthy person is one who is free of illness, injury, or mental and emotional problems that impair normal human activity. However, the question of exactly what is healthy or normal behavior is open to interpretation. Health management practices maintain the overall well-being of an individual.

Typically, **safety** concerns physical well-being instead of mental or emotional well-being. The main purpose of effective safety programs in organizations is to prevent work-related injuries and accidents.

Health and safety policies focus on the safe interaction between people and the work environment. Because many employers' efforts in the past were inadequate in providing healthy and safe work environments, Congress passed Occupational Safety and Health Act in 1970. This act has had a tremendous impact on the workplace; therefore, any person interested in P/HR management must develop a knowledge of the act's provisions and implications. The Occupational Health and Safety Administration (OSHA) administers the act.

Health and Safety Responsibilities

As Figure 16–1 indicates, the primary health and safety responsibilities in an organization usually fall on supervisors and managers. A P/HR manager or safety specialist can help investigate accidents, produce safety programs materials, and conduct formal safety training. However, department supervisors and managers play key roles in maintaining safe working conditions and a healthy work force. A supervisor in a ball bearing plant has several health and safety responsibilities: reminding employees to wear safety glasses; checking on the cleanliness of the work area; observing employees for any alcohol, drug, or emotional problems that may affect their work behavior; and recommending equipment changes (such as screens, railings, or other safety devices) to specialists in the organization.

A P/HR safety specialist in the same plant has other safety responsibilities: maintaining government-required health and safety records; coordinating a safety training class for new employees; assisting the supervisor in investigating an accident in which an employee was injured; and developing a plantwide safety communication

HEALTH
refers to a general state of physical, mental, and emotional well-being.

SAFETY
refers to protection of the physical well-being of people.

Figure 16–1
Health and Safety Responsibilities

P-HR UNIT	MANAGERS
■ Coordinates health and safety programs ■ Develops safety reporting system ■ Provides accident investigation expertise ■ Provides technical expertise on accident research and prevention	■ Monitor health and safety of employees daily ■ Coach employees to be safety conscious ■ Investigate accidents ■ Observe health and safety behavior of employees

program and informational materials. The interface between the supervisor and the P/HR specialist is crucial to a coordinated health and safety maintenance effort.

A Changing View of Safety

Before the passage of workers' compensation laws (see Chapter 15), an employee could *not* recover damages if:

■ The injury was caused by his or her negligence or the negligence of a fellow worker.
■ The injury happened because of hazards inherent in the job.
■ The worked died or became disabled as a result of occupational injury or disease.

Employers had always acted on the assumption that safety was the employee's responsibility. In 1911, with the passage of the first workers' compensation law in Wisconsin, the attitude of society began to change. Society's concerns were expressed by the passage of workers' compensation laws in all states and the Occupational Safety and Health Act at the national level. Employers once thought that accidents and occupational diseases were avoidable byproducts of work. This idea has been replaced with prevention and control concepts that minimize or eliminate health and safety risks and hazards in the workplace.

■■ ■■ ISSUES IN OCCUPATIONAL SAFETY

Tangible benefits of a well-managed safety program include: (1) reduction in insurance premiums, (2) savings of litigation costs, (3) fewer wages paid for lost time, (4) less expense in training new workers, (5) less overtime, and (6) greater productivity.

Every year employers lose an astounding amount of money and other resources because of accidents and the figures have increased since 1983. The following shows some recent figures on annual accident rates *per 100 employees* for the United States:

Total accidents	8.6
Total lost work cases	4.0
Total lost workdays	69.9

There were a total of 6.4 million injuries and illnesses and 3,300 workplace deaths for the reported year.[2] Safety and labor officials tie the rate of injury increase to competition and the pressure for more productivity. Smaller work crews, overtime, faster assembly lines, all equate to more *speed* in working and less concern for safety.[3]

Hazardous Jobs

Certain jobs and industries are more hazardous than others. Farming, mining, construction, and transportation are the most dangerous industries, in that order. The most dangerous single jobs are:[4]

- Timber logger
- Airline pilot
- Asbestos and insulation worker
- Structural metal worker
- Electrical power-line/cable installer
- Fire fighter
- Garbage collector
- Truck driver
- Bulldozer operator
- Earth driller

Criminal Prosecution of Executives

In an effort to assign individual responsibility for corporate practices, several legal cases across the country have taken aim at executives in companies that have had serious workplace injuries. In the Chicago Magnet Wire case, five senior executives in the firm were charged with aggravated battery, reckless conduct, and conspiracy. They were accused of allowing more than forty workers to become ill and suffer nerve and lung damage through exposure to hazardous chemicals at the company's plant. In the Film Recovery Systems Inc. case, murder charges were filed against three senior executives after a worker died from inhaling cyanide fumes. Both cases are on appeal.[5]

In New York, PYMM Thermometer Company owners were convicted on charges of assault and reckless endangerment for exposing workers to mercury. The verdict was overturned and is on appeal. In Austin, Texas, the president of Sabine Consolidated Inc. was convicted of criminally negligent homicide when two employees died in the collapse of a trench in which they were working. The case is on appeal.[6]

There is another side of the issue, of course. Employer groups contend that it is unfair for companies that comply with OSHA regulations to be prosecuted for criminal conduct. "The issue here is whether we have a clear standard for employers to follow or whether we are going to be at the mercy of the whims and caprices of every county attorney in the U.S." says Thomas Reid of the Illinois Manufacturing Association.[7]

Child Labor

Another safety concern is reflected in restrictions affecting younger workers, especially those under the age of 18. Child labor laws, found in Section XII of the Fair Labor Standards Act, set the minimum age for most employment at 16 years. For "hazardous" occupations, 18 years is the minimum. Figure 16–2 presents a list of 17 hazardous occupations.

The law is quite strict for 14–16 year-olds, who may essentially hold only clerical, office, and retail food service jobs, pump gas, or do errand and delivery work. They can work only between 7 A.M. and 7 P.M. during the school year, 3 hours per day on school days, and are restricted to an 8-hour day on weekends. These provisions do not apply to newspaper delivery, theatre performances, and children working for their parents in farming and similar occupations.

Many employers require age certificates for employees because the Fair Labor Standards Act places the responsibility on the employer to determine an individual's age. Asking for an age certificate helps an employer avoid unknowingly hiring

Figure 16–2
Child Labor and Hazardous Occupations

1. Manufacturing or storing explosives

2. Driving a motor vehicle and being an outside helper

3. Coal mining

4. Logging and sawmilling

5. Using power-driven woodworking machines*

6. Exposure to radioactive substances and to ionizing radiations

7. Operating power-driven hoisting apparatus

8. Operating power-driven metal-forming punching and shearing machines*

9. Mining, other than coal mining

10. Slaughtering, or meat packing, processing, or rendering*

11. Using power-driven bakery machines

12. Operating power-driven paper-products machines*

13. Manufacturing brick, tile, and related products

14. Using power-driven circular saws, band saws, and guillotine shears*

15. Wrecking, demolition, and shipbreaking operations

16. Roofing operations*

17. Excavation operations*

*In certain cases, the law provides exemptions for apprentices and student learners in these occupations.

SOURCE: Employment Standards Administration, Wage and Hour Division, U.S. Department of Labor, *Child Labor Requirements in Nonagricultural Occupations*. WH Publication No. 1330 (Washington D.C.: U.S. Government Printing Office).

someone who is too young to perform hazardous jobs. These certificates may be issued by a representative of a state labor department, education department, or by a local school official. In various states they are referred to as *age certificates, employment certificates, work permits*, or *working papers*. Figure 16-2 shows hazardous occupations as defined by Federal Law.

Recently, child labor has been rediscovered. About 500 federal agents conducted more than 3,400 investigations of child labor violations during a nationwide three-day probe. About 43 percent of employers were found to be in apparent violation. The major violations were with 14 and 15 years-olds working too many hours and 16 and 17 year-olds working hazardous jobs. The fast-food industry and New York's garment industry were those industries most frequently cited for violations.[8]

Worker Attitudes and Accidents

Attitudinal variables, as well as equipment and work design, affect accident rates. Attitudes toward working conditions, accidents, and safe work practices are very important because more problems are caused by careless employees than by machines or employer negligence.

At one time, workers who were dissatisfied with their jobs were thought to have higher accident rates. However, this assumption has been questioned in recent years. One study of accident proneness found that younger and less-experienced employees were involved in more injuries and accidents. This same study suggested

Researchers Michael Schuster and Susan Rhodes of Syracuse University examined the records at three New York manufacturing firms to see if there is a relationship between overtime and accidents.

The logic of a relationship between overtime and accidents is as follows: Fatigue based on physical factors rarely exists in today's industrial workplace. But fatigue, which is defined as boredom, occurs when a person is required to do the same tasks for a long period of time, and boredom is rather common. As fatigue of this kind increases, motivation is reduced; along with decreased motivation, workers' attention wanders and the likelihood of accidents increases.

The researchers examined 462 accidents and the amount of overtime preceding each in the three firms. As reported in *Industrial Relations*, the study results tentatively support the hypothesis that overtime work *is* related to accident incidence. Further, the more overtime worked, the more severe the accident appeared to be. In conclusion, the authors caution that this study is not the final work, although it is the first one using an individual level of analysis *and* looking at the overtime that preceded accidents.[9]

that there were some differences in personality and emotional characteristics between people who had no accidents and those who had repeated accidents.[10] Although employees' personalities, attitudes, and individual characteristics have an effect on accidents, the exact cause-and-effect relationship is difficult to establish.

BOREDOM AND MONOTONY.   Employees doing the same job repeatedly each day frequently become bored. They either begin to pay less attention to their tasks or they develop bad habits that can cause accidents and injuries, as the study in P/HR: Research indicates. Redesigning a job to relieve monotony is a way of dealing with worker boredom. Elements of job design such as job scope and job depth should be assessed continually.

Engineering Approach to Safety

Employers can prevent some accidents by designing machines, equipment, and work areas so that workers who daydream periodically or who perform mechanical jobs cannot injure themselves or others. Providing safety equipment and guards on machinery and installing emergency switches often forestall accidents. To prevent a punch-press operator from mashing her finger, a safety guard is attached to a machine so her hand cannot accidentally slip into the machine. Actions such as installing safety rails, keeping aisles clear, and installing adequate ventilation, lighting, or heating and air conditioning can all help make the work environment safer.

A **safety hierarchy** represents the order in which actions should be taken to eliminate danger effectively:[12]

- *First priority:* To eliminate hazard completely
- *Second priority:* To use safeguards
- *Third priority:* To use warning signs
- *Fourth priority:* To train and instruct
- *Fifth priority:* To prescribe personal protection

Notice that three of the five methods are engineering approaches to safety.

SAFETY HEIRARCHY
the order in which actions should be taken to eliminate work safety problems.

P/HR: Practice *and* Research

Cutting Corners, Losing Lives

On a drilling rig near Gillette, Wyoming, the top priority was saving time and money. The oil industry was deep in a depression and despite state safety regulations prohibiting the practice, Exeter Drilling Company began a test for oil and natural gas long before it was light enough to see. To have waited for daylight each day would have cost another $6,000,

an Exeter official claimed, because the rig and crew would sit idle until then. However, using artificial lighting raises the chances of a stray electrical spark igniting the hydrocarbons for which the crew was searching.

John E. Nelson, 39, was killed and four other people were injured in an explosion caused by such use of lighting. Also, just one month

after the fatal accident, a huge piece of drilling pipe came loose and crushed another Exeter employee to death. "In hurrying to do a job fast, someone must have done something in the wrong sequence," says Douglas Basey, Exeter's administrative manager. "You've got to cut corners out there."[11]

ERGONOMICS.   Ergonomics is a specialized field that has as its task the proper design of the work environment. Ergonomics comes from the Greek *ergon* meaning "work" and the suffix *-omics* meaning "management of." An ergonomist studies the physiological, psychological, and engineering design aspects of a job, including such factors as fatigue, lighting, tools, equipment layout, and placement of controls. Human factors engineering is a related field.

Behavioral Approach to Safety

Engineers approach safety from the perspective of redesigning the machinery or the work area. Industrial psychologists see safety differently. They are concerned with the proper match of people to jobs and emphasize employee training in safety methods, fatigue reduction, and health awareness.

Industrial psychologists with the St. Paul (insurance) Companies have conducted numerous field studies with thousands of employees. The results show a definite relationship between emotional factors, such as stress, and accidents.[13] Other studies point to the importance of individual differences, motivation, attitudes, and learning as key factors in controlling the human element in safety.

■ ■ ACCIDENT RATES AND COST

Occupational safety experts say that workplace safety has become less urgent to employers than it was. One argues that accident trends seem to run in cycles and lag by three to five years behind changes in federal safety policy.[14] The industries where safety conditions appear to have deteriorated most seem to be those that have been depressed or in which severe competition exists. P/HR: Practice shows how Exeter Drilling Company cut corners and lost lives.

Nationally, highway vehicle accidents account for 27 percent of the job-related deaths, heart attacks rank second as 12 percent, industrial vehicles accidents third at 11 percent, and electrocutions fourth at 10 percent. In addition, industrial accidents cost more than $32 billion each year in direct and indirect costs to employers.[15] Calculating the cost of accidents is desirable because top management can easily understand such data, and expenditures for improving worker health and safety are justified more easily.

▬ ▬ HEALTH

Employee health problems are inevitable—and varied. They can range from minor illnesses such as a cold to serious illnesses related to the jobs performed. Some employees have emotional problems; others have drinking or drug problems. Some problems are chronic; others are transitory. But all may affect organizational operations and individual employee productivity.

Four major health problems have direct relevance to P/HR management: physical illness, emotional illness, alcoholism, and drug abuse (see Figure 16–3). Employers who are concerned about maintaining a healthy work force must engage in problem solving in these areas. In the paragraphs that follow, these and other health-related issues are discussed.

Physical Health and Illness

Because physical illnesses often reduce an employee's ability to perform a job, most employers help employees who have physical illnesses and health problems by providing hospitalization and health insurance. But sound health programs focus on prevention as well as on treatment of illness.

Health and the Work Environment

Many people have heard of the health problems developed by asbestos workers, coal miners, and some chemical workers. Cancer, black lung disease, and radiation poisoning are among the many health concerns of employers and employees. For example, it has been estimated that over 150,000 U.S. workers in fifty-six different occupations are exposed to mercury on the job.[16]

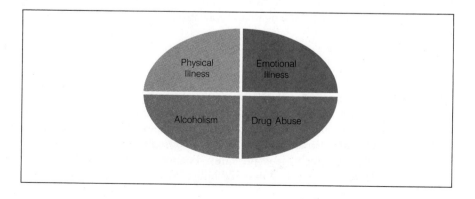

Figure 16–3
Major Health Problems

Other health problems can be caused by an environment that exposes workers to excessive noise or harmful lighting. New technology has created its own hazards. For instance, some employees who work at computer video display terminals have complained of a number of problems that have been labeled "VDT syndrome."[17]

Problems attributed to "VDT syndrome" include dizziness, eye strain, headaches, backaches, or muscle spasms. Skin problems, cataracts, and stress are also mentioned as part of VDT syndrome. However, there is little evidence to prove that such health problems are associated with VDT use.[18] Proper design of work stations and adjusting the height of chairs may eliminate some of the problems.[19]

Recent interest in VDT syndrome has spotlighted another area of concern: repetitive motion disorders, or cumulative trauma disorders. Thousands of repetitive tappings, grippings, or twistings can cause inflammation of tendons, nerves, blood vessels, and ligaments around the hand and forearm. The resulting disability, called *carpal tunnel syndrome*, is very painful and debilitating. Affecting a range of workers from typists to fish filleters to grocery checkers, repetitive motion disorders are getting significant attention.[20]

Threats to Reproductive Health

A very recent health concern is the threat to unborn children and a person's ability to reproduce that may be caused by exposure to certain chemical hazards in the workplace. In so-called "clean rooms," where computer chips are etched with acid and gases at Digital Equipment Corporation, miscarriage rates among women were 39 percent, nearly twice the national average. Responses to Digital's report have differed sharply. Digital "strongly urged" pregnant women to leave such jobs. AT&T has relocated all pregnant women out of computer chip reproduction jobs. Intel, National Semiconductor Corporation, and others have left the decision to the employees.[21]

In limited legal tests, it appears that the following should guide policies relating to reproductive health. If an employer has a fetal policy that applies to only one sex, it violates Title VII of the Civil Rights Act of 1964 unless the employer can show:[22]

■ Substantial harm exists.
■ The risk is *only* to one sex.
■ Employers demonstrate there are no acceptable alternatives.

It is far from certain that isolating females from chemical exposure risks ensures against reproductive and fetal health problems. Employees working with toxic chemicals face known reproductive risks, but employers are caught in a legal limbo between EEO concerns about job rights and concerns for the health of employees.[23]

Stress

The pressures of modern life, coupled with the demands of a job, can lead to emotional imbalances that are collectively labeled *stress*. Evidence of stress can be seen everywhere, from the 35-year-old executive who dies of a sudden heart attack to the dependable older worker who unexpectedly commits suicide. One indicator of stress is *hypertension* (high blood pressure). Twenty-five million U.S. workers suffer from hypertension, resulting in a $20 billion loss in wages and productivity every year.[24] Many experts believe that people who abuse alcohol and drugs do so to help reduce stress.

Until recently, most companies reasoned that if their managers could not handle stress, they were not tough enough for the job. But now many companies offer counseling programs aimed at stress reduction.[25]

Not all stress is unpleasant. To be alive means to respond to the stimulation of achievement and the excitement of a challenge. In fact, there is evidence that people *need* a certain amount of stimulation and that monotony can bring on some of the same problems as overwork. What is usually meant by the term *stress* is excessive stress, or distress.

WHAT IS STRESSFUL? Many factors determine what a person will find stressful. Those who have a hard time adjusting to change are more susceptible. Other factors, including biochemistry, physical strength, psychological makeup, values, and habits, affect individual reactions. Other major contributors to stress have been found to be:

- Lack of control
- Inability to predict
- Inaccurate perceptions of events
- Intense responsibility

Two recent cases have found that stress, including mental depression resulting in suicide, may be an "occupational illness" and compensable under workers' compensation statutes.[26] In a recent Maine case, a police officer, an 18-year veteran of the municipal police force, became depressed over his failure to be promoted, and committed suicide. Evidence introduced before the state Workers' Compensation Appeal Board confirmed that the officer became severely depressed over this failure and disappointment was a major factor in his resultant suicide. The court found suicide to be a compensable claim where the claimant establishes a causal connection between the work-related activity and the resulting death.

A Nebraska case also allowed compensation benefits to be awarded to an employee who suffered severe anxiety and mental depression following a work-related injury. The Supreme Court agreed with the Workers' Compensation Court's finding that the mental depression was either caused by or aggravated by the accident. The decision relied on several earlier Nebraska cases that allowed the compensation court to consider all factors, mental and physical, in determining the amount of compensation to which the employee was entitled.

STRESS: A SURVEY. A survey done for the *Wall Street Journal* uncovered several interesting facts about stress and business.[27] Of executives who do complain of stress, a large percentage are young, suggesting that as people grow older they may learn to handle stress better (or perhaps people who do not handle stress well do not grow older).

Executives in the survey attributed more stress to certain industries. Commodity trading, advertising, and investment banking were considered by many to be stressful industries. Executives cited employees under their direction as the biggest cause of stress in large and middle-sized organizations. At smaller firms, financial problems were the main source. Strategies used by executives to cope with stress can include physical exercise (golf, tennis, hunting or fishing, aerobics, and running), a change of scene, reading, and hobbies.[28]

MANAGEMENT'S ROLE.   When an emotional problem (stress-related or otherwise) becomes so severe that it disrupts an employee's ability to function normally, the employee should be directed to appropriate professionals for help. Because emotional problems are difficult to diagnose, supervisors and managers should not become deeply involved. If a worker is emotionally upset because of marital difficulties, a supervisor should not personally try to solve the employee's problems. Even though most supervisors and managers are concerned about employees' problems, they should realize that appropriate professionals are better qualified to help troubled employees.

Employee Assistance Programs

EMPLOYEE-ASSISTANCE PROGRAM (EAP) provides counseling and other help to employees having emotional, physical, or other personal problems.

One method that organizations are using to respond to employees' emotional, physical, and personal problems is an **employee assistance program (EAP)**. In such a program, an employer establishes a liaison relationship with a social service counseling agency. Employees who have problems may then contact the agency, either voluntarily or by employer referral, for assistance with a broad range of problems. Counseling costs are paid for by the employer in total or up to a pre-established limit.

Employee assistance programs are attempts to help employees with their most difficult problems. Some P/HR managers feel that EAPs make their other P/HR programs more effective. For example, in one large company the vice president of personnel found that much of his department's time was being consumed by such problems as employee anxiety reactions, suicide attempts, alcohol- and drug-related absences, and family disturbances. Further, the medical department was not able to provide accurate information on whether affected employees could successfully return to work. The vice president decided an EAP might save a great deal of time and money.

Increased interest in EAPs is due in part to the increase in the incidence of physical and emotional problems in the working population. Slightly less than half the companies responding to one survey offer EAPs. Median cost to the company is about $18 per worker.[29]

Alcoholism

Alcoholism is costly. It has been estimated that problem drinkers on payrolls cost American industry approximately $89.5 billion a year in lost production, mismanagement of resources, sick pay, and absenteeism. Up to 10 percent of the American work force suffers from various degrees of alcoholism.[30] Alcoholism and other substance abuse problems rank at the top of the problems dealt with in employee assistance programs (EAPs) (see Figure 16–4).

ALCOHOLISM AND EAPS.   EAPs got their start as alcohol treatment programs.[31] Because of the human and financial costs of the problem, management in a growing number of organizations is sponsoring programs to deal with alcoholic managers and workers. In this way, employers are able to retain otherwise good workers disabled by drinking. Usually, these programs are supported enthusiastically by unions. Insurance companies have been active in offering comprehensive programs to help treat alcoholism. The Kemper, Equitable, Traveler's, and Prudential insurance companies have employee programs that classify alcoholism as a treatable

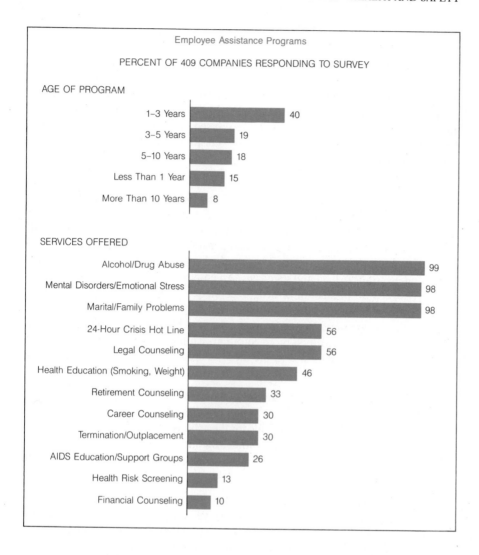

Figure 16–4
**Problems Addressed by Employee
Assistance Programs**

SOURCE: SHRM–BNA survey, 1990.

disease. The director of an alcoholism assistance program for Union Pacific Railroad reports that more than 1,500 employees have used the program. The success rate has been about 86 percent.[32]

The United States is not the only country with alcohol-related problems. The Soviet Union recently cracked down on its twin (and related) productivity problems: absenteeism and alcoholism. Now anyone found drunk on the job can be fired and has to pay for damaged goods and lost production.

Managers and supervisors should encourage employees with drinking problems to seek specialized treatment.[33] This treatment can be made available through an EAP, a cooperative program between an employer and a union, a private agency, state or local health and social service agencies, or voluntary organizations such as Alcoholics Anonymous.

Assisting employees who have drinking problems is part of good P/HR management. Although some alcoholic employees may resist treatment at first, alcohol rehabilitation programs generally have had excellent success rates. Instead of immediately firing employees with a drinking problem, employers may confront them, which helps alcoholics admit their problem. They then can be directed to a treatment program.[34]

Drug Abuse

Drug abuse is pervasive throughout society, from the inner-city ghetto to the affluent suburb and from legal drugs, such as barbituates and tranquilizers, to illegal hard drugs, such as heroin and crack cocaine. Some organizations have found employees selling drugs to other employees at work. Management at one computer firm discovered a drug ring in which employees grossed $10,000 a week. In a California firm some employees were observed drying cocaine in a microwave oven in the company cafeteria.[35]

DEALING WITH EMPLOYEE DRUG PROBLEMS.   Managers faced with employee drug abuse should be aware of drug-induced changes in an employee's behavior. Possible tip-offs to drug abuse are excessive absenteeism, increased tardiness, decreased job performance, and unexplained personality and behavior changes.[36]

Chemical dependency or abuse of controlled substances is considered a "handicap" under various federal and state laws. An employer cannot discriminate against employees because of alcohol or drug dependency if, after reasonable accommodation for their condition, they can do the job despite the handicap.

However, requirements that employees submit to blood tests, urinalysis, or polygraph tests are becoming much more common. Employers are willing to risk battles with employee-rights advocates in the areas of drug and alcohol abuse for several reasons:

1. Employees who are substance abusers cost more to keep, are more often involved in accidents, and are more likely to require discipline.
2. Employers are frequently held liable for the actions of employees who are known (or should have been known) to be under the influence of chemical substances.
3. Security concerns, including theft and confidential information, are greater with substance abusers.

Some drug-screening methods are problematic. For example, general tests for urine screening are very imprecise and positive results may discriminate against individuals, including those who once had drug problems but have overcome them. The issue of protecting the rights of employees is discussed in greater detail in Chapter 17.

Obviously, smoking marijuana occasionally is a different matter from being hooked on heroin. To address drug problems, employers should: (1) develop an awareness of drug problems and (2) develop policies and responses to cope with drug abuse. Because of increasing evidence that links drug abuse with accidents or shoddy work, more organizations are addressing the problem.

Other employers, although alarmed by the consequences of substance abuse, do not want to create an investigative atmosphere. These employers believe that instituting employee assistance programs and quick confrontation are more appropriate actions. However, companies doing business with the federal government must ensure that they have drug-free workplaces.[37]

AIDS

Employers are increasingly confronted by the problems associated with employees having AIDS. Obviously, there are health risks to the person with AIDS and the eventual decline in productivity and attendance brought on by the inevitable diseases that follow. Potentially much greater problems exist with the fear and panic in the workplace born of misunderstanding and misinformation. A survey conducted by the Georgia Institute of Technology underscored the problems stemming from misinformation, rumor, and myth generated by AIDS. Two-thirds of all respondents said they would be concerned about sharing a bathroom with a person with AIDS. Nearly half expressed concern about using the same cafeteria, and more than a third expressed unwillingness to use the same office equipment. Comments Georgia Tech professor David M. Herald, "If people are 'catatonic' because they have a co-worker with AIDS, the impact on productivity and efficiency is going to be great."[38]

Very few firms have a policy to deal with AIDS. The firms that have lost an employee are more likely to have a policy than those who have not, by 35 to 8 percent according to another survey. Nearly 56 percent said they did not believe a uniform policy to be possible.[39]

Many companies are unwilling to deal with the HR management problems involved with an AIDS-infected staff member. No matter what experts might say, an employee with AIDS, whether on the shop floor or in the executive offices, creates feelings of anxiety and unrest among other employees, suppliers, and customers. To meet this problem and yet address the needs of an afflicted employee, some companies are electing to continue to pay the employee's full salary, medical, and retirement benefits on the stipulation they not return to work.

Many companies feel that it is unnecessary to adopt specific policies that deal solely with AIDS for the following reasons: (1) They do not want to draw attention to the problem and unnecessarily alarm employees. (2) Current company policy on life-threatening illnesses probably covers the situation, so there is no reason to treat AIDS any different from any other illness. (3) A specific AIDS policy may prove too restrictive since flexibility is needed as changes in scientific knowledge and the law occur.[40]

Wellness Programs

Unlike EAPs that deal with problems after they have occurred, corporate wellness programs are designed to maintain or improve employee health before problems arise. Employer desires to improve productivity, decrease absenteeism, and put a lid on health costs have come together in the "wellness" movement. Wellness programs encourage self-directed lifestyle changes. Early wellness programs were aimed at reducing the risk of disease. The newer programs have emphasized healthy lifestyles and environment.[41]

Specific components of wellness programs may include physical fitness, hypertension control, nutrition and weight control, smoking cessation, and stress management. Organizations have entered the "wellness business," not because they have suddenly developed a more active social conscience, but because in one recent year business spent $65 billion in group life and health insurance premiums. Much of that money goes to finance care after emergencies (like heart attacks) that are, at least to some degree, preventable.

Almost half of all worker deaths are from cardiovascular diseases, such as heart attacks or strokes. But employers requiring employees to participate in wellness programs can make a difference. Two examples are instructive. In Belgium 19,400 factory workers (men between the ages of 40 and 59) were divided into two groups. Men in group A were counseled in smoking reduction, exercise, cholesterol intake, and weight and blood pressure control. Group B got no such counseling. After five years, group A showed a death rate 17.5 percent lower than group B and a heart attack rate 24.5 percent lower.

An experiment in Mankato, Minnesota, aimed at reducing heart disease in that city through counseling and publicity. Five hundred adults each year were randomly chosen to have their cholesterol levels, blood pressure, and other health indicators checked. Classes in exercise, eating patterns, and smoking withdrawal were offered, and the school system began a physical education curriculum that promotes cardiovascular fitness.

Two companies in Mankato have begun a similar program companywide. First National Bank of Mankato imposed a ban on employee smoking during office hours. It also sponsored exercise classes. Hubbard Milling is working toward eliminating smoking at work. This firm also caters "health" lunches, requires managers to take annual physical exams, and subsidizes exercise programs and weight-loss counseling. While the results are not yet known, early indications are that the wellnessess effort is paying off for employers and employees in Mankato.

Many agree that wellness programs will become increasingly popular as employers try to reduce health-costs. Some evidence exists that such programs are associated with improved health, reduced absenteeism, turnover, and stress, although not conclusively.[42]

■ ■ OCCUPATIONAL SAFETY AND HEALTH ACT

The Occupational Safety and Health Act, which became effective in 1971, was passed "to assure so far as possible every working man or woman in the Nation safe and healthful working conditions and to preserve our human resources."[43] Every employer engaged in commerce who has one or more employees is covered by the act. Farmers having fewer than ten employees are exempt from the act. Covered under other health and safety acts are employers in specific industries such as coal mining. Federal, state, and local government employees are covered by separate provisions or statutes.

Basic Provisions

The act established the Occupational Safety and Health Administration, known as OSHA. The act also established the National Institute of Occupational Safety and Health (NIOSH) as a supporting body to do research and develop standards.

ENFORCEMENT STANDARDS.   To implement the act, specific standards were established regulating equipment and working environment. The Occupational Safety and Health Administration often uses national standards developed by engineering and quality control groups. Employers are required to meet the provisions and standards under OSHA. Figure 16–5 gives examples of some specific OSHA standards.

"GENERAL DUTY" CLAUSE.   Section 5a(1) of the act is known as the "general duty" clause. This section requires that in areas in which no standards have been adopted, the employer has a *general duty* to provide safe and healthy working conditions. Employers who know of, or who should reasonably know of, unsafe or unhealthy conditions can be cited for violating this clause. The existence of

§ 1910.151 Medical services and first aid.

(a) The employer shall ensure the ready availability of medical personnel for advice and consultation on matters of plant health.

(b) In the absence of an infirmary, clinic, or hospital in near proximity to the workplace which is used for the treatment of all injured employees, a person or persons shall be adequately trained to render first aid. First aid supplies approved by the consulting physician shall be readily available.

(c) Where the eyes or body of any person may be exposed to injurious corrosive materials, suitable facilities for quick drenching or flushing of the eyes and body shall be provided within the work area for immediate emergency use.

§ 1910.157 Portable fire extinguishers.

(a) General requirements—(1) Operable condition. Portable extinguishers shall be maintained in a fully charged and operable condition, and kept in their designated places at all times when they are not being used.

(2) Location. Extinguishers shall be conspicuously located where they will be readily accessible and immediately available in the event of fire. They shall be located along normal paths of travel.

(3) Marking of location. Extinguishers shall not be obstructed or obscured from view. In large rooms, and in certain locations where visual obstruction cannot be completely avoided, means shall be provided to indicate the location and intended use of extinguishers conspicuously.

(4) Marking of extinguishers. If extinguishers intended for different classes of fire are grouped, their intended use shall be marked conspicuously to insure choice of the proper extinguisher at the time of a fire.

(5) Temperature range. Extinguishers shall be suitable for use within a temperature range of at least 40° to 120° Fahrenheit.

SOURCE: General Industry Standards, USDOL Pamphlet OSHA NO. 2206, OSHA Safety & Health STDS (29CFR 1910).

Figure 16–5
Sample OSHA Standards

standard practices or of a trade association code, which is not included in OSHA standards, often is used as the basis for citations under the "general duty" clause.

Employers are responsible for knowing about and informing their employees of safety and health standards established by OSHA and for putting up OSHA posters in prominent places. In addition, they are required to enforce the use of personal protective equipment and to provide safety communications to make employees aware of safety considerations. Employees who report safety violations to OSHA cannot be punished or discharged by their employers.

HAZARD COMMUNICATION.   The federal Hazard Communication Standard requires manufacturers, importers, distributors, and users of hazardous chemicals to evaluate, classify, and label these substances. Employers must also make available to employees, their representatives, and health professionals information about hazardous substances. The "right to know" has survived legal challenges from some industry and union groups. The new regulations were held to be a "standard" within the meaning of the Occupational Safety and Health Act.[44] The right to know of hazards is covered in more detail with employee rights in the next chapter.

REFUSING UNSAFE WORK.   Both union and nonunion workers have refused to work when the work was unsafe. Although such actions may appear illegal, in many cases they are not.

Two important Supreme Court cases have shed light on this issue. In "*Whirlpool v. Marshall*" (1980), employees and unions won a major victory. The U.S. Supreme

Court unanimously ruled that workers have the right to walk off a job if they believe it is hazardous without fear of reprisal from the employer. The Court ruled that "employees have the right not to perform an assigned task because of a reasonable apprehension of health or serious injury coupled with a reasonable belief that no less drastic alternative is available."[45] *Gateway Coal v. the United Mine Workers* clarified the necessary requirements by which employees could refuse unsafe work.[46] Current legal conditions for refusing work because of safety concerns are:

- The employee's fear is objectively reasonable.
- The employee tried to get the dangerous condition corrected.
- Using normal procedures to solve the problem has not worked.

Record-Keeping Requirements

The Occupational Safety and Health Administration established a standard national system for recording occupational injuries, accidents, and fatalities. Employers are generally required to maintain an annual detailed record of the various types of accidents for inspection by OSHA representatives and for submission to the agency.

Employers who have had good safety records in the previous years and who have less than ten employees are not required to keep detailed records. Only those small organizations meeting the following conditions must complete OSHA form 200, the basic reporting document:

- Firms having frequent hospitalization injuries or illnesses
- Firms having work-related deaths
- Firms included in OSHA's annual labor statistics survey

No one knows how many industrial accidents go unreported. It may be many more than anyone suspects, despite the fact that OSHA has now increased its surveillance of accident-reporting records. OSHA guidelines state that facilities whose accident record is less than the national average rarely need to be inspected, which gave organizations an incentive to become lax with safety standards. While investigating a death at Chrysler's Belvedere, Illinios, plant, OSHA inspectors found that 812 job-related injuries were not reported in a one-year period. The plant had shown an unusually low number of injuries during that time. Chrysler representatives said that the charges were based on "interpretations of government guidelines on the handling of paperwork." Nevertheless, Chrysler agreed to pay OSHA fines of over $200,000.[47]

ACCIDENT FREQUENCY RATE.   Accident frequency and severity rates must be calculated. Regulations from OSHA require organizations to calculate injury frequency rates per 100 full-time employees on an annual basis. The accident frequency rate is figured as follows:

$$\frac{N}{EH} \times 200,000$$

where N   =   number of occupational injuries and illnesses
EH   =   total hours worked by all employees during reference year
200,000   =   base for 100 full-time equivalent workers (working 40 hours per week 50 weeks per year)

Employers compute accident severity rates by figuring the number of lost-time cases, the number of lost workdays, and the number of deaths. These figures are

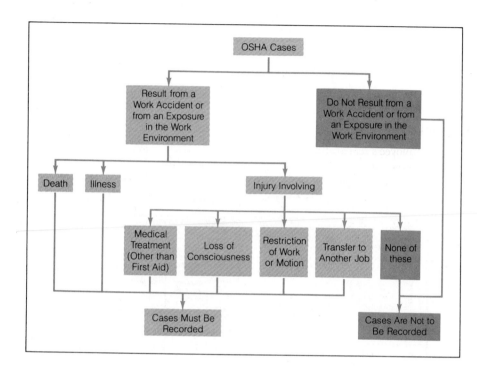

Figure 16–6
Guide to Recordability of Cases Under the Occupational Safety and Health Act

SOURCE: U.S. Department of Labor Statistics, *What Every Employee Needs to Know About OSHA Record Keeping* (Washington D.C.: U.S. Government Printing Office).

then related to total work hours per 100 full-time employees, and compared with industrywide rates and other employers' rates.

REPORTING INJURIES/ILLNESSES. There are four types of injuries or illnesses defined by the act:

1. *Injury- or illness-related deaths*
2. *Lost-time or disability injuries:* disabling or job-related injuries that cause an employee to miss his or her regularly scheduled work on the day following the accident.
3. *Medical care injuries:* injuries that require treatment by a physician but do not cause an employee to miss a regularly scheduled work turn
4. *Minor injuries:* injuries that require first-aid treatment and do not cause an employee to miss the next regularly scheduled work turn

The record-keeping requirements under OSHA are summarized in Figure 16–6. Notice that only minor injuries do not have to be recorded for OSHA. Managers may attempt to avoid reporting lost-time or medical care injuries. For example, if several managers are trained in first-aid, some injuries can be treated on the work site. In one questionable situation, an employee's back injuries were treated with heat packs by the plant P/HR manager to avoid counting the accident as a medical care injury. (Figure 16–7 is the OSHA form that employers use to summarize annual injuries and illnesses.)

Employers sometimes move injured employees to other jobs to avoid counting an injury as a lost-time injury. For example, if a seamstress in a clothing factory injured her hand on the job so that she could not operate her sewing machine, her employer might ask her to carry thread to other operators and perform other "make-work" jobs so that she did not miss work, and the injury would not have to be reported. Current regulations attempt to control this kind of subterfuge by

Figure 16–7
OSHA Form 200

U.S. Department of Labor

For Calendar Year 19 _____   Page ____ of____

	Form Approved
Company Name	O.M.B. No. 1220-0029
Establishment Name	
Establishment Address	

Extent of and Outcome of INJURY						Type, Extent of, and Outcome of ILLNESS												
Fatalities	Nonfatal Injuries					Type of Illness							Fatalities	Nonfatal Illnesses				
Injury Related	Injuries With Lost Workdays				Injuries Without Lost Workdays	CHECK Only One Column for Each Illness *(See other side of form for terminations or permanent transfers.)*							Illness Related	Illnesses With Lost Workdays				Illnesses Without Lost Workdays
Enter DATE of death. Mo./day/yr.	Enter a CHECK if injury involves days away from work, or days of restricted work activity, or both.	Enter a CHECK if injury involves days away from work.	Enter number of DAYS away from work.	Enter number of DAYS of restricted work activity.	Enter a CHECK if no entry was made in columns 1 or 2 but the injury is recordable as defined above.	Occupational skin diseases or disorders	Dust diseases of the lungs	Respiratory conditions due to toxic agents	Poisoning (systemic effects of toxic materials)	Disorders due to physical agents	Disorders associated with repeated trauma	All other occupational illnesses	Enter DATE of death. Mo./day/yr.	Enter a CHECK if illness involves days away from work, or days of restricted work activity, or both.	Enter a CHECK if illness involves days away from work.	Enter number of DAYS away from work.	Enter number of DAYS of restricted work activity.	Enter a CHECK if no entry was made in columns 8 or 9.
(1)	(2)	(3)	(4)	(5)	(6)	(a)	(b)	(c)	(d)	(e)	(f)	(g)	(8)	(9)	(10)	(11)	(12)	(13)
										(7)								

INJURIES   ILLNESSES

Certification of Annual Summary Totals By _____ Title _____ Date _____

OSHA No. 200   **POST ONLY THIS PORTION OF THE LAST PAGE NO LATER THAN FEBRUARY 1.**

requiring employees to perform the same type of job they performed before being injured.

Inspection Requirements

The act provides for on-the-spot inspection by OSHA agents, known as *compliance officers* or *inspectors*. Under the original act, an employer could not refuse entry to an OSHA inspector. Further, the original act prohibited a compliance officer from notifying an organization before an inspection. Instead of allowing an employer to "tidy up," this *no-knock provision* permits inspection of normal operations. The provision was challenged in numerous court suits. Finally, in 1978, the U.S. Supreme Court ruled on the issue.

MARSHALL V. BARLOW'S INC. An Idaho plumbing and air conditioning firm, Barlow's, refused entry to an OSHA inspector.[48] The employer argued that the no-knock provision violated the Fourth Amendment of the U.S. Constitution, which deals with "unreasonable search and seizure." The government argued that the no-knock provision was necessary for enforcement of the act and that the Fourth Amendment did not apply to a business situation in which employees and customers have access to the firm.

The Supreme Court rejected the government's arguments and held that safety inspectors must produce a search warrant if an employer refuses to allow an inspector into the plant voluntarily. However, the Court ruled that an inspector does not have to prove probable cause to obtain a search warrant. A warrant can be obtained if a search is part of a general enforcement plan.

CONDUCT OF INSPECTION. When the compliance officer arrives, the manager should request to see the inspector's credentials. After entering, the OSHA officer typically requests a meeting with the top representative or manager in the organization. The officer also may request that a union representative, an employee, and a company representative be present as the inspection is conducted. The OSHA inspector checks organizational records to see if they are being maintained and the number of accidents that have occurred. Following this review of the safety records, the inspector conducts an on-the-spot inspection and may use a wide variety of equipment to test compliance with the standards. After the inspection, the compliance officer can issue citations for violations of standards and provisions of the act.

SAFETY CONSULTATION. In conjunction with state and local governments, OSHA has established a safety consultation service. An employer can contact the state agency and have an authorized safety consultant conduct an advisory inspection. The consultant cannot issue citations or penalties and generally is prohibited from providing OSHA with any information obtained during the consultation visit. Such a visit provides an employer with safety information to help prevent future difficulties when OSHA does conduct an inspection.

Citations and Violations

The OSHA violation and citation notices issued depend on the severity and extent of the problems and on the employer's knowledge of them. There are basically five types, ranging from minimal to severe.

DE MINIMIS. A *de minimis* condition is one that does not have a direct and immediate relationship to the employees' safety or health. A citation is not issued but the condition is mentioned to the employer. Lack of doors on toilet stalls is an example of a *de minimis* violation.

OTHER-THAN-SERIOUS. Other-than-serious violations could have an impact on employees' health or safety but probably would not cause death or serious harm. Having loose ropes in a work area on which people could trip and hurt themselves might be classified as a nonserious violation.

SERIOUS. When a condition could probably cause death or serious physical harm, and the employer should know of the condition, a serious violation is issued. Examples are the absence of a protective screen on a lathe (which could easily allow an employee to mangle a hand) or the lack of a blade guard on an electric saw.

WILLFUL AND REPEATED. Willful and repeated violation citations are issued to employers who have been previously cited for violations. If an employer knows about a safety violation or has been warned of a violation and does not correct the problem, a second citation is issued. The penalty for a willful and repeated violation can be as high as $10,000. If death results from a willful violation, a jail term of six months can be imposed on responsible executives or managers.

IMMINENT DANGER. If there is reasonable certainty that the condition will cause death or serious physical harm if it is not corrected immediately, an imminent danger citation is issued and a notice posted by an inspector. Imminent danger situations are handled on the highest priority basis. They are reviewed by a regional OSHA director and must be corrected immediately. If the condition is serious enough and the employer does not cooperate, a representative of OSHA may go to a federal judge and obtain an injunction to close the company until the condition is corrected. The absence of any guard railings to prevent an employee from falling three stories into heavy machinery could be classified as an imminent danger violation.

PENALTIES. In place of a rather rigid system of imposing fines, OSHA inspectors now use a regulated penalty calculation process. This process, which is somewhat complex, considers the probability of occurrences and the severity of possible injury. Then a penalty is calculated.

Fines are levied only if more than ten violations (except *de minimis* conditions) are found. Thus, a machine shop owner who has eight other-than-serious violations is not penalized if unsafe conditions are corrected by the next inspection. On the other hand, USX Corp. was fined a record $7.3 million for more than 2,000 violations.[49]

Effects of OSHA

By making employers and employees more aware of safety and health considerations, OSHA has had a significant impact on organizations. But how effective the act has been is not clear. It does appear that OSHA regulations have been able to reduce the number of accidents and injuries in some cases. Some studies have shown that OSHA has had a positive impact; others have shown that OSHA has had no impact.

Criticisms of OSHA

Most employers agree with the act's intent to provide healthy and safe working conditions for all employees. However, criticism of OSHA has emerged for several reasons.

VAGUE STANDARDS.   Some OSHA standards are vague, especially the "general duty" clause. It is difficult for an employer to know whether or not it is complying. In one case, a standard required that plants with a certain number of workers have qualified medical personnel "in near proximity" to the work area. This standard has been the subject of several OSHA violations and cases. What is meant by "near proximity"? Is it in the work area? In the plant? Is it a hospital ten minutes away?

HIGHLY TECHNICAL RULES.   OSHA rules often are very complicated and technical. Small business owners and managers who do not have a safety specialist on staff find the standards difficult to read and understand. The presence of many minor standards also hurts OSHA's credibility. To counter such criticism, OSHA has revoked about 900 minor or confusing standards.

NEED FOR SAFETY COUNSELING.   Another major criticism is that an OSHA inspector cannot serve as a safety counselor. However, with the establishment of the consultation program this criticism has lost some of its strength. Officials from OSHA also can meet with employers who are designing and building new facilities to review blueprints and plans. This review enables the employers to design their facilities to comply with OSHA regulations.

COSTS OF COMPLIANCE.   An additional concern is that the cost of correcting violations may be prohibitive for many employers. For a small company to make major structural changes in a building may be financially impossible. The cost of compliance may not be realistic given the cost of the violation.

   In one case, the U.S. Supreme Court indicated that OSHA regulations limiting the exposure of workers to cotton dust do not have to meet a cost–benefit test. The decision in the case indicated that congressional intent of establishing OSHA was to provide maximum worker protection. Use of a cost–benefit approach would lead to less protection because of high costs, which would violate the law.[50] As a result of this decision, some efforts have been made to amend the act to include cost–benefit considerations. But such efforts have been strongly resisted by the AFL–CIO and other labor organizations.

PROBABILITY OF INSPECTION.   Because OSHA has so many work sites to inspect, many employers have only a relatively small probability of being inspected. Some suggest that many employers pay little attention to OSHA enforcement efforts for this reason. Labor unions and others have criticized OSHA and Congress for not providing enough inspectors.

■■ ■ A SYSTEMS APPROACH TO SAFETY

Effective safety management considers the type of safety problems, accidents, employees, and technology in the organizational setting. Furthermore, the systems approach to safety recognizes the importance of the human element in safety. Simply attempting to engineer machines, without dealing with the behavioral reactions of employees and without trying to encourage safe behavior, compartmentalizes the safety effort. Several basic components are involved in a systematic approach to safety.

Organizational Commitment

Any systematic approach to safety begins with organizational commitment to a comprehensive safety effort. This effort should be coordinated from the top to include all members of the organization. It should also be reflected in management's actions and work. One study of five plants that won safety awards showed that "active management involvement in occupational safety makes the major difference between success and failure."[42] If the president of a small electrical manufacturing firm does not wear a hard hat in the manufacturing shop, he can hardly expect to enforce a requirement that all employees wear hard hats in the shop. Unfortunately, sincere support by top management is often missing from many safety programs.

Coordinated Safety Efforts

Once a commitment is made to safety, planning efforts must be coordinated, with duties assigned to supervisors, managers, safety specialists, and P/HR specialists. Naturally, the duties vary according to the size of the organization and the industry. For this reason, it is impossible to suggest a single proper mixture of responsibilities. The focus of any systematic approach to safety is the continued diligence of workers, managers, and other personnel. Employees who are not reminded of safety violations, who are not encouraged to be safety conscious, or who violate company safety rules and policies are not likely to be safe employees.

SAFETY COMMITTEES.   Workers frequently are involved in safety planning through safety committees, often composed of workers from a variety of levels and departments. At least one member of the committee is usually from the P/HR unit. A safety committee generally has a regularly scheduled meeting, has specific responsibilities for conducting safety reviews, and makes recommendations for changes necessary to avoid future accidents.

The safety emphasis must be consistently made and enforced. Properly coordinated efforts between P/HR units and managers will aid in developing safety-conscious and safety-motivated employees.

EMPLOYEE SAFETY MOTIVATION.   Encouraging employees to keep safety standards continuously in mind while performing their jobs is difficult. Often, employees think that safety measures are bothersome and unnecessary until an accident or injury occurs. For example, requiring employees to wear safety glasses in a laboratory may be necessary most of the time. But if the glasses are awkward, employees may resist using them, even when they know they should have protection. Some employees may have worked for years without them and think this new requirement is a nuisance.

SAFETY DISCIPLINE.   Enforcing safety rules and disciplining violators are important components of safety efforts. Frequent reinforcement of the need for safe behavior and feedback on positive safety practices are extremely effective in improving worker safety.

Consistent enforcement has been used by employers as a defense against OSHA citations. In one situation, a utility foreman was electrocuted while operating an overhead crane. However, the company was exonerated because it had consistently enforced safety rules and penalized violators. The employee who was killed violated a safety rule for grounding equipment even though the company had given him regular safety training, had posted signs prominently, and had warned all employees about grounding equipment. The OSHA district director ruled that the employee's action was an isolated incident and management was not the blame.

SAFETY INCENTIVES.   Some organizations have used safety contests and given incentives to employees for safe work behavior. Jewelry, clocks, watches, and even vacation trips have been given as a reward to employees for good safety records. For example, safe driving awards for drivers in a trucking firm have been quite successful in generating safety consciousness. Belt buckles and lapel pins are especially popular with the drivers.

SAFETY TRAINING AND COMMUNICATIONS.   One way to encourage employee safety is to involve all employees at various times in safety training sessions and committee meetings and to have these meetings frequently. In addition to safety training, continuous communication programs to develop safety consciousness are necessary. Posting safety policies and rules is part of this effort. Contests, incentives, and posters are all ways employers can heighten safety awareness.[54] Changing safety posters, continually updating bulletin boards, and posting safety information in visible areas are also recommended. Merely sending safety memos is not enough. Safety films and videotapes are common ways to communicate safety ideas.

SAFETY INSPECTION.   It is not necessary to wait for an OSHA inspector to inspect the work area for safety hazards. Such inspections may be done by a safety committee or by the safety coordinator. They should be done on a regular basis because OSHA may inspect organizations with above-average lost workday rates more frequently.

In investigating the *scene* of an accident, it is important to determine the physical and environmental conditions that contributed to the accident. Poor lighting, poor ventilation, and wet floors are all possible considerations at the scene. Investigation at the scene should be done as soon as possible after the accident to ensure that conditions under which the accident occurred have not changed significantly. One way to obtain an accurate view of the accident scene is with photographs or videotapes.

The second phase of the investigation is the *interview* of the injured employee, his or her supervisor, and witnesses to the accident. The interviewer attempts to determine what happened and how the accident was caused. These interviews may also generate some suggestions on how to prevent similar accidents in the future.

The third phase of any good accident investigation is the *accident investigation report*. This report form provides the necessary data required by OSHA.

As a part of an investigation, recommendations should be made on how the accident could have been prevented and what changes could prevent further accidents. Identifying why an accident occurred is useful, but identifying steps to prevent it from occurring again is an important part of a systematic safety program.

ACCIDENT RESEARCH.   Closely related to accident investigation is research to determine ways to prevent accidents. Employing safety engineers or having outside experts evaluate the safety of working conditions is useful. If a large number of the same accidents seem to occur in an organizational unit, a safety education training program may be necessary to emphasize safe working practices. For example, a publishing company reported a greater than average number of back injuries caused by employees lifting boxes. Safety training on the proper way to lift heavy objects was then initiated to prevent back injuries.

Evaluation of Safety Efforts

Organizations need to monitor their safety efforts. Just as organizational accounting records are audited, periodic audits of a firm's safety efforts should be made also. Accident and injury statistics should be compared with previous accident patterns to determine if any significant changes have occurred. This analysis should be designed to measure progress in safety management. A manager at a hospital might measure its safety efforts by comparing the hospital's accident rate with hospital industry figures and with rates at other hospitals of the same size in the area.

Another part of safety evaluation is updating safety materials and safety training aids. The accident investigation procedures and accident-reporting methods also should be evaluated continually to make sure these are actually generating ideas useful in reducing accidents. Safety policies and regulations should be reviewed and made to comply with both existing and new standards set up by OSHA, state, and professional agencies.

SUMMARY

- Health is a general state of physical, mental, and emotional well-being.
- Safety is protection of a person's physical health.
- Accidents and industrial health concerns are a major problem.
- Worker attitudes play a major role in accidents and accident prevention.
- Accident prevention can be approached from an engineering or behavioral perspective, but both should be considered.
- Stress is a major concern today because of its relationship to physical distresses. However, not all stress is bad.
- People find that situations in which they cannot control, accurately predict, accurately perceive, or escape intense responsibility are very stressful.
- Alcoholism affects about 10 percent of the American work force.
- Alcoholism and drug abuse are extremely expensive to industry. Many employers are reacting by getting tough or by increasing use of EAPs.
- OSHA is designed to help improve the accident-prevention and health situation in business and industry.
- The Occupational Safety and Health Act requires record-keeping, reporting of injuries, and inspection of work sites.

■ Criticisms of OSHA range from charges of vague standards to a lack of effectiveness.

■ A good safety program that considers accident prevention from a systems perspective includes organizational commitment, coordination, employee motivation, accident investigation, accident research, and evaluation of safety efforts.

REVIEW AND DISCUSSION QUESTIONS

1. Differentiate between health and safety as P/HR activities. Then identify some factors that affect health and safety.
2. Discuss the following statement by a supervisor: "I feel it is my duty to get involved with my employees and their personal problems to show that I truly care about them."
3. Why should an employer be concerned about employee alcohol and drug usage?
4. Describe the Occupational Safety and Health Act and some of its key provisions about standards, record keeping, and inspection requirements.
5. Discuss the following comment: "OSHA should be abolished because it just serves to harass small businesses."
6. Why is a systems approach to safety important?

CASE | **Stress At Gulf Oil**

Several years ago Texas oilman T. Boone Pickens waged a bitter takeover battle for Gulf Oil Corporation. The battle lasted months before Gulf was finally acquired by another firm.

The proxy contest and takeover attempt was the largest in corporate history, and resulted in excessive work loads as armies of investment bankers, lawyers, and public relations consultants descended on the company. Only a small percentage of the company's employees were directly involved in the day-to-day activities of the proxy fight, but all Gulf employees, from top management down were affected, if only by picking up the duties of a co-worker involved in the fight.

Gulf officials acknowledged that the situation placed unprecedented pressure on every employee in the firm. "Intense emotions, round-the-clock hours, and an all out fight" is how one executive at the company's Pittsburgh headquarters characterized the atmosphere that enveloped Gulf Oil.

The ability of individuals to cope with the changing events varied widely. The intense atmosphere, countless tasks, and unrelenting hours caused a high degree of stress for those involved. During the proxy fight, much of the stress was the adrenaline-pumping type, which kept morale high and pushed employees to work late nights, weekends, and even holidays voluntarily. It was a "campaign" that resulted in a tremendous coming together of people working for the same cause. An intense loyalty and identification with their company emerged among employees.

Once Gulf was taken over, a high stress level remained, but the cause changed to uncertainty about jobs. Some employees complained of classic symptoms such as decreased energy levels or sleeping problems.

Throughout the period, management recognized the problems of high stress and the need for increased communication with employees. Frequent desk-top information sheets and videotapes on the progress of the situation were prepared and distributed. A "hot-line" was established during the most intense period of the proxy fight so that employees could follow events on a daily basis. Stress management seminars were set up following the merger to give employees better skills to cope with the pressures that had been created.[55]

QUESTIONS

1. Why was it important for Gulf Oil to aid employees in handling stress?
2. Identify both positive and negative facets of stress that appear in the case.

NOTES

1. "Smokers at Houston Firm Pay $10 a Month for Lighting Up," in the *Omaha World-Herald*, January 7, 1990, 16.
2. "6.4 Million Workers Reported Injuries." *Omaha World-Herald*, November 17, 1989, A4.
3. C. Ansberry, "Workplace Injuries Proliferate as Concerns Rush People to Produce," *Wall Street Journal*, June 16, 1989, 1.
4. "Jobs That Are Most Hazardous," *USA Today*, January 6, 1989, 2B.
5. M. Verespej, "Execs Could Be Tried for Murder," *Industry Week*, March 6, 1989, 61; M. Geyelin, "Verdict Upheld for Workers in Personal Injury Case," *Wall Street Journal*, June 2, 1989, B1.
6. S. Garland, "Safety Ruling Could Be Hazardous to Employer's Health," *Business Week*, February 20, 1989, 34.
7. Ibid.
8. "Investigation of Child Labor Hits Thousands," *Omaha World-Herald*, March 15, 1990, 1. "Child Labor Violations on the Rise," *Omaha World-Herald*, February 11, 1990, 8–G.
9. Adapted from M. Schuster and S. Rhodes, "The Impact of Overtime Work on Industrial Accident Rates," *Industrial Relations* 26 (1985): 234–246.
10. John B. Miner and Mary G. Miner, *Personnel and Industrial Relations*, 4th ed. (New York: Macmillan, 1985), 485–487.
11. Adapted from J. Ptak, "What Price Injury?" *Business Industry Magazine*, January 1987, 90.
12. R. L. Barnett and D. B. Brickman, "Safety Hierarchy," *Journal of Safety Research* 17 (1986): 50.
13. J. W. Jones et al., "Promoting Safety by Reducing Human Error," *Personnel*, June 1986, 41.
14. R. L. Simpson, "Safety Last," *Wall Street Journal*, March 18, 1986, 1.
15. "Auto Accidents Lead Job-Realted Deaths," *Chicago Tribune*, January 5, 1987, 36.
16. U.S. Department of Labor, Occupational Safety and Health Administration, *Mercury*, OSHA Pamphlet No. 2234 (Washington, D.C.: U.S. Government Printing Office).
17. W. Bellis, "How Safe Are Video Terminals?" *Fortune*, August 28, 1988, 66.; D. Jordan, "The VDT Peril," *Computer Dealer*, October 1988, 28.
18. D. Jordan, "VDT Health and Safety: A Summary of Medical Opinion," *Computer Dealer*, October 1988, 35.
19. A. Weber, "Minimizing VDT Risks . . .," *Human Resources Professional*, May/June 1989, 37.
20. "No. 1 Work Hazards of the 1990's," *Omaha World-Herald*, June 7, 1989, 2.
21. B. Meier, "Companies Wrestle with Threats to Worker's Reproductive Helath," *Wall Street Journal*, February 5, 1987, 25; "Childbearing: The Dangers of High Tech," *U.S. News & World Report*, January 26, 1987, 12; and "Profile of a Warning," *Wall Street Journal*, January 13, 1987, 1.
22. "Equal Employment Opportunity," *Employee Relations Law Journal* 11 (1986): 735; "EEOC Fetal Protection Policy Guidelines," *Personnel Journal*, March 1989, p. 28.
23. C. Zielinski, "The Toxic Trap," *Personnel Journal*, February 1990, 40.
24. S. Modic, "Surviving Burnout," *Industry Week*, February 20, 1989, 29.
25. J. Wylie, "A Manager's Guide to Stress Management," *Meeting Destinations*, February 1989, 51.
26. HRAM Newsletter, February 1990, 2.

27. R. Ricklefs, "Many Executives Complain of Stress," *Wall Street Journal*, September 29, 1989, 27.

28. For example, J. Hyatt, "All Stressed Up and No Place to Go," *INC*, January 1987, 74–79.

29. "Personal Help," *Wall Street Journal*, November 11, 1986, 1.

30. D. M. Podolsky, "RIT Report: Economic Costs of Alcohol Abuse and Alcoholism," *Alcohol Health and Research World*, Winter 1984–85, 34.

31. M. Major, "Employee Assistance Programs: An Idea Whose Time Has Come," *Modern Office Technology*, March 1990, 76.

32. Robert McMorris, "Workers and V. P. Benefits from Programs to Aid Those Derailed by Drinking," *Omaha World-Herald*, February 12, 1990, 8.

33. M. Cavanagh, "Myths Surround Alcoholism," *Personnel Journal*, February 1990, 112; R. Weiss, "Writing Under the Influence . . .," *Personnel Psychology* 40 (1987): 341.

34. M. Markowitz, "The Organization and Alcohol Abuse," *Human Relations* 40 (1987): 833–852; J. Castelli, "Employer-Provided Programs Pay Off," *HRM Magazine*, April 1990, 55.

35. S. Jordon, "Workplace Drug use 'Common,' " *Omaha World-Herald*, September 17, 1989, 2M.

36. S. Bergeman, "Help Employees Who Help Themselves," *HRM Magazine*, April 1990, 46.

37. J. Deming, "Drug Free Workplace Is Good Business," *HRM Magazine*, April 1990, 61.

38. D. Harper, "Overcoming the Fear of AIDS," *ABA Banking Journal*, June 1988, 49–61.

39. T. Tyrer, "AIDS, AA Survey Shows Workplace Concern," *Advertising Age*, April 3, 1989, 1, 22, 27; T. Tyrer, "Why Formal AIDS Policy Is Important," *Advertising Age*, April 3, 1989, 27; T. Tyrer, "How AIDS Views Differ in Business World," *Advertising Age*, April 3, 1989, 27.

40. A. Gini, "Meeting AIDS at Work," *Advertising Age*, April 3, 1989, 36.

41. S. Caudron, "Assessments Rescue Health Programs," *HRM Magazine*, April 1990, 64.

42. J. Work, "How Healthy Are Corporate Fitness Programs?," *The Physician and Sportsmedicine*, March 1989, 226–237.

43. U.S. Department of Labor, Occupational Safety and Health Administration, *All About OSHA*, OSHA Pamphlet No. 2056 (Washington DC: U.S. Government Printing Office), 3.

44. W. J. Goldsmith, "Current Developments in OSHA," *Employee Relations Law Journal* 11 (1986): 348–354.

45. *Whirpool v. Marshall*, 78–1870 (1980).

46. *Gateway Coal Co. v. the United Mine Workers of America*, 94 S.Ct. 641 (1981).

47. "Chrysler Is Cited in Case Involving Job-Injury Reports," *Wall Street Journal*, November 6, 1986, 14; and *USA Today*, July 7, 1987, B1.

48. *Marshall v. Barlow's Inc.*, 76–1143 (1978).

49. F. Swoboda and C. Skryzycki, "OSHA Fines USX Corp. Record $7.3 Million," *Washington Post*, November 2, 1989.

50. *American Textile Manufacturing Institute, Inc., et al. v. Donovan, et al.* 101 S.Ct. 2478; 69 LEd.2d 185 (1981).

51. M. Geylin, "Study Faults Federal Effort to Enforce Worker Safety," *Wall Street Journal*, April 28, 1989, B1.

52. "NIOSH: Management Is the Key," *National Safety News*, September 1987, 41.

53. B. Leonard, "Taking a Big Risk," *HR Magazine*, January 1990, 52.

54. J. Jenkins, "Self-Directed Workforce Promotes Safety," *HR Magazine*, February 1990, 54.

55. Used with permission of Susan LeBon, Gulf Oil Company.

Employee Rights and Discipline

After you have read this chapter, you should be able to:

1. Explain how views on the nature of employee rights have changed
2. Identify three exceptions to employment at-will-used by the courts
3. List elements necessary to maintain an employee handbook as part of an implied employment contract
4. Discuss the concept of just cause and how it is determined
5. Explain the issues and problems associated with drug tests
6. Identify the major concerns about polygraph and honesty testing
7. Outline a progressive discipline sequence

P/HR: Today *and* Tomorrow

Monitoring or Performance Measurement?

Eavesdropping is on the rise, both on and off the job, thanks to advances in surveillance technology. Although companies doing the monitoring have few qualms, right-to-privacy advocates, employees, and some lawmakers are concerned. Employers are using sensitive instruments to check supermarket checkers, bank tellers, stockbrockers, IRS agents, hotel reservation agents, hospital workers, and airline pilots.

This surveillance is called *monitoring,* and is usually aimed at measuring the performance of service workers. It may take many forms, from counting the number of keystrokes a secretary makes per hour to tallying the lines of copy a programmer writes per day. Although it has been used in the past, monitoring has been made much easier by the computer. Monitoring has resulted in some real cost savings. Equitable Life Assurance Society, which uses a computer to check on how much work each employee is producing, has cut its claims-processing force significantly and is paying 20 percent more claims with 30 percent fewer people. In the financial industry, Kidder Peabody and Co. says it monitors bond-trading conversations between brokers and customers to safeguard order accuracy.

Despite such success stories, the negative effects of monitoring are a growing concern. Some people don't like it!! The fight is becoming a power pull and the strong undoubtedly will win. Through collective bargaining, airline pilots won the right not to be monitored. Monitoring has become an issue for Equitable Insurance Co., too, as claims processors bargain for a say in the standards use.

A Michigan Bell spokesman says that the company monitors a random sampling of calls to operators and customer service representatives. He says the practice is "Essentially the only quality control tool we have. We don't have a product like a car that rolls off the assembly line and can be inspected."

In part, opposition to monitoring has come from an organization called "9-to-5," which set up a hot-line for employees who suspect they are being monitored by their employer. 9-to-5 says, "With the computerized work force approaching 40 million, as many as 26 million workers may be under electronic scrutiny."

That organization wants restriction on the use of monitoring, notification of employees, and then limitations placed on employers. What will happen in this area will depend on congressional or state legislative action—but it should be interesting to watch the debate develop![1]

"While the right to talk may be the beginning of freedom, the necessity of listening is what makes the right important."

Walter Lippman

Although the Constitution of the United States grants citizens rights to freedom and due process, such rights are not always present in the workplace. Federal, state, and local laws or labor–management contracts grant employees such rights at work. Without these items, the right of management to run its business has been so strong that employee's rights are not guaranteed.[2]

Major exceptions are in areas where new laws have changed traditional management prerogatives: EEO, collective bargaining, safety, sexism, etc. These laws and their recent interpretations have caused more confusion in the area of employee rights than ever before. The yet unresolved nature of employee rights at work are considered in this chapter.

A **right** is that which belongs to a person by law, nature, or tradition. Of course, there is considerable potential for disagreement as to what really is a right. Employer pressures on employees with "different" lifestyles illustrate areas in which conflicts occur. Rights are sometimes divided into moral and legal categories. Legal rights may or may not correspond to certain moral rights, and the reverse is true as well.[3] Rights are offset by **responsibilities** or obligations.

Some rights have applications both on and off the job. Health and safety rights, free speech, and the right to due process are three examples. Other rights might apply in one arena, such as in the workplace, but not in the other. Restrictions on employees smoking at work versus smoking at home are examples. Additionally, there is a difference between a right and a privilege. Sometimes management and employees do not have a clear agreement as to which rights do exist in the workplace. Unions have tried over the years to define employer–employee rights, often through confrontation. Unionism has declined but increased restrictions on employer P/HR practices through state legislation and court decisions have increased employee rights.

The proliferation of court-backed employee rights mirrors a change in society's attitude toward work. To live within the new employee-rights environment, employers must ensure that the P/HR procedures are fair and not applied in an arbitrary and capricious manner. Figure 17–1 shows a possible division of responsibilities between the P/HR unit and operating managers over employee rights and discipline.

A RIGHT
is that which belongs to a person by law, nature, or tradition.

RESPONSIBILITY
is a duty or obligation to be accountable for an action.

P/HR UNIT	MANAGERS
■ Design P/HR procedures that incorporate employee legal and moral rights	■ Keep informed of employee rights concerns
■ Design progressive discipline process if nonunion	■ Operate under the discipline system—make disciplinary decisions, dismiss employees who violate policies and rules
■ Train managers on the protection and limits of employee rights and discipline process	■ Provide feedback to the process situations not covered by the disciplinary process

Figure 17–1
Rights and Discipline Responsibilities

■ ■ EMPLOYEE RIGHTS AND RESPONSIBILITIES

Having a job includes responsibilities of the employee to the employer. These responsibilities may be spelled out in a job description, in an employment contract, or in P/HR policies, but many are not. They also exist as employer expectations about what is acceptable behavior or performance on the part of the employee.

Some scholars and courts of law argue that if an *employee* has obligations in the employment relationship, then the *employer* has obligations toward the employee.[4] Employment as a reciprocal agreement (both sides have obligations) suggests that employee moral rights arise in exchange for such employee actions as loyalty, service, accountability, etc.

The Current Situation

Workplace litigation has reached epidemic proportions as employees who feel their rights have been violated sue their employers. Advocates for expanding employee rights warn that management policies abridging free speech, privacy, or due process will lead to national legislation to regulate the relationship. At the same time, P/HR professionals are under pressure to maintain a lean, efficient, flexible, drug-free work force. They argue that to remain competitive they must protect management's traditional employment-at-will prerogatives. To maintain efficiency and quality, "dead wood" cannot be tolerated.[5]

As employees increasingly regard themselves free agents in the workplace—and the power of unions declines—a struggle between employee and employer "rights" is taking place. For example, when David Stikes reported to work at the Chevron Oil field near Coalinga, California, management announced a surprise search of workers. He emptied his lunch pail and locker, but refused to allow his car to be searched and he was fired. Stikes sued for lost wages, damages, and the return of his job. The surprise search was prompted by the company's discovery of drug paraphernalia in a company truck. Workers at Chevron sign statements agreeing to the company's right to search and test for drugs.[6]

Employers have not fared very well in many of these cases. One study of claims of wrongful discharge found the employee had a 86% chance of winning a case brought against a private employer and a 33% chance against a governmental entity.[7] Another study showed that workers who sued for invasion of privacy, sexual harassment, or slander won an average jury award of $375,000. The invasion-of-privacy verdicts included cases of drug and alcohol abuse, unlawful surveillance, and use of polygraph tests. As in the previous study, a high percentage of the cases were won by employees (72%).[8]

Further, it is not only the company that is liable in many cases. Individual managers and supervisors have been found liable when hiring or promotion decisions are based on discriminatory factors or when they have knowledge of such conduct and do not take steps to stop it.[9] The P/HR: Research shows the extent of policies designed to protect employees and employers in the United States.

Employee rights defined in various state laws are divided here into three major categories:

1. Rights affecting the employment agreement
   ■ Employment-at-will
   ■ Implied employment contracts

Ben Rosen and Catherine Schwoerer reported in *HR Magazine* on a survey of 785 Society for Human Resource Management members on policies in effect to protect employee and employer rights. About 44 percent of those responding characterized their companies' policies as striking a balance between employee and employer rights. Thirty-seven percent said the policies emphasized employer rights, and 19 percent said employee rights were emphasized.

The following chart shows typical protection policies for each group and the percentage of firms who have such a policy, deem it successful, and feel it is needed.[10]

	Exist	Successful	Needed
Access to records	89.8%	93%	77%
Privacy protection	83.2%	96%	88%
Health–safety information	79.0%	91%	78%
Disciplinary policy	71.7%	95%	79%
Company ombudsman	39.8%	91%	54%
Free speech protection	26.3;%	85%	45%
Impartial arbitrators	23.3%	87%	31%
Background investigation	80.9%	89%	91%
Avoid "implied contract"	79.7%	95%	87%
Termination at will	51.1%	93%	71%
Medical screening	40.6%	88%	56%
Drug testing	37.0%	93%	66%
Psychological-polygraph testing	10.5%	74%	24%
Electronic surveillance	7.4%	73%	18%

- ■ Due process
- ■ Dismissal for just cause
2. Employee privacy rights
   - ■ Employee rights to records
   - ■ Substance abuse and drug testing
   - ■ Polygraph and honesty testing
3. Other employee rights
   - ■ Rights in workplace investigation
   - ■ Rights to know of potential hazards and unsafe working conditions
   - ■ Employee free speech and whistle-blowing
   - ■ Notification of plant closings

■■ ■■ RIGHTS AFFECTING THE EMPLOYMENT AGREEMENT

Although it can be argued that all the employee rights issues affect the employment relationship, four basic issues predominate: employment-at-will, implied contracts, due process, and dismissal for cause.

Employment-at-Will (EAW)

Employment-at-will (EAW) is a common law doctrine stating that employers have the right to hire, fire, demote, or promote whomever they choose, unless there is a law or contract to the contrary. Employers often defend EAW for one or more of the following reasons:

1. The right of private ownership of a business guarantees EAW.
2. EAW defends employees' rights to change jobs, as well as an employer's rights to hire and fire.
3. Interfering with EAW reduces productivity in our economy.

HISTORY OF EAW.   EAW is a by-product of the nineteenth-century Industrial Revolution.[11] Laissez-faire social thought encouraged rapid economic expansion and granted business complete flexibility in the way employees were handled. Very little changed until the twentieth century when unionized labor gained protection from arbitrary and capricious discharge through grievance arbitration procedures in most union contracts. In disputed cases, a neutral arbitrator ruled whether or not there were adequate grounds for dismissal. Over time, both management and unions generally became familiar with restraints placed on employers who discharged employees. Many public sector employees are granted due process protection under civil service regulations, whether or not employees are represented by a union. Nonunion employees remained under the EAW doctrine. In the 1960s, however, an increasing number of state courts began to create exceptions to EAW ideas. Courts questioned the *fairness* of an employer's decision to fire an employee without just cause and due process. The suits imply that employees have job rights that must be balanced against EAW.

The courts in California and New York have taken two very different approaches to EAW. These positions represent the extreme ends of a continuum of approaches being taken nationwide. In New York, courts have refused to take EAW cases, saying that EAW is a legislative concern, not one for the courts to decide. On the other hand, in California, courts will take EAW cases almost without exception.

WRONGFUL DISCHARGE   The courts have recognized three different rationales for hearing EAW cases.

1. *Public Policy Exception*. This exception to EAW holds that an employee can sue if he or she is fired for action against public policy. For example, if an employee refused to commit perjury and was fired, he could sue. Or, if an employee refused to engage in a price-fixing arrangement and was fired, she could sue the employer.
2. *Implied Employment Contract*. This approach holds that the employee *will not* be fired as long as he or she does the job. Long service, promises of continued employment, lack of criticism of job performance, and how the employer has handled similar cases are such events.
3. *Good Faith and Fair Dealing*. This approach suggests that a covenant of good faith and fair dealing exists between the employer and at-will employees. If the employer has broken this covenant by unreasonable behavior, the employee has legal recourse.[12]

A landmark court case in this area is *Fortune v. National Cash Register Company*. The case involved the firing of a salesman (Fortune) who had been with NCR for

25 years.[13] Fortune was fired shortly after winning a large order that would have earned him a big commission. From the evidence, the court concluded that he was fired because NCR wanted to avoid paying him the commission, which violated the covenant of good faith.

The courts generally have conceded that unionized workers cannot pursue EAW actions as at-will employees because they are covered by an alternative remedy: the grievance arbitration process. Nearly all states have adopted one or more statutes that limit an employer's right to discharge. The universal restrictions include race, age, sex, national origin, religion, and handicap. Restrictions on other areas vary so much from state to state that local conditions must be considered unique.

Figure 17–2 shows a breakdown of those who have filed wrongful discharge suits. The lesson of wrongful discharge suits is that employers should take care to see that dismissals are handled properly and that all P/HR management systems are in order. One lawyer has suggested the following:[14]

- Put grounds for dismissal in writing and distribute them to all employees.
- Keep good written records on termination actions.
- Make sure performance appraisals give an honest picture of a person's performance.
- Warn employees of problems that possibly could lead to termination before someone is dismissed.
- Involve more than one person in termination decisions.

Rights in the Employment Contract (Employee Handbooks)

Like employment-at-will, the idea that a contract (even an implied, unwritten one) exists between workers and employer affects the employment relationship. Several courts have held that if an employer hires someone for an indefinite period, and promises job security, or gives specific procedures for discharge, the employer has lost the right to terminate at-will. These actions establish employee expectations. When the employer fails to follow up on them, employees have recourse in court.

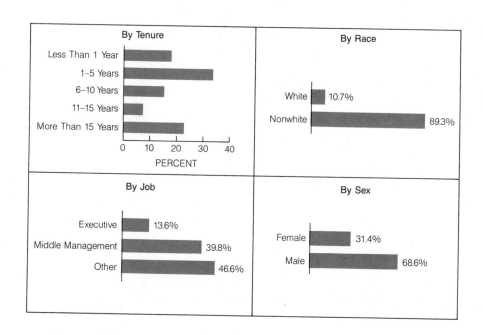

Figure 17–2
Wrongful Discharge Suits

SOURCE: *Wall Street Journal*, September 7, 1989, B1.

P/HR: **Practice *and* Research**

Implied Contracts: Employee Handbooks

Legal research identifies the *Pine River State Bank v. Mettile* case as the classic case on employee handbooks and employee rights. In this case, Pine River State Bank (PRSB) hired Mettile as a loan officer. Mettile moved to Pine River, Minnesota, to take the job. Nothing was said about the length of service expected. The bank distributed a handbook to all employees, drafted by the bank president, which contained information regarding PRSB's employment policies about such provisions as working hours, time-off, vacation, and sick leave. It also contained specific provisions on job security and disciplinary action.

Mettile received a performance appraisal and a 7 percent raise after he had been on the job a year. In the second year of his employment, bank officials found that Mettile had made numerous errors in complying with banking laws; he was responsible for fifty-seven "serious technical exceptions." For example, Mettile's files on car loans showed that he had mishandled vehicle certificates, collateral, insurance, and financial statements, amounting to over $600,000 in loans.

Consequently, the president fired Mettile without following the disciplinary procedures outlined in the employee handbook. Mettile sued claiming that the bank had violated the procedures in the handbook by dismissing him without cause, which constituted a breach of the employment contract. The jury found that Mettile *had* been dismissed without cause and awarded him $27,675.

When the matter reached the Minnesota Supreme Court on appeal, the central question was, "Can a personnel handbook be part of an employee's contract of employment?" The court found that the four-step disciplinary procedure spelled out in the handbook created a unilateral contract, consideration for which is continued employment, although the employee is free to leave at any time.[16]

In essence, the courts have held that such promises constitute a contract between an employer and employees, even though there is no signed document. A landmark case is *Pine River State Bank v. Mettile*, but many other cases have led to similar conclusions: that handbooks are implied contracts (see the P/HR: Practice). The legal remedy for a broken contract requires the party breaking the contract to perform and keep its contracted obligation. However, courts also have imposed liability if such contracts are broken. Tort liability carries with it the threat of compensatory and punitive damages—a potentially costly situation for an employer who has broken the implied contract.[15]

Guidelines For An Employee Handbook

An employee handbook gives employees a reference source for all company policies and rules. Employee handbooks can be a positive tool for effective management of human resources. Management should consider several factors when preparing handbooks.

READABILITY.   Specialists who prepare employee handbooks may not write on the same level as those who will read them. A study of 50 company handbooks revealed that the average level of most handbooks was the third year of college, which is much higher than the typical reading level in any company. One solution is to test the readability of the handbook on a sample of employees before it is published.

USE. Another important factor to be considered in preparing an employee handbook is its method of use. Simply giving an employee a handbook and saying, "Here's all the information you need to know," is not sufficient. In one study, employee handbooks ranked third behind a supervisor and "the grapevine" as a source of information.

Some organizations distribute handbooks as part of their orientation process. One company periodically gives all employees a written test on the company handbook. P/HR managers use questions that are consistently missed to focus their communication efforts. These tests also are used to update the handbook.

LEGAL REVIEW OF LANGUAGE. The current legal trend is no reason to abandon employee handbooks as a way to communicate with employees. Violating one's own P/HR policies erodes employees' confidence in the organization as an employer. Many smaller employers do not have employee handbooks with P/HR policies, thus leaving themselves open to costly litigation and out-of-court settlements.

A more sensible approach is to develop employee handbooks and P/HR policies, then have legal counsel review the language contained in them. Some recommendations include:

- *Eliminate controversial phrases.* For example, the phrase "permanent employee" often is used to describe those people who have passed a probationary period. This wording can lead to disagreement over what the parties meant by "permanent." A more appropriate phrase is "regular employee."
- *Use disclaimers.* Contract disclaimers have been upheld in court. However, there is a trade-off between disclaimers and the image presented by the handbook, so disclaimers should not be overused. A disclaimer also should appear on application forms. A disclaimer in the handbook can read as follows:

This employee handbook is not intended to be a contract or part of a contractual agreement between the employer and the employee. Employer reserves the right to modify, delete, or add to any policies set forth herein without notice and reserves the right to terminate an employee at any time with or without cause.

- *Keep the handbook current.* Many employers simply add new material to handbooks rather than delete old inapplicable rules. Those old rules can become the bases for new lawsuits. Consequently, handbooks and P/HR policies should be reviewed periodically and revised every few years.[17]

Due Process

Due process, or the opportunity to defend oneself against charges, is guaranteed in the U.S. Constitution. For unionized employees, due process usually refers to their rights to use the grievance procedure specified in the union contract. It may include steps in the grievance process, time limits, arbitration procedures, and knowledge of disciplinary penalties.

Compared with due process procedures specified in union contracts, at-will employee procedures are more varied and can address a broader range of issues. However, according to critics, employee attempts to use their rights of due process often run into difficulties:

1. Employees do not get enough help in preparing their defenses.
2. There is little protection for the person who uses the process against management.
3. The final decision maker may not be independent from management.

DUE PROCESS
gives one the opportunity to defend oneself against charges.

These three issues must be addressed if due process procedures are to be perceived as fair. Employees must be given the opportunity to present their sides of the story during the disciplinary process.

Nonunion organizations are well advised to have a grievance procedure for their employees. Just the presence of an equitable grievance procedure can be a positive indication that an employee has been given due process. The design of grievance procedures is covered in Chapter 19.

ORGANIZATIONAL OMBUDSMAN.   The ombudsman, a concept originating in Sweden, is a person outside the normal chain of command who serves as a "public defender" a problem solver for management and employees. For example, one firm uses an ombudsman to resolve complaints from employees that cannot be settled through the employee's supervisor or the P/HR department. The ombudsman reviews the employee's information and complaint. After the problems are discussed with other individuals, such as the employee's supervisor or a representative of the P/HR department, the ombudsman recommends a solution to the problem. Making such an individual available gives employees the opportunity to talk freely about complaints and frustrations that may not otherwise surface until they become serious problems. Using an ombudsman also can be a way to make sure that employees are given a fair hearing and due process in attempting to address their problems.

Dismissal for Just Cause

Like due process, dismissal for *just cause* usually is spelled out in a union contract, but often is not as clear in an at-will situation. While the definition of just cause varies from case to case, the criteria used by courts have become well-defined over time from arbitration awards. They appear in Figure 17–3.

Related to just cause issues is the concept of "**constructive discharge.**" Under normal circumstances, an employee who resigns rather than being dismissed may *not* later collect damages for violation of legal rights. An exception to this rule does occur when the courts find that the working conditions are so intolerable as to force a reasonable employee to resign. Then, the resignation is considered a discharge. Constructive discharge is most often found when an employer *deliberately* makes conditions intolerable in an attempt to get the employee to quit.

Discharge for just cause is especially difficult to establish when the case involves an employee's off-the-job behavior. The basic premise is that an employer should not control the lives of its employees off the job. But certain conditions can arise that make the concern of the employer appropriate.

In one case, the Baltimore Transit Company fired the Acting Grand Dragon of the Ku Klux Klan. The arbitrator upheld the dismissal and said that there was a

CONSTRUCTIVE DISCHARGE is most often found when an employer deliberately makes conditions intolerable in an attempt to get the employee to quit.

Figure 17–3
Just Cause

- ■ Was the employee warned of the consequences of his/her conduct?
- ■ Was the company's rule reasonable?
- ■ Did management investigate before disciplining?
- ■ Was the investigation fair and impartial?
- ■ Was there evidence of guilt?
- ■ Were the rules and penalties applied in an evenhanded fashion?
- ■ Was the penalty reasonable, given the offense?

clear danger of physical violence and an economic boycott to the company if the man were retained. In another case, Southern California Edison Company fired an employee because he lied about his arrest for possession of marijuana. The arbitrator upheld the dismissal because the company's need for accurate information from the employee was important in his job.

Arbitrators use four tests to determine whether off-the-job behavior is just cause for dismissal:[18]

1. Injury or harm to the employer's business
2. Inability or unsuitability of the employee to do the job
3. Other employees' refusal to work with the offender
4. Adverse effect on the employer–employee relationship

The case of General Telephone of Kentucky illustrates the last point. An employee verbally and physically assaulted his supervisor at a restaurant while both were off-duty and was dismissed. The arbitrator upheld the discharge because the incident would carry over into the employment relationship.[19]

■■ ■ EMPLOYEE PRIVACY RIGHTS

Under employee privacy rights, three categories of employee rights are considered: (1) employee rights to records, (2) substance abuse and drug testing, and (3) polygraph and honesty testing.

Employee Rights to Records

As a result of concerns about the protection of individual's privacy rights, the Privacy Act of 1974 was passed. It includes provisions affecting P/HR record systems. This law applies only to federal agencies and organizations supplying services to the federal government, but similar state laws, somewhat broader in scope, also have been passed. Regulation of private employers on this issue for the most part is a matter of state rather than federal law.

Several legal issues are involved in employee rights to privacy and P/HR records:

■ Right to access personal information
■ Opportunity to respond to unfavorable information
■ Right to correct erroneous information
■ Right to be notified when information is given to a third party
■ Right to know how the information is being used internally
■ Right to reasonable precautions, assuring the individual that the information will not be misused

In the past, it was not unusual or considered improper for employers to collect personal data on employees that ranged from marriage information to political party affiliation. Employees were not allowed to see their P/HR files, but such information often was released to third parties at an employer's discretion without the employee's permission. Criticism of such practices in many states has led to legislation covering employee rights in this area. States define what is a personnel record differently, but Pennsylvania provides a comprehensive definition: A "personnel file" includes applications for employment; wage or salary information; notices of commendations, warning, or discipline; authorizations for a deduction or withholding of pay; fringe benefit information; leave records; and employment history with the employer, including salary information, job title, retirement record, attendance records, and performance evaluations.[20]

Probably the most frequent way for an employer to run afoul of laws on employee records is when another employer asks for information about a former employee. Lawyers recommend that only the most basic employment history such as job title, dates of employment, and ending salary data be given. Although that information may be safe, it probably is not especially helpful to the employer seeking the reference, since such information doesn't answer questions a potential employer may have about an employee's suitability.

Although most employees do not feel their employers are engaged in improper collection of personal information, they do favor a new system of rules to handle sensitive information that is collected. Further, they want decisions on promotions, job assignments, and discipline made on the basis of information that they can examine if a dispute arises.

A study found that employees have rather limited knowledge about what information their employers keep on file. Also employees are more concerned about disclosure of personal information to parties outside the firm than they are about how the information is used inside the firm.[21] These findings may require rethinking and reorganizing of many existing record-keeping systems in P/HR units (see Figure 17–4). Doing so can minimize problems later.

Several years ago, the U.S. Privacy Protection Commission recommended that companies make voluntary efforts to improve the way they treated employee information. Recently, the chairman of that committee surveyed Fortune 500 firms and found that some changes had been made since the previous recommendation but that progress has been slow. However, he is urging Congress to pass additional legislation to protect employees' privacy.[22] The most recent survey found that:

- 87% of employers allow employees to look at their P/HR files, but only 27 percent let employees look at their supervisor's P/HR files on them
- 57% use private investigators to collect or verify information
- 38% have no policy covering release of data
- 80% will give information to potential creditors
- Since the last survey, more employers evaluate their record-keeping periodically and forward corrections to anyone given false information
- More employers collect medical records for use in employment decisions, probably because of concerns about AIDS, smoking, and drug abuse.

Substance Abuse and Drug Testing

The issues of substance abuse and drug testing at work is getting increased attention at all levels of government. There are difficult issues regarding the trade-off between a safe workplace and rights to privacy, but the scope of the problem is clear. Substance abuse results in sixteen times the normal absenteeism, four times the accident rates, one-third more illness benefits, and five times as many workers' compensation claims.[23]

Two misconceptions about privacy in the workplace should be cleared up. First, federal constitutional rights, such as unreasonable search and seizure, protect an individual only against the activities of the government. Thus, employees can be searched at work. This principle was reaffirmed by a U.S. Supreme Court decision that even employers in government workplaces may search desks and files without search warrants if they believe that a work rule was violated.[24] Second, employer

1. *Develop Policies about Personnel Records*

   Policies should be developed that cover the gathering, use, disclosure, and retention of records covering employment, personnel and payroll, security, medical, and insurance matters. The policies should:
   a. limit the collection, use, and retention of such records
   b. set up procedures to ensure the accuracy, timeliness, and completeness of information collected, maintained, and disclosed
   c. allow current employees, former employees, and applicants to see, copy, correct, and amend records maintained about them
   d. limit internal use of access to records
   e. limit external disclosure of information in records
   f. restrict use of arrest and conviction records except to the extent necessary to comply with governmental regulations, and maintain such records separately from other personnel files
   g. restrict use of military discharge records if other than honorable
   h. notify applicants and employees about sources used for information and record-gathering purposes
   i. designate records of employees, former employees, and applicants that the employer will allow to be reviewed and copied, and will not allow to be reviewed and copied
   j. notify employee, former employees, and retirees about any fees for copying and mailing records and documents
   k. explain to them any records kept separately from personnel files, such as medical and benefits information

2. *Disclosure Statement*

   A disclosure statement should be developed for distribution to employees, former employees, and job applicants that includes the following:
   a. the type and number of records maintained on all workers—past, present, and prospective
   b. the usage, disclosure, and retention period for each record.

3. *Review Files Regularly*

   An employer should review all current personnel files individually to ensure that outdated, unnecessary, and potentially damaging documentation is removed and destroyed.

4. *Designate File Custodian*

   An employer should designate a file custodian either within its personnel department or some other officer of the organization.

5. *Restrict Separate Files*

   As much as possible, an employer should restrict, if not eliminate, the maintenance of any separate employee files by managers.

6. *Base Decisions on File Information*

   All decisions to transfer, promote, or discipline employees should be made solely on the basis of information maintained in the personnel department's master employee file.

7. *Train Managers*

   All managers should be trained on how to structure and draft effective, liability-free documentation for employees' personnel files.

Figure 17–4
Guidelines for the Privacy Protection of Personnel Records

SOURCE: Mary P. Carlton, "Workers' Privacy: A Call for Voluntary Action," p. 19. Reprinted by special permission from the July 1980 issue of *ABA Banking Journal,* Copyright 1980 by the American Bankers Association.

due process *does not* have to include the criminal standard of "beyond a reasonable doubt." Termination of an employee because of substance abuse problems must be in keeping only with the due process described in an employer's policy.

Unless state or local law prohibits testing, employers have a right to require employees to submit to a blood test or urinalysis. But court decisions generally have indicated that random drug testing may be unconstitutional and that public agencies must have "probable cause" to test.[25]

There are several arguments against drug testing: (1) It violates employees' rights. (2) Drugs may not affect job performance in every case. (3) Employers abuse the results of tests. (4) Such tests are often inaccurate or the results are misinterpreted. The last argument deserves more inspection.

The accuracy of some drug tests does vary widely, even when conducted by professional laboratories. The Center for Disease Control found that virtually all laboratories in its ten-year study had unacceptably high error rates. Largely because of human error, all labs failed to identify correctly even half the samples for four out of the five drugs tested.[26] More troubling is the fact that some employee drug testing is done with test kits on site. Samples are easily contaminated, mishandled, or sabotaged. For example, "clean" urine is being sold so individuals can pass drug tests. Further, tests are not accurate unless confirmed by a second test. Because of cost, some employers fail to use the confirming test.[27] Finally, factors other than human error can contribute to false positive test results. For example, one of the most common drug tests (EMIT) may be made false positive by using aspirin, eating poppy seeds, or by inhaling a little of someone else's marijuana smoke.

Some arithmetic quickly shows the potential for abuse in drug testing. In the case of drug urinalysis, a test with 90 percent accuracy would be considered unusually good.[28] If a group is screened with a 90 percent accurate test, and 1 percent of employees use drugs, there could be as many as nine false positive readings for every true one. The lives of the 9 persons falsely accused might be affected negatively.

Drug testing has caused an emotional outpouring of pros and cons in the media. However, if certain requirements can be met, testing is both appropriate and legal. Those requirements are:[29]

- Job consequences of abuse are so severe they outweigh privacy concerns.
- Accurate test procedures are available.
- Employees' consent in writing is obtained.
- Results are treated confidentially, as any medical record.
- Employers have a complete drug program including counseling assistance to drug users.

The U.S. Supreme Court has ruled that certain drug-test plans do not violate the Constitution. But private employer programs are governed mainly by state laws which currently are a confusing hodge-podge. Federal agencies are moving ahead rapidly despite legal challenges. Passage of the Drug-Free Workplace Act in 1989 placed requirements on employers that are government contractors to take steps to eliminate employee drug-usage. The Transportation Department has tested truck and bus drivers, train crews, mass transit employees, airline pilots and mechanics, pipeline workers, and licensed seamen. Eight to 30 percent of truck driver tests have proved positive. On the other hand, out of 35,000 air traffic controllers tests, 161 were positive. Thirty-four were fired and the rest were reassigned or returned to duty after rehabilitation.[30]

Both NASA and the U.S. Air Force have used a simple test of critical tracking ability to detect impairment due to drug use. The test is easier and quicker than urinalysis. It can be used to assess a worker's fitness on the spot before he or she goes to work. The test operates much like a video game. It measures the ability to use fine hand-eye coordination and reaction time and takes less than a minute.[31]

Polygraph and Honesty Testing

The late Senator Sam Ervin called them "twentieth-century witchcraft," but until recently employers continued to use polygraph or "lie detector" tests. The theory behind a polygraph is that the act of lying produces stress which in turn causes observable physical change. The examiner can then interpret those physical responses to specific questions and make a judgment as to whether the person being tested is practicing deception.

However, the Office of Technology Assessment determined that the validity of lie detector tests could not be established. The American Psychological Association contends that an "unacceptable number of false positives" occur. [32] For these reasons, few American courts will admit polygraph data as evidence. As mentioned in Chapter 9, in 1988 Congress passed the Polygraph Protection Act, which prohibits the use of polygraphs for most pre-employment screening and judging a person's honesty. [33]

HONESTY TESTS.   "Pencil-and-paper" honesty tests have gained popularity recently. They are not restricted by the polygraph law nor by most states. It is estimated that 5,000 organizations are using this alternative to polygraph testing, and over two dozen such tests are being sold. [34]

Like personality tests, honesty tests were developed from test items that differentiated between people known to be honest and those known to be dishonest. But it is not always easy to determine who is honest for the purpose of validating the test, and serious questions can be raised about the validity of the tests. The only major study done on honesty tests found a large body of flawed but consistently supportive research validating them. [35]

Polygraphs and honesty tests do not violate any legal rights of employees if private sector employers adhere to state laws. The Fifth Amendment (which prohibits self-incrimination) may be a basis for prohibiting such tests in public sector employment.

■■ ■ MISCELLANEOUS EMPLOYEE RIGHTS

Four other areas of employee rights should be mentioned briefly: (1) Employee rights in workplace investigations, (2) Employee rights to know of potential hazards, (3) Employee free speech, and (4) Employee notification of plant closing.

Workplace Investigations of Employees

Employers have increased their attempts to investigate employee theft and substance abuse in their organizations. For example, General Motors operated a "sting" operation to identify drug users in some of its plants. As a result, some 200 persons were arrested. Drug abuse, dishonesty, and unethical behavior are the focus of such investigations.

Public-sector employees are protected by the Constitution in the areas of due process, searches and seizure, and privacy. But employees in the private sector have raised some major concerns during such investigations. [36]

- *Defamation* can occur when remarks are made during an investigation. For example, if an employee is referred to as a thief, the employer may be sued for slander and defamation of character.
- *Invasion of privacy* results when private facts discovered in an investigation, are disclosed publicly. Physically entering another's personal property (home, purse, or shopping bag) may constitute invasion of privacy also.
- *Emotional distress* can occur when one person knowingly engages in "outrageous conduct" that results in severe emotional distress. For example, one employer announced it would fire people, one by one, until the thief confessed. This tactic produced several successful "emotional distress" lawsuits.
- *False imprisonment* occurs when an individual is wrongfully restrained physically. Denying an employee permission to leave the room when an interview is being conducted may qualify.
- *Assault and battery* results if a person is touched or fears being touched without permission. Physical detention may violate assault and battery restrictions.

Employee Rights to Know of Hazards

The public's increased awareness of hazards associated with workplace chemicals has been reflected in legislation designed to inform and train employees in the use of hazardous materials. The Hazard Communications Standard, an OSHA regulation (29 CFR 1910.1200), places specific responsibilities on employers to inform employees about the hazards of chemicals with which they work. The standard was first issued in 1983 and targeted the manufacturing sector; later it was expanded to cover *all* employers engaged in the handling and use of hazardous materials. Over the years it has become known as the "worker's right-to-know" law. The Federal OSHA Act provides for states to develop their own occupational safety and health regulations that meet or exceed federal standards.

Chemical manufacturers must provide a material safety data sheet for every hazardous substance. Employer hazard communication programs have several requirements. Employers are required to evaluate chemicals that employees are exposed to and inform them of any hazardous properties. Employers also are required to post a list of all hazardous chemicals in the workplace. For example, welding fumes, wood dust, paints, solvents, sterilizing chemicals and cleaners, carbon monoxide from vehicles, etc. are considered hazardous.[37] Hazardous chemicals must bear identifying labels that state the hazard and employees must be trained in the recognition of hazards and the safe handling and use of chemicals.

Free Speech (Whistle-Blowing)

A person who reports a real or perceived wrong done by his or her employer is called a "whistle-blower." Two key questions are: (1) When do employees have the right to speak out with protection from retribution? (2) When do employees violate the confidentiality of their jobs? Often the answers are difficult to determine. A widely publicized case involved an employee in the U.S. Defense Department who revealed that significant cost overruns on an airplane contract were being concealed from the U.S. Congress. Attempts were made by his superiors to transfer him, demote him, or fire him. The whistle-blower ultimately left the Defense Department, but not before Congress held a series of public hearings and investigations.

Whistle-blowing is an important right, although one that can be abused. But whistle-blowers are less likely to lose their jobs in public employment than in

<table>
<tr><td>

P/HR: Practice *and* Research

</td><td>

Whistle-Blowing

</td></tr>
</table>

One of the few empirical examinations of whistle-blowing was done by Janet Near and Marcia Miceli and reported in the *Journal of Applied Psychology*. Through the U.S. Merit Systems Protection Board, they mailed a questionnaire to 13,000 employees of 15 federal agencies. Approximately 8,600 were returned, for a response rate of 66 percent.

Respondents were asked if they had seen wrong doings in the agencies during the last 12 months and if so, had they blown the whistle? Respondents reported affirmatively to both questions. The respondents were then asked if they had experienced retaliation as a result of whistle-blowing. Many had and an analysis of that retaliation was undertaken.

Those persons who had gone outside the organization with their information suffered more severe retaliation than those who took their complaints to management. Retaliation was related to the whistle-blower's decision in some cases to leave the organization. For those whistle-blowers who stayed, retaliation did not keep them from insisting that they would do it again. In summary, whistle-blowers appear committed to bringing about change, and retaliation simply does not keep many of them from acting.

The research paints a picture of employers lashing out at a "stool pigeon." If that is the case, the idea that employers should *encourage* valid whistle-blowing may be difficult to implement.[38]

private employment because most civil service systems have rules protecting whistle-blowers.

However, rights to free speech are not protected by a comprehensive whistle-blowing law that applies to both public and private employees. If an individual is fired or made miserable for reporting a perceived wrongdoing, that person may not receive proper redress. One study revealed that whistle-blowers are more likely to suffer retaliation if they lack support of their managers. Retaliation was more severe if the employee used channels outside the organization for blowing the whistle (see the P/HR: Research).

Employee's Right to Know of Plant Closings

When an employer chooses to close a facility, the employees usually experience severe economic and psychological problems.[39] The federal government requires a sixty-day notice before "massive layoff" or "plant closing" involving more than fifty people. The WARN Act (Worker Adjustment and Retraining Notification) imposes stiff fines on employers who do not give such notice.

▉ ■ P/HR POLICIES, PROCEDURES, AND RULES

It is useful at this point to consider some guidelines for making P/HR policies, procedures, and rules. Where there is a choice among actions, policies act as guides to choosing the appropriate actions. **Policies** are general in nature, while procedures and rules are specific to the situation. The important role of policies in guiding organizational decision making requires that they be reviewed regularly because obsolete policies can result in poor decisions and poor coordination. Policy pro-

POLICIES
are general guidelines that regulate organizational actions.

PROCEDURES
are customary methods of handling
activities.

RULES
are specific guidelines that regulate
and restrict the behavior of individuals.

liferation also must be carefully monitored. Failure to review, add to, or delete policies as situations change may lead to problems.

Procedures are customary methods of handling activities and are more specific than policies. For example, policy may grant that an employee will be given a vacation. Procedures will establish a specific method for authorizing vacation time without disrupting work.

Rules are similar to procedures in that they guide action and typically allow no discretion in their application. They may be part of a procedure, but seldom constitute the entire procedure. A rule reflects a management decision that action be taken—or not taken—in a given situation and provides more specific behavioral guidelines than policies. For example, one welding company has a policy stating that management intends to provide the highest quality welding service in the area. The rule that a welder with fewer than five years of welding experience will not be hired carries out this policy. This rule constrains P/HR selection decisions.

P/HR Policy Coordination Responsibilities

For policies, procedures, and rules to be effective, coordination between the P/HR unit and other managers is vital. As Figure 17–5 shows, managers as the main users and enforcers of rules, procedures, and policies should receive some training and explanation in how to carry out the policies. The P/HR unit supports other managers. It is critical that any conflict between the two entities be resolved so that employees receive a fair and coordinated response.

Guidelines for P/HR Policies and Rules

The following guidelines suggest that well-designed P/HR policies and rules should be consistent, necessary, applicable, understandable, distributed and communicated, and reasonable. A discussion of each characteristic follows.

CONSISTENT.   Rules should be consistent with organizational policies, and policies should be consistent with organizational goals. The principal intent of policies is to provide written guidelines and to specify actions. If some policies and rules are enforced and others are not, then all tend to lose their effectiveness.

NECESSARY.   P/HR policies and rules should reflect organizational philosophy and directions. To this end, managers should confirm the intent and necessity of proposed rules and eliminate obsolete ones. Policies and rules should be reviewed whenever there is a major organizational change. Unfortunately, this review is not always done, and outdated rules are still on the books in many organizations.

APPLICABLE.   Because P/HR policies are general guidelines for action, they should be applicable to a large group of employees. If they are not, then the appropriate areas or people must be identified. For instance, if a sick leave policy is applicable only to nonexempt employees, it should be specified in the company handbook. Policies and rules that apply only to one unit or type of job should be developed as part of specific guidelines for that unit or job.

UNDERSTANDABLE.   P/HR policies and rules should be written so that employees can clearly understand them. One way to determine if policies and rules are

P/HR UNIT	MANAGERS
■ Designs formal mechanisms for coordinating P/HR policies ■ Provides advice in development of organization-wide P/HR policies, procedures, and rules ■ Provides information on application of P/HR policies, procedures, and rules ■ Explains P/HR rules to managers ■ Trains managers in carrying out policies, procedures, and rules	■ Help in developing P/HR policies and rules ■ Review policies and rules with employees ■ Apply P/HR policies, procedures, and rules ■ Explain rules and policies to employees

Figure 17–5
P/HR Policy Coordination Responsibilities

understandable is to ask a cross section of employees with various positions, education levels, and job responsibilities to explain the intent and meaning of a rule. If the answers are extremely varied, the rule should be rewritten.

DISTRIBUTED AND COMMUNICATED.   P/HR policies must be distributed and communicated to employees to be effective. Employee handbooks can be creatively designed to explain detailed policies and rules so that people can refer to them at times when no one is available to answer a question. Supervisors and managers can maintain discipline by reminding their employees about policies and rules.

REASONABLE.   Ideally, employees should be able to see policies as being fair and realistic. Policies and rules that are so inflexible or penalize individuals unfairly should be reevaluated. For example, a rule forbidding workers to use the company telephone for personal calls may be unreasonable if emergency phone calls are occasionally necessary. Limiting the amount of time the telephone can be used for personal business and the number of calls might be more reasonable.

Some of the most ticklish policies and rules involve employee behavior. Dress codes are frequently controversial, and organizations that have them should be able to justify them to the satisfaction of both employees and outside sources that might question them. No-smoking policies also can generate considerable heat.

■■ ■ EMPLOYEE DISCIPLINE

Employee rights are an appropriate introduction to the topic of employee discipline because employee rights are often an issue in disciplinary cases. **Discipline** is a form of training that enforces organizational rules. The goal of preventive discipline is to heighten employee awareness of organizational policies and rules. Knowledge of disciplinary actions may prevent violations. The emphasis on preventive discipline is similar to the emphasis on preventing accidents. Counseling by a supervisor in the work unit can have positive effects. Many times people simply need to be made aware of a rule.

The disciplinary system (see Figure 17–6) also can be viewed as an application of behavior modification to marginal or unproductive employees. The best discipline is clearly self-discipline. Once most people understand what is required at work, they can usually be counted on to do their jobs effectively. Yet some find that the prospect of external discipline helps their self-discipline. Even though an

DISCIPLINE
is a form of training that enforces organizational rules.

Figure 17–6
The Disciplinary System

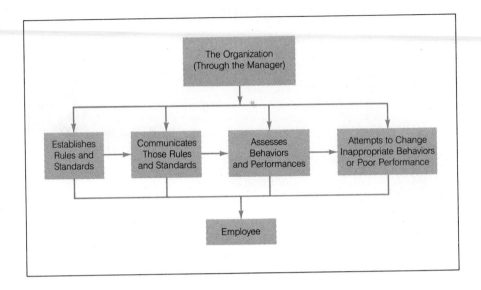

employer's description of discipline is purposely upbeat and nonnegative in tone, there are times when discipline involves the use of punishment. Under such circumstances, managers must see to it that punishment is *corrective* in nature and not purely punitive.

Marginal Employees

The marginal employee is typically one of a small number of employees who cause the most problems. If the employer fails to deal with marginal employees, they can have adverse effects on the entire work group. Disciplinary problems caused by marginal employees include absenteeism, tardiness, productivity deficiencies, alcoholism, and insubordination.[40]

Counseling and Discipline

Counseling can be an important part of the discipline process. The focus is on fact finding and guidance to encourage desirable behavior, instead of using penalties to discourage undesirable behavior. The philosophy is that violations are actions that can be constructively corrected without penalty.

Typically, there is a sequence of events in counseling and discipline. Often, an employee's first violation results in a meeting with the immediate supervisor. A second violation brings another discussion with the supervisor on how this kind of behavior can be avoided in the future. The next violation leads to counseling with the same manager and that manager's immediate superior. A fourth infraction results in "final counseling" with top management. The offender is typically sent home for the rest of the day without pay and told that any further violation will result in termination. If the employee has no further violations for a year, his or her personnel file is wiped clean. Any new violations start the process all over again. Certain serious offenses are exempted from the procedure and may result in immediate termination. Stealing or coming to work intoxicated are common offenses leading to immediate termination. Certain offenses typically carry more severe penalties than others, as can be seen in Figure 17-7.

PROBLEM	TYPICAL HANDLING		
	WARNINGS	SUSPENSION	DISCHARGE
Attendance	X	XX	XXX
Intoxication at work		XX	XXX
Fighting		O	XXX
Failure to use safety devices	X	O	XXX
Sleeping on the job	X		XXX
Possession of weapons			XXX
Theft			XXX
Drug use at work			XXX
Falsifying employment application			XXX
Outside criminal activities			XXX

Note: O means this step *may* be omitted.

Figure 17–7
Offenses and Penalty Patterns

Progressive Discipline

Progressive discipline incorporates a sequence of steps into the shaping of employee
behaviors. Progressive discipline suggests that attempts to modify behavior get progressively more severe as the employee continues to show improper behavior. Figure
17–8 shows a typical progressive discipline system. Progressive discipline, which
foregoes counseling may be used for somewhat more serious offenses. At one
manufacturing firm failure to call in when a employee is to be absent from work,
may lead to a suspension after the third offense in a year.

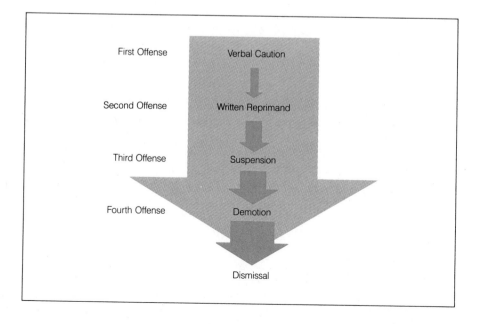

Figure 17–8
Progressive Discipline Procedures

An employee is given every opportunity and help, as appropriate, to correct deficiencies before being dismissed. Following the progressive sequence ensures that both the nature and the seriousness of the problem have been clearly communicated to the employee. Not all steps in the progressive discipline procedure have to be followed in every case. The idea is to impress on the offender the seriousness of the problem and the manager's determination to see that the behavior is changed. Most progressive discipline procedures include verbal and written reprimands and suspension before dismissal occurs.

The Use of Threat

Changes in society have made it increasingly difficult to make employees fear failure and punishment. Many limitations on negative sanctions have been imposed during the last century. Management's ability to use punishment has not disappeared, but it is less subject to control by the individual manager. However, under certain circumstances, threats and discipline can work.[41]

Threats appear to be most effective when individuals have a strong fear of failure and low personal standards of conduct or productivity. Punishment does *not* work when inappropriate behavior is caused by intellectual or physical factors. In fact, under those circumstances, punishment can actually do considerable harm and should not be used.

One area in which threats have been used with positive results is in controlling absenteeism. Threats and discipline do not work as direct solutions to alcohol and drug-related problems, but they might be used to motivate employees to seek assistance and treatment.

For discipline to work, it must focus on a specific problem and indicate how employees can change or improve their behavior to avoid further discipline. In addition, the manager must make it clear that threats will be carried out (bluffing will not work) and that administration of discipline is a legitimate part of a manager's responsibility. This kind of communication requires coolness under emotionally tense conditions, as well as management expertise in diagnosing and resolving the situation.

Why Discipline May Not Be Used

Sometimes managers are reluctant to use discipline. There are several reasons why discipline may not be used.

1. *Lack of training*: Many managers have little background in using discipline and have no idea how to administer it effectively. They should avoid using discipline.
2. *Lack of support*: Many managers do not want to use discipline because they fear that their decisions will not be backed by higher management.
3. *Fear of acting alone*: A manager may feel that he or she is the only one who is enforcing a rule. For example, an employee protests discipline by saying, "You are the *only manager* that makes us arrive at eight o'clock."
4. *Guilt*: Some managers feel that before they became managers, they filled the same shoes as their employees, so they cannot discipline others for doing something they used to do.
5. *Loss of friendship*: If managers allow themselves to become too friendly with employees, they might fear losing that friendship if they use discipline.

6. *Time loss:* Discipline, when done properly, does require a lot of time. There are many steps involved and many interviews with the employee. Sometimes, it is easier for managers not to spend the time disciplining especially if their actions may be overturned by higher management.

7. *Loss of temper:* Managers may be afraid that they will lose their tempers when talking about a rule violation with the employee.

8. *Rationalization:* Many managers rationalize that employees know when they have done something wrong and that they (managers) do not really need to talk to the employees because the employees realize that they were wrong.

9. *Lack of appropriate policies:* Absence of appropriate policies within the organization for disciplinary action may dissuade managers from taking action otherwise deserved.

10. *Fear of lawsuits:* Managers are increasingly concerned with being *sued* for disciplining someone, particularly for taking the ultimate disciplinary step of dismissal (see the P/HR: Practice).

If managers do not take disciplinary action when gross infractions occur, there is a chance that some individuals who usually would *not* get into trouble will do so. Some organizations take a lenient attitude toward theft of company property. A major felony may result in nothing more than a reprimand or disciplinary suspension. The drastic step of calling in the police is almost never taken unless a sizable permanent cash loss is involved. Yet it is clear that anything short of drastic action tends to encourage some people to steal.

Effective Discipline

Because of the legal aspects, managers must understand discipline and know how to administer it properly. Good discipline always should be aimed at the behavior, not at the employee personally. The reason for discipline is to improve performance.

The manager administering discipline must consider the effect of actions taken by other managers and actions taken in the past. *Consistency* and *precedent* are important if employees are to preceive discipline as equitable. For example, if two people commit the same offense, but one person is more severely disciplined, the latter may rightfully complain about differential treatment and favoritism. Consistent discipline helps to set limits and informs people about what they can and cannot do. Inconsistent discipline leads to confusion and uncertainty. The purpose of discipline is not to get revenge or satisfaction for wrongs that have been committed; rather it is to change undesirable behavior.

Effective discipline in our society requires that people know the rules. When people perceive discipline as unfair, they often do not realize that they have broken a rule. This situation is different from the legal system in which "ignorance of the law is no excuse." Where employee discipline is concerned, honest ignorance often is an acceptable excuse, which puts the pressure on management to see to it that employees have been informed of all rules as well as of any changes that might have occurred.

Good discipline is *immediate.* The longer the time that transpires between the offense and the disciplinary action, the less effective the discipline will be. For example, an employee who has a poor record for wearing safety gear fails to wear his goggles one day. His supervisor notices it, but is busy with another problem so he does not confront the employee about it. Just before quitting time, the supervisor calls the employee into the office to give him a two-day suspension without pay. This tactic is a poor way to handle discipline.

P/HR: Practice *and* Research

The Risks of Firing

In the comics, Mr. Dithers always shakes a finger at Dagwood Bumstead and fires him on the spot, but the funny papers no longer follow reality. Firing is not that easy anymore. The right to fire employees, a manager's ultimate weapon, is coming under unprecedented legal attack. A number of lawsuits have been settled *for the complainant*, and these cases usually are based on the court's assessment that the complainant has been *unfairly treated*.

Some organizations are pressing managers to be more truthful when they give employees performance appraisals. These employers insist that managers use progressive discipline and document reasons for dismissals more thoroughly. One management lawyer cautions that managers may have *personal liability* if they do not give honest appraisals.

In a recent case involving Bissell Incorporated, an executive's performance began to slip after he was passed over for promotion to vice president. He received neither dismissal warnings nor an opportunity to improve before he was fired. He accused Bissell of negligence and a federal judge partially agreed, saying that Bissell had a duty to inform the executive more fully about the reasons for the termination decision. The judge ultimately awarded the man over $60,000. The decision has led Bissell to put greater emphasis on tough, honest performance appraisals. Now, before dismissals can occur, the general manager says he asks the supervisor, "Has he been warned properly and notified and does the person's personnel file reflect the justification?"[42]

Good discipline is handled *impersonally*, although the person being disciplined may often be resentful and aggressive. Managers can help minimize these feelings by being as objective and honest as possible.

Managers cannot make discipline an enjoyable experience, but they can minimize the unpleasant effect somewhat by presenting it impersonally and by focusing on behaviors, not on the person. Effective discipline also must be clearly linked to job-related behavior or performance. Punishment presented in an inconsistent manner has a negative effect on employees' job satisfaction.[43]

Discharge: The Final Alternative

The manager may feel guilty when dismissing an employee. If an employee fails, it may be because the manager was not able to create an appropriate working environment. Perhaps the employee was not adequately trained or management failed to establish effective policies. Managers are responsible for their people and they share the blame for failures.

General Electric, Union Carbide, and S. C. Johnson and Sons have adopted systems that require employees who have been warned about deficiencies to create their own improvement plans. Firing a worker because she does not keep her own promises is more likely to appear equitable and defensible to a jury. Also, the system seems to reduce the emotional reactions that lead fired workers to sue in the first place.[44]

Discipline and Productivity

That discipline and sanctions are positively related to performance surprises some who feel that punishment can only harm behavior. Yet employees look to other people to learn appropriate behaviors and attitudes (modeling). In work organizations, standards become institutionalized through roles, operating procedures, and group norms. The work group may feel uncertain or perceive that an inequity has taken place if one individual violates these standards. Those individuals who violate organizational rules may violate group norms as well, so lack of discipline can cause problems for the group as well as for the manager.

If a manager tolerates unacceptable behavior, the group may feel further threatened. Although employees may understandably resist unjustified discipline from a manager, actions that are taken to maintain legitimate standards may actually reinforce productive group norms and result in increased performance.

SUMMARY

- Ideas about normal and legal employee rights have changed considerably in the last 20 years.
- The employment relationship is viewed as a reciprocal one in which the employee, in return for loyalty, service, etc., has moral rights.
- Employee rights affecting the employment agreement include employment-at-will, implied contracts, due process, and dismissal for cause.
- Employment-at-will relationships are changing in the courts. At-will employees have found protection under public policy exceptions, implied contract exceptions, and good faith/fair dealing exceptions.
- An employee handbook and P/HR policies have been viewed as contracts by the courts, which presents no problem as long as the handbook conforms to certain standards.
- Although due process is not guaranteed for at-will employees, the courts expect to see evidence of due process in employee discipline cases. It is good management to do so anyway.
- Dismissal for cause has been tested through arbitration and court cases.
- Employee rights to their own records vary considerably from state to state. Government employees have consistent rights and guarantees in this regard.
- Drug testing generally *is* legal and thus is widely used as employers try to deal with increasing drug problems at work.
- Polygraph testing appears to be relatively inaccurate and its use has declined. In its place are pencil-and-paper honesty tests that employers use to deal with high levels of employee dishonesty.
- Miscellaneous employee rights include workplace investigations, right to know of hazards, whistle-blowing and plant closings.
- Discipline is best thought of as a form of training. Although self-discipline is the goal, sometimes counseling or progressive discipline are necessary to encourage self-discipline.
- Threat works to change behavior in certain situations. In others, it does not.
- Managers may fail to discipline when they should for a variety of reasons. The end point in the dismissal process—termination—has been drastically changed as a result of redefinition of employee rights.
- Good discipline can have a positive effect on productivity.

REVIEW AND DISCUSSION QUESTIONS

1. From where do employee rights originate?
2. Explain the public policy exception to employment-at-will.

3. Discuss the differences and similarities between the issues of due process and just cause.
4. What are the pros and cons of giving a prospective employer honest information on a former employee of yours who stole from the company?
5. Design a checklist of items to remember in doing an investigation of an employee in your company.
6. What does it mean for discipline to be internal as opposed to external? Which is best?

CASE	To Honk or Not to Honk

Dominic Garcia, a delivery truck driver for United Parcel in Stockton, California, believes in standing up for his rights. Mr. Garcia is a Teamster activist, not beloved by his bosses at United Parcel. One day he was making his rounds with a supervisor in the cab of his truck. As he pulled up in front of a house to deliver a package, the supervisor ordered him to "honk the horn" to call out the customer. Instead, Garcia got out and rang the customer's doorbell.

The law in California (and most states) says drivers of delivery trucks are to use their horns only for emergencies. But United Parcel had a policy ordering drivers to honk their horns to save time. "It rubbed me the wrong way," said Garcia, "that they would order me to violate the law."

The district manager told Garcia that the company would pay any fine for honking, but Garcia still said no and was dismissed for insubordination. His case progressed through arbitration (he was temporarily reinstated with a ten day suspension), to the National Labor Relations Board, to the Federal Appeals Court.[45]

QUESTIONS

1. How do you suppose the court ruled?
2. What is the employee rights issue here?
3. If the company had not been unionized, what recourse would Garcia have had?

NOTES

1. "Supervisors Using Electronic Scrutiny," *Omaha World-Herald*, February 18, 1990, 12–G. M. Verespej, "How Much Can You 'Bug' Employees?" *Industry Week*, August 7, 1989, 65; J. Abramson, "Mind What You Say; They're Listening," *Wall Street Journal*, October 25, 1989, 51; P. Amend, "High Tech Surveillance," *USA Today*, March 14, 1990, 11B.
2. Patricia H. Werhane, *Persons, Rights, and Corporations* (Englewood Cliffs, N.J.: Prentice-Hall, 1985), 78.
3. Mary Gibson, *Worker's Rights* (New York: Rowman and Allanheld, 1983), 124.
4. Werhane, op. cit., 102–104.
5. B. Rosen and C. Schwoerer, "Balanced Protection Policies," *HRM Magazine*, February 1990, 59.
6. C. Skrzycki, "Just Who Is in Charge Here, Anyway?" *Washington Post*, January 29, 1989, H1.
7. D. Bacon, "See You in Court," *Nation's Business*, July 1989, 17.
8. "50 State Survey," *Omaha World-Herald*, September 17, 1989, 16.
9. L. Lorber et al., "The Manager's Individual Liability in the Workplace . . .," *Legal Report*, *Society for Human Resource Management*, Winter 1989, 4.

10. Rosen and Schwoerer, op. cit., 61.

11. Adapted from R. M. Smith, "Exemptions to the Employment-at-Will Doctrine," *Labor Law Journal* 366 (1985): 875–876.

12. William H. Holley and Roger S. Wolters, "An Employment-at-Will Vulnerability Audit," *Personnel Journal*, April 1987, 130–138.

13. M. Wald and D. Wolf, "Recent Developments in the Law of Employment-at-Will," *The Labor Lawyer* 36 (1985): 541–542.

14. Adapted from K. Decker, "At-Will Employment in Pennsylvania," *Dickinson Law Review* 87 (1983): 504–505.

15. P. K. Gillette, "The Implied Covenant of Good Faith and Fair Dealing: Are Employers the Insurers of the Eighties?" *Employee Relations Law Journal* 11 (1986): 440.

16. Adapted from J. D. Coombe, "Employee Handbooks: Asset or Liability?" *Employee Relations Law Journal* 12 (1987): 6–9.

17. *Ibid.* 14–16.

18. M. Hill, Jr. and D. Dawson, "Discharge for Off-Duty Misconduct in the Private and Public Sectors," *Arbitration Journal*, June 1985, 24–25.

19. Ibid, 31.

20. S. C. Kahn, "Employee Access to Personnel Records," *Employment Relations Today* 12 (195–86): 315.

21. R. W. Woodman et al., "A Survey of Employee Perceptions of Information Privacy in Organization," *Academy of Management Journal* 25 (1982): 660.

22. J. Solomon, "As Firms' Personnel Files Grow, Worker Privacy Falls," *Wall Street Journal*, April 19, 1989, B1.

23. B. Murphy, "Drug Testing in the Utility Industry," *Management Quarterly*, Summer 1989, 16–30.

24. *Omaha World-Herald*, April 1, 1987, 14.

25. *Industry Week*, February 9, 1987, 20–21.

26. J. Bloch, "So What? Everyone Is Doing It?" *Fortune*, August 11, 1986, 102.

27. J. Redeker and J. Segal, "Profits Low? Your Employees May Be High!" *Personnel*, June 1989, 72–77.

28. W. H. Anderson, "Too Many Bugs in Screening Measures," *Wall Street Journal*, June 16, 1986, 22.

29. W. Green, "Drug Testing Becomes a Corporate Mine Field," *Wall Street Journal*, November 21, 1989, B1.

30. "Labor Letter," *Wall Street Journal*, May 8, 1990, 1.

31. "Job Test Screens for Impairment, Protects Privacy," *Omaha World-Herald*, March 11, 1990, G1.

32. S. Dentzer et al., "Can You Pass the Job Test?" *Newsweek*, May 5, 1990, 47.

33. "How to Comply with the Polygraph Law," *Nation's Business*, December 1989, 36–37.

34. C. Gorman, "Honestly, Can We Trust You?" *Time*, January 21, 1989.

35. Paul R. Sackett and Michael M. Harris, "Honesty Testing for Personnel Selection: A Review and Critique," *Personnel Psychology* 37 (1984): 221–245.

36. G. Hensbaw and K. Youmans, "Employee Privacy . . .," *SHRM Legal Report*, Spring 1990, 2–5; and D. J. Duffy, "Conducting Work Place Investigations: Potential Liabilities for Employers," *Employment Relations Today*, Spring 1985, 64–68.

37. P. Tyson, "Hazard Communications for Nonmanufacturing Employees," *SHRM Legal Report*, Spring 1988, 1–4.

38. Adapted from J. P. Near and M. P. Miceli, "Retaliation Against Whistleblowers: Predictors and Effects," *Journal of Applied Psychology* 71 (1986): 137–145.

39. J. Bracher and A. Kinicki, "Strategic Management, Plant Closings, and Social Responsibility: An Integrative Process Model," *Employee Responsibilities and Rights Journal* 1, (1989) 203.

40. J. Braham, "Difficult Employees," *Industry Week*, June 19, 1989, 30–35.

41. The following discussion is adapted from J. Miner, *The Challenge of Managing* (Philadelphia: W. B. Saunders, 1975), 75–76.

42. Adapted from J. S. Lublin, "Legal Challenges Force Firms to Revamp Ways They Dismiss Workers," *Wall Street Journal*, September 13, 1986, 1.

43. C. Greer and C. Labig, Jr., "Employee Reactions to Disciplinary Action," *Human Relations* 40, (1988) 507–524.

44. S. Herman, "Ready, Aim or Fire?" *Personnel Administrator*, June 1989, 132–134.

45. Adapted from D. Meister, "Hero Hunting," *Christian Science Monitor*, May 29, 1986, 12.

Union–Management Relations

After you have read this chapter, you should be able to:

1. Identify what a union is and state the two major purposes of unions in the United States
2. Trace the evolution of American labor unions from 1800 to 1935
3. Explain the acts that compose the National Labor Code
4. Describe the different structure levels of unions
5. Identify and discuss the stages in the unionization process
6. Explain the decline in the percentage of U.S. workers represented by unions

P/HR: Today *and* Tomorrow

Nissan Workers Reject Unionization

One of the most widely publicized efforts by a union to represent a group of employees took place in 1989 at the Nissan Motor Manufacturing Corporation Plant in Smyrna, Tennessee. The union election received extensive media coverage for several reasons.

First, this effort by the United Auto Workers (UAW) was the first union election conducted by the National Labor Relations Board at Japanese-owned auto plants in the United States. Second, more and more Japanese automobile firms have established plants in the United States, and the Nissan election was seen by many as a test of some of the Japanese management strategies used in those plants. The only previous effort by the UAW to organize a Japanese automobile plant was at the Honda plant in Marysville, Ohio, in 1985. However, the union withdrew its request for an election shortly before voting was to occur. The UAW did win representation at some plants that are jointly owned by U.S. and Japanese firms, such as the Mazda–Ford plant in Flat Rock, Michigan, and the Toyota–General Motors plant in Fremont, California. But the Nissan election vote was the first one in which no U.S. partner was involved. A third reason for the attention given to the Nissan election was that the plant was the first of a number of new Japanese-owned plants to open in the southern United States, which traditionally has been hostile to unions.

The results of the election represented a major setback to efforts to unionize Japanese-owned auto plants. By more than a two-to-one margin, Nissan workers rejected the union. The vote was 1,622 against and 711 for the union. The reasons for the decisive rejection of the union provide some interesting insights on why unions in the United States have had increasing difficulty recruiting members in the 1980s and how an employer's style of management can affect workers' views of the need for union representation.

The primary reason that the union lost the election can be summarized in remarks by Nissan members such as Dotty Lachert, a production technician, who said, "The UAW can't give us anything we don't already have." Bucky Kahl, the director of human resources at Nissan, said, "We pride ourselves in being a company that functions in a participatory way . . . The vote was a statement of support for strongly participative management."

In the effort to persuade workers to vote one way or the other, the company and the union used different appeals. The UAW campaigned on the issues of workplace safety and the fast pace of the assembly line at Nissan. To convey its message, the UAW president, Owen Bieber, led the organizing campaign, aided by thirty professional organizers.

The company countered the union campaign by emphasizing the good benefits, pay levels, and participative management climate. During the last few weeks before the election, Nissan management held small-group meetings with workers at which managers stated that the teamwork atmosphere in the plant would be threatened if the union won. Also, management showed videos on strike violence at union-represented plants in other industries. The company also emphasized that in the six years since the plant had been open, no workers had been laid off and that it expected continued expansion and addition of jobs.

Following the election, the Nissan plant manager, Jerry Berefield, said, "I'm more convinced than I ever have been that the UAW is never going to organize this plant." Whether that prediction holds true depends on a number of factors, not the least of which is the continued economic strength of Nissan.[1]

"You can play 'Solidarity Forever' until your banjo string breaks, but it won't solve the lousy problems."

Cass Alvin

Some people contend that a **union**, as a formal association of workers that promotes the interests of its members through collective action, represents an outside force. Certainly, Nissan was able to create this image of the UAW. Others argue that a union is an internal force of employees within an organization. Regardless of the internal–external issue, it is undeniable that unions or unionization pressures present an additional challenge for managers and P/HR professionals.

Figure 18–1 shows the P/HR unit and operating managers' responsibilities in dealing with unions. This pattern may vary in different organizations. In some organizations, the P/HR is not involved with labor relations because the operating management handles them. In other organizations, the P/HR unit is almost completely in charge of labor relations. The division of responsibilities shown in Figure 18–1 is a midpoint between these extremes.

This chapter takes a broad look at union–management relations. Specific information on how unions become employee representatives is also presented.

When employees choose a union to represent them, management and union representatives enter into formal collective bargaining over certain issues such as pay scales, benefits, etc. Once these issues are resolved into a labor contract, management and union representatives must work together to manage the contract and deal with grievances. Grievances are formal complaints filed by workers with management. Collective bargaining and grievance procedures are two important interfaces that occur between management and labor unions once a union has gained recognition as a legal representative of employee interests. Both areas are examined in Chapter 19.

A UNION
is a formal association of workers that promotes the interests of its members through collective action.

UNIONISM IN THE UNITED STATES

Unionism in the United States has followed a somewhat different pattern than unionism in other countries. In such countries as Italy, England, and Japan, the union movement has been at the forefront of nationwide political trends. For the most part, this politicalization has not occurred in the United States. Perhaps workers in the United States tend to identify with the American free enterprise system. Further, class consciousness and conflict between the working class and the management class is less in the United States than in many other countries. Ownership of private property by both management and workers is a further mediating influence in the United States.

P/HR UNIT	MANAGERS
■ Deals with union organizing attempts at the company level ■ Monitors "climate" for unionization and union relationships ■ Helps negotiate labor agreements ■ Provides detailed knowledge of labor legislation as may be necessary	■ Provide conditions conducive to a positive relationship with employees ■ Avoid unfair labor practices during organizing efforts ■ Administer the labor agreement on daily basis ■ Resolve grievances and problems between management and employees

Figure 18–1
Labor Relations Responsibilities

Purposes of Unions

Unions in the United States have several roles. These roles reflect the purposes of the unions in the American capitalist system. The two major roles are discussed next.

JOB-CENTERED ROLE.   The primary purpose of unionism in the United States has been the collective pursuit of "bread-and-butter" economic gains. Unions have emphasized helping workers obtain higher wages, shorter working hours, job security, and safe working conditions from their employers.

Achieving their goals has meant that unions have had to be politically active in order to get supportive laws passed. Such political activity traditionally was oriented more toward workplace issues such as health and safety, minimum wage increases, and pension protection. But, increasingly, unions have taken positions on broad social and economic issues. For example, unions have been in the forefront of those pushing for mandatory parental leave, universal health insurance for most workers, and child-care tax credits for working parents. In a period of economic and demographic change, unions likely will continue to press for broader worker-oriented laws. In summary, labor unions see themselves as ensuring that the needs of workers are considered when governmental laws and issues affecting workers are addressed.

COUNTERVAILING FORCE ROLE.   Another role unions see for themselves is as a countervailing force that keeps management "honest" and makes management consider the impact of its policies on its employees. However, a rather delicate balance exists between management power and union power in an organization. It is easy for this balance to be tipped one way or the other.

Through their respective representatives, management and unions spend a great deal of time and effort disagreeing with each other. Because of their built-in adversarial roles, disagreement is to be expected. Yet it is naive to suppose that either position or group is right all the time or to assume that there are many serious disagreements that lead to strikes. Work lost because of strikes or lockouts has constituted a relatively small percentage of total work time. The U.S. figures are considerably lower than those of many other countries.

These two philosophical purposes of unions, focusing on jobs and serving as a countervailing force, can be seen throughout the evolution of the union movement in the United States. An overview of major milestones in that evolution follows.

▬ ▬ EVOLUTION OF U.S. UNIONS

It has been suggested that the labor movement in the United States arose when craft workers in similar occupations banded together voluntarily to protect their jobs.[2] Voluntary union membership is based on *job consciousness*: Jobs are a scarce resource and union members must protect them. Following this line of reasoning, the union's chief concern is *job control*. A union is expected to control the jobs under the union's jurisdiction, such as plumbing, electrical work, or carpentry. Job control has been one of the cornerstones of American unionism.

Early Union Efforts

As early as 1794, shoemakers organized a union, picketed, and conducted strikes. However, in those days, unions in the United States received very little support from the courts. In 1806, when the shoemaker's union struck for higher wages, a Philadelphia court found union members guilty of engaging in a *criminal conspiracy* to raise wages.

COMMONWEALTH V. HUNT.   In 1842 the Massachusetts Supreme Court handed down a decision in the case of *Commonwealth v. Hunt* that became an important legal landmark. The court ruled, "For a union to be guilty of conspiracy, either its objective of the means used to reach it must be criminal or unlawful."[3] As a result of this decision, unions were no longer seen as illegal conspiracies in the eyes of the courts, and the conspiracy idea lost favor.

Major Labor Organizations

The end of the Civil War in 1865 was followed by rapid industrial expansion and a growth of giant business trusts. The 1870s were characterized by industrial unrest, low wages, long hours, and considerable unemployment. In 1877, great railroad strikes spread through the major U.S. railroad companies as union members protested against the practices of railroad management. Eight years later, a group of workers formed the Knights of Labor.

KNIGHTS OF LABOR.   The goals of the Knights of Labor were: (1) to establish one large union embracing all workers, and (2) to establish a cooperative economic system to replace capitalism. The leaders of the Knights of Labor believed that a large, national union was necessary to counterbalance the huge business trusts of that time. They emphasized political reform and establishment of work cooperatives. But after their peak in 1885, the Knights soon faded from the labor scene.

AMERICAN FEDERATION OF LABOR.   In 1886, the American Federation of Labor (AFL) was formed as a federation of independent national unions. Its basic principle was to organize *skilled craft workers*, like carpenters and plumbers, and to bargain for such bread-and-butter issues as wages and working conditions. Samuel Gompers was the AFL's chief spokesman and served as president until his death in 1924.

At first, the AFL grew slowly. Six years after its formation, its total membership amounted to only 250,000. However, it managed to survive in the face of adversity while other labor groups withered and died.

Earlier, the Civil War had given factories a big boost. Factory mass-production methods, which used semiskilled or unskilled workers, were necessary to supply the armies. Though factories provided a potential area of expansion for unions, they were hard to organize. Unions found that they could not control the semiskilled workers entering factory jobs because such workers had no tradition of unionism. It was not until 1938, that the Congress for Industrial Organization (CIO) was founded to provide a labor union organization focusing on semiskilled and unskilled workers.

Early Labor Legislation

The right to organize workers and engage in collective bargaining is of little value if workers are not free to exercise it. As historical evidence shows, whereas management has developed practices calculated to prevent workers from using this right, the federal government has taken action to both hamper unions and protect them.

SHERMAN AND CLAYTON ACTS.   The passage of the Sherman Antitrust Act in 1890 forbade monopolies and certain efforts to restrain trade. Later, as a result of a 1908 Supreme Court case, *(Loewe v. Lawlor)*, union boycott efforts were classed as attempts to restrain trade.

In 1914, the Clayton Act, which limited management's use of legal injunctions to stop labor disputes, was passed. But it had little effect because of a Supreme Court interpretation of the Act. As a result, union strength declined throughout the 1920s.

RAILWAY LABOR ACT.   The Railway Labor Act (1926) represented a shift in government regulation of unions. As a result of a joint effort between railroad management and unions to reduce transportation strikes, this act gave railroad employees "the right to organize and bargain collectively through representatives of their own choosing." In 1936, airlines and their employees were added to those covered by the act. Both these industries are still covered by this act instead of by others passed later.

The act outlines a rather complex series of steps to prevent work stoppages. Although a detailed explanation is beyond the scope of this book, it should be noted that many labor experts today feel that the airline and railroad industries should be covered under the same laws as all other industries. Because times have changed, they argue, the Railway Labor Act should be eliminated.[4]

NORRIS–LAGUARDIA ACT.   In 1932, Congress passed the Norris–LaGuardia Act, which guaranteed workers some rights to organize and restricted the issuance of court injunctions in labor disputes. The Norris–LaGuardia Act substantially freed union activity from court interference and made the infamous *yellow dog contract* illegal. Under this type of contract, signed by the workers as a condition of employment, the employee agreed not to join a union on penalty of discharge. It was called a yellow dog contract because, according to union sympathizers, only a "yellow dog" would take a job under such conditions.

In 1933, the National Industry Recovery Act (NIRA) was passed. It contained, among other clauses, provisions extending the policies of the Railway Labor Act for railroad employees into interstate commerce. Also, the act set up election machinery permitting employees to choose collective bargaining representatives. However, the NIRA was declared unconstitutional in 1935, and was replaced by the Wagner Act.

■ ■ NATIONAL LABOR CODE

Union progress from the 1930s to the mid-1950s provided the basis for the development and passage of several acts: (1) the *Wagner Act*, (2) the *Taft–Hartley Act*,

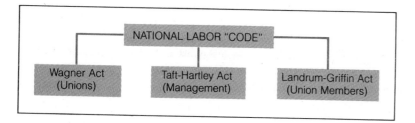

Figure 18–2
National Labor Code

and (3) the *Landrum–Griffin Act*. These acts have had the most direct and continuing impact on employers and unions and form the National Labor Code, the legal basis for today's labor relations in the private sector. Each of the acts in the code was enacted to protect some entity in the union–management relationship. Figure 18–2 shows each segment of the code and which entity receives the greatest protection. The nature of this protection will become clearer as each act is discussed.

A fourth law, the Federal Service Labor–Management Statute of 1978, applies only to U.S. governmental employees and unions representing them. That act became the model for labor codes covering state governmental workers. Also, the act used many provisions in the National Labor Code to tailor a law specifically for federal workers.

Wagner Act (National Labor Relations Act)

The Wagner Act has been called the Magna Carta of labor and was, by anyone's standards, *pro-union*. Passed in 1935, the Wagner Act was an outgrowth of the Great Depression. With employers having to close or cut back their operations, workers were left with little job security. Unions stepped in to provide a feeling of solidarity and strength for many workers. Their success in organizing workers for common goals dramatically increased union membership during the period from 1935 to 1947 to 14 million members, an approximately fourfold increase.

The Wagner Act declared, in effect, that the official policy of the U.S. government was to encourage collective bargaining. It helped union growth in three ways:

1. It established workers' right to organize, unhampered by management interference.
2. It defined unfair labor practices on the part of management.
3. It established the National Labor Relations Board (NLRB) to see that the rules were followed.

The NLRB, although set up as an impartial umpire of the organizing process, has changed its emphasis depending on which political party is in power to appoint members. This body administers all of the provisions of the Wagner and subsequent labor relations acts.

The Wagner Act established the principle that employees would be protected in their rights to form a union and to bargain collectively. To protect union rights, the act prohibited employers from undertaking the following five unfair labor practices:

1. Interfere with, restrain, or coerce employees in the exercise of their rights to organize, bargain collectively, and engage in other concerted activities for their mutual aid or protection
2. Dominate or interfere with the formation or administration of any labor organization or contribute financial or other support to it

3. Encourage or discourage membership in any labor organization by discrimination with regard to hiring or tenure or conditions of employment, subject to an exception for a valid union security agreement
4. Discharge or otherwise discriminate against an employee because he or she filed charges or gave testimony under the act
5. Refuse to bargain collectively with representatives of the employees[5]

Taft–Hartley Act (Labor Management Relations Act)

When World War II ended, the pent-up demand for consumer goods was frustrated by numerous strikes—about three times as many as before the war. The passage of the *Taft–Hartley Act* in 1947 answered the concerns of many who felt that the power had become too strong.

The Taft–Hartley Act was an attempt to balance the collective bargaining equation. It was designed to offset the prounion Wagner Act by limiting union actions; therefore, it was considered to be *pro-management*. It provided the second part of the National Labor Code.

The new law amended or qualified in some respect all of the Wagner Act's major provisions and established an entirely new code of conduct for unions. The Taft-Hartley Act forbade a series of unfair labor practices by unions. It became unlawful for a *union* to:

1. Retain or coerce employees in the exercise of their rights under the act; restrain or coerce any employer in the selection of his bargaining or grievance representative
2. Cause or attempt to cause an employer to discriminate against an employee on account of membership or nonmembership in a labor organization, subject to an exception for a valid union shop agreement
3. Refuse to bargain collectively in good faith with an employer if the union has been designated as bargaining agent by a majority of the employees
4. Induce or encourage employees to stop work for the object of forcing an employer or self-employed person to join a union or forcing an employer or other person to stop doing business with any other person (boycott provisions)
5. Induce or encourage employees to stop work for the object of forcing an employer to assign particular work to members of a union instead of to members of another union (jurisdictional strike)
6. Charge an excessive or discriminatory fee as a condition to becoming a member of the union
7. Cause or attempt to cause an employer to pay for services that are not performed or are not to be performed (featherbedding)

NATIONAL EMERGENCY STRIKE is one that affects an industry or a major part of it such that the national health or safety would be impeded.

NATIONAL EMERGENCY STRIKES.　The Taft–Hartley Act also allows the president of the United States to declare a strike a national emergency. A **national emergency strike** is one that affects an industry or a major part of it such that the national health or safety would be impeded. Under the Taft–Hartley Act, such strikes can be delayed up to eighty days by the action of the president. The national emergency provisions of the act require: (1) the appointment of a fact-finding board, (2) resumption of bargaining by the parties, (3) obtaining an injunction against the strike from federal courts, and (4) a report to Congress. These provisions were upheld following a challenge by the United Steel Workers in 1959.[7]

"RIGHT-TO-WORK." One specific provision (Section 14b) in the Taft–Hartley Act deserves special explanation. The so-called right-to-work provision outlaws the closed shop, except in construction-related occupations, and allows states to pass right-to-work laws. A **closed shop** requires individuals to join a union before they can be hired.

The act did allow the **union shop,** which requires that an employee join the union, usually thirty to sixty days after being hired. **Right-to-work laws** are *state* laws that prohibit both the closed shop and the union shop. They were so named because they allow a person the "right to work" without having to join a union. Approximately twenty states have enacted these laws (see Figure 18–3).

CLOSED SHOP
requires individuals to join a union before they can be hired.
UNION SHOP
requires that an employee join a union, usually 30 to 60 days after being hired.
RIGHT-TO-WORK LAWS
are state laws that prohibit both the closed shop and the union shop.

Figure 18–3
Right-to-Work States

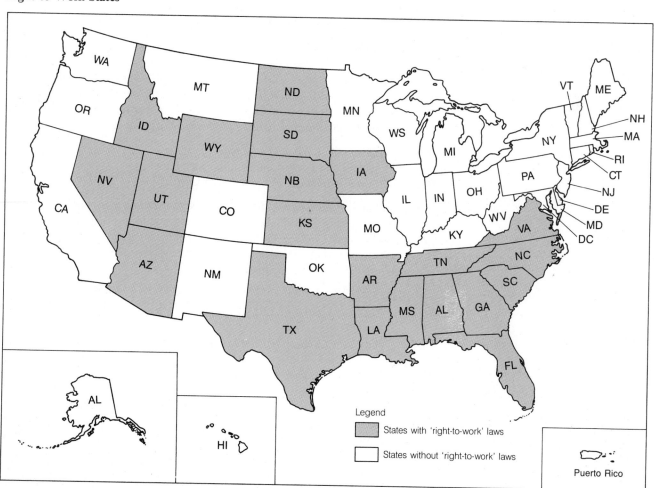

Legend

Shaded: States with 'right-to-work' laws

White: States without 'right-to-work' laws

Puerto Rico

Landrum–Griffin Act
(Labor/Management Reporting and Disclosure Act)

In 1959, the third segment of the National Labor Code, the Landrum–Griffin Act, was passed as a result of a congressional committee's finding on union corruption. The Teamsters union headed by Dave Beck and James Hoffa was investigated by the committee, and the law passed was aimed at protecting individual union members. Among the provisions of the Landrum–Griffin Act are:

1. Every labor organization is required to have a constitution and by-laws containing certain minimum standards and safeguards.
2. Reports on the union's policies and procedures, as well as an annual financial report, must be filed with the Secretary of Labor and must be disclosed to the union's members.
3. Union members must have a bill of rights to protect their rights within the union.
4. Standards are established for union trusteeship and union elections.
5. Reports on trusteeships must be made to the Secretary of Labor.
6. A fiduciary relationship is imposed upon union officers.
7. Union leaders are required to file reports with the Secretary of Labor on conflict-of-interest transactions.
8. The Secretary of Labor is made a watchdog of union conduct, is a custodian of reports from unions and their officers, and is given the power to investigate and prosecute violations of many of the provisions of the act.[8]

UNION MEMBER RIGHTS.   A union is a democratic institution in which union members vote on and elect officers and approve labor contracts. The Landrum–Griffin Act was passed to ensure that the federal government protects those democratic rights. Some important rights guaranteed to individual union members are:

- Right to nominate and vote on officers
- Right to attend and participate in union meetings
- Right to have pension funds properly managed

In a few instances, union officers have attempted to maintain their jobs by physically harassing or attacking individuals who try to oust them from office. In other cases, union officials have "milked" pension fund monies for their own use. Such instances are not typical of most unions, but illustrate the need for legislative oversight to protect individual union members.

Federal Service Labor–Management Relations Statute

Passed as Title VII of the Civil Service Reform Act of 1978, this statute made major changes in how the federal government dealt with unions. The act also identified areas that are and are not subject to bargaining.[9]

The act established the Federal Labor Relations Authority (FLRA) as an independent agency similar to the NLRB. The FLRA was given authority to oversee and administer union–management relations in the federal government and to investigate unfair practices during union organizing efforts. The three-member FLRA is appointed on a bipartisan basis and each member is appointed for five years. In addition, the act gave the Federal Service Impasse Panel (FSIP) the authority to investigate situations in which union–management negotiations reach impasse.

■■ ■ UNION STRUCTURE

American labor is represented by many different unions. Some of them represent workers who do the same kind of job, whereas others represent employees in a particular industry. Some are small, others are large. Some are national, others international. Regardless of size and geographic scope, there are two basic types of unions that have developed over time.

Type of Unions

The two types of unions that exist have different historical roots. A **craft union** is one in which its members do one type of work, often using specialized skills and training. Examples include the International Association of Bridge, Structural, and Ornamental Iron Workers and the American Federation of Television and Radio Artists.

An **industrial union** is one that includes many persons working in the same industry or company, regardless of jobs held. Examples are the United Food and Commercial Workers, United Auto Workers, and the American Federation of State, County, and Municipal Employees.

CRAFT UNION
is one in which its members do one type of work, often using specialized skills and training.

INDUSTRIAL UNION
is one that may include many persons working in the same industry or company, regardless of jobs held.

Union Hierarchy

Labor organizations have developed complex organizational structures with multiple levels. The broadest level is a **federation,** which is a group of autonomous national and international unions. The federation allows for individual unions to work together and present a more unified front to the public, legislators, and their members. The most prominent federation in the United States is the AFL–CIO. The AFL–CIO is a rather loose confederation of national and international unions. Altogether, the labor organizations in the AFL–CIO represent over 14 million workers. The structure of the AFL–CIO is shown in Figure 18–4.

FEDERATION
is a group of autonomous national and international unions.

National Unions

The national or international unions are autonomous from the federation though they often are affiliated with it. They collect dues and have their own boards, specialized publications, and separate constitutions by bylaws. Such national–international unions as the United Steel Workers (USW) or the American Federation of State, County, and Municipal Employees (AFSCME) determine broad union policy and offer services to local union units. They also help maintain financial records, provide a base from which additional organization drives may take place, and control the money for strike funds.

Intermediate union organizational units coordinate the activities of a number of local unions. All local unions in a state, or in several states, may be grouped together with some type of joint governing board. Such organizations may be citywide, statewide, or multistate-wide.

Local Unions

Local unions may be centered around a particular employer organization or around a particular geographic location. For example, the Communication Workers of

Figure 18–4
Structure of the AFL–CIO

SOURCE: U.S. Department of Labor, Bureau of Labor Statistics, *Directory of National Unions and Employee Associations,* published annually.

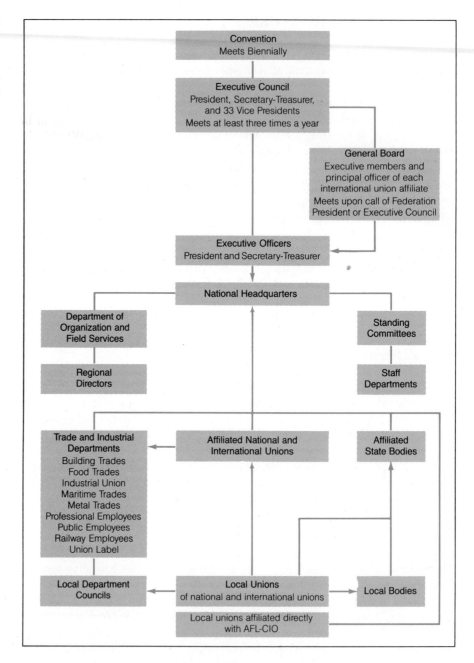

American local in Dallas, Texas, might include all the nonexempt Southwestern Bell telephone company employees in Dallas. (Nonexempt employees are subject to the overtime provisions of federal wage and hour laws.)

The policy-making process of the local union is generally democratic in form. Members vote on suggestions by either the membership or the officers. Normally, secret ballots are used. Officers in local unions are elected by the membership and are subject to removal if they do not perform satisfactorily. For this reason, local union officers tend to be concerned with the effect of their actions on the membership. They tend to react to situations as politicians do because they, too, are concerned about obtaining votes. The importance of preserving *union democracy* was the reason for the passage of the Landrum–Griffin Act (discussed earlier in this chapter).

Recently, some local unions have been defying their national unions in the belief that national leaders are giving up hard-won benefits under management pressure. For example, in Iowa, South Dakota, and Nebraska, disagreement by local members of the United Food and Commercial Workers (UFCW) with the national union over a contract settlement led to worker walkouts and disagreements with both the national union and several meat packers. Further, the locals are becoming more independent as pattern bargaining falls apart nationally. The era of big-time national labor talks is waning. Work rules are the major issue today and negotiation is accomplished at the local level.

BUSINESS AGENTS AND UNION STEWARDS.   Some unions have *business agents,* who are full-time union officials and usually are elected. The agent may run the local headquarters, help negotiate contracts with management, and may become involved in attempts to unionize employees in other organizations.

Union stewards are usually elected by local union members and represent the lowest elected officer in the union. Stewards negotiate grievances with the supervisors and generally represent employees at the worksite. The union steward is the "first-line" union representative for employees. As would be expected, one study found that union stewards had a higher degree of commitment to the union than did rank-and-file members. The study also found that the higher the commitment to the union by its members, the more positive the view of union decision making. Interestingly, an individual's higher union commitment also was related to having lower job satisfaction.[10]

▬ ▬ THE UNIONIZATION PROCESS

The process for a group of employees to gain union representation can begin for two primary reasons: 1) targeted industry or company, or 2) employee requests. A look at both follows:

1. *Targeted industry or company:* The local or national union identifies a firm or industry in which it believes unionization can succeed. In the chapter-opening example, the UAW targeted the Nissan plant in Smyrna, Tennessee. Usually, the industry has a significant number of employees who may be amenable to organizing. For example, the insurance industry in several midwestern cities was targeted because many of its workers were women in lower-paying clerical jobs, almost all of whom were not represented by a union. The logic for targeting is that if the union is successful in one firm or a portion of the industry, then many other workers in the industry will be more willing to consider unionizing.

2. *Employee requests:* Individual workers in an organization may contact a union to indicate a desire to unionize. The employees themselves or the union then may begin a campaign to win support among the other employees. Whether the union pursues the unionization effort is determined by such factors as the size of the potential employee unit, how expensive it will be to campaign for support, whether the requesting employees' complaints truly are an accurate gauge of employee feelings, and others.

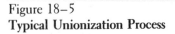

Figure 18–5
Typical Unionization Process

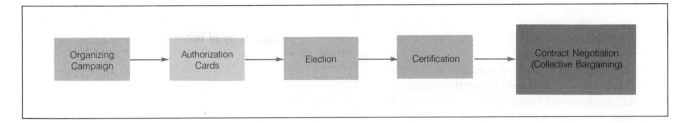

Why Employees Unionize

Whether the union targets a group of employees or the employees themselves request union assistance, the union still must win sufficient support from the employees. Research studies consistently reveal that employees join unions for one primary reason: They are dissatisfied with their employers and how they are treated by their employers and feel the union can improve the situation. Important factors seem to be employee dissatisfaction with wages and benefits, job security, and supervisory treatment. The type of work done does not seem to be as great a factor in unionization as working conditions.[11]

As the Nissan example indicates, the primary determinant of whether or not employees unionize is management. If management treats employees like valuable human resources, then employees generally feel no need for outside representation. That is why providing good working conditions, fair treatment by supervisors, responsiveness to worker complaints and concerns, and reasonably competitive wages and benefits are antidotes to unionization efforts. As would be expected, individuals who tend to be more independent or who generally view unions negatively are the most likely to oppose unionization efforts.

One study found that the pressures and views of co-workers, family members, and others in their job categories influence an individual's intention to vote for or against union representation.[12] As the P/HR: Research indicates, both general and specific beliefs about unions are important.

Once the unionization efforts begin, all activities must conform to the requirements established by labor laws and the National Labor Relations Board for private-sector employees or the appropriate federal or state governmental agency for public-sector employees. Both management and the unions must adhere to those requirements or the results of the effort can be appealed to the NLRB and overturned. With those requirements in mind, the union can embark on the first stage of the typical union organizing effort, shown in Figure 18–5.

Organizing Campaign

Like other organizations seeking members, unions usually mount an organized campaign to persuade individuals to support the union's efforts. This persuasion takes many forms, ranging from personal contacts with employees outside of work, mailing materials to employees' homes, inviting employees to attend special meetings away from the company, or publicizing the advantages of union membership.

P/HR: Practice *and* Research

Workers' Beliefs about Unions

A study by Deshpande and Fiorito offers some interesting insights on how people view unions and voting for union representation. As reported in the *Academy of Management Journal*, the authors used data gathered from almost 1,500 individuals in an opinion survey sponsored by the AFL–CIO. The individuals were surveyed regarding both their general and specific beliefs about unions. The questions about general beliefs included positive and negative statements about whether unions improved wages and working conditions, stifled individual initiative, and the like. The specific beliefs dealt with the effect of unions or such factors as recognition, advancement, pay, and job security at the individuals' own workplaces. Data also were obtained on the demographic charac-

teristics of respondents such as age, gender, education, and others.

Analyses of the data revealed that antiunion voting intentions were highest among people with more education, southerners, and white-collar workers. Also, both extrinsic factors, such as pay and working conditions, and intrinsic factors, such as recognition and participation in decisions, affect voting intentions.

Additional statistical analyses of all of the data found that individuals' specific beliefs about how a union would impact their own workplaces was the most important determinant for a person's intention to vote for or against a union. Those results are what one would expect. But the implication for unions' attempting to attract members is important. Previous studies had found that a large major-

ity of nonunion employees feel that unions do, in fact, improve pay and working conditions of employees. Yet only about a third of those employees indicated that they would vote for the union in a representative election if it were held at their organization.[13]

According to the authors, unions must show workers that they will benefit at their own workplaces. Even if workers have general beliefs that are positive toward unions, they must believe that unions can help them at their own jobs. Unions must be able to show workers that unions can assist with issues such as workplace participation, more meaningful work, and other intrinsic factors, not just with the extrinsic factors of wages, benefits, and working conditions.[14]

Handbilling is one common type of publicity. Brochures, leaflets, and circulars are all handbills. These items can be passed out to employees as they leave work, mailed to their homes, or even attached to their vehicles, as long as they comply with the rules established by laws and the NLRB. Their purpose is to convince employees to sign authorization cards.

HANDBILLING
is written publicity given to employees by unions to convince the employees to sign authorization cards.

Authorization

An **authorization card** is signed by an employee to designate a union as his/her collective bargaining agent. At least 30 *percent* of the employees in the targeted group of employees must sign authorization cards before an election can be called. If at least 50 percent of the targeted employees sign authorization cards, the union can request that the employer recognize the union as the official bargaining agent for all of the employees, and no election is held. However, as would be expected, most employers refuse this request. Consequently, the union must petition the NLRB to hold a representation election.

In reality, the fact that an employee signs an authorization card does not mean that the employee is in favor of a union, but that he or she would like the opportunity to vote on having one. Employees who do not want a union still might sign authorization cards to attract management's attention to the fact that employees are disgruntled.

AUTHORIZATION CARD
is signed by an employee to designate a union as his/her collective bargaining agent.

The care that unions and management must take to avoid committing an unfair practice during a representation election can be seen in the experience of the United Food and Commercial Workers (UFCW), in its attempt to organize a union at Mailing Services, Inc., in Hillside, N.J. The UFCW won a representation election by a 151 to 113 margin. However, the firm filed an unfair practices charge against the UFCW.

It seems that three days before the election, the union sent out a handbill to publicize what it labeled as the "first union benefit"—free medical screening tests for cholesterol, blood pressure, etc. The handbill said, "Please take advantage of your first union benefit. It's for your health." Eighty employees did so.

The National Labor Relations Board (NLRB) ruled that offering such a benefit was an improper inducement to vote for the union and ordered a new election to be held. The NLRB decision indicated that it would have ruled against the employer if a similar program had been offered by the company. The NLRB decision said, "It is reasonable to conclude . . . that the recipient of this gift would likely have felt a sense of obligation to the donor, the union . . . Therefore, we find the union's announcement and subsequent provision of free medical screening within three days of the representation election to be objectionable conduct that impaired the employees' exercise of free choice."[15]

Representation Election

An election to determine if a union will represent the employees is supervised by the NLRB (private sector) or another legal body (public sector). If two unions are attempting to represent employees, the employees will have three choices: union A, union B, or no union.

BARGAINING UNIT.   Before the election is held, the appropriate bargaining unit must be determined. A **bargaining unit** is composed of all employees eligible to select a single union to represent and bargain collectively for them. If management and the union do not agree on who is and who is not included in the unit, then the NLRB must make a determination.

One of the major criteria used in deciding the composition of a bargaining unit is what the NLRB has called a "community of interest." This concept means that there is a mutuality of interests of employees in the following areas:

■ Wages, hours, and working conditions
■ Traditional industry groupings for bargaining purposes
■ Physical location of employees and the amount of interaction and working relationships among employees groups
■ Supervision by similar levels of management

BARGAINING UNIT
is composed of all employees eligible to select a single union to represent and bargain collectively for them.

UNFAIR PRACTICES.   Both before the election when authorization cards are being solicited and after an election has been requested, unfair practices identified in both the Wagner and Taft–Hartley acts place restrictions on employer and union actions in this process. The P/HR: Practice describes how a union had a successful election overturned due to an unfair practice.

A number of tactics may be used by management representatives to try to defeat a unionization effort. Such tactics often begin when handbills appear or when authorization cards are being distributed. Figure 18–6 contains a list of the more common tactics that management can and cannot use. Several of the "Do's" were part of the aggressive effort made by Nissan to combat the UAW's efforts.

One example illustrates the possible consequences when management engages in an unfair practice. The owner-manager of a small manufacturing firm fired a worker who was soliciting authorization cards from other employees at lunch. The reason given was poor job performance, but the worker's poor performance was not documented adequately and the company was asked why the worker's performance became so poor so quickly. As a result of the company's tactics in dealing with the employee, the employee was reinstated and a representation election was ordered. However, the company won the election 28 to 3. If the hasty and illegal action had not been taken by management, the union effort would have died a natural death and no election would have been held.

Some organizations have experts who specialize in helping management combat unionization efforts. They have had a measure of success. One study found that unions had won 48 percent of the elections in which management consultants were used and 65 percent in which consultants had *not* been used.[16]

ELECTION PROCESS.   Assuming an election is held, the union only needs to receive the votes of a *majority of those voting* in the election. For example, if a group of 200 employees is the identified unit and only 50 people vote, only 26 employees would need to vote yes in order for a union to be named as the representative of all 200. If either side believes that unfair labor practices have been used by the other side, the election results can be appealed to the NLRB. If the NLRB finds that unfair practices were used, it can order a new election. Assuming that no unfair practices have been used and the union obtains a majority in the election, the union then petitions the NLRB for certification. Over the years unions have won representation elections about 45 to 50 percent of the time. Statistics

DO	DON'T
■ Tell employees about current wages and benefits and how they compare with other firms	■ Promise employees pay increases or promotions if they vote against the union
■ Tell employees you will use all legal means to oppose unionization	■ Threaten employees with termination or discriminate when disciplining employees
■ Tell employees the disadvantages of having a union (especially cost of dues, assessments, and requirements of membership)	■ Threaten to close down or move the company if a union is voted in
■ Show employees articles about unions and negative experiences others have had elsewhere	■ Spy on or have someone spy on union meetings
■ Explain the unionization process to your employees accurately	■ Make a speech to employees or groups at work within 24 hours of the election (before that, it is allowed)
■ Forbid distribution of union literature during work hours in work areas	■ Ask employees how they plan to vote or if they have signed authorization cards
■ Enforce disciplinary policies and rules in a consistent and fair manner	■ Urge employees to persuade others to vote against the union (such a vote must be initiated solely by the employee)

Figure 18–6

Management Do's and Don'ts in the Unionization Process

from the NLRB consistently indicate that the smaller the number of employees in the bargaining unit, the higher the percentage of elections won by unions.[17]

Certification and Decertification

Official certification of a union as the legal representative for employees is given by the NLRB, or the relevant body, after reviewing the results of the election. Once certified, the union attempts to negotiate a contract with the employer. The employer *must* bargain, as it is an unfair labor practice to refuse to bargain with a certified union.

Employees who have a union and no longer wish to be represented by it can use the election process called **decertification.** The decertification process is similar to the unionization process. Employees attempting to oust a union must obtain decertification authorization cards signed by at least 30 percent of the employees in the bargaining unit before an election is called. If a majority of those voting in the election want to remove the union, the decertification effort succeeds. One caution: Management may not assist the decertification effort in any way by providing assistance or funding.[18]

Decertification elections generally result in the union losing. According to data from the NLRB, unions have lost about three-fourths of all decertification elections in recent years. Some of the reasons that employees decide to vote out a union include:[19]

- Better treatment by employers, so employees do not believe they need a union to protect their interests
- Efforts by employers to discredit the union, resulting in employees initiating decertification
- The inability of some unions to address the changing needs of a firm's work force
- Declining image of unions, coupled with the lack of confidence in aging labor leaders by younger, more educated workers

After election and certification of the union comes negotiation of a labor contract, one of the most important methods that unions use to obtain their major goals. A general discussion of collective bargaining is contained in Chapter 19.

■■ ■■ TRENDS IN UNION MEMBERSHIP

For organized labor in the United States, the statistics tell a disheartening story. Unions represent fewer than 17 percent of all workers, down from 40 percent in the mid-1950s. Since 1980, one-fifth of the large unionized companies have gone into bankruptcy. Union wage hikes have been sharply lower, and the members in many unions have had to "give back" the gains of earlier times to comply with management's need to restrain labor costs and to increase productivity.

Management took a much more activist stance during the 1980s. Economists speculate on the issues that have sparked union decline: deregulation, foreign competition, a larger number of people looking for jobs, and a general perception by firms that dealing with unions is expensive compared with the nonunion alternative.

The decline in union representation of the labor force also can be attributed to many of the changes discussed in Chapter 1. The decline of manufacturing jobs has occurred in the industries that traditionally had the highest percentage of union

DECERTIFICATION
is a process whereby a union is removed as the representative of a group of employees.

members.[20] Consequently, the number of union jobs has declined, although at the same time the overall number of jobs has grown. One study found that during 1988, the number of manufacturing jobs increased by 335,000, but union membership declined by 113,000. From 1980 to 1988 the decline in union membership in manufacturing was two million.[21] The primary growth in jobs in the United States has been in service industries having large numbers of white-collar jobs. Also, the influx of more women into the work force and the growth in part-time workers indicate the changing mix of jobs. But unions traditionally have had the greatest difficulty convincing white-collar workers and women to join unions. The only area where unions have had some measure of success is with public-sector employees. A look at some of these trends follows.

White-Collar Unionism

White-collar workers include clerical workers, insurance agents, keypunchers, nurses, teachers, mental health aides, computer technicians, loan officers, auditors, and salespeople. Efforts to organize white-collar workers are increasing for several reasons. Advances in technology have boosted the number of white-collar workers in the work force. With the proportion of employees in white-collar jobs increasing relative to employees in manufacturing jobs, unions have had to focus on white-collar employees in order to obtain new members.

Union leaders feel that white-collar workers and professionals have the same employment concerns as manufacturing workers—pay, job security, and working conditions. Professionals in areas such as nursing, teaching, and engineering are seen as potential union members for this reason. But white-collar organizing has not lived up to its promise.

One major difficulty that unions face in organizing white-collar workers is the image of unions themselves. Many white-collar workers see unions as resistant to change and not in touch with the concerns of the more educated workers in white-collar technical and professional jobs. One study found that union membership is less likely on jobs requiring higher levels of education. Also, union membership tends to be more prevalent in occupations that are less complex, having less varied, more routine tasks.[22] In addition, many white-collar workers, including professionals, exhibit quite a different mentality and set of preferences from those held by blue-collar union members. For example, one study revealed that professionals define fairness in pay differently than blue-collar workers. The professionals saw fairness as pay based on individual performance, while the blue-collar workers always have preferred pay based on equality and seniority, two basic tenets of traditional unionism.[23]

Some even believe that many of the traditional principles of labor laws governing union–management relations, developed primarily for industrial workers, are not appropriate for professional jobs.[24] Consequently, unions must redefine their rules and how they operate if they are to appeal to large number of white-collar workers.

Unions and Women Workers

Unions generally have not been as successful in organizing women workers as they have men. Figure 18–7 indicates that although the percentage of women who are union members or who are represented by unions did not decline as much as that for men workers over a five-year period, the actual number of women workers

Figure 18–7
Percentages of Men and Women in Unions

SOURCE: Bureau of Labor Statistics, U.S. Department of Labor, 1990.

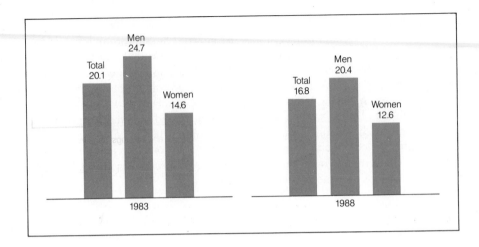

represented by unions changed little, even though many more women were working than in earlier years.

If unions are to reverse the decline in their membership, both in percent and in total members, they will have to develop strategies and approaches to appeal more effectively to women workers.[25] There are some indications that unions are doing this. Unions have been in the forefront in the push for legislation on such family-related goals as child care, maternity and paternity leave, pay equity, and flexible work arrangements. Unions in the garment and service industries, which have a high concentration of female workers, generally emphasize the conflicting demands of work and family and the inequality of women's wages compared with men's.[26]

Unionism in the Public Sector

Unions have been somewhat more successful in finding members in the public sector than in the private sector. As Figure 18–8 shows, a much higher percentage of governmental workers are union members than are private workers.

STATE AND LOCAL GOVERNMENT UNIONISM.   Unionization of state and local government employees presents some unique problems and challenges. First, many unionized local government employees are in exclusive and critical service areas. Police officers, fire fighters, and sanitation workers all provide essential services in most cities. Allowing these workers to strike endangers public health and safety. Consequently, over 30 states have laws prohibiting public employee work stoppages. These laws also identify a variety of ways to resolve negotiation impasses, including arbitration.

The impact of public employee wage increases on taxes is another concern. As taxpayers, the general public is increasingly critical of state and local government tax expenditures. Thus, wage demands by public employees often become political issues. One study of 700 cities found that collective bargaining increased expenditures in the departments covered by union contracts. But collective bargaining did not affect the total expenditures, total revenues, or property taxes of the cities.[27] A possible explanation for these results is that even though the departments represented by unions had increasing costs, the cities adjusted other expenditures to

INDUSTRY	PERCENT UNION MEMBERS	
	1983	1988
Agriculture workers	3.4	2.0
Private nonagriculture workers	16.8	12.9
Government workers	36.7	36.7

SOURCE: Bureau of Labor Statistics, U.S. Department of Labor, *Employment and Earnings*, January 1989, 226.

Figure 18–8
Union Strength in the Private and Public Sectors

keep costs in line. Also, the study only examined property taxes, whereas many cities have raised their sales taxes to generate additional revenues.

State and local government unions operate under laws and hiring policies that vary widely from city to city and state to state. Civil service and so-called merit systems make the public sector vastly different from the private sector. State and local laws, not federal labor laws, take precedence, so unique legal situations often occur. Local and state officials who lack experience with unions and collective bargaining processes may hamper union–management relations. Consider a farmer and a dentist serving on a county board; their limited knowledge of union-related activities and processes might easily stand in the way of effective union–management decisions.

UNIONISM AND THE FEDERAL GOVERNMENT.   Although unions in the federal government hold the same basic philosophy as unions in the private sector, they do differ somewhat. Through past executive orders and laws, realistic methods of labor–management relations that consider the special circumstances present in the federal government have been established. The Office of Personnel Management has considerable control over P/HR policies and regulations. For example, because of limitations on collective bargaining, federal government unions cannot bargain over wages.

SUMMARY

- A union is a formal association of workers that promotes the interests of its members through collective action.
- Unions in the United States primarily have been concerned with job-centered issues and acting as a countervailing force to management.
- Labor unions in the United States have survived many ups and downs but saw their greatest growth from 1935 to 1947.
- The National Labor Code is composed of three laws that provide the legal basis for labor relations today. The three laws are the Wagner Act, Taft–Hartley Act, and Landrum–Griffin Act.
- The Wagner Act was designed to protect the unions and workers. Taft–Hartley restores some powers to management, and Landrum–Griffin protects individual union members.
- The Federal Labor–Management Services statute, passed in 1978, made major revisions in the union–management relations process in the federal government.

- The structural levels of a union include a federation, the national or international union, the local union, business agents, and union stewards.
- Workers join unions primarily because of management's failure to address major job-related concerns.
- The process of organizing includes an organizing campaign, authorization, a representation election, NLRB certification, and collective bargaining.
- The process can be reversed through decertification.
- Union membership as a percentage of the work force is down from 25 percent in 1970 to about 17 percent currently.
- For unions to reverse this decline in membership, they must organize more white-collar, women, and government workers.

REVIEW AND DISCUSSION QUESTIONS

1. How effective do you believe U.S. unions are in fulfilling their two self-identified roles: a job-centered role and a countervailing force role?
2. List five key events that occurred in U.S. labor history before 1935.
3. Identify the three parts of the National Labor Code and the key elements of each act.
4. What is the meaning of a "confederation" of unions? What are the levels within a union confederation?
5. A co-worker has just brought you a union leaflet that urgest employees to sign an authorization card. What events would you expect to occur from that point?
6. Discuss the following comment by an internationally-known management consultant: "I think anybody who anticipates that unions will exist in any major role or in major quantities as bargaining units in the U.S. in the year 2000 is dreaming."

| CASE | **Unionization At the Youth Home** |

Attempts to unionize employees in smaller firms frequently meet resistance by owners and managers. However, that resistance must comply with provisions in the acts of the National Labor Code. When unfair practices are believed to exist, then complaints can be filed by either management or the union with the National Labor Relations Board, which then conducts an investigation and makes a ruling. What follows are the facts of an unfair practices charge that was filed in an actual case involving a youth home in Maryland in the mid-1980s.[28] The home was operated as a nonprofit entity by a religious organization. Much of the descriptive material below is taken directly from the NLRB order and decisions on the case, but the real names of individuals have been changed.

The executive director of the home at the time of the case was Pamela Williams. The employees at the home had contacted representatives of the Maryland State Employees Council 92, American Federation of State, County, and Municipal Employees (AFSCME), about organizing the employees of the home for union representation.

During the two-month period of time during which the unionization efforts were under way, Williams let employees know how disappointed and angry she was at their attempt to unionize. In early November, Williams met with several of the employees and told them that the home was in poor financial condition. She then accused them of being irreligious for considering unionization and "greedy." She suggested that if the employees were unhappy, they just should resign. Otherwise she might have to discharge them. She had already discharged Jerry Gordon during the last week of October, supposedly for work-related reasons, although Gordon was one of those who had actively supported the unionization effort.

Several days after the first meeting, Williams again met with several employees and again emphasized that the home was in a financial crisis. If the unionization efforts were successful and wage costs rose, employees could expect their benefits to be reduced. Also, some services for the youth at the home would be cut, reducing the need for staff. A few weeks later Williams followed through with a staff reduction by discharging James Wooten, who also was active in supporting the unionization effort.

Nothing more happened for several months, but the unionization effort continued. Finally, about four months later, the union filed an unfair practices charge with the NLRB, alleging that the actions of the executive director violated Section 8 (a) (1) and (3) of the National Labor Relations Act.

QUESTIONS

1. If you were on the National Labor Relations Board, what decision would you make and why? (Note: Your instructor has the NLRB decision in the accompanying instructor's guide)
2. What lessons does this case have for managers when discussing issues with employees during unionization efforts.

NOTES

1. Adapted from a variety of news stories, including David Landis, "Union Again Fails to Make Gain in South," *USA Today*, July 28, 1989, B1–2; "The UAW vs. Japan," *Business Week*, July 24, 1989, 64–65; Gregory A. Patterson, "Nissan Workers Reject UAW Bid to Organize Plant in Tennessee," *Wall Street Journal*, July 28, 1989, A3; Stephanie Overman, "Nissan Sees Union's Loss as Management Style's Win," *Resource*, September 1989, A12; Sal Vittolino, "Nissan Drives 'Em Away," *Human Resource Executive*, October 1989, 1, 24–27.

2. S. Perlman, *A History of Trade Unionism in the United States* (New York: Macmillan, 1929).

3. *Commonwealth of Massachusetts v. Hunt*, Massachusetts, 4 Metcalf 3 (1842).

4. Jonathan Clements, "Stopped in Their Tracks," *Forbes*, May 30, 1988, 224.

5. "National Labor Relations Act" (PL x, 5 July 1935) *United States Statutes at Large* 49, 449.

6. "Labor-Management Relations Act, 1947" (PL 101, 23 June 1947), *United States Statutes at Large* 61, 136–162.

7. *United Steel Workers v. United States*, 45 LRRM 2066 (1959).

8. "Labor-Management Reporting and Disclosure Act of 1959." (PL 86–257, 14 September 1959), *United States Statutes at Large* 73, 519–546.

9. For more details, see William H. Holley, Jr. and Kenneth M. Jennings, *The Labor Relations Process*, 3rd ed. (Chicago: Dryden Press, 1988), 579–586.

10. John M. Magenau, James E. Martin, and Melanie M. Peterson, "Dual and Unilateral Commitment Among Stewards and Rank-and-File Union Members," *Academy of Management Journal* 31 (1988): 359–376.

11. Jeanne M. Brett, "Why Employees Want Unions," *Organizational Dynamics*, Spring 1980, 47–59.

12. B. Ruth Montgomery, "The Influences of Attitudes and Normative Pressures on Voting Decisions in a Union Certification Election," *Industrial Relations* 42 (1989): 263–279.

13. T. A. Kochan, H. C. Katz, and R. B. McKersie, *The Transformation of American Industrial Relations*, (New York: Basic Books, 1986).

14. Adapted from Satish P. Deshpande and Jack Fiorito, "Specific and General Beliefs in Union Voting Models," *Academy of Management Journal* 32 (1989): 883–897.

15. Adapted from *Resource*, May 1989, 61; *Mailing Services, Inc.* 293 NLRB N. 58 (March 31, 1989).

16. J. J. Lawler, "The Influence of Management Consultants on the Outcome of Union Certification Elections," *Industrial and Labor Relations Review* 40 (1984): 38–51.

17. "Unions Won 48.6 Percent of 1988 Elections," *Resource*, May 1989, 16.

18. William J. Bigoness and Ellen R. Pierce, "Responding to Union Decertification Elections," *Personnel Administrator*, August 1988, 49–53.

19. Marvin J. Levine, "Double-Digit Decertification Activity: Union Organizational Weakness in the 1980s," *Labor Law Journal* 40 (1989): 311–315.

20. Alan I. Murray, "American Manufacturing Unions Stasis: A Paradigmatic Perspective," *Academy of Management Review* 13 (1988): 639–652.

21. "More Factory Workers—But Fewer with Union Cards," *Business Week*, June 12, 1989, 18.

22. Greg Hundley, "Things Unions Do, Job Attributes, and Union Membership," *Industrial Relations* 28 (1989): 335–355.

23. F. S. Hills and T. Bergmann, "Professional Employees: Unionization Attitudes and Reward Preferences," *Personnel Administrator*, July 1982, 50–73.

24. David M. Rabbin, "Professional Employees, Collective Bargaining, and the Law," *ILR Report*, Spring 1989, 29–33.

25. J. H. Foegen, "Labor Unions: Don't Count Them Out Yet," *Academy of Management EXECUTIVE* 3 (1989): 67–69.

26. C. Trost, "More Family Issues Surfacing at Bargaining Tables . . .," *Wall Street Journal*, December 2, 1986, 66.

27. Robert G. Valleta, "The Impact of Unionism on Municipal Expenditures and Revenues," *Industrial and Labor Relations Review* 42 (1989): 430–442.

28. Adapted from 283 NLRB120.

Collective Bargaining and Grievance Management

After you have read this chapter, you should be able to:

1. Define collective bargaining and identify at least four bargaining relationships and structures
2. Explain the three categories of collective bargaining issues
3. Identify and describe a typical collective bargaining process
4. Define and explain the differences among conciliation, mediation, and arbitration
5. Discuss two major collective bargaining trends
6. Define a grievance and describe the importance and extent of grievance procedures
7. Explain the basic steps in a grievance procedure
8. Discuss arbitration as the final phase of a grievance procedure

P/HR: Today *and* Tomorrow

Bargaining for Health-Benefit "Give-Backs"

During collective bargaining, negotiators increasingly are occupied with issues that reflect the changing relationship of union members and management. One issue is the effort by management in many firms to have workers assume a greater share of health-care benefit costs by asking workers to "give back" some of the health benefits that have appeared in previous labor contracts. The responses from union workers have been vehemently negative, as several examples illustrate.

One of the largest union-management confrontations over health benefits occurred with AT&T and the seven "Baby Bell" telecommunications companies (Ameritech, Bell Atlantic, Bell South, U.S. West, Nynex, Southwestern Bell, and Pacific Telesis), on the one hand, and the Communications Workers of America (CWA), on the other. The battle lines were clearly drawn, as shown by the comment of a CWA spokesman:

> We have the best health benefits in the country. It has taken us years to build them up and we are proud of them. And, we don't intend to give them up just because the company is screaming about the high cost of health premiums.

The Baby Bells, as well as AT&T, faced health-care benefit cost increases as high as 49 percent over a three-year period, so management had major reasons for requesting changes in the labor contracts with the CWA.

During negotiations, AT&T demanded that CWA members give up first-dollar coverage of all health-care costs. To replace that plan, AT&T proposed that workers pay a $25–$50 monthly fee, as well as accept deductibles of $150–$200. After tough negotiations, the CWA was able to retain first-dollar coverage, but it accepted the company's proposal to establish preferred-provider networks of hospitals and doctors who would charge AT&T lower rates than normal. Under the new contract, if employees do not use the preferred providers, then they will pay the higher rates with $150–$200 deductibles. At the seven "Baby Bell" companies, similar demands were met by major resistance, including strikes at several of the firms. The strike at Nynex lasted several months. In the end, the companies had to retreat and accept settlements similar to the one reached by AT&T.

Other industries have seen labor and management conflict over health-care benefit costs, also. For instance, in Seattle, 12,000 members of the United Food and Commercial Workers International Union (UFCW) went on strike for twelve weeks against large supermarket chains in the area. One of the major issues was an employer demand for an eight-cent-an-hour per employee deduction to be applied to health-care benefit costs. Again, the union was able to beat back the effort by agreeing to a preferred-provider network. Benefit give-backs also were at the heart of negotiations in the steel, aluminum, and coal-mining industries. As part of continuing cost-containment efforts, undoubtedly benefit give-backs will continue to be an issue during collective bargaining negotiations in the 1990s.[1]

"Collective bargaining should be more than a fistfight, more than rulemaking. It must be more than merely adversarial. And there is ample evidence that it can be."

D. Quinn Mills

Union-management relations take center stage in an organization following a successful unionization attempt. The final stage of the unionization process is the negotiation and signing of a contractual agreement between a union and an employer. In this chapter, the process of contract negotiation through collective bargaining is discussed. Also, one of the most important areas of day-to-day union-management relations—grievances—is examined.

▇▇ ■ COLLECTIVE BARGAINING

In the United States, collective bargaining is somewhat different from the process seen in other countries because of the different philosophical and political origins of the collective bargaining systems. Different legal frameworks for collective bargaining also exist in different countries.

Collective bargaining is the process whereby representatives of management and workers negotiate over wages, hours, and other terms and conditions of employment. It is a give-and-take process between representatives of two organizations for the benefit of both. It is also a power relationship. As the opening discussion about negotiations over health benefit "give-backs" indicates, the power relationship in collective bargaining involves conflict, and the threat of conflict seems neccessary to maintain the relationship.[2] But perhaps the most significant aspect of collective bargaining is that it is an ongoing relationship that does not end immediately after agreement is reached.

COLLECTIVE BARGAINING
is the process whereby representatives of management and workers negotiate over wages, hours, and other terms and conditions of employment.

Types of Bargaining Relationships

The attitude of management toward unions is one major factor in the relationship between union and management. This attitude plays a crucial role in management's strategic approach to collective bargaining.[3] Management-union relationships in collective bargaining can follow one of several patterns. Figure 19–1 shows the relationship as a continuum, ranging from conflict to collusion. On the left side of the continuum, management and union see each other as enemies. On the right side, the two entities join together illegally. There are a number of positions in between, and a discussion of the six strategies follows.[4]

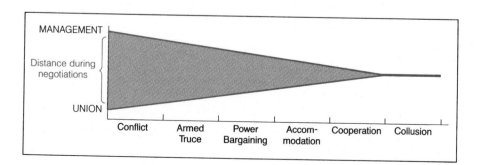

Figure 19–1
Collective Bargaining Relationship Continuum

CONFLICT.　In the conflict strategy, management takes a totally uncompromising view. A desire to "bust the union" may underlie the use of the conflict strategy. To paraphrase a saying from old western movies, management's attitude is that "the only good union is a dead union!"

ARMED TRUCE.　Management representatives who practice the armed-truce strategy take the position that they are well aware of the vital interests of the organization, while the union is poles away and always will be. However, management realizes that forcing head-on conflict is not in the best interests of either party and that the union is not likely to disappear. Consequently, management is willing to negotiate a basic agreement. Many union-management relationships, especially in smaller businesses, have not progressed beyond this armed-truce stage.

POWER BARGAINING.　Managers engaged in a power bargaining relationship can accept the union; many even pride themselves on the sense of "realism" that forces them to acknowledge the union's power. Managerial philosophy here assumes that management's task is to increase its power, then use it whenever possible to offset the power of the union. The union engages in power bargaining, using tactics that have an impact on the employer's pocketbook-lawsuits, public hearings, demonstrations, appeals to legislators, etc.[5] This relationship characterized the negotiations between the Communications Workers of America and the Baby Bell telecommunications firms.

ACCOMMODATION.　In accommodation, management and the union learn to adjust to each other and attempt to minimize conflict, to conciliate whenever necessary, and to tolerate each other. The accommodation strategy in no way suggests that management goes out of its way to help organized labor. However, it does recognize that the need to reduce confrontation is helpful in dealing with common problems often caused by external forces, such as imports and government regulations.

COOPERATION.　The cooperation strategy involves full acceptance of the union as an active partner in a formal plan. This strategy rarely occurs because management must support both the right and the desire of unions to participate in certain areas of decision making. The two parties jointly resolve P/HR and production problems as they occur. Labor-management committees and codetermination are examples of cooperation.

COLLUSION.　Collusion, which is relatively rare in American labor history, has been deemed illegal. In the collusion strategy, union and management engage in labor price fixing designed to inflate wages and profits at the expense of the general public.

Bargaining Structures

Collective bargaining can be structured in several different ways. The most common ones are:

- One employer, one union
- One employer, multiplant
- One employer, multiunion
- Multiemployer, one union
- Multiemployer, multiunion

The *one-employer, one-union* structure is the simplest and most common; it occurs when an employer has just one unionized operating facility. If the union represents employees at other facilities of the firm, then the collective bargaining structure is *one-employer, multiplant.* For example, if a printing company has three facilities, each located in different states, then a collective bargaining contract can be negotiated for all plants at the same time. The *one-employer, multiunion* structure may be used when a large employer has employees represented by different unions, and contracts with each union are negotiated at the same time. This model is common in the construction industry where one employer may face several different building trade unions representing a number of different crafts.

Another variation, *multiemployer, one-union structure,* was developed in the coal-mining and similar industries. This structure has been used extensively in the steel industry in the form of a *master contract* that applies to all companies. This master agreement then is supplemented by a *local contract* dealing with individual company and/or plant issues.

The final bargaining structure is the *multiemployer, multiunion* structure. This structure has been used in the construction industry in which a group of unions negotiate with a contractor's association representing all of the unionized construction companies in a geographic area.

The choice of a bargaining structure is made by the parties involved. A union may favor dealing with all employers in an area at the same time in order to put equal pressure on all employers. Or the union may favor negotiating with one company, and then using the contract gained as a model for other firms in the same industry. This approach has been labeled *pattern bargaining,* and has been used by the United Auto Workers with General Motors, Ford, and Chrysler.

Employers may prefer structures other than one-employer, one union, for a variety of reasons. If an employer has multiple unions with which to bargain, the company may spend less time and get more consistent contracts by negotiating with all unions at once. Or an employer may prefer a one-employer, multiplant structure in order to get similar contracts at widely diverse plants, which also may put pressure on individual plant locals to agree to similar concessions and work rule adjustments.

In summary, the choice of a bargaining structure is made for a variety of reasons, many of which reflect the bargaining power and pressures that each party believes it can exert. A bargaining structure may change over time as unions attempt to stay up-to-date with changes in organizational or industry growth and technology. Such changes are similar to those that often occur in corporate organizations in response to similar pressures.

Issues for Bargaining

A wide range of issues can be the subject of collective bargaining between union and management representatives. The three categories of issues that are identified in the Wagner Act are as follows:

- *Illegal issues* are those that require either party to take illegal action, such as giving preference to individuals who have been union members when hiring employees.

■ *Mandatory issues* are those that are identified specifically by labor laws or court decisions as being subject to bargaining. If either party demands that issues in this category be bargained over, then bargaining must occur. Generally, mandatory issues relate to wages, benefits, nature of jobs, and other work-related subjects. That broad view means that many issues have been ruled to be mandatory subjects for bargaining, as the list below indicates:[6]

- ■ Discharge of employees
- ■ Security
- ■ Grievances
- ■ Work schedules
- ■ Union security and dues checkoff
- ■ Retirement and pension coverage
- ■ Vacations
- ■ Individual merit raise plans
- ■ Christmas bonuses
- ■ Rest- and lunch-break rules
- ■ Safety rules
- ■ Profit-sharing plans
- ■ Required employee physical exams

■ *Permissive issues* are those that are not mandatory but relate to the jobs. These issues can be bargained over if both parties agree. For example, giving benefits to retired workers has been ruled to be a permissive issue by the U.S. Supreme Court.[7] The right of management to drop a product line has also been ruled a permissive subject for bargaining. In general, permissive issues are those that are under the control of one party, but that party decides that it is advantageous to bargain over them. Finally, neither party can insist on bargaining over the permissive issues to the point of causing a strike or lockout of workers.[8] However, the dividing line between what issues are mandatory and what are permissive often is difficult to determine, and various court decisions have taken somewhat different directions on some issues.[9]

Typical items included in a formal labor contract are shown in Figure 19–2. Notice how wide a range of issues the contract covers. The primary areas covered are wages, benefits, working conditions, work rules, and other necessary legal conditions. It is important for the contract to be written clearly and precisely. Unclear or imprecise wording often leads to misunderstandings that result in grievances or other problems. To ensure that the contract is understandable, as well as legally accurate, both parties should check the readability and clarity of the wording in labor contracts. Two areas of common concern in contract bargaining are *management rights* and *union security* agreements.

MANAGEMENT RIGHTS.   Virtually all labor contracts include a management rights clause. That provision often reads as follows:

The employer retains all rights to manage, direct, and control its business in all particulars, except as such rights are expressly and specifically modified by the terms of this or any subsequent agreement.[10]

By including such a provision, management is attempting to preserve its unilateral right to decide or make changes in any areas not identified in a labor contract. Some labor contracts spell out in more detail the issues that fall under management rights, while others use the general language above. As would be expected, man-

1. Purpose of agreement	11. Separation allowance
2. Nondiscrimination clause	12. Seniority
3. Management rights	13. Bulletin boards
4. Recognition of the union	14. Pension and insurance
5. Wages	15. Safety
6. Incentives	16. Grievance procedure
7. Hours of work	17. No-strike or lockout clause
8. Vacations	18. Definitions
9. Sick leave and leaves of absence	19. Terms of the contract (dates)
10. Discipline	20. Appendices

Figure 19–2
Typical Items in a Labor Contract

agement representatives want to have as many issues defined as management rights as they can.[11]

UNION SECURITY.   A major concern of the union representatives when bargaining is to negotiate **union security** provisions to aid the union in obtaining and retaining members. One major union security agreement is the *dues check-off*, which is a provision that union dues will be deducted automatically from the payroll checks of members. This provision makes it much easier for the union to collect its funds. Otherwise, the union must bill and collect the dues each month from each of its members.

Another form of union security is *requiring union membership* of all employees, subject to state right-to-work laws (see Chapter 18). The following types of union security agreements can be negotiated in states without right-to-work laws:[12]

■ *Union shop:* Employee must join the union after a waiting period or be terminated.
■ *Modified union shop:* After a waiting period all new employees must join the union. Present union members must maintain their memberships, but present employees who are not members do not have to join the union.
■ *Maintenance of membership:* Workers joining a union must maintain their memberships or be terminated.
■ *Agency shop:* Employees who are not union members must pay dues and fees equivalent to those paid by union members.

Union security agreements are very common in labor contracts. For example, over 80 percent of all labor contracts surveyed contained some union security provisions. Dues check-off and union shop agreements were the most common.[13]

UNION SECURITY
are provisions to aid the union in obtaining and retaining members.

■■ ■ PROCESS OF COLLECTIVE BARGAINING

The collective bargaining process has a number of stages. Over time, each union and management situation develops slight modifications that are necessary for effective bargaining. The process shown in Figure 19–3 is typical.

Preparation

Especially after a bitter organizing campaign, a union may take months to win an initial contract. Some unions never reach contract agreement and voluntarily re-

Figure 19–3
Typical Collective Bargaining Process

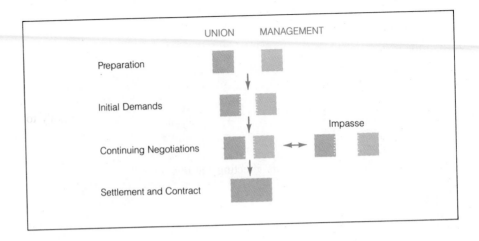

linquish their certification. Both labor and management representatives spend much time preparing for negotiations. If a previous contract is expiring, the grievances filed under the old contract will be reviewed to identify contract language changes to be negotiated. Employer and industry data concerning wages, benefits, working conditions, management and union rights, productivity, and absenteeism are gathered. Once the data are analyzed, each side identifies what its priorities are and what strategies and tactics it will use to obtain what it wants. Each tries to allow itself some flexibility in order to trade off less important demands for more critical ones.

The courts have stated that unions cannot represent workers in a competent manner if they do not have necessary company information. Therefore, management must provide the necessary data. If the organization argues that it cannot afford to pay what the union is asking, the employer's financial situation and accompanying data are all the more relevant. However, the union must request such information before the employer is obligated to provide it.[14]

Initial Demands

Typical bargaining includes an initial proposal of expectations by both sides. The amount of rancor or calmness exhibited will set the tone for future negotiations between the parties. Union and management representatives who have been part of previous negotiations may adopt a pattern that has evolved over time. In negotiations for the first contract between an employer and a union, the process can be much more difficult. Management representatives must adjust to dealing with a union, and employees who are leaders in the union must adapt to their new roles.

Continuing Negotiations

After opening positions have been taken, each side attempts to determine what the other values highly so the best bargain can be stuck. For example, the union may be asking the employer to pay for dental benefits as part of a package that also includes wage demands and retirement benefits. However, the union may be most interested in the wages and retirement benefits and willing to trade the dental payments for more wages. Management has to determine what the union wants more and decide exactly what to give up.

During negotiations, both management and union must evaluate cost proposals concerning changes in wages, benefits, and other economic items quickly and accurately. A mathematical modeling system tied to a computer spreadsheet will perform the calculations and produce a total cost figure almost immediately. Such issues as an extra day off or a 10¢ an-hour pay raise can be converted easily to annual cost figures for comparison.

BARGAINING POWER.   The factors affecting the outcomes when collective bargaining occurs are shown in Figure 19–4. As that model shows, there are four sets of factors that impact the bargaining power of a management and a union, all of which must be considered by the negotiators in their give-and-take discussions.

Obviously, *economic factors* are important. What a firm can afford without jeopardizing its economic health is important to both the management and the union. The various *organizational factors* reflect the relative strength or weaknesses of the union. The *sociodemographic factors* will affect the types of proposals made by management and union. For example, if the workers represented by the union are older and predominately male, then certain benefits such as maternity coverage or child-care assistance may not be desired as much as additional pension contri-

Figure 19–4
Determinants of Collective Bargaining Actions

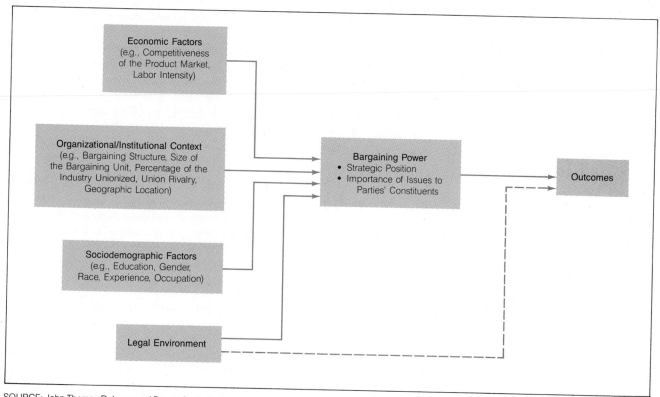

SOURCE: John Thomas Delaney and Donna Sochell, "The Mandatory–Permissive Distinction and Collective Bargaining Outcomes," *Industrial and Labor Relations Review* 42 (1989): 571. Used with permission.

butions. Both parties must comply with all of the appropriate *legal restraints and regulations* on bargaining procedure and outcomes. Depending on the analyses of those factors, the parties make use of their bargaining power to obtain concessions from the other party. Ultimately, the outcomes are represented as provisions in the labor contract.

BARGAINING BEHAVIOR. Collective bargaining is not simply a logical and rational process. The behavior of the negotiators is critical. Representatives can exhibit any of four behavior subprocesses in collective bargaining.[15]

1. *Distributive bargaining* occurs when one party must win and the other lose over a conflicting issue. If a union wants a dues check-off, and the employer does not want a check-off, only one side can win. Either there will or will not be a check-off.
2. *Integrative bargaining* occurs when both management and union face a common problem and must work together for a solution. If a steel company and the United Steelworkers union are concerned about employee absenteeism and discipline problems caused by worker alcoholism, the parties might negotiate a joint program that identifies how alcoholism and the problems it presents can be handled. In an integrative bargaining process, both parties will agree to provide some funds to pay for alcoholic treatment activities.
3. *Attitudinal structuring* occurs when each side attempts to affect the tone or "climate" of the negotiations. The climate created and the attitudes of the other path often determine which of the six bargaining strategies identified earlier is adopted during negotiations.
4. *Intraorganizational bargaining* occurs when disagreements exist *within* labor or management. Union negotiators may not be addressing the same concerns that union members have in some areas. Such differences often arise.[16] If some union members feel that dental insurance should be included in a union proposal and other union members feel that higher retirement benefits are more important than dental insurance, some consensus about dental insurance would have to be reached within the union membership. Sometimes, union negotiators will have the members rank their preferences for specific benefits.[17] Whatever the method, the union negotiation team must work to develop consensus before going to the bargaining table.

"GOOD FAITH." Provisions in federal labor law require that both employer and employee bargaining representatives negotiate in "good faith." In *good faith*, the parties agree to send negotiators who are in a position to bargain and make decisions, rather than people who do not have the authority to commit either group to a decision. Meetings between the parties cannot be scheduled at absurdly inconvenient hours. Some give-and-take discussions also must occur. After decisions are made in good faith, neither party can renege on the agreement. Blatant antiunion or antimanagement propaganda cannot be used during the bargaining process. The specifics of the collective bargaining "good faith" relationship are defined by a series of NLRB and court rulings.

Settlement and Contract Agreement

After an initial agreement has been made, the two sides usually return to their respective constituencies to determine if what they have informally agreed on is acceptable. A particularly crucial stage is **ratification** of the labor agreement. In this stage, the union negotiating team explains the agreement to the union members and presents it for a vote. If approval is voted, the agreement is then formalized into a contract.

Bargaining Impasse

Regardless of the structure of the bargaining process, labor and management do not always reach agreement on the issues. In such cases, a deadlock may lead to union strikes or management lockouts. During a **strike**, union members stop work and often picket, or demonstrate against, the employer outside the place of business by carrying placards and signs.

In a **lockout**, management shuts down company operations to prevent union members from working. This action also may avoid possible damage or sabotage to company facilities and employees who continue to work. One of the more publicized lockouts occurred in 1987, when the owners of the National Football League teams locked out players and hired replacement players for several weeks.

Both strikes and lockouts are forms of pressure on the other party. By striking, the union attempts to pressure management into making some concessions and signing a contract. However, management may respond and hire replacement workers or operate the company by using supervisors and managers to fill in for striking workers. By locking out workers, an employer puts economic pressure on union members in the hope that they will make concessions and support a contract agreement.

TYPES OF STRIKES. Workers' rights vary depending on the type of strike. For example, in an economic strike an employer is free to replace the striking workers. But during unfair-labor-practice strikes, workers who want their jobs back at the end of the strike must be reinstated. The types of strikes include:

- *Economic strikes* occur when the parties fail to reach agreement during collective bargaining.
- *Unfair-labor-practice strikes* occur when union members walk out of work over what they feel are illegal employer actions, such as refusal to bargain.
- *Wildcat strikes* occur during the life of the collective bargaining agreement without approval of union leadership and violate a no-strike clause in a labor contract. Strikers can be discharged or disciplined.
- *Jurisdictional strikes* occur when one union's members walk out to force an employer to assign work to them instead of to another union.
- *Sympathy strikes* express one union's support for another involved in a dispute, even though the first union has no disagreement with the employer.

Generally, work stoppages due to strikes and lockouts are relatively rare. Figure 19–5 shows that during the 1980s strikes actually declined, except for a slight rise in 1986. The decline can be traced to many factors. Overall, there has been a decline in union power, paralleling the decline of heavy industry in the United States and decreased public support of unions. Thus, many unions are reluctant to go on strike because of the financial losses they would incur, whereas others fear that the financial losses would cause the employer to go bankrupt. In addition, management has shown its willingness to hire replacements, and some strikes have ended with union workers losing their jobs. Efforts to forestall such drastic actions on the part of either party can take the form of conciliation/mediation or arbitration.

RATIFICATION
occurs when union members vote to accept the terms of a negotiated labor agreement.

STRIKE
occurs when workers refuse to work in order to put pressure on an employer.

LOCKOUT
occurs when management shuts down company operations to prevent union members from working.

Figure 19–5
Amount of time lost in work stoppages during strikes of the 1980s

SOURCE: Bureau of Labor Statistics, U.S. Department of Labor, 1990.

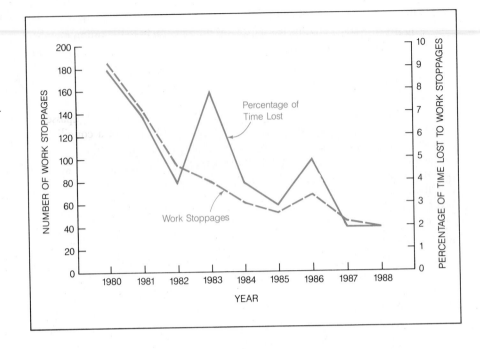

IN CONCILIATION
the third party attempts to keep the union and management negotiators talking so that they voluntarily can reach a settlement.

IN MEDIATION
the third party assists the negotiators in their discussions and also suggests settlement proposals.

ARBITRATION
is a means to decide disputes in which negotiating parties submit a dispute to a third party to make a decision.

CONCILIATION OR MEDIATION.   Conciliation or mediation occurs when an outside individual attempts to help two deadlocked parties continue negotiations and arrive at a solution. In **conciliation** the third party attempts to keep the union and management negotiators talking so that they voluntarily can reach a settlement. In **mediation** the third party assists the negotiators in their discussions and also suggests settlement proposals. In neither conciliation nor mediation does the third party attempt to impose a solution.

Conciliators and mediators usually are experienced neutrals who act as counselors to reopen communication, clarify problems, and try to find areas in which the two parties can agree. The success of mediators often is linked to their having significant previous experience, being flexible, and taking an active role in keeping the parties negotiating.[18]

Often, mediators and conciliators are provided by the Federal Mediation and Conciliation Services (FMCS). This agency, created by the Taft-Hartley Act assists union and management negotiations when labor disputes arise. The FMCS has offices in most major U.S. cities and employs several hundred trained labor experts. Employees of the FMCS sit down with the negotiators from both union and management and attempt to forestall strikes or lockouts.

ARBITRATION.   **Arbitration** is a means to decide disputes in which negotiating parties submit a dispute to a third party to make a decision. Arbitration can be conducted either by an individual or a panel of individuals.

Arbitration can be used in various settings, but in labor-management relations it has two uses. The most frequent, called *grievance arbitration*, occurs when disputes arise about the meaning of a contract that has been negotiated. More on grievance arbitration appears later in the chapter. Settling disputes about the terms and conditions in a labor contract that is being negotiated is called *interest arbitration*, which is used relatively infrequently in the private sector because employers generally do not want an outside party making decisions about their rights, wage levels, benefits offered, or other matters.[19]

But interest arbitration is used regularly in the public sector. Because many governmental employees, especially those who provide essential services to the general public, are prohibited by law from striking, some means of evening out the bargaining power is needed. Therefore, many governmental entities have laws or regulations requiring arbitration when contract negotiations reach impasse.

An arbitrator is an impartial person whose job, unlike that of a conciliator or mediator, is to determine the relative merits of each argument and then make a decision, called an *award*. Most arbitration decisions are binding on both the union and management.

Different types of arbitration are used. In *final-offer arbitration*, the arbitrator must select either the employer's or the union's final contract offer without making any changes. This approach is taken in disputes between major league baseball players and club owners, in which an arbitrator identifies the salary to be paid to a player based on the last offer from the player and the baseball club. In other types of arbitration, the arbitrator evaluates the positions and data submitted by each party and makes a decision, which often is different from the final offer of either party.

TRENDS IN COLLECTIVE BARGAINING

During the 1980s, management in many organizations and industries took deliberate steps to reduce costs. The opening discussion on bargaining health-benefit give-backs is an example. Because labor costs represent significant expenditures in many industries, management efforts to reduce such costs ran into union resistance. Throughout the 1980s, in many unionized firms, management succeeded in forcing unions to accept changes. There is every reason to believe that management will continue its efforts to lower labor costs during the 1990s, especially in light of the growing competition from goods produced in countries such as Japan, Taiwan, South Korea, Germany, Great Britain, and others. Several of the most prominent union-management bargaining trends are discussed next.

Union-Management Cooperation

The 1980s saw an increase in what have been called "cooperative initiatives" between organized labor and management. These efforts have taken several forms.

UNION OWNERSHIP. Unions have become active participants in the restructuring of American industry by encouraging workers to become partial or complete owners of their employers. These efforts were spurred by concerns that firms were preparing to shut down or to prevent mergers or buyouts by financial investors whom the union feared would cut union jobs.

Unions have been active in assisting members to put together an employee stock ownership plan (ESOP) to purchase all or part of some firms. For example, in 1983 when closure of Weirton Steel in West Virginia was announced, the unionized employees purchased the firm through an ESOP and the firm has continued to operate satisfactorily since then. However, not all union-led ESOPs have been successful, as the collapse of the Hyatt Clark Industries ESOP takeover of a General Motors plant, led by the United Auto Workers union, illustrates.[20]

Unions also have made offers to purchase firms to head off financially leveraged takeovers by other investors. For example, the unions representing United Airlines employees made a counteroffer to a takeover attempt of that firm. In conjunction with the top management group at United Airlines, the pilots union also persuaded the unions representing flight attendants and machninists to back the buyout offer.

Some firms also have union representatives on their board of directors. The best known example is Chrysler Corporation, in which a representative of the United Auto Workers was given a seat on the board in exchange for assistance in getting federal government financial help in the late 1970s. Such a practice is very common in European countries, and is called *co-determination*.

Most situations in which unions become involved in ownership either occur with troubled firms or are defensive in nature to prevent some other party from buying the firm. It will be interesting to see if union ownership efforts continue in the 1990s.

PRODUCTIVITY COOPERATION.   One approach has found union and management representatives bargaining to identify cooperative ways that will ensure the economic survival of the company, while also providing job security for workers.[21] Often the bargaining results in union agreement to reduce or freeze its wages and benefits and to change work rules that impede productivity. In turn, management provides job security guarantees to union workers.

Several examples, in addition to the P/HR: Practice on A. O. Smith, illustrate how such union-management cooperation has worked. At Xerox a study revealed that over $3 million could be saved by contracting some subassembly work out to nonunion firms. Xerox brought its problem to the Amalgamated Clothing and Textile Workers union, representatives of the workers who would lose their jobs if the subcontracting was done. After six months of meetings, the joint management-union team identified ways to save $3.7 million and keep the unionized workers employed.[22]

Other union-management efforts follow the Japanese or European models and exist in U.S. organizations under a number of different names: autonomous work teams, quality circles, or quality-of-work-life teams. For example, LTV Steel Company has nearly 300 "labor-management participation teams" in its plants. The teams evolved out of an agreement with the United Steelworkers of America and attempt to break down the adversarial barriers between union and management. The teams have achieved several successes in improving quality and cutting costs.

A similar approach has been adopted by the United Auto Workers in dealing with General Motors, Ford, and Chrysler.[24] The Ford plant in Louisville, Kentucky, almost closed in 1979 because of low productivity, poor quality, and low sales of the light trucks and Bronco IIs made there. At that point, UAW Local 862 and Ford management met to discuss ways to save the 3,000 jobs and make the plant more competitive. As a result of changes suggested by the joint union-management committee and implemented throughout the plant, the facility had 3,300 workers in 1988, and the quality and productivity levels had increased dramatically.[25]

Studies of such efforts are somewhat mixed in their assessment of the effectiveness of cooperative initiatives.[26] Managers of unionized Wisconsin firms felt that participation programs had played a role in improving company performance.[27] Another study found that the success of collaborative efforts dwindled over time, particularly when employment levels continued to decline despite joint union-management activities.[28] These findings reinforce observations of a counter trend, worker skepticism, and resistance to cooperative efforts.

P/HR: Practice *and* Research

Labor-Management Cooperation at A. O. Smith

The benefits of labor-management cooperative efforts on productivity are illustrated at A. O. Smith, a Milwaukee-based automotive parts manufacturing firm. Beginning in the early 1980s, both management and union leaders recognized that major problems existed at Smith. Bored workers doing repetitive tasks were directed by dictatorial supervisors. Grievances over work rules were common, and the piecework wage system was based on quantity, not quality. For instance, about 20 percent of the truck frames produced for Ford had to be repaired before shipment to Ford.

Skip ahead six or seven years, and the defect rate on the Ford truck frames was about 3 percent and productivity had doubled. What happened to turn around the situation at Smith can be tied to joint labor-management efforts to involve workers in improving productivity, change work rules, and transform the management practices used.

Beginning in the early 1980s, Smith formed employment involvement (EI) groups to discuss ways of improving quality and lowering costs. But those EI groups were set up by management without union input, so the unions representing workers refused to support the efforts and little productivity or quality enhancement resulted. However, in 1984, General Motors, one of Smith's larger customers, began reducing its purchases. Both union representatives and management knew radical steps were needed to prevent loss of jobs and company revenues. Thus, the seven unions representing Smith employees and management agreed to participate in new EI efforts. Problem-solving groups were established at all levels, beginning with the plant floor, at which both management and union officials participated along with workers. EI made some progress, but by 1986–87 further reductions in orders from automakers forced Smith to lay off 1,300 workers and threaten to close the Milwaukee plant unless major work rule changes were made.

During contract negotiations in 1987, both sides agreed to drop the piecework pay system and to make many work rule changes. The company also agreed to freeze worker pay rates at the 1987 level instead of cutting workers' pay $3.00 per hour. The work rule changes allowed the installation of the work-team approach. These teams are composed of five to seven workers who perform a group of jobs on a rotating basis. The teams designated their own leaders who can request maintenance as needed, schedule production and overtime, and stop production to fix quality problems. Using teams in this way meant that Smith could reduce the number of first-line supervisors. For the remaining supervisors and managers, management training programs were instituted.

The unions and management continue to discuss changes in seniority rules and job security guarantees for workers. But no longer do workers or managers worry about the plant closing because of low productivity or quality problems.[23]

WORKER RESISTANCE TO COOPERATION. In spite of the numerous successes of labor-management cooperation, a growing number of workers are questioning the value of such cooperation if it means that workers must take cutbacks in wages or jobs. Some union dissidents have labeled labor-management cooperation efforts "a management plot."

One group that has been particularly vocal is UAW Local 594 in Pontiac, Michigan. Joint efforts led by top local leaders had agreed to changed work rules and team production arrangements as a way to reduce costs and save union jobs. But the local union members voted against the changes because they did not feel that there were sufficient job security guarantees for members.[29] In 1990, a documentary movie called *Roger and Me* captured some of the distrust of union members about cooperating with General Motors.

Concessionary Bargaining

In many industries, unions have engaged in **concessionary bargaining,** which occurs when the union agrees to reduce wages, benefits, or other factors during collective bargaining. Unions have agreed to concessions in such industries as auto, airline, rubber, meat processing, steel, and trucking. When the unions have refused to grant concessions, companies have simply shut down or hired replacement non-union workers at lower wage and benefit levels.

Economic survival and/or competitiveness have been the driving forces behind employers' demands for concessions from unions. Another cause is industry de-regulation, which gave the competitive edge to the lower-cost firms. Deregulation has occurred in such widely varied industries as telecommunications, railroads, airlines, financial services, and others. For instance, deregulation of the telecom-munications industry led to increased competition and ultimately to resistance by members of the Communication Workers of America to increasing their health-benefit costs with the seven Baby Bell telecommunications firms.

The willingness of a union to negotiate cutbacks depends on pressures from the public as well as from management. Also, the package of concessions must appear to provide a legitimate solution to a company's problem and to give some job security guarantees for the union to be willing to concede previous bargaining gains.[30] However, when unions engage in concession bargaining, union solidarity, credibility of union leaders, and union effectiveness all may be affected negatively.

TWO-TIER BARGAINING.   Another approach taken to reduce labor costs and pro-vide job security for union members is two-tier bargaining. A *two-tier wage structure* is one in which new union members receive lower wages and fewer benefits than existing members performing similar jobs. This approach was used extensively in the airline industry. For example, pilots hired after November 1983, at American Airlines earned half the salary as pilots hired before them. American Airlines estimated that two-tier contracts saved $100 million dollars in one year alone.

As unionized firms negotiated two-tier contracts, they brushed aside the predic-tion by some that such plans would inevitably cause friction on the job. Significant problems did arise several years later. For instance, Hughes Aircraft Company, a military contractor, used such a plan in Tucson, Arizona. Raises were given to Hughes workers at its missile factory, but the wages for new hires were frozen so much lower that pay scales for the newly hired would never match the current employee pay rates. The plan flopped! New workers did not stay and workmanship became so sloppy that the Air Force suspended contract payments. As a result, Hughes backed away from the plan by raising starting wages by 24 percent and removing the cap on new workers' future wages.

There is little comfort in being in the top tier of a two-tier plan because top-tier workers are always concerned about a "backlash." The plans are not popular with the new employees, and the longer-service workers fear that their high wages give management an incentive to get rid of them.

Formal studies on the phenomenon suggest that newly hired employees may be less productive. Also, the programs are seen quite differently by new employees, managers, unions, and senior workers.[31] In summary, two-tier wage schemes, which may have been a triumph of collective bargaining when they were negotiated, now seem to have lost much of their appeal.[32] Resistance to such settlements likely will continue, especially when the cooperative efforts do not prevent loss of union jobs or plant closings.

Bankruptcy and Closings as Bargaining Tactics

One management tactic affecting collective bargaining is filing for bankruptcy. In 1983, Continental Airlines declared bankruptcy and then continued to operate in reorganization, having voided an expensive union contract. Unions argued that this tactic took away their ability to negotiate with employers. Employers, on the other hand, felt that it was necessary for their survival in deregulated industries that permit open competition and often engage in price-cutting wars. Frank Lorenzo, chairman of Continental, relied on a decision of the U.S. Supreme Court which ruled that a New Jersey building materials company (Bildisco) could declare bankruptcy and immediately ignore its labor contracts. The Court also set broad standards whereby federal judges can decide if companies are justified in dismantling a labor agreement.

Congress finally decided the issue in 1984 when it passed a new bankruptcy law. The law basically represents a compromise between the positions of employers and labor unions. Under the law, an employer must petition the courts for a hearing on proposed changes in a labor contract and must provide financial data to the union. If the court finds that the union rejected the proposal without good cause and evidence clearly supports the employer's plea for relief, the employer has the right to reject the labor contract.

Again in 1989, Lorenzo used bankruptcy as a way to void expensive labor contracts at Eastern Airlines, owned by Texas Air Company, the parent company of both Continental and Eastern. He then received court support to hire nonunion workers at lower wage and benefit levels.

Other firms less well known also have used bankruptcy or closing a plant as the ultimate bargaining threat. Also, the National Labor Relations Board (NLRB) has expanded the law so that organizations are now relatively free to move to another location. Unions contend that such decisions will lead to a wave of plant closings in order to escape union influence; but management feels such steps are part of management rights. However, employers must comply with the provisions of the Worker Adjustment and Retraining Notification Act passed in 1988.

▬ ▬ GRIEVANCE MANAGEMENT

Alert management knows that active dissatisfactions, whether real or imaginary, expressed or unexpressed, are a potential source of trouble. Hidden dissatisfaction grows and soon arouses an emotional state that may be completely out of proportion to the original complaint. Before long, workers' attitudes can be seriously affected. Therefore, it is important that complaints and grievances be handled properly.

A **grievance** is a specific, formal notice of employee dissatisfaction expressed through an identified procedure. A **complaint,** on the other hand, is merely an indication of employee dissatisfaction, which has not taken the formal grievance settlement route. Management should be concerned with both grievances and complaints because many complaints can become grievances.[33] Complaints are good indicators of potential problems within the work force.

One study concluded that an effective grievance procedure improves productivity, because the procedure reduces the magnitude of workers' reactions to real and imagined slights.[34] Without a formal mechanism to air perceptions of inequitable treatment, employees harbor adverse reactions longer. Also, with a grievance procedure, formal work practices based on clearly understood precedents develop over

A GRIEVANCE
is a specific, formal notice of employee dissatisfaction expressed through an identified procedure.

A COMPLAINT
is an indication of employee dissatisfaction which has not taken the formal grievance settlement route.

time. Finally, without a grievance procedure, there is seldom an arbitration (neutral third party) step, and management ends up imposing the decision.

UNION V. NONUNION GRIEVANCE MANAGEMENT.   There are differences in how grievances are handled between firms whose workers are represented by unions and those whose workers are nonunion. In an organization in which a union exists, grievances might occur over any of several matters: interpretation of the contract, disputes not covered in the contract, and grievances of individual employees. In nonunionized organizations, complaints also tend to relate to a variety of concerns, such as wages, benefits, working conditions, and equity. Whether such complaints can be termed grievances depends on whether there is a formal procedure in a nonunion firm for handling them. Grievance procedures almost always are included in labor–management contracts. One review found that 99 percent of labor contracts in all industries contained grievance procedures.[35] However, the pattern is significantly different in organizations where employees are not unionized. Relatively few nonunion firms have grievance procedures, although their numbers are growing.

GRIEVANCE MANAGEMENT AT UNIONIZED EMPLOYERS.   Grievance procedures are important for effective employee–employer relations in unionized firms. From the standpoint of the union, grievance systems allow employees a way to dispute management's implementation of the collective bargaining agreement. Further, without a grievance procedure, management may be unable to respond to employee discontent in important areas because managers are unaware of the dissatisfaction. Such information does not always come to the attention of management automatically. A great deal of discontent is dismissed at lower levels and never rises to managers who have the authority to make decisions that can rectify problems. For these reasons, a formal grievance procedure is a valuable communication tool for the organization because it provides workers a fair hearing for their problems.

A crucial measure of the performance of a grievance system is the rate of grievance resolution. Those resolved grievances then become feedback to help resolve future grievances at an earlier stage.[36]

DISPUTE RESOLUTION PROCESS IN NONUNION EMPLOYERS.   Managers commonly insist that they have an "open-door" policy—if anything is bothering employees, all they have to do is come to management and talk. However, employees are often skeptical of this approach, feeling that their complaint would probably be viewed as unnecessary "rocking the boat." An open-door policy is not sufficient as a grievance procedure. A "super manager" should be able to maintain open channels of communication and quickly spot and rectify any troubles that might become grievances. However, managers who have this degree of communication ability are relatively rare.[37]

A growing number of nonunion firms have established formal grievance procedures because of the legal issues raised in Chapter 17. Increasingly, court decisions reflect concerns about protecting employee rights and providing employees due process. Some of the key issues that must be addressed when establishing a nonunion grievance procedure are as follows:[38]

■ Purposes of a grievance procedure
■ Availability of the system to employees
■ Identification of grievance issues
■ Identification of grievance mechanisms and procedures

Nonunion firms with formal grievance procedures often call the process "dispute resolution."[39] One firm that has established a nonunion grievance system for the group of its employees not represented by a union is Houston Lighting and Power. In this system, nonunion employees are encouraged to discuss complaints with their supervisors or trained mediators in the P/HR department.[40] One survey of seventy-eight nonunionized firms that have formalized grievance procedures found that six of them even use arbitration by a neutral third party to address grievances not otherwise resolved.[41]

Many organizations, dissatisfied with little-used open-door policies, are instituting *peer-review boards* to resolve disciplinary and promotion disputes. The technique is also becoming a way to reduce lawsuits, especially frivolous ones. The typical peer review panel consists of five members: three employees and two managers. The peer review comes into play as the last step in a grievance procedure, when all other avenues have been exhausted.

At General Electric, three names are selected from a pool of hourly workers who have volunteered for peer-review duty. Each member of the pool has had 12 hours of basic law and peer-review training. The five-person panel hears the case and hands down a decision. Aggrieved employees are given assistance in preparing their cases if necessary, but lawyers are excluded from the process.[42]

About 100 companies now use peer-review boards, including Federal Express, Digital Equipment, Citicorp, and Borg-Warner. The system has been used successfully to resolve cases ranging from sexual discrimination to wrongful discharge. An employee whose firing is upheld by a peer-review board is less likely to file suit, and a judge may be less disposed toward the employee who ignores a review board in favor of a lawsuit.[43]

Grievance Responsibilities

The division of responsibilities between the P/HR unit and line managers for handling grievances is shown in Figure 19–6. These responsibilities vary considerably from one organization to another, even between unionized firms. But the P/HR unit usually has a more general responsibility. Managers must accept the grievance procedure as a possible constraint on some of their decisions.

Causes of Grievances

Grievances can be filed for different reasons on many different issues, both large and small. Once a collective bargaining contract is signed, that contract becomes the main governing document in union-management relations. The typical con-

P/HR UNIT	MANAGERS
■ Assists in designing the grievance procedure	■ Operate within the grievance procedure
■ Monitors trends in grievance rates for the organization	■ Attempt to resolve grievances where possible as "person closest to the problems"
■ May assist preparation of grievance cases for arbitration	■ Document grievance cases at own level for the grievance procedure
■ May have responsibility for settling grievances	■ Have responsibility for grievance prevention

Figure 19–6
Grievance Responsibilities

tract details what management can and cannot do, as well as the responsibilities of the union.

CONTRACT VIOLATIONS.   The day-to-day administration of a contract most often focuses on employee and employer rights. When a unionized employee feels his or her rights have been infringed on under the contract, that employee can file a grievance. Therefore, one major cause of grievances is that the employee and union believe the employer has violated the contract.

PROBLEM IDENTIFICATION.   Another reason why a grievance may be filed is to identify that a problem exists in the organization. For example, an employee might file a grievance to draw attention to some unsafe working conditions, even though specific contract provisions may be vague on this score.

PROTECTION OF JOB SECURITY.   Because many workers and unions are concerned with protecting jobs, formal grievances often concern job rights. Suppose that Paula Goldberg filed a grievance when an employee with a lower job classification was promoted instead of her. Paula claimed that the contract stipulated seniority would be the first consideration in promotion. Paula really is not concerned about the meaning and intent of the contract, because she knows that employees in higher job classifications are less likely to be laid off during slack periods. The basis for her grievance is her own long-term security. A person's need for security is a recognized behavioral fact, and formal grievance procedures can help reduce these fears.

PERSONAL ENHANCEMENT.   Grievances also can be filed by employees and pursued by union stewards to enhance their own status and importance. In one company a union steward encouraged employees to file a number of grievances, thereby providing him the opportunity to work on resolving the grievances instead of his own job assignment. Also, because the steward was planning to run for president of the union local, he could show that he was actively involved in representing the union members. One study found a relationship between the encouragement of grievances and union election rivalries.[44]

Approaches to Grievances

A formal grievance procedure sometimes leads management to conclude that the proper way to handle grievances is to abide by the "letter of the law." Therefore, management does no more nor less than what is called for in the contract. Such an approach can be labeled the *legalistic approach* to the resolution of grievances. A much more realistic approach, the *behavioral approach*, recognizes that a grievance may be a symptom of an underlying problem that management should investigate and rectify.

It is important to consider the behavioral aspects of grievances in order to understand why grievances are filed and how employees perceive them.[45] Management should recognize that a grievance is a behavioral expression of some underlying problem. This statement does not mean that every grievance is symptomatic of something radically wrong. Employees do file grievances over petty matters as well as over important concerns, and management must be able to differentiate between the two. However, to ignore a repeated problem and take a legalistic approach to

| P/HR: | Practice *and* Research | Employee Attitudes about Grievance Processes |

Throughout most discussions about grievance procedures, it has been stated that grievances should be resolved at the lowest levels of the process. But a research study by Gordon and Bowlby raised some interesting questions about those generalizations.

In a study published in *Personnel Psychology*, the researchers surveyed grievance processes in seven unions. Members of these unions, which represented both public sector and private sector employees, were sent surveys containing attitudinal questions about the grievance systems at their places of employment. Areas probed included the fairness of the grievance process and the procedures used.

Also, if an individual had filed a grievance, he or she was asked to describe the characteristics of the grievance and the outcomes of the grievance procedure.

Analyses of the responses of the 324 individuals who reported having filed grievances offer some insights. One unexpected finding was that the level at which grievances were settled had little relationship to the attitudes that the employees had about the grievance system. Although it may be less time consuming to have grievances settled earlier, settling grievances at the first stage does not appear to make the attitudes of those filing grievances more positive. The

study also found that the type of grievance filed was important. Grievances on work assignments tended to affect the working relationships of grievants with first-line supervisors. As would be expected, if an employee won the grievance, his or her job satisfaction was higher.

What this study highlights is that grievances and grievance procedures have a impact on the attitudes of the employees and managers in organizations, beyond the resolution of the immediate problem. Consequently, effective grievance management can contribute to effective continuing working relationships in organizations.[46]

grievance resolution is to miss much of what the grievance procedure can do for management. The P/HR: Research on employee attitudes about grievance procedures reveals that the grievance process also has continuing effects on attitudes of grievants.

Individual Rights in a Grievance

A unionized employee generally has a right to union representation if he or she is being questioned by management and if discipline may result. If these so-called Weingarten rights (named after the court case that established them) are violated and the employee is dismissed, he or she usually will be reinstated with back pay.[47]

However, individual union members do not always feel that their best interests are properly served by the union. Workers and unions may not agree on the interpretation of a contract clause. For example, a worker might feel strongly that his suspension for drinking was not sufficiently represented by the union because the shop steward (his union representative) is a teetotaler.

If an individual does not feel the union has properly and vigorously pursued the grievance, he or she may have recourse to the federal court system. Such cases attempt to pinpoint individual rights inside the bargaining unit and determine what those rights are if a person has been denied due process through the grievance procedure. In fact, an individual can pursue a grievance against an employer on his or her own if a union does not back the claim.

■ ■ GRIEVANCE PROCEDURE

GRIEVANCE PROCEDURE
is a formal channel of communication
used to resolve formal complaints
(grievances).

Grievance procedures are formal communications channels designed to settle a grievance as soon as possible after the problem arises. First-line supervisors are usually closest to a problem; however, the supervisor is concerned with many other matters besides one employee's grievance and may even be the subject of an employee's grievance.

Supervisory involvement presents some real problems in solving a grievance at this level. For example, William Dunn, a 27-year-old lathe operator at a machine shop, was approached by his supervisor, Joe Bass, one Monday morning and told that his production was lower than his quota. Bass advised him to catch up. Dunn reported that there was a part on his lathe needing repair. Bass suggested that Dunn should repair it himself to maintain his production because the mechanics were busy. Dunn refused and a heated argument ensued, which resulted in Bass ordering Dunn home for the day.

This illustration shows the ease with which an encounter between an employee and a supervisor can lead to a breakdown in the relationship. This breakdown, or failure to communicate effectively, could be costly to Dunn if he lost his job, a day's wages, or his pride. It could be costly to Bass, who represents management, and to the owner of the machine shop if production was delayed or halted. Grievance procedures can resolve such conflicts.

However, the machine shop had a contract with the International Brotherhood of Lathe Operators, of which Dunn was a member. The contract specifically stated that company plant mechanics were to repair all manufacturing equipment. Therefore, Bass appears to have violated the union contract. What is Dunn's next step? He may use the appeals machinery provided for him in the contract. The actual grievance procedure is different in each organization. It depends on what the employer and the union have agreed on and what is written into the labor contract.

Steps in a Grievance Procedure

As Figure 19–7 shows, several steps exist in most grievance procedures. The grievance can be settled at any stage.

1. The employee discusses the grievance with the immediate supervisor.
2. The employee then discusses the grievance with the union steward (the union's representative on the job) and the supervisor.
3. The chief union steward discusses it with the supervisor's manager.
4. The union grievance committee discusses the grievance with the unit plant manager or the employer's P/HR department.
5. The representative of the national union discusses it with the company general manager.
6. The final step may be use of an impartial umpire or arbitrator for ultimate disposition of the grievance.

EMPLOYEE AND SUPERVISOR.   In our example, Dunn has already discussed his grievance with the supervisor. The first step should eliminate the majority of gripes and complaints employees may view as legitimate grievances.

Supervisors are generally responsible for understanding the contract so that they can administer it fairly on a day-to-day basis. They must be accessible to employees for grievance investigations and must gather all the pertinent facts and carefully investigate the causes, symptoms, and results. But the filing of grievances does

Figure 19–7
A Grievance Procedure.

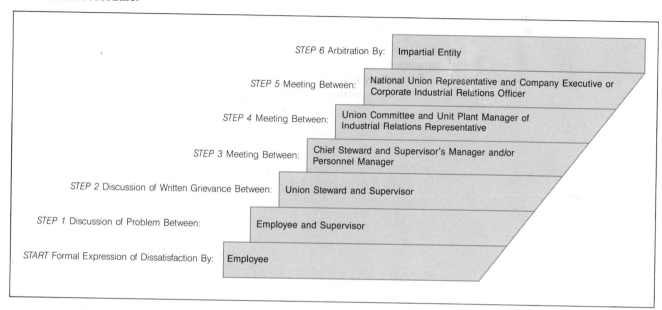

STEP 6 Arbitration By: Impartial Entity

STEP 5 Meeting Between: National Union Representative and Company Executive or Corporate Industrial Relations Officer

STEP 4 Meeting Between: Union Committee and Unit Plant Manager of Industrial Relations Representative

STEP 3 Meeting Between: Chief Steward and Supervisor's Manager and/or Personnel Manager

STEP 2 Discussion of Written Grievance Between: Union Steward and Supervisor

STEP 1 Discussion of Problem Between: Employee and Supervisor

START Formal Expression of Dissatisfaction By: Employee

create some risks for employees. The reactions of supervisors to employees who file grievances may affect the employees' performance ratings. This reaction may be even more pronounced if the supervisor is the target of the grievance.[48]

UNION STEWARD AND SUPERVISOR.   The second step involves the union steward, whose main task is to present the grievance of a union member to management. However, the responsibility rests not only with the individual steward, but also, to a large degree, with the union membership as a whole. The effect of this grievance on the relationship between a union and management must be determined.

Assume that Dunn's grievance remains unsettled after the second step. The steward takes it to the chief steward who contacts Bass's boss and/or the unit's P/HR manager. In most grievance procedures, the grievance is documented and, until it is settled, much of the communication between management and the union is in writing. This written communication is important because it provides a record of each step in the procedure and constitutes a history for review at each subsequent step.

One study found that an employee's previous work history with an organization influences managerial decisions on grievances at the second and third stages. An employee whose work history shows he/she has been disciplined less, has more tenure on the job, and has compiled a better performance record is more likely to have a grievance upheld by management. This study underscores the impact of behavioral factors on the grievance process.[49]

UNION GRIEVANCE COMMITTEE AND UNIT MANAGER.   Pressure tends to build with each successive step because grievances that are not precedent setting or difficult are screened out earlier in the process. If the department manager (who is supervisor Bass's boss) backs Bass against the chief steward, the grievance goes to the next step. The fourth step brings in the local union management grievance commmittee. In our case, the grievance committee of the union convinces the plant manager that Bass violated the contract and Dunn should be brought back to work and paid for the time he missed. The plant manager gave in partly because he thought the company had a weak case and partly because, if the grievance continued past him, it would probably go to arbitration, and he did not feel the issue was worth the cost. Although in Dunn's case a grievance committee was used, not all grievance procedures use committees.

NATIONAL REPRESENTATIVES AND ARBITRATORS.   If the grievance had remained unsettled, representatives for both sides would have continued to meet to resolve the conflict. Although relatively rare, a representative from the national union might join the process. Or a corporate executive from headquarters (if the firm is a large corporation) might be called on to help resolve the grievance so that it does not go to arbitration.

■■ ■ GRIEVANCE ARBITRATION

Arbitration is flexible and can be applied to almost any kind of controversy except those involving criminal matters. Advisory or voluntary arbitration may be used in the negotiation of agreements, in the interpretation of clauses in existing agreements, or in both. Because labor and management generally agree that disputes over the negotiation of a new contract should not be arbitrated, the most important role in labor relations played by arbitration is as a final step in the grievance procedure.

GRIEVANCE ARBITRATION
is a means of settling disputes arising from different interpretations of a contract using a third party.

Grievance arbitration is a means of settling disputes arising from different interpretations of a contract using a third party. This dispute resolution is not to be confused with contract arbitration, which is arbitration to determine how a contract will be written. Grievance arbitration is a deeply ingrained part of the collective bargaining system, although it was not always so. In earlier times, arbitration was not considered a useful part of the process in settling labor disputes.

However, in 1957, a court decision that established the right of unions to sue for specific performance arbitration awards gave arbitration new strength.[50] Later court cases added more powers to the arbitration process. It was ruled that a company had to arbitrate all issues not specifically excluded in the contract. Courts were directed not to rule on the appropriateness of an arbitration award unless misinformation, fraud, or negligence was involved.[51]

One alternative to arbitration, using *mediation* to settle grievances, has been tested successfully in some industries. But mediation is more frequently used to help solve problems between labor and management arising out of attempts to reach a collective bargaining agreement.

Grievance Arbitration Process

The wording of the contract clause to express accurately each party's intent relative to arbitration is a common arbitration issue. It is important to spell out the types of disputes that may be taken to arbitration. Most collective bargaining contracts suggest that either party may start arbitration proceedings. Others state that only the union can initiate arbitration proceedings. Still others permit arbitration only when both parties agree.

Assuming that a grievance has not been resolved and the labor contract calls for arbitration, the arbitration process begins with the selection of a single arbitrator or a panel of arbitrators, usually three in number. The manner of selecting arbitrators varies, but usually each party eliminates names from a list of potential arbitrator candidates until only one name remains. If a panel is used, then the union selects one name, the management selects one name, and the "neutral" is selected in the manner just noted. Most contracts call for union and management to share equally in the cost of arbitration.

An arbitration hearing is conducted somewhat like a judicial hearing. Each side submits a written brief describing its views and citing the evidence to support those views. The arbitrator can call witnesses to testify and can request other evidence.

Following the hearing, each side may be asked to submit a post-hearing brief. The arbitrator then reviews all the evidence, including the applicable section of the labor contract, and makes a decision. This decision also is called an *award* and is enforceable in federal court if the labor contract indicates that arbitration decisions are binding on both parties.

Grievance arbitration presents several problems. It has been criticized as being too costly, too legalistic, and too time-consuming.[52] Also, one study found that arbitrators generally treated women more leniently than men in disciplinary grievance situations.[53] Many feel that there are too few qualified and experienced arbitrators. Nevertheless, grievance arbitration likely will continue to be a useful tool in union-management relations.

Preventive Arbitration

Labor and management sometimes tend to ignore potential problem areas in a relationship until it is too late. The result can be an explosive dispute that does a great degree of harm. Preventive arbitration can minimize this sort of difficulty. It is the duty of a preventive arbitrator to meet periodically (at least monthly) with union and management representatives to discuss areas of potential trouble between the parties. Although the use of a preventive arbitrator is not a panacea for resolving difficulties in labor-management relations, it can be a useful tool. The plan calls for adherence by both parties to the arbitrator's recommendations during a 60-day period, during which time, the problem can be solved in a calm and considered manner.

SUMMARY

- Collective bargaining occurs when management negotiates with representatives of workers over wages, hours, and working conditions.
- Different collective bargaining relationships exist. Conflict, armed truce, power bargaining, accommodation, cooperation, and collusion are recognized as special relationships.
- Different collective bargaining structures are used, ranging from one employer and one union to multiple employers bargaining with multiple unions.
- The issues subject to collective bargaining fall into three categories: illegal, mandatory, and permissive.

- Provisions on management rights and union security typically appear in labor contracts.
- The collective bargaining process includes preparation, initial demands, negotiations, and settlement.
- Once an agreement (contract) is signed between labor and management, it becomes the document governing what each party can and cannot do.
- Bargaining power of both the management and union is determined by economic, organizational, sociodemographic, and legal factors.
- During bargaining different types of behavior can be used, ranging from distributive to intraorganizational in nature.
- When impasse occurs, work stoppages through strikes or lockouts can be used to pressure the other party.
- Efforts to resolve impasses can include conciliation, mediation, or arbitration.
- One major trend in collective bargaining has been union-management cooperation, either through union ownership or productivity assistance.
- Concessionary bargaining occurs when the union agrees to wage, benefit, or other reductions during the bargaining process.
- Grievances express worker dissatisfaction or differences in contract interpretations. Grievances follow a formal path to resolution.
- A formal grievance procedure is usually specified in a union contract, but it should exist in any organization to provide a system for handling such problems.
- Grievances can be approached by management from either a behavioral or a legalistic viewpoint; however, the behavioral approach is recommended.
- A grievance procedure begins with the first-level supervisor—and ends (if it is not resolved along the way) with arbitration.

REVIEW AND DISCUSSION QUESTIONS

1. Why do collective bargaining strategies and structures differ?
2. Give several examples of illegal, mandatory, and permissive bargaining issues.
3. What are the stages in a typical collective bargaining process?
4. Assume that a bargaining impasse has occurred. What would be the differences between using mediation and arbitration to resolve the impasse?
5. Discuss why union-management cooperation and concessionary bargaining has led to a backlash from some unionized workers.
6. Give an example of a grievance and how both unionized and nonunion firms might handle it.
7. What steps would be followed in a typical grievance process? Why is arbitration, as the final step of a grievance process, important and useful?

CASE	The "Stolen" Orange Juice

Grievances can be filed on actions on large or small matters. The following case represents a grievance that was decided by an arbitrator hired by Greyhound Food Management (Warren, Michigan) and the United Catering Restaurant, Bar, & Hotel Workers, Local 1064.[54]

The grievance was filed by the union on behalf of Tom, a union member working as a fast-food attendant at a Greyhound-operated cafeteria. The Greyhound Food Service provided food service management on a contract basis for many firms, including Hydra Matic, a manufacturing company located in Warren, Michigan.

Tom had been working for Greyhound for almost a year, and was working the 1 P.M.–8:30 P.M. shift making $5.25 an hour at the time of his discharge from the company. The company justified Tom's employment termination by asserting that he had attempted to steal a six-ounce container of orange juice, which normally sold for fifty-eight cents. Tom's supervisor testified that from his office he observed Tom attempting to leave the premises with the container of orange juice hidden under his jacket. After stopping Tom, the supervisor accused him of attempting to steal the orange juice. Then the supervisor telephoned the assistant manager for instructions. The assistant manager told the supervisor to document the incident and stated that he (the assistant manager) would take care of the matter the next morning. The supervisor's written report stated that he had heard the refrigerator door slam, followed by Tom's walking toward the door. The supervisor asked Tom twice what Tom had in his coat, after which Tom pulled the juice out of his coat, dropping and spilling it over the floor.

The following morning the assistant manager called Tom and the union steward into his office and confronted them with the supervisor's written description of the incident. Tom denied that he attempted to steal the orange juice, saying that the supervisor just saw some orange juice on the floor. At a meeting later that morning, the assistant manager terminated Tom's employment. Tom filed a grievance, which was immediately denied. Tom and the union then requested arbitration, as was allowed under the company-union labor contract.

The arbitrator reviewed several documents including statements from the supervisor, the assistant manager, a former employee, and the union steward. Also, he had to review the relevant sections of the labor contract on management rights, seniority, and the grievance procedure. Finally, the arbitrator reviewed the list of company rules and regulations that were posted by the time clock, one of which said that disciplinary action ranging from reprimand to immediate discharge could result from rule violation. The first rule prohibited "stealing private, company, or client's property."

Company position

The company's position was that Tom had knowledge of posted work rules, the first of which clearly prohibited theft. The company also had a policy that no company property was to leave the restaurant. The testimony of the supervisor established that Tom attempted to steal and remove company property. It was not relevant that Tom's impermissible act did not succeed. The detection by management of the theft before Tom left the premises did not excuse the act. Also, the company said that the size or dollar amount of the theft was immaterial. Therefore, because the company followed the terms of the union contract that provided for dismissal of employees for "just cause," and because Tom knew, or should have known, of the rule against stealing, the arbitrator should rule for the company.

Union position

The act of attempting to steal a container of orange juice valued at fifty-eight cents does involve moral turpitude and therefore requires the application of a "high degree of proof." In addition, the employer carries the burden of convincing the arbitrator beyond a reasonable doubt through the witnesses that Tom did attempt to steal the orange juice. Even though Tom had been subject to some other minor disciplinary actions in the past, termination was too harsh a penalty and therefore the arbitrator should rule for Tom and the union.

QUESTIONS

1. How important is the value of the item in comparison to the alleged act of stealing?
2. Because Tom never actually left the company premises with the juice, did he actually steal?
3. How would you rule in this case? (Your instructor can give you the actual decision by the arbitrator, which is contained in the instructor's manual that accompanies this text.)

NOTES

1. Adapted from "Union Workers Are Digging In On Health Costs," *Omaha World-Herald*, August 20, 1989, 1G;. James Fraze, "Six of Seven Baby Bell Contracts Signed," *Resource*, October 1989, 1, 4; and James Fraze, "Health Benefits Key Issue in Strikes," *Resource*, September 1989, 1, 4.

2. T. L. Leap and D. W. Grigsby, "A Conceptualization of Collective Bargaining Power," *Industrial and Labor Relations Review* 39 (1986): 202–212.

3. Grant T. Savage, John D. Blair, and Ritch L. Sorenson, "Consider Both Relationships and Substance When Negotiating Strategically," *Academy of Management EXECUTIVE* 3 (1989): 37–48.

4. The six strategies are adapted from R. E. Allen and T. B. Keavany, *Contemporary Labor Relations* (Reading, Mass.: Addison-Wesley, 1988) 126.

5. Michael A. Verespej, "The New Battleground," *Industry Week*, April 6, 1987, 40.

6. John J. Kenny, *Primer of Labor Relations*, 23rd ed. (Washington, D.C.: Bureau of National Affairs, 1986), 46–47.

7. *Allied Chemical and Alkaline Workers of America, Local No. 1 v. Pittsburgh Plate Glass Co.* 404 U.S. 157 (1971).

8. *NLRB v. Wooster Division of Borg-Warner Corp.* 356 U.S. 342 (1958).

9. John Thomas Delaney and Donna Sochell, "The Mandatory-Permissive Distinction and Collective Bargaining Outcomes," *Industrial and Labor Relations Review* 42 (1989): 566–583.

10. Adapted from William H. Holley and Kenneth M. Jennings, *The Labor Relations Process*, 3rd ed., (Chicago: Dryden Press, 1988), 395.

11. Martin M. Perline and David J. Poynter, "Managerial Perceptions of Collective Bargaining Issues," *Personnel Administrator*, August 1989, 73–75.

12. Edward Brankey and Mel E. Schnake, "Exceptions to Compulsory Union Membership," *Personnel Journal*, June 1988, 114–122.

13. *Basic Patterns in Union Contracts* (Washington D.C.: Bureau of National Affairs, 1986), 101.

14. P. A. Susser, "Union Access to Company Information," *Personnel Administrator*, April 1986, 32–36.

15. Richard E. Walton and Robert B. McKersie, A *Behavioral Theory of Labor Negotiations* (New York: McGraw-Hill, 1965).

16. Stephen R. G. Jones, "The Role of Negotiators in Union-Firm Bargaining," *Canadian Journal of Economics* 22 (1989): 630–642.

17. James B. Dworkin, et al., "Worker's Preferences in Concession Bargaining," *Industrial Relations* 27 (1988): 7–20.

18. Steven Briggs and Daniel J. Keys, "What Makes Labor Mediators Effective?" *Labor Law Journal* 40 (1989): 517–520.

19. Dennis H. Loberson, "Long-Term Agreements at Philip Morris," *Personnel Journal*, December 1989, 36–39.

20. Everett M. Kassalow, "Concession Bargaining: Towards New Roles for American Unions and Managers," *International Labour Review* 127 (1988): 573–592.

21. Michael A. Verespej, "Bargaining for Economic Survival," *Industry Week*, February 20, 1989, 19–26.

22. John G. Belcher, Jr., "The Role of Unions in Productivity Management," *Personnel*, January 1988, 54–58.

23. Adapted from John Hoerr, "The Cultural Revolution at A. O. Smith," *Business Week*, May 29, 1989, 66–68.

24. Donald F. Ephlin, "Revolution By Evolution: The Changing Relationship Between GM and the UAW," *Academy of Management EXECUTIVE* 2 (1988): 63–66.

25. "Teamwork Spirit Keeps Ford Plant Rolling," *Omaha World-Herald*, December 4, 1988, 16G.

26. Anil Verma, "Joint Participation Programs: Self-help or Suicide for Labor?" *Industrial Relations* 28 (1989): 401–410.

27. P. B. Voos, "Managerial Perceptions of the Economic Impact of Labor Relations Programs," *Industrial and Labor Relations Review 41* (1987): 195–208.

28. William N. Cooke, "Improving Productivity and Quality Through Collaboration," *Industrial Relations* 28 (1989): 299–310.

29. Wendy Zellner, "The UAW Rebels Teaming Up Against Teamwork," *Business Week*, March 27, 1989, 110–114.

30. Brian. E. Becker, "Concession Bargaining: The Meaning of Union Gains," *Academy of Management Journal 31* (1988): 377–387.

31. Marvin J. Levine, "The Evolution of Two-Tier Wage Agreements: Bane or Panacea in Labor-Intensive Industries," *Labor Law Journal 40* (1989): 12–20.

32. David J. Walsh, "Accounting for the Proliferation of Two-Tier Wage Settlements in the U.S. Airline Industry, 1983–1986," *Industrial and Labor Relations Review 42* (1988): 50–62.

33. Henry J. Pratt, "Employee Complaints: Act Early and Be Concerned," ARMA *Records Management Quarterly*, January 1989, 26–28.

34. C. Ichniowski, "The Effects of Grievance Activity on Productivity," *Industrial and Labor Relations Review 39* (1986): 86.

35. *Basic Patterns in Union Contracts* (Washington, D.C.: Bureau of National Affairs, 1986), 33.

36. BNA *What's New in Collective Bargaining*, June 5, 1986, 4.

37. E. T. Suturs, "Hazards of an Open Door Policy," *INC*, January 1987, 99–102.

38. George W. Bolander and Harold C. White, "Building Bridges: Nonunion Employee Grievance Systems," *Personnel*, July 1988, 62–65.

39. *Employment Guide* (Washington, D.C.: Bureau of National Affairs, 1988), 10–221.

40. "Solving Employees' Problems," *Personnel Administrator*, July 1988, 20–22.

41. Douglas M. McCabe, "Corporate Nonunion Grievance Arbitration Systems: A Procedural Analysis," *Labor Law Journal 40* (1989): 432–437.

42. J. Tasini, "Letting Workers Help Handle Worker's Gripes," *Business Week*, September 15, 1986.

43. L. Reibstein, "More Firms Use Peer Review Panel to Resolve Employees' Grievances," *Wall Street Journal*, December 3, 1986, 33.

44. C. E. Labig, Jr. and I. B. Helburn, "Union and Management Policy Influences in Grievance Initiation," *Journal of Labor Research 7* (1986): 269–284.

45. Brian S. Klaas, "Determinants of Grievance Activity and the Grievance System's Impact on Employee Behavior: An Integrative Perspective," *Academy of Management Review 14* (1989): 445–458.

46. Adapted from Michael E. Gordon and Roger L. Bowlby, "Propositions about Grievance Settlements: Finally, Consultation with Grievants," *Personnel Psychology 41* (1988): 107–123.

47. Neal Orkin and Louise Schmoyer, "*Weingarten*: Rights Remedies and the Arbitration Process," *Labor Law Journal 40* (1989): 594–599.

48. Brian S. Klaas and Angelo D. DeNisi, "Managerial Reactions to Employee Dissent: The Impact of Grievance Activity on Performance Ratings," *Academy of Management Journal 32* (1989): 705–717.

49. Brian S. Klaas, "Managerial Decision Making About Employee Grievances: The Impact of the Grievant's Work History," *Personnel Psychology 42* (1989): 53–68.

50. *Textile Workers Union of America v. Lincoln Mills of Alabama* 353 U.S. 448 (1957).

51. The legal standing of grievance arbitration was clarified in a series of cases involving the United Steelworkers union, called the "Steelworkers Trilogy." The cases involved are *United Steelworkers of America v. American Manufacturing Co.* 363 US 564 (1960); *United Steelworkers of America v. Warrior and Gulf Navigation Co.* 363 US 574 (1960); and *United Steelworkers of America v. Enterprise Wheel and Car Corp.* 363 US 593 (1960).

52. Arthur Eliot Berkeley, "The Most Serious Faults in Labor–Management Arbitration Today, and What Can Be Done to Remedy Them," *Labor Law Journal 40* (1989): 728–733.

53. Brian Bemmels, "Gender Effects in Discipline Arbitration: Evidence from British Columbia," *Academy of Management Journal 31* (1988), 699–706.

54. 89 LA 1138 (1987).

Evaluation of the P/HR System

The various P/HR activities that must be performed in any organization have been examined to this point in the text. The last section considers P/HR management in different environments and assesses P/HR effectiveness.

P/HR activities vary from one organizational setting to another. For example, in a small business there is often no formal P/HR department; operating managers perform these function. Sometimes family members are deeply involved in the business. In addition to highlighting some unique facets of P/HR in smaller organizations, Chapter 20 also discusses P/HR activities that may have to be managed somewhat differently by public sector P/HR professionals.

Chapter 20 also examines the considerations that affect P/HR decisions for employees working in international environments. As more and more organizations begin or expand their international operations, it will be important for all managers and P/HR staff members to be knowledgeable about staffing, training, and compensation in an international environment.

Chapter 21 describes the issues involved with assessing P/HR effectiveness. Through records and collected data, P/HR practices are analyzed. Having a computerized human resource information system enhances the retention and retrieval of P/HR data. This final portion of the chapter discusses several formal means of assessing P/HR effectiveness.

P/HR Management in International and Other Environments

After you have read this chapter, you should be able to:

1. List and define several types of international employees

2. Explain why staffing activities for international jobs are more complex than for domestic ones

3. Discuss three areas of international training and development

4. Identify several international compensation practices

5. Explain at least four differences between public and private sector P/HR management

6. Discuss the evolution of P/HR activities in small organizations and how family factors affect them

P/HR Management and Maquiladoras

Many firms based in highly developed nations such as the United States have attempted to maintain competitively priced products by establishing manufacturing plants in less-developed countries having lower labor costs. One illustration is the establishment of *maquiladora* plants located along the U.S.–Mexico border. The plants are called *maquiladoras* from the Spanish for "someone who makes goods for market." In many of the *maquiladoras,* parts are shipped to Mexico and then the goods are assembled in the plants for shipment to the United States. Wage rates for Mexican workers at *maquiladoras* average about $30 per week ($.80/hour), depending on the currency exchange rate, compared with U.S. wages of $200 per week or more for comparable work.

Such diverse corporations as Outboard Marine, RCA, General Motors, Zenith, Sunbeam, and R. G. Barry have established *maquiladoras*. One estimate is that over 1,400 plants employing approximately 400,000 Mexican workers have been established in Mexican border towns.

Firms that establish *maquiladoras* are required by Mexican government regulations to offer such benefits as health insurance, vacation time, holiday pay, and a fifteen-day cash bonus at holiday time. Other benefits that are not government-mandated include subsidized or free lunches, free transportation to and from work, and others.

But the *maquiladoras* have some negative impacts. First, the wage rates are even lower than the typical wage rates of about $1.60/hour in assembly plants in the interior of Mexico. Thus, U.S. labor union officials and others criticize *maquiladoras* as being "sweatshops." Second, the growth of the number of plants, has resulted in bordertown housing shortages, transportation problems, and even labor shortages. For example, in Acuna, Mexico (across the border from Del Rio, Texas), sixteen new plants opened up in a six-month period in 1989.

More and more U.S. firms will be tapping Mexico's labor supply as a result of economic trade arrangements between the U.S. and Mexico. Whether the *maquiladoras* continue to proliferate and where have significant human resource implications.[1]

"To be trained as an American manager is to be trained for a world that is no longer there."

Lester Thurow

Management of human resources is not restricted to large private sector corporations operating in one country. The organization that operates internationally must make many changes in the type and manner of its P/HR activities. Likewise, there are some unique environmental pressures and characteristics that make modifications of such P/HR activities as staffing and training in the public sector necessary. Finally, there are many small organizations in which the management of P/HR activities must be adapted to reflect the limited financial resources and work force in smaller organizations. This chapter focuses on how organizations in different environments adapt in order to manage their human resources more effectively.

■■ ■ INTERNATIONAL P/HR MANAGEMENT

Today, U.S. firms are competing in a global economy. As the opening discussion on *maquiladoras* illustrates, these firms are using a variety of approaches to maintain competitiveness. Likewise, foreign firms are establishing operations in the United States. The degree of internationalization that has occurred is illustrated by the following facts:[2]

- The 100 largest U.S. multinational corporations had foreign sales of over $500 billion in one year.
- Foreign firms have direct investments in the United States of about $250 billion.
- Many U.S. firms receive a sizable share of their sales and profits outside the United States (see Figure 20–1).
- Foreign firms own 100 percent of such firms as People's Drug Store, Shell Oil, Central Soya, CBS Records, Giant Food Stores, and Firestone Tire & Rubber.

The growth overseas by U.S. firms is illustrated by McDonald's Corporation International, whose operations provide about one-third of the corporate revenues. About 40 percent of all new McDonald's restaurants are being opened outside the United States, including such new markets as Hungary and the U.S.S.R.

Types of International Employees

As individual firms develop and expand their international operations, they are identified as *multinational firms*. These multinational firms typically employ individuals from both inside and outside the country in which the operations occur. Several different classifications of individuals can be employed by multinational firms:

- Individuals who are not citizens of the countries in which they work are **expatriates.**
- A **host-country national** is an employee who is a citizen of a country in which a branch or plant is located, but the organization is headquartered in another country.
- A **third-country national** is someone who is a citizen of one country, working in a second country, and employed by an organization headquartered in a third country.

AN EXPATRIATE is a person working in a country who is not a national citizen of that country.

A HOST-COUNTRY NATIONAL is an employee who is a citizen of a country in which a branch or plant is located, but the organization is headquartered in another country.

A THIRD-COUNTRY NATIONAL is someone who is a citizen of one country, working in a second country, and employed by an organization headquartered in a third country.

Figure 20–1
Foreign Sales and Profits of U.S. Firms

FIRM	FOREIGN AS % OF TOTAL REVENUE	FOREIGN AS % OF TOTAL OPERATING PROFIT
Johnson & Johnson	50.0	55.5
Dow Chemical	54.1	45.1
Coca Cola	54.5	68.7
NCR	59.0	76.0
H. J. Heinz	40.1	41.4
Colgate Palmolive	63.7	56.1
Gillette	64.7	73.7
McDonald's	36.1	30.1

SOURCE: *Forbes*, July 23, 1990, 207–210.

Each of these individuals presents some unique P/HR management challenges. Because each may be a citizen of a different country, different tax laws and other factors apply. P/HR professionals have to be knowledgeable about the laws and customs in each country. They must establish appropriate payroll and record-keeping procedures, among other activities, to ensure compliance with varying regulations and requirements.

One survey of 30 multinational corporations found that these firms are reducing the use of expatriates and increasing the use of host-country nationals. Among the reasons cited for this shift are to increase the familiarity and knowledge about host-country customs and business practices and to reduce the higher costs associated with expatriates.[3]

The actual annual costs of an executive located outside the United States who is paid $100,000 in salary is more likely to be $250,000 when housing costs, school subsidies, and tax equalization payments are considered.[4] If an executive quits prematurely or insists on a transfer home, costs can equal or exceed the person's annual salary. Consequently, international P/HR management practices focus heavily on staffing and selection, training and development, compensation and safety. Each of these areas is examined next.

International Staffing and Selection

Many companies have the misguided notion that a good employee in a domestic operation will make a good expatriate. This idea has cost companies many thousands of dollars in mistakes. About 20 percent of all U.S. expatriates fail to complete their foreign assignments, so their firms incur more costs replacing them, relocating the expatriates home, and other costs. Costs for the parent company per-failure range from $55,000 to $150,000.[5]

Poor staffing for international assignments occurs for several reasons. A study by Tung suggests the following reasons why those selected by U.S. firms for international assignments did not succeed:[6]

■ Inability of spouse to adapt to international environment or other family-related problems
■ Inappropriate personality or maturity of selected individual
■ Inability of international manager to handle the expanded responsibilities faced overseas
■ Lack of technical competence and/or motivation to work overseas

P/HR: Practice *and* Research	TRW Installs an HRIS

TRW, Inc., is a highly diversified worldwide corporation employing over 90,000 people. Its primary business activities fall into three operating groups: (1) automotive, (2) electronics and defense, and (3) industrial and energy. To track all P/HR activities of its far-flung empire, TRW developed an integrated, automated human resource information system (HRIS).

Before beginning the project, TRW had over fifty separate payroll systems and ten other P/HR systems. To start, TRW pulled together computer-systems experts, management information systems (MIS) representatives, and human resource staff members from throughout the company. The team recommended that a consulting firm specializing in HRIS be hired to develop a needs analysis questionnaire. This 31–page questionnaire requested information on ten P/HR areas: (1) basic record keeping, (2) benefits planning and administration, (3) pension planning and administration, (4) compensation, (5) human resources planning and development, (6) labor relations, (7) employment and recruitment, (8) time reporting and attendance, (9) equal employment opportunity and affirmative action, and (10) health and safety. Once the results were compiled, the technical components of the system could be identified.

The team then obtained information and bids from various HRIS software suppliers. The list of twelve vendors was narrowed to three finalists, and team members visited the finalists' offices and talked with other firms using the products.

After a final selection was made, pilot installation programs were established at several TRW locations. Throughout the installation and evaluation process, the supplier provided technical support and training assistance. The pilot programs were judged successful, and the team recommended that TRW install the system corporation-wide.

Implementing the system throughout the corporation required another three years. However, with its installation, TRW was able to have a decentralized business structure with centralized coordinated human resource information processing. TRW Project Director Rick Marshall said, "Our hope is that instead of spending time on manual efforts, employees will be performing more analytical work, and TRW people at the group, sector, and company levels will be able to access data needed to fulfill such needs as compensation surveys and EEO reporting on a consolidated basis.[10]

organization attempts to ensure that the HRIS fulfills its potential, is accepted by users, and is implemented in an organized manner.

TRAINING.   Training those who will be using the system is critical to the successful implementation of an HRIS. This training is at several levels. First, everyone within the organization concerned with data on employees has to be trained to use new recording forms compatible with the input requirements of the system. In addition, in the P/HR department, staff members, including the executive in that area, must be trained on the system. For many P/HR professionals, this training may be their first exposure to computers, yet they must learn the "nitty-gritty" details.[11] Support and instruction from hardware and software vendors also are important in order for the organization to realize the full benefits of the system.

SECURITY AND PRIVACY.   Two other issues of concern are security and privacy. Controls must be built into the system to restrict indiscriminate access to the HRIS data on employees.[12] For example, health insurance claims information might identify someone who has undergone psychiatric counseling or treatment for alcoholism. Likewise, performance appraisal ratings on employees must be guarded.

Often, data disks are kept in specially locked cabinets. In addition, closely restricted passwords are needed to access different parts of the HRIS data base.

◼◼ ◼◼ PERSONNEL/HUMAN RESOURCE COMMUNICATIONS

HR Information not only means data on people and their performance but also communication of information within the organization as well. Communication affects the management of people as much as, or more than, any other process over which management has influence. Through communications, new policies are explained, changes are implemented, and instructions are given.

Downward and Upward Communications

Just as an HRIS is built on data and information, P/HR communication is built on using the P/HR data and information to communicate down the organization so that employees have the P/HR information they need. Likewise, employees must have ways to communicate upward so that their ideas are made available for P/HR management decision making. The communications process is built on transmittal of information both downward and upward in the organization.

Downward communication flows from top management and is essential so that employees know what is and will be happening in the organization and what top management expectations and goals are. For example, Great American Bank of San Diego acquired other banks during the past several years. The P/HR division of the bank developed communication programs to discuss each merger as it occurred with current Great American employees. For those working in the newly acquired bank, communication efforts were crucial in dealing with the anxieties and stress caused by the mergers. P/HR managers held orientation and discussion sessions in each branch location and employees were encouraged to bring their spouses. Questions were solicited and answered by a panel of existing Great American employees and managers.[13]

Upward communication also is important so that managers know what the ideas, concerns, and information needs of employees are. Both formal means to encourage upward communication, such as a suggestion system, and informal means are used. However, upward communications can be a threatening experience for both managers and employers.[14]

As anyone who has ever worked in any organization knows, an important part of organizational communication is carried out through informal information channels, referred to as the *grapevine*. Just as jungle drums in old Tarzan movies indicated trouble, activity along the grapevine may reflect employee concerns and organizational problems, and supervisors and managers should monitor it.

Managers should be aware of current grapevine messages and listen for major distortions. Activity in the grapevine depends on how important a topic is and on the presence (or absence) of official communication about it. Studies show that a minority of employees account for a majority of the information brought into and discussed throughout the organization.[15]

It is impossible to eliminate the grapevine. Absence of a grapevine in an organization might indicate that employees are either too scared to talk or that they care so little about the organization that they do not want to talk about it. Because the grapevine is a fact of organization life, it is important that managers share information and communicate details to reduce the need for the rumors and gossip that naturally spread on the grapevine. Some of the common formal upward and downward communication means are highlighted next.

Employee Publications and Media

Organizations communicate with employees through internal publications and media, including newspapers, company magazines, organizational newletters, videotape, and intensive computer technology. Other formal communication methods include bulletin boards, posters, movies, and slides.

Whatever the formal means used, managers should make an honest attempt to communicate information employees need to know. Communication should not be solely a public relations tool to build the image of the organization. Bad news, as well as good news, should be reported objectively in readable style.

For example, an airline publication has a question-and-answer section in which employees anonymously can submit tough questions to management. Management's answers are printed with the question in every issue. Because every effort is made to give completely honest answers, this section has been very useful. The same idea fizzled in another large company because the questions were answered with "the company line" and employees soon lost interest in the less-than-candid replies.

PUBLICATIONS. Various newsletters, magazines, and other internal publications are produced to aid formal P/HR communications. Such publications frequently contain feature stories on employees and their families, promotions, retirements, and awards, and on the organization and its operations. Some elaborate publications in larger organizations require full-time public relations staff. In smaller organizations, a secretary in the P/HR department may prepare a mimeographed newsletter.

AUDIOVISUAL MEDIA. As audiovisual technology has developed, many employers have added audiovisual methods of communication with employees. Some employers produce *audiotapes* or *videotapes* explaining benefit programs, corporate reorganizations, and revised P/HR policies and programs, which are shipped to each organizational branch. At those locations, the tapes are presented to employees in groups, then questions are addressed by a manager or someone from headquarters. Other organizations have used *teleconferencing*, in which satellite technology links facilities and groups in various locations. In this way, the same message can be delivered simultaneously. For example, Domino's Pizza uses a satellite network to communicate information on new products, store operations, ideas, and other information. Others using satellites are J. C. Penney's, Texas Instruments, and Federal Express.

Computers can be used for employee communications also. One large food-processing company installed computers at each of the firm's major work locations. Employees with questions about their benefits could obtain answers about coverage options and other details almost instantly. Such a service is especially useful for employers that have flexible benefits plans.[10]

Suggestion Systems.

A **suggestion system** is a formal method of obtaining employee input and upward communication. Giving the employees the opportunity to suggest changes or ways in which operations could be improved can encourage loyalty and commitment

A SUGGESTION SYSTEM
is a formal method of obtaining employee input and upward communication.

Ms. Peoples, the box says "Suggestions", not "Filing".

to the organization. Often an employee in the work unit knows more about how waste can be eliminated, how hazards can be controlled, or how improvements can be made than do managers who are not as close to the actual tasks performed. Many suggestion systems give financial rewards to employees for cost-saving suggestions. In such organizations it is important to calculate the anticipated savings because payments to employees often are tied to a percentage of savings, up to some maximum level.[17]

Suggestions systems have been saving money for employers for almost 100 years. Beginning in 1898, at Eastman Kodak Corporation, the first suggestion award was a $2.00 payment to a worker who pointed out the advantages of washing windows in the production department. A survey of over 900 employers by the National Association of Suggestion Systems found the average net savings per suggestion implemented to be $7,663.[18] In the U.S. government, worker suggestions resulted in a savings of $1.2 billion in one year. The top award paid was $35,000 to a National Guard member who suggested using an $8.70 electronics part purchased at a local electronics store to test helicopter navigation lights, instead of buying some costly equipment designed specifically for that task.[19]

MAKING SUGGESTION SYSTEMS WORK. Suggestions seldom appear as fully developed plans. They are usually "ideas" that need some work before they can be implemented. Figure 21–3 summarizes some important do's and don'ts for suggestion systems.

DO	DON'T
■ Commit management to answer every suggestion ■ Publicize the program ■ Reward successful suggestions ■ Respond to *all* signed suggestions ■ Use locked boxes and printed forms, and pick up routinely	■ Reject a suggestion because it is not polished ■ Allow the suggestions to get lost in the system ■ Fail to institute a suggestion system simply because it isn't sophisticated

Figure 21–3
Do's and Don'ts for Suggestion Systems

A suggestion system should be publicized, and good suggestions should be implemented. Suggestions should be collected often and evaluated by a committee, usually composed both of managers and nonmanagers. The committee passes on the suggestions it approves to upper management, who accepts or rejects them and determines the rewards to be given.

One major reason that suggestion programs fail is the inattention of management to feedback. Prompt feedback is important to all employees submitting suggestions. If employees are not told if or why their suggestions are accepted or rejected, much of the underlying momentum will be lost.[20] At one firm in Massachusetts, all individuals submitting suggestions receive specific feedback and discussion by appropriate managers. Also, those implemented are posted on bulletin boards in each work area. Squibb Corporation even uses computerized suggestion terminals so that employees can input their suggestions. The employees are told that they can omit their names if they wish and that they do not need to be concerned about grammatical errors.[21]

FAILURE OF SUGGESTION SYSTEMS.   Suggestion systems can fail if the employees see the suggestions programs as a waste of time because they believe that little will change, or if they distrust management who may view suggestions as criticisms. At General Electric's appliance division, salaried employees were asked to submit cost-cutting ideas. However, in the same request there were implied threats that if too few ideas and too little savings were identified, employees could expect staff cuts and layoffs. As would be expected, the program was not received positively and few employees participated.[22] What this example and others indicate is that the success of a suggestion system is linked to the amount of trust and communication associated with management, particularly top management.

■■ ■ P/HR RESEARCH

P/HR research analyzes past and present P/HR practices by using collected data and records. P/HR research data can be used in four main ways:[23]

■ Monitoring current P/HR activities
■ Identifying P/HR problem areas and possible solutions to these problems
■ Forecasting trends and their impact on P/HR management
■ Projecting the costs and benefits of future P/HR activities

Conducting research is often crucial to solving P/HR problems because it is often difficult to make good decisions without accurate information. Just as a physician must make a diagnosis before treating an illness, current P/HR practices must be

P/HR RESEARCH
analyzes past and present P/HR practices by using collected data and records.

researched and analyzed to ensure that future P/HR programs and activities are more effective. Many managers are intimidated by the word *research* and its academic implications. But research can be quite simple and straightforward, such as using a questionnare to ask employees about work scheduling options. For example, employees in a state education agency completed such a survey in their unit. This survey pointed out problem areas that would otherwise not have been discovered, so that the revised work schedules offered were made compatible with the desires of employees.

Primary vs. Secondary Research

Research in many fields can be categorized as *primary* or *secondary*. In researching P/HR areas, both types are useful, as the following discussion indicates.

PRIMARY RESEARCH
is the method by which data is gathered directly on problems and issues.

PRIMARY RESEARCH.   In **primary research,** data are gathered directly on problems of concern. Attitude surveys, questionnaires, interviews, and experiments are all primary research methods. Individuals who plan to do primary research should first decide what phenomenon they wish to study. Examples of primary research topics are causes of nursing employee turnover, employee attitudes about flex-time, extent of flexible benefit plans, and the relationship of a pre-employment physical exam to worker's compensation claims.

A common presentation format for primary research studies and articles includes the following sections:

- *Statement of the problem research area:* What is being studied and why is it important that it be researched now?
- *Literature review:* What have other researchers and writers said about the problem under study?
- *Hypotheses and research methods used:* What is this study expected to add to knowledge of the subject and what research methods are to be used? Why?
- *Results:* What do the collected data mean once they have been analyzed? What was found and how do the results relate to the hypotheses and the findings from previous research? What was not found and what are the weaknesses of the study?
- *Conclusions and recommendations:* What courses of action are suggested by the research results? What future research directions does the research suggest?

Examples of research presented in this format on P/HR topics and issues can be found in the *Academy of Management Journal, Personnel Psychology,* or other research-oriented journals listed in Appendix A. The primary research studies presented in these journals can offer guidance on factors affecting P/HR problems, the impact of various management approaches to P/HR issues, or other topics beneficial to P/HR academicians and practitioners.

SECONDARY RESEARCH
uses research done by others and reported in articles in professional journals or books.

SECONDARY RESEARCH.   **Secondary research** uses research done by others and reported in articles in professional journals or books. One approach that has grown in popularity is the use of *literature reviews* on a topic area. For instance, a literature review on employee selection interviews examines much of the primary and secondary research done by other researchers to produce a summary of findings on various facets of selection interviewing.[24] Also, there are several different computerized literature data bases available to P/HR researchers. Pay and benefits surveys prepared by governmental agencies or management consulting firms illustrate another common use of secondary research on P/HR activities.

Some of the most important methods of conducting P/HR research are experiments, employee questionnaires, research interviews, and using research done by other organizations. Each of these methods is discussed briefly.

Experiments

Experiments can provide useful P/HR insights. An **experiment** involves studying a factor responds when changes are made in one or more variables, or conditions. For instance, to test the impact of flextime scheduling on employee turnover, a firm might allow flexible scheduling in one department on a pilot basis. If the turnover rate of the employees is that department drops in comparison with the turnover in other departments still working set schedules, then the experiment may indicate that flexible scheduling can reduce turnover. Then the firm may try flexible scheduling in other departments.

The biggest problem with experiments in P/HR research is that P/HR management is practiced in the "real world." Unlike chemistry or other pure sciences, P/HR management is an applied science, and in real organizations it may be very difficult to control outside factors. Using the flexible scheduling example, other factors may be influencing turnover in the firm. But by having the other department as a *control group* (a similar population to that of the experimental group but in which no changes were introduced) the effects of the flexible scheduling change in the pilot department, can be compared with those in the control departments, and it is reasonable to assume that any differences are the result of the experimental group variable (flextime).

P/HR experiments also can be conducted in laboratory settings using simulated P/HR situations. For example, a group of M.B.A. students can be shown sample resumes on potential candidates for a specific job. If all of the resumes contain similar qualifications, but the gender of the "applicants" is changed from male to female, the effect of gender on applicant suitability can be studied. The problem with such laboratory studies is that practicing managers filling actual jobs may or may not act in the same manner as the students in a laboratory setting. Nevertheless, laboratory experiments are used extensively in P/HR research, and they may suggest other research experiments that can be conducted in the "real world."

EXPERIMENTAL DESIGNS.   There are several different designs for setting up experiments. People trained in experimental design and statistics usually are needed to conduct such studies and interpret the results. As mentioned in Chapter 10, three common designs are:

1. *Post-measure:* Gathering data after an experiment has been conducted
2. *Pre-post-measure:* Gathering data from the same subjects before and after a change is made
3. *Pre-post-measure with control group:* Having some employees perform a job in a new way while others perform the same job in the old way, and comparing the results before and after the change

The last design is preferred and more widely used because the differences in the performance of the groups can be identified more clearly and related to the experiment, assuming other conditions are maintained. However, the two groups must be similar if the comparisons are to be as meaningful as possible. See the hospital incentive and absentee experiment in P/HR: Research for an example of pre-post-measure with a control group.

P/HR:	Practice *and* Research	An Incentive and Absenteeism Experiment

Scholtzhauer and Rosse conducted a field experiment at a nonprofit hospital over a five-year period on the effect of an incentive program on absenteeism. The results were reported in *Personnel Psychology*. The subjects of the study were randomly selected from among the full-time workers at the hospital, which employed about 3,000 employees. A comparison group of unionized employees and an experimental group of nonunion employees were used. However, in spite of the union–nonunion difference, the groups were similar on many demographic factors such as age, marital status, education, etc.

An incentive program for the experimental nonunion group was developed, based on the employees' annual use of 96 hours of sick leave. At year end, employees who were eligible could convert up to 24 hours of sick leave into additional pay or vacation time. However, those in the union group were not eligible for the incentive program. Data on total hours of absence was gathered for several years: the year before the introduction of the incentive program, the three years of the program, and the year after it was discontinued.

The results showed that the two groups had similar absenteeism records before the start of the incentive program. Once the incentive program began, the experimental group had an increase in the number of employees with perfect attendance and a decrease in the number with 20 or more hours of absence. However, little change occurred in the comparison group of union workers.

The end result of the program was an estimated decline in average absence of 32 percent during the incentive period. Savings attributed to the program averaged more than the costs of the incentives.[25]

Employee Questionnaires

One type of research uses questionnaires to give employees opportunities to voice their opinions about specific P/HR activities. Employee opinion questionnaires can be used to diagnose specific problem areas, identify employee needs or preferences, and reveal areas in which P/HR activities are well received.[26] For example, questionnaires may be sent to employees to collect ideas for revising a performance appraisal system. Or employees may be asked to evaluate specific organizational communication methods, such as the employee handbook or the company suggestion system. One common use of a questionnaire is to determine if employees are satisfied with their benefit programs. In addition, some organizations survey employees before granting new benefits to see if they are desired.

Questionnaires can be distributed and collected by supervisors, given out with employee paychecks, or mailed to employees' homes. More accurate information usually is obtained if employees can give information anonymously.[27] A new way to obtain employee survey information is through computerized systems, as described in the P/HR Practice.

ATTITUDE SURVEYS focus on employees' feelings and beliefs to pinpoint the underlying opinions about their jobs and the organization.

ATTITUDE SURVEYS.   Attitude surveys focus on employees' feelings and beliefs that underly their opinions about their jobs and the organization. Some employers conduct attitude surveys on a regularly scheduled basis (such as every year), while others do it intermittently. These surveys, which serve as a sounding board for employees to air their feelings about their jobs, supervisors, co-workers, and organizational policies and practices, can be a starting point for improving productivity.

P/HR:	Practice *and* Research	Electronic Mail Research

With the evolution of new technologies, additional ways of conducting P/HR research are available. One of the most intriguing use of an electronic mail system (EM) is to obtain survey information from employees.

Large and medium-sized organizations increasingly are turning to EM. These systems allow anyone with a computer account to compose and send memos, leave messages, and otherwise communicate with others in the organization. Such firms as AT & T, IBM, Westinghouse, 3M, and others have EM systems.

Electronic mail is a feasible way to conduct employee surveys because a researcher can electronically transmit a questionnaire to all or selected EM addresses. The respondents then provide their answers and "send" them back to the researcher. The responses can be made in an anonymous manner.

One study that made use of EM found that the major advantage of the system was the reduction in the transmission costs and response times required to gather data. Also, respondents liked being able to respond in a more convenient manner. As EM systems become more widespread, this method of gathering employee survey data is likely to expand. [28]

Various types of attitude surveys can be conducted, depending on the issues to be explored. For instance, in one company a survey revealed that employees liked the work they did, but problems with the company's structure and policies hampered their job performance and satisfaction. In this case, employee satisfaction with work differed from satisfaction with the company.

The value of such a study is that it can be used to identify the culture of an organization, reveal the current state of an organization, and indicate areas in which changes are needed. [29] Other studies survey employees about the leadership styles used by their bosses and employee morale problems. Selected sample questions from an attitude survey conducted for an insurance company are contained in Figure 21–4 .

Attitude surveys can be custom-designed to address specific issues and concerns in an organization. But only surveys that are valid and reliable can measure attitudes accurately. Often a "research" survey that is developed in-house is poorly structured, asks questions in a confusing manner, or leads employees to respond in a manner

An attitude survey conducted for an insurance company asked employees to identify how much they agreed or disagreed with statements on a number of areas. Sample statements from various areas were:

- My immediate supervisor seeks out the thoughts and feelings of others.
- I find real enjoyment in my job.
- I would not consider taking another job with another firm.
- In this firm, high standards for performance are set.
- If you do good work, you will receive rewards and recognition.
- Unnecessary requirements and rules are kept to a minimum.
- I am rewarded fairly for the experience I have.
- I have little control over how I carry out my daily tasks.
- I think top management makes an effort to get opinions from the employees.
- Right now, staying with this organization is a matter of necessity as much as desire.

Figure 21–4
Sample Questions from an Attitude Survey

that will give the desired results. For these reasons, consultants often are hired to develop and conduct customized attitude surveys.

Prepared attitude surveys also are available from a wide variety of vendors. One drawback to the use of standardized surveys is that they may not cover special concerns.[30] If P/HR managers choose a standardized survey, they should check published reliability and validity statistics before using it.

By asking employees to respond candidly to an attitude survey, management is building up employee's expectations that action will be taken to do something about the concerns identified.[31] Therefore, a crucial part of conducting an attitude survey is to provide feedback to those who participated in it. It is especially important that negative survey results be communicated so as not to foster the appearance of hiding the results or placing blame.[32] Generally, it is recommended that employee feedback be done through meetings with managers, supervisors, and employees, often in small groups to encourage interaction and discussion. That approach is consistent with the most common reason for conducting an attitude survey—to diagnose strengths and weaknesses so that actions can be taken to improve the P/HR activities in an organization.

Research Interviews

A research interview is an alternative to a survey and may focus on a variety of problems. One widely used type of interview is the exit interview.

EXIT INTERVIEW
asks those leaving the organization to identify the reasons for their departure.

EXIT INTERVIEW.   During an **exit interview,** those who are leaving the organization are asked to identify the reasons for their departure. This information can be used to correct problems so that others will not leave. P/HR specialists rather than supervisors usually conduct exit interviews, and a skillful interviewer can gain useful information.

A wide range of issues can be examined in exit interviews. According to one study, most exit interviews gather information about the following issues:[33]

- Reasons for leaving
- Adequacy of and improvements needed in supervision
- Salary treatment and experiences
- Best-liked and least-liked aspects of the job
- Adequacy of training[33]

Departing employees may be reluctant to divulge their real reasons for leaving because they may wish to return to their jobs some day. They may also fear that candid responses will hinder their chances of receiving favorable references. One major reason an employee commonly gives for leaving a job is an offer or more pay elsewhere. Although this reason is acceptable, the pay increases may not be the only factor. Consequently, to tap other reasons it may be more useful to contact the departing employee a week or so later. Former employees may be more willing to provide information on a questionnaire mailed to their homes or in telephone conversations conducted some time after they leave the organization.

Research Using Other Organizations

P/HR specialists can gain new insights from managers and specialists in other organizations by participating in professional groups. The most prominent professional organizations are the Society for Human Resource Management (SHRM) and the International Personnel Management Association (IPMA). These organizations publish professional journals and newsletters, conduct annual meetings and conferences, and offer many other services, often through local chapters. SHRM is composed primarily of private sector P/HR professionals, whereas members of IPMA are P/HR managers from local, state, and federal government agencies.

Private management consulting firms and local colleges and universities also can assist in P/HR research. These outside researchers may be more knowledgeable and unbiased than people inside the organization. Consultants skilled in questionnaire design and data analysis can give expert advice on P/HR research. Appendix B contains a list of organizations and agencies having information useful to P/HR specialists and other managers.

NATIONAL OR AREA SURVEYS.   Surveys by other organizations can provide some perspectives for an organization. Other organizations, such as the Bureau of National Affairs and the Conference Board, sponsor surveys on P/HR practices in different communities, states, and regions. The results are distributed to participating organizations. An organization also may conduct its own comparative outside surveys, such as wage surveys.

CURRENT LITERATURE.   Professional P/HR journals and publications are a useful communication link among managers, P/HR specialists, researchers, and other practitioners. Appendix A contains a list of journals that often publish P/HR management information. Such publications help professionals learn about current changes in the field and what other organizations are doing.

Importance of P/HR Research

P/HR decisions can be improved through research because better information leads to better solutions. Effective management comes through analyzing problems and applying experience and knowledge to particular situations. A manager who just "supposes" that a certain result may occur is not likely to be effective. In some organizations, systematic programs of P/HR research are used to assess the overall effectiveness of P/HR activities.

▮ ▮ ASSESSING AND MEASURING P/HR ACTIVITIES

As in other areas of an organization, it is important to review P/HR activities for effectiveness. Because effectiveness is concerned with how well an organization reaches its objectives over time, research on, and assessment of, P/HR activities contribute to the long-term effectiveness of the organization. Efficiency of P/HR activities is determined through measurements of cost/benefit factors.

Generally, management does not see expenditures on P/HR activities and programs as contributing directly to the profit or "bottom-line" results of an organization. Instead, P/HR efforts have been viewed solely as costs. According to Cascio, there are several reasons why assessment of P/HR effectiveness and efficiency has been difficult and deficient.:[34]

■ Top management believes that the effectiveness of P/HR activities cannot be measured.
■ P/HR professionals may not want to have their own effectiveness and efficiency assessed with quantifiable measures.

■ Those professionals who do want to do P/HR assessments do not know how to measure their own activities.

Yet assessment of P/HR effectiveness and efficiency is just as necessary as it is in other areas of an organization. These assessment efforts should look both inside and outside the P/HR department. Inside the P/HR department, the P/HR staff must be efficient and productive in handling the internal workings of the department. Outside the department, P/HR staff members must serve their "clients" effectively and efficiently. The P/HR clients are the employees and managers in the organization, as well as those outside the organization who deal with the P/HR staff.

P/HR Assessment Approaches

A variety of approaches can be used to conduct assessments of P/HR management in an organization. Some approaches rely mainly on the measurement of direct costs, whereas others give greater weight to indirect costs in their measurement efforts.

DIRECT AND INDIRECT MEASURES.   Measurement of P/HR activities can be classified as either *direct* or *indirect*. *Direct* measures deal with dollar costs that are spent by the organizations. For instance, recruiting costs will include direct expenditures such as advertising, recruiter travel, and other expenses. *Indirect* measures rely on measurement of time, quality, or quantity. For example, what is the value of reducing the time spent recruiting a key technical employee, such as a biochemistry researcher for a pharmaceutical firm, compared with the additional direct costs of this effort? Or, if selection interviewers are able to reduce the number and time of interviews by using a structured interview, what is the value of developing that interview? In this case, the indirect measures can be changed to direct measures by converting the interviewer's pay per hour and the number of interviews conducted.

Absenteeism and turnover costs are two areas that are commonly measured. As mentioned in Chapter 4, the absence of a clerical worker for one day costs up to $100 in reduced productivity and additional management efforts. Turnover also is costly. In one midwestern city, having a data-entry operator leave within the first six months of employment was estimated to cost the firm approximately $1,100, when hiring, training, benefit, and lost productivity were all considered. For specialized professionals and executive positions, turnover can cost over $50,000. Such calculations require consideration of a number of variables, including employment advertising costs, relocation expenses, and recruiting and interviewing time.

UTILITY ANALYSIS
builds economic or other statistical models to identify the costs and benefits associated with specific P/HR activities.

UTILITY AND COST/BENEFIT ANALYSES   In **utility analysis,** economic or other statistical models are built to identify the costs and benefits associated with specific P/HR activities.[35] These models generally contain equations that identify the relevant factors impacting the P/HR activity under study. According to Jac Fitz-Enz, a pioneer in measuring P/HR effectiveness, formulas and measures should be derived from a listing of activities and the variables associated with those activities.[36] Figure 21–5 contains an example, designed by Fitz-Enz, that quantifies selection interviewing costs.

The examples noted in the chapter-opening discussion of costs and benefits of various programs, such as the child-care program at Union Bank, illustrate why

Here is an example of how P/HR costing models can be developed, according to Jac Fitz-Enz,[37] The following equations show how to compute interviewing costs.

$$C/I = \frac{ST + MT}{I}$$

C/I = cost of interviewing

ST = total *staff time* spent interviewing (interviewer's hourly rate $\times$ hours)

MT = *management time* spent interviewing (manager's hourly rate $\times$ hours)

I = number of applicants interviewed

An example helps to illustrate the formula. Assume that an employment interview specialist is paid $12 an hour and interviews eight applicants for a job an hour each. Following the personal interview, the applicants are interviewed by a department manager paid $20 an hour for 30 minutes each. The interview costs would be:

$$\frac{\overset{ST}{(\$12 \times 8 \text{ hours})} + \overset{MT}{(20 \times 4 \text{ hours})}}{8 \text{ interviews}} = \frac{96 + 80}{8} = \frac{176}{8} = \$22 \text{ per applicant}$$

What this equation might indicate is the benefit of reducing the number of applicants interviewed by using better employment screening devices. Obviously, the costs of those screening items, such as a paper-and-pencil test, would have to be included when calculating the total selection costs.

Figure 21–5
Selection Interviewing Costs

top management may view the value of P/HR activities incorrectly if only direct costs are examined.

■■ ■ COMPREHENSIVE P/HR ASSESSMENT

In addition to studies of costs and benefits of selected P/HR activities, other assessment methods take a comprehensive look at the performance of P/HR activities. Two of them, P/HR audits and human resource accounting, are examined briefly.

P/HR Audit

A P/HR audit, similar in purpose to a financial audit, is a formal research effort to evaluate the current status of P/HR management in an organization. Through the development and use of statistical reports and research data, P/HR audits attempt to evaluate how well P/HR activities have been performed, so that management can identify what needs to be improved.[38]

A P/HR audit begins with management determining the objectives it wants to achieve in the P/HR area. The audit then compares the actual state of P/HR activities with the objectives. Often a checklist is used. A simplified P/HR Audit is shown in Figure 21–6.

A variety of research sources may be used during a P/HR audit. Review of all relevant P/HR documents is helpful. Common documents to be reviewed include employee handbooks, organization charts, job descriptions, and many of the forms used such as performance appraisals, benefit statements, and labor union contracts. Also, interviews are conducted with a cross-section of executives, managers, supervisors, and P/HR staff members to obtain information about P/HR practices and problems.[39]

P/HR AUDIT
is a formal research effort to evaluate the current state of P/HR management in an organization.

Where appropriate, data can be gathered on specific facets of P/HR management. This data can be obtained more easily if the organization has an HRIS in place. Attitude survey data also can provide valuable insights. One study found that some of the P/HR data that are used most frequently as indicators of P/HR performance include the following:[40]

- Total compensation as a percentage of firm income (net before taxes)
- Percentage of work force unionized
- Number or percentage of management positions filled internally
- Firm dollar sales per employee
- Benefits as a percentage of payroll costs

In some organizations, the P/HR staff members conduct the P/HR audit. However, a more objective assessment may be achieved if the organization uses external consultants for this task. Regardless of who conducts the P/HR audit, it is important to prepare a written report. This report should identify the methods used, the

Figure 21–6
P/HR Audit Checklist

Score **Work Analysis**
_____ Current job descriptions (at least 80% of jobs)
_____ Job specifications/qualifications
_____ Job design considerations
Staffing
_____ Human resource planning procedures and forecasts
_____ Use of internal recruiting sources
_____ Use of external recruiting media
_____ EEO compliance recruitment
_____ Legal application blank
_____ Validation of testing procedures
_____ Privacy concerns and reference checking
_____ Affirmative action plan
_____ Employment of women/minorities/disabled
_____ Training of interviewers (including supervisors)
Training and Development
_____ Orientation of new employees
_____ Job-skill training programs
_____ Career planning programs
_____ Management development programs

Appraisal
_____ Job-related appraisal
_____ Appraisal feedback training for managers
_____ Internal equity of appraisal program
_____ Tie between appraisals and compensation
Compensation
_____ Formal wage and salary system
_____ Consistency with external wage/salary survey
_____ Incentive program
_____ Employee recognition program
_____ Benefit programs
_____ Retirement plan and counseling
Employee Relations
_____ Safety compliance/investigation
_____ Discipline policies and procedures
_____ Turnover/absenteeism analysis and control
_____ Personnel records/employee privacy protection
_____ Employee-related activities and programs
_____ Exit interview procedures
_____ Staffing and budgetary requirements
Union
_____ Formal grievance procedure
_____ Union problem prevention training
_____ Collective bargaining procedures

Scoring: Where you think your personnel department is doing a *very good* job, give yourself a score of 3. For an *adequate* job (one that needs some improvement) score 2. If you are *weak* in an area (and need major improvement) score 1. Score a minus 1(−1) where the activity is basically nonexistent. Typically, a small company's personnel department should score at least 90 if it is to be effective. How much work do you have to do?

SOURCE: Robert L. Mathis and Gary Cameron, "Auditing Personnel Practices in Smaller-Sized Organizations: A Realistic Approach," *Personnel Administrator,* April, 1981, as adapted.

specific observations on the state of P/HR activities, and recommendations for improvements. The report should go to top management, as well as P/HR staff members, to obtain greater commitment to implementing the recommendations.

Human Resource Accounting

Human resource accounting is similar to preparation of a financial accounting statement. Just as financial accounting reflects the cost of capital assets such as machinery and buildings, human resource accounting attempts to place a value on organizational human resources by formulating a human resource "balance sheet." In this way, human resources are considered an asset instead of an expense, and are computed as part of the total worth of an organization.[41] However, because of its complexity and difficulty, human resource accounting has been used very rarely.

HUMAN RESOURCE ACCOUNTING attempts to place a value on organizational human resources.

SUMMARY

- P/HR records provide a basis for government compliance, documentation, and research on P/HR actions.
- An HRIS is an integrated system designed to make records more useful to management as a source of information.
- A typical HRIS is composed of input, a data base, and output, and often makes use of computer software and hardware.
- An HRIS offers a wide range of P/HR uses, with payroll, benefits administration, and general record keeping and administration being the most prevalent.
- Establishment of an HRIS generally is done by a project team. Once the key components are identified, training must be done and security–privacy issues must be addressed.
- A variety of employee publications and audiovisual media can be used to enhance formal personnel communication efforts.
- Suggestion systems can be a good source of new ideas if employee suggestions are handled properly.
- Research on P/HR activities answers questions with facts, not guesswork.
- Primary researchers gather data directly on issues, whereas secondary researchers use research done by others and reported elsewhere.
- Research information can be gathered from several sources: questionnaires, attitude surveys, climate surveys, exit interviews, experiments, and comparisons with other organizations.
- P/HR activities typically have not been assessed because of a perceived inability to measure their effectiveness, and/or a lack of desire to have them assessed.
- Measurement of P/HR activities can include direct and indirect costs.
- Turnover and absenteeism costs are two areas in which there is great interest in measuring costs and benefits.
- P/HR audits can be used to gather comprehensive information on the state of P/HR matters in an organization.
- Human resource accounting attempts to place a value on organizational human resources by formulating a human resources "balance sheet."

REVIEW AND DISCUSSION QUESTIONS

1. "Record-keeping is a necessary but mundane part of P/HR management." Discuss.
2. Using the area of employee benefits as an example, identify the major components of an HRIS and give illustrations of each.
3. If you had to establish a suggestion system for a firm with 500 employees, what would you include in the program?
4. Give some examples of primary and secondary research sources you might ·use to obtain information on the training needs of first-level supervisors.
5. You are P/HR director for Consolidated Widgets. What means would you use to conduct P/HR research on turnover and absenteeism problems in your firm?
6. Why is assessing and measuring the effectiveness and efficiency of P/HR programs so important?
7. How would you conduct a P/HR audit in a bank with 150 employees?

CASE | **Stemming Turnover in Retail EDP Departments**

The national average for employee turnover in data processing is about 30 percent annually. For data-processing jobs in the retailing industry, turnover historically has been much higher. It took that industry some time and research to discover what would keep these highly mobile and difficult-to-replace people around.

Many retailers now recognize that they are in competition with banks and manufacturing companies for data processors and have to pay competitive wages. But companies found that it takes more than just money to keep turnover in line. For example, some firms have discovered the role of training in obtaining and retaining these employees. Some retailers hire people with no data-processing background and train them to their systems and standards. One firm's research showed that people trained this way tended to remain with the company longer.

Questionnaire research has shown that EDP employees feel they are under a constant deluge of assignments. (That problem can be addressed by setting benchmarks so that people know what is expected of them and by when, rather than having a continually–increasing stack of projects that are all high-priority.) One firm dealt with the problem by setting up a buffer team to handle 75 to 80 percent of the emergencies that cause the feeling of being swamped.

P/HR research, both formal and informal, has helped managers to improve the turnover situation in retail EDP. Retailing once was second choice or worse for trained EDP people, but as retailers have changed reward systems, adopted more advanced computer systems, and learned what it takes to keep these people, the situation has improved.[42]

QUESTIONS

1. Describe why continuing P/HR research is important for retailers with EDP employees.
2. What methods of research are identified in the case, and what others might be useful?

3. Give two examples of specific P/HR research projects that might address the problem of turnover in retail EDP departments.

NOTES

1. Adapted from Julie Solomon, "Companies Try Measuring Cost Savings From New Types of Corporate Benefits," *Wall Street Journal*, December 29, 1988, B1.

2. Adapted from W. E. Blundell, "Equal Employment Records: To Know Them Is to Love Them," *Wall Street Journal*, March 19, 1984, 24.

3. Adapted from "Many Control and Limit Access to Personnel Files, Survey Finds," *Resource*, June 1989, 2; and "Access to Employee Records," *Employment Guide*, July 10, 1989, 79.

4. Mike Bowker "A Glimpse at Tomorrow's Technology," *Human Resource Executive*, March 1989, 33–36.

5. Stephen G. Perry, "The PC-Based HRIS," *Personnel Administrator*, February 1988, 60–63.

6. Adapted from "HRIS Software Buyers' Guide," *Personnel Journal*, April 1990, 143–156; "Systems Supermarket," *Human Resource Executive*, October 1989, 52–61; and "Speciality Software Buyer's Guide," *Human Resource Executive*, April 1989, 36–48.

7. Janet Bensu, "Use Your Data in New Ways," *HR Magazine*, March 1990, 33–34.

8. John E. Sprig, "Payroll and Personnel: The New Interface," *Personnel Journal*, April 1989, 56–63.

9. Judith I. Dunnington, "Successful HRIS Implementation," *Personnel Journal*, February 1990, 78–84.

10. Adapted from Sharon A. Stahlheber and Barbara Levin, "How TRW Unified Its Decentralized Personnel System," *Personnel Journal*, August 1986, 140–146.

11. Mike Bowker, "HRIS Enters the Decade of the Upgrade," *Human Resource Executive*, February 1990, 28–31.

12. Joan E. Goodman, "Does Your HRIS Speak English?" *Personnel Journal*, March 1990, 77–83.

13. James F. Kelly, "Talk Eased Merger Stress for Great American Employees," *Personnel Journal*, October, 1989, 77–83.

14. Alan Zaremba, "The Upward Network," *Personnel Journal*, March 1989, 34–39.

15. R. Keller and W. Holland, "Communications and Innovations in Research and Development Organizations," *Academy of Management Journal* 26 (1983): 278–286.

16. Barbara Jean Gray, "The Kiosk Connection," *Human Resource Executive*, January 1989, 39–41.

17. Donna Burnette and Tim C. Bousum, "Calculate Suggestion Program Savings," *Personnel Journal*, February 1989, 33–35.

18. "Suggestions Save Money," *USA Today*, August 9, 1989, B1.

19. "Workers Save $1.2 Billion in '88," *USA Today*, December 1, 1989, 4A.

20. "Got Suggestions?" *Omaha World-Herald*, February 11, 1990, G1, 5.

21. "Squibb's Prescription for Success," *Human Resource Executive*, April 1989, 30–31.

22. Lisa Collins, "GE Solicits Staff Advice," *USA Today*, May 30, 1989, 2B.

23. Jac Fitz-Enz, *Human Value Management* (San Francisco: Jossey-Bass Publishers, 1990), Chap. 9.

24. For an example of a literature review on selection interviewing, see Michael M. Harris, "Reconsidering the Employment Interview: A Review of Recent Literature and Suggestions for Future Research," *Personnel Psychology* 42 (1989): 691–726.

25. Adapted from Dale L. Scholtzhauer and Joseph G. Rosse, "A Five-Year Study of a Positive Incentive Absence Control Program," *Personnel Psychology* 38, (1985): 575–585.

26. Howard M. Pardue, "Is the Team on Your Side?" *Personnel Administrator*, November 1989, 64.

27. Thomas Rotondi, "The Anonymity Factor in Questionnaire Surveys," *Personnel Journal*, August 1988, 42–43.

28. Adapted from Lee S. Sproull, "Using Electronic Mail for Data Collection in Organizational Research," *Academy of Management Journal* 29, (1986): 159–169.

29. Robert L. Desatnick, "Management Climate Surveys: A Way to Uncover an Organization's Culture," *Personnel*, May 1986, 49–55.

30. George Gallup, "Employee Research: From Nice to Know to Need to Know," *Personnel Journal*, August 1988, 42–43.

31. Paul Sheibar, "The Seven Deadly Sins of Employee Attitude Surveys," *Personnel*, June 1989, 66–71.

32. Louis E. Tagliaferi, "Taking Note of Employee Attitudes," *Personnel Administrator*, April 1988, 96–102.

33. D. A. Drost, F. P. O'Brien, and Steve Marsh, "Exit Interviews: Master the Possibilities," *Personnel Administrator*, February 1987, 104–110.

34. W. F. Cascio, *Costing Human Resources: The Financial Impact of Behavior in Organizations*, 2d ed. (Boston: Kent Publishing, 1987), 7–8.

35. Brian D. Steffy and Steven D. Maurer, "Conceptualizing and Measuring the Economic Effectiveness of Human Resource Activities," *Academy of Management Review 13* (1988): 271–286.

36. Jac Fitz-Enz, *How to Measure Human Resources Management* (New York: McGraw-Hill, 1984).

37. Adapted from Jac Fitz-Enz, *How to Measure Human Resources Management*.

38. Bruce Ellig, "Improving Effectiveness Through an HR Review," *Personnel*, June 1989, 56–63.

39. Jonathan A. Segal and Mary A. Quinn, "How to Audit Your HR Programs," *Personnel Administrator*, May 1989, 67–70.

40. Robert O. Hansson, Nancy D. Smith, and Pamela Mancinelli, "Monitoring the HR Job Function," *HR Magazine*, February 1990, 76–78.

41. Robert B. Rogow and Charles P. Edmonds, "Tallying Employees as Assets," *Personnel Administrator*, June 1988, 168–170.

42. Adapted from "EDP Department Turnover," *Chain Store Executive*, January 1982, 7–8.

Current Literature in P/HR Management

Students are expected to be familiar with the professional literature in their fields of study. The professional journals are the most immediate and direct communication link between the researcher and the practicing manager. Two groups of publications are listed below:

A. *Research-Oriented Journals.* These journals contain articles that report on original research. Normally these journals contain either sophisticated writing and quantitative verifications of the author's findings or conceptual models and literature reviews of previous research.

Academy of Management Journal
Academy of Management Review
Administrative Science Quarterly
American Journal of Psychology
American Behavioral Scientist
American Journal of Sociology
American Psychologist
American Sociological Review
Annual Review of Psychology
Applied Psychology: An International Review
Behavioral Science
Behavior Science Research
British Journal of Industrial Relations
Cognitive Studies
Decision Sciences
Group and Organization Studies
Human Organization
Human Relations
Industrial & Labor Relations Review
Industrial Relations

Interfaces
Journal of Abnormal Psychology
Journal of Applied Behavior Analysis
Journal of Applied Behavioral Science
Journal of Applied Business Research
Journal of Applied Psychology
Journal of Business
Journal of Business and Psychology
Journal of Business Communications
Journal of Business Research
Journal of Communications
Journal of Counseling Psychology
Journal of Experimental Social Psychology
Journal of Industrial Relations
Journal of International Business Studies
Journal of Management
Journal of Management Studies
Journal of Occupational Psychology
Journal of Personality and Social Psychology
Journal of Social Issues
Journal of Social Psychology
Journal of Vocational Behavior
Labor History
Labor Relations Yearbook
Labor Studies Journal
Management Science
Occupational Psychology
Organizational Behavior and Human Decision Processes
Personnel Psychology
Psychological Monographs
Psychological Review
Social Forces
Social Science Research
Sociology Perspective
Sociometry
Work and Occupations

B. *Management-Oriented Journals.* These journals generally cover a wide range of subjects. Articles in these publications normally are aimed at the practitioner and are written to interpret, summarize, or discuss past, present, and future research and administrative applications. Not all the articles in these publications are management-oriented.

Academy of Management Executive
Administrative Management
Arbitration Journal
Australian Journal of Management
Business
Business Horizons
Business Management
Business Month
Business Quarterly
Business and Social Review
California Management Review
Canadian Manager
Columbia Journal of World Business
Compensation and Benefits Review
Directors and Boards
Employee Benefits Journal
Employee Relations Law Journal
Employment Decisions Practices
Employment Relations Today
Enterpreneurship Theory and Practice
Forbes
Fortune
Harvard Business Review
Hospital & Health Services Administration
HR Magazine
Human Resource Executive
Human Resource Management
Human Resource Planning
Human Behavior
INC.
Industry Week
International Management
Journal of Pension Planning
Journal of Business Strategy
Labor Law Journal
Long-Range Planning
Manage
Management Consulting
Management Planning

Management Review
Management Solutions
Management Today
Management World
Managers Magazine
Michigan State University Business Topics
Monthly Labor Review
National Productivity Review
Nation's Business
Organizational Dynamics
Pension World
Personnel
Personnel Journal
Personnel Management
Psychology Today
Public Administration Review
Public Opinion Quarterly
Public Personnel Management
Research Management
SAM Advanced Management Journal
Security Management
Sloan Management Review
Supervision
Supervisory Management
Training
Training and Development Journal
Working Woman

C. *Abstracts & Indices.* For assistance in locating articles, students should check some of the following indices and abstracts that often contain subjects of interest.

Applied Science and Technology Index
Business Periodicals
Dissertation Abstracts
Employee Relations Index
Index to Legal Periodicals
Index to Social Sciences and Humanities
Management Abstracts
Management Contents
Management Research Abstracts
Personnel Management Abstracts
Psychological Abstracts
Reader's Guide to Periodical Literature
Sociological Abstracts
Work-Related Abstracts

Important Organizations in P/HR Management

Appendix *B*

Administrative Management Society
4622 Street Rd.
Trevose, PA 19047
(215) 953-1040

AFL-CIO
815 16th St., NW
Washington, DC 20006
(202) 637-5000

American Abritration Association
140 W. 51st St.
New York, NY 10020
(212) 484-4800

American Compensation Association
14040 N. Northsight Blvd.
Scottsdale, AZ 85260
(602) 951-9191

American Management Associations
135 W. 50th St.
New York, NY 10020
(212) 586-8100

American Society for Healthcare
Human Resources Administration
840 N. Lakeshore Dr.
Chicago, IL 60611
(312) 280-6111

American Society for Industrial Security
1655 N. Fort Meyer Dr., Suite 1200
Arlington, VA 22209
(703) 522-5800

American Society for Public Administration
1120 "G" St., NW, Suite 500
Washington, DC 20005
(205) 393-7878

American Society for Training and Development
1630 Duke Street
Alexandria, VA 22312
(703) 683-8100

American Society of Pension Actuaries
1700 K St., NW, Suite 404
Washington, DC 20006
(202) 659-3620

American Society of Safety Engineers
1800 East Oakton
Des Plaines, IL 60018
(312) 692-4121

Association of Executive Search
Consultants, Inc.
151 Railroad Ave.
Greenwich, CT 06830
(203) 661-6606

Association for Health and Fitness
965 Hope St.
Stamford, CT 06902
(203) 359-2188

Bureau of Industrial Relations
University of Michigan
Ann Arbor, MI 48104

Bureau of Labor Statistics (BLS)
Department of Labor
3rd Street & Constitution Ave, NW
Washington, DC 20210

Bureau of National Affairs (BNA)
1231 25th Street, NW
Washington, DC 20037

Canadian Public Personnel Management Association
220 Laurier Ave., West, Suite 720
Ottawa, Ontario
Canada K1P 5Z9
(613) 233-1742

Employee Benefit Research Institute
2121 K St., NW, Suite 860
Washington, DC 20037
(202) 659-0670

Employee Relocation Council
1627 K St., NW
Washington, DC 20006
(202) 857-0857

Employment Management Association
5 West Hargett, Suite 1100
Raleigh, NC 27601
(919) 828-6614

Equal Employment Opportunity Commission (EEOC)
2401 E Street, NW
Washington, DC 20506

Human Resource Certification Institute (HRCI)
606 N. Washington
Alexandria, VA 22314
(703) 548-3440

Human Resource Planning Society
P.O. Box 2553
Grand Central Station
New York, NY 10163
(212) 837-0632

Human Resource Systems Professionals
P.O. Box 8040-A202
Walnut Creek, CA 94596
(415) 945-8428

Industrial Relations Research Association
7726 Social Science Bldg.
Madison, WI 53706
(608) 262-2762

Internal Revenue Service (IRS)
1111 Constitution Ave., NW
Washington, DC 20224
(202) 566-3171

International Association for Personnel Women
194-A Harvard St.
Medford, MA 02155
(617) 391-7436

International Foundation of Employee Benefit Plans
18700 Blue Mound Rd.
Brookfield, WI 53005
(414) 786-6700

International Personnel Management Association
1617 Duke St.
Alexandria, VA 22314
(703) 391-7436

International Society of Pre-Retirement Planners
2400 South Downing St.
Westchester, IL 60153
(617) 495-4895

Labor Management Mediation Service
1620 I St., NW, Suite 616
Washington, DC 20006

National Association for the Advancement of Colored People
(NAACP) 4805 Mt. Hope Dr.
Baltimore, MD 21215
(212) 481-4800

National Association of Manufacturers (NAM)
1331 Pennsylvania Ave., NW
Suite 1500N
Washington, DC
(202) 637-3000

National Association of Personnel Consultants
3133 Mt. Vernon Ave.
Alexandria, VA 22305
(703) 684-0180

National Association of Temporary Services
119 South St. Asaph
Alexandria, VA 22314
(703) 549-6287

National Employee Services & Recreation Association
2400 S. Downing Ave.
Westchester, IL 60153
(312) 562-8130

National Public Employer Labor Relations Association
1620 I Street, NW, 4th Floor
Washington, DC 20006
(202) 296-2230

Occupational Safety and Health Administration (OSHA)
200 Constitution Ave., NW
Washington, DC 20210
(202) 523-8045

Office of Federal Contract Compliance Programs (OFCCP)
200 Constitution Ave., NW
Washington, DC 20210

Pension Benefit Guaranty Corporation
P.O. Box 7119
Washington, DC 20044

Profit Sharing Council of America
200 N. Wacker Drive, Suite 1722
Chicago, IL 60606
(312) 372-3411

Society for Human Resource Management (SHRM)
606 N. Washington
Alexandria, VA 22314
(703) 548-3440

U.S. Chamber of Commerce
1615 H Street, NW
Washington, DC 20062

U.S. Department of Labor
200 Constitution Ave., NW
Washington, DC 20210

Validating Selection Instruments and Using Regression to Predict Performance from Test Scores

Appendix **C**

Any good statistics text will provide greater explanation of the concepts and mathematics. The intent here is to provide a brief summary and listing of critical formulas that will allow you to predict performance from test scores, and to validate selection instruments.

To validate a selection instrument, scores on the instrument (the predictor) are correlated with job performance (the criterion). Pearson Product Moment Correlation is most frequently used. The procedure can use data in columns or standard deviations. Data in columns briefly will be shown here.

X (Test Score)		Y (Performance Score)
Joe Jones	86	5
Sam Smith	50	2
Becky Brown	74	3
Fred First	60	2
Andrew Armejo	69	3
X = 329		Y = 15

Correlation Coefficient $r = \dfrac{\Sigma\, xy}{\sqrt{\Sigma\, x^2 \cdot \Sigma\, y^2}}$

$$x = X - \overline{X}$$
$$y = Y - \overline{Y}$$

To interpret the resulting coefficient, use the table of r values that follows. The table uses the .05 level of significance, and the T-Test to tell us the nature of the relationship. That may be enough, but to predict performance from a known test score, regression can be used.

Table of r Values

Number of Pairs of Items	To Be Significant r Must at Least Be:
10	.63
15	.51
20	.44
25	.39
30	.36
35	.33
40	.31
45	.29
50	.28
75	.23
100	.19
200	.15

The general formula is $Y = a + bx$

Y = the predicted value for performance given a test score of X

$$a = \overline{Y} - b(\overline{X})$$
$$b = \frac{\Sigma\, XY - (\Sigma X)\,(\Sigma Y)}{N\, \Sigma X^2 - (\Sigma X)^2}$$

N = the number of pairs of data points

To Summarize the process:

1. Begin with good test and performance data.
2. Calculate validity (correlation).
3. Check for significance.
4. Calculate regression equation for the data.
5. Plug in actual test score (X) to predict performance for a given individual.

Starting a Career

Questions asked by students in P/HR management classes often reflect their concerns about getting a job. This appendix, prepared with the assistance of a senior student, provides an overview of some of the activities involved in getting a job.* Throughout this section, specific tips and suggestions are made. No attempt has been made to direct you to specific references, as similar points are made in many sources. Instead, you should conduct your own research to identify readings on specific ideas highlighted in the following discussion.

■ ■ KNOW THYSELF

Before you can tell anyone what your skills, knowledge and abilities are, you have to understand them yourself. Prior to writing your resume, you should sit down and identify your strengths. There are four primary areas that you need to explore: the skills you possess; activities that interest you; your personal attributes; and past job and activity results.

Your Skills. In defining your skills, you should make a list of what you do well. Keep the list basic and do not leave out the obvious; reading and writing well do count. Now go back and check off those skills that you are willing to use in your work. For example, if you are good at research, would you be willing to take a job that required you to spend time sorting through information to prepare a report? Next get specific. Pick 10 or 12 of the skills that you have checked and define them in more detail. Describe how you have applied or could apply these skills in either work or non-work activities. Finally, pick out the skills that are most

*The authors acknowledge the assistance provided by Steven Howell.

valuable to you, write them down, and set that list aside. The next step is to identify your areas of interest.

Your Interests. What do you like to do? What would you like to do if you had the chance? What kind of people do you like? These items do not have to be work-related because this listing is meant to identify activities that give you pleasure. Be honest and do not include items just to make your list "look better." Now narrow the list down to the 10–12 interests you would like to have included in your job. Then, put this list with your list of skills and move on to an exploration of your personal attributes.

Your Attributes. "I am _____ ." Now fill in the blank. This is how to identify your attributes. You try to identify who are you, not just the you that people think you are, or the you that you let other people see. The "you" that must be identified here is how you see yourself. Are you hard-working, temperamental, creative, energetic, honest, shy? If so, put all of them down, but be honest with yourself. If you think you are intelligent, then write it down. Be careful not to list "labels" you've been given by others if you do not think they are true.

The next step is the same as in the first two areas: narrowing your list down. You should identify your 5 strongest and most positive attributes. Now put this list (you guessed) with the others and move on to the final area: your results.

Your Results. What important accomplishments have you had? What have you done of which you are proud? Did you work part-time while you were in school? Did you write a paper or build something? Did you organize and lead some project? If the results are there, then write them down. You may need to use your list of skills and interests to get started. Do not leave any area out. Work, school, military service, community service, hobbies, are all areas from which you may show the results of your activities.

Now you should identify the 10 accomplishments you consider to be most relevant to the type of work you want to do in the future. By writing them down and putting that list with the other three, you now have the foundation for your resume and you are about ready to prepare it. There is just one more bit of background work to do: Find out about your targetted job.

■ ■ RESEARCH THE EMPLOYER

By now you have a good idea of what you want to do, but you must identify what a future employer will expect you to do. The best way to find out is to ask. Contact some organizations in the area that employ people in the fields or jobs in which you would like to work. Talk to a wide range of people, including supervisors or managers, and individuals who are working in those areas. Also, you should talk to the career counselors and professors at your college or university and read books and articles about your field of interest. Make a special effort to find out what kinds of tasks you will be expected to perform and what types of responsibilities you will have. You may think you know all there is to know about the job you want, but you might be wrong. If you are wrong, then your resume also may be wrong (and useless). While you are asking all of these questions, do not forget to find out what kind of person most employers are interested in hiring.

Then, take the information you have gathered and compare it with the lists you have already prepared. The items that match should go on your resume.

■ ■ THE RESUME

Preparation of a resume starts you on the road to employment. A resume is a summary of your academic accomplishments, your work experiences, and your expectations for employment. It is the first "picture" that most employers will have of you. Because those doing the hiring do not have the time to try to understand what you are trying to say in your resume, you must ensure that your resume shows them, simply and precisely, what contributions you would make to their operations.

As with everything else in life, there are hard and fast rules governing the preparation of a resume—except for the exceptions.

Rule #1: Your resume should be concise; many experts recommend no more than one page. Two pages at the absolute maximum.

Rule #2: Your name, address, and phone number are printed at the top, 1½ inches down, and they are centered on the page.

Rule #3: Your resume should be typed on a high-quality typewriter or letter-quality printer. If you do not have one, find one. If you cannot find one, hire someone who has one to type your resume.

Rule #4: NO MISTAKES! Have two or three people critique it. If there is an error, retype it. A sloppy resume will lose you jobs.

Rule #5: Use action verbs. "Supervised 5-member work crew" looks and sounds much better than "I was in charge of the supervision of the day-to-day workings of a 5-person crew."

Rules #6: Keep your resume simple and uncluttered. If your resume is direct and to the point and the sections are separated with plenty of white space, it stands a much better chance of being read seriously.

Rule #7: No personal data. Your personal description, any references to your age, sex, national origin, religion, material status, or a photograph have no place on your resume. In addition, requests for information in these areas are not legal and should be tactfully denied. No exceptions.

Rule #8: No references. You should have a separate sheet listing your references often that sheet is presented later. The last line of your resume should read: "References available upon request." No exceptions.

By now you must be thinking that if you follow these rules, your resume will look just like everyone else's. While this may be possible, it is not very probable.

A resume can follow several forms: chronological, functional, targeted, the resume alternative, or the creative resume. The choice of form depends upon the specific situation, but for the majority of newly graduated college students the chronological or functional formats are the most appropriate. Examples of both are shown in Figure D–1 and D–2. While the spacing between sections depends upon the individual resume, some specific guidelines for preparing your resume follow:

First, below your name and address, along the left margin (one inch from the left edge of the paper), type the word "OBJECTIVE:" followed by a one-or two-sentence description of what job (or career field) for which you are applying. It should be single-spaced and no more than two-three lines.

The next area presented is your educational background. The word "EDUCATION:" should appear along the left margin, followed by the degree or degrees you earned, your major, the school you attended (if more than one, list them in chronological order starting from the most recent, one to a line) and the year of your graduation. For people with more experience, education probably should follow the skills section discussed next.

The center sections of your resume are where you tell the employer what you will bring to his/her company. You should get your preparatory lists from before. Can the skills required by the employer for this job be grouped into two or three major categories? If so, then group your skills and accomplishments under

---

Figure D–1
Chronological Resumé

```
DEBRA JAMES
5421 Dodge Avenue
Omaha, Nebraska 68104
(402) 221-9908


*  OBJECTIVE

     Entry-level management position in marketing/sales.

*  EDUCATION

     University of Nebraska at Omaha
     Bachelor of Science in Business Administration, May, 1992
     Specializing in Marketing    Cumulative GPA: 3.4 (4.00)

     Participated in two special research projects with Small
     Business Administration: 1) to assist Boardwalk Shopping
     Center, Omaha, to become more visible to the public and
     increase sales, 2) to study the feasibility of opening an
     interior designer showcase in the Omaha area.

*  EXPERIENCE

     Corral Western Wear, Omaha, Nebraska, 7/90-present (part-time).
     Salesperson. Average twenty-five hours per week involving
     customer contact. Formulated a marketing research proposal
     relating to different lines of western clothing not currently
     in stock.

     University of Nebraska at Omaha, 5/89-7/90 (part-time). Student
     Programming Organization (SPO), Student Director. Planned and
     implemented 10 educational and cultural programs. Selected
     programs for presentation, negotiated contracts with booking
     agents, managed tickets sales based on budgeted expenses.

     Clothing, Inc., Omaha, Nebraska, 10/86-11/88 (full-time). Sales
     Associate. Originated, planned and supervised new fashion show
     presentations. Identified, selected, and assisted in training
     of part-time sales force. Suggested several advertising
     campaigns that were implemented.

*  ACTIVITIES

     President, Phi Chi Theta, professional women's business
       fraternity, Spring, 1992: Vice President, Fall, 1991
     Student Orientation Leader (3 semesters)
     Member, American Marketing Association
     Member, Moving Company, modern dance group

*  REFERENCES

     Available upon request
```

Figure D-2
Functional Resumé

William Smith
2020 Jackson Blvd.
Omaha, NE 68111
(402) 664-9496

EDUCATION:

B.S. Journalism, University of Nebraska at Omaha, 1990

WRITING:

* Wrote articles for the sports section of college newspaper.
* Had three articles published in Omaha Sun Newspaper.
* Served as assistant editor of the sports section of college newspaper.
* Editor of high school student newspaper.

SPORTS:

* Played collegiate basketball four years.
* Captain and starting center for UNO's defending North Central Conference champion basketball team.
* Voted most improved player by teammates as a junior and chosen to All-Conference tournament team during senior year.
* Nominated to the NCC All-Academic squad.
* Coached high school basketball players at summer clinic.

COMMUNICATION/RADIO/VIDEO:

* Announced live broadcasts of football games on college radio.
* Wrote and delivered nightly sports news for radio on football weekends.
* Assisted in developing basketball training via video.
* Delivered sports promotional spots on local college radio station.

WORK HISTORY:

1989-90	KVNO, Campus Radio, University of Nebraska at Omaha. Reporter
Summer 1989	Smietrews Restaurant, Omaha, Nebraska. Night Manager.
Summer 1986-1987	Mutual of Omaha, Omaha, Nebraska. Pressman.

REFERENCES:

* Available upon request

these categories and list them from most important to less important (the *least important* does not belong in your resume). If not, then list your skills under the heading "CAPABILITIES:" and your accomplishments under "ACHIEVEMENTS:". Start with the items that best match the requirements listed by your outside sources. In either case, remember Rule #5: Use action verbs. These sections can be single- or double-spaced, depending on the room you have. The word "I" should not appear anywhere on your resume.

The last two sections of your resume should be your WORK HISTORY and REFERENCES. As with the other sections, these headings should appear in capital letters at the left margin. Start the work history section with your most recent job and go back in time for four or five jobs. If you had a job more than five years ago but it is extremely relevant to this job, include it also. Start with the dates that you worked at that job. Next list the job title and the name of the company or organization for which you worked. If you performed any duties that are relevant to the job you are applying for, list them on separate lines. The reference section was covered by Rule #8. If employers want your references, they can ask for them later.

You should always remember that your resume is your "paper picture." Taking the time to insure that it looks good, and experimenting with layout and spacing may force you to revise your draft resume. A third draft will almost always be better than the first.

Now your are ready to use your "perfect" resume. The cover letter transmitting the resume may be as important as the resume itself.

THE COVER LETTER

Whenever you send your resume to a company, you should include a cover letter. The cover letter is your personalized introduction to the company and is just as important as your resume. Sending a resume without a cover letter is like sending a piece of junk mail and will almost guarantee that your resume will not be read.

The letter should be addressed to a specific person, by name and position. In general, it is better if you send your letter and resume to the director or supervisor of the department or section for which you would expect to be working. P/HR departments receive countless resumes every week and many of them can become "lost in the shuffle." In addition, it is usually the department head that has the final decision on whether or not you get the job.

Rules for the preparation of the cover letter are similar to those for the resume. Use a quality (20-lb.) bond paper. You should include the date at the top, along the right margin and the complete address of the recipient along the left margin. As with any standard business letter, never, never, never send a generic cover letter with the name and address of the individual filled in at the top. This innocent shortcut only succeeds in giving the impression that the recipient is just another name on your list.

The body of the letter should be about half a page long. It should point out two or three facts from the resume and expand upon them. The letter should state your reason for sending it, but it should contain something more than "I think I would like to work for your company."

You should always include some personal comment directed specifically to the individual and the company. For example, you might mention a problem that you are aware they are having, and a possible solution that you have. Or, if the individual's name appeared in a newsarticle and that is where you got the idea to contact him or her, say that.

You should always close your cover letter with the suggestion of a meeting but do not just say "I would like to talk to you about this further." Include a time frame. If the company is out of town, you should tell the individual when you will be in that area. In any case, give a date when you will be in contact with her or him again. A statement like "I will be interviewing in your area on May 14 and 15 and would appreciate the opportunity to speak with you further on this subject. I will call the week before I am there to set up a time that is convenient for you" is a very good closing for a cover letter. Then end your letter with an appropriate closing and your signature. Also, it is a good idea to include your address and telephone number above the date, in case the letter and resume are separated.

THE APPLICATION

Some college graduates will not be required to complete an application form when they apply for a job. Most college placement offices supply the companies who will be interviewing their graduates with data sheets that contain all of the relevant information on the candidate. Nevertheless, many graduates will be required at some time to complete a standard application form for a job. The most frequent concern voiced by students is how to handle one problem: illegal questions.

As was mentioned in the text of this book, many of the job application forms in use today contain questions that, by law, do not have to be completed by the applicant. These questions are ones that concern race, sex, age, national origin, religion, and mental and physical limitations not relevant to the performance of the job. In addition, application forms should not ask questions concerning arrests, as people are not judged guilty of a crime solely on the basis of arrests. Questions concerning criminal convictions should be asked only insofar as they pertain to the performance of the job. Questions concerning credit ratings or current financial situation may not be asked unless they have a direct relationship to the job (i.e., if the job will place you in a situation of being unsupervised and around sums of money). Questions about any political or ideological affiliations may not be asked. It is also illegal to ask questions about physical descriptions unless they can be shown to be *Bona Fide* Occupational Qualifications (BFOQ). Also questions concerning marital status and family may not be asked.

As a general rule, it is best if you, as the applicant, leave blank or put a dash (-) for any of these illegal questions on application forms. If the employers are asking questions for the purpose of maintaining EEO compliance records, they should have a separate form or obtain appropriate information after you have been hired.

■■ ■ THE INTERVIEW

You have submitted your resume, contacted the company, and have been invited in for an interview, or you have made an appointment with one of the recruiters who will be visiting your campus. Either way, there are four areas of knowledge that may help you have a better interview: preparation for the interview; behavior during the interview; your rights in the interview; and following up on the interview.

■■ ■ PREPARATION FOR THE INTERVIEW

Once you know that you have an interview, you need to begin preparing for it. As with your resume, a little preparation can set you far above the other applicants in the race for the job. First, find out all the information you can about the company with which you will be interviewing. Questions include: What do they do? What are their markets? Who are their competitors? How are they doing financially? Most of this information is available from the company itself, especially if the company is large enough and publicly-traded. Quite often you will be able to find articles concerning the company in newspapers and magazines. If nothing else, you can call and ask questions of someone working for the company. In addition, you should also try to gather as much information concerning the job for which you are applying. Find out what the duties are for that position, what the salary range is (if possible), why the position is open, and what happened to the last person who had the job.

As the day of the interview draws near, you need to begin preparing yourself for the interview. The appropriate clothing often is a vested suit for men and a skirted suited for woman. Your clothing makes a state-

ment about yourself and it should say what you want it to say (for a detailed discussion of the proper clothing, see *Dress for Success* or *The Woman's Dress For Success Book* both by John T. Molloy). Your personal appearance—whether your hair is neatly groomed, whether you are clean-shaven (men) or tastefully made-up (women)—is also critical. You should make sure you look as sharp and crisp as you can before arriving for the interview.

■■ ■ BEHAVIOR DURING THE INTERVIEW

On the day of the interview, it is vital for you to arrive on time. If necessary, give yourself a half-hour head start, just in case. By arriving at the site of the interview, 10 minutes or so before your appointment, you give yourself time to relax. Arriving just in the nick of time, out of breath and flushed, is almost as bad as arriving late. Also, it is generally recommended that you curb your desire for a cigarette and spit out your gum before you walk in the door.

When the person with whom you will be interviewing comes to get you (being called in the office usually is not done), stand, smile, and extend your hand. At that point, the interview has just begun and you can lose the job before the first question is even asked. You should exude confidence and your handshake should be firm, but not a crusher. Also you may wish to take along a small note card with questions you want to ask printed on it.

During the interview you should sit in an erect but comfortable manner. As much as possible, try to avoid any unnecessary body movement such as drumming your fingers, swinging your legs, or squirming in your seat. All of these actions will be distracting to the interviewer and may be the first and major fact that is remembered about you. You should maintain eye contact with the interviewer, but not to the point that you are staring. When asked a question, answer it in an even voice at a conversation level. Above all, remember that an interview is a two-way experience. The interviewer is checking you out and you are checking out the company.

It is important for you to assert yourself during the interview. If the company does offer you a position, you want to be sure that it will suit you as much as you will suit it. By asking questions, you can put the information you gathered prior to the interview to use. Avoid emphasizing questions about benefit plans for employees. Instead focus on questions concerning the job. You should try to answer all questions precisely, but if you feel that the wrong impression has been given from your response, do not hesitate to add to your answer. Never forget that you too have rights in the interviewing process.

■■ ■ YOUR RIGHTS

At some point in the interview, a question may be asked of you that you do not feel is job-related and that may be illegal. However, you should not let yourself be intimidated. If the interviewer asks if you have ever been arrested, you can decline to answer. You should explain that you have never been convicted of any crime and that you have never missed any work time as a result of an involvement with the authorities (provided that it is true). You can, of course, answer any question that you wish, but remember, the interviewer is not legally authorized to ask those types of questions and he or she should know that. However, the interview is not the time to try to correct any illegal practices on the part of the interviewer.

■■ ■ FOLLOWING UP THE INTERVIEW

At the close of the interview, you should be sure to thank the interviewer and shake hands once again. When you return home, make a note or two about the facts discussed during the interview. Then, a day or two after the interview, write a brief thank-you note. The note should thank the interviewer once again for the time spent and should mention something of importance that was brought up in the interview, especially if it was favorable for you.

In summary, remember that you are an equal partner in any interview and you have rights. Prepare in advance for the interview. Focus on your positive attributes during the interview and know your rights. Then, follow the interview up with a brief thank-you note. The tips in this appendix should help you to get many more second interviews and job offers. Good luck.

SECTION CASES

<table>
<tr><td>CASE: Section I</td><td>Downsizing</td></tr>
</table>

Northeast Power, NP, a public utility, provides electricity for a city of 800,000 and its surrounding areas. Power is produced by traditional methods and in one nuclear plant located north of the city along a large river. The company employs approximately 1800 people.

As a result of environmental concerns involving the operation of nuclear power plants, NP decided to reduce its staff. The goal was to achieve cost containment by reducing staff in the non-nuclear areas. Three hundred employees had to be cut, a goal established by upper level management representing a major cultural change. Previously, the company enjoyed a family atmosphere with strong job security. It had never reduced its staff, even in the Depression years, employees and jobs were not terminated.

The reduction in staff was designed to release more funds for the purpose of upgrading the nuclear plant since The Nuclear Regulatory Commission had required such upgrades in order to meet stricter standards. The new standards were a result of the general public's concerns about safety. The same kind of impact was felt by all nuclear power plants. Shutting down was not a viable option because millions of dollars and several years are required to close an operating nuclear plant.

To effect a reduction in costs, each division of the power company (except the nuclear division) was assigned a portion of the total number of jobs to be cut. The division manager was given the responsibility of selecting the positions to eliminate in his or her area.

To achieve staff reduction, the company's first step was to institute an early retirement program. One hundred and thirteen employees took advantage of the option, creating a problem for one of the seventeen divisions. This division lost 63 employees, all journeymen electricians, to early retirement. The positions had to be refilled with less experienced workers. (Approximately ten years of training are required to become a journeyman.)

The next step was to eliminate selected positions from which the occupant had not retired. This step was more difficult because of the distribution of people taking early retirement. The division that included the journeymen electricians had openings to be filled, while other divisions needed to terminate employees. Transferring employees from other divisions into open positions of a technical nature was not possible.

Terminations in other divisions did not occur all at the same time. As each division manager decided on a position to be eliminated, a letter of termination was sent out to the incumbent. Eliminating positions stretched out over eight months since no time table had been set for completion of the process. Fear was rampant among the employees; morale reached an all-time low for the company. Productivity among workers declined. Considerable time was spent speculating on who was going to be terminated next. The quality of the work being performed was poor.

During this time, the nuclear division, too, was undergoing changes. As upgrading the plant began, many new jobs were created. Unfortunately, these positions were difficult to fill because of the technical nature of the work, and poor communication about internal transfers. The openings were not posted in such a way to allow all employees access to job information.

Conflict and resentment developed between the employees of the non-nuclear and those of the nuclear divisions. Employees in the non-nuclear divisions resented the fact that their jobs were being sacrificed to create new jobs in the nuclear division. The nuclear division employees felt that they were working overtime to keep up with the changes. Voluntary employee turnover rates doubled in the company. Many valuable long-term employees who had not been targeted for termination resigned, creating more open positions.

Downsizing, which went on for almost a full year, left a residue of morale and turnover problems. The stability of the company with many long-term employees was gone.

The goal of cutting costs to upgrade the nuclear plant was achieved, and the commitment to the nuclear plant remained intact. The money that was saved has enabled needed capital improvements to be made at the nuclear power plant. But would this utility want to pay the price a second time?

Questions:

1. What was the main problem with downsizing at NP?
2. What could have been done differently to avoid the morale and unnecessary turnover problems?
3. What should be done to avoid similar problems if a further reallocation of resources becomes necessary?

CASE: Section II   **Warehousing EEO Problems?**

When Frances Miles looks at her desk after completing her first month at Lynch Warehousing Company (LWC), she knows why she was hired to be the firm's first corporate coordinator of employment and affirmative action. Several interesting situations with equal employment implications she has learned about in the past few weeks stare up at her.

Her new employer is a Dallas-based warehouse and distribution company which manages such facilities throughout the South and Southwest. LWC owns the warehouses and rents or leases space to various firms who need warehouse and distribution space, but who prefer not to own their own facilities. As part of its revenue, the firm also manages and staffs the warehouses where about 300 employees work. During the past year, LWC has sought contracts with several federal and state agencies, which in turn have contracted with LWC for warehouse storage services. As a result, LWC has an affirmative action plan, written six months ago by a consultant with expertise in the area. The consultant and Richard Castro, LWC's Personnel Director, recommended that an employment coordinator be hired to be affirmative action compliance officer. In that role, Frances is now dealing with one EEO problem in the company.

The firm had received notice that the state equal employment agency of Texas had selected one LWC location to be audited as part of a compliance review. During her second week with LWC she visited the location and its manager, Larry Jensen, to help him prepare for the audit. She performed an adverse impact analysis on employees at the location and on the selection ratio for applicants according to minority status and gender. The worst case of adverse impact was in the warehouse technician job, a second-level job which requires some special equipment operations skills and experience. Over the past two years non-minorities were promoted or hired in the job at a rate of 20% per number of applicants, whereas minority individuals were hired at a rate of 5%. Frances recognized that this disparity definitely constituted adverse impact. She then checked on the selection process for warehouse technician to ensure that all criteria used were specifically related to the job.

Frances had to search through several filing cabinets in order to locate all of the application blanks and selection interview documentation (if it existed) for each rejected minority applicant. Based on her review, Frances concluded that in eight separate instances minority candidates were equally or more qualified than the non-minority individuals selected. She then met with Jensen, or his assistant manager who had conducted some of the interviews, to discuss those selection decisions which Frances knew the state agency investigator might examine. If, when the investigator conducts an analysis, there is inadequate justification, the firm could be liable for back pay with interest, and have to offer employment to some of the minority applicants not selected.

Much to Frances' dismay, she found out that another selection criterion was being used only with minority applicants—a credit check. According to Jensen, he had experienced several problems with minority employees having financial problems, having wages garnished, or being sued for non-payment of debts. Consequently, for any minority applicant, Jensen was obtaining credit reports. However, no credit checks were run on non-minority applicants. Frances knew that the credit check could not be considered a job-related and business necessity, because the warehouse technicians had no contact with financial affairs, except to check merchandise for proper receiving and shipping of correct quantities. Larry argued that the credit check was a business necessity because personal financial problems of employees led to absenteeism and took additional managerial time. But, when Frances asked him if non-minority employees had experienced financial problems, Larry said, "Well, maybe one or two, but not nearly as often and as many of them caused problems as the minorities. Therefore, I didn't see any need to waste the company's money getting credit reports on everyone because of one or two problems, when 20 or 30 of the minority workers have had financial problems."

Frances then asked Jensen if he used any other criteria to select warehouse technicians. Jensen told her that during the interview he always asked about lifting objects up to seventy pounds and any previous back injuries. The firm also required all warehouse workers

to get a physical exam prior to official hiring. If an applicant seemed to be acceptable after an interview, the applicant was taken to the warehouse and asked to maneuver a fork-lift truck through several aisles, off-load some pallets of merchandise onto an upper shelf, and back the forklift truck to the starting point. Frances learned that if the forklift "test" could not be completed in five minutes, or if the applicant ran into a shelf or dropped the merchandise pallets, then he/she was rejected.

Frances, back at her office, is trying to decide how she and LWC should prepare for the upcoming EEO investigation. She meets with Castro and the corporate legal counsel tomorrow, so she does not have much time to develop her recommendations.

Questions:

1. What EEO compliance strategies are highlighted in the case?
2. What approaches should be used to validate and/or defend the various selection "tests" that Jensen is using?
3. What course of action should Frances Miles, Richard Castro, and Larry Jensen follow in planning for the investigator's visit?

CASE: Section III	Selection at Its Worst!

Lenore Johnson responded to the following advertisement in a local newspaper:

> Repair Supervisor
> 12 repairmen,
> major brands
> LARGE RADIO & TV CO.
> address
> phone number
> An Equal Opportunity Employer

Johnson is a young, aggressive black woman. She has been employed by an electronics manufacturing company as an assembly person for three years and as a

line leader for the last year. She has an amateur radio operator's license and is studying for a commercial radio telephone license. Her work record at the ABC Electronics plants has been good. Her department manager's comments on her last performance appraisal indicated that she had good potential for promotion.

The owner of LARGE RADIO & TV is an elderly gentleman who started the business many years ago. He has 16 employees—4 salespeople and 12 repairmen. He is proud of his accomplishments and is very much "his own man."

Johnson filled out the application blank (Figure 1) and was given an interview. The interview was held at the repair shop complete with several interruptions, phone calls from customers, and questions from sales-

Figure 1
LARGE RADIO AND TV CO.
Application for employment.

LARGE RADIO AND TV CO.
APPLICATION FOR EMPLOYMENT

1. Name: _____
2. Background in Radio/TV:
3. Your working habits:
4. What is your driving record?
5. Why do you want this job?
6. Do you realize if we get any collection calls or garnishment of wages on you, that you will be immediately dismissed? Yes   No
7. Do you use tobacco?
8. Are you in debt?
9. What are your hobbies?

I hereby affirm that my answers are true and correct.

Signed _____

---

people and repairmen. The owner described the job by making references to the previous supervisor in glowing terms. ("He was a great guy. He was always in here early to open up and make coffee, and he usually was the last one to leave.") The previous supervisor was retiring because of health problems, and the owner did not want to run the shop by himself again. He was planning to semiretire and wanted someone who would keep the place going, so he only had to "check in on things" once a day.

The owner asked Johnson to take a four-page "electronics knowledge" test that had been developed by a local trade association. She completed the test while he attended to another interruption. When the owner returned, he briefly scanned the test. He asked her who her boss was at ABC Electronics because "I know most of the guys over there." She told him who her boss was and stated that she had written performance reviews reflecting her good work as a supervisor. When asked why she wanted to leave ABC Electronics, Johnson stated that she wanted to advance herself and hoped to have a business like LARGE RADIO & TV someday.

The owner then asked her if she would have any difficulty supervising 12 men. Although most of the people she had been supervising were women, Johnson indicated that she also had supervised several men at the plant and felt that she would have no more problems than anyone else.

She inquired about the normal working hours for the shop. He replied that the shop was open from 7:30 A.M. to 4 P.M. every day except Sunday. "However," the owner said, "most of the men are still here at 5 or 5:30 P.M." He added that occasionally they would have a sale and the shop would be open until 9 P.M.

Noticing the wedding band on her finger, he asked, "Will your husband mind if you have to work late once in a while?" Johnson replied that she didn't think that had anything to do with the job, and that she expected to have to work some extra hours.

The owner asked if she was good with figures "since the previous supervisor had done almost all the paperwork." He added, "You women are usually good with numbers." She said that she felt her arithmetic skills were adequate and that she had been responsible for the assembly line paperwork at ABC Electronics. "My line produced 13 different models of televisions sets last year, and I was responsible for meeting production goals and making sure that the levels of inventory for my line were sufficient," Johnson said.

"Do you know anything about trucks?" the owner asked. "Glen used to take care of little problems with the service vans. Of course, we always sent the trucks to a repair shop if it was something serious." She replied that she had little automotive experience.

The owner concluded the interview by thanking Johnson and indicated he would make his decision "soon." After two weeks without word from the owner, she called to find out if she was still being considered. She was told that he had hired someone else.

When Johnson inquired why she had not received the job, the owner said that he felt the young man whom he had hired had stronger technical skills and would become a good supervisor. She pressed for details and found out that the young man was a recent graduate from an area technical school, but had no supervisory experience. The owner had interviewed the young man over lunch at a cafe and had accepted his technical school diploma as a substitute for the test Johnson had taken.

Questions

1. Identify the specific selection criteria that the owner was using in this case and whether or not they are job-related.
2. What grounds, if any, does Johnson have for an EEO complaint?
3. How should she proceed?

Empire Savings and Loan

Empire Savings and Loan is the fourth largest financial institution in a moderately sized city. It employes 150 people and relies heavily on part-time employees, especially college students. Empire has three facilities in the city, the maximum allowed by state law. Its main facility has the largest number of employees and contains all major departments of the organization.

There are two branch facilities. One is located near the rail lines and stock yards. It accounts for a substantial portion of the firm's deposits. The other facility is in the fast-growing western section of the city where Empire hopes to attract new customers and "sell" the bank's services to them.

The state legislature currently is considering a bill to allow financial firms to open another branch facility in the same city. The banking community has lobbied for many years to get this bill passed, and last year the bill was narrowly defeated. This year, however, because of changes in the federal laws, the bill has a good chance of passage. If it is passed, Empire and other financial firms will be allowed to open an additional facility 30 days after the bill is signed by the governor.

Top management at Empire is excited at the prospect of a new facility, and wants to be prepared to move quickly after the bill is passed. Therefore, the manager of the west branch facility has been directed to select and train a person to be night manager and to prepare and move two tellers to the new facility once it is opened.

Although the manager of the new facility will be chosen from the staff at the main facility, top management wants the other staff members to come from the west branch. The feeling is that employees of the west branch will be better prepared for the task of opening a new branch because branch facilities can only take loan applications and forward them to the main facility. They cannot approve loans.

John Wilson has been chosen as the person to be trained as night manager. For the past three months, Wilson has trained in this capacity and is now able to perform the duties expected of him with little supervision. He still works as a teller when the need arises (because of illness or vacation), but this is not unusual. All bank representatives at the west facility are expected to perform teller duties when necessary.

However, in Wilson's opinion, management is using this situation as a basis for not giving him a full promotion. Management still classifies Wilson as a teller and not as a bank representative. There is a significant difference in responsibilities and salary between the two positions. The Director of Operations, Pat Knust, says that he is not willing to promote Wilson fully until he assumes his duties at the new facility. If the bill is not passed and the new facility not opened, Wilson will re-assume his job as a teller and be promoted when a position opens up.

Wilson is unhappy with this situation and has had numerous discussions with Knust about his predicament. Management has not yet made a decision. Wilson has decided to give Knust an ultamatum: either they must promote him fully to bank representative or he will look elsewhere for employment. His boss does not want him to leave because Wilson is an excellent employee and is already trained for the position. Furthermore, Wilson is admired and well respected by nearly all the employees with whom he works. His leaving under such circumstances would have a negative impact on other employees.

A second employee in the west branch facility, Mildred Pierce, is a part-time college student who has been hired recently for a full-time job in the bookkeeping department at Empire. When she left the interview, Pierce thought it was going to be the perfect job. She was told that her hours would be from 8:30 A.M. to 4:30 P.M., four days a week, and from 8 A.M. to 5 P.M., Saturdays. The duties of the job were filing checks, answering the phone, and operating a CRT. The bank provided full training and told her that in a few months Pierce would have the opportunity to lean how to run the proof machine or move into a teller position. She was also assured of a raise from $5.10 an hour to $5.50 or more after a review in three months.

During the first week, everything went well for Pierce. She filed checks, observed the other employees on the job, and learned her way around the facility. The second week she was given her own desk and told she was on her own. The check filing was simple, but when it came to the phone and CRT, everything went wrong. Customers asked her questions about which she had no information, and many CRT procedures had been changed. When she informed the supervisor of her problems, the supervisor told Pierce that she would help her "later." Later never came and Pierce ended up training herself by trial and error, while upsetting quite a few customers along the way.

On the first Tuesday of the second month, Pierce came into work at 8:30 and was immediately called into her supervisor's office. She was told that everyone was expected to come in as early as possible on statement day (first Tuesday of each month) to help get the statements out on time. Because Pierce was a part-time student, it was very difficult for her to come in early. When she informed her supervisor, she was told to change her class schedule if she wanted a good review. Pierce changed her schedule and began coming in early on statement day. When she went in for her review a month later, she was told that a new policy had gone into effect and it would be another three months before she would receive a raise. It would also be impossible to train her for another position for a few months. Consequently, Pierce put in her two-week notice the next day.

Since Pierce quit two months ago, five other part-time employees have left, in addition, several managers including the P/HR director, have quit.

Questions

1. Discuss John Wilson's selection for the promotion (if it occurs) and how he is being trained.
2. What are the advantages of developing employees internally (such as with John) instead of looking externally?
3. What are the problems associated with recruiting and training college students as full-time employees?

CASE: Section V

New Project Compensation Blues

Robles Company is the second largest wholesaler of office supplies in the area. Julie Phillips has been working for the Robles company as a sales trainer for exactly one year. She was responsible for training all of the sales people on procedures, quotas, and sales techniques.

Recently Julie's boss, Joe Dumars, Director of Sales, and his boss, Gerald Hawes, Vice President of Sales, have been discussing a new project, Officelink. The project has the potential to create a great amount of revenue for the organization. Officelink could be a factor in positioning Robles Company as number one in the area in sales. The project would allow area retailers to link up with the Robles mainframe computer system through personal computers from their offices, which would give them the ability to order supplies online. Officelink would simplify the ordering process, encourage repeat business, give immediate feedback concerning supply availability and restock inventory levels directly into the retailer's records kept on the personal computer.

Joe and Gerald know that all the retailers would need to be trained on Officelink, and Julie was viewed as the logical choice to do the training. Because Julie was interested in automation, and had the experience and education to lead the project, the two upper managers asked her to help with the business plan and to research different aspects of Officelink. Julie, always willing to take on new responsibilities and try new challenges, jumped at the chance to help. Even though this assignment would be in addition to her training duties, Julie felt that it presented a great opportunity. Gerald and Joe assured Julie that if the project was approved, she would fill the position of Officelink Director.

After two months of working on the project, Julie and the two managers presented the business plan to the Robles Board of Directors. The Board approved the project, and Joe and Julie began to work on the job description for the Officelink Director. Gerald checked with the Human Resources department about posting the job. He explained that the person he wanted to fill the position had been doing the job of researching and working on the project from the beginning. However, Human Resources indicated that the position should be posted within the division. Gerald therefore posted a description of the job, pay grade, location, education, and skills required. Everyone in the division wondered why the job had been posted since Julie had already been working on the project.

There was also concern among some employees within the division because of the pay grade offered. This pay grade, a 14, was well above what many employees in the division were currently earning. Two employees in the division voiced their concerns about the pay grade to Human Resources. The pay grade listed was what Gerald felt the job was worth, given the revenue potential of Officelink and the responsibility and experience required. The pay grade had not been formally assigned or agreed upon by Human Resources.

At the Robles Company, pay grades are assigned by a committee of employees which evaluate job descriptions and determines which pay grade a position will receive. This is done by looking at the responsibility, experience, and skills required for the position. When the committee met concerning the Officelink Director, the committee assigned a pay grade four grade levels lower (10) than that posted with the position. Gerald contacted the Vice President of Human Resources to discuss the pay grade and position decision. The Vice President of Human Resources asked him why the position had been posted in the first place, since a person had already been selected for the job. Gerald explained that he was instructed to post the position by someone in Human Resources. The Vice President agreed to reevaluate the position if some market comparison would show the position warranted a higher salary.

Market research in Chicago, and the surrounding areas was done to determine the current market salary for a comparable position. Results indicated that many positions were at the pay level proposed and above.

No comparable positions paid less than what had been proposed. The committee met again with the benefit of this new information, and this time awarded a pay grade of eleven.

Gerald Hawes was not satisfied. He scheduled another meeting with the Vice President of Human Resources, but she was not willing to over-ride the committee. The President of Robles was finally asked to make a decision on the proper salary level. The President decided to leave the pay grade at an 11, but to pay Julie the difference between her current pay grade, a 9, and pay grade 14. The net impact was to put her in a red-circled position.

The process took over five months. During this time, Julie worked at her regular job, as well as working on the new project. She was aware of all the controversy surrounding the new position and was very disappointed with the final pay grade assigned. She also discovered some jealous co-workers who believed Julie was overpaid.

When the final decision was made, Julie agreed to take the job at an increase retroactive to the date the Board approved the position.

Questions

1. Discuss whether or not Julie should have begun to work on the project before she was hired for the position?
2. Discuss whether or not Gerald should have posted the position?
3. What is the purpose of using pay grades and did the system get in the way of the objective in this case?

CASE: Section VI | **Success vs. Failure to Follow Rules**

Owning a business had been a dream of Bob and Sue Rowlands. After several years of planning, the time was right to open their own computer store. The loans were in place, suppliers had been arranged, and a list of potential clients had been drawn up. As expected, business began slowly. The primary market for this "mom and pop" operation was small industrial firms, but retail sales also played a part. After two years of hard work, they were in the black.

Bob and Sue investigated the possibility of buying into a franchise, after several years of mediocre profits.

They thought better earnings could be expected because of lower wholesale costs and improved marketing techniques that came with being a part of a franchise. They deliberated several months before they decided to buy into a successful national franchise.

In the beginning, the husband and wife team were the only company employees. Bob ordered and solicited business sales, while Sue took care of the books and helped with retail sales when needed. As a result of buying into the franchise, their business grew and so did their need for additional sales help. Recruiting was very difficult. Advertisements in the paper went unanswered for months and leads at the area's technical schools dried up, and they were becoming desperate.

Their daughter knew a young man named Rick Smithson. He had a background as a sales representative for a herbicide manufacturer and experience with computers; he seemed to be a likely candidate. Although he was not qualified exactly as they would have preferred for the sales position, Rick was hired. Bob and Sue felt they probably wouldn't find a better candidate in the area, given their recruiting results, and that with some intense training, Rick should be able to learn the computer business without too much trouble. Rick was sent to several conferences that gave in-depth training on personal computers, software packages, and computer repair. The training came easily to him because of his interest in the subject.

Initially, the pay scale was structured to allow Rick a base salary while he was training. After training was over and he began selling, a base salary plus a commission on his total sales was to be the compensation method. Rick seemed pleased with the arrangement because he could affect his paycheck by the amount of effort he was willing to put into it.

By contacting acquaintances from his previous job, Rick established an impressive network of clients. Many of these clients referred other customers which further increased sales. The owners were delighted with how well Rick was working out and because he was having so much success with the business market, they decided to let him take over that entire segment, only stepping in when requested. Bob set to work on improving the retail side of the business. He developed new marketing strategies specific to the demographics of the area and offered free informational meetings that were well attended by the public. Slowly, the retail segment began to see an improvement in sales.

The owners did not foresee their market expanding greatly in this area because potential was somewhat limited, but they expected business to remain steady as their clients upgraded their systems. They were generally content with the way the business was progressing. As part of their strategy to keep costs low, Bob and Sue avoided hiring anyone else. When necessary, other family members would work at the store to help out.

Business went along as usual for several years with profits remaining relatively constant which was acceptable to the owners. Bob used a hands-off approach with Rick, as he had proven himself to be an exceptional employee. Rick's schedule kept him out of the office most of the time. He stopped by only to turn in orders and pick up equipment that was ready to be installed.

Upon arriving at the office one morning, there was a message for Bob to call one of Rick's clients, Mr. Barrett from Crystal Plastics, because Rick was on a two-week vacation. Mr. Barrett was inquiring about the software package and printer he was suppose to have received with the delivery of his local area network system. Bob thought this sounded odd, so he told Mr. Barrett he would check and then call him back.

Bob referred to his copy of the bill of sale and found no mention of a printer or software package. He couldn't understand how Rick could have forgotten to record these items on the bill of sale. To find out specifically what should have been delivered, he called Mr. Barrett again. Bob told Mr. Barrett that Rick must have had all the documentation with him, so he needed some clarification as to what was missing from the delivery. Mr. Barrett stated that a dot matrix printer and the Column Pro accounting software package were missing. These had been promised as an incentive to buy the network.

Bob was shocked because the company did not offer "incentives" to buy. He wondered how long this practice had been going on. He and his wife had always prided themselves on low prices with no gimmicks and Rick knew that. Sales incentives were simply not a part of their business policy. Nor did the owners want it to be. With their current inventory/ordering system, however, he saw how easily this practice could be hidden. Software was bought in large quantities and kept in the storeroom. Restocking occurred only when the shelf was low. A similar situation existed with the inexpensive printers. More expensive equipment was brought in only when orders had been placed. No tracking of inventory was done because Bob and Sue trusted the integrity of the only non-family member of the firm.

To determine the extent of the practice, Sue compared actual sales quantities to inventory ordered the past year. Because this comparison had never been done before, it took several days. During that time, Bob called several other accounts to inquire if incentives had been offered as a part of the sales package. He found out that it was occurring frequently. Sue quantified the sales losses to be in excess, of $10,000, but Rick had generated over $250,000 in sales. He had been giving away, at minimum, a software package per purchase.

Rick was to arrive back from vacation the following day. The owners had to make an important personnel decision overnight.

Questions:

1. What caused Rick to deviate from the established policy?
2. Why did it take so long to discover Rick's use of incentives?
3. Discuss whether or not a valuable employee should be lost by enforcing appropriate policies.
4. What alternatives are available?
5. If you were Bob and Sue which alternative would you choose, and why?

CASE: Section VII | **The Furniture Store**

Fifteen years ago Fred Sterbenz opened his own retail store and sold unpainted furniture. The Furniture Store (TFS) was located in Lakeside, a small city in the south-eastern part of the United States. Although Sterbenz's business was somewhat slow at first, it grew steadily. Sales rose, inventory expanded, and more clerical personnel were hired. However, it soon became evident that Mr. Sterbenz was not able to service all potential customers effectively. Warehouse space also was badly needed.

Because TPS was well located, Fred was hesitant about moving into a larger facility elsewhere. As an alternative to relocating, he opened a satellite store in an outlying district to attract new customers, as well as to provide better service to his current ones. Mr. Sterbenz eventually expanded his business into several neighboring towns until he had a total of six stores. When Martin Furniture, a small manufacturing firm that supplied some furniture for Sterbenz, became financially unstable, Fred was able to gain control of the manufacturing plant. The acquisition proved to be a good one.

With a favorable economy, Sterbenz's company has grown very rapidly and has been quite sensitive to its employees. In the changing times of the 1980s, TFS has continued to manage its human resources creatively.

At two plants all employees, including production workers, are on salary; these plants also have no unionized employees. Only one-third of TFS's entire work force is unionized, whereas the company's competitor has a much higher percentage of unionized workers. When TFS has negotiated with unions, it has been able to cut the number of job classifications, gain more flexibility in making work assignments, and

work out agreements so employees can do maintenance on their own machines.

However, TFS's creative management of human resources has not been limited to production workers. Changes also were made to improve the productivity of designers. The designers were put in individual, windowless offices with state-of-the-art computer equipment, unlike the large "bullpen" area in which they had worked previously. Productivity jumped 39 percent the year in which these changes were initiated. The head of design said that the results were so good the company was "reluctant to believe them."

The reasons given for the improvements were surprising. Predictably, the designers loved their new electronic gadgets, but simple changes such as privacy and comfortable chairs helped too. Dennis Hacker relates, "I'd close the door and grind away at my work; the next thing I knew I was getting hungry. I'd realize it was 6 P.M. and I'd worked right through the day."

The Furniture Store has expanded into overseas production but the bulk of its work force still remains in this country. As the U.S. work force changes, efforts to increase productivity will have to be focused more on white collar employees. By the year 2000, they will make up 77 percent of the work force. Improvement of white-collar productivity depends on how people use their time; therefore TFS wants to analyze and eliminate time employees waste on filing, attending meetings, or staring out the window. The employees themselves were asked what it would take to generate more productivity. The result was the radically redesigned work environment and a computer that performs many activities on which people had wasted time before.

The long-range effects of TFS's efforts to improve employee productivity over its whole range of products remains to be seen in the future. Fred Sterbenz is still very much in charge of the company but he realizes that the transformation from owner/manager to professional management is well underway. His commitment to his employees has resulted in upgrading the P/HR function to the vice presidential level in the company and hiring an experienced P/HR person to give the company direction. Previously, all managers handled most of their own P/HR activities, usually on a "casual" basis. Mr. Sterbenz said: "It's time for us to get our personnel activities organized, and we need a qualified person to do it."

The following reports are a part of the information available to the applicants that Mr. Sterbenz wants to consider. He has asked each to devise a short plan for auditing the P/HR function, with specific recommendations on what areas should be examined given the company's growth. He is aware of some concerns in the safety and hiring areas already.

TFS GROWTH 1980–1987		
	Employees	**Sales**
1980	150	3 million
1981	375	8 million
1982	550	10 million
1983	750	11 million
1984	1,027	20 million
1985	1,897	25 million
1986	2,521	50 million
1987	3,136	55 million

TFS ANNUAL TURNOVER 1980–1987	
Year	**Percent of Turnover**
1980	10%
1981	12%
1982	12%
1983	18%
1984	18%
1985	22%
1986	25%
1987	25%

Questions:

1. If you were applying for the P/HR job, what areas for audit would you recommend given what you know about the company and its growth?
2. Write a report describing the P/HR audit you would recommend to Mr. Sterbenz.

ABSOLUTELY, POSITIVELY HUMAN RESOURCES: A Case Study of the Evolution of the Personnel/Human Resource Division at FEDERAL EXPRESS

Prepared by: James E. Coleman

■ ■ A STAR IS BORN

The history of Federal Express Corporation is, at least vaguely familiar by now, to even the most casual reader of business literature. Possessing the classic attributes of the American success story—the innovative, risk-taking entrepreneur against entrenched powers; the mystique associated with buying a fleet of jet aircraft; the frequent brushes with financial collapse during the company's infancy—Federal Express has generated business school case studies, press coverage and television documentaries.

This publicity is not surprising. After all, it is an exciting tale. FedEx's first night of operations produced only six packages. Although volume grew steadily, the company incurred substantial financial losses for over two years. Frederick W. Smith, the company's founder and current chairman, and his associates scrambled to raise additional funding, while calming the increasingly frayed nerves of investors. Couriers who picked up and delivered packages hocked their wrist watches to pay for gas for their vans. Pilots charged aviation fuel on their personal credit cards.

Notes: Special thanks for support in the development of this case are expressed to James A. Perkins and Anne W. Manning of Federal Express, Memphis, TN.

Author background: James E. Coleman currently is pursuing a Ph.D. in Marketing and Strategic Logistics at the University of Alabama. His business career has included positions with Arthur Andersen as a CPA, as well as extensive management experience with Federal Express Corporation, most recently as Managing Director of Public Relations.

These early difficulties obviously were overcome. Federal Express now produces nearly seven billion dollars of revenue annually, transports almost 1.5 million packages daily, operates a worldwide fleet of more than 375 aircraft, and employs over 87,000 people.

Many studies have elaborated on the company's operational characteristics, such as the "hub-and-spokes" system or the ownership of its own aircraft, to explain the turn in fortune. Others have cited its aggressive, entertaining TV advertising. Nearly all agree that Fred Smith's visionary and focused leadership was an essential ingredient.

While acknowledging the obvious importance of these factors, Federal Express executives consistently provide a different primary reason for the company's success. The success "secret" of FedEx lies in its employees and their determination to serve the customer. In Smith's words: "The way I see it, leadership does not begin with power but rather, with a compelling vision or goal of excellence. One becomes a leader when he or she is able to communicate that vision in such a way that others feel empowered to achieve excellence. Federal Express has no secret formula for success. The 'secret' is in all of the management books. The difference is that we really try very hard to do what they say."

What exactly is this difference that enabled Federal Express to inspire such loyalty, to create a perception of excellence and to achieve profitable and rapid growth? Federal Express's people philosophy had its roots in the prevailing management literature which Fred Smith studied. The implementation of the philosophy reflects Smith's experiences in Vietnam: "I came back with a tremendous desire to do something positive for people. The difference is perhaps best suggested by the opening remarks on corporate philosophy contained in the Federal Express Manager's Guide, a comprehensive document developed by the company's Employee Communications group in close consultation with Smith:

The Elevation of Human Dignity

Beginning with the American revolution, the rights and value of a single human life, regardless of heritage, have become the central focus of social evolution in the industrialized world. The U.S. Constitution and Bill of Rights, and important legislation—particularly in the U.S. since the depression—mark steady progress in the elevation of human dignity. Modern behavioral scientists such as Abraham Maslow and Frederick Herzberg have shown that virtually every person has a hierarchy of emotional needs from basic safety, shelter, and sustenance to the desire for respect, satisfaction, and a sense of accomplishment.

Slowly these values have appeared as the centerpiece of progressive company policies, always with remarkable results. Simultaneous improvements in the laws protecting individual rights, combined with improved education and mass communications, have created a workforce that must be led rather than "bossed." The coincidence of changed attitudes on the part of many corporate managers and an astute workforce has led to a number of spectacular business successes. Energies formerly wasted by workplace strife have been redirected towards satisfying the only real boss—the customer. By making business a team effort, offering excellent remuneration and security, and providing an outlet for people's desire to create and contribute, a number of large Japanese and American enterprises have become dominant in their fields.

Federal Express, from its inception, has put its people first, both because it is right to do so and because it is good business. Our corporate philosophy is succinctly stated: People-Service-Profit (P-S-P).

On April 17, 1973—first night of operations—however, this eloquent statement of FedEx's people philosophy was a full *thirteen years* from being written. The development of the company's efforts in human resources directly correlates with the conceptualization, definition and application of innovations derived from the P-S-P philosophy.

■ ■ RECRUIT AND ADMINISTER INSURANCE CLAIMS

The Conceptual Stage

When James A. Perkins, now Senior Vice President and Chief Personnel Officer, reported to work in 1974,

total FedEx employment was under 1,000; the company served fewer than 30 cities; and the personnel division consisted of fewer than 10 people. Five of them reported to the Vice President of Industrial Relations, who was also responsible for the operation of the package sorting hub at the company's headquarters in Memphis.

The main duties of the five personnel representatives consisted of processing insurance claims and payroll information for newly hired employees. The others, like Perkins were located in field offices and reported directly to one of the regional vice presidents of operations. Perkins was given copies of a general promotional brochure about Federal Express as orientation material. A file drawer in his desk served as his personnel information system.

One of the company's primary objectives, he was told, was to expand the current base of about 30 cities, adding another 20 or so during the next twelve months. After he received his list of expansion cities, he was instructed to "hire the best people you can, because their performance will determine the success or failure of FedEx. Explain to them that we are going to be a Fortune 500 company one of these days, and it will really pay off for them if they're willing to sign on with us now. We believe in treating our people right. We'll ensure they are treated fairly, receive good benefits, and are rewarded for outstanding performance—once we're successful."

Although explanations like the above didn't always happen exactly like that, it is illustrative of the "sophisticated" state of human resources efforts during the early years of the company's history. Challenges were numerous. Expansion plans called for the number of cities served to nearly double annually for several consecutive years. Couriers and station managers had to be recruited rapidly, even though the name Federal Express was hardly a household word at that time. Pay and benefits were slightly below market, and the company's survival was far from assured. Thus, the persuasion skills of the regional personnel advisors were much in evidence as they described the exciting potential for rapid advancement offered by "getting in on the ground floor" of Federal Express' development.

In the early days there were no company-wide personnel standards. Each region and division operated almost autonomously. In fact, there were very few written policies, even within divisions. In almost all cases, implementation of those policies that did exist was left to management at the various local operations without central monitoring.

The message was espoused everywhere in the company, however, with remarkable consistency: "Take care of our people and they, in turn, will deliver the impeccable service demanded by our customers who will reward us with the profitability necessary to secure our future—People-Service-Profit."

A sense of adventure and optimism about FedEx's ultimate success permeated the organization. Obviously, the "compelling vision" Smith referred to as a prerequisite for leadership had been clearly communicated to, and adopted by, the employees of the fledgling company. In many cases, the employees had received the message directly from Smith during one of his frequent trips to the stations and departments. He was always particularly clear about one thing: "Use all the available talent out there,"—in essence, Smith's own version of an EEO statement. In fact, he said since, "If the EEOC were to go out of business today, it wouldn't change the way we do things one bit . . . we do what we do because it is right."

By the late 1970's the number of employees exceeded 6,000. Rapid growth accentuated the need for a new *modus operandi* for personnel. No longer could personnel needs be met by "throwing bodies" at the problem.

Among the many changes during this period was the initiation of several centralized departments comprising what was then referred to as the Industrial Relations division. A corporate training group was established by recruiting operations people from the field and from customer service. Trainers designed, produced, and taught separate courses based on their experience.

In the compensation areas, formal pay system based upon a job evaluation system was instituted to provide some consistency to pay scales across divisional lines and geographical locations. As Federal Express became profitable, stock distribution plans for all employees, profit-sharing, and a management-by-objectives bonus program achieved the long-promised financial rewards.

For the first time, the hodgepodge of intra-divisional personnel policies was documented and standardized into the "Federal Express Employee's Handbook." To develop this handbook, a small group of recently hired personnel professionals worked long hours for months on end interviewing and negotiating with the various department heads. Yet, detailed personnel procedures were still far from being agreed upon, much less standardized throughout the company.

However, perhaps the most significant change for the personnel advisors, was the 1978 reorganization in which personnel functions were, for the first time, brought together into a single organizational unit. Previously, the headquarters personnel groups reported to the Vice President of Industrial Relations, while the regional personnel advisors reported to one of the four Regional Vice Presidents of Operations. Following the reorganization, all of the company's personnel employees reported administratively through the department's chain of command, although the regional personnel advisors retained a "dotted line," or matrix reporting relationship, to the operating departments.

Concurrent with these changes, airline deregulation gave Federal Express the authority to operate larger jet aircraft. With this restriction out of the way, the seemingly rapid growth to-date would pale in comparison to expansion plans for the upcoming years.

■ ■ BUILDING UPON THE BASE

The Definition Stage

During the early 1980's, Federal Express's employee count rose fivefold, from about 6,000 in 1979 to over 32,000 in 1985. Although no one was able to make precise predictions at the start of this period, it was clear to Perkins, Smith, and most other managers that the recently reorganized division was ill-prepared for the expected growth. The division's structure was so new and the variations in personnel procedures from one operating division to another so great, that the situation was at best chaotic, and in some cases, approached instability.

This state of affairs was faced by Jim Perkins when he was named senior vice president of the personnel division in 1979. With several years of experience as a P/HR professional, Perkins began to recruit a team of top-notch P/HR professionals—a "novel" approach compared to the free-wheeling days of transferring weak operations managers to "personnel" simply because they were "good with people". To upgrade the P/HR staff, Perkins had his work cut out for him.

As employees transferred from region to region to satisfy the demand for experienced couriers and managers at the ever-expanding number of operating stations, complaints about inequity of treatment regarding compensation, time-off, sick days, and other personnel programs were heard with increasing frequency. Although an embryonic procedure allowing escalation of complaints, at employees' discretion, to successively higher management levels existed for handling these situations, most had to be resolved on a case-by-case basis by Perkins as the Senior Vice President of Personnel. The company's emphasis on promotion from within often resulted in promotions for individuals who performed well in courier and customer service agent positions. While this emphasis created intense employee loyalty, personnel issues and problems were becoming more common because of the relative inexperience of the management group and the lack of a comprehensive management training program.

In a company which prided itself on its nearly flawless ability to solve customers' more complex logistical problems literally overnight, operations people had little patience for explanations about the subtle complexities associated with personnel matters. "If we can deliver packages from New York City to Los Angeles overnight, why can't you get the paychecks for new employees started on time?" was an oft-repeated phrase.

Clearly, swift and radical action was necessary to prevent serious problems from developing. If the existing ratio of personnel advisors to operations employees was going to be maintained, staggering increases in human resources staffing would be required. Senior management felt this was far too costly to be considered a viable solution.

A dramatic shift in personnel's operating procedures ultimately provided the answer. Front-line managers had to become the purveyors and keepers of the Federal Express P-S-P philosophy. The plan not only called upon first-level managers to assume responsibility for the recruiting, hiring, performance development, and pay administration of their own employees, but it also required the managers to take charge of the copious paperwork associated with these roles. To say that this proposition received a cool reception by the field operating managers would be an understatement.

The various managers in operations were unhappy because they believed they were being called upon to "do personnel's job" in addition to their own, already heavy, responsibilities. Personnel representatives were concerned: they felt that they were now expected to become advisors to line management for all types of technical questions and problem situations without line authority to implement the proposed solution. The "revised job description" required different skills; persuasion topped the list. The conversion process was long and drawn-out, requiring a steady, step-by-step transfer of the responsibilities, all of which had to be accompanied by improved management support systems.

The most compelling task, and the one to be tackled before any transfer of authority, was the creation and documentation of procedures which were truly company-wide to support the many policies contained in the Employee Handbook. To ensure the highest level of acceptance possible, task forces were formed to develop all major procedures. Each of these groups included people from every affected operating and staff group, as well as legal staff and personnel representatives. Although it was a grinding and sometimes painful process, FedEx produced its first authentic personnel policy and procedure guide—called the People Manual—which arrived on each manager's desk in mid-1981. To provide a more efficient means of processing the voluminous paperwork required to keep track of the ever-expanding work force, automation was introduced. Because Federal Express was already a heavy user of high technology on the operation side, this technological innovation did not meet with the usual resistance.

However, two significant hurdles still had to be overcome. First, an extraordinary return on the investment had to be justified to compete with the operating divisions' appetite for investment capital. Second, despite the general comfort Federal Express employees felt with new technologies, a suspicion developed that the personnel information system somehow could be used to their detriment—a fear of "big brother" was the usual first reaction.

The solution to both problems occurred quite naturally, however. Given the phased-in approach required by funding and data processing limitations, the system was introduced piece-by-piece. Gradually, managers increasingly relied on it and even thought of innovative and money saving uses for PRISM—as the new system came to be known. Employees also came to appreciate PRISM because the timeliness and accuracy of their performance reviews and merit increases improved.

The introduction of the system was eased by a massive training effort. In addition to supplying a comprehensive, yet easy-to-use guide to the features of PRISM, each department's personnel representative conducted training sessions for managers and discussed the purposes and features of the system with all employees in open, department-wide meetings.

With the procedural matters documented and an efficient systems solution to the 'paper blob' established, Perkins and his P/HR professionals turned their attention to the more strategic concern of maintaining the P-S-P philosophy throughout the company's now far-flung operations. An enhanced training effort was viewed as part of the solution. After several reorganizations, a not uncommon phenomenon at Federal Express, skills training became the responsibility of the operating divisions. This shift left the headquarters group free to concentrate on career planning and management development, while coordinating multi-divisional training programs.

However, were properly trained managers, information systems, policies and procedures, enough to ensure that all employees received the respect and fair treatment that lay at the heart of the FedEx People Philosophy? This question led to three of the company's unique programs.

- The Guaranteed Fair Treatment Procedure—the formalization of an employee grievance procedure
- Survey-Feedback-Action (SFA)—the development of an *action-oriented* "people" management information system
- The Open Door Program—a practical "real-world" Open-Door Program

The GFTP accomplished much more than its original purpose of guaranteeing executive attention to every employee complaint not receiving a satisfactory response at the first level of the process. It became a vehicle for change and a barometer indicating which company policies were either poorly communicated or, in some cases, in need of revision or rethinking.

While most of GFTP cases were settled in the first stage of the three-step process, quite a few reached the last stage, the Appeals Board. (See Exhibit I for a summary of the process). Consisting of the Chief Executive Officer, Chief Operating Officer, Chief Personnel Officer, and two other senior officers serving rotating terms, the Appeals Board meets every Tuesday morning. The presence of the CEO and COO continues to send a resounding signal that people and their concerns are a priority. In some cases, adjudication is delegated to a Board of Review composed of the employee's peers. Either board may overturn management decisions.

Time and again, the GFTP has brought employee concerns and workable solutions to the surface—not just for an individual employee, but for the entire company. The attendance policy, the Ground Operations Accident Prevention policy, and even the GFTP itself were modified as a result of concerns brought up during GFTP cases.

SFA was begun in 1979 as a "people" management information system. It had the twin objectives of measuring employee attitude trends and facilitating workgroup problem-solving on human resource issues. For example, the "action" phase of the annual survey helped managers bring up and resolve potential work group problems before they reached the crisis stage.

The Leadership Index comprises certain questions (see Exhibit II, first ten questions) which measure each

Exhibit I
Guaranteed Fair Treatment Procedure

GUARANTEED FAIR TREATMENT PROCEDURE

The Guaranteed Fair Treatment Procedure affirms your right to appeal any eligible issue through a process of systematic review by progressively higher levels of management. Though the outcome is not assured to be in your favor, your right to participate within the guidelines of the process is guaranteed.

The Guaranteed Fair Treatment Procedure is a three-step process which requires specific actions to be performed by specific individuals within a designated time frame. The steps are identified as follows:

1. **Management Review**
   - **Complainant**
     - Submits written complaint to a member of management (manager, senior manager, or managing director) within seven (7) calendar days of occurrence of the eligible issue.
   - **Manager, Senior Manager and Managing Director**
     - Review all relevant information.
     - Hold a telephone conference and / or meeting with the complainant.
     - Make decision to either uphold, modify, or overturn management's action.
     - Communicate their decision in writing to complainant and personnel matrix.

   NOTE: When multiple levels of management exist, a consensus decision will be rendered. All of the above should occur within ten (10) calendar days of receipt of the complaint, unless written notice of time extension is provided the complainant and personnel.

2. **Officer Review**
   - **Complainant**
     - Submits written complaint to an officer (Vice President or Senior Vice President) of the Division within seven (7) calendar days of the Step 1 decision.
   - **Vice President and Senior Vice President**
     - Review all relevant information.
     - Conduct additional investigation, when necessary.
     - Make a decision to either uphold, overturn, modify management's action, or initiate a Board of Review.
     - Communicate their decision in writing to complainant with copy to personnel matrix and the complainant's management.

   NOTE: When multiple levels of management exist, a consensus decision will be rendered. All of the above should occur within ten (10) calendar days of receipt of the complaint, unless written notice of time extension is provided the complainant and personnel.

3. **Executive Review**
   - **Complainant**
     - Submits written complaint within seven (7) calendar days of the Step 2 decision to the Employee Relations department who investigates and prepares the GFTP case file for Appeals Board review.
   - **Appeals Board**
     - Reviews all relevant information.
     - Makes decision to either uphold, overturn, or initiate a Board of Review, or take other appropriate action.
     - All of the above should occur within fourteen (14) calendar days of receipt of the complaint, unless written notice of time extensions are provided the complainant and personnel.
     - Responds in writing to complainant within three (3) calendar days of the decision with copy to personnel matrix and the complainant's chain of command.

   NOTE: It may be necessary for the Appeals Board to adjust or recommend that lower management adjust the remedy already imposed upon an employee, including the imposition of more severe or greater discipline in order to protect the Company, other employees, the general public and the safety of our operation.

   For more details, refer to Personnel Policy & Procedure Manual P7-43, or contact your personnel representative or Employee Relations.

manager's performance as perceived by the workgroup. In effect, employees give their managers an annual performance appraisal by completing the confidential, computer-scored SFA form provided and collected by the workgroup's personnel representative. Managers were, and still are, required to meet with their staffs within six weeks after the distribution survey results in order to develop an action plan for dealing with workgroup concerns. When the concern was widespread, some of the action plans have been implemented company-wide.

Exhibit II
Survey-Feedback-Action (SFA) Index

HOW TO ANSWER: Read each statement carefully. Then to the right of each statement mark the bubble which best expresses your agreement or disagreement with the item. Mark only one answer for each item, and remember to respond to all items. Remember that "workgroup" means all persons who report to the same manager as you do regardless of job title.

Rating scale columns (left to right): STRONGLY AGREE (SA), AGREE (A), SOMETIMES AGREE/DISAGREE (AD), DISAGREE (D), STRONGLY DISAGREE (SD), UNDECIDED/DON'T KNOW (U)

1. I feel free to tell my manager what I think.
2. My manager lets me know what's expected of me.
3. Favoritism is not a problem in my workgroup.
4. My manager helps us find ways to do our jobs better.
5. My manager is willing to listen to my concerns.
6. My manager asks for my ideas about things affecting our work.
7. My manager lets me know when I've done a good job.
8. My manager treats me with respect and dignity.
9. My manager keeps me informed about things I need to know.
10. My manager lets me do my job without interfering.
11. My manager's boss gives us the support we need.
12. Upper management (directors and above) lets us know what the company is trying to accomplish.
13. Upper management (directors and above) pays attention to ideas and suggestions from people at my level.
14. I have confidence in the fairness of management.
15. I can be sure of a job as long as I do good work.
16. I am proud to work for Federal Express.
17. Working for Federal Express will probably lead to the kind of future I want.
18. I think Federal Express does a good job for our customers.
19. All things considered, working for Federal Express is a good deal for me.
20. I am paid fairly for the kind of work I do.
21. Our benefit programs seem to meet most of my needs.
22. Most people in my workgroup cooperate with each other to get the job done.
23. There is cooperation between my workgroup and other groups in Federal Express.
24. In my work environment we generally use safe work practices.
25. Rules and procedures do not interfere with how well I am able to do my job.
26. I am able to get the supplies or other resources I need to do my job.
27. I have enough freedom to do my job well.
28. My workgroup is involved in activities to improve service to our group's customers.
29. The concerns identified by my workgroup during last year's SFA feedback session have been satisfactorily addressed.

LOCAL QUESTIONS

(Please do not use these spaces unless instructed to do so by your SFA administrator. Refer to a separate sheet for the questions.)

L1.................LOCAL ITEM #1.................L1. SA A AD D SD U
L2.................LOCAL ITEM #2.................L2. SA A AD D SD U
L3.................LOCAL ITEM #3.................L3. SA A AD D SD U
L4.................LOCAL ITEM #4.................L4. SA A AD D SD U
L5.................LOCAL ITEM #5.................L5. SA A AD D SD U
L6.................LOCAL ITEM #6.................L6. SA A AD D SD U
L7.................LOCAL ITEM #7.................L7. SA A AD D SD U
L8.................LOCAL ITEM #8.................L8. SA A AD D SD U
L9.................LOCAL ITEM #9.................L9. SA A AD D SD U
L10.................LOCAL ITEM #10.................L10. SA A AD D SD U

The Open Door Program channels employee concerns about corporate policies and the rationale behind them directly to the manager most knowledgeable in the area, up to and including the CEO. That person then has 14 days to respond in writing, with a copy going to the Personnel department.

With these 'safety valves' in place, the P/HR professionals believed they had established core programs that would carry the Federal Express P-S-P philosophy for the foreseeable future. Subsequent events demonstrated that establishing a base of critical personnel programs was merely the starting point. Several significant tests of the People Philosophy lay ahead.

■ ■ INNOVATION AND EMPLOYMENT

The Creative Application Stage

In the mid '80's Federal Express had to recruit numerous communications technology specialists to support its launch of ZapMail, a facsimile-based electronic transmission system. The central personnel problem at that time was that pay scales for computer specialists tended to be higher than those for the airline and general industry groups with which FedEx were normally favorably compared. Innovative strategies, such as an incentive program for professionals similar to the more familiar MBO/MIC (Management by Objective/Management Incentive Compensation), were instituted to achieve parity. The MBO program required most professional employees—in conjunction with their managers—to develop a set of specific, measurable objectives for their efforts. Progress toward these objectives was evaluated quarterly and documented through the number of points awarded. The final value of the points was determined at the end of the year, depending upon such factors as the company's service level to customers and its profitability. Thus, in a good year, professionals who earned all of their potential points were eligible for bonus checks.

However, the acid test for the human resources division came about two years later, when FedEx decided to discontinue ZapMail—leaving about 1300 "techies" wondering about their future. Wall Street security analysts were overjoyed and quickly set about calculating how much more FedEx stock would be worth without the product's operating losses and payroll expenses. A long standing promise to the employees, however, was the 'No Layoff Philosophy' for those who performed their assigned tasks competently.

Any doubt that management meant what it said was eliminated when, the very afternoon of the announcement, Jim Barksdale, the Chief Operating Officer, told the assembled ZapMail employees that comparable jobs at Federal Express would be found for each of them. Nobody lost or received a pay decrease during the several months it took to find comparable positions. The relocation of ZapMail employees was a massive effort. An external hiring freeze was instituted immediately. Lists were compiled of available open positions and the background and career interests of the affected employees were identified. A "match game" of tremendous proportions ensued as personnel advisors negotiated with, and persuaded, each other in order to find reasonable positions for the displaced employees.

During this period, package volume nearly tripled and employees rose from 32,000 in 1985 to almost 90,000 by 1990. Perhaps even more challenging to the (now renamed) Human Resources division, Federal Express launched a major international expansion program that included the acquisition of more than 20 offshore corporations and Flying Tigers, a U.S. company with over 6,000 employees around the world.

The employees acquired were not steeped in the FedEx People Philosophy. Rapid growth and expansion required innovative refinement of the company's long standing P-S-P philosophy. For example, implied in the basic P-S-P statement was the belief that an employee with the proper training, a feeling of job security, and a strong sense of self-respect, would feel empowered to deliver the best possible service to the customer.

The question for the P/HR professionals was how best to create this sense of empowerment and the resulting quality of service. In other words, how could Federal Express's unique P/HR programs be deployed to support the company's overall business strategy more directly?

One approach was to tie employees goals to company goals as closely as possible through performance-based pay plans, as opposed to the more common "length of service" methodologies. Although pay-for-knowledge/performance is common in many companies in professional positions, its application to a traditional group of 'hourly' employees, such as couriers and customer service agents, was not so common.

The transition was made slowly, beginning with the linking of performance-related criteria to profit sharing. Next, a bonus plan was instituted that allowed couriers and other customer-contact employees to receive additional cash compensation for any 6-month period during which they excelled in certain crucial areas. Another major step was taken as courier promotions were linked to performance criteria. Eventually, all employees at Federal Express will be required to pass periodic "knowledge certification" exams in order to remain in customer or package-contact positions.

However, extensive training was a prerequisite to testing if employees were to perceive the programs as fair. The P-HR professionals at FedEx had to determine how to train the tens of thousands of customer-contact employees effectively and efficiently, not only initially, but with enough frequency that they remained current on the rapidly changing services and procedures detailed by the changing company service manuals.

FedEx relied upon its predisposition toward using technology to resolve the dilemma. Interactive video units were purchased and curriculum developed to train and update employees on all aspects of services and procedures. Virtually every station, convenience center and customer service center, across the nation was equipped with the video units. Paid training time was made a required part of every employee's regular responsibilities. The program has been not only accepted, but also applauded by most of the affected work groups.

Management capabilities were the focus of the human resources department during this phase. Given the emphasis being placed on self-management, training and empowerment for front-line employees, those expected to lead the charge had to be even better prepared.

Dramatic strides were made via three major initiatives: the Federal Express Manager's Guide, the Leadership Institute and the Leadership Evaluation and Awareness Program (LEAP). The Manager's Guide comprehensively states the P-S-P philosophy. It includes sections not only on P-S-P, but also on the corporate mission and strategy, the general expectations of the company's various constituencies, the definition of "management" and most importantly, an extensive discussion of all aspects of leadership, which FedEx clearly believes is the most important aspect of management.

The task assigned to the Leadership Institute—a central training facility for Federal Express managers worldwide—was to ensure that managers didn't treat this information lightly. Now, each group of incoming managers is thoroughly indoctrinated before being assigned a position of authority over other people. All classes are taught by selected, seasoned and successful,

FedEx managers capable of discussing from experience the situations that managers are likely to encounter.

The courses (see Exhibit III) range from the immediately practical to topical business and social issues. Advanced courses are offered to managers on more in-depth topics such a the GFTP or interpersonal dynamics

The most recent addition to the management training effort is known as LEAP, or the Leadership Evaluation and Awareness Program. This process ensures that only candidates possessing basic leadership abilities and the will to succeed as a manager at Federal Express be considered for management positions.

It is essentially an extended training and evaluation which helps employees determine whether or not they want to be a manager. The evaluation process includes a peer review which is weighed heavily in determining LEAP endorsement, a prerequisite to applying for any management position.

Will the Federal Express management style be appropriate as it extends its service around the world? After a period of trial and error following its initial foray into the international arena, Federal Express has discovered an approach they believe will be effective and appropriate throughout the world—namely to export the *philosophy*, not the policies and procedures.

Two of the more successful exports have been the SFA and the GFTP, although both require modification on a country-by-country basis. For example, in the Netherlands, termination is not "GFT-able" since government approval is required prior to terminating an employee. But the process was implemented there for all other issues.

Japan also has proved a challenging environment for introduction of the GFTP. When FedEx's Japanese employees were asked if they would use the process, the resounding response was "no." One employee articulated what seemed to be the entire group's concern: "The limb that sticks too far from the tree is cut off." Because of the Japanese cultural value placed on group consensus and harmony with the company, it became obvious that the employees believed they or their work-group, would become an exception by filling a complaint under the GFTP.

But the personnel representatives have persisted, dividing the workforce into small groups to explain the process and its objectives in great detail. The groups are then asked to appoint a leader, discuss the pros and cons, reach a consensus and report their decision to the overall workforce. In every group the decision has been to retain the GFTP. However, modifications have been made. In the event of termination, the

Exhibit III
Leadership Institute Courses

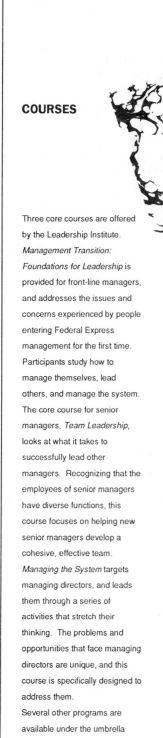

COURSES

Three core courses are offered by the Leadership Institute. *Management Transition: Foundations for Leadership* is provided for front-line managers, and addresses the issues and concerns experienced by people entering Federal Express management for the first time. Participants study how to manage themselves, lead others, and manage the system. The core course for senior managers, *Team Leadership*, looks at what it takes to successfully lead other managers. Recognizing that the employees of senior managers have diverse functions, this course focuses on helping new senior managers develop a cohesive, effective team. *Managing the System* targets managing directors, and leads them through a series of activities that stretch their thinking. The problems and opportunities that face managing directors are unique, and this course is specifically designed to address them.

Several other programs are available under the umbrella title, "The Leadership Series." Managers can choose from courses such as *Race Relations*, *Participative Leadership*, *Ethics*, *Human Needs*, and *Special Problems of Minorities*. These programs offer an intensive study of the topic in an environment that encourages challenging the status quo.

Two courses offered by the Leadership Institute move out of the traditional classroom setting and into a variety of locations where nature is the classroom. *Exploring Leadership*, available to all levels of management,

uses the woods and mountains to create a metaphoric learning lab.

Another non-traditional program, *Exploring Teamwork* takes intact management groups to the outdoors also. There, again, experiential activities allow the teams to assess their effectiveness, and identify opportunities for improvement.

The Leadership Institute is constantly reassessing the needs of the corporation, and developing new programs for management. It is always recognized that managing at Federal Express is different from any other corporation, and that what succeeds in other companies won't necessarily work here. This is the common theme that is seen in all Leadership Institute courses.

Board of Review (a peer review step) would not be used since this would be contrary to the Japanese culture. Instead, one of the steps of the GFTP provides the option for a manager to seek the collective wisdom of the workforce on rights and work rule issues. Thus, there is a delicate balance between "doing it the FedEx way" and following the local customs. In essence, it requires that particular policies and procedures be modified to fit whatever the local culture defines as "excellent treatment of employees and uncompromising customer service."

In other words, "Take care of our people; they, in turn, will deliver the impeccable service demanded by our customers who will reward us with the profitability necessary to secure our future: People-Service-Profit." With this sound business philosophy and the elements of its human resources strategy in place, Federal Express believes it is prepared for the challenges that lie ahead as the company's extraordinary growth continues in the 1990's.

Questions:

1. Discuss how the corporate culture of Federal Express was established by Smith, Perkins, and others.
2. How did the P/HR division at Federal Express evolve to include both the administrative/operational role and the strategic HR role?
3. Identify how the various programs at Federal Express reinforce the importance of employee rights and relations in P/HR management.
4. Identify how each of the eleven major P/HR activities listed in Figure 2-6 (page 34) appear as part of the case.
5. Discuss why Federal Express P/HR policies and practices had to be adapted to reflect additional factors present when operating internationally.
6. Compare and contrast the various P/HR activities at Federal Express with those of an organization at which you have worked.
7. How would you go about evaluating the effectiveness of the various P/HR activities at Federal Express? What do you think the results would show?

GLOSSARY

Adverse Impact occurs when there is a substantial difference in employment decisions (hiring, laying off, promoting) that works to the disadvantage of members of protected groups.

Affirmative Action requires employers to identify problem areas in the employment of protected group members and to set goals and take steps to overcome those problems.

Arbitration is a means to decide disputes in which negotiating parties submit a dispute to a third party to make a decision.

Attitude Surveys focus on employees' feelings and beliefs to pinpoint the underlying opinions about their jobs and the organization.

Authorization Card is signed by an employee to designate a union as his/her collective bargaining agent.

Availability Analysis identifies the number of protected group members available to work in the appropriate labor market.

Bargaining Unit is composed of all employees eligible to select a single union to represent and bargain collectively for them.

Behavior Modeling is copying someone else's behavior.

Benchmark Job is one performed by several individuals with similar duties that are relatively stable, requiring similar KSAs and found in many other organizations.

Benefit is additional compensation given to employees as a reward for organizational membership.

Bonafide Occupational Qualification (BFOQ) is a legitimate reason why an employer can exclude persons on otherwise illegal bases of consideration.

Business Necessity is a business practice necessary for safe and efficient organizational operations.

Career is the sequence of work-related positions occupied throughout a person's life.

Central Tendency Error is rating persons in a narrow band in the middle of the rating scale.

Centralization is the extent to which decision-making authority/responsibility is concentrated upward in the organization.

Chronology is a structured review of activities during a period of time.

Closed Shop requires individuals to join a union before they can be hired.

Codetermination is a practice whereby union or worker representatives are given positions on a company's board of directors.

Collective Bargaining is the process whereby representatives of management and workers negotiate over wages, hours, and other terms and conditions of employment.

Commission is compensation computed as a percentage of sales in units or dollars.

Comparable Worth requires that jobs with comparable knowledge, skills, and abilities be paid similarly.

Compa-Ratio is a pay level divided by the midpoint of the pay range.

Compensation Committee usually is a subgroup of the board of directors composed of outside directors.

Compensatory Time-Off is time-off given in lieu of payment for the time worked.

Complaint is an indication of employee dissatisfaction, which has not taken the formal grievance settlement route.

Compressed Work Week is one in which a full week's work is accomplished in fewer than five days.

Concessionary Bargaining occurs when the union agrees to reduce wages, benefits, or other factors during collective bargaining.

Conciliation occurs when a third party attempts to keep the union and management negotiators talking so that they voluntarily can reach a settlement.

Constructive Discharge is most often found when an employer deliberately makes conditions intolerable in an attempt to get the employee to quit.

Contingent Worker is one who is employed as a temporary or part-time worker.

Contrast Error is the tendency to rate people relative to other people rather than to performance standards.

Contributory Plan is one in which the money for pension benefits is paid in by both employees and employers.

Co-payment requires employees to pay part of insurance premium costs.

Cost/Benefit Analysis is comparing what efforts will cost with benefits received to see which is greater.

Craft Union is one in which its members do one type of work, often using specialized skills and training.

Database is the stored data used by the computer.

Decentralization is the extent to which decision-making

authority/responsibility is dispersed downward through the organization.

Decertification is a process whereby a union is removed as the representative of a group of employees.

Defined-Benefit Plan is one in which an employee is promised a pension amount based on age and service.

Defined-Contribution Plan is one in which the employer makes an annual payment to an employee's pension account.

Discipline is a form of training that enforces organizational rules.

Discrimination (EEOC definition) is the use of any test that adversely affects hiring, promotion, transfer or any other employment or membership opportunity of classes unless the test has been validated and is job related, and/or an employer can demonstrate that alternative hiring, transfer, or promotion procedures are unavailable.

Disparate Treatment occurs when protected group members are treated differently from other employees.

Downsizing is reducing the size of an organizational work force.

Draw is an amount advanced to an employee and repaid from future commissions earned by the employee.

Due Process gives one the opportunity to defend oneself against charges.

Duty is a larger work segment composed of several tasks performed by an individual.

Employee-Assistance Program (EAP) provides counseling and other help to employees having emotional, physical, or other personal problems.

Employee Skills Inventory is a compilation of data on the skills and characteristics of employees.

Employee Stock Ownership Plan (ESOP) is a stock bonus plan whereby employees gain ownership in the organization for which they work.

Encapsulated Development occurs when an individual learns new methods and ideas in a development course and returns to a work unit that is still bound by old attitudes and methods.

Entrepreneur is a creative and energetic individual who also encourages these characteristics in others.

Environmental Scanning is the process of studying the environment of the organization to pinpoint opportunities and threats.

Equity is defined as the perceived fairness of what the person does (inputs) compared with what the person receives (outcomes).

Exempt Employees are those who are not required to be paid overtime under the Fair Standards Act.

Expatriate is a person working in a country who is not a national citizen of that country.

Experiment involves studying how a factor responds when changes are made in one or more variables or conditions.

Exit Interview is an interview during which those who are leaving the organization are asked to identify the reasons for their departure.

Extinction is the absence of a response to a situation.

Federation is a group of autonomous national and international unions.

Flexible Benefits System allows employees to select the benefits they prefer from groups of benefits established by the employer.

Flexible Spending Account allows employees to contribute pre-tax dollars to buy additional benefits.

Flextime refers to variations in starting and ending times, but assumes that a number of hours (usually 8) is worked each day.

Forecasting uses information from the past and present to identify expected future conditions.

Four-Fifths (4/5th) Rule states that discrimination generally occurs if the selection rate for a protected group is less than 80 percent of their representation in the relevant labor market or 80 percent less than the majority group.

401 (k) Plan allows employees to receive cash or to have employer contributions from profit-sharing and stock-bonus plans placed into a tax-deferred account.

Funded Method provides pension benefits over a long period from funds accumulated ahead of time.

Gainsharing sharing with employees of greater-than-expected gains in profits and/or productivity.

Garnishment is a court action in which a portion of an employee's wages is set aside to pay a debt owed to a creditor.

Graphology is an analysis of an individual's handwriting in order to identify personality characteristics.

Green-Circle Job is one in which the incumbent is paid below the range set for the job.

Grievance is a specific, formal notice of employee dissatisfaction expressed through an identified procedure.

Grievance Arbitration is a means of settling disputes arising from different interpretations of a contract using a third party.

Grievance Procedure is a formal channel of communication used to resolve formal complaints (grievances).

Halo Effect is rating a person high or low on all items because of one characteristic.

Handbilling is written publicity given to employees by unions to convince the employees to sign authorization cards.

Hardware is the actual computer equipment used, such as computers, disk drives, monitors, printers, and optiscanners.

Health refers to a general state of physical, mental, and emotional well-being.

Health Maintenance Organization (HMO) is a form of health care which provides services for a fixed period on a prepaid basis.

Host-Country National is an employee who is a citizen

of a country in which a branch or plant is located, but the organization is headquartered in another country.

Human Resource Accounting attempts to place a value on organizational human resources.

Human Resource Development focuses on increasing capabilities of employees for the continuing growth and advancement in the organization.

Human Resource Information System (HRIS) is an integrated system designed to provide information used in P/HR decision making.

Human Resource Planning consists of analyzing and identifying the need for and the availability of the human resources required for an organization to meet its objectives.

Immediate Confirmation indicates that people learn best if reinforcement is given as soon as possible after training.

Incentive is compensation that rewards employees for efforts beyond normal performance expectations.

Individual Retirement Account (IRA) allows an employee to set aside funds in a special account which are tax-deferred until the employee retires.

Industrial Union is one that may include many persons working in the same industry or company, regardless of jobs held.

Insured Plan is one administered through insurance companies or similar institutions which buy retirement annuity policies.

Interfaces are areas of contact between the P/HR unit and other managers in an organization.

Intrapreneuring describes employees acting in an independent manner within an organization.

Involuntary Part-time Workers are individuals who work less than 35 hours per week, but normally would be working full time if possible.

Job is a grouping of similar positions having common tasks, duties, and responsibilities.

Job Analysis is a systematic way to gather and analyze information about the content of jobs, human requirements, and the context in which jobs are performed.

Job Criteria are the elements of a job to be evaluated during performance appraisal.

Job Depth is the amount of planning and control responsibilities in a job.

Job Description specifies in written form the tasks, duties, and responsibilities of a job.

Job Design refers to a conscious effort to organize tasks, duties, and responsibilities into a unit of work.

Job Enlargement is broadening the scope of a job by expanding the number of different tasks to be performed.

Job Enrichment is increasing the depth of a job by adding employee responsibility for planning, organizing, controlling, and evaluating the job.

Job Evaluation is the systematic determination of the relative worth of jobs within an organization.

Job Rotation is the process of shifting a person from job to job.

Job Satisfaction is a pleasurable or positive emotional state resulting from the appraisal of one's job or experiences.

Job Scope refers to the number and variety of tasks performed by a job holder.

Job Sharing is a work arrangement in which two part-time workers share one full-time job.

Job Specifications list the skills, knowledge, and abilities an individual needs to do the job satisfactorily.

Keogh Plan (H.R.10 Plan) allows self-employed individuals to establish an individualized pension plan.

Lockout occurs when management shuts down company operations to prevent union members from working

Line Function generally is the operating branch of the organization or that part directly concerned with producing the product or service.

Loyalty is commitment to and allegiance with an organization.

Mandated Benefits means that employers are required by law to provide certain benefits previously offered voluntarily.

Market Price is the prevailing wage rate paid a job in the immediate job market.

Massed Practice occurs when a person does all of the practice at once.

Maturity Curve depicts the relationship between experience and pay raise.

Mediation occurs when a third party assists the negotiators in their discussions and also suggests settlement proposals.

Mentoring is a relationship between a manager at midpoint in his or her career and a young adult in the first stage of a career.

Merit System is one in which P/HR activities are governed by uniform and impersonal policies and procedures.

Microcomputers are the smallest computers and often are referred to as personal computers (PC's).

Motivation is derived from the word "motive" and is an emotion or desire causing a person to act.

National Emergency Strike is one that affects an industry or a major part of it such that the national health or safety would be impeded.

Negative Reinforcement occurs when an individual works to avoid and undesirable reward.

Noncontributory Plan is one in which all the funds for pension benefits are provided by the employer.

Nondirective Interview uses general questions, from which other questions are developed.

Organization is a goal-oriented system of coordinating relationships between people, tasks, resources, and managerial activities.

Organizational Climate is a composite view of the characteristics of an organization as seen by employees.

Organizational Culture is a pattern of shared values and beliefs giving members meaning and providing them with rules for behavior.

Organizational Development is a value-based process of self-assessment and planned change, involving specific strategies.

Orientation is the planned introduction of employees to their jobs, co-workers, and the organization.

Outplacement is a group of services provided displaced employees to give them support or assistance.

Patronage occurs when an individual is appointed to a position based upon past political support or friendship.

Pay is the basic compensation an employee receives, usually as a wage or salary.

Pay Compression occurs when pay differences among individuals becomes small.

Pay Grades are used to group together individual jobs having approximately the same job worth.

Pay Survey a collection of data on existing compensation rates for workers performing similar jobs in other organizations.

Performance Appraisal is the process of determining how well employees do their jobs compared with a set of standards and communicating that information to the employees.

Perquisites ("perks") are special benefits for executives that are usually noncash items.

Personnel/Human Resource (P/HR) Audit is a formal research effort to evaluate the current state of P/HR management in an organization.

Personnel/Human Resource (P/HR) Generalist is a person with responsibility for performing a variety of activities.

Personnel/Human Resource (P/HR) Research analyzes past and present P/HR practices by using collected data and records.

Personnel/Human Resource (P/HR) Specialist is a person with in-depth knowledge and expertise is a limited area.

Personnel/Human Resource (P/HR) Management is the strategic and operational management of activities focusing on the human resources within an organization.

Piece-Rate System is one in which an employee is paid for each unit of production.

Policies are general guidelines that regulate organizational actions.

Portability is a pension plan feature that allows employees to move their pension benefits rights from one employer to another.

Position is a collection of tasks, duties, and responsibilities performed by one person.

Positive Reinforcement occurs when a person receives a desired reward.

Preferred Provider Organization (PPO) is a health-care provider that contracts with an employer or an employer group to provide health-care services to employees at a competitive rate.

Primary Research is the method by which data is gathered directly on problems and issues.

Procedures are customary methods of handling activities.

Productivity is most often defined as the ration of output to input.

Profit sharing distributes a portion of the profits of the organization to employees.

Protected Group Member is an individual who falls within a group identified for protection under equal employment laws.

Punishment is action taken to repel the person from the undesired action.

Quality Circles are small groups of employees that meet on a regular basis to discuss ways to improve productivity and cut costs.

Ratification occurs when union members vote to accept the terms of a negotiated labor agreement.

Realistic Job Preview (RJP) is the process through which an interviewer provides a job applicant with an accurate picture of a job.

Recruiting is the process of generating a pool of qualified applicants for organizational jobs.

Red-Circle Job is one in which the incumbent is paid above the range set for the job.

Reliability refers to the consistency with which a test measures an item.

Repatriation is the process of bringing expatriate employees home.

Responsibilities are obligations to perform certain tasks and duties.

Responsibility is a duty or obligation to be accountable for an action.

Reverse Discrimination may exist when a person is denied an opportunity because of preferences given to protected group individuals who may be less qualified.

Right is that which belongs to a person by law, nature, or tradition.

Right-to-Sue Letter is issued by the EEOC and notifies the person that he or she has ninety days in which to file a personal suit in federal court.

Right-to-Work Laws are state laws that prohibit both the closed shop and the union shop.

Rules are specific guidelines that regulate and restrict the behavior of individuals.

Safety refers to protection of the physical well-being of people.

Safety Hierarchy the order in which actions should be taken to eliminate work safety problems.

Salary is payment that is consistent from period to period.

Secondary Research uses research done by others and reported in articles in professional journals or books.

Selection is the process of choosing individuals who have relevant qualifications to fill jobs in an organization.

Self-funding occurs when an employer sets aside funds to pay health claims in excess of the amount provided by funding in lieu of insurance coverage.

Sexual Harassment refers to actions that are sexually directed, unwanted, and subject the worker to adverse employment conditions.

Software contains the program instructions that tell the computer how to process the data.

Spaced Practice occurs when several practice sessions are spaced over a period of hours or days.

Staff Functions refer to people or positions that provide an advisory, control, or support role to the organization.

Standard is an expected level of performance.

Status social ranking of a person in relation to others.

Stock Option gives an employee the right to buy stock in a company, usually at the fixed price for a period of time.

Strategic Planning is the process of identifying organizational objectives and actions needed to achieve those objectives.

Stress Interview is used to create pressure and stress on an applicant to see how the person responds.

Strike occurs when workers refuse to work in order to put pressure on an employer.

Structured Interview uses a set of standardized questions that are asked all job applicants.

Suggestion System is a formal method of obtaining employee input and upward communication.

Task is a distinct identifiable work activity composed of motions.

Telecommuting is the process of going to work via electronic computing and telecommunications equipment.

Third-Country National is someone who is a citizen of one country, working in a second country, and employed by an organization headquartered in a third country.

Title VII is that portion of the 1964 Civil Rights Act prohibiting discrimination in employment.

Training is a learning process whereby people acquire skills or knowledge to aid in the achievement of goals.

Turnover occurs when employees leave the organization and have to be replaced.

Unfunded Plan pays pension benefits out of current income to the organization.

Uninsured Plan is one in which the benefits at retirement are determined by the employer based upon calculations that consider the age of the employee, years worked, and other factors.

Union is a formal association of workers that promotes the interests of its members through collective action.

Union Security are provisions to aid the union in obtaining and retaining members.

Union Shop requires that an employee join a union, usually 30 to 60 days after being hired.

Unit Labor Cost is the total labor cost per unit of output. The unit labor cost is equal to the average wage divided by the level of productivity.

Utility Analysis builds economic or other statistical models to identify the costs and benefits associated with specific P/HR activities.

Utilization Analysis identifies the number of protected group members employed and the types of jobs held in an organization.

Utilization Review is an auditing of the services and costs billed by health-care providers.

Validity means that a "test" actually measures what it says it measures.

Vesting is the right of employees to receive benefits from their pension plans.

Voluntary Part-time Workers are individuals who wish to work less than 35 hours per week.

Wage and Salary Administration is the group of activities involved in the development, implementation, and maintenance of a base pay system.

Wages are payments directly calculated on the amount of time worked.

Work Group is a collection of individuals brought together to perform organizational work.

Work Sharing occurs when an employer reduces work hours and total pay for all or a segment of the employees.

Workers' Compensation provides benefits to a person injured on the job.

NAME INDEX

SUBJECT INDEX